# SPONSORS OF THE PAST. FLEMISH ART AND PATRONAGE 1550-1700

# SPONSORS OF THE PAST. FLEMISH ART AND PATRONAGE 1550-1700

Proceedings of the symposium organized at the
Katholieke Universiteit Leuven
December, 14-15, 2001
Faculteit Letteren
Departement Archeologie, Kunstwetenschap en Musicologie

Edited by HANS VLIEGHE and KATLIJNE VAN DER STIGHELEN

BREPOLS

Cover illustration:
Michaelina Woutiers, Triumph of Bacchus (detail), before 1659. Vienna, Kunsthistorisches Museum.

Copy-editor Hans Devisscher



D/2005/0095/26

ISBN 2-503-51500-2

Printed in the E.U. on acid-free paper

# Foreword

*Kunst is iets dat je deelt. Als je het niet deelt is het helemaal niets. (Art is something to be shared. Unless you share it, it loses its value entirely).* These are the words of Ronald de Leeuw, head of the Rijksmuseum in Amsterdam. *Kunst gaat over de grote thema's van het leven. De belangstelling voor kunst ontwikkelt zich in de loop van je leven steeds meer. Het is net als vis eten, dat vind je ook niet lekker als je jong bent. Als je ouder wordt, ga je dat steeds meer waarderen (Art deals with the major issues in life. People become more and more interested in art as they grow older. It is like eating fish. People don't enjoy fish when they are young, but appreciate it all the more as they advance in age).* This view was expressed by Antony Burgmans, Chairman of the Board of Unilever. Both quotations are to be found in the anthology just published entitled *Passie voor kunst. 31 interviews met prominente kunstliefhebbers* by Koos de Wilt (Wormer, 2003). There are many similarities between the way people lived with art in the past and how they do so today. The sponsors of the past are the collectors of today. They collect to live and live to collect.

On December 14 and 15, 2001 the *Wetenschappelijke Onderzoeksgemeenschap Vlaamse Renaissance- en Barokkunst*, funded by the Fund for Scientific Research, Flanders (*Fonds voor Wetenschappelijk Onderzoek-Vlaanderen*), organized a colloquium at the University of Leuven entitled 'Commissioned Art. Flemish Art and Patronage, 1550-1700.' The aim of this colloquium was to give an idea of the many-sided character of patronage in relation to Flemish art. The organizers sought to cast further light on the specific differences between princely, aristocratic, ecclesiastic and civil forms of art patronage. The outcome of our appeal to potential speakers was a wide variety of well-documented case studies, which not only examined the changing relations between artists and their patrons, but also dealt with the specific ways in which individual artists were able to respond to the wishes of their employers.

All but one of the revised texts of these lectures are included in this volume. It is our sincere wish that these articles will enhance our insight into a relatively neglected aspect of the historic framework in which Flemish art was developed.

The Editors

# Contents

# A Model Court Architect. Mary of Hungary and Jacques Du Brœucq (1545–1556)

*Krista De Jonge*

In 1593 the architect, surveyor and military engineer Pierre le Poivre petitioned governor Pierre Ernest count of Mansfeld as follows:

> 'A Son excellence, remonstre en toute humilité maistre Pierre le Poyvre, architecte et géographe de Sa Majesté, comme ayant continué ès l'espace de treize ans à l'exerce de Sadicte majesté et de Vostre Excellence...; ores comme le suppliant at entendu que ung nommé maistre Jacques de Breucque ayant servy du mesme estat d'architecte feu Marie, royne d'Hongerie, duquel ledict maistre Jacques fut pourveu d'une pension de IJ^C livres de xl groz, monnoye de Flandres, en recompense de ses bonnes services qu'il avoyt faict assistant les ingénieurs de Sadicte majesté en faysant les modelles de Philippeville, Marienbourch et Charlemont, lequel pension luy fut assignee sur le recepveur es domaines de Mons, lequel il at tire jusques l'an iiijxxv qu'il trespassoit, prie partant ledict suppliant qu'il plaise à Vostre Excellence luy colloquer en recompense de ses bonnes et longues services en la place dudict maistre Jacques de Breucque ...'[1]

This document suggests that Du Brœucq's pension, and the position it was related to at court, served as a reference to the artist's successors in the service of the King and His representatives at the close of the century, years after Du Broeucq's death. Lepoivre took care to refer to Du Brœucq's activities in the military domain, the better to present his own case in a favourable light: by the time Albert of Austria and the Infanta Isabella assumed the regency, the military engineers of the King in fact dominated architectural practice at the court.[2] Du Brœucq's contemporary and acquaintance Lodovico Guicciardini, the well-known Florentine chronicler living in Antwerp, on the contrary sums up his œuvre by referring to Boussu and Mariemont,[3] two buildings, lost nowadays, which stand for Du Brœucq's most important connections to the court milieu and which perfectly represent the close interaction between the architect and his patron.

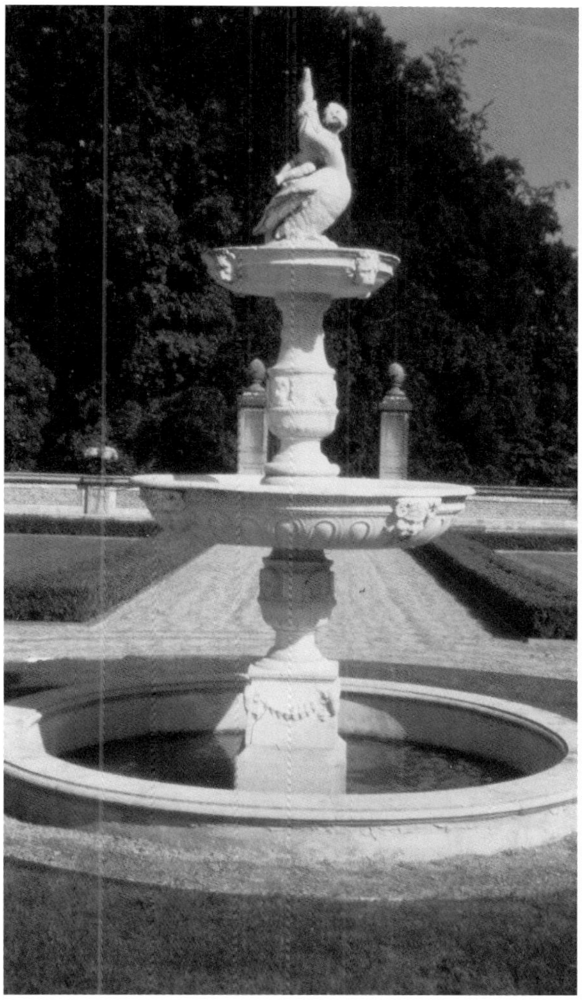

Fig. 1. Gaasbeek, fountain in Carrara marble bearing the arms of Boussu (photo author, 1999)

Very probably, Du Brœucq had gotten his first entrée into the network of court patronage at Boussu, where work on the new castle started officially on 24 March 1540. Jean de Hennin-Liétard, 'premier et grand écuyer' (First Master of Horse) to the Emperor, may have employed the young sculptor from Saint-Omer already in the mid-1530's, i.e. before Du Brœucq established his workshop in Mons (1539–1540), when he obtained the commission of creating the alabaster sculptures for the rood-screen of Sainte-Waudru.[4] Already before demolishing the ancestral keep, Jean de Hennin had ordered Genuese marble artefacts to embellish the new building he planned to raise on the same site: two chimney-pieces modelled upon the one in the Sala del Naufragio in the villa Doria at Fassolo and a doorway decorated with figures, to be delivered by the sculptors Giovanni Maria da Passallo and Antonio di Nova da Lancio before October 1534; a fountain basin copied after the one in the garden of the Spanish ambassador in Genua, ordered on 26 May 1535 of Niccolò da Corte; the *Three Graces* – probably meant to adorn the same fountain –, four putti and a life-size *Ceres* by Guglielmo della Porta, shipped, as Vasari reports it, to Flanders before 1537; another marble fountain decorated with a putto holding a swan and the arms of Boussu, not dated, conserved at Gaasbeek (fig. 1), and maybe other pieces unknown to us.[5] It is possible that Du Brœucq, as a talented sculptor, was asked to inspect the pieces upon delivery in Boussu, or in Antwerp, the main port of transit, or even in Genua itself, before they started the arduous journey to the North: such a procedure would be consistent with contemporary practice. The confrontation with these pieces must have left a lasting impression upon the sculptor. Du Brœucq's formal repertory is not without elements, which are typical for the standard Genuese export product of the time (fig. 2).[6] For instance, the chimney-piece crowned with a pyramidal hood flanked by figures, and supported by claw-footed male herms, counts among the sources of the herms carrying antique weaponry sculpted by Du Brœucq in Avesnes stone for the great hall in the palace of Binche (fig. 12).[7]

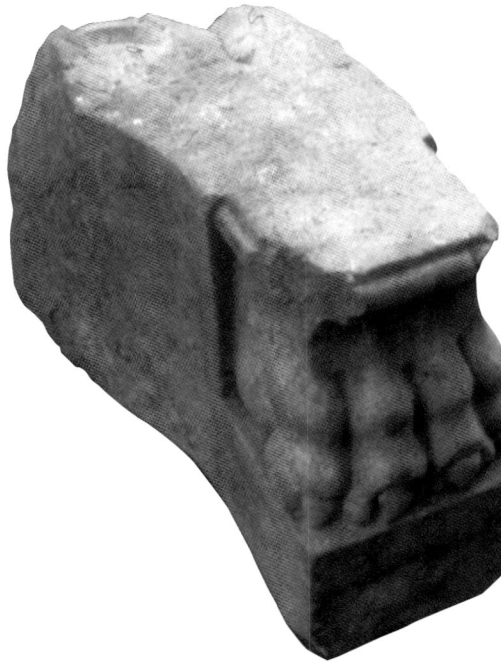

Fig. 2. Boussu, clawed foot in Bray sandstone, part of a chimney-piece possibly inspired by a Genuese model (photo author, 1996)

Jean de Hennin-Liétard's personality as a patron of the arts still remains to be defined: there is no entry in the *Biographie nationale*, which is all the more astounding when one considers his exalted position at court.[8] He became a Knight of the Golden Fleece in 1531 and apparently held the position of 'premier et grand écuyer', or 'gran scudiere' as Vasari puts it, from 1538. The court ordinance of Nicolas Mameranus of Luxemburg, dated 1546–1547, confirms these titles: 'Ioannes ab Hennin, Dominus à Bossu, supremus Præfectus stabuli, Eques ordinis Aurei-Velleris'.[9] He also inherited the title of 'grand bailly' (sheriff) 'des bois de Hainault et prevost' (provost) and 'conte de Vallenciennes', positions which like the former one, implied that he was well versed in matters military and indeed was partially responsible for the defence of this exposed border region.[10] The Venetian ambassador Bernardo Navagero confirms this in his report of July 1546 to the Venetian Senate.[11] Jean de Hennin was an extremely well connected member of the 'supra-national' nobility, which in the 15th century had taken root in the Low Countries thanks to the favour of the dukes of Burgundy of the House of Valois. The unpublished genealogical manuscript by Jacques Le Boucq, *Recueille des antiquites de la noble maison de Hennin Lietart* (Valenciennes 1571) shows ties to the Croÿ, Merode, Montmorency, Lannoy, Barbançon, and other families.[12] His wife, Anne of Burgundy, whom he married in 1532, was the eldest daughter of Adolf of Burgundy, lord of Veere, a descendant on the illegitimate side of the 'Grand Duc d'Occident' Philip the Good.[13] His eldest son Maximilian de Hennin would inherit the positions of admiral of Flanders and 'stadhouder' of Holland held by Anne's brother Maximilian of Burgundy from 1542 to 1558, when he died without issue.[14] Pierre Du Mont or Montanus the Elder reports in his notes to a late French translation of Guicciardini's *Descrittione* that these illustrious family ties were represented in the castle by a series of family portraits, following the Habsburg example.[15]

All of Jean de Hennin's titles were in fact represented unequivocally in the new residence at Boussu. Montanus also describes the 'paintures artificielles de toutes sortes de chevaux tirées au vif, qui y furent mises lors de l'entrée de l'Empereur', i.e. on 2 February 1545. These portraits of horses seem to have survived in the *Album de Croÿ* dedicated to the princedom of Porcian and the marquisate of Montcornet, where they appear together with the four main façades of the castle.[16] The identifying inscriptions – one of them, accompanying a piebald mare, informs us that she was a present of the duke of Medina to the Emperor, who in his turn donated her to the king of France in 1539 – show that these famous animals symbolize diplomatic relationships at the imperial court. As such they were the 'grand écuyer''s immediate responsibility and indeed, a symbol of his status. Also, recent excavations at Boussu have led to the discovery of an enormous bulwark or 'boulevard', which preceded the gatehouse with its Tuscan triumphal arch (figs. 3-4).

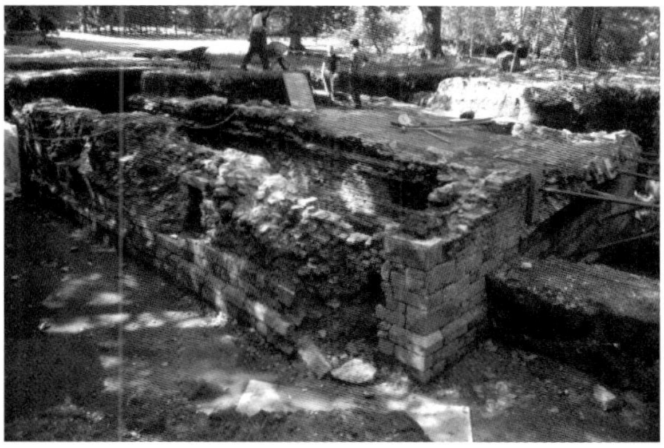

Fig. 3. Boussu, lower part of the bulwark in front of the first gate, with vaulted galleries and lateral gunports commanding the ditch in front of the gatehouse (photo author, 2000)

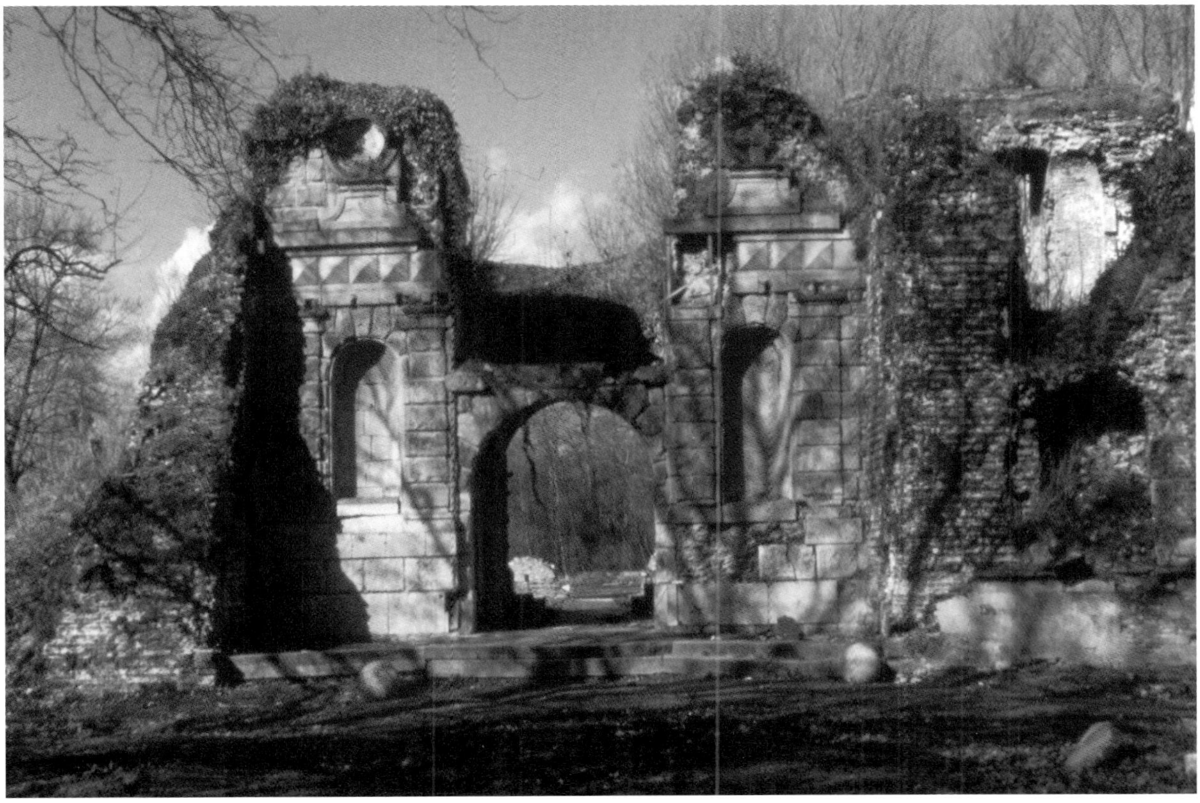

Fig. 4. Boussu, gatehouse with Tuscan triumphal arch (photo author, 1995)

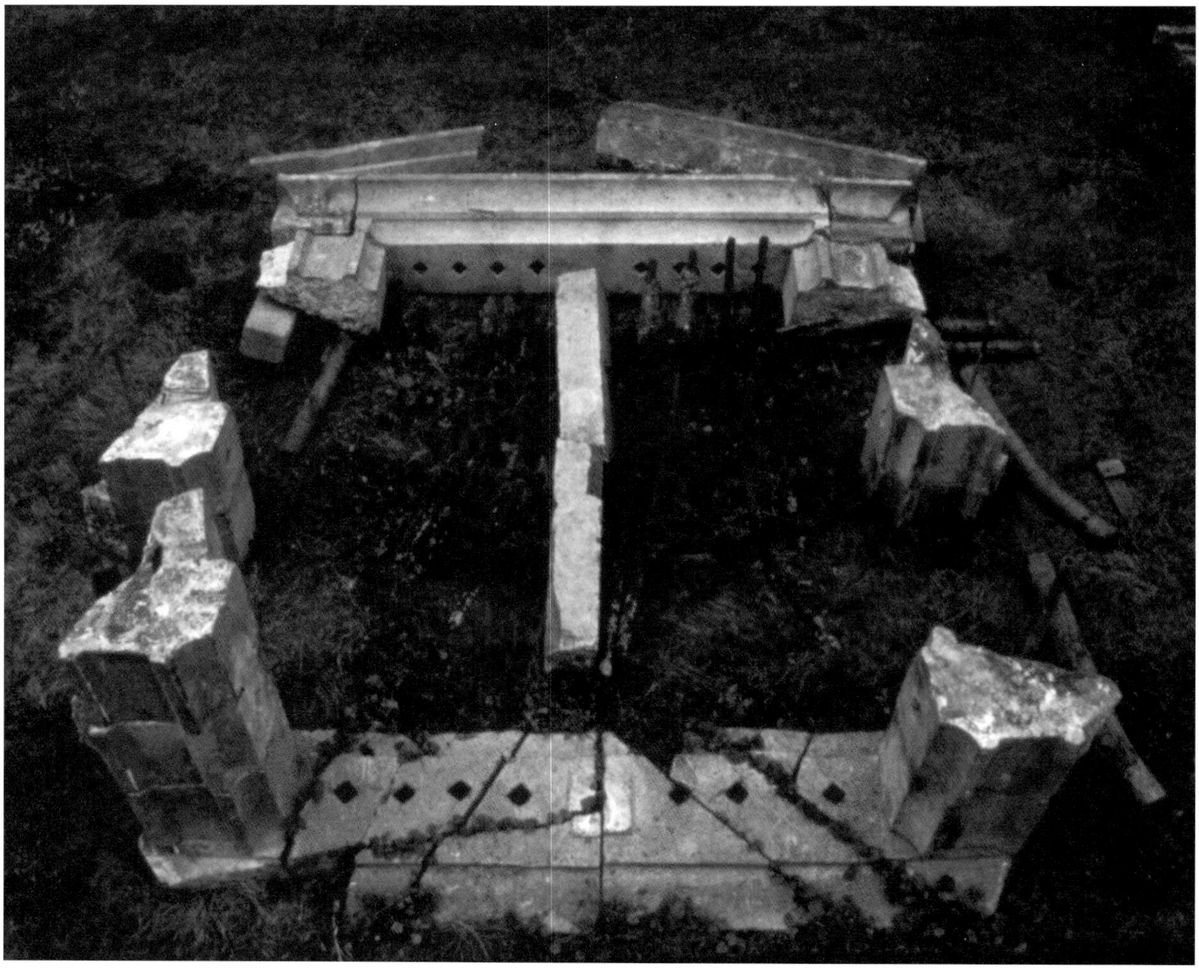

Fig. 5. Boussu, pedimented window recovered from the north ditch (photo Cécile Ansieaux, 1995)

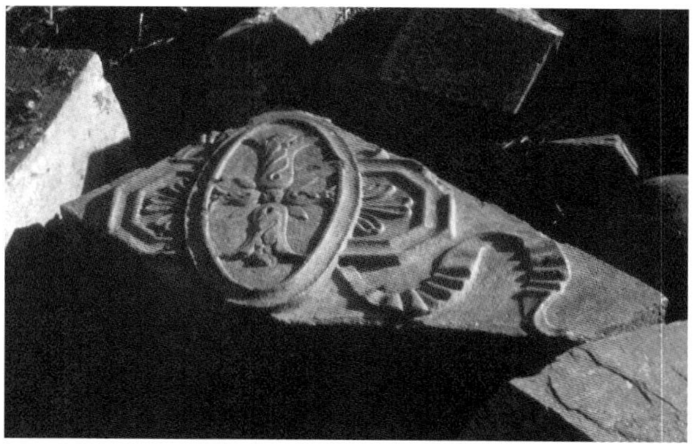

Fig. 6. Boussu, arcade fragment in Ecaussines limestone decorated with crossed shields in the antique manner (photo author, 1995)

It is something of an anomaly as far as its defensive function goes, because by 1540 the Italianate bastionated fortification system had been introduced into the Low Countries, and no one better than the well-traveled 'grand écuyer' would have been aware of the fact that the old-fashioned 'boulevard', which was invented around 1400, would not have withstood the new, heavy artillery. The elaborate entrance system in fact refers to Jean de Hennin's position as provost and sheriff. The 'boulevard', together with the two drawbridges, the squat, completely vaulted towers of the gatehouse, and the colonnaded entrance gallery with its elevated archers' walkway on both sides afforded some defence against a small-arms attack, but that was not their primary function. They were meant to express the idea of fortification and its connotations of nobility, and to refer to prestigious examples of the past generation, which still abounded in the border region (e.g. Anto-

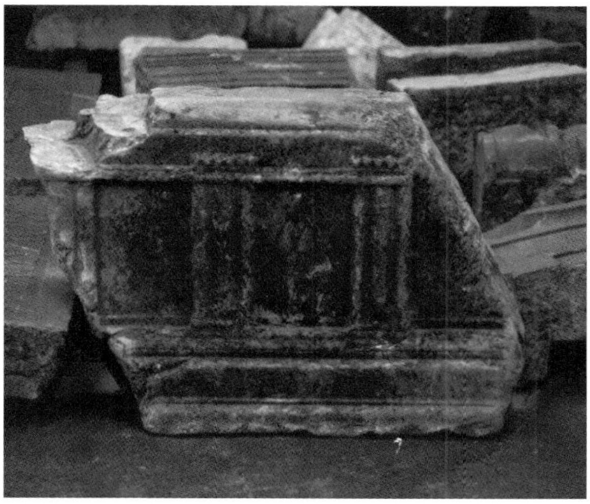

Fig. 7. Boussu, Doric entablature fragment in Ecaussines limestone (photo author, 1998)

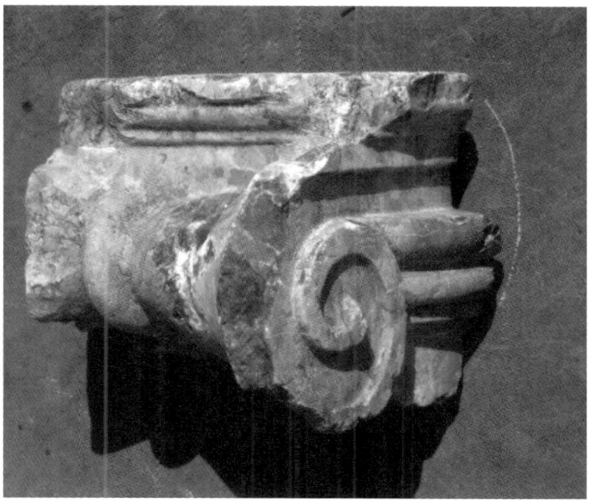

Fig. 8. Boussu, fragment of a Ionic capital in red marble of Rance (photo author, 1997)

ing, Hainaut and Montcornet, Ardennes).[17] The medieval predecessor of the residence at Boussu, ruined in 1478, also possessed such a defence work.[18]

Du Brœucq's task as 'maistre des ouvrages a Boussut', i.e. as designer and executive architect,[19] had been to find a suitable architectural expression for his patron's ambitions and there is no doubt that he succeeded very well. Not only the residence's large size, but also the 'antique' repertory of forms Du Brœucq used throughout and its sumptuous finishing made it into a prodigy house admired by professionals – like Philip II's architect Gaspar de Vega[20] – and casual visitors alike, in spite of the fact that it was left unfinished in a damaged state at Jean de Hennin's death in 1563. In recent studies we have concentrated on the many fragments excavated at the site in an attempt to define the artistic personality of the architect more accurately (figs. 5–9).[21] The example of the 'boulevard', however, goes to show that this is only half the story and that the patron played an active role in the designing process. The main building was, like the gatehouse, built of brick judiciously strengthened by cut stone at the corners, window surrounds, cornices and doorframes. Modern scholars have identified this manner of building with the whole of the Low Countries, so it is easy to forget that at the time it was still perceived as the 'Brabantine manner of building', exported everywhere by favoured building masters of the elite like the Keldermans family.[22] Some features – like the tall

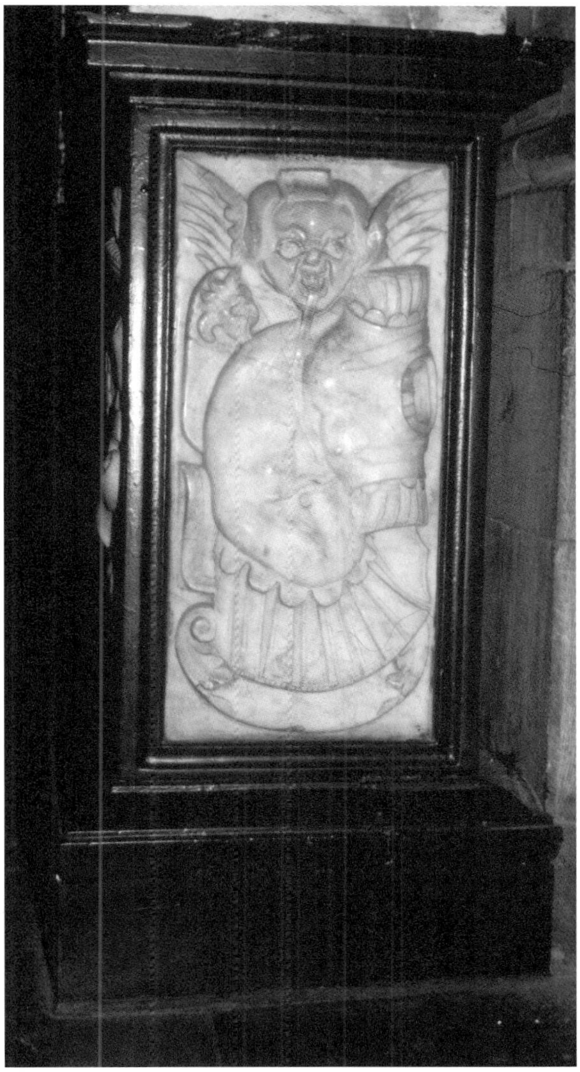

Fig. 9. Mons, Sainte-Waudru, pedestal from Boussu in black Dinant touchstone and white marble, decorated with trophies in the antique manner (photo author, 1993)

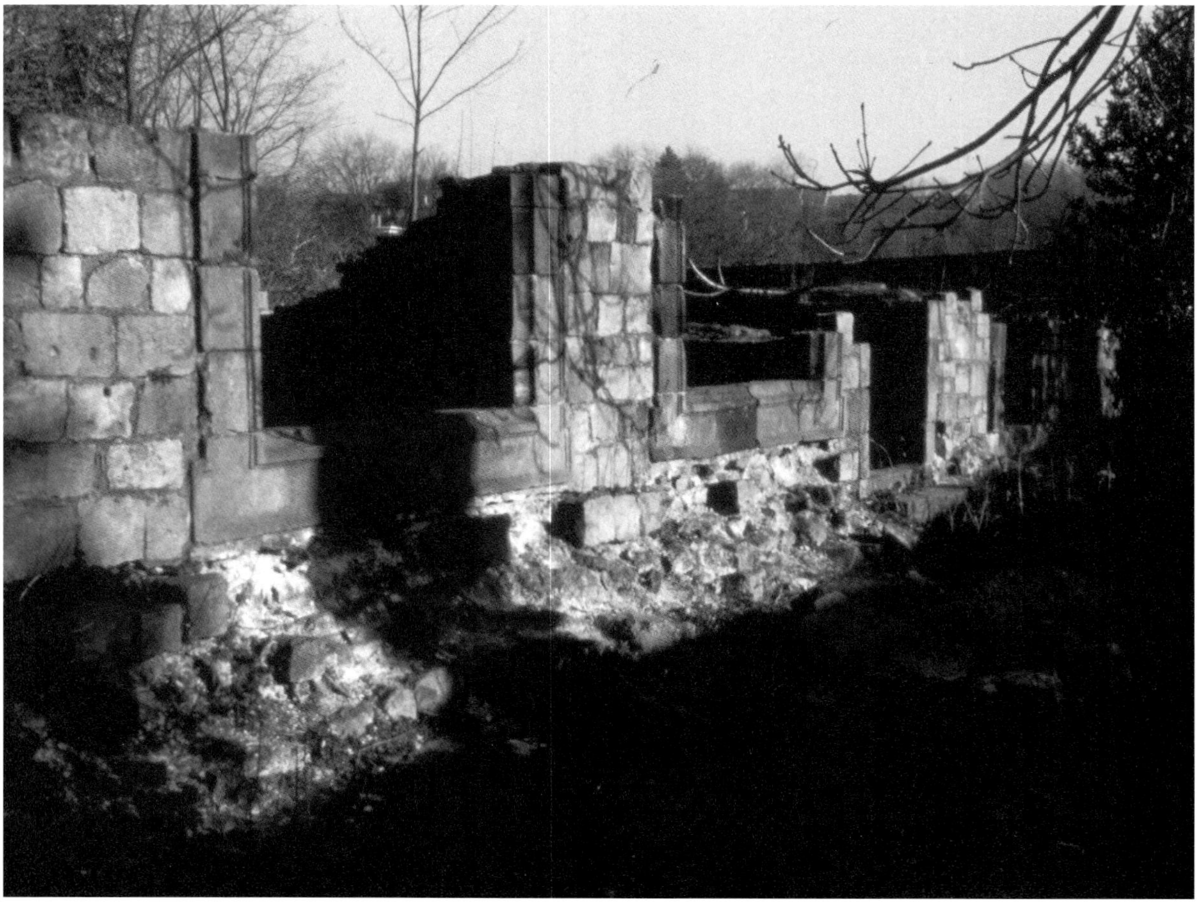

Fig. 10. Binche, ruins of the cross wing renovated by Du Brœucq. Window surrounds with "ears" after a Raphaëlesque model (photo author, 1993)

pavilion-like towers crowned by fanciful spires and indeed the idea of a symmetrical, colonnaded quadrangle with complex staircases placed upon the main axis – referred to the residences of the principal members of the elite, the castle at Heverlee built for Guillaume of Croÿ, lord of Chièvres († 1521), and the castle at Breda, built for Henry III of Nassau, Guillaume's successor as First Lord of the Chamber ('grand chambellan'), in particular.[23] Because he had great power both over the personal household and affairs of state, the 'grand chambellan''s position at court was so powerful, that Charles V declined to nominate a successor to Henry III of Nassau in 1539; in the future, the 'mayordomo mayor' of Spanish origin would take his place.[24] Thus Du Brœucq's building offered a synthesis of extremely precise references to the architecture of the highest nobility in the Burgundian-Habsburg realm. To what extent this is borne out by Jean de Hennin's activities as a collector, unfortunately remains a matter of conjecture. Karel van Mander mentions in his *Schilder-Boeck* (1603–1604) that Pieter Aertsen, at the age of 17 or 18 years, travelled from Amsterdam to Boussu to look at the famous collection of paintings there.[25] Another fragment of evidence can be found in the account books of Binche. At the end of the year 1552, the 'molleur en plattre' (stucco worker) Luc Lange or Luca Lancia di San Germano made stucco copies of several 'testes desdits anticquaiges', which belonged to Mary of Hungary, for Jean de Hennin.[26] Finally, Constantin Huygens the Younger mentions the sale, on 24 May 1676, in Mons of several 'bustes modernes faits en Italie', which allegedly had belonged to Jean de Hennin.[27]

In the building accounts of Mary of Hungary's new palace at Binche, a town which she received as a personal gift from her brother in 1545, Du Brœucq is styled 'maistre des ouvrages a Boussut'. This indeed suggests that his work at Boussu brought him to the atten-

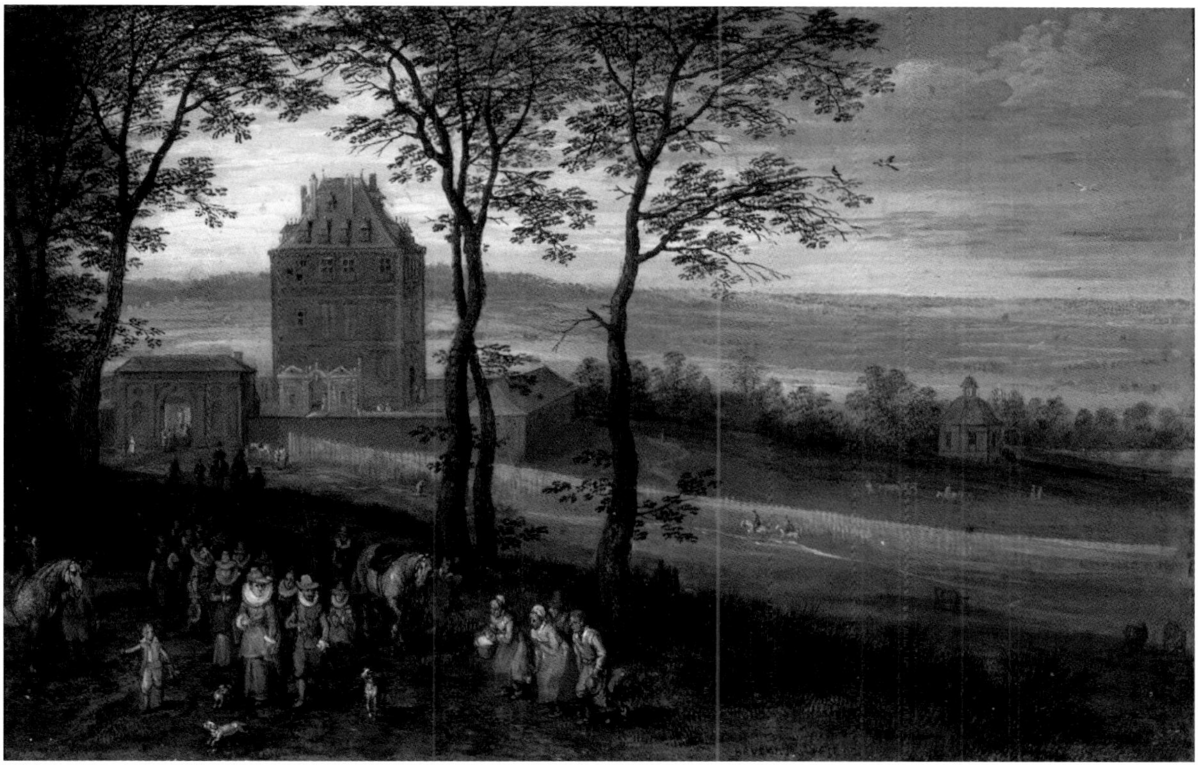

Fig. 11. Jan Brueghel I, known as Fluwelen Brueghel, Mariemont seen from the north (entrance) side, 1611. The original terraced roof with balustrade had to be replaced in 1567 already. Munich, Alte Pinakothek, cat. 1893

tion of the regent. The accounts also testify to the close relationship between Boussu, which was still under construction at the time, and the new construction site at Binche, where work on the 'nouveau et riche logis' started in 1546.[28] The building fragments in Ecaussines stone at both sites closely resemble each other not only as to their form, but also in workmanship (fig. 10).[29] At both sites, it seems the Le Prince family was responsible for the stonework, true to the privileged role they played since a generation at least on the most important building sites in the Southern Low Countries.[30] Mary of Hungary also borrowed the 'grand écuyer''s prized German woodworkers and their tools: between 1548 and 1552, Hans and Michel Wisrutter joined Balthasar Bruye's team to work on carved wood panelling, inlaid window shutters and parquet floors in precious 'bois de bresil, bois de barbarin, oliviers', and 'bois dalmarche' or Baltic oak.[31] Work on the new wing at Binche progressed in parallel with the construction of Mary's hunting lodge at Mariemont, some miles distant; indeed, master Balthasar Bruye can be found there, too, and so does the master mason of Binche, Guillaume Le Naing (fig. 11).[32] In François de Rabutin's words, 'la magnifique maison de Mariemont, construite curieusement pour le singulier plaisir et delectation de la reine Marie, appropriée de tant de singularités qu'il est possible de penser' was an original creation, which carried the personal stamp of its patron, a lover of the hunt famous even in a period and in a milieu known for its hunting excesses.[33] Situated in a private hunting park, this 'palagio a guisa di castello'[34] was not meant to be an official court residence, lacking sufficient kitchen space, the usual dormitories for the young ladies of the court and even a large chapel, capable of accommodating the whole entourage. It took the form of a cube, placed in the exact centre of a square artificial pond, and accessible only across a rusticated bridge. Its richly decorated, flat roof offered a marvellous view of the terraced gardens sloping down to the river at the south and the west side.[35] There was nothing like it in the Low Countries at the time, which probably explains why Henry II of France singled it out for destruction in the campaign of 1554.[36]

Throughout the account books, Jacques Du Brœucq is consistently called 'maistre Jacques lartiste' (the artist).[37] This must be understood as a specific reference to the title created for Jean Mone, the sculptor from Metz who can be credited with having been the first to emancipate himself from the constraints of the guild system by virtue of his position as court artist.[38] Mone could indeed be found, together with Rombout Keldermans II, building master to the emperor, at all the major construction sites of the elite, from Hoogstraten, where they worked on Antoine de Lalaing's castle, to Heverlee, where they created the Celestin priory as a personal mausoleum for Guillaume de Croÿ, and to Brussels itself, where they worked on the new court chapel.[39] The second to carry the title was Pieter Coecke van Aelst, painter, entrepreneur and the first to publish theoretical texts on the new 'antique' architecture in the Low Countries.[40] He is mentioned in this manner in the documents relating to the construction of a new staircase in front of the main range at the Coudenberg palace in Brussels, where he acted as a consultant for the imperially themed sculptures on top of the triumphal arch.[41] The title 'artist' seems to have been used to single out the major specialists in 'antique works' ('anticse wercken') active in court circles. Thus it also serves as a measure of Jacques Du Brœucq's position and renown as Model Court Architect from 1545 onwards.

However, documents from a later period seem to contradict the privileged status suggested by this title. Du Brœucq did not enjoy the complete independence, which we would nowadays associate with his position: artistic freedom in design apparently went hand in hand with complete submission to the comptroller's approval on matters of choice of materials, workmen, and remuneration. At some point between 1622 and 1627, the comptroller of Finance Cornelis De Backer found himself forced to reject a request for a raise from the painter and court architect Jacques Francart, which he felt overstepped the bounds not a little.[42] He indignantly pointed out that the court architect only had to 'faire desseigns, plans reliefs et aultres choses depandans de l'architecture', but that all other matters relating to the construction site and its management were the responsibility of the comptroller and of the supervisors nominated by the finance administration; indeed, these civil servants upon occasion had drawn up simple plans, elevations and perspective views themselves. Francart wanted to take too much upon himself, contrary to his colleagues Hardouin, Mathieu Boullin, Wenzel Cobergher, Henry Meerte and others who had served the archdukes before him in the duchy of Brabant, and contrary to 'the famous architect Jacques Du Brœucq at the time of Mary of Hungary'. The building accounts for Binche and Mariemont bear this out, but only to a certain degree. Du Brœucq is paid for designs and works of sculpture he carries out personally, e.g. the design for the coffered ceiling and the panelling executed by Philippe de Nivelles, and the famous arm-bearing herms and the marble chimneypieces in the great hall at Binche, which he himself sculpted (fig. 12).[43] On the other hand, he drew his famous wage of 200 pounds right from the start, i.e. from 12 May 1545, when clearance work on the site at Binche had only just begun.[44] Nevertheless, taken all in all, De Backer is guilty only of a slight exaggeration. As Rafael Domínguez Casas has shown in a recent article, the administration of construction work for the duke of Burgundy, especially in Brabant, had evolved by Du Brœucq's time into a strictly regulated, hierarchical and centrally managed service, and only the fragmented governing system of the Low Countries made it impossible to extend this system to the whole of the territory.[45] In Spain, however, no such impediment existed; the centralised 'Junta de Obras de casas y bosques', created after the Brabantine model, would serve Charles V and especially Philip II well. Within this system, the designer was indeed relegated to a relatively subordinated position.

On one level only, the artist reigned supreme. In matters of design, patron and architect were able to discuss 'mesures et ornemens d'architecture' (De Backer's words) on an equal footing. 'Architecture' – a new-fangled term, introduced into the Flemish language in 1539, and which should rightly be translated as 'architectural design' rather than as 'the art of construction' – interested both the patron and the architect, according to the theoretical texts current in the court milieu: Pomponius Gauricus's *De Sculptura* (Antwerp 1528, published by Cornelis and Johannes Grapheus); Alberti's treatise (in the Latin, 1485 version); various Vitruvius

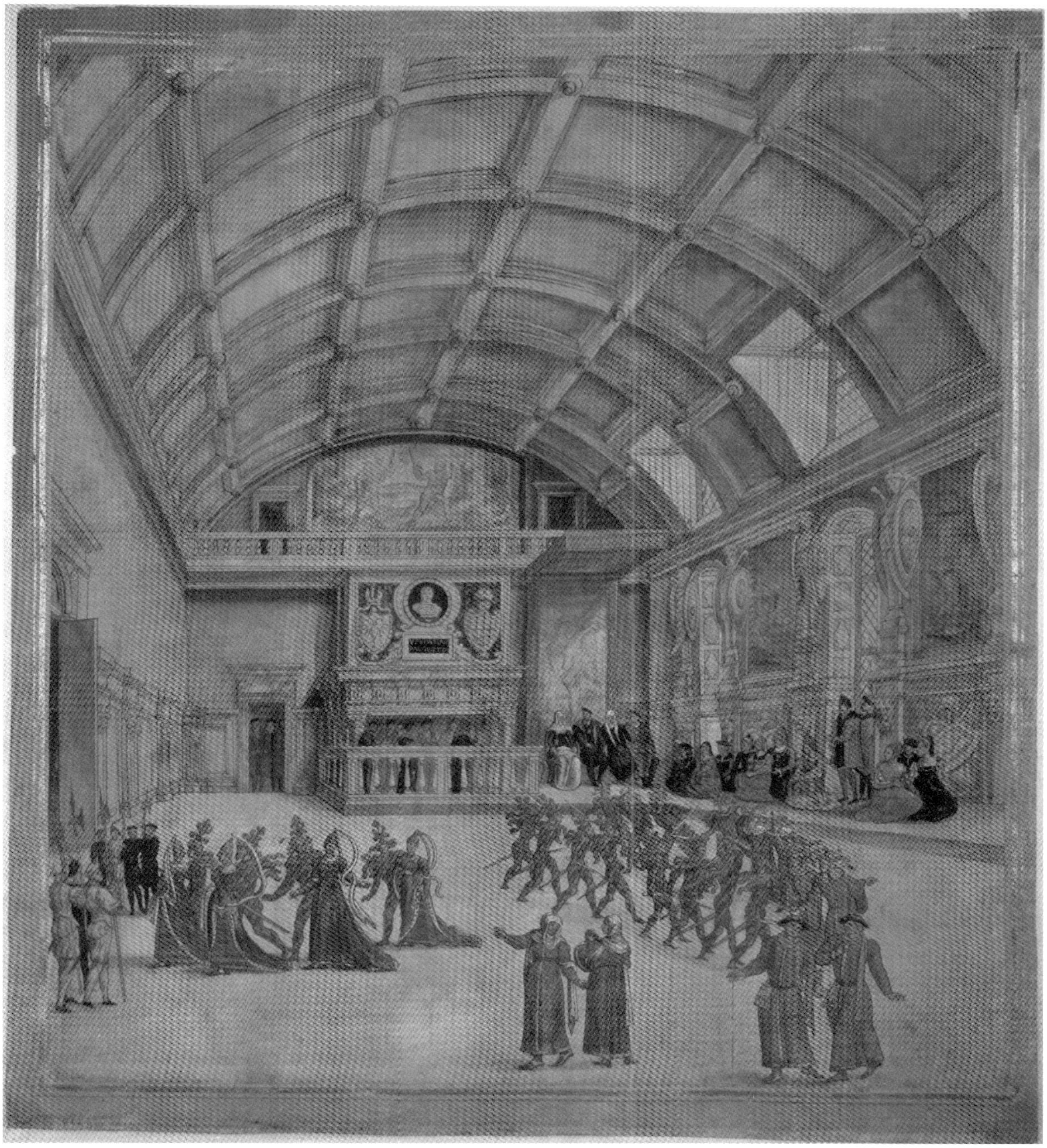

Fig. 12. Binche, great hall on the upper floor, shown during the masked ball on August 28, 1549. Anonymous artist, pen and ink, washed drawing, 398 x 379 mm. Brussels, Royal Library Albert I, Drawings collection, F 12930 plano C

editions, among which the Como, 1521, edition by Cesare Cesariano, and the Strasburg, 1543, edition based on the former; Diego de Sagredo's *Medidas del romano* (French version, Paris ca. 1530); and especially Pieter Coecke van Aelst's publications, his Vitruvian excerpt *Die inventie der colommen* (Antwerp 1539) and his translations of Serlio's books.[46] The latter – expensive in-folios – specifically addressed themselves to all 'lovers of architecture', i.e. the patrons rather than the various craftsmen interested in the right way to construct antique ornament.[47] Most of Coecke's Serlio translations were present in Mary of Hungary's library, as befitted the works of the 'libraire de l'Imperialle Maiesté'.[48] Coecke aptly dedicated his French translation of Serlio's Fourth Book (Antwerp 1542) to her, since she appreciated 'choses anticques et authenticques'.[49] Indeed, the subtle transformation Serlio's Fourth Book

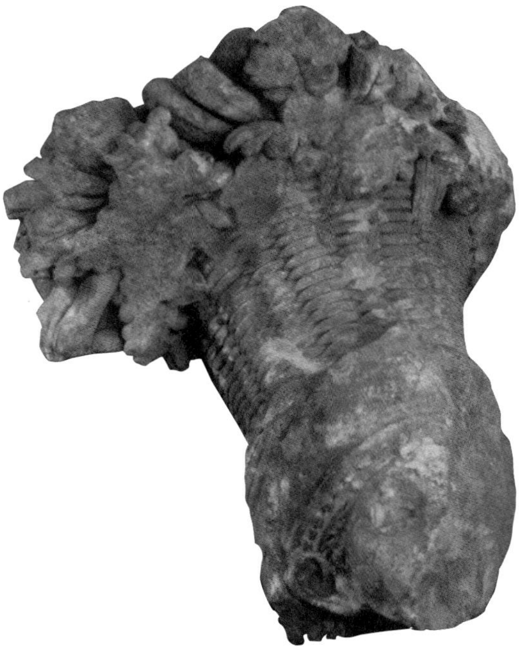

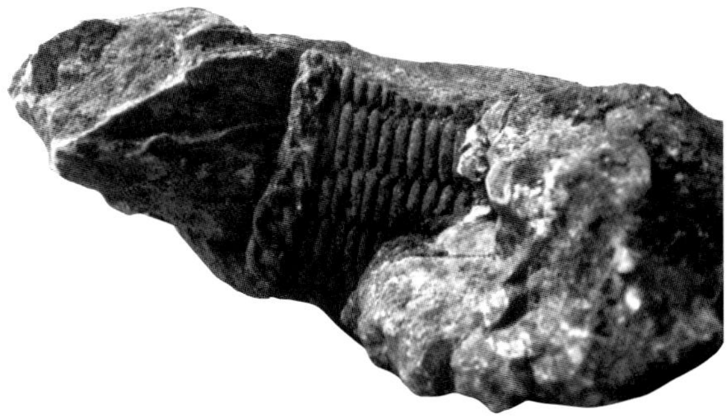

Fig. 13. (a. and b.) Boussu, Caryatid's heads in Avesnes stone, recovered from the north ditch (photo author, 1995)

underwent at Coecke's hands, tellingly speaks of Mary's specific interests in architecture. The revised text does not speak about the essentially modern character of the five-order system: Coecke took care to present the treatise as a purely Vitruvian text, in which the true principles of antique architecture would be revealed, or, as he put it, 'translaté au prouffit de ceulx, qui en leurs Edifices veullent ensuyvre l'Anticquite Romaine: car par ce pourront cougnoistre toutz ordres d'edifices, & aussi avoir elucidation des plusieurs secretz dudict Vitruvius'.[50] He also corrected Serlio's vision of antiquity on numerous points, and added comments in a Vitruvian key, which evolved from one edition to another.[51]

The architecture Jacques Du Brœucq created for the regent, however, was truly modern, as was recognised by Hans Vredeman de Vries in his treatise *ARCHITECTURA Oder Bauung der Antiquen auss dem Vitruvius, woellches sein funff Colummen orden* (Antwerp 1577).[52] De Vries writes that although authors like Serlio and Vitruvius have demonstrated how to build according to the 'Italian antique manner' ('naer de antiquiteyte Italiaense maniere'), it is necessary to adapt this architecture to the customs of the Low Countries, and he cites Du Brœucq as one of the 'strong, ingenious masters and architects of great experience' who was capable of 'accomodating this architecture to this country's situation and necessities'.[53] This modern architecture could indeed accommodate the personal preferences of the regent, while appearing 'antique'. In Mariemont, the image of the Italian villa dominating its surroundings blended with the vision of the fairy-tale castle of chivalric romance, enhanced by the enchanted garden full of marvels in the best Burgundian-Habsburg tradition (fig. 11). The best example of 'modern antiquity', however, was offered by the great hall on the upper floor at the Binche palace (fig. 12). For the decoration of the wall opposite the entrance, Du Broeucq used the system invented only a short time before by Rosso and Primaticcio for Francis I's private gallery at Fontainebleau (1533–1540)[54], but now its theme is a celebration of imperial power, in keeping with Mary's status as regent and as a representative of Habsburg imperial rule.[55] Titian's and Coxcie's *Damned* (*Titius* or *Prometheus*, *Sisyphus*, *Tantalus* and *Ixion*), placed between the windows, were framed by figures sculpted in the round, i.e. herms bearing antique weaponry; underneath ran panelling carved with antique trophies and subdivided by pilasters topped by lions' heads. Du Brœucq used the traditional, easily worked white Avesnes stone for the herms, instead of the Italian 'stucco duro'. In addition, the monumental chimneypieces, one at each end of the room, followed the model of the so-called 'cheminées de Castille' in Francis I's château de Madrid in the Bois de

Boulogne (1541–1545); they were the only examples of this type to be found outside France.[56] Obviously, Mary of Hungary closely followed the artistic developments at the French court.[57] At the time, she was indeed still trying to obtain the use of the molds Primaticcio had made of the famous Cleopatra/Ariadne and the Nile in the Vatican, so that Leone Leoni could also provide her with bronze copies of these antiques.[58] She finally had to be content with stucco copies, made by Luca Lancia di San Germano between 1550 and 1553, and placed in the garden grotto at Binche.[59] In Mariemont, the 'sallette' or dining room on the first floor was decorated with thirteen stucco statues by Luca Lancia, one of them a Venus in the antique manner.[60] This decoration seems to have been closer in spirit to the gentle nymphs of Fontainebleau. Du Brœucq's chimneypieces in the great hall at Binche served to display the antique busts of Hadrian and Julius Cæsar, placed in the central tondo; Mary of Hungary had acquired these antiques – for far too much money, as she was wont to complain, according to Cabanillas – in Rome.[61] The Fontainebleau repertory must have influenced the work at Boussu, too, as one of the finds made eight years ago seems to suggest. The two caryatids' heads, which must have decorated the back door leading, across a bridge, to a circular island with grotto pavillon, follow Fontainebleau models (figs. 13a–b): this is shown by their elongated eyes and lowly placed, big ears, which evoke Rosso's Egyptian herms at the Pavillon des Armes, and by the baskets with fruit and flowers on their heads, which are close to the caryatids in the Chambre du Roi.[62]

After the devastation wrought by the French army upon Binche, the regent briefly toyed with the idea of a grandiose restoration, which would have meant demolishing part of the town houses surrounding the palace. Du Brœucq visited her several times in September 1554 and March 1555 to discuss these plans, travelling to Antwerp, Turnhout and Arras to do so.[63] However, in 1556, when the first restoration work in Binche and Mariemont was under way, Du Brœucq's pension was reduced by half to 100 pounds a year: his patron left the Low Countries for Spain, to retire from public life.[64] She no longer needed a Court Architect.

## Abbreviations

ARAB : Brussels, Algemeen Rijksarchief

BNP: Bibliothèque nationale, Paris

KBB: Brussels, Royal Library Albert I

# NOTES

1. ARAB, *Audiëntie*, document dated on 4 August 1593. Cited after Auguste Pinchart in Robert Hedicke, *Jacques Dubrœucq de Mons*, Brussels 1911 (*Annales du cercle archéologique de Mons*, XL), pp. 433–434. On Lepoivre, see Charles van den Heuvel, 'Pierre Le Poivre (1546–1626), Engineer of the King, and the Representation of Architecture', in Werner Thomas and Luc Duerloo (eds.), *Albert and Isabella 1598–1621. Essays*, Turnhout, 1998, pp. 198–202.

2. Krista De Jonge, 'Court Residences and Court Architects', in Thomas and Duerloo 1998 (as in note 1), pp. 191–198. Philippe Bragard, 'The Archducal Engineers', *ibidem*, pp. 213–215.

3. 'Et di presente vivono Jacopo Bruecq nato vicono a S. Omero gentilhuomo grande scultore, & famoso architettore; ordin/ Bossu & poi Marimont, & altri superbi edifitij alla Regina d'Ungheria Reggente del paese ...'. Lodovico Guicciardini, *Descrittione... di tutti i Paesi Basi, altrimenti detti Germania inferiore*, Antwerp, Guglielmus Silvius, in-fol., 1567, p. 101.

4. See in general Hedicke 1912 (as in note 1), pp. 19–165, 362–373. Jan-Karel Steppe, *Het koordoksaal in de Nederlanden* (*Verhandelingen van de Koninklijke Vlaamse Academie voor Wetenschappen, Letteren en Schone Kunsten van België. Klasse der Schone Kunsten*, nr. 7), Brussels, 1952, pp. 314–233. Micheline Sonkes, 'Jacques Dubrœucq et le jubé de Sainte-Waudru à Mons', *Revue des archéologues et historiens d'art de Louvain*, III, 1970, pp. 121–130. Robert Didier, 'Les œuvres du sculpteur Jacques Du Brœucq', in [cat. exh.] *Jacques Du Brœucq, sculpteur et architecte de la Renaissance*, Mons, 1985 pp. 31–102.

5. Documents cited by William Eisler, *The Impact of the Emperor Charles V upon the Visual Arts*, Ph.D. Thesis, The Pennsylvania State University, 1983, pp. 85–85, 303–306. Krista De Jonge and Marcel Capouillez (eds.), *Le château de Boussu* (*Monuments et Sites, Etudes et Documents*, 8), Jambes, 1998, pp. 136–141. Krista De Jonge, 'Les jardins de Jacques Du Brœucq et de Jacques Hollebecque à Binche, Mariemont et Boussu', in Carmen Añón Feliú (ed.), *Felipe II, el rey íntimo. Jardín y Naturaleza en el siglo XVI*, Madrid, 1998, pp. 212–213.

6. About this export phenomenon, see Hanno Walter Kruft, 'Un cortile rinascimentale italiano nella Sierra Nevada: La Calahorra', *Antichità Viva*, 1969, 2, pp. 35–51. Elena Parma Armani, 'Il secolo d'oro dei Genovesi: il Cinquecento. Una svolta internazionale', in *La scultura a Genova e in Liguria dalle origini al Cinquecento*, Genua, 1987, I, pp. 267–345. Franco Renzo Pesenti, 'Portali del manierismo a Genova', *ibidem*, pp. 347–365. Rosa López Torrijos, 'La scultura genovese in Spagna', *ibidem*, pp. 366–393. Beatriz Tejero Villareal, 'Las fuentes genovesas en los jardines de Felipe II', in *Felipe II, el rey íntimo* (as in note 5), pp. 399–420. Rosa López Torrijos, 'La relación del primer Marqués de Santa Cruz con las Artes. Datos inéditos sobre obras y colecciones', in *El arte en las cortes de Carlos V y Felipe II. IX jornadas de arte del Centro de Estudios Históricos*, Madrid, 1999, pp. 409–418.

7. Krista De Jonge, 'Le langage architectural de Jacques Du Brœucq: entre Rome et Fontainebleau', in De Jonge and Capouillez 1998 (as in note 5), pp. 182–185.

8. There is scant information on Jean de Hennin in the biography of his son Maximilian. J. Lefèvre, 'Maximilien de Hénin-Liétard, comte de Boussu', in *Biographie Nationale, Supplément 4*, XXXII, Brussels, 1964, pp. 63–64.

9. Cologne 1550, republished in Antonius Sanderus, *De (...) Catholici Reges in Belgio Conciliis dissertatuncula*, 1659, part: *Status Aulicus*, Brussels, 1660, p. 18. We consulted a copy bound with Antonius Sanderus, *Presbyteri Chorographia sacra Brabanti (...)*, Brussels, 1659–1669, in KBB, VH 27225[2] C RP.

10. Like his father Philip and his grandfather Pierre de Hennin-Liétard before him. Hans Cools, *Mannen met macht. Edellieden en de moderne staat in de Bourgondisch-Habsburgse landen (1475–1530)*, Zutphen, 2001, pp. 232–233. Alain Salamagne, 'Philippe II de Croÿ, seigneur d'Arschot, l'organisation défensive des Pays-Bas méridionaux au début du XVIe siècle et la genèse de la fortification bastionnée (1521–1528)', *Mémoires de la Société archéologique & historique de l'Arrondissement d'Avesnes (Nord)*, XXXII, 1992, pp. 36–37.

11. E. Albèri (ed.), *Relazioni degli ambasciatori veneti al Senato, Ser. I, Relazioni degli stati europei, tranne l'Italia*, Florence, 1839–1863, I, pp. 294–296.

12. BNP, ms. fr. 31836, first part.

13. L. Sicking and R. Fagel, 'In het kielzog van Columbus. De heer van Veere en de Nieuwe Wereld, 1517–1527', *Bijdragen en mededelingen betreffende de geschiedenis der Nederlanden*, CXIV, 1999, pp. 313–327. J.J. Pérez Preciado, 'Cañón Hercules del señor de Veere Maximilian de Borgoña', in Fernando Marías and Felipe Pereda (eds.), *Carlos V. Las armas y las letras*, Madrid, 2000, pp. 340–341. Cools 2001 (as in note 10), pp. 163–165.

14. Lefèvre 1964 (as in note 8).

15. Loys Guicciardin, *Description de touts les Pays-Bas, autrement appellez la Germanie inférieure, ou Basse Allemagne*, Calais, Abraham Maire, in-8°, 1609, pp. 445–446. Dagmar Eichberger and Lisa Beaven, 'Family Members and Political Allies: The Portrait Collection of Margaret of Austria', *Art Bulletin*, LXXVII, 1995, pp. 225–248.

16. De Jonge and Capouillez 1998 (as in note 5), pp. 141–142.

17. Krista De Jonge, 'L'image de la *domus* noble dans les anciens Pays-Bas de la Renaissance: le cas de Boussu', in Jean Guillaume (ed.), *Vraie et fausse fortification: les 'signes militaires' dans l'architecture de la Renaissance. Actes du colloque tenu à Tours du 13 au 16 juin 2000*, Paris, in preparation. Alain Salamagne, 'Aux origines de la fortification bastionnée. Le boulevard d'Antoing et la famille monumentale des boulevards de plan polygonal', *Revue des archéologues et historiens d'art de Louvain*, XXV, 1992, pp. 31–62.

18. AEM *Cartes et plans* 32. De Jonge and Capouillez 1998 (as in note 5), p. 45.

19. He is defined as such in the account books pertaining to Binche (1545–1549), e.g. ARAB *Rekenkamer* 27302, fol. 200verso. Hedicke 1911 (as in note 1), p. 404.

20. Report of 16 May 1556 (Archivo General de Simancas, Obras y Bosques: Segovia, Leg. 1). F. Iñiguez Almech, *Casas reales y jardines de Felipe II* (*Cuadernos de Trabajo de la Escuela española de história y arqueología, secunda época*, I), Rome 1952, p. 165.

21. De Jonge and Capouillez 1998 (as in note 5).

22. *Up die maniere van Brabant*: source from the Mosan valley (1542) cited by Ruud Meischke, *et al.*, *Huizen in Nederland.*

*Utrecht, Noord-Brabant en de oostelijke provincies. Architectuurhistorische verkenningen aan de hand van het bezit van de Vereniging Hendrick de Keyser,* Zwolle, 2000, p. 75, after Eduard Van Even, *Renseignements inédits sur la construction du refuge de l'abbaye de Herkenrode à Hasselt (1542–1545)*, s.l., 1874.

23. De Jonge 1998 (as in note 7), pp. 161–170. Krista De Jonge, 'Aktuelle Probleme der Renaissanceforschung in den Niederlanden. Hof und Hofarchitekten – der Casus Jacques Du Brœucq', in Günter Bers and Conrad Doose (eds.), *Italienische Renaissancebaukunst an Schelde, Maas und Niederrhein. Stadtanlagen – Zivilbauten – Wehranlagen*, Jülich, 1998, pp. 51–70.

24. As commented upon by Bernardo Navagero. Albèri 1839 (as in note 11), I, pp. 294–296. Christina Hoffmann, *Das Spanische Hofzeremoniell von 1500 to 1700 (Erlanger Historische Studien*, 8), Frankfurt a.M., 1985, pp. 34, 57–73.

25. Fol. 243verso. A.F. Mirande and G.S. Overdiep (eds.), *Het schilder-boek van Carel van Mander. Het leven der doorluchtige Nederlandsche en Hoogduitsche schilders*, Amsterdam, 1943, pp. 306–307.

26. ARAB *Rekenkamer* 27309, fol. 37verso. Hedicke 1911 (as in note 1), p. 414. Jacques Debergh, 'Luc Lange "molleur en plattre" actif en Hainaut entre 1550 et 1553', *Belgisch Tijdschrift voor Oudheidkunde en Kunstgeschiedenis*, LIX, 1990, pp. 75–90.

27. J.F. Heijbroek, D. Roorda, M. Schapelhouman and E. de Wielde (eds.), *Met Huygens op reis: tekeningen en dagboeknotities van Constantijn Huygens jr. (1628–1697), secretaris van stadhouder-koning Willem III*, Zutphen, 1983, p. 151.

28. ARAB *Rekenkamer* 27302, 27305, 27306 vol. 1–2. Hedicke 1911 (as in note 1), pp. 252–293, 398–424. Krista De Jonge, 'Le palais de Charles Quint à Bruxelles. Ses dispositions intérieures aux XVe et XVIe siècles et le cérémonial de Bourgogne', in Jean Guillaume (ed.), *Architecture et vie sociale. L'organisation intérieure des grandes demeures à la fin du Moyen Age et à la Renaissance (De Architectura)*, Paris, 1994, pp. 114–116.

29. De Jonge and Capouillez 1998 (as in note 5), pp. 109–113, 145–158.

30. In Mechelen, for instance, Eustache Le Prince made the stone pillars for the Palace of the Great Council designed by Rombout Keldermans (deliveries between 1526 and 1532). Frieda van Tyghem, 'Bestuursgebouwen in Brabant en Vlaanderen', in Herman Janse (ed.), *Keldermans. Een architectonisch netwerk in de Nederlanden,* Den Haag, 1987, p. 123. Jean-Louis Van Belle, *Les maîtres de carrière d'Arquennes sous l'Ancien Régime. Un métier. Des hommes*, Brussels, 1990, p. 39. See also *id.*, *Nouveau dictionnaire des signes lapidaires – Belgique et Nord de la France*, Louvain-la-Neuve, 1994.

31. ARAB *Rekenkamer* 27306, part 2, fol. 435verso, fol. 438verso.

32. Krista De Jonge, 'Nouvelles perspectives sur 'une maison de moult grand plaisance' royale: Mariemont', *Revue de l'Art*, in preparation. ARAB *Rekenkamer* 27306, part 2, 2nd account, fol. 597verso.

33. *Commentaires* ..., 1554, cited by Samuel Glotz, 'De Marie de Hongrie aux Gilles de Binche. Introduction critique aux *Triomphes* de Binche célébrés du 22 au 31 août 1549', *Les cahiers binchois*, XIII, 1995, p. 123. Mary of Hungary personally took over the position of grand master of the hunt ('grand veneur') in Brabant. Jacqueline Kerkhoff, "Het hof van Maria van Hongarije in de Nederlanden", in Jacqueline Kerkhoff and Bob van den Boogert (eds.), (exh. cat.) *Maria van Hongarije 1505–1558. Koningin tussen keizers en kunstenaars* (Utrecht, 's-Hertogenbosch, 1993*)*, Zwolle, 1993, pp. 173–174.

34. Guicciardini (as in note 3), p. 267.

35. See also Krista De Jonge, 'L'environnement des châteaux dans les Pays-Bas méridionaux au XVIe siècle et au début du XVIIe siècle', in Jean Guillaume (ed.), *Architecture, jardin, paysage. L'environnement du château et de la villa aux XVe et XVIe siècles (De Architectura)*, Paris, 1999, pp. 185–206 and Krista De Jonge 1998 (as in note 5), pp. 198–206.

36. Guicciardini (as in note 3), p. 267. Other sources cited by Glotz 1995 (as in note 33), pp. 122–124, 133–135.

37. ARAB *Rekenkamer* 27305, fol. 157verso; 27306, vol. I, fol. 275recto. Hedicke 1911 (as in note 1), pp. 406, 409. Krista De Jonge, 'Architekturpraxis in den Niederlanden in der frühen Neuzeit: Die Rolle des italienischen Militärarchitekten; der *status quaestionis*', in Günter Bers and Conrad Doose (eds.), *Der italienische Architekt Alessandro Pasqualini (1493–1559) und die Renaissance am Niederrhein: Kenntnisstand und Forschungsperspektiven*, Jülich, 1994, pp. 363–383. Krista De Jonge, 'Exemplum di progettazione rinascimentale nei Paesi Bassi: l'opera di Jacques du Brœucq', *Annali di architettura*, IX, 1997, pp. 218–232. On Mary of Hungary's court artists, see in general Bob van den Boogert, 'Macht en pracht. Het mecenaat van Maria van Hongarije', in Kerkhoff and Van den Boogert 1993 (as in note 33), pp. 273-276.

38. Jozef Duverger, M.J. Onghena and P.K. van Daalen, 'Nieuwe gegevens aangaande XVIde eeuwse beeldhouwers in Brabant en Vlaanderen', *Mededelingen van de Koninklijke Vlaamse Academie voor Wetenschappen, Letteren en Schone Kunsten van België, Klasse der Schone Kunsten*, XV, 1953, 3, pp. 3–95, especially pp. 6–26. Domien Roggen, 'Jehan Mone, artiste de l'empereur', *Gentse Bijdragen tot de Kunstgeschiedenis*, XIV, 1953, pp. 207–245.

39. J. Lauwerys, 'De kerk van Hoogstraten, I (tot 1555)', *Jaarboek van de Koninklijke Hoogstratens Oudheidkundige kring*, XXX, 1960. J. Lauwerys, 'De kerk van Hoogstraten, II. Symboliek en iconografie', *Jaarboek van de Koninklijke Hoogstratens Oudheidkundige kring*, XXXIX, 1971. J. Lauwerys, 'Het kasteel van Hoogstraten', *Jaarboek van de Koninklijke Hoogstratens Oudheidkundige kring*, XLVI, 1978 and XLVII, 1979. Johanna Leys, 'De invloed van Anthonis I en Rombout II Keldermans op de kasteelfortificaties', in Janse 1987 (as in note 30), pp. 161–162. Raymond De Ceulaer, *De Sint-Catharinakerk te Hoogstraten* (Inventaris van het kunstpatrimonium van de provincie Antwerpen 2), Gent, 1988, pp. XII–XIII. Patrick Valvekens, *Bijdrage tot de studie van het Celestijnenklooster te Heverlee. Het mecenaat van de families van Croÿ-van Arenberg. Reconstructie van het kerkinterieur en nader onderzoek van het werk van Jan Mone in deze kerk*, M.A., Leuven 1980. *Id.*, 'Nieuwe gegevens over het Celestijnenklooster te Heverlee, gevolgd door een nader onderzoek van de sculptuur van Jan Mone voor de Celestijnenkerk', *Jaarboek van de Geschied- en Oudheidkundige Kring voor Leuven en omgeving*, XXIII, 1983, pp. 3–69. *Id.*, 'Iconografische bronnen voor de studie van het Celestijnenklooster te Heverlee', *De vrienden van Heverleebos en Meerdaalwoud. Jaarbulletin*, 1985, pp. 31–60. *Id.*, 'De Celestijnenpriorij', in *Leuven & Croÿ. Een stad en een geslacht*, Brussels–Leuven, 1987, pp. 18–23. Raymond van Uytven, 'Leuvense glazeniers in het Celestijnenklooster te Heverlee tijdens de zestiende eeuw', *Arca Lovaniensis artes atque historiae reserans documenta. Jaarboek*, 1974, pp. 174–176, 182–184. Bart Minnen, *Het hertogdom Aarschot onder Karel van Croÿ (1595–1612). Kadasters en gezichten (Albums de Croÿ)*, Brussels, 1993, pp. 178–237. Ruud Meischke and Frieda van Tyghem, 'Huizen en hoven gebouwd onder leiding van Anthonis I en Rombout II', in Janse 1987 (as in note 30), pp. 150–153. Dirk Van Eenooge, Thierry Delcommune and Marcel Celis, 'Onder het Koningsplein te Brussel: de hofkapel van Karel V', *Monumenten en Landschappen*, XIX, 2000, 1, pp. 4–38.

40. Georges Marlier, *La Renaissance flamande. Pierre Coeck d'Alost*, Brussels, 1966, pp. 21–31, 45–46, 379–390. H. De la Fontaine Verwey, 'Pieter Coecke van Aelst en zijn boeken over architectuur', in H. de la Fontaine Verwey (ed.), *Uit de wereld*

*van het boek I. Humanisten, dwepers en rebellen in de zestiende eeuw*, Amsterdam 1975, pp. 51–68. *Id.*, 'Pieter Coecke van Aelst and the publication of Serlio's book on architecture', *Quaerendo*, VI, 1976, pp. 167–194. Rudy Rolf, *Pieter Coecke van Aelst en zijn architectuuruitgaves van 1539 (P.R.A.K. 1)*, Amsterdam, 1978. Jacques Offerhaus, 'Pieter Coecke et l'introduction des traités d'architecture aux Pays-Bas', in Jean Guillaume (ed.), *Les traités d'architecture de la Renaissance (De Architectura)*, Paris, 1988, pp. 443–452. John B. Bury, 'Serlio. Some bibliographical notes', in Ch. Thoenes (ed.), *Sebastiano Serlio*, Milan, 1989, pp. 92–101. Krista De Jonge, 'Vitruvius, Alberti and Serlio. Architectural Treatises in the Low Countries 1530–1620', in V. Hart and P. Hicks (eds.), *Paper Palaces. The rise of the Renaissance architectural treatise*, New Haven–London, 1998, pp. 281–296. Krista De Jonge, '*"Anticse wercken"*: la découverte de l'architecture antique dans la pratique architecturale des anciens Pays-Bas. Livres de modèles et traités 1517–1599', in Michèle-Caroline Heck, Frédérique Lemerle, Yves Pauwels (eds.), *Théorie des arts et création artistique dans l'Europe du Nord du XVIe au début du XVIIIe siècle. Actes du colloque international*, Lille, 2002, pp. 55–74.

41. Statues by Jean Guilgot or Wilho. Duverger, Onghena and van Daalen 1953 (as in note 38), pp. 49–50. Eddy D'Hondt, *Extraits des comptes du domaine de Bruxelles des XVe et XVIe siècles concernant les artistes de la Cour (Miscellanea archivistica Studia*, 4), Brussels, 1989, pp. 66–68. De Jonge 1994 (as in note 28), pp. 113–114.

42. ARAB *Hofwerken* 192, *Correspondance*, dossier 7, document 2. Annemie De Vos, 'Hof van Den Haag en hof van Brussel (1590–1630). Structurele organisatie van de bouwprojecten tijdens de regering van prins Maurits en van de aartshertogen Albrecht en Isabella', *Bulletin van de Koninklijke Nederlandse Oudheidkundige Bond*, XCVIII, 1999, 5–6, pp. 201–204.

43. De Jonge 1997 (as in note 37).

44. ARAB *Rekenkamer* 27302, fol. 204verso. Hedicke 1911 (as in note 1), p. 421.

45. Rafael Domínguez Casas, 'Carlos V y la introducción del sistema administrativo y estético del ducado de Brabante en los palacios reales españoles', in *Bruxelles et la vie urbaine. Archives, art, histoire. Recueil d'études dédiées à la mémoire d'Arlette Smolar-Meynart*, Brussels, 2001, pp. 749–791.

46. Floris Prims, 'Het eigen werk van Cornelis Grapheus (1482–1558). I. II.', in Floris Prims (ed.), *Antwerpiensia. Losse bijdragen tot de Antwerpsche geschiedenis*, Antwerp, 1938, pp. 172–190. Gerard van Wezel, *Het paleis van Hendrik III graaf van Nassau te Breda* (De Nederlandse Monumenten van Geschiedenis en Kunst), Zeist–Zwolle, 1999, pp. 163–184. E.M. Kavaler, 'Being the Count of Nassau. Refiguring identity in space, time and stone', *Beeld en zelfbeeld in de Nederlandse kunst, 1550–1750 / Image and Self-Image in Netherlandish Art, 1550–1750 (Nederlands Kunsthistorisch Jaarboek*, 46), 1995, pp. 13–51. S. Muller Fz., 'Getuigenverhoor te Antwerpen over het maken van ontwerpen van gebouwen in de 16e eeuw door schilders, goudsmeden, timmerlieden en metselaars', *Archief voor Nederlandsche Kunstgeschiedenis*, ed. by F.D.O. Obreen, IV, Rotterdam 1881–1882, pp. 227–245. Hessel Miedema, 'Over de waardering van architekt en beeldende kunstenaar in de zestiende eeuw', *Oud Holland*, XCIV, 1980, pp. 71–84. See also note 40.

47. *Generale Reglen der Architecturen op de vyve manieren van edificien, te weten, thuscana dorica, ionica, corintha ende composita, met den exemplen der antiquiteiten die int meeste deel concorderen met de leerinhge van Vitruvio*, Antwerp, 1539, dedicatory note.

48. ARAB *Ms divers* 391, 19th-century copy with translation of the Simancas inventory. Claudine Lemaire, 'La bibliothèque des imprimés de la reine Marie de Hongrie régente des Pays-Bas, 1505–1558', *Bibliothèque d'Humanisme et Renaissance*, LVIII, 1996, 1, pp. 119–139.

49. *Reigles generales de l'Architecture, sur les cincq manieres d'edifices, ascavoir, Thuscane, Doricq[ue]; Ionicq[ue]; Corinthe, & Co[m]posite, avec les exemples danticquitez, selon la doctrine de Vitruue*, Antwerp, 1542, dedicatory note.

50. *Ibidem.*

51. The first Flemish edition of the Fourth Book (as in note 47) has comments added between asterisks on fol. Bi verso, Biiii verso, Diiii recto, Diiii verso, Ei recto, Eiiii verso, Iii verso, Iiii recto, Iiii verso, Ki recto, and Riiii recto. The second Flemish edition of the Fourth Book (*Reglen van Metselrijen op de vijve manieren van Edificien te wetene Thuscana Dorica Ionica Corinthia ende Composita, ende daer by gesedt die exemplen vanden Antijcquen die in demeeste deel met de leeringe van Vitruvio overcommen*, Antwerp, 1549) has different comments, which are more strictly Vitruvian: Coecke insists even more upon the importance of following the right rules. The first French edition of the Fourth Book (as in note 49) also has different comments, as has the third, revised French edition (1550).

52. Hans Mielke, *Hans Vredeman de Vries: Verzeichnis der Stichwerken und Beschreibung seines Stils sowie Beiträge zum Werk Gerard Groennings*, Berlin, 1967, pp. 48–51. Peter Fuhring, *The New Hollstein. Dutch & Flemish Etchings, Engravings and Woodcuts 1450–1700. Vol. XLVII. Vredeman de Vries, Part II, 1572–1630*, Rotterdam, 1997, pp. 56–85, nos. 408–431. Henk Nalis *et al.*, *The New Hollstein. Dutch & Flemish Etchings, Engravings and Woodcuts 1450–1700. The Van Doetecum Family, Part III. The Antwerp Years, 1554–1575, The Years of Refuge 1576–c. 1583*, Rotterdam, 1998, pp. 190–201, nos. 739–762. Petra Sophia Zimmermann, *Die Architectura von Hans Vredeman de Vries. Entwicklung der Renaissance-architektur in Mitteleuropa*, Munich–Berlin, 2002. *Id.*, 'Der Vitruvianismus und die *Architectura* von Hans Vredeman de Vries', in Heiner Borggrefe *et al.* (eds.), *Hans Vredeman de Vries und die Renaissance im Norden*, Munich, 2002, pp. 71–80.

53. *ARCHITECTURA* ..., chapter on the Doric order, s. fol.: 'Hoe wel dat den vermaerden Vitruvius, Sebastiaen Serlio, ende den experten Iacobus Androuetus Cerseau, ende meer andere diversche sorten der facien, edeficien, fronten oft gevels, naer de antiquiteyte Italiaense maniere en gebruyc haerder architecturen en bouwinghen ghestelt hebben, alsoomen in haerlieden en meer anderen meesters, baecken en patroonen bevindt, naer dien s' landts aert, wesen en ghebruyc, sonder cruys-vensters, en sonderlinghen groot licht soeckende, noch hooge verdiepinghen, dan breet en weynich verdiepens: maer in dese Nederlanden heeftmen een ander conditie, namelijck in steden van grooter negotien, daer de plaetsen cleyn en dier sijn, moetmen al in de hoochde tot veel gheriefs, met veel lichts te crijgen, inventeren en soecken, elck na sijn gheleghentheyt en plaetse, tsy groot oft cleijn, de meeste commodite ende dienst der edificien oft logamenten der architecturen soecken ende ghebruycken op sijn ghelegen plaetse, sulcx wel ghebruyct en gheobserveert hebben dese naergenoemde en meer andere cloecke ende ingenieuse meesters ende vervaren architecteurs deser Nederlanden ter eeren, als meester A. Floris, de vader van Cornelis Floris, meester Jacques van Berghen, meester Jan Gilgho, meester Anthonis Mockaert, M. Jan de Heere, superalij Cornelis Floris, tot Luyck M. Thomas voor Guilliame Paludani, ende noch meer andere die ick niet en kenne, dan haer wercken wel betoonen, hun ingenie int bewijs der architecturen, te weten t' accomoderen naer gheleghentheyt deses landes ghebruycinghe en dienst, meer dan opt de Antiquen van noode is gheweest, sulcx men in elck deel oft partije bevinden mach, en ondersoecken t' mijne om een beter.'

54. 'La galerie François Ier au château de Fontainebleau', *Revue de l'Art*, 1972, pp. 16–17. Henri Zerner, 'Le système décoratif de la Galerie François Ier à Fontainebleau', in André Chastel (ed.), *Actes du colloque international sur l'art de Fontainebleau*, Paris, 1975, pp. 31–35. Wolfram Prinz, *Galleria. Storia e tipologia di uno spazio architettonico*, Ferrara, 1977. Michael Mezzatesta, 'The Façade of Leone Leoni's House in Milan, the

Casa degli Omenoni: The Artists and the Public', *Journal of the Society of Architectural Historians*, XLIV, 1985, 3, pp. 233–249. Bob van den Boogert, 'Macht en pracht. Het mecenaat van Maria van Hongarije', in Kerkhoff and Van den Boogert 1993 (as in note 33), p. 337. Krista De Jonge, 'Le langage architectural de Jacques Du Brœucq: entre Rome et Fontainebleau', in De Jonge and Capouillez 1998 (as in note 5), pp. 180–185.

55. See in general Kerkhoff and Van den Boogert 1993 (as in note 33).

56. Monique Chatenet, *Le château de Madrid au bois de Boulogne. Sa place dans les rapports franco-italiens autour de 1530*, Paris, 1987, pp. 117–118. *Id.*, 'Une nouvelle 'cheminée de Castille' à Madrid en France', *Revue de l'Art*, 91, 1991, pp. 36–38.

57. Jozef Duverger, 'Marie de Hongrie, gouvernante des Pays-Bas, et la Renaissance', in *Evolution générale et développements régionaux en histoire de l'art. Actes du XXIIe congrès international d'Histoire de l'Art, Budapest 1969*, Budapest, 1972, p. 722.

58. Maurice Van Durme, 'Antoon Perrenot van Granvelle en Leone Leoni', *Belgisch Tijdschrift voor Oudheidkunde en Kunstgeschiedenis*, XXVII, 1949, 3–4, pp. 653–678. *Lettere di artisti italiani ad Antoine Perrenot de Granvelle, Tiziano, Giovan Batista Mantovano, Primaticcio, Giovanni Paolo Poggini ad altri* (*Documenti e ricerche*, 7), Madrid, 1979, pp. 57–62.

59. Hedicke 1911 (as in note 1), pp. 413–414. Sylvie Pressouyre, 'Les fontes de Primatice à Fontainebleau', *Bulletin Monumental*, CXXVII, 1969, pp. 223–239. Debergh 1990 (as in note 26). Jacques Debergh, 'Luc Lange et Jacques Du Brœucq. Quatre considérations', *Belgisch Tijdschrift voor Oudheidkunde en Kunstgeschiedenis*, LXIII, 1994, pp. 63–72. De Jonge 1998 (as in note 5), p. 197.

60. Robert Wellens, 'Le domaine de Mariemont au XVIe siècle (1546–1598)', *Annales du Cercle archéologique de Mons*, LXIV, 1958–1961, pp. 105–107. Debergh 1990 (as in note 26).

61. Hedicke 1911 (as in note 1), pp. 409–410. Robert Petit (ed.), *Le très heureux voyage fait par très haut et puissant Prince don Philippe, fils du grand empereur Charles-Quint depuis l'Espagne jusqu'à ses domaines de la Basse-Allemagne... par Juan Cristoval Calvette de Estrella* (Société des Bibliophiles de Belgique), Brussels, 1873–1884, XI, p. 85. Hieronymo Cabanillas, *Relacion muy verdadera de las grandes fiestas que la Serenissima Reyna doña Maria ha hecho al Príncipe nuestro señor en Flandes*. Medina del Campo, Juan Rodríguez, 1549, republished by C. Pérez Pastor, *la Imprenda en Medina del Campo*, Madrid, 1895, p. 57.

62. De Jonge and Capouillez 1998 (as in note 5), pp. 133, 185. The caryatids in the Chambre du Roi date from 1534–1535, as does the Porte Egyptienne of the pavillon des Armes. Sylvie Béguin, 'Remarques sur la chambre du Roi', in Chastel 1975 (as in note 54), pp. 199–231. Françoise Boudon and Jean Blécon, *Le château de Fontainebleau de François Ier à Henri IV. Les bâtiments et leurs fonctions*, Paris, 1998, pp. 38–39.

63. Hedicke 1911 (as in note 1), pp. 419–421.

64. *Ibidem*, pp. 421–422.

# Aarschot and Solre. The Collections, Patronage and Influence in Spain of two Flemish Noblemen

*José Juan Pérez Preciado*

Jean de Croÿ, second count of Solre, and Philip of Aremberg, sixteenth duke of Aarschot, were two of the most important Flemish politicians at the Spanish court during the first half of the seventeenth century. Both of them spent part of their lives in Madrid, dedicating themselves to political affairs and forming a strong link between the courts of the Archdukes and Philip IV. From the Spanish capital they had contact with the Flemish artistic world through patronage or purchase of some of the best paintings by the best artists of that period. By the time they died in 1638 and 1641, respectively, these two noblemen had assembled excellent collections of paintings in their Spanish houses that were later sold on the local market. Some of these paintings and the artists who made them were until that moment unknown in Spain. The influence of the Solre and Aarschot collections in Madrid, the collectors who bought works at auction and the way the paintings were brought into Spain are the main subjects of this paper. Also of topical interest are the patronage of Croÿ and Aremberg in Flanders via their agents, their patronage of Spanish artists, their relationship to Spanish politics and collectors, and their influence on royal and court taste. All of these considerations offer an interesting approach to the study of the development of interest in Flemish art and artists in mid-century Spanish artistic circles.

Jean de Croÿ belonged to one of the most important families in Flanders, which had served the Spanish kings since the sixteenth century. He had been a member of the Order of the Golden Fleece since 1613, having been appointed by Philip III. But his closest relations with the Spanish crown began in the second decade of the seventeenth century.[1] While acting as governor and bailiff of the Hainaut region, he was one of the main collaborators of the cardinal of Cueva, who led the Spanish government in Flanders. Croÿ moved to the Spanish court soon after, and in 1624 he was appointed member of the Spanish Council of State, playing an important role in the *Junta de Almirantazgo*, an institution which dealt with Spanish maritime politics in northern Europe. Because of this activity, he was sent to the Baltic region as a diplomat in 1626 in order to combat Dutch naval power.

The titles and posts held by Croÿ in Spain suggest his privileged position as a link between Spain and Flanders. In 1624 he was appointed captain of the Archers of the Burgundian Royal Guard, an honorific position in the highly complicated world of palatine influence. It was entirely composed of Flemish members, most of them painters. These painters formed a network of Flemish artists in the Spanish court, with Croÿ as its influential head.[2] The highest point in Croÿ's career came in 1628 when he was appointed a member of the newly renovated Supreme Council of Flanders, thereby becoming an indispensable intermediary between Madrid and Brussels.

Croÿ's diplomatic activities allowed him easy access to the king. Moreover, he improved such circumstances with periodical gifts to Philip. For instance, in 1626 while Croÿ was in Germany, he sent Philip IV a certain number of horses. At other times, his consignments to Madrid included chests and boxes that Isabella Clara Eugenia sent to the queen of Spain.[3] Croÿ's position as intermediary of Isabella's dispatches is very interesting, since it is well-known that some of these dispatches contained Flemish paintings of the highest quality that she sent to the Spanish court.[4] Croÿ maintained contacts not only with the king, but also with other influential politicians and collectors, such as the marquis of Leganés. Although we have no direct document which demonstrates any exchange of paintings between these two

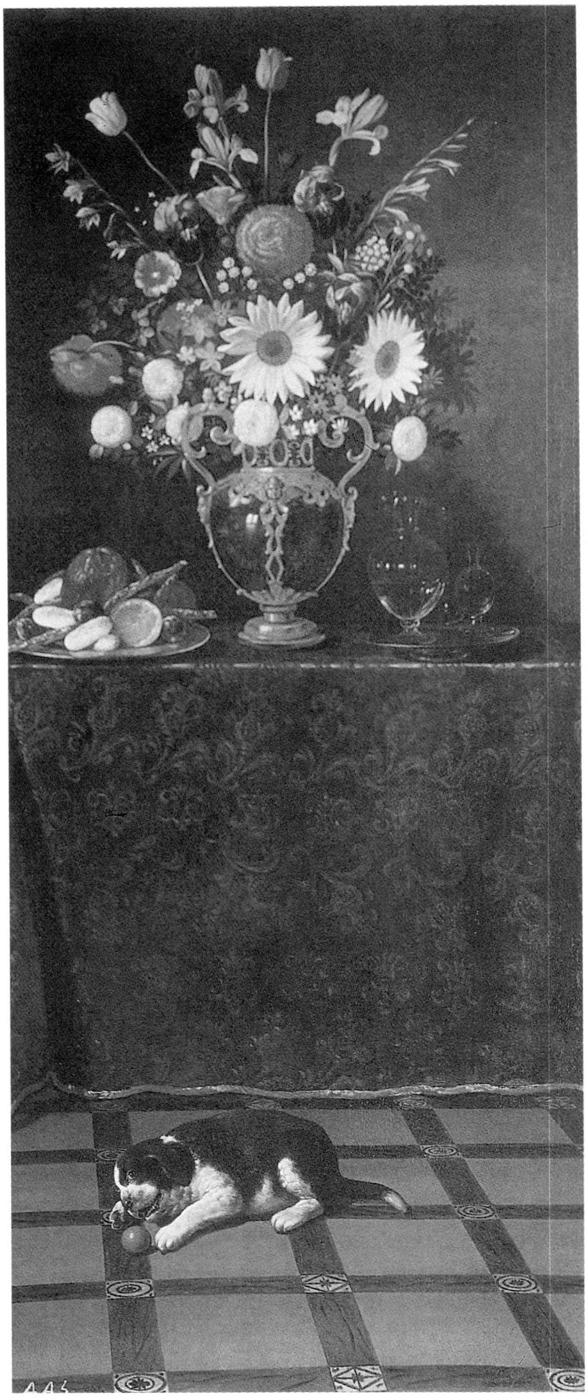

Fig. 1. Juan van der Hamen, *Still Life with Dog*. Madrid, Museo del Prado

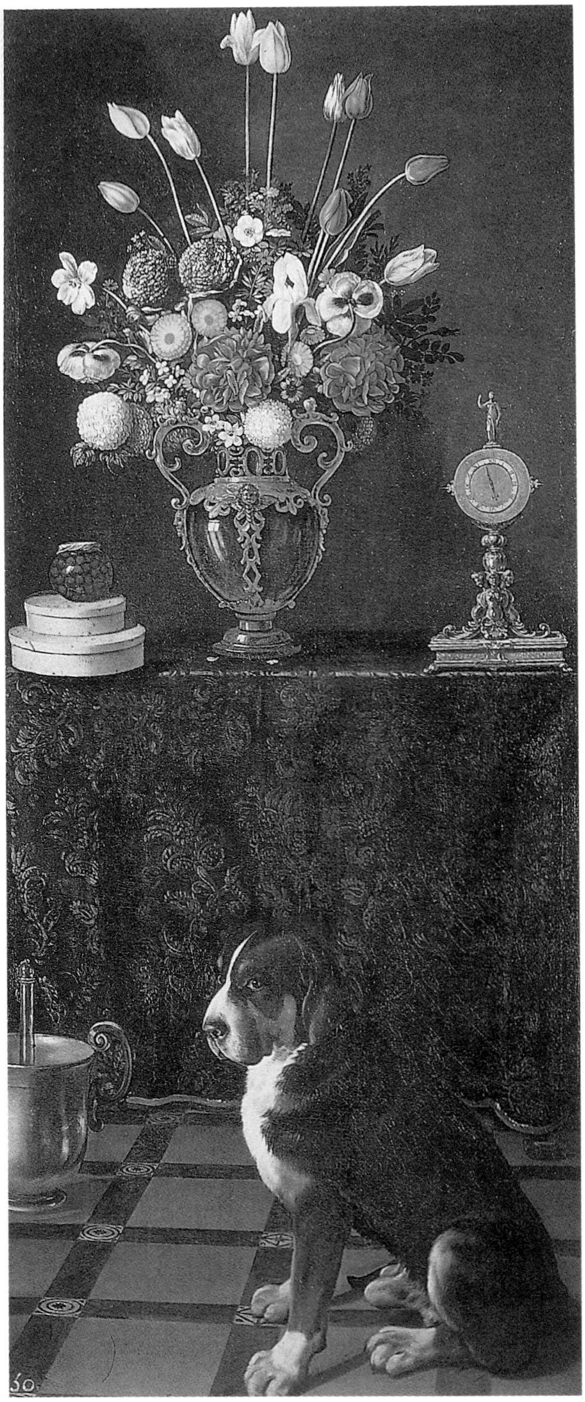

Fig. 2. Juan van der Hamen, *Still Life with Dog*. Madrid, Museo del Prado

noblemen, we can easily suppose it given that Croÿ sent the marquis' wife a shipment containing a large number of books in 1626.[5] Furthermore, Leganés supported Croÿ's candidature in the Flemish government in the event of Isabella's death, saying that Croÿ was the best candidate due to his *claro talento e intención*.[6] Other members of the Council of Flanders were also clearly tied to Croÿ, including Nicolas Bastón, secretary of the Council of Flanders, himself also a minor collector.[7]

Croÿ's position as intermediary between Flanders and Spain had special importance with respect to importing certain Flemish paintings into the Spanish court during the nobleman's journeys. On June 9, 1624, for instance, the earl brought jewellery, furniture and chests to Spain 'for his personal enlightenment'. The chests contained an uncertain number of paintings that unfortunately the customs documents do not specify.[8] Although we do not know the specific themes of the paintings, we do know Croÿ's predilections for genre scenes, hunts and still lifes – at least during his early years in Spain. On March 1, 1625, he received some other goods from Flanders that enriched his collections. On this occasion the documents are more eloquent. Together with a magnificent tapestry depicting the history of Hercules and another depicting the history of David, five paintings arrived for Croÿ in Madrid. These are described as *one hunting scene, another of a deer hunt, another of a kitchen scene, another of a deer hunt with two figures on horseback, another of a wild boar with a hunter on horseback.* [9] These descriptions remind us of the hunting scenes painted by Snyders, Paul de Vos and Rubens in preceding decades. We must assume that the first appearance of this type of painting in Spain is due to collectors like Croÿ.

As a whole, Croÿ's collection was magnificent. It was composed of one hundred and sixty-nine pictures, with paintings on canvas, panel and copper. When Solre died in 1638 his paintings were appraised by Philippe Diriksen, a Spanish painter of Flemish origin and member of the Archers' Guard, and by Felix Castello, a painter of Italian origin. Unfortunately the documents reveal nothing about the authorship of the paintings, but two small works on copper, '*Luzbel Fal*' and *'The Salutation'*, were said to be from Rubens. Another work, however, *Moses and the Brazen Serpent,* may be the canvas by Van Dyck now in the Prado (cat. 1637). In the same way, a *Card Game* and a *Dentist* are easily connected with two paintings with the same subjects by Theodoor Rombouts, also in the Prado (cat. 1635 and 1636, figs. 4 and 5).[10]

While Croÿ's taste for Flemish painting is clear, there are some data which suggest the patronage of Spanish artists. Juan van der Hamen (1596–1631) was a highly successful artist in Madrid who was evidently of Flemish origin. His father and grandfather had also been members of the Archers' Guard,[11] demonstrating their good standing with the Spanish kings for generations. It has been proven that two pictures of vertical format, described in the Solre collection as *Flower vases on tables with dogs,*

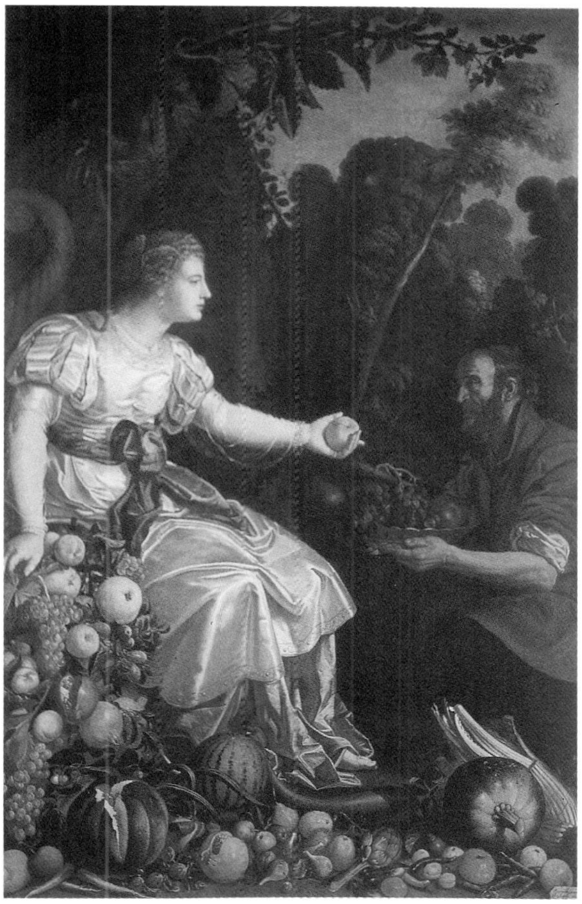

Fig. 3. Juan van der Hamen, *Flora Offering*. Madrid, Museo del Prado

are the two Van der Hamen paintings now in the Prado (cat. 4158 and 6413, figs. 1 and 2). Moreover, three other works in the Croÿ collection were also paintings by Van der Hamen. They depicted human figures and were described in the inventory as *Gods receiving an offering of flowers and fruit*, evidently an allegory of the seasons. Two of them can be connected to the *Homage to Flora* in the Prado (cat. 2877, fig. 3) and the so-called *Vertumnus and Pomona,* now owned by the Bank of Spain.[12]

The sale of Croÿ's collection offered Spanish collectors, especially Philip IV, the opportunity to purchase Flemish paintings of high quality by Rubens, Van Dyck, Rombouts, Snyders, Paul de Vos, or the Spaniard Van der Hamen. Even before Croÿ's goods were sold, twenty-nine of the best paintings passed into royal possession. Considering their high prices, they were some of the best paintings in the collection. These royal acquisitions prove that the Prado's paintings are the same ones formerly in Croÿ's collection. The 'vases of flowers with

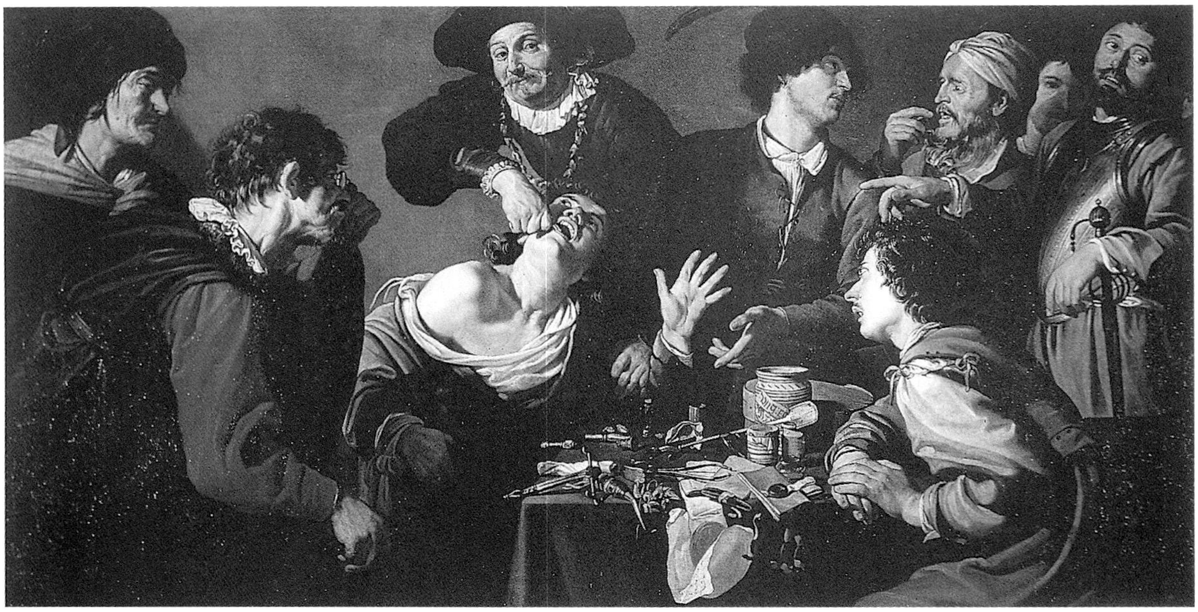

Fig. 4. Theodoor Rombouts, *The Dentist*. Madrid, Museo del Prado

dogs' and the two Rombouts fell into royal hands and passed into the royal collections which formed the nucleus of the Prado in the nineteenth-century. The king also acquired two of the hunting scenes that Croÿ had brought into Spain. These two pictures, described as deer and boar hunts, were appraised at 5000 *reales* each, demonstrating Philip's fondness for hunting scenes. We must also consider that in the same years, many of Snyders' hunting scenes were arriving in Madrid to decorate the royal hunting lodge, La Torre de la Parada.

During the 1630s the royal palace of Buen Retiro was also being decorated. Hence, it is not unusual that most of the king's acquisitions from Croÿ's sale were decorative paintings like landscapes. Six landscapes on panel, another six on copper and four on canvas passed into royal possession. But the king also chose another kind of painting, namely genre painting. One such piece is described as *a night conversation where some people are paying cards,* and this could be related to the kind of small genre scenes painted by Brouwer and Teniers. Another of the king's acquisitions, described as *a hunting larder where there is a monkey ruining a basket,* is evidently a scene by Snyders. This artist may also have been the author of other paintings bought by the king, who was a real fan of Snyders. The king also acquired a picture of some fish, valued at the high price of 7000 *reales*, and another depicting a *bird larder with a swan* valued at 6000 – together the highest prices in Croÿ's collection. Presumably these pictures were also painted by Snyders. Another highly-valued painting, described as *a fruit garland where there are some children*, can be identified with those that Rubens and Snyders had designed depicting the same subject. The version that today resides in the royal palace at Granja could be the same painting owned by Croÿ.[13] Finally, a painting described as *the martyrdom of saint John*, also acquired by the king, is almost impossible to identify with any existing picture.

The documents reveal that other paintings in the Croÿ collection, like the history of Moses and the brazen serpent, actually belonged to the marquis of Aytona. Once Croÿ died this painting was returned to Aytona. The marquis of Aytona, Francisco Moncada, was the interim governor of Flanders after the death of Isabella Clara Eugenia, so he had close ties to Flanders. Although we know nothing about Aytona's collection or his taste in paintings, we must assume a certain interest in Flemish art, since he was portrayed by Van Dyck.[14] The fact that he had a painting from the Croÿ collection implies the possibility of an exchange of paintings between these two noblemen.

Once the best paintings had passed into the royal collection, and those like that of Aytona were given back to their legitimate owners, the rest of the Solre collection was sold at a public auction beginning July 1, 1638. Many buy-

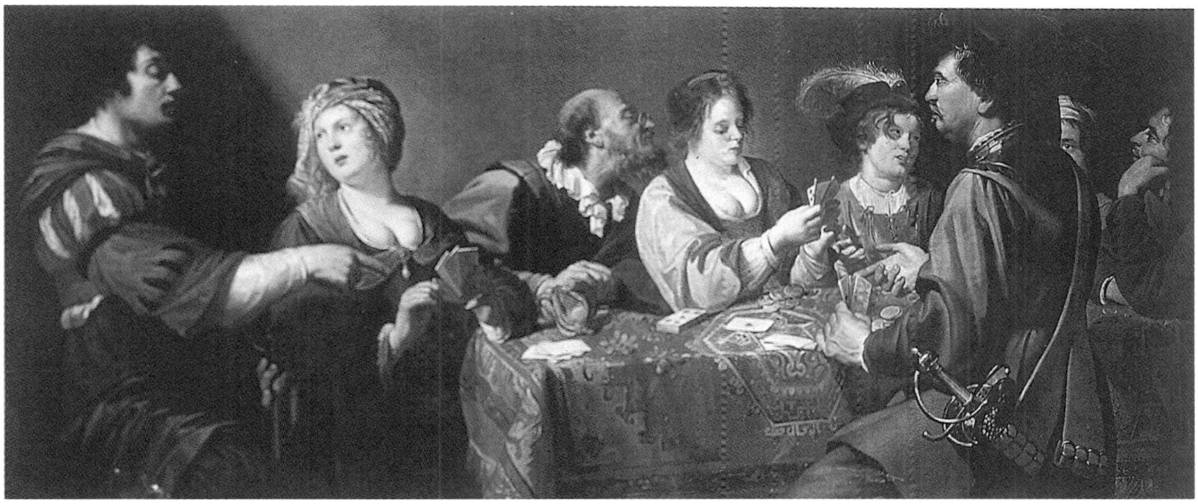

Fig. 5. Theodoor Rombouts, *The Card Players*. Madrid, Museo del Prado

ers of varying social status attended the auction, all interested in acquiring high-quality paintings and goods. Surprisingly enough, however, most of them are unknown in the historiography of art collecting in Spain. The majority of essays on art collecting focus on aristocratic collections. For this reason, little is known about the Solre buyers because for the most part they were members of the royal bureaucracy: palace employees, bankers, merchants, and royal tenants.

Many of the buyers came from the royal councils, where their political affairs afforded them contact with politicians and diplomats like Croÿ. For instance, Diego Abarca Maldonado, who bought some of the battle and landscape paintings,[15] was a lawyer and accountant for the Crusade Council.[16] Not very much is known about Abarca's relationship to art collecting: only a few works ordered from the Spanish painter José Lanchares,[17] and a painting of Christ with Mary Magdalen from Eugenio Cajés.[18] Although the artistic approach of Eugenio Cajés is quite different from what is found in the Flemish paintings that Diego Abarca would have been able to buy at the Croÿ auction, Cajés was not unknown to collectors of Flemish painting, since the duke of Aarschot also possessed a work by him, as we will see below.

Other palace functionaries also acquired goods from the Croÿ sale. The doctor Marco Antonio Gussio, an Italian who led the royal chapel,[19] bought six tapestries depicting the history of Abraham with vegetal decoration.[20] The royal secretary Juan Lucas Manzolo bought four small works on copper depicting landscapes.[21]

The sale also interested officials who dealt with Flemish politics. Some of them were of Flemish origin, such as Diego L'Hermitte, son of a military official who had served both Philip II and Philip III.[22] L'Hermitte wanted to serve in the royal palace as a member of the king's chamber, but he was only able to enter the administration in relation to nordic affairs. He went to Brussels as treasurer of the Council of Flanders in 1644. [23] Thus, there is nothing unusual in the fact that he acquired some of the maps in Croÿ's collection.[24] Similarly Jean Becquet, secretary of Council of Flanders, also purchased goods under similar circumstances, preferring twelve landscapes in tempera.[25]

Merchants installed in Madrid, especially those who had made their fortunes lending money to the king, were another important group at the Croÿ auctions. Some of them were only small-scale lenders who had advanced the royal exchequer in the administration, like the Portuguese Diego Rodríguez de Morais,[26] who bought a small work on copper representing the Annunciation.[27] But many others, like Julio Cesar Scazuola, were indeed professional bankers who lent large amounts of money to Philip IV at high rates of interest, and to the Cardinal-Infante Don Fernando of Austria as well.[28] Scazuola was of German origin and he had been one of the main suppliers of the king. He had been in Madrid since 1617, where he was the main agent of the powerful German bankers, the Fugger family.[29] This activity guaranteed him a great deal of social status, which he improved by owning paintings and luxury goods. The inventory of his possessions at the time of his death on January 31, 1640, lists 130 paintings.[30] He also had others in his two villas near Madrid, which together with his wife's collection amounted to at least 200 paintings,[31] plus another 40 in the family chapel.[32] The importance of Scazuola as a collector runs parallel with his taste for Flemish painting. Although no particular artists are mentioned in the documents concerning his collection, they do tell us something about the possible Flemish origin of some of his many battles, landscapes, seascapes, genre scenes, and pastoral paintings. Conclusive proof of Scazuola's interest in Flemish art, however, is his receipt of a shipment of sixty paintings in 1640, described in the documents as coming from Flanders: *que ultimamente vinieron de Flandes para el dicho Julio Cesar Scazuola.*[33] Among these seventy paintings were marine and seaport scenes, religious works, at least eight hunting scenes taking place in a forest, and eight landscapes. Although some of the paintings are said to have been sold before they arrived in Spain, such documents clearly highlight Scazuola's activity as an importer of Flemish painting into Spain. The position of this banker as a mediator between Flemish painting and Spanish collecting can be traced not only through the aforementioned envoy, but also through the sale of his own collection. This enables us to take a look at those people who bought his Flemish paintings. Some of them were the same people who bought paintings at Croÿ's sale. This is true in the case of Jacinto Lamini, who at the Scazuola auction bought *a larder with a boar, with dear and a grape basket next to a lobster,* clearly a Flemish painting.[34] Moreover, at Croÿ's sale Lamini bought one of the three scenes depicting the gods with fruit by Van der Hamen.[35]

The two other works with similar iconography, allegories or gods with fruit by Van der Hamen, were bought by Bartolome Barrilano, whose professional occupation remains unknown, but whose fondness for collecting paintings is well-established.[36] When he married in 1655, he owned a small collection with no more than sixty-five works.[37] Most of them were small paintings on copper, but he also had paintings by artists such as Bassano, El Greco, Raphael, Dürer, Andrea del Sarto, Maximo Stanzione, the so-called Antiveduto, and Spanish paintings by Francisco Collantes and Juan Fernández, El Labrador. More interesting still is the presence of Flemish paintings and painters in his collection. Among them were two works on copper and a *banquet* said to be by Rubens, a portrait by Van Dyck, and a vase of flowers by Seghers – in Spain known as 'el teatino'. Although the value of his paintings was not very high, Barrilaro's growing taste for collecting was confirmed seven years later when his pictures were inventoried again. By 1658 his collection had grown to one hundred and fifty works. Some of them are cited as Flemish battle scenes, reminiscent of those by Snayers or Vrancx, which were very well-known in Madrid, but he also owned other Flemish paintings like flower pieces and landscapes.[38]

Bartolomé Barrilaro also bought two religious scenes on copper and a canvas depicting the Virgin at the Croÿ sale[39] which are easily identified in his own inventories of paintings. It is astonishing, however, that his two major purchases, the two Van der Hamen paintings, were not inventoried. We may suppose that he purchased these two paintings only to sell them immediately afterwards. Here, we may imagine Barrilaro as a commercial intermediary for paintings. In fact, there is information to suggest that Barrilaro did in fact work as an intermediary in the art market in Madrid. In 1655 a member of the clergy reclaimed almost fifty pictures which he had previously given to Barrilaro for the purpose of finding a buyer. Some paintings by Caravaggio were included in this operation.[40] His activity as a dealer, along with the sale of his own collection, made Barrilaro one of the most important figures present at the Solre auction.

It would be fairly safe to assume that some of the other purchasers at the Croÿ sale were also intermediaries. The presence of a certain number of completely unknown people who bought the best and most expensive paintings and goods can be explained if we assume that they were working for other collectors. This may have been the case with Gregorio de Vega, who is unknown in the historiography of Spanish collections but who is indeed one of the main purchasers at Croÿ's auction. He bought twenty-five of the best paintings, particularly some of the more opulent hunting scenes and still lifes, along with eight cheaper works on copper.[41] The possibility that this man worked for a more important collector remains open. In fact this seems to be the case for many of the names of painters appearing in the auction document about whom we have no information, but who could have worked for others. This circumstance could also explain the absence of the big names in Spanish collecting at the Croÿ sales. Purchasers like Alonso Velasco, who bought six marine paintings and two large hunting scenes,[42] or Diego Contreras, who bought four landscapes,[43] may have been jewellery keepers, or butlers, or simply servants of important aristocratic families.

In fact when the major Spanish collectors of the moment attended the Croÿ auction, they did not buy paintings. Noblemen such as the admiral of Castilla,[44] the count of Oñate[45] and Luis de Haro[46] visited the auction but preferred objects such as weapons, silver, or bits for their horses. These purchases reveal their lack of interest in Flemish painting, since they did not take advantage of the opportunity that the Croÿ sales offered.

From a social and economic point of view the most important purchaser at the Croÿ auction was Don Pedro Valle de la Cerda, who bought twenty-three paintings of birds and landscapes. He was very closely linked to the faction of the prime minister – the count-duke of Olivares – through his marriage to the sister of Jerónimo de Villanueva, one of the members of the Olivares group. Pedro Valle de la Cerda had managed to garner important political appointments, being a counsellor of the treasury and member of War and Crusade Councils.[47] His fondness for painting was rewarded in 1630 when he inherited the outstanding collection formed by his father, Don Luis Valle de la Cerda.[48] This collection was focused almost exclusively on religious painting, the only secular themes being portraits of family and the emperors. Pedro Valle de la Cerda improved the collection of his father in the area of non-religious subject matter with his purchase of decorative paintings of birds and landscapes from the Croÿ auction.

Philip Charles of Aremberg, duke of Aarschot and prince of Aremberg (1597–1640), was also a member of one of the most important provincial families in Flanders. His family had joined the Habsburg cause during the time of Emperor Charles I. From the government of Namur, Aremberg reached the court at Brussels, initially backing a slightly hostile policy towards Spain which is reflected in his opposition to Chancellor Boisschot, president of the supreme court in Flanders. In spite of this situation he held a high position in Spanish politics; he was state chancellor and took part in many government councils (called *Juntas* in Spain). In 1633, Isabella Clara Eugenia sent him to Madrid, where he is supposed to have maintained good relationships with the Dutch and headed a rebellion of the nobility in Flanders against Spanish rule.[49] Even so, Aremberg established personal links with some of the major Spanish politicians, such as the marquis of Leganés, who supported his nomination within the framework of the political reforms of 1629 due to the position of his family.[50] In fact, Aarschot initially lodged at the house of Leganés, stating that there he felt himself in paradise due to the large number of paintings and works of art decorating its halls.[51] He had a difficult and rebellious personality, and the suspicion of fostering the 1632 rebellion of the nobility resulted in Aremberg's being found guilty of treason; he was imprisoned in April 1634.[52] He was at first moved to the fortress of Pinto, near the court, and he was later imprisoned at his house in the centre of Madrid, the Seven Chimneys. He was imprisoned for six years, until his death in September 1640. In 1637 he was joined by his wife Marie Cléophée of Hohenzollern and his son Philippe-François of Aremberg.

In spite of being involved in complex judicial proceedings and in spite of the lack of liberty that resulted, Aremberg refused to resign either his noble status or his pleasure in painting. During his imprisonment he regularly corresponded with his contact persons in Brussels through letters that were scrupulously controlled, translated and given to the Council of State, which monitored his activities closely. Thanks to this surveillance we know that he continued to receive shipments of paintings for the decoration of his palace, produced by some of his favourite artists. We know, for example, that artists like Salomon Noveliers were painting for Aarschot at this time. In a letter sent by the translator to the council on April 15, 1636, Aarschot wrote to an addressee whose identity remains unknown: '*take care to receive from the painter Noveliers the number of paintings according to the money*

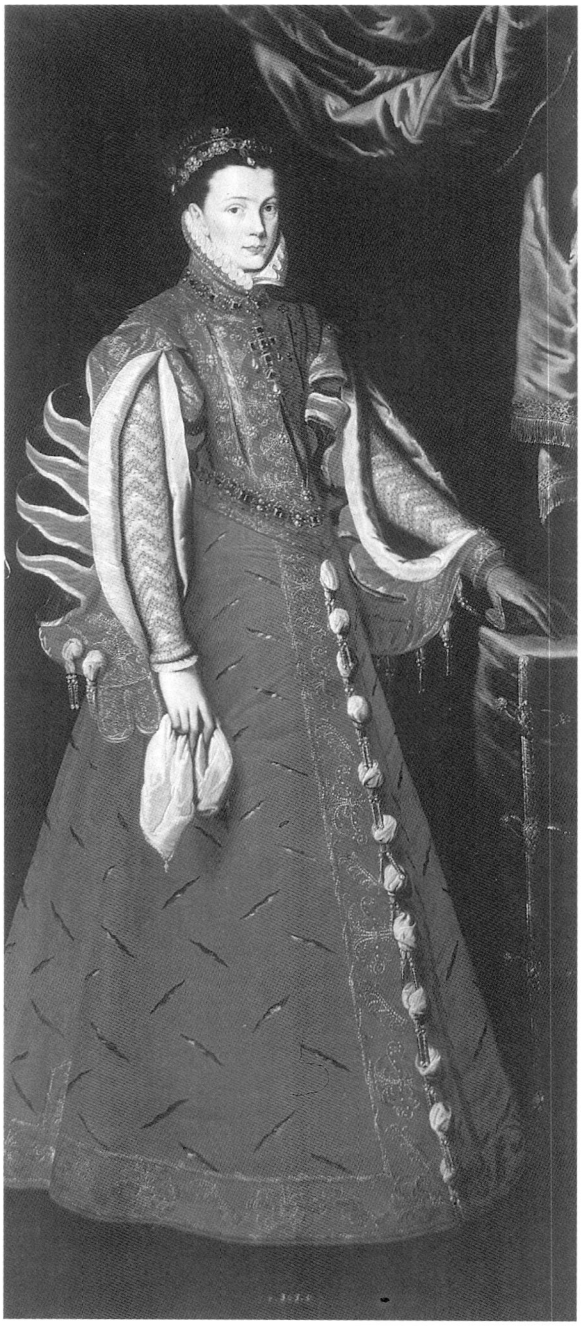

Fig. 6. Salomon Noveliers, *Portrait of Isabelle de Valois*, Private collection

*he has received'*.[53] Because of the date, the painter in question is to be identified as Salomon Noveliers, son of Pierre Noveliers, court painter to Albert and Isabella and restorer of the archducal collections.[54] Salomon Noveliers had set the prices for the collection of Charles de Croÿ, the predecessor of Philippe of Aremberg in the duchy of Aarschot.[55] We may suppose, then, that he had a fluent relationship with this family. Noveliers was at that time also known for being an intermediary in the sale of Rubens' paintings. For this reason, the executors of the estate gave him a painting of a nymph with a basket of fruit.[56] Noveliers' involvement in the Spanish market was not restricted to the sale of the Aarschot paintings. The marquis of Leganés himself had a group of portraits of Spanish kings painted by him.[57] One of those works, a portrait of Isabelle de Valois, recently appeared on the Spanish market (fig. 6).[58]

Aarschot's commissions to Flemish painters also included works by Jacob van Hulsdonck. On April 14, 1639, Felipe d'Ursel wrote to the duke from Brussels concerning '*The painting of flowers and other things that the duke had asked'*,[59] and the following day Antonio Lasser wrote him another letter from Antwerp relating to the same topic, which he sent together with a piece of paper on which Jacques van Hulsdonck offered to do the painting himself for a reasonable price.[60] Unfortunately the Hulsdonck text was never translated and does not appear in the documents of the council. By that time, however, Aarschot no longer valued Hulsdonck's work. On May 12, 1639, the duke rejected this painter, offering his opinion about him in writing: '*with regard to Hulsdonck's paintings, his work is very clean but it has not brightness enough to ask for such a high price for it, that is why I will not get it'*.[61]

The letter of May 12 is addressed to Canon Tassis, one of Aarschot's intermediaries in Brussels. Thanks to this letter we know of Aarschot's penchant for Dutch paintings, which he had expected to get despite the scarcity of such pictures on the market and lack of security in sending them from Flanders. This ultimately caused him to desist: '*I have received your letter and I have seen what you write about the Dutch paintings, about their scarcity and the lack of security to have them well and faithfully finished'*.[62] Due to the difficulties involved and the high price of the small paintings he wanted, he had to resign himself to what was available in Spain: '*since the small things are so expensive and so scanty, I have to be resigned to the things I have here'*.[63]

In spite of these problems, Aarschot nevertheless decided to order paintings from Brussels and Antwerp. At least 3900 florins were sent to Canon Tassis as a payment for other new paintings. Aarschot decided that this lot should have the same size as some of the other paintings ordered previously from Paul de Vos. However, the topics would be quite different. The duke preferred paintings of landscapes and views: *'I am sure that in order to make pretty landscapes with good and grand figures, with good perspective and other such things, there is no lack of good masters in Antwerp and Brussels to choose among'*.[64] He also wrote in detail how the paintings were to be executed: *'requesting you that the paintings were of the same size, always in pairs on canvas, and in one piece without seams, and well made so the painting does not jump'*. Such statements demonstrate the degree of direct control Aarschot exercised in his commissions.

At that time, it was impossible to know who painted the works, but according to the contents of the letter they may have been painted by the same artist who had already painted another five pictures in Brussels, ordered shortly before. The agent who took charge of this new job was Jan Battista Van Delen. The relationship between Van Delen and Aarschot was interesting due to the fact that Van Delen participated soon after in the sale of Rubens' own collection, which demonstrates his active involvement with the art market in Flanders. In a letter to Van Delen dated May 12, Aarschot specified the size the five pictures should have. They should be no bigger than the piece of paper on which his letter was written: *'...the size of this letter, the longest side of the sheet is the length* [of the painting], *the shortest side of the sheet is the height'*. He further specified the size of the figures: *'the bigger figures must have four feet less one fifth'*, and that the author of these five pictures should be the same who had painted another work depicting a blind man: *'the same master who did the Blind man that you sold me'*. But above all, he specified the topic, which was to be a gallant company or genre painting.[65] The orders to Flanders probably coincided either with the arrival of a shipment of paintings for the duke in December of 1639,[66] or with the lot that arrived after his death in 1641.[67] In this last shipment there were works by an artist called Brum (perhaps Antoni de Bruyn) and by Alexander Adriaenssen.

With the paintings he ordered from his imprisonment, Aremberg complemented the group of hunting scenes he had previously ordered from Paul de Vos with landscapes, views and genre paintings. Before his trip to Spain, Aarschot paid De Vos for several paintings, and in 1638 the costs for another twenty pictures for the duke were paid, along with two fables of Aesop, which were all sent to Spain, and an additional thirty-two paintings thereafter. Even though it is possible that many of these paintings were sold before arriving in Spain,[68] we know from documents found in Madrid that at least on May 12, 1639, the duke was still anxiously awaiting the works by Paul de Vos: *'I am waiting for news of the De Vos paintings, which I consider there would be many finished and on their way'*.[69] In any case, the work of this artist was in Spain when the duke died, and its acquisition disputed by some Italian and Spanish collectors.[70] In addition, many works which arrived in Spain after Aarschot's death may have been by this painter.[71]

In addition to Paul de Vos, other Flemish artists were patronised by Aarschot while he was imprisoned in Madrid. Gaspar de Crayer painted eight pictures before July 1639, whose subjects are unfortunately not mentioned in the documents.[72] Besides De Crayer, other painters like the still life painter Adriaen van Utrecht, a still life painter, worked for Aarschot during the same period,[73] as did other minor artists like Agustin van Venne[74] and Gherard van Hoechstal.[75] In the same way, using agents in Brussels, Aarschot paid a certain amount of money to Pierre Cra for two miniatures,[76] to François van den Hecke for some tapestries, [77] and to the engraver Michiel van den Berghe for some unspecified works.[78] These payments demonstrate that Aarschot continued his activities as a collector even though he was in prison.

As we have seen in the letters written from Spain, the duke acquired and made payments for paintings in Flanders through the intermediaries or agents he had there. One of them was Canon Tassis. In addition to the above mentioned shipments, Tassis received 228 florins for four more paintings on February 19, 1639.[79] In 1640, he was in charge of finding prints or engravings for the duke in Antwerp.[80] Another intermediary was Cornelio Barbé or Monsieur Warbe, who regularly sent objects, tapestries and paintings to Spain.[81] Barbé was in Spain in 1638, where he bought a painting of the Tower of Babel from Croÿ for 330 *reales*. He then sold it to Aarschot for the same price.[82] However, the duke's main intermediary was Juan Enriquez Gobelinos or Monsieur Goblinus. He sent some paintings to Spain, including a portrait of the archduchess Isabella,[83] and he was responsible for negotiating with and paying Paul de Vos[84] in Antwerp. Finally, it is necessary to mention Aarschot's own brother, the priest Charles de Aremberg, who also sent him some engravings and prints in 1635.[85]

The duke of Aarschot's interest in collecting Flemish paintings during his painful sojourn in Spain was reflected not only in his orders to Brussels but also in his relations with Italy. In 1640, six paintings by Cornelis de Wael (1592–1667) were sent to the duke from Genoa. De Wael was not only a battle and marine painter but an art dealer in Italy as well. This set of paintings entered Spain through the seaport of Alicante on the east coast. The intermediaries in this case were the Lavana (or Savana) brothers, and Aarschot paid them 2844 *reales*.[86]

Other Flemish artists patronised by Aarschot while he was in Spain were Gaspar van Eyck and Jean Duchamps. The former painted at least six pictures for the duke, for which there are payments in 1638 and 1639.[87] Through the accounts of his administrator in Madrid we understand that by this time Gaspar van Eyck was painting in Spain and that he probably painted marines for Aarschot's collection.[88] Jean Duchamps painted a portrait of Aremberg's son, François Philippe d'Aremberg. For this work he received 1100 *reales* in September 1639.[89] Aarschot's sponsorship of Duchamps is quite important, because this painter had been in Italy with the *Bamboccianti* and was therefore an important link between Flemish and Italian genre painting and the Spanish market. Even so, other collectors like the marquis of Leganés maintained a good relationship with this painter, and donated him a painting when he died.[90]

Aarschot sponsored not only Flemish painters, but also Spanish painters. Thus Antonio Puga made a portrait of the duchess and a copy of Rubens' *Wolf Hunt*, now in the Metropolitan Museum.[91] Puga was apparently one of Aarschot's favourite Spanish artists, since it seems that he had many works by him in his collection. The inventory lists some genre subjects that have been identified with paintings like *The Knifegrinder* (St Petersburg, Hermitage), *The Oil Seller* (Castres, Musée Goya, fig. 7) and the *Tavern Scene with Wine Seller and Smokers* (Pontevedra, City Museum).[92] And we can probably also add a painting called *Blind Man Playing the Guitar*, which today is in a private collection in Spain.[93]

Aarschot's interest in Puga explains why he was chosen to set the prices of the duke's collection when he died. He was assisted in this task by Juan de la Corte.[94] The latter was a painter of Flemish origin who lived in Spain and who had also produced works for Aremberg. Born in 1597, he was trained in the late mannerist style in Flanders, and in 1613 he was already in Spain working for King Philip III.[95] As De la Torre himself pointed out in 1627, when he opted to become a royal painter, the main subjects of his work tended toward architecture, battles and landscapes. For this reason he was a possible candidate for making the kind of small painting already mentioned by the duke in the letter expressing his resignation to what was available in Spain.

Francisco Collantes, another Spanish painter favored by Aarschot, also produced the same kind of small-format paintings with light subjects like landscapes and perspectives. The document from the sale of his collection includes ten paintings by this artist, at least two of which were landscapes.[96] Francisco Collantes was a specialist in landscapes, although he also made some religious paintings and still lifes during the course of his artistic career. Perhaps the most interesting aspect of his art was the Flemish flavor of his landscapes, which was closely related to the late mannerism of the 16th century, but updated by the inclusion of classical or anecdotal elements like ruins. In this he was nearer to the Roman landscape painters of the early 17th century. His landscapes recall those of Paul Bril or Adam Elsheimer, and he seems to have known the works of Moses van Uyttenbroeck (1600–1648).[97] His most profitable period was during the 1630s, when he made decorative paintings for the new palace of Buen Retiro. It would have been around this time that Aarschot became interested in his work. Collantes was widely accepted in the Spanish market and was one of the painters most valued by the critics of the moment. In fact he was always warmly received by Spanish critics, and it seems certain that the treatise writer Vicente Carducho refers to Collantes when he describes the way Spanish painters portrayed Madrid's surroundings: '*the beautiful landscape pieces that these banks shape... have [been] imitated [by] those who [do the] best work in this Court, and I certify to you that they can be envied by the best of Flanders*'.[98] Thus, the pseudo-Flemish painter Collantes was able to attract the attention of an experienced connoisseur like Aarschot.

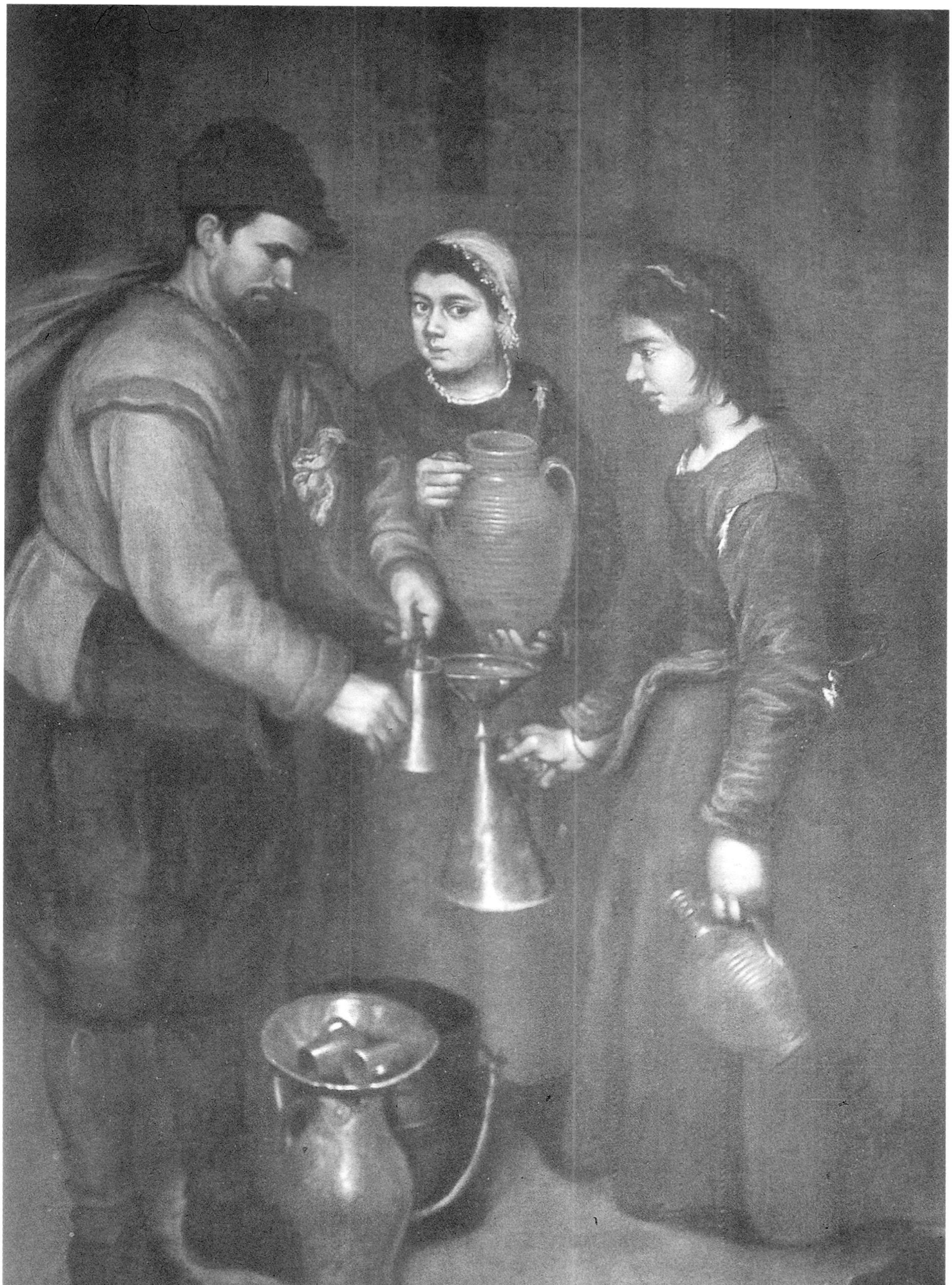

Fig. 7. Antonio Puga, *The Oil Seller*. Castres, Musée Goya

It is more difficult to understand why Aarschot liked the work of Eugenio Cajés, whose work does not possess similar affinities with Flemish painting. Aarschot had some small religious paintings by this artist, as well as a few portraits and what is presumed to be a self-portrait of Cajés.[99] Antonio Puga was Cajés' pupil, and even finished some of his paintings. Puga could therefore have been the connection between this painter and Aarschot.[100] In the thirties he was one of the most appreciated artists in Madrid, and was represented in all the major collections. As a royal painter his most successful work was that found in the main hall of the palace of Buen Retiro, where he portrayed the glory of Spanish military power in *The Conquest of Puerto Rico.*

Finally, mention should be made of other artists cited in the accounting documents from Aarchot's stay in Madrid. These documents include payments to unknown artists like Jacques de León, who was asked to repair two crucifixes in wood and bronze,[101] or the carpenter Diego Perales, who repaired the damage to his paintings and made frames for them.[102]

Nevertheless, the Aremberg collection presupposes the presence of Flemish and Spanish paintings of high quality in Madrid. The inventory lists some paintings by Rubens, like the *Wolf Hunt* now in the Metropolitan Museum, as well as many others by Brueghel, Bloemaert,[103] Paul de Vos – according to the consignments seen above – and Snyders – if we trust the descriptions made by the appraisers.[104] His fabulous collection and his noble spirit made Aarschot one of the most important connoisseurs in Madrid. There is some information on the exchange of paintings with other Spanish collectors that deserves further study. One such collector was the marquis of Povar, Pedro Antonio Dávila y Aragón, who was a member of the Royal Chamber and captain in the German Guard. In September 1638 he bought thirty-four pictures from Aremberg, for which he paid 20,000 *reales.*[105] In the inventory made by his wife in 1641, these paintings were described as 'animal paintings bought from the count of *Ariscote*'.[106] These animal paintings were probably fables or hunt scenes and either by Paul de Vos or Snyders. This fact implicates Aarschot directly in the development of Spanish taste for this kind of painting. But Aarschot not only sold paintings, he also bought them. In 1639 he acquired four paintings from the admiral of Castilla, an important Spanish collector,[107] and he even bought a painting from the Solre sale through Cornelius Barbé.[108]

Because of Aremberg's magnificent collection and his good relationship with other collectors, it was not difficult to find a large number of collectors and other people buying paintings during the days in which the auction took place. Some paintings had been valued so highly that it was necessary to request a second appraisal to reduce the prices, but even so, there were some famous collectors at the auction, such as the marquis of Leganés. The purchases of Leganés included Rubens' *Wolf Hunt*, one tiger hunt and four highly valued still lifes.[109] Moreover, Leganés' own inventory of paintings listed some other hunting scenes that are mentioned as proceeding from the Aarschot collection.[110]

Many other aristocratic collectors, such as the marquis of Carpio, are conspicuous for their lack of purchases. This connoisseur, whose own collection would have been of an enormous size just a few years before, only bought one small genre painting depicting a servant in a kitchen.[111] The auction was also attended by other, less significant aristocrats. For instance, the count of Cantillana acquired two small works on copper,[112] while the count of Medellin and the marchioness of Cortes bought nothing but luxury goods and silver.[113]

Much more interesting is the presence of foreign ambassadors at the auction, suggesting that some of the Aremberg pictures may have travelled to other locations in Europe. The German ambassador acquired four paintings: two landscapes, two flower pieces and a genre scene with a blind man – perhaps the one mentioned by Aarschot in his letters.[114] This ambassador may have been Enrico Ottone, marquis of Grana, who arrived in Spain in June 1641,[115] the same man who in 1682 became governor general of the Low Countries. The Danish ambassador acquired a painting representing Avarice, a Crucifixion and a miniature with 'the tower of Nebronte'.[116]

Members of the clergy also bought pictures from Aremberg. Some of them, like the bishop of Panama, acquired several, probably for his own collection. The bishops of Evora and Portoalegre in Portugal were also at the auction.

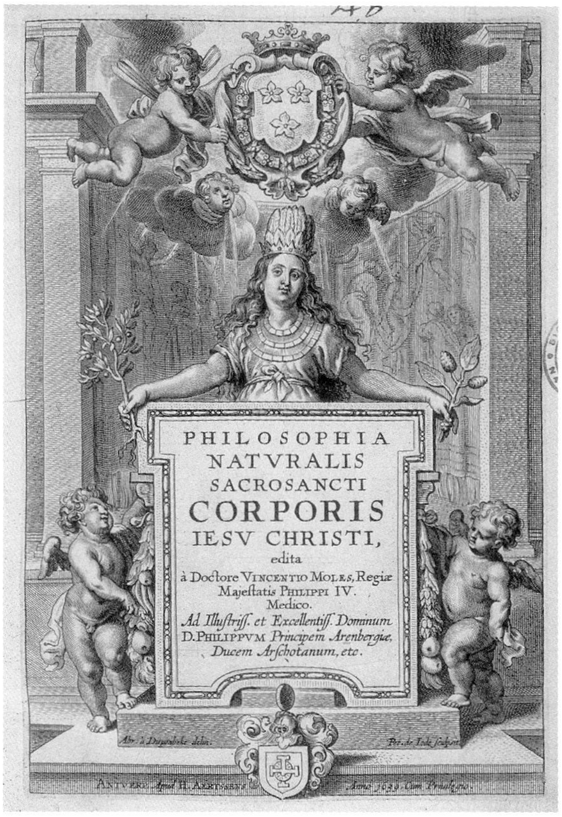


Fig. 8. Peter de Jode, Title-page of Vicente Moles' *Philosophia Naturalis Sacrosanti Corporis Christi*

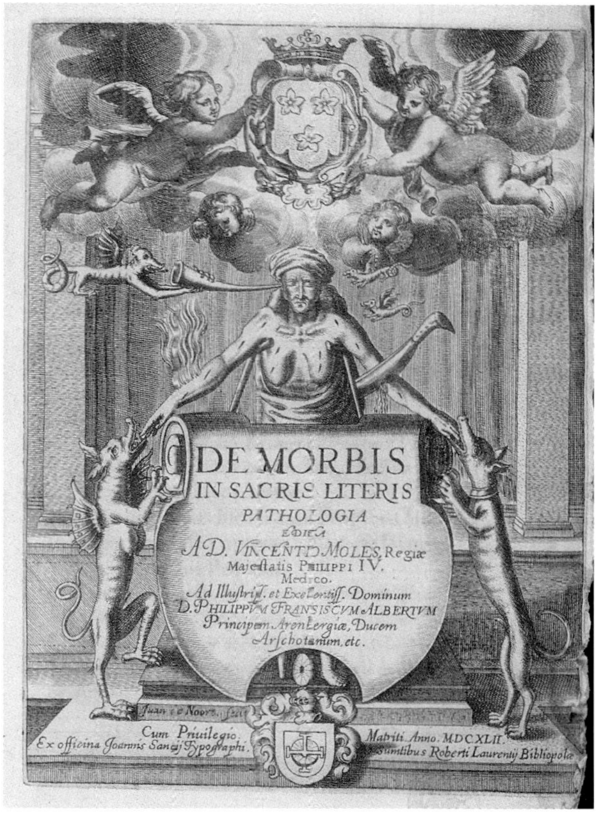


Fig. 9. Jean de Noort, Title-page of Vicente Moles' *De Morbis in Sacris Literis Pathologia*

We can assume that the paintings they bought were sent to their respective dioceses in Portugal.[117] The purchases of the inquisitor of Aragón are curious indeed. Surprisingly, he did not purchase religious paintings but a still life with a porcelain plate and fruit on panel, similar to the ones created by Jan Bruegel.[118]

However, it was the middle class who was best represented with regard to the Aarschot sales. Some of them were palace officials like Fructuoso Pique, secretary of the Supreme Council of Aragon, himself a minor collector, who acquired a small picture of the Virgin, the price and quality of which were in keeping with his modest collection.[119] Another such buyer was Pedro de Tapia, Doorkeeper of the Council of Italy. Although not a very rich man, he spent the considerable sum of 6300 *reales* on five pictures: a market scene, a religious scene, a fruit seller and an image of a duke's servant, called Mundino. His purchase of such highly valued works suggests the possibility that he was working for some other anonymous and more powerful collector.[120] We could easily apply this theory to purchasers like Nicolas Droipe, a servant of the queen with Flemish ancestors.[121] It could also be applied to Domingo Herrera de la Concha, who was custodian of the royal painting and tapestry collections, or *Mozo de la Furriera* y *Ujier* of the royal chamber. Unfortunately, the relative insignificance and vague descriptions of his purchases make it impossible to identify the works in the royal collections.[122]

Of far greater relevance was the presence at the auction of Vincencio Moles.[123] Moles was the physician of the king, and he is known in artistic historiography for having assisted the painter Velázquez at his death.[124] Moreover Moles was the physician of the Aarschot family while they were in Spain, and Aarschot even sponsored some of the doctor's publications, such as the *Philosophia Naturalis Sacrosancti Corporis Christi* (Antwerp, 1639, fig. 8).[125] The front page of this work is based on a design by Abraham van Diepenbeeck and engraved by Peter de Jode; it includes *putti* taken from Rubens' compositions. Aarschot's sponsorship of Moles' written work indirectly promoted engravings by or after Flemish artists in Spain. Similarly, another book written by Moles, *De*

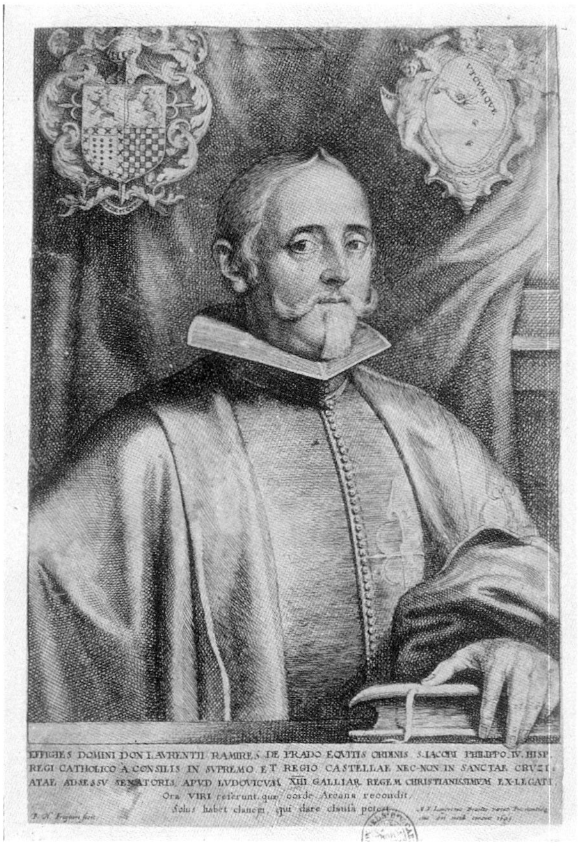

Fig. 10. Anonymous, *Portrait of Lorenzo Ramirez del Prado*, engraving. Madrid, Biblioteca Nacional

*morbis in sacris literis pathologia* (Madrid, 1642, fig. 9), displayed a print by the Fleming Jean de Noort on its front page.

In other cases, the purchasers were more or less connected to Flemish politics, like the secretary of the Council of Flanders, Jaques de Breth,[126] or the Jesuit Hermann Hugo, Aarschot's confessor, and the chaplain of Ambrosio Spinola, author of *Obsidio Brediana* (Antwerp, 1626), a work relating the conquest of the city of Breda by the forces of Philip IV.[127] Hugo can be included in another group of purchasers at the Aremberg auction: the intellectuals. It was interesting to deal with the erudite members of society who visited the auctions and bought various pictures. Some of them, like Sancho Hurtado de la Puente, were official historians charged with creating propaganda.[128] Chief among them was Lorenzo Ramírez del Prado (fig. 10), a political writer who in 1617 had written *Consejo y Consejero de Príncipes* (Madrid, 1617), a treatise concerning the ideal qualities of royal advisers based on previous works by Jean Coquier. In the main chapter of that book he pointed out that a good councillor must renounce the hoarding of properties and goods: '*if there is something that the councillor must avoid it is the desire for possessions and wealth*'.[129] However, he did not apply such principles to himself, for he had a magnificent library and art collection.[130] Ramírez had relations with other famous collectors like Juan de Lastanosa, who wrote about him: '*and before he left, he said to me that if I went to Madrid, he would give me the key of his library to see how much was there; and it is certain that this gentleman has brought together very many unique things and seeing them in Madrid is worth a trip*'. Those 'unique' things were not only books but also paintings, of which Ramírez was an obsessive buyer, as proven by the opinion of a certain chaplain who, during a visit by Ramírez, avoided showing him the library so that he did not '*desire any manuscripts or any fine picture*'.[131]

Moreover, Ramírez del Prado was a cultivated man whose knowledge and taste for art was exemplified by his own library, in which there was a section dedicated to the liberal arts with works by Vitruvius, Alberti, Leonardo da Vinci, Ortelius, and some editions of the *Treatise on Painting* by the Spaniard Vicente Carducho, alongside books on geography, arithmetic, astrology, music, and navigation.[132] It is therefore not surprising that such extensive visual and intellectual knowledge was pressed into service for the ephemeral architecture erected when queen Mariana of Austria entered Madrid in 1649. The designs included ten golden sculptures of kings and emperors, including the current monarchs, and eight more paintings with inscriptions.[133] In such designs Ramírez del Prado would have been able to put into practice his knowledge of Flemish art, which he could have improved through his visits to collections rich in Flemish painting like the one owned by Aremberg.[134]

In connection with the erudite, we should also mention the lawyers and men of letters. Some of them, such as Diego de Altamirano, had worked for Aarschot during the duke's defence against the political charges levelled at him. At the auction Altamirano acquired four works on copper and a Christ figure, possibly sculpted.[135] Another such buyer was Tomás Onis Portocarrero, a lawyer on the Royal Council, [136] who preferred genre paintings as they were appropriate to his social condition.[137]

The most interesting group represented at the Aremberg auction, however, was that of the businessmen, moneylenders and royal suppliers. We can easily distinguish a clear relationship between their acquisition of paintings and their desire for social advancement. One of these men was Sebastian Baez Martinez of Seville, who worked for the important banker Octavio Centurion, marquis of Monesterio, resident in Madrid.[138] Another was Duarte Díaz de Olivares, a minor Portuguese lender[139] who does not seem to have been an avid collector of paintings. In his inventory of 1658 only six religious paintings and two female portraits are mentioned,[140] none of them from Aremberg purchases.[141] A more important figure was Bartolome Spinola, who was a highly active royal lender in the thirties and very well connected to politic power. He became a member of the Treasury Council and the War Council and in his later years acquired a few titles, clearly reflecting his rising social career.[142] Financially, he was one of the main guarantors of the finances of the Spanish crown, but he also worked as an administrator for a number of courtiers, which accorded him a high economic position.[143]

The most important of the businessmen was Manuel Cortizos. He was of Portuguese origin and he held important posts in Spanish public finances, including that of chief royal accountant and treasurer during the golden years of the Portuguese bankers at the Spanish court. Because of his personal qualities, he was also present at all palace events, and documents show that he made flattering gifts to the king.[144] Socially, he achieved noble status in 1668 after a vigorous propaganda campaign in which the acquisition of paintings played a significant role. At the Aremberg auction he bought at least seven flower pieces, some of them described as tulips, recalling works by Jan I Bruegel or his followers.[145] With these purchases he complemented other important acquisitions that he had made a few years before at the sale of Juan de Fonseca, an important collector who had been a major patron of Velázquez. At the Fonseca auction, Cortizos bought many still lifes, three pictures of flowers and birds and sixteen portraits. All of his purchases consisted of decorative paintings to be hung in his purportedly ostentatious mansions.[146]

The use of paintings and collections as a means of social display was also favored by other influential people present at the Aremberg sale. Some of these were important politicians like Jeronimo de Villanueva, protonotary of the Aragon region and one of the most powerful men in the Olivares administration. Villanueva had inherited a collection from his father in 1610, which was composed of religious paintings and portraits. He increased this collection by purchasing decorative Flemish paintings at the Aremberg auction.[147] There, Villanueva bought two large still lifes with hare and deer, and two religious paintings depicting the Resurrection and the Magdalen washing Christ's feet, plus a scene from the history of Mucius Scaevola.[148] All of these pictures are described in the 1653 inventory of his own collection.[149] Moreover, Villanueva's taste already showed some inclination toward Flemish painting. During his second visit to Spain in 1628, Rubens executed a sketch for the altar of a Benedictine monastery of which Villanueva was a patron. Although Rubens never made the final painting for the altar – only a small sketch – it seems that the model was conceived by Claudio Coello, who made the final version in 1668.[150]

In the same way, two other purchasers mentioned as Joseph Gonzalez and Juan Gonzalez may have been the famous counsellor of Castilla, also factotum of Prime Minister Olivares, and his son. Although their purchases were not significant, their presence at the Aremberg sale was further evidence of the social repercussions generated by the auction at the Spanish court.[151] In fact, many other great collectors attended the sale, such Suero de Quiñones,[152] whose personality as collector and connoisseur was explained by Vicente Carducho in his *Dialogues on Painting* (Madrid, 1633) when he wrote: '*Don't miss a look at the ones* [paintings] *of Suero de Quiñones, . . because he has very good ones'*.[153] Rodrigo de Tapia is another well-known collector who was present at the Aremberg auction. He was a member of a very old family residing in Madrid, and in his youth he had sponsored the works of Miguel de Cervantes.[154] The quality of his collection was also recorded by Vicente Carducho, who said: '*I also see the ones* [houses] *of Rodrigo de Tapia, whose galleries and rooms we admire so for their quantity, goodness and good taste'*.[155] Tapia had inherited the collections from his father, Pedro de Tapia, a powerful member of the Supreme Council of the Inquisition, who owned four portraits by a Flemish painter and a large number of hunting scenes. His was a very modern collection which his son enriched with purchases from the Aremberg auction that included five of the best still lifes and a painting with birds.[156]

Finally, we should mention the ways in which artists were able to profit from the Aremberg sales. The presence of the duke's favourite, Antonio Puga, is by no means unusual. He bought many frames and mouldings, as well as three engravings cited as '*a satyr with a farm worker woman; a woman milking a goat,*' and '*a satyr playing the flute*'.[157] These purchases suggest that Puga may have used the engravings as models for his own compositions. This would have been in accordance with the practice, widespread among Spanish artists, of using Flemish engravings to compose their own pictures. Similarly, another purchaser, listed as Pedro de la Torre, may have been the famous architect of the same name. He bought one of the portraits of horses and a court scene '*with the Queen and her ladies as a perspective*',[158] an appropriate acquisition for an architect and altarpiece designer.

As we have already seen in the case of the Croÿ auction, the Aarschot sales hosted a large number of anonymous purchasers whose names, as they were common ones, makes it almost impossible to identify them. Some of them made purchases of high quality and extreme costliness. This is true in the case of Juan de Velasco, who bought a group of five genre paintings made by Antonio Puga.[159] And it is also true of Juan Bervel (or Bergel), who in December 1642 acquired eight canvases with equestrian portraits of the Austrian house, eight portraits of the Spanish royal house, fourteen large hunting scenes, a bird concert, a picture of the five senses, and some Biblical scenes. He spent the extraordinary sum of 33,400 *reales*, a sum never before spent by any of the other purchasers at the Aremberg auction.[160] Another such case was Diego Jiménez, who was interested in a series of miracles related to the Habsburg family and six equestrian portraits related to the wars of Flanders, along with other minor pictures, decorative objects and books.[161] But this was also true of many others, such as Juan Ferrer, who bought seven equestrian portraits valued at 3,500 *reales*;[162] Jaime Ferrer, who bought two battle paintings, a sculpture of Saint Jerome in wood, and a landscape with a carriage by Bruegel;[163] Juan Garrido, who bought three fables of Aesop, two bird concerts and a wolf hunt;[164] Juan Rodriguez, who acquired the self-portrait of Eugenio Cajés;[165] and Francisco Mendese, who spent more than four thousand *reales* on a series of sixteen portraits of the Habsburgs.[166] As in the case of the Croÿ sales, the possibility remains that those unknown purchasers were working for other, bigger collectors, including the king. Another possibility is that the unknown purchasers were dealers themselves, although this is only speculation. But the presence of at least one dealer at the Aremberg auctions has been proven. He was Juan Enriquez van Vucht, an interesting figure not only for his mercantile activities but also for his collection of paintings. He owned works by Hendrick van Balen and two hunting scenes by Rubens. Moreover, he was also responsible for bringing Rubens' *Martyrdom of St Andrew* to Spain for the main chapel of the Flemish hospital in Madrid, where it still remains.[167]

In conclusion it is necessary to emphasize the role played by the Croÿ and Aarschot collections at the Spanish court, where they became an example of modernity via the acquisition of Flemish paintings. The list of purchasers who attended their auctions helps us to understand the phenomenon of collecting and the market for painting in Madrid during the first half of the century. In the same way, the relations established by Croÿ and Aarschot with artists like Peter Paul Rubens, Antoon van Dyck, Gaspar de Crayer, Frans Snyders or Paul de Vos made them an essential vehicle for importing high quality Flemish paintings into Spain. This fact should furthermore be seen against the background of Philip IV's own taste for Flemish painting and the decoration of the royal palaces.

Moreover, the activities of Croÿ and Aarschot while they were in Spain help us to understand some of the ways in which paintings by artists such as Adriaen van Utrecht, Cornelis de Wael and others arrived in Spain. Finally, the study of these two cases has highlighted the role of intermediaries in the acquisition of paintings at the sales, and it has furthermore pointed up the importance of agents in Flanders, like those in the service of Aarschot, with respect to the patronage of Flemish paintings destined for Spain.

# NOTES

1. For Solre's biography see: *Biographie Nationale de Belgique,* Brussels, 1921–1924, XXIII, pp. 121–126, supplement, 1959, vol. 2, pp. 303–306; see also the briefs in M. Burke and P. Cherry, *Documents for the History of Collecting: Collections of Paintings in Madrid 1601–1755,* Ann Arbor, 1997, and P. Cherry, *El bodegón español en el Siglo de Oro,* Madrid, 1999; for Solre's political relations with Spain see: A. Esteban Estringana, 'La crise politique de 1629–1633 et le début de la prééminence institutionelle de Pierre Roose dans le gouvernement général des Pays-Bas Catholiques', *Belgisch tijdschrift voor filologie en geschiedenis,* LXXVI, 1998, p. 958, n. 48.

2. In fact it would be Jean de Croÿ who made major reforms in the guard. He gave it modern statutes, looked after the nationality of its members and prevented them from working at servile jobs. These reforms improved the social prestige of the members, which included painters like Philip Diriksen, Pedro Perrer, Francisco de la Corte and Cornelius van de Beer; see Cherry 1999 (as in note 1), pp. 148–150.

3. Archivo Histórico Nacional, Madrid (AHN), Consejos, libro 365, fol. 358v.

4. B. J. Garcia Garcia, 'Los regalos de Isabel Clara Eugenia y la Corte española. Intimidad, gusto y devoción', *Reales Sitios,* 143 (2000), pp. 16–27.

5. AHN, Consejos, libro 636, fol. 103.

6. 'High intelligence and good intentions', Archivo General de Simancas (AGS), Estado, 2237, consultation of December 8, 1629.

7. Solre's gifts to Bastón, mainly books, are cited in AHN, Consejos, libro 366, fol. 103. Bastón had relations with other collectors such as Fray Íñigo de Brizuela, president of the Council of Flanders, from whom he bought a painting of *St Peter Denying Christ* valued at 2618 *reales*. Bastón's own inventory of paintings, although no artists are cited, seems focused on Flemish painting, with landscapes, battles etc. The collection was appraised by Jan Appelmans, painter and member of Archers' Guard, Archivo Histórico de Protocolos de Madrid (AHPM), 7104, fol. 147v–149v.

8. AHN, Consejos, libro 635, fol. 132.

9. AHN, Consejos, libro 635, fol. 200.

10. Burke & Cherry 1997 (as in note 1) I, p. 319–326, where the paintings were already identified.

11. His father, also named Juan van der Hamen, came from Brussels and was a member of the guard, as was his grandfather, Pedro van der Hamen, who had served in the military under the emperor Charles V in Flanders; see Cherry 1999 (as in note 1), p. 145 ff.

12. Burke Cherry 1997 (as in note 1), I, p. 319 ff.

13. For all the copies from this composition see H. Robels, *Frans Snyders, Stilleben- und Tiermaler 1579–1657,* Munich, 1989, p. 366 and 368.

14. Nothing was known about the Aytona collection until 1681, when the pictures of Ana de Silva y Corella, marchioness of Aytona, were appraised; for this collection see Burke & Cherry 1997 (as in note 1), I, p. 708. The Aytona portrait by Van Dyck is now in Vienna, Kunsthistorisches Museum, and is dated 1634.

15. Archivo Histórico de Protocolos de Madrid (AHPM), 5328, fol. 136.

16. His professional activities are cited in his will, dated 1640, AHPM, 8221, fol. 496. His activities as a lawyer are well-known through a document from a lawsuit he worked on, today in the History Academy of Madrid, 14/11532 (13).

17. Lanchares' will demonstrates that Maldonado owed the painter the price of a painting he had made. Unfortunately nothing else is said about the subject of it. Cited in M. Agulló, *Más noticias sobre pintores madrileños de los siglos XVI al XVII,* Madrid, 1981, p. 37.

18. As Cajés write in his own will: *declaro que don Diego de Abarca me tiene dado docientos reales para quenta de vn quadro de vn Christo que boy haciendo y de la Magdalena,* cited in M. Agulló, *Noticias sobre pintores madrileños de los siglos XVI y XVII,* Granada, 1978, p. 37.

19. He came from one of the main Sicilian families and was a theologian and Apostolic Protonotary of the Pope in Spain. His palace career began in 1630 when he asked for the post of honorable royal chaplain, the person in charge of the royal chapel; Archivo General de Palacio, Madrid (AGP), Expedientes Personales (PER), 7795/8.

20. AHPM, 5328, fol. 153.

21. AHPM, 5328, fol. 146

22. He was the son of Deonis L'Hermitte, who had served in the battle of Dunkirk (1594) under the leadership of Archduke Albert and the count of Fuentes, AGP, PER, 549/10.

23. AGS, Cámara de Castilla, libro 369, fol. 55v.

24. AHPM, 5328, fol. 147v.

25. AHPM, 5328, fol. 146 and 147v. He also acquired luxury objects like fans and silver pieces.

26. According to the document of the sale, Morais was exchequeur of the royal councils.

27. AHPM, 5328, fol. 143v.

28. AGS, Cámara de Castilla, leg. 1205.

29. For an in-depth economic and social biography of Scazuola, see C. Álvarez Nogal, *Los banqueros de Felipe IV y los metales preciosos americanos (1621–1665),* Madrid, 1997, p. 29.

30. AHPM, 7805, fol. 1046v The appraisal was made by the painter Jusepe Leonardo.

31. AHPM, 7805, fol. 1077v. Appraisal made on June 6, 1640, by Jusepe Leonardo.

32. AHPM, 7805, fol. 1122. This group of paintings along with a few others in the so-called desk-room and children's room was inventoried and appraised some time after the first two groups.

33. AHPM, 7805, fol. 1067v.

34. The sale of Scazuola's goods began in February 1640, AHPM, 7805, 1156 y. For the Lamini purchases see fols. 1177v–1178. He also acquired one series of decorative paintings composed of twelve ovals depicting birds.

35. AHPM, 5328, fol. 132; Burke & Cherry 1997 (as in note 1), p. 321. He acquired moreover three works on copper described as *from Humanity with a Bacchus god,* which is very strange iconography indeed.

36. AHPM, 5328, fol. 131. Burke & Cherry 1997 (as in note 1), pp. 321.

37. Agulló 1981 (as in note 17), p. 217.

38. Inventoried by the painter Angelo Nardi on February 28, 1658, AHPM, 9077, fol. 244.

39. AHPM, 5328, fol. 149–149v.

40. *Declaro que tengo en poder del dicho Bartolome Barrilaro quarenta y siete o quarenta y ocho pinturas, que no me acuerdo fixamente las que son, que se las entegué prestadas, que me las pidió para con ellas açer algunas ferias y asta haora no las ha echo, por no auernos conbenido el susodicho ni yo en el precio en que auian de ser, y asta ora no me las a entregado y están en su poder. Mando que se cobren = y declaro que el susodicho me presto quatroçientos y çinquenta reales en vellon. Y para este efecto tiene en su poder por prenda un quadro de* ~~*Nicolas*~~ (sic) *de Caravacho de la ystoria del Cambio de San Matheo* ~~*que*~~ (sic) *es un quadro grande. Mando se le pague a el susodho la dicha cantidad y se cobre el dicho quadro.* Last will of Francisco Miracles Sotomayor, Minor Orders Clergy, opened on September 9, 1655, cited in M. Agullo y Cobo and M.T. Baratech Zalama, *Documentos para la Historia de la Pintura Española,* Madrid, 1996, p. 135.

41. AHPM, 5328, fol. 128–130 and 132–133v.

42. AHPM, 5328, fol. 132–131v.

43. AHPM, 5328, fol. 131v.

44. AHPM, 5328, fols. 135–137v.

45. Ibidem, fols. 143v–144.

46. Ibidem, fol. 140.

47. His biography in Alvarez y Baena, *Hijos Ilustres de Madrid,* Madrid, 1791, p. 212.

48. The collection was appraised on August 30, 1630, by Juan de Fontecha, AHPM, 2499, fol. 669.

49. For his biography and family ancestors see *Bibliographie Nationale de Belgique,* I, Brussels, 1866, pp. 388–401, and 406, 410; and J.-P. Tytgat, 'Charles, prince et comte d´Aremberg, duc d´Aarschot, baron de Zeverberg, seigneur de Enghien (1550–1616)', in *Une ville et ses seigneurs Enghien et Aremberg 1607–1635,* Enghien, 1994, pp. 7–20. On his role in Spanish politics see Esteban Estringana 1998 (as cited on note 1), pp. 948 and 95; J. Elliot, *The Count-duke of Olivares*, London, 1986, pp. 463, 467–472.

50. Leganés would say of Aarschot: *q aunque verde y arojado de condiciones es grande de tan conoçida calidad y es rendida parentela en aquellas prouincias a quienes seria de sumo dolor su arrimo sus antepasados confirmaron su fidelidad con notorias fineças y en esto tengo por sin duda lo seguira el duque.* AGS, Estado, 2237, December 1629.

51. L. P. Gachard, *Actes des Etats Généraux de 1632,* II, Brussels, 1856, p. 455.

52. For the circumstances surrounding Aarschot's emprisonment in Madrid see H. Soly and R. Vermeir, 'Le duc d´Arschot et les conséquences de la conspiration des nobles (1632–1640)', in *Beleid en Bestuur in de oude Nederlanden. Liber Amicorum Prof. Dr. M. Baelde,* Ghent, 1993.

53. AHN, Consejos. Leg. 12444, exp 5.

54. On Noveliers' role in the archducal court see the text by Sabine van Sprang in these proceedings (pp. 37-46).

55. S. Speth-Holterhoff, *Les peintres flamands de cabinets d'amateurs,* Brussels, 1957, pp. 38 and 204, n. 52.

56. J. Denucé, *De Antwerpsche Konstkamers. Inventarissen van Kuntverzamelingen te Antwerpen in de 16 en 17 eeuwen (Bronnen voor de geschiedenis van de Vlaamsche kunst,* II), Antwerp, 1932, p. 76.

57. J.L. López Navío, 'La gran colección de pinturas del Marqués de Leganés', *Analecta Calasanctiana,* 1962, pp. 287–288.

58. Caylus Gallery, Madrid, on sale in the spring of 2000.

59. Resumen que hace Andrés Gutiérrez de Haro, traductor de las cartas que recibía y enviaba Aarschot, de las cartas enviadas a mediados de Abril, AHN, Consejos, leg. 12444, exp 6.

60. Ibidem.

61. Haro's translation of Aarschot's letter to Canon Tassis on May 12, 1639, AHN, Consejos, leg. 12444, exp. 6.

62. Ibidem.

63. Ibidem.

64. Ibidem.

65. Haro's translation of the letter written by Aarschot to Baptista van Dalen on May 12, 1639, AHN, Consejos, leg. 12444, exp. 6.

66. On May 14 Aarschot paid the customs duty to Eduard Coronel for *paintings that came from Flanders,* AHPM, 5985, fol. 716.

67. Cited in Burke & Cherry 1997 (as cited on note 1), II, p. 343.

68. A. Balis, *Landscapes and Hunting Scenes, II* (*Corpus Rubenianum Ludwig Burchard,* XVII-2), London, 1986 p. 25, n. 20.

69. Letter from Aarschot to Tassis, AHN, 124444, exp. 6.

70. Camilo Guido, duke of Mantua's agent in Spain, wanted to acquire fourteen hunting scenes from the Aarschot collection; see J. Southorn, *Power and display in the seventeenth century,* Cambridge, 1988, p. 42.

71. Some of the paintings that arrived Madrid after duke's death may have been by Paul de Vos: *another canvas (....) that is a boar hunt; plus eleven canvases on hunting,* Burke & Cherry 1997 (as cited on note 1), I, p. 344, nº 10 and 20.

72. Some of the books recording Aarschot's accounts in Flanders for the period during which he was in Spain are conserved in the Archives Générales du Royaume in Brussels (AGR). On July 13, 1639, 84 florins were paid to Gaspar de Crayer as part of the 384 florins agreed upon as the price of the eight paintings. AGR, LA 4683, book from June 1, 1639–October 17, 1639, fol. 11v.

73. Van Utrecht received 156 florins in July 1640, Ibidem, fol. 10v

74. He is paid the sum of 32 florins for non-specified works on August 5, 1639, Ibidem, fol. 17v.

75. Ibidem, fol. 24v.

76. AGR, LA 4682, book from August 9, 1640, to November 2, 1640, fol. 13v.

77. AGR, LA 4682, book from November 2, 1640, to August 31, 1644, fol. 18.

78. AGR, LA 4682, book from June 1, 1639, to October 17, 1639.

79. AGR, LA 4682, book from January 29 to May 30, 1639, fol. 13.

80. AHPM, 5985, fol. 762.

81. AGR, LA 4682, book from August 9, 1640, to November 2, 1640, fol. 14.

82. AHPM, 5328, fol. 132, for the purchases from the Croÿ collection; AHPM, 5985, fol. 651, for the sale to Aarschot.

83. AHPM, 5985, fol. 598.

84. AGR, LA, 4682, book from January 29 to May 30, 1639, fol. 14v.

85. 104 *reales* were paid for them in March, AHPM, 5985, fol. 828v.

86. AHPM, 5985, fol. 739v–740.

87. Some payments to Van Eyck appeared among the papers of Aarschot's accountant Diego Tomlison: 2000 *reales* for six paintings for the duke on November 9, 1638 (AHPM, 5985, fol. 556); 600 *reales* for the same paintings on December 5, 1638 (fol. 556v); 900 *reales* on January 2, 1639 (fol. 626); 800 *reales* on April 10, 1639 (fol. 650v); and 900 *reales* in May 1639. Cited as payments to Gaspar de Crayer in Burke & Cherry 1997 (as cited on note 1), I, p. 347. Probably 'Gaspar van Eyken' or 'Gaspar van Ecke' is to be identified with the marine painter Gaspar van Eyck.

88. Burke & Cherry 1997 (as cited on note 1), I, p. 349, n° 16. The Prado has three marine paintings by Gaspar van Eyck (cat. nos. 1507, 1508 and 1509); one of them is dated 1649, which makes impossible its having any relation to the Aarschot paintings.

89. Ibidem, fol. 692v.

90. See López Navio 1962 (as in note 57), p. 280.

91. There are many payments to Puga: 50 *reales* in August 1638 plus 400 *reales* on February 16, 1639, both for a portrait of the duchess of Aarschot, Ibidem, fol. 554 and fol. 635v; 1900 *reales* for his services during September and October 1638 (idem 554v–555); another 800 *reales* on November 19, 1639 (fol. 708). For the copy he made from the Rubens picture he was paid 1500 *reales*. For this work there is a receipt dated April 11, 1640, after the duke had already died (AHPM, 5993, fol. 1181). See also Burke & Cherry 1997 (as in note 1), I, p. 345.

92. Burke & Cherry 1997 (as cited on note I), II, p. 346.

93. The Aarschot paintings by Puga included a Blind man playing guitar, for which no dimensions are mentioned in the document; see Burke & Cherry 1997 (as cited on note 1), II, n° 67.

94. There are some payments to Juan de la Corte on January 2, April 24, and July 12, 1639, AHPM, 5985, fols. 552–554.

95. On Juan de la Corte see D. Angulo and A. E. Pérez Sánchez, *Pintura Madrileña del primer tercio del siglo XVII*, Madrid, 1969, pp. 349 ff; and D. T. Kinkead, 'El testamento de Juan de la Corte', *Boletín del Seminario de Estudios de Arte y Arqueología de la Universidad de Valladolid*, 1986, p. 461.

96. The sale document cites ten paintings by Collantes, but their topic is not mentioned, AHPM, 5993, fol. 1272v. However, the inventory document states that two landscapes with black frames had been pawned, AHPM, 5993, fol. 1134.

97. For the best study of his oeuvre see D. Angulo and A.E. Pérez Sánchez, *Pintura Madrileña del segundo tercio del siglo XVII*, Madrid, 1983, p. 36 ff.

98. V. Carducho, *Diálogos de la pintura*, Diálogo Cuarto, fol. 47, ed. Calvo Serraller, 1979, p. 177. See also Angulo & Pérez Sánchez 1983, (as in note 97), p. 37.

99. See Burke & Cherry 1997 (as in note 1), I, pp. 349, n° 14, 17 and 354, n° 110 and 111.

100. For Cajés see Angulo & Pérez Sánchez 1969 (as in note 95), p. 212 ff.

101. Paid on August 6, 1637, AHPM, 5985, fol. 507.

102. He was paid on January 6, 1639, for the repair of the equestrian portraits in the Aarschot collection, AHPM, 5985, fol. 632v; on February 4, 1639, for some frames (fol. 508); and in August 1640 for mending a painting (fol. 771v).

103. See Burke & Cherry 1997 (as cited on note 1), I, pp. 351, n° 65; 353, n° 84, 86, 90; 354, n° 106; 355, n° 134–136; 356, n° 162 and 353, n° 94, respectively.

104. For instance, there are many described as bird concerts, like numbers 52 and 59.

105. *Del s^r l^do Juan Antonio Elasco a quenta del veinte mil R^s en belllon que el s^r marques de povar deue a su Ex^a para algunas pinturas que a feriado de su Ex^a a pagar en quatro terminos el 1° en el mes de 7^bre 1638 y los otros de tres en tres meses cinco mil reales de Bellon, AHPM, 5985, fol. 550.*

106. AHPM, 6208, fol. 911–911v, where it is said that there were thirty-four paintings.

107. *En el mes de enero 1639 de Su Ex^a el señor admirante de Castilla mil y ochocientos Reales de bellon por quatro pinturas que su Ex^a le a feriado*, AHPM, 5985, fol. 623.

108. In a letter written by Aarschot on May 12, 1639, he ordered: *como de la misma manera a sido pagado a los 28 de abril deste año de 330 reales de bellon por una pintura que hauia comprado de la cassa mortuoria del Difunto s^r conde de sora* (Aarschot to Andrés Ghestel, AHN, Consejos, Leg. 12444, exp. 6). We assume he meant the painting of the Tower of Babel which Cornelius Warbe bought from Solre and then sold to Aarschot. The Spanish language made 'Sora' from the sound of 'Solre'.

109. AHPM, 5993, fol. 1267. They were purchased on October 7. The inventory said the still lifes came from Holland. See Burke & Cherry 1997 (as in note 1), I, p. 348.

110. See López Navio 1962 (as in note 57), n° 1141–1144.

111. AHPM, 5993, fol. 1277v. It was purchased on November 14. For a view of the Carpio collection see: M. Burke, *Private Collections of Italian Art in Seventeenth Century Spain*, Ph.D. New York University, 1984, I, pp. 131–201, II, pp. 212–380; and Burke & Cherry 1997 (as in note 1), I, pp. 726–786, 462–483.

112. It was acquired on October 7, 1641, AHPM, 5993, fol. 1266.

113. AHPM, 5993, fol. 1241v and 1246. The marchioness of Cortes was the sister of the count of Castrillo, who played an important role in the importation of painting for the king from Italy in the thirties.

114. AHPM, 5993, fol. 1283.

115. AGS, Cámara de Castilla, libro 369, fol. 18

116. AHPM, 5993, fol. 1283.

117. Ibidem, fol. 1245 and 1242v respectively.

118. Ibidem, fol. 1268

119. He died in 1657; the inventory of his possessions describes small bronze objects and only a few paintings, all of them on copper, AHPM, 9158, fol. 387 ff.

120. AHPM, 5593, fol. 1266, October 6, 1641.

121. In 1619 an archer with the same name died who is supposed to have been related to him, AHPM, 5230, fol. 87.

122. Duprie bought two canvases depicting the Ecce Homo and the Virgin on September 12 Herrera de la Concha bought a representation of the Christ Child sleeping on November

16; none of them had a high price, AHPM, 5993, fol. 1243 y 1246.

123. He bought an image of the Virgin on September 12, AHPM, 5993, fol. 1243.

124. A. Palomino, *Vidas*, ed. Nina Ayala, Madrid, 1986, p. 193.

125. AGR, LA 4682, book from June 1 to October 17, 1639, fol. 20.

126. He bought a cheap clock on September 12, AHPM, 5993, fol. 1243

127. Although he did not buy any paintings – only two decorative pyramids on ivory and ebony – on September 19, his presence testifies to the intellectual occupations of some of the collection purchasers, AHPM, 5993, fol. 1250.

128. He bought a small sculpture in copper and a carving or painting of Christ, AHPM, 5993, fol. 1267.

129. L. Ramirez de Prado, *Consejo y Consejero de Principes,* ed. Juan Beneito, Madrid, 1958, p. 35.

130. J. Entrambasaguas, *La Biblioteca de Ramírez de Prado,* Madrid, 1943.

131. Entrambasaguas 1943 (as in note 130), p. XIII.

132. One of the divisions of his library was described as follows: *De artes liberales, en que estan mathematicos, con todas sus especies, geográphos, arithmeticos, chronographos, astrologos, musicos, pintores, architectonicos, militares, nauticos, hidrografos &c* (Ibidem, p. 95 ff).

133. Cherry 1999 (as in note 1), p. 506; Marqués de Saltillo, 'Prevenciones artísticas para acontecimientos regios en el Madrid secentista (1640–1680)', *Boletin de la Real Academia de la Historia*, CXXI, 1947, pp. 375–378; and AHPM, 7881, fol. 153.

134. His purchases were religious, including an ebony carving of the Virgin and other carvings with Ercole, purchased on September 17, AHPM, 5993, fol. 120.

135. September 13 and 19, 1641, AHPM, 5993, fols. 1244 and 1249.

136. He died on June 18, 1642; during his life he had been a judge in Ávila and Court Councils lawyer. See his will in AHPM, 5990, fol. 655.

137. In fact, one of his purchases is described as a painting with burgundian people at table; the other was an interior of a tavern. Both of them were purchased on September 16, 1641, AHPM 5993, fol. 1247.

138. AGP, Alcázares de Sevilla, C$^{a}$ 222/18. His purchases included a religious painting with Christ, Saint Mary Magdalen and Saint John, and were made on October 23, 1641, AHPM, 5993, fol. 1274.

139. See C. Sanz Ayan, *Los Banqueros de Carlos II,* Valladolid, 1989, p. 526; and C. Alvárez Nogal, *Los banqueros de Felipe IV y los metales preciosos americanos (1621–1665),* Madrid, Banco de España, 1997, pp. 107 and 176.

140. AHPM, 11302, fols. 470v and 471.

141. A carving of the Virgin and a carving of the Trinity, purchased in September 1641, AHPM, 5993, fol. 1242.

142. Álvarez Nogal 1989 (as in note 139) p. 28 and 55.

143. Según refleja su testamento era administrador del marqués de Cañete y tenia numerosos bienes materiales AHPM, 4530, fol. 248. En la almoneda Aremberg, sin embargo, apenas compra una imagen de la Virgen, AHPM, 5993, fol. 1242.

144. Sanz Ayan 1989 (as in note 139), pp. 199, 454, 459 and 472.

145. September 13, AHPM, 5993, fol. 1244–1244v.

146. His houses were reputed to have been decorated in a magnificent way, owing to his improving social status, Sanz Ayán 1989 (as in note 139), pp. 475–476.

147. AHPM, 8126, fol. 853.

148. AHPM, 5993, fol. 1265–1265v. Purchased on September 30, 1641, Burke & Cherry, 1997 (as in note 1), I, p. 522.

149. Burke & Cherry 1997 (as in note 1), I, pp. 521–526.

150. A. Vergara, *Rubens and his Spanish Patrons,* Cambridge, Cambridge University Press, 1998, *p.* 97, n. 127 and 128.

151. Three small paintings, a religious scene and a tapestries series depicting the history of Samson on September 19 and 23, 1641, AHPM, 5993, fols. 1250v and 1257; for Juan González, fol. 1247.

152. AHPM, 5993, f 1257.

153. Carducho 1979 (as in note 98), p. 425. His contemporaries did not believe the attibutions of his paintings. The poet Ulloa y Pereira, referring to certain works by Pedro de Orrente, said that if they were in Suero de Quiñones collection they would be by Bassano, cf. A.E. Pérez Sánchez, *La pintura italiana en España,* Madrid, 1965, p. 66, n. 13.

154. Saltillo, 'Dos mecenas de Cervantes: El duque de Béjar y don Rodrigo de Tapia', *Boletín de la Real Academia de la Historia,* CXXX, 1952, pp. 7–58.

155. Carducho 1979 (as in note 98), p. 424.

156. AHPM, 5993, fol. 1266, October 3, 1641.

157. AHPM, 5993, fol. 1278, November 20, 1641.

158. AHPM, 5993, fol. 1285. December 24, 1641.

159. AHPM, 5993, fol. 1267v, October 7, 1641.

160. AHPM, 5993, fols. 1281v, 1288v, 1291v, 1282.

161. AHPM, 5993, fol. 1288v, December 30, 1641. He also bought a painting with Saint Benedict, two paintings of the Virgin, one boar hunt with a dog, two landscapes, a martyrdom of Saint Sebastian and a painting with Christ tied to the column, ibidem, fol. 1286v.

162. AHPM, 5993, fol. 1289, December 30, 1641. He may have been related to Jerónimo Ferrer, who on the following day purchased three equestrian portraits, a painting on copper depicting Christ and Nicodemus, another painting on copper depicting Saint Peter in prison, a small landscape painted on paper, a genre painting on panel, a canvas with birds and a painting with a monkey and a cat on panel.

163. AHPM, 5993, fol. 1283v, December 17, 1641.

164. AHPM, 5993, fol. 1283v, December 19, 1641.

165. AHPM, 5993, fol. 1290v, December 31, 1641.

166. AHPM, 5993, fol. 1280, December 10, 1641.

167. His collection found in AHPM, 5185, fol. 409, first published in Burke and Cherry, 1997 (as in note 1), I, p. 367. For the arrival of this picture in Spain see Vergara, 1998 (as in note 150), p. 137.

# Les peintres à la cour d'Albert et Isabelle: une tentative de classification*

*Sabine van Sprang*

Avec l'intronisation d'Albert et Isabelle (1598–1633), les Pays-Bas sont à nouveau dotés de souverains en résidence, après quarante ans de troubles et de gouverneurs se succédant à un rythme parfois effréné. Leur présence marque également l'essor d'une «société de cour» revitalisée. Les arts devaient y jouer un rôle important: conformément à l'esprit de leur temps, les archiducs considéraient que collectionner les oeuvres d'art – en particulier, des œuvres flamandes – et offrir leur protection aux artistes constituaient deux activités essentielles à leur magnificence princière.

Plusieurs peintres furent ainsi attachés à leur service. Tous ne jouissaient cependant pas du même statut. Si la position exceptionnelle qu'occupait Rubens, nommé chevalier à la fin de sa carrière, est communément reconnue par les chercheurs – encore que rarement située dans l'organisation globale de la cour –, ses collègues sont généralement qualifiés, sans autre distinction, de «peintres des archiducs». Or, il existait clairement des différences de rang et de traitement. Dans son ouvrage de référence sur les peintres œuvrant pour la cour (1955), Marcel De Maeyer a récolté, avec une rigueur qui force l'admiration, l'essentiel des données relatives à leur charge. Cependant, en fin de volume, il propose une classification de leur condition qui ne tient pas suffisamment compte, selon nous, de la logique de la cour et paraît dès lors erronée sur certains points[1]. Il en vient ainsi à négliger la spécificité des privilèges octroyés par les souverains, qui, dans bien des cas, revêtent une forme foncièrement originale. C'est pourquoi nous nous proposons de réexaminer les catégories établies par l'auteur à partir des sources qu'il a lui-même récoltées pour une grande part, et que nous avons pu compléter par quelques inédits.

Selon Marcel De Maeyer les peintres qui travaillaient pour les souverains, puis au nom d'Isabelle ou de Philippe IV sous la régence de l'infante, peuvent être classés en trois catégories: ceux qui ont œuvré pour la cour sans bénéficier de privilèges particuliers; ceux qui reçurent, généralement après un certain nombre d'années, l'exemption de contraintes liées au droit de bourgeoisie par gratitude envers leur prestation, mais ne furent jamais nommés à la cour à proprement parler; et enfin ceux qui furent effectivement élevés au rang de «peintre de cour». À la première catégorie appartenaient, d'après lui, des peintres tels que Gisbertus Venius ou Antoon Sallaert (il y en eut d'autres); à la deuxième, Jan Brueghel l'Ancien, Joos de Momper et sans doute le Malinois Hans Verbeeck; et à la troisième: Hendrik de Clerck, Denijs van Alsloot, Pieter, Salomon et peut-être David Noveliers, Jacques Francart, Willem van Deynum, Peter Paul Rubens, bien sûr, et probablement Antoon van Dyck (sous l'infante; fig. 1). Le statut et la fonction de ces deux derniers artistes étaient toutefois disproportionnés comparés à ceux de leurs collègues. Enfin, citons le cas particulier d'Otto Venius, qui, tout en exécutant des tableaux pour les souverains, la ville d'Anvers et le clergé, fut attaché à la cour en tant que *«ingéniaire du chasteau»* de la métropole portuaire (avant 1604), puis en tant que *«guardain* (waerdeyn) *de la monnoye de leurs altezes en Bruxelles»* (1612)[2].

La première catégorie pose peu de problèmes: de tout temps les cours ont employé des artistes de manière occasionnelle sans pour autant les nommer officiellement ou leur octroyer le moindre privilège[3]. Ainsi, Antoon Sallaert, peintre d'histoire et portraitiste, semble n'avoir été engagé que de façon ponctuelle sous la régence d'Isabelle pour exécuter au palais des travaux d'ordre essentiellement décoratif[4]. Quant à Gisbertus Venius (frère d'Otto Venius), l'archiduc lui refusa explicitement l'exonération des maltôtes alors que l'artiste avait réalisé plusieurs portraits à sa demande au début de son gouvernement[5].

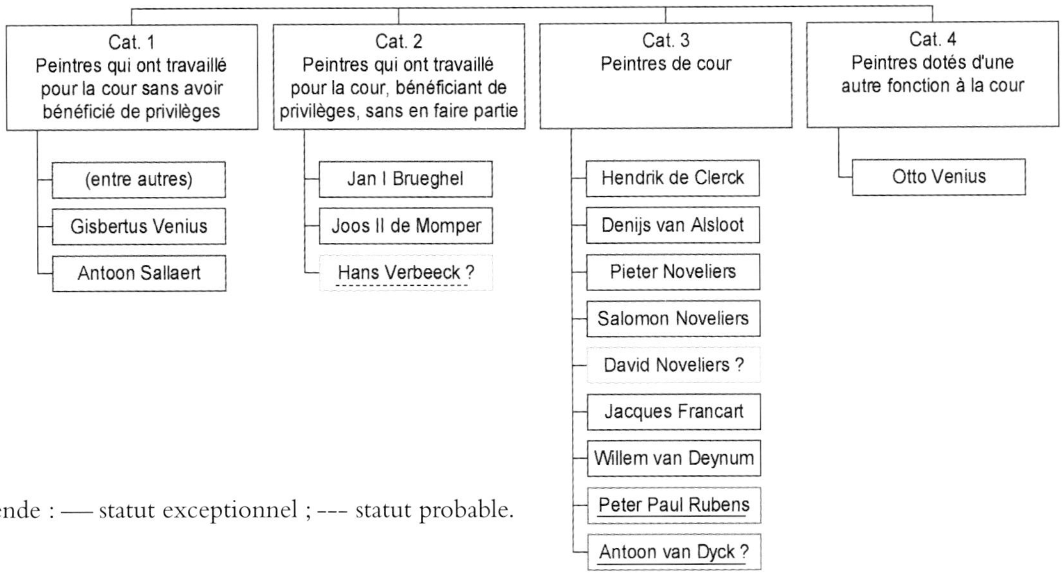


Légende : — statut exceptionnel ; --- statut probable.

Fig. 1. Classification des peintres qui ont travaillé pour la cour d'Albert et Isabelle selon Marcel De Maeyer

Les deuxième et troisième catégories établies par De Maeyer nous paraissent, en revanche, plus problématiques: si nous adhérons au principe de subdivision, nous ne pouvons suivre l'auteur dans son classement des peintres, ni dans les critères qui l'y ont poussé.

La nomination à la cour instaurait traditionnellement une allégeance personnelle confirmée par serment, quelle que soit la fonction[6]. Elle s'assortissait d'un certain nombre d'avantages juridiques, ecclésiastiques[7] et sociaux ainsi que du droit éventuel de percevoir des traitements fixes. S'il était d'origine bourgeoise, le candidat faisait ainsi son entrée dans la *maison* du souverain, en devenant son *serviteur domestique* – appelé aussi *officier*[8]. Cette désignation était commune à tous les employés et valait donc pour les artistes également. Appartenaient à la cour, tous ceux qui étaient consignés dans les états journaliers (*les escroues*) et – pour autant qu'ils soient salariés – dans les registres aux gages, comme le stipule une ordonnance promulguée par l'archiduc en 1613:

«.... *Et comme il y pourroit tomber doubte quelz nous tenons pour noz domestiques et courtisans, nous déclarons pour telz tous ceux qui se trouveront enrollez ou assentéz es livres de nostre cour et maison, de quelle qualité, nation ou condition qu'ilz soyent, mesmes aussi tous ceulx qui suyvront nostre cour et n'auront gaiges, par voye de l'exercito* (...)»[9]

Qu'en était-il des peintres appelés à la cour mentionnés dans les deuxième et troisième catégories établies par De Maeyer? Comme celui-ci ne manque pas de le faire remarquer, l'analyse de leur statut est d'autant plus difficile qu'à quelques exceptions près, les patentes de leur nomination sont perdues[10]. Les *escroues* manquent également pour la période concernée et les registres aux gages sont incomplets. Toute étude comparative s'avère délicate, puisque nous ne disposons pour chacun de ces artistes que de documents épars et souvent divers.

Parmi les sources qui nous renseignent de façon utile, figurent les *Livres de raison* (*Libros de la Razon*) contenant l'enregistrement des ordres de paiement prescrits de 1612 à 1618 par l'archiduc Albert pour le compte de sa maison. Il s'agit donc de rétributions effectuées sur la secrétairerie particulière du souverain[11]. Deux peintres y sont mentionnés régulièrement: Jacques Francart (le même qui en 1622 sera promu *architecte et ingéniaire* du roi d'Espagne Philippe IV, et auteur de plusieurs églises baroques) et Willem van Deynum, un portraitiste et enlumineur dont l'œuvre reste largement à découvrir. Le nom de Francart apparaît pour la première fois sous la date du 20 mars 1613 avec l'épithète *mi pintor*, un titre qui exprime clairement la nature du lien entre l'artiste et le souverain. Le registre précise en outre que le peintre reçoit des gages annuels s'élevant à 300 florins[12]. Ce revenu n'empêchait pas que l'artiste soit payé au surplus pour des commandes spécifiques, comme de nombreux récépissés l'ont démontré[13]. Un an plus tard, le 31

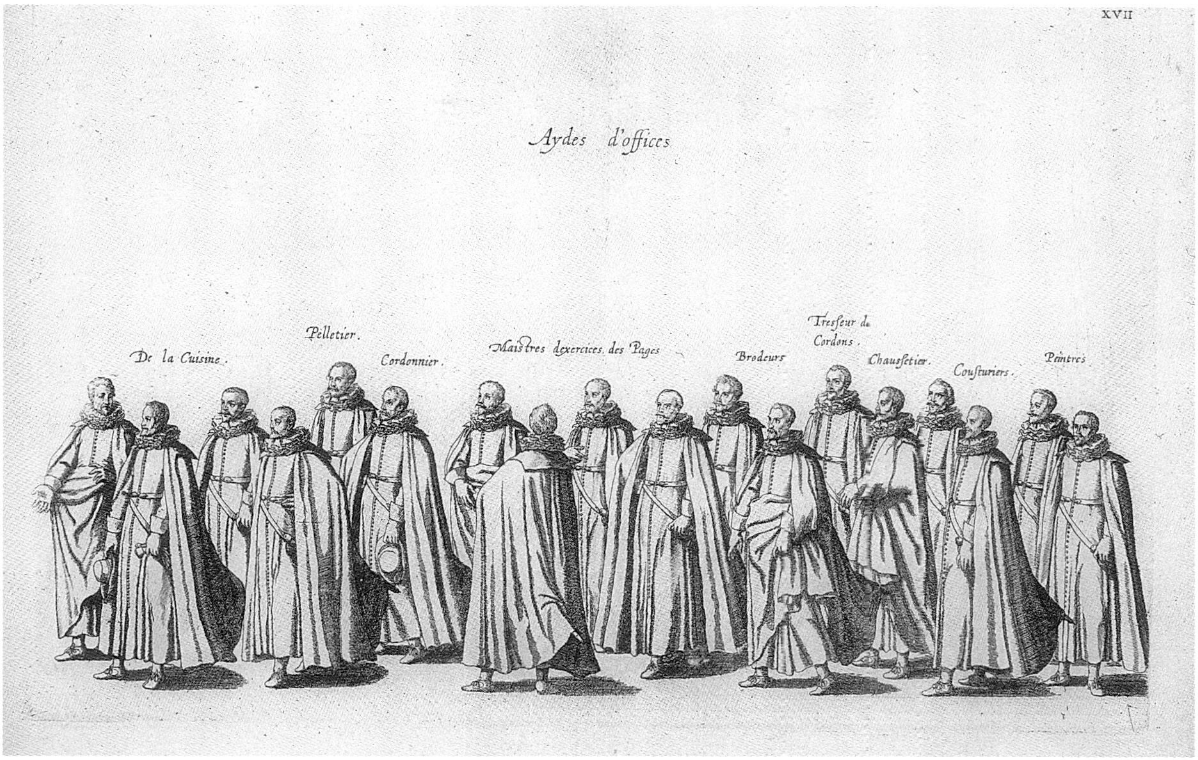


Fig. 2. J. Francart, *Pompe funèbre de l'archiduc Albert*, gravure, extrait de J. Francart, *Pompa Funebris optimi potentissimi princeps Albert Pii*…, Bruxelles, 1623

août 1614 ou peu après, c'est au tour de Willem van Deynum d'être inscrit dans le *Livre de raison* de l'archiduc en tant que *mi pintor y yluminador*, son salaire étant fixé à 250 florins l'an[14].

Un échange de courrier en 1618 entre la cour et la ville de Bruxelles nous apprend par ailleurs que Van Deynum, en sa qualité de *domestique* de cour, n'était pas assujetti à la gilde des peintres[15]. Ce privilège, que le magistrat tenta de contester, ne présentait pas que des avantages: exonéré de ce fait des obligations et contributions corporatives, l'artiste se voyait contraint en contrepartie à ne travailler que pour les souverains et leur entourage direct, la vente libre de ses œuvres lui étant interdite. Le respect de cette disposition, attachée à la condition initiale de l'officier artisan, apparaît cependant comme exceptionnelle: le déficit chronique des finances princières avait amené depuis longue date déjà les peintres de cour aux Pays-Bas à s'affilier au métier plutôt qu'à limiter leur clientèle[16], même s'il fallait pour cela (en principe) s'acquitter du droit de bourgeoisie et satisfaire à toutes les corvées civiles[17].

Il est probable toutefois que Jacques Francart travailla dans les mêmes conditions que Van Deynum. Nous retrouvons en effet l'un de ses élèves, Théodore de Sany, originaire de Valenciennes et devenu citoyen de Bruxelles, admis comme maître à la gilde bruxelloise des peintres en 1620, par autorisation expresse du magistrat[18].

Les *Libros de la Razon* nous renseignent aussi sur la position que Francart (fig. 2) et Van Deynum occupaient dans l'organisation de la cour. À l'instar des principales cours européennes de l'époque fondées sur le modèle bourguignon, celle des archiducs se composait de quatre sections: la *Chapelle*, l'*Hostel*, la *Chambre* et enfin l'*Écuyerie*. La Chambre, suivant l'étiquette espagnole, était partagée à son tour entre celle de l'infante et celle d'Albert[19]. C'est sous cette dernière section que nous retrouvons les deux peintres, rangés parmi les artisans qualifiés, appelés ailleurs *officiers des mains*[20]. Ils dépendaient de la *Garderobe,* qui avait dans ses attributions la garde des objets précieux appartenant à la chambre et à la chapelle (fig. 3)[21]. Leur poste était donc relativement modeste, ce dont témoigne également le montant de leurs gages, égal ou à peine supérieur à celui des simples archers et gardes du corps[22].

Le rang du peintre François Verbeelen à la cour devait être plus modeste encore. Il est

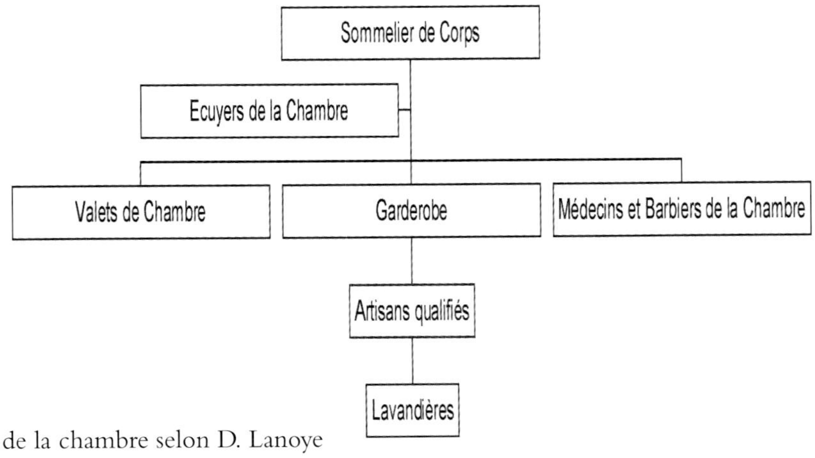


Fig. 3. Le Service de la chambre selon D. Lanoye

significatif à cet égard que De Maeyer se contente de citer l'artiste en note, le jugeant indigne de figurer dans l'une de ses catégories[23]. En 1601, Verbeelen succède à un certain Cornelis Witler comme *peintre ordinaire de la court*[24]. D'après les sources disponibles (la commission et quelques paiements), son mandat semble s'être limité à l'exécution de travaux de peinture et de décoration (y compris des décors de théâtre), non seulement pour le Coudenberg, mais aussi pour le château de Tervuren. Sans doute faisait-il partie du menu personnel, ressortissant à l'*Hostel* et attaché directement au service du palais (*la court*)[25]. Gratifié d'un salaire fixe dont nous ignorons le montant[26], mais qui ne devait pas être très élevé, il exerça sans aucun doute des activités en dehors de la cour également, puisque nous le retrouvons mentionné à la gilde des peintres de Bruxelles dès 1603[27].

La condition de Peter Paul Rubens à la cour était, on le sait, d'une tout autre nature. Il est aussi l'un des rares peintres dont les patentes ont été conservées. Sollicité par les archiducs pour devenir leur *officier* et élevé à la dignité de *paintre de* [leur] *hostel* le 23 septembre 1609, Rubens bénéficie des «*droitz, honneurs, libertez, exemptions et franchises accoustumez et y appertenans, et dont joyssent aultres noz domesticques et serviteurs*»[28]. Mais ses gages sont nettement supérieurs à ceux perçus par ses confrères (500 livres par an) alors qu'il ne travaille que de manière ponctuelle pour les souverains. En outre, il peut résider à Anvers et «*enseigner à ses serviteurs et aultres qu'il voudra sondict art, sans estre assubjecti à ceulx du mestier*», tandis qu'il exerce librement et réalise des œuvres pour qui lui plait[29]. L'artiste semble néanmoins avoir servi, à l'occasion, de conseiller *audict office*[30], à l'instar de l'architecte Wensel Cobergher dans le domaine de la construction[31]. Rappelons toutefois que Rubens s'était inscrit comme maître à la gilde des peintres d'Anvers en 1598. En cela sa situation diffère de celle de Van Deynum qui ne s'est jamais fait membre du métier de Bruxelles. Libéré des contraintes corporatives, Rubens continua d'ailleurs à entretenir des relations avec sa gilde, dans le but, sans doute, de la ménager[32]. En 1633, il fut même élu au poste de doyen, une charge qu'il refusa, mais non sans avoir offert à la corporation une *Vierge au perroquet*[33]. Contrairement à ce que prétendit son neveu Philips, Rubens n'était donc aucunement lié à la cour par «*des chaînes*», fussent-elles «*dorées*»[34]. Son titre, comme sa rémunération paraissent avoir été essentiellement honorifiques. Anobli en 1624 par Philippe IV, Rubens occupa ensuite, de 1625 à 1629, le poste de «ayuda de camera» de l'infante Isabelle, une charge indubitablement peu élevée, mais qui fut régulièrement allouée à des membres de la noblesse[35].

Il est probable, comme le suggère De Maeyer, que l'exemple du grand maître inspira la situation de Van Dyck à la cour, avant son départ pour l'Angleterre en 1632. Gratifié d'une chaîne d'or dès 1628 pour avoir réalisé le portrait de l'infante, l'artiste fut exempté de certaines corvées et taxes civiles d'Anvers par mandement du 22 mars 1629[36]. Bénéficiant apparemment d'une pension par la suite, il continua à résider, tout comme son aîné, dans la ville portuaire. Sa rémunération annuelle ne semblait toutefois pas dépasser les 250 livres, un montant comparable aux gages que percevait Van Deynum en son temps, mais il s'agit sans doute, une fois encore, d'une rétribution principalement honorifique[37].

Restent les autres peintres cités par De Maeyer. Nous l'avons dit, la perte de certains documents clés, comme les lettres patentes, rend l'interprétation des données souvent ardue. Ainsi en est-il des Noveliers: Pieter le père, et David et Salomon, les fils. Les sources nous apprennent que ceux-ci furent principalement affectés à la restauration et à la conservation des tableaux de la collection ducale du Coudenberg et du château de Tervuren, ce qui devait les occuper beaucoup. Ils paraissent, en outre, avoir exercé des activités de marchand auprès des souverains. Pourtant, seul Salomon semble avoir joui de gages (200 livres l'an) sous la régence d'Isabelle[38]. Son titre, *peintre de l'hostel de la court,* reflète par ailleurs sa position hiérarchique au palais: il permet de ranger l'artiste parmi les membres de l'*Hostel* qui avaient dans leurs compétences la maintenance des biens du palais (*la court*) et dont dépendaient peut-être les *peintres ordinaires,* tel un François Verbeelen évoqué plus haut[39].

Est-ce à dire que Pieter et David ne faisaient pas partie du personnel de cour? Tout porte à le croire. De Maeyer se trompe en affirmant que le père est cité comme tel par Gisbertus Venius en 1608, dans l'espoir de bénéficier du même privilège[40]: celui-ci se borne à mentionner Pieter Noveliers aux côtés des peintres Hendrik de Clerck et Denijs van Alsloot «*quy ont la franchise et exemption* [des maltôtes]» alors qu'ils «*n'ont pas tant travaillé pour leursdictes Altezes*» que le plaignant[41]. Le même type de dispenses est encore invoqué par Noveliers père en 1618 dans sa demande à la cour de le relever de ses fonctions au profit de son fils Salomon (avant que celui-ci ne devienne «*peintre de l'hostel*»)[42] et accordé en 1619 à son autre fils David[43]. Nous n'y trouvons aucune référence à un salaire, ni même à un office particulier. Certes, il existait depuis le XVe siècle déjà des *domestiques* nommés uniquement *aux honneurs,* sans rémunération fixe[44]. Sous les archiducs, cela sera encore le cas du sculpteur Robert de Nole, qui reçut pourtant le titre prestigieux, comparable à celui de Rubens, de *Sculpteur de* [leur] *hôtel*[45]. Il nous semble cependant que Pieter autant que David Noveliers appartenaient à une autre classe de *serviteurs,* ceux que nous appellerions volontiers les *fournisseurs de la cour*[46]. Ils rejoignent ainsi les peintres qui ne faisaient pas partie de la cour à proprement parler, rangés dans la deuxième catégorie de De Maeyer, à savoir, Jan Brueghel l'Ancien, Joos de Momper et Hans Verbeeck (peintre dont on ne connaît à ce jour aucun tableau – voir fig. 4). Tous ont en commun d'avoir été libérés, entièrement ou partiellement, des contraintes communales (mais non corporatives: ils sont tous inscrits à la gilde), souvent à leur propre requête, après avoir travaillé plusieurs années pour les archiducs et sans avoir jamais perçu de rentes. En outre, certains sont exemptés du paiement de leur résidence. Mais, ni les mandements de la cour dépêchés au magistrat ni aucun autre document officiel ne les désignent par un titre spécifique; ils se bornent à stipuler qu'ils sont ou furent *retenus au service* des souverains, sans que n'apparaisse l'épithète *domestique,* ou un qualificatif équivalent, tel que *aux escroues*[47]. Le cas de Jan Brueghel, qui, en 1610, demande explicitement aux archiducs de devenir leur *peintre domestique,* mais ne reçoit des souverains que les dispenses civiles, étant «*quelque fois occupé en ouvrages de* [leur] *service*», peut servir dans ce contexte d'exemple paradigmatique[48]. Il en va de même de celui de Joos de Momper, qui sera dispensé des obligations civiles en 1626, après avoir livré des œuvres à la cour pendant près de vingt-sept ans[49]!

Ces peintres semblent donc avoir bénéficié de certains avantages *à l'instar* des membres de la cour, mais sans en être pour autant. La missive que l'infante Isabelle adresse en 1629 à la ville de Bruxelles afin que les franchises de David Noveliers soient renouvelées ne laisse aucun doute à ce propos: elle y fait mention d'exemptions «(...) *en la forme et manière qu'en jouyssent les serviteurs de nostre hostel*» au lieu de «*ainsi qu'en jouissent les autres nos serviteurs et domestiques*», qui était la formule d'usage[50]. À ce type de fournisseur appartenait également, selon nous, le peintre d'histoire Hendrik de Clerck, «*retenu au service* » des archiducs et confirmé dans ses privilèges en 1606, par un mandement comparable à celui libérant les autres artistes que nous venons de citer[51].

La position de Denijs van Alsloot se présente, en revanche, sous une forme plus complexe. Le paysagiste est inscrit à la gilde des peintres de Bruxelles et nous n'avons trouvé aucun indice qui puisse laisser croire qu'il percevait des gages de la cour. L'artiste semble toutefois avoir

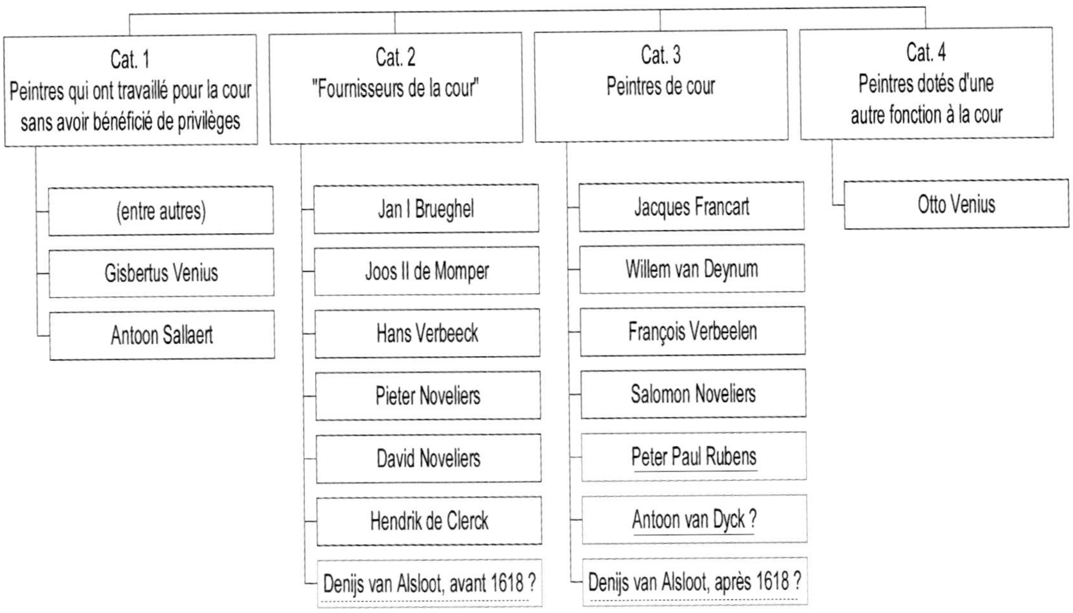


Fig. 4. Nouvelle classification proposée ici des peintres qui ont travaillé pour Albert et Isabelle. Légende voir Fig. 1

été dispensé de ses devoirs de citadin en 1606 sans en avoir fait la demande officielle, donc peut-être à l'initiative des archiducs. L'ordre l'émancipant le désigne en outre explicitement comme *leur serviteur* – mais sans ajouter le qualificatif *domestique* – qui a œuvré pour eux à leur *grand contentement*[52]. Lui-même signe fréquemment ses tableaux avec la mention «peintre de Son Altesse [l'archiduc]» dès 1606/08.

Cependant, aucun document officiel à son sujet, émanant du palais ou de la ville, ne lui confère d'autre distinction que celui de *peintre* ou de *maître peintre*. En 1608, Gisbertus Venius, espérant bénéficier, comme Van Alsloot, de l'exemption des maltôtes, le qualifie simplement de «paysagiste»[53]. L'artiste ne paraît donc pas avoir porté de titre spécifique, ni occupé d'office déterminé, même *aux honneurs*.

Pourtant, le registre des Chambres des Comptes à Lille signale en 1628 que Van Alsloot fut *en son vivant peinctre de Son Alteze Sérénissime*, raison pour laquelle l'infante Isabelle avait acheté deux tableaux à la nièce de l'artiste afin que celle-ci puisse entrer au couvent[54]. De plus, le nom de Van Alsloot figure parmi les *officiers* et *paiges officiaus* à qui la cour fournit un vêtement de deuil à l'occasion de la pompe funèbre en l'honneur de l'archiduc Albert en mars 1622[55]. Or le cahier des dépenses pour les obsèques ne cite pas l'artiste parmi les peintres et artisans qui participèrent de façon active à son élaboration, ce qui paraît écarter la possibilité qu'il y assista par nécessité professionnelle. Van Alsloot aurait-il tout de même fait partie du personnel de la cour, sans salaire fixe, ni titre particulier[56]? Il faut alors admettre qu'il fut nommé après avril 1618, soit après son procès où il comparaît comme simple *maître* devant la Chambre des Tonlieux, et non devant le Conseil Privé, dans une affaire de servitude qui l'oppose à son voisin Jan Mattens[57]. Le peintre serait-il devenu membre de la cour suite aux séries monumentales des *Festivités du papegai en 1615 à Bruxelles* qu'il réalisa pour les archiducs entre 1615 et 1619/20? Ou occupait-il une autre fonction officielle dont nous ignorons la teneur?

Si Van Alsloot finit effectivement par appartenir à la domesticité des souverains, son cas formerait une exception à la règle. Car tous les peintres qui furent enrôlés à la cour, hormis Rubens et sans doute Van Dyck, le furent essentiellement pour des raisons pratiques. Leur statut leur permettait de percevoir des gages, mais les obligeait parallèlement à être en permanence à la disposition des archiducs, même pour la simple exécution d'ouvrages de peinture: en 1621 encore, Jacques Francart est rétribué pour avoir polychromé un reliquaire destiné à l'oratoire de l'infante[58]. Le privilège de faire partie de la *maison* des souverains s'accompagnait ainsi de contraintes qui répondaient aux besoins parfois les plus ordinaires de la cour. La place occupée par Francart et Van Deynum parmi les *officiers des mains* confirme cet état de choses, tout comme celle de François Verbeelen, *peintre ordinaire*. Même Salomon Noveliers, *peintre de l'hôtel de la cour*, paraît avoir restauré plus de tableaux pour le palais, que d'en avoir peints. En ce sens, le statut des peintres de cour avait peu évolué depuis le XVe siècle où cette fonction concernait essentiellement des tâches décoratives[59].

Or aucun versement des archiducs à Van Alsloot ne concerne un travail qui puisse s'apparenter à une simple prestation d'ordre utilitaire. Il s'agit toujours de tableaux – essentiellement des *paysages*, comme nous le rappelle Gisbertus Venius. On comprend aussi mieux pourquoi le très admiré Jan Brueghel, établi à Anvers, se vit refuser le poste de *domestique*, devant se contenter des dispenses communales: il ne venait à Bruxelles que de façon occasionnelle, ce qui ne peut légitimer un traitement fixe; le titre et la rente essentiellement honorifiques de Rubens, et, plus tard, de Van Dyck, devaient rester de l'ordre de l'exception.

La position du *fournisseur de la cour* n'en était pas moins enviable: en plus d'avantages financiers appréciables, elle assurait la protection des archiducs[60]. Il semble aussi qu'elle donnait le droit à l'artiste d'approcher ses souverains[61] et de se proclamer attaché à leur service. Lorsqu'en 1629, David Noveliers s'adresse au magistrat de Bruxelles pour prolonger son droit à l'exonération de l'impôt communal et d'autres privilèges, il se dit être ainsi *schilder van Haere Doorluchtichste Hoocheyt*[62]. Il semble donc que les peintres furent les premiers à tirer parti de l'ambiguïté de leur statut. Le fait que Van Alsloot signe ses tableaux avec la mention «peintre de l'archiduc» ne peut donc pas constituer une preuve de son appartenance au personnel de la cour.

Mais si nous pouvons admettre que la concession de franchises participait d'une forme de distinction particulière, toutes les exemptions n'avaient pas la même valeur. Autant qu'une reconnaissance, certaines d'entre elles, comme la libération de la garde, représentaient une condition de travail indispensable. Le cas échéant, c'est d'ailleurs sur cette nécessité que les archiducs s'appuyaient pour argumenter leur décision auprès des autorités municipales: Brueghel est d'abord relevé de la garde civile à Anvers, étant *«continuelement occupé en ouvraiges de nostre service»* (1609)[63]; Hans Verbeeck, bourgeois de Malines, reçoit le même privilège (1600) pour pouvoir *«plus commodément vaquer à ce que de nostre part lui sera enchargé»*[64]. En 1629 encore, l'infante Isabelle s'exprime dans des termes analogues à propos de Jacob Jordaens *«occupé à peindre des cartons de tapisseries»*, dans un mandement qui, par ailleurs, avait échappé récemment encore à l'attention des chercheurs[65].

L'exonération de l'impôt communal, en revanche, participait pleinement de la *faveur princière*. De Maeyer en sous-estime la portée lorsqu'il l'assimile à un simple dédommagement, pourtant très convoité par les artistes. Il s'agissait d'une faveur d'autant plus remarquable qu'elle relevait en principe de la seule compétence des autorités urbaines et non des archiducs[66]. Les souverains semblent donc avoir outrepassé leur droit en proclamant qu'être retenu à leur service, même temporairement, autorisait les mêmes types de dispenses et prérogatives qu'une nomination à la cour[67]. Ils forçaient en quelque sorte le magistrat à reconnaître à la fois leur *bon vouloir* et le statut privilégié de leur protégé. Il est vrai que le geste ne coûtait rien à la cour et il est probable que les archiducs l'auraient commis plus encore si les villes elles-mêmes n'avaient pas opposé leur forte résistance. Albert refusa ainsi d'affranchir Gisbertus Venius *à cause de la conséquence* qu'un tel acte pouvait entraîner chez d'autres citoyens et c'est cette même *conséquence* qui fit patienter De Momper près de vingt-sept ans[68]. Il n'en demeure pas moins que ce passe-droit permettait à celui qui en bénéficiait de sortir du rang *à la manière* des serviteurs domestiques de la cour, voire de se confondre avec ceux-ci. Peut-être est-ce la raison pour laquelle Van Alsloot figure parmi les officiers dans les comptes concernant la pompe funèbre d'Albert alors qu'il ne paraît pas avoir occupé d'office particulier. Peut-être, après tout, n'était-il alors qu'un *fournisseur* de la cour. En outre, il s'agissait d'une reconnaissance foncièrement originale, dans le sens où elle fut délivrée à plusieurs artistes dont les souverains appréciaient particulièrement les œuvres. En témoignent les nombreux tableaux de Brueghel et de De Momper (plus de dix de ses peintures sont répertoriées au château de Tervuren en 1620) qui composaient leurs collections. Le statut de *fournisseur de la cour* permit donc aux archiducs de gratifier les qualités artistiques, sans y adjoindre d'impératif. Vue sous cet angle, la fonction valait bien une nomination au palais.

# NOTES

*Nous tenons à remercier vivement les professeurs d'Histoire Luc Duerloo, de la Economische Hogeschool Sint-Aloysius Brussel, Paul Janssens, de la Katholieke Universiteit Brussel et Alain Dierkens, de l'Université Libre de Bruxelles, qui ont bien voulu relire notre texte et nous faire part de leurs commentaires. Cette étude a été menée dans le cadre de notre thèse de doctorat, *Denijs van Alsloot (vers 1568?–1625/26) et son atelier. Exemple d'un peintre actif à Bruxelles au service des archiducs Albert et Isabelle* (titre provisoire), que nous effectuons sous la direction du professeur Catheline Périer-D'Ieteren, auprès de l'Université Libre de Bruxelles.

1. M. De Maeyer, *Albrecht en Isabella en de schilderkunst. Bijdrage tot de geschiedenis van de XVIIe-eeuwse schilderkunst in de Zuidelijke Nederlanden* (*Verhandelingen van de Koninklijke Vlaamse Academie voor Wetenschappen, Letteren en Schone Kunsten van België*), Bruxelles, 1955, pp. 248–250.

2. Ibidem, pp. 65–66.

3. Un exemple célèbre est celui de Rogier van der Weyden, qui, suite au décès de Jan van Eyck, travailla à la cour de Philippe le Bon sans engagement officiel. Voir D. De Vos, *Rogier van der Weyden. Het volledige oeuvre*, Anvers, 1999, pp. 53–57.

4. Les archives des Chambres des Comptes à Bruxelles mentionnent un paiement, en 1624–1625, de 182 florins 1 sou 6 patards à «*Jan Vanden Venne, Anthoen Sallaerts, Mertene Vanden Venne*» et leurs compagnons (*medegesellen*), pour des travaux exécutés à la cour, lesquels sont détaillés dans huit «*distincte billetten*» qui ont malheureusement disparu. La même année, un nouveau paiement de 83 livres fut versé à «*Jan Vanden Venne et Anthoni Sallaerts*». Il s'agissait très vraisemblablement de travaux de décoration, car si le premier paiement n'évoque que des «*peintures*» pour la *Warande,* le second précise que Vanden Venne et Sallaerts s'étaient chargés de peindre et de dorer «*diverses figures*» dans la grande grotte, ainsi que de nettoyer et de vernir les bords de la fontaine adjacente. Voir Bruxelles, Archives Générales du Royaume (ci-après AGR), Chambres des Comptes, n° 27512 (*Ouvrages de la Cour,* 1621–1629), fol. 31v° et 61. Passages reproduits dans M. Van der Vennet, «Le peintre bruxellois Antoine Sallaert», *Bulletin des Musées royaux des Beaux-Arts de Belgique*, 1974–1980, 1–3, pp. 188–189. Enfin, De Maeyer a publié un troisième paiement de 557 florins 19 patards à «*Merten Vanden Venne, Jan Vanden Venne, Anthoen Sallaerts et Jacques Francquart*», pour plusieurs travaux de peinture effectués en 1630 et 1631 (Bruxelles, AGR, Chambres des Comptes, reg. 27513, fol. 66v°, voir De Maeyer 1955 (voir note 1), p. 398, doc. 242).

5. Bruxelles, AGR, Archives de l'audience et papiers d'état, liasse 1893/2. Publié par De Maeyer 1955 (voir note 1), p. 288, doc. 52.

6. Voir M. Warnke, *L'artiste et la cour. Aux origines de l'artiste moderne*, Paris, 1989, pp. 11–17 en particulier.

7. Tout membre ressortit au chapelain de la cour. Voir Bruxelles, AGR, Archives de l'audience et papiers d'état, n° 33/1, cour, n° 25, *Privilèges des domestiques de son Alteze* (1613), art. VIII et IX.

8. Voir Bruxelles, AGR, Conseil d'état, n° 157.

9. Bruxelles, AGR, Archives de l'audience et papiers d'état, n° 33/1, cour, n° 25, art. XII. Cité par J. Duverger, «Het statuut van de zestiende-eeuwse hofkunstenaar in de Nederlanden», *Jaarboek Koninklijk Museum voor Schone Kunsten Antwerpen*, 1982, p. 79, note 97.

10. De Maeyer 1955 (voir note 1), p. 249.

11. Bruxelles, AGR, Chambres des Comptes, reg. 1837 et 1838. Voir J. Lefèvre, «Les livres de raison de l'archiduc Albert (1612–1618)», *Archives et bibliothèques de Belgique*, 1971, n° 42, pp. 156–163.

12. Bruxelles, AGR, Chambres des Comptes, reg. 1837, fol. 112. Publié par De Maeyer 1955 (voir note 1), p. 306, doc. 90.

13. Voir Ibidem, passim.

14. Bruxelles, AGR, Chambres des Comptes, reg. 1837, fol. 314. Publié par De Maeyer 1955 (voir note 1), p. 312, doc. 98.

15. Voir Ibidem, pp. 228–230. Le registre des dépenses de la maison de l'archiduc mentionne Van Deynum comme étant le peintre de l'archiduc Albert alors que les lettres citées ici le nomment parfois «*verlichter van Henne Hoogheden*» (Ibidem, p. 339) ou «*peintre illuminateur des archiducqz*» (A. Pinchart, *Archives des arts, sciences et lettres. Documents inédits, publiés et annotés*, II, Gand, 1863, pp. 218–219). Dans la pratique, il ne semble donc pas y avoir eu de réelle différence entre le titre de peintre de l'archiduc Albert et celui de peintre des archiducs Albert et Isabelle.

16. Voir De Maeyer 1955 (voir note 1), p. 248; Duverger 1982 (voir note 9), pp. 78–79 et Warnke 1989 (voir note 6), p. 84 sqq. En ce qui concerne Van Deynum, ses activités semblent s'être limitées à la réalisation de portraits et d'enluminures, deux types d'art particulièrement prisés par l'aristocratie. C'est sans doute parce que celle-ci constituait l'essentiel de sa clientèle, qu'il considérait avantageux de ne pas s'inscrire à la gilde. Parmi la littérature récente sur l'œuvre de Van Deynum, voir Cl. di Fabio, «Due generazioni di pittori fiamminghi a Genova (1602–1657) e la bottega di Cornelis de Wael», [cat. exp.] *Van Dyck a Genova. Grande pittura e collezionismo*, Gênes, Palazzo Ducale, 1997, pp. 84–87.

17. Bruxelles, AGR, Archives de l'audience et papiers d'état, n° 33/1, cour, n° 16: «*de gevrijde pensionarissen soe wanneer zij hun begeven tot poirters en neeringhe of tot eenigen ambachten binnen deser stadt (...) soe worden sy daarmede subject tot alle diensten ende lasten van der selven stadt, gelyck zulcx by vonnisse van mijn vrauwe van Parme, moeder van zijn Hoocheyt voleert*». Cité Duverger 1982 (voir note 9), pp. 78–79.

18. A. Pinchart, «La corporation des peintres de Bruxelles», *Messager des Sciences Historiques ou Archives des arts et de la bibliographie de Belgique*, 1877, p. 313.

19. Voir D. Lanoye, «Structure and Composition of the Household of the Archdukes», in W. Thomas et L. Duerloo (eds.), *Albert and Isabella 1598–1621*, Turnhout, 1998, pp. 107–119. Nous nous sommes principalement fondée sur cette étude pour refléter la structure générale de la cour.

20. Tant Francart que Van Deynum sont, de manière systématique, cités successivement devant Antonio de la Barra, *brodeur* de l'archiduc et Juan Pinto, chaussetier. Voir Bruxelles, AGR, Chambres des Comptes, reg. 1837 et 1838, passim. Le

rang de Van Deynum est confirmé par la *Liste des serviteurs domesticques reformez de feu S: A: le Sérénissime archiduc Albert*, datant de 1624, où il est mentionné explicitement sous la rubrique «*officiers des mains*», tout comme Juan Pinto d'ailleurs. Voir Bruxelles, AGR, Conseil d'état, n° 157.

21. Lanoye 1998 (voir note 19), pp. 114–115. Nous tenons à remercier vivement D. Lanoy de nous avoir permise d'utiliser son tableau.

22. Les gages des gardes du corps s'élevaient en 1612 à 255 florins l'an. Voir, pour un tableau comparatif des gages à la cour de Bruxelles, K. Proesmans, *Het muziekleven aan het hof van Albrecht en Isabella (1598–1621)* (mémoire de licence), Louvain (KUL), 1988, p. 90.

23. De Maeyer 1955 (voir note 1), p. 249, note 1.

24. Bruxelles, AGR, Chambres des Comptes, reg. 366 (*Registre de la commission des officiers resortissans sous la chambre des comptes en Brabant depuis 1600 à 1604*), fol. 20v°.

25. Voir, pour comparaison, Lanoye 1998 (voir note 19), pp. 112–113.

26. La commission (voir note 24) révèle en effet que l'artiste est nommé au poste de *peintre ordinaire de la court « aux sallaires et franchises y attenans »*.

27. En 1603, Verbeelen prend son propre fils, Johannes, en apprentissage. Voir Pinchart 1877 (voir note 18), p. 294. Dans une requête adressée au commis des finances du roi et datée du 23 décembre 1595, l'artiste se définit également comme «*marchand de painctures*». Voir Bruxelles, AGR, Archives de l'audience et papiers d'état, liasse 1235.

28. Document non localisé. Voir De Maeyer 1955 (voir note 1), pp. 293–295, doc. 62. Les gages de Rubens équivalent à ceux d'un maître de chapelle. Voir Proesmans 1988 (voir note 22), loc. cit.

29. De Maeyer 1955 (voir note 1), pp. 96–97.

30. Rubens donne ainsi son avis sur la valeur de tableaux exécutés par David Noveliers. Lille, Archives départementales du Nord, reg. B 2890, fol. 395v°. Publié par De Maeyer 1955 (voir note 1), p. 337, doc. 134.

31. Voir A. de Vos «Jacques Francquart (1583–1651), Architect of the Court, and the Rue Isabelle in Brussels», in Thomas et Duerloo 1998 (voir note 19), p. 211.

32. Entre septembre 1621 et septembre 1622, Rubens y inscrit même un élève du nom de Jacques Moermans. Les circonstances qui l'ont amené à agir de la sorte sont inconnues. Peut-être le peintre a-t-il a voulu se montrer prudent face au changement de régime à Bruxelles, suite au décès de l'archiduc Albert.

33. Rubens délégua sa charge à son ami Hans van Mildert. Voir L. Wuyts, in *P.P. Rubens. Catalogus schilderijen – olieverfschetsen. Antwerpen, Koninklijk Museum voor Schone Kunsten*, Anvers, 1990, pp. 38–39, cat. 5.

34. Voir C. Brown, «Rubens and the Archdukes», in Thomas et Duerloo 1998 (voir note 19), p. 121.

35. Voir L. Duerloo, «A Court in a Country of Painters. The Habsburg Policies of Patronage in the Netherlands», *The Court Painter in Early 17th Century* (sous presse).

36. De Maeyer 1955 (voir note 1), p. 194 et Bruxelles, AGR, Archives de l'audience et papiers d'état, n° 2026/3 (cité dans M. Forrier, [cat. exp.] *Autour de J. Brueghel l'Ancien, P.P. Rubens, A. van Dyck. L'art et les artistes aux Archives de l'Etat*, Bruxelles, Archives générales du Royaume, 1999, pp. 80–81, cat. 105). Van Dyck est exempté de la gabelle, des maltôtes, de garde et de guet. Il ne nous a pas été permis de voir le document, mais d'après la description qu'en fait le catalogue de l'exposition, il semblerait que Van Dyck ne portait pas à l'époque de titre spécifique. Il est probable qu'il ne fit partie de la cour à proprement parler que plus tard, lorsqu'il bénéficia d'une pension

37. F.J. Van den Branden, *Geschiedenis der Antwerpsche Schilderschool*, Anvers, 1883, p. 718, cite un document, daté du 27 mai 1630, dans lequel «*Anthonio van Dijck, schilder van Heure Hoocheyd*» charge le peintre bruxellois Pieter Snayers d'obtenir auprès de diverses personnes l'arriéré de plusieurs commandes ainsi que «*het jaerelijcx pensioen van 250 gulden tsjaers, daermede Heure Hoocheydt hem, Anthonio van Dijck, heeft gebeneficieert*».

38. Bruxelles, AGR, Chambres des Comptes, reg. 46012, fol. 362. Publié par De Maeyer 1955 (voir note 1), pp. 411–412, doc. 258.

39. Remarquons que ce titre évoque celui de Rubens, *Peintre de l'hôtel des archiducs,* devenu «vacant» depuis que le maître anversois était devenu «ayuda de camera». Noveliers aurait-il, en quelque sorte, pris la succession de Rubens (en tenant compte qu'il s'agissait alors d'une cour de «gouvernante» et non plus «souveraine»)? Si c'est le cas, il n'en va que du titre: ni les gages, ni même la fonction ne sont comparables. L'acte cité en note 39 stipule clairement, en effet, que les gages de Salomon comprennent «*l'entretien des peinctures de la Court et maison de la Vuere*», le peintre étant payé «*par voye du fourier mayor*». Voir, pour comparaison, Lanoye 1998 (voir note 19), pp. 110–112.

40. De Maeyer 1995 (voir note 1), pp. 221–222.

41. Bruxelles, AGR, Archives de l'audience et papiers d'état, liasse 1893/2. Publié par De Maeyer 1995 (voir note 2), p. 288, doc. 52.

42. Bruxelles, AGR, Archives de l'audience et papiers d'état, liasse 1895/2. Publié par Pinchart 1863 (voir note 15), II, pp. 322–323. La requête porte sur «*la franchise et exemptions des maltotes et gabelles sur vin, bierre et pareilles choses, ensamble de guet et garde, et contribution*».

43. Bruxelles, AGR, Conseil privé espagnol, carton 1247. Publié par De Maeyer 1955 (voir note 1), p. 345, doc. 147. David Noveliers est «*francq et exempt des assises, guet et garde, logement et contribution pour iceluy*».

44. Voir J. Duverger, «Jan Mostaert, Ereschilder van Margareta van Oostenrijk», *Aachener Kunstblätter*, 1971, pp. 113–117 et Duverger 1982 (voir note 9), pp. 80–81.

45. Lettre patente datée du 24 mars 1604, édité par Pinchart 1863 (voir note 15), II, p. 303. De Nole fut, tout comme Rubens, dispensé d'inscrire ses élèves à la gilde.

46. Warnke a lui aussi utilisé cette dénomination pour désigner les artistes qui ne résidaient plus à la cour. Le fait que certains d'entre eux percevaient néanmoins des gages rend toutefois le terme inapproprié, selon nous, dans ce cas. Voir Warnke 1989 (voir note 6), pp. 88–93.

47. Le mandement que les archiducs adressent le 20 janvier 1610 au magistrat d'Anvers pour dispenser Rubens des mêmes charges et corvées précise ainsi « *nostre intention et volonté est que le faciez jouir de l'exemption et franchise des impostz et assises, ainsi qu'en jouissent tous aultres* [serviteurs] *exemptz par les escroeues de nostre hostel* (...)». Document non localisé, publié par Pinchart 1863 (voir note 14), II, p. 170. Nous avons vu plus haut qu'à l'exception des courtisans, les *serviteurs* inscrits aux *escroues* étaient nécessairement des *domestiques*.

48. Bruxelles, AGR, Archives de l'audience et papiers d'état, liasse 1894/1. Pour la publication de la requête de Jan Brueghel et du mandement des archiducs aux magistrats d'Anvers, voir Ch. Duvivier, «Documents concernant le peintre Jean Breughel», *Revue d'histoire et d'archéologie*, II, 1860, p. 440. Voir également

De Maeyer 1955 (voir note 1), pp. 148–149. Brueghel sera exempté des accises, des maltôtes, de garde et de guet.

49. Bruxelles, AGR, Archives de l'audience et papiers d'état, liasse 1993/1. Édité par De Maeyer 1955 (voir note 1), p. 377, doc. 203 et doc. 204. Voir aussi Ibidem, pp. 160–162. De Momper obtiendra les mêmes exemptions que Jan Brueghel.

50. Bruxelles, AGR, Conseil privé espagnol, n° 1247. Édité par De Maeyer 1955, p. 392, doc. 232. Voir, pour comparaison, note 48 ci-dessus.

51. De Clerck avait déjà bénéficié de «*la franchise tant de logement, garde que des maltotes*» par ordre de l'archiduc Ernest en 1594, pour lequel il avait travaillé. Ces prérogatives furent toutefois contestées par la ville de Bruxelles, raison pour laquelle l'artiste demanda aux archiducs d'intervenir. Il est significatif que dans le mandement que ceux-ci adressent au magistrat pour renouveler les privilèges du peintre, il ne soit référé à aucun titre de cour: De Clerck est qualifié de *paindre résident en ceste ville.* En outre, les souverains stipulent clairement qu'ils désirent voir l'artiste bénéficier de la «*grâce*» que lui avait octroyée Ernest (voir Bruxelles, AGR, Conseil privé espagnol, carton 1245 ; publié par De Maeyer 1955 (voir note 1), p. 281, doc. 42).

52. Bruxelles, AGR, Conseil privé espagnol, liasse 1245. Voir M. De Maeyer, «Denijs van Alsloot (vóór ca. 1573–1625 of 1626) en de tapijtkunst», *Artes textiles. Bijdragen tot de geschiedenis van de tapijt-, borduur-, en textielkunst*, I, 1953, pp. 3–11 et De Maeyer 1955 (voir note 1), pp. 280–281, doc. 41. Van Alsloot est exempté de garde et du paiement des maltôtes et des accises.

53. Voir références note 41.

54. Lille, Archives Départementales du Nord, reg. B. 2951, fol. 800r°–v°.

55. Bruxelles, AGR, Manuscrits divers, 415 (*Quayer des frais et dépens engendrez pour le deuil et funérailles à cause du trespas de feu l'archiducq Albert célébré à Bruxelles au mois de mars xvi^c xxij*), fol. 7r°.

56. Wensel Coeberger fut reçu ainsi, sans titre particulier, au nombre «*des serviteurs domestiques*» des souverains en 1604, avant d'être élevé en 1605 à la dignité «*d'architecte et ingénieur des archiducs*». Voir, pour l'acte de 1604, Bruxelles, AGR, Archives de l'audience et papiers d'état, liasse 1892/3, publié par De Maeyer 1955 (voir note 1), pp. 277-278, doc. 36 et pour l'acte de 1605 (non localisé), Ibidem, pp. 279–280, doc. 40.

57. Bruxelles, AGR, Chambre des Tonlieux de Bruxelles, 499, liasse 1262. L'ordonnance concernant les affaires de justice des membres de la cour promulguée par Albert en 1613 précise en effet, à l'article VII, que «*pour les matières civiles qui toucheront auxdits de nostre cour et maison, nous déclarions que lesdits de notre Conseil Privé en seront les juges compétens*». Bruxelles, AGR, Archives de l'audience et papiers d'état, n° 33/1, cour, n° 25.

58. Bruxelles, AGR, Chambre des Comptes, reg. 50564, fol. 21. Édité par De Maeyer 1955 (voir note 1), p. 351, doc. 158. Voir également la note 4 ci-dessus.

59. Voir l'étude magistrale de M.P.J. Martens, *Artistic Patronage in Bruges Institutions, ca. 1440–1482* (Thèse de doctorat), Ann Arbor, U.M.I., 1992.

60. Même après la mort de Jan Brueghel, sa veuve continua de jouir des exemptions et franchises qu'avait reçues son mari. Bruxelles, AGR, Archives de l'audience et papiers d'état, liasse 1246. Publié par De Maeyer 1955 (voir note 1), p. 372, doc. 193.

61. Aubertus Miraeus (1622) relate ainsi que Brueghel aurait été invité à s'entretenir avec l'archiduc Albert pendant son temps libre. De Maeyer 1955 (voir note 1), p. 62. Il va de soi que ces propos doivent se lire comme un motif panégyrique qui renvoie à la relation d'amitié entre Alexandre et Apelle (voir à ce propos Warnke 1989 (voir note 6), pp. 51–52). Mais ceci n'exclut nullement qu'ils contiennent une part de vérité.

62. Bruxelles, AGR, Conseil privé espagnol, liasse 1247. Publié par De Maeyer 1955 (voir note 1), pp. 388–389, doc. 226a et b.

63. Bruxelles, AGR, Archives de l'audience et papiers d'état, liasse 1237. Publié par Duvivier 1860 (voir note 48), II, p. 333.

64. Document non localisé, publié par E. Neeffs, *Histoire de la peinture et de la sculpture à Malines*, Gand, 1876, p. 233. L'acte ne parle pas de dispenses de taxe, comme c'est habituellement le cas. Le texte suggère cependant qu'à l'époque l'artiste travaillait régulièrement pour les archiducs, de sorte que nous pouvons considérer que son statut équivalait à celui d'un *fournisseur.* Voir aussi De Maeyer 1955 (voir note 2), pp. 233–234.

65. Bruxelles, AGR, Archives de l'Audience et papiers d'état, n° 2026/4. Voir Forrier 1999 (voir note 38), pp. 80–81, cat. 105.

66. Nous remercions vivement le professeur Paul Janssens de nous avoir éclairée sur les compétences juridiques des archiducs par rapport aux autorités citadines.

67. Dans un document demeuré inédit et daté de 1602, l'archiduc Albert énumère les personnes qui ont droit d'office, par leur fonction ou leur statut, à l'exemption de «*tous gabelles, ausi les maltôtes, daces et imposte mis ou à aultres par la ville de Brusselle ou par l'Estat de Brabant, sur vins et bierres et semblables vivres et composition*». Il s'agit des «*Embasadeurs*», de la «*Ducesse de Branswijck*» et du «*Ducque de Malle, comme prince du sang*», des «*chevalier*[s] *de l'ordre*», des «*consiliers d'esta privez et des finances ensemble, leurs vefves, suivant la promes d'accorde faict à iceux par le Magistrat et membres de ceste ville le premier febvrier 1506* (...)», des «*Maistres générales des postes, de «l'Auditeure générales»* [sic], des «*Commissaires générales et ordinaires des monstres*», des «*Trésoriers des guerres*», des «*Contrôleures et Receveurs de l'Artillerie*» et de «*tous ceux de la Maison de Leurs Alteze* [sic], *aultres lesquels seront comprins, ceux de la Chapelle, tant prédicateurs de la Courte que Chapelijns et Musiciens, ensamble, les archiers, et Halbardiers de leurs gardes*». Voir Bruxelles, AGR, Archives de l'audience et papier d'état, n° 33 / 1, n° 62.

68. En 1610, Anvers tente d'opposer son refus au mandement d'Albert d'affranchir Brueghel du paiement des assises et maltôtes, en invoquant «*la mauvaise conséquence*» d'un tel acte et cela d'autant plus que Rubens et Otto Venius en ont déjà été dispensés par leur fonction à la cour. La ville va même jusqu'à espérer que le souverain se «*contentera*» de ces deux exemptions à l'avenir (Bruxelles, AGR, Archives de l'audience et papiers d'état, liasse 1894/1, publié par Duvivier 1860 (voir note 48), II, pp. 440–441). Sans doute est-ce là le principal motif pour lequel De Momper insistera, dans sa requête auprès d'Isabelle en 1626, sur le fait que Brueghel est alors décédé (motif qui échappe à De Maeyer 1955 (voir note 1), p. 161 et p. 377, doc. 203). La ville essaiera d'ailleurs de s'opposer également aux privilèges de De Momper, prétextant notamment que «plus de cent personnes» jouissent déjà de prérogatives analogues à Anvers (et non «plus de cent *artistes*», comme le mentionne Roland Baetens dans son article «La relance d'une dynamique culturelle sous le règne des archiducs» in Thomas et Duerloo 1998 (voir note 19), p. 149). Voir Anvers, Stadsarchief, Gilden en Ambachten, liasse 4578.

# Rubens and Philip IV: a Reappraisal*

*David Howarth*

Over several years I have been working on a corpus of manuscripts which provide new information about Rubens, Van Dyck and the Anglo-Flemish art world of the early seventeenth-century. This body of material consists of what are known as *State Papers Flanders* and by way of a complement to these, the hitherto overlooked private papers of the confidante and close friend of Rubens, Sir Balthazar Gerbier, English Agent in Flanders, 1631–1642 (fig. 1). The two sets of papers are to be found in the Public Record Office in London. Prompted by what these parallel series yield, the intention of this essay is to look afresh at Rubens' relationship with Philip IV of Spain.

The Gerbier papers are to be found in these two parallel sequences: the first constitutes what is largely official material in the form of dispatches for Charles I's two secretaries of state in London. These are now to be found in *State Papers Flanders*. This is the series which provided W. Nöel Sainsbury with the material published in 1859 as *Original Papers Relating to Rubens*. What has not been appreciated hitherto however, is that despite the bulk and value of Sainsbury's book for a study of Rubens and his contemporaries, Sainsbury himself seems to have overlooked further significant material contained within *State Papers Flanders*. Some of this unnoticed information will appear in what follows.

In addition to what Sainsbury did unearth in *State Papers Flanders*, are manuscripts which complement what he published in *Original Papers*, but which seems not to have been available at the time his book came out.[1] I refer to what are described in the Public Record Office catalogues as the *Letter Books* of Gerbier. These contain rough drafts and copies of the official dispatches and letters encountered in the official run of *State Papers Flanders*, but also documents often of an altogether more private nature. Predictably, the latter are by no means always to be found in duplicate in *State Papers Flanders*. *The Letter Books*, as they are known, contain new material about 'mon ami', as Gerbier describes Rubens. However there are too references to Antony Van Dyck, Antonis Mor,[2] Jacob Jordaens, Gaspar de Crayer and the English miniaturist, Isaac Oliver. In addition the *Letter Books* also contain material about patrons of the visual arts.

Now it is specifically what Gerbier has to say about the relationship between Philip IV and Rubens which will concern us in this essay. The purpose of this paper is to consider some passing references not identified by Sainsbury in State Papers Flanders, together with other material in the *Letter Books* which may perhaps suggest a slightly different nuance to what we might fairly call, the 'orthodox' view of the relationship between Philip IV and Rubens.

How then might we characterise this orthodoxy? To begin with it might be helpful to identify those who have created the 'view' about the relationship between Spanish king and Flemish painter. These scholars are: Svetlana Alpers, Jonathan Brown, John Elliott, John Rupert Martin, Steven Orso and Alejandro Vergara. Among this array of distinguished writers it is Brown and Elliott in partnership who have done most to stamp the coin with the sharpest profile of Philip IV as a patron. It is therefore appropriate to begin by acquainting ourselves with what these pre-eminent scholars of Golden Age Spain have to tell us. Here we must turn to Brown and Elliott's book, *A Palace for a King* (Yale University Press, 1980); a study in cultural archaeology which examines the genesis of the Buen Retiro. This was the palace on the outskirts of Madrid created in 1632–1633, by the Conde-Duque de Olivares for the delectation of Philip IV.

In *A Palace for a King*, Brown and Elliott argued that Philip IV was a patron of exceptional percipience from an early age. They tell us how in the 1620s, Philip had 'begun to develop both as a patron and a connoisseur'.[3] As the two historians turn their attention to the visit of Rubens to Madrid between the late summer of 1628 and the spring of 1629, they go on to suggest how then Rubens had a power-

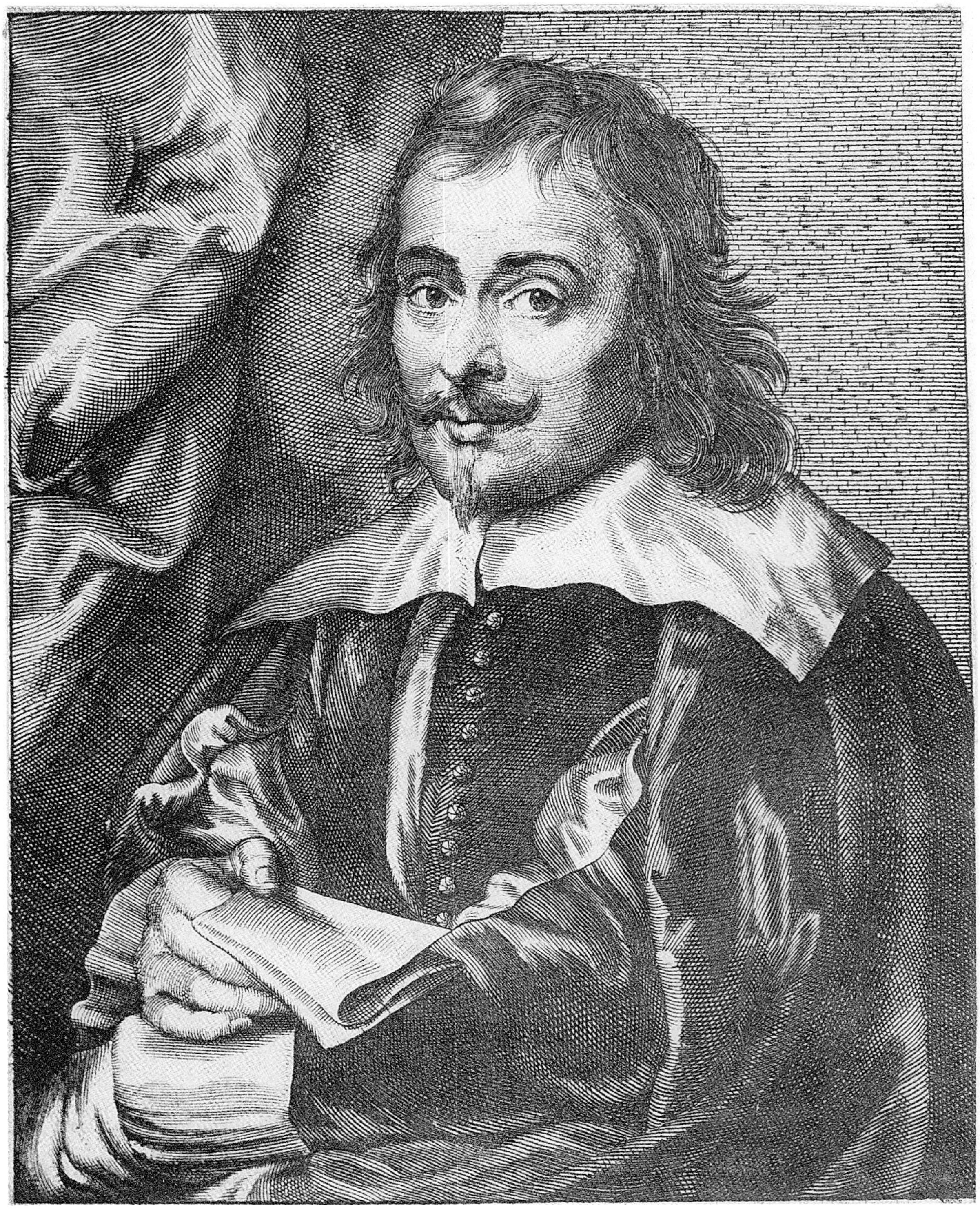

Fig. 1. Paulus Pontius after Anthony van Dyck, *Portrait of Balthasar Gerbier*, engraving

ful affect on Philip IV. They argue that for the king, 'Rubens now became his most devoted admirer and patron' whilst for Philip IV and Velázquez, 'With his [Rubens'] example before their eyes, they were inspired to make the Spanish court into a showplace for masterpieces of painting old and new'.[4] Much as I admire *A Palace for a King*, and no one has done more to add to our understanding of the culture of Golden Age Spain than Brown and Elliott, I have my doubts as to whether their view of the farsightedness of Philip as a patron is altogether justified.

I do not see Philip IV in the 1620s developing as a patron of the visual arts quite as rapidly as Brown and Elliot have argued. Velázquez was hired to paint portraits; about as exciting an assignment as Van Dyck was to receive ten years later from his equally unimaginative English patrons. Where we might ask, are all the religious, mythological, and history pieces by Velázquez which we might expect Philip to have ordered, if we are to accept Brown and Elliott's view that Philip was a precocious patron who was to see immediately the pre-eminence of Rubens as soon as the artist arrived in Madrid by mid September 1628. As matters stand, all we actually have certain knowledge of outwith the bounds of portraiture, and from the brush of Velázquez in the six years between his arrival in Madrid in 1623 and the appearance there of Rubens in 1628, is the *Expulsion of the Moors*; the lost large scale propaganda piece. What happened then to the man who painted *Christ in the House of Mary and Martha* before he ever saw the skyline of Madrid?

Now as for Rubens, when he arrived as emissary from the archduchess Isabella in the early autumn of 1628, he came with a medley of eight paintings for the king which it would appear Philip had ordered, and not as was previously thought, merely accepted in the role of passive recipient.[5] These eight pictures, some of which at least may perhaps have been in Rubens' stock for perhaps six or seven years, then came to hang in the *salón nuevo* of the Alcázar in Madrid were clearly they would have displayed the versatility of Rubens to the king and his entourage.[6] But let us pause for a moment. This very transaction serves to point up something of a paradox; at least at this juncture of Philip's career as art patron. The really intriguing thing is just how little interest Philip *then* came to take in commissioning Rubens when he had the world's most productive painter, a captive under his roof. Why was it that despite presumably being the grateful recipient of choice canvases, Philip conspicuously failed to take advantage of all that talk we are told went on? Why did Philip not commission pictures; pictures of the same ambition as certainly he became much later to welcome at the Torre de la Parada; moved so to do, as I shall argue, by the inspiration of Philip's youngest brother, the Cardinal-Infante Ferdinand? As matters stood however in that autumn of 1628, years would pass before Philip IV asked anything beyond portraiture of Rubens.

With Rubens' visit to Madrid of 1628 we are faced with one of the great conundrums of the artists' career: what Pacheco describes as Rubens' campaign of copying all the Titians in the royal collection in Madrid.[7] Actually I do not believe for a moment Rubens did such a thing; how could he when there were even vaster numbers of Titians in Madrid then than there are now? I think Vergara put it very well when he describes Pacheco's claim as 'rhetorical'. Assuming therefore that Pacheco was indeed exaggerating when describing the extent to which Rubens worshipped Titian, the prodigious number of Titians Rubens certainly did copy, remains a curious episode which we still do not wholly understood; despite Vergara's illuminating comments on this strange episode in the life of the artist.[8] For my part, I confess I have never really understood what this exercise represented for Rubens. Some argue that it was only now in 1628–1629, and whilst in Madrid, that Rubens truly came to terms with Titian. But can that really be the case with a man who as keeper of the ducal collections in Mantua, had had responsibility for a number of remarkable masterpieces of Titian? Surely ten years in Italy for an artist of Rubens' talents was quite enough to get on equal terms even with Titian. No, I suspect the *raison d'etre* for all those copies has a bearing on Rubens' relationship with Philip, or should we say more accurately, Rubens' lack of one. In Madrid in 1628, Rubens waited and waited for Philip to actually ask him to do something large scale, ambitious and interesting, and still nothing was forthcoming.[9] Perhaps then Rubens said to himself, that in copying Titian, he could promote himself, cement Hispano-Flemish relations, and flatter the household gods of the Austrian Habsburgs, by appearing to pay homage to Philip IV's grandfather, Charles V, and that man's great role as a patron of the famous Italian master. Stuck in Madrid with not enough painting to do in 1628, Rubens needed to overcome frustration and disappointment, to fill his time, and to flatter a man on whom he had called in the first instance let us remember, not as a painter but as a diplomat.

What then of the period when the Buen Retiro was being jerry built: that is to say c. 1632–1633? Rubens was the most successful painter in the world at this moment and he was a Spanish subject; the only painter besides Velázquez of whom it could be said Philip IV had a really close personal acquaintance.[10] If however we now walk into the Hall of Realms, the centrepiece of the Buen Retiro, what do we find? There is no Rubens. John Elliott has suggested that there is nothing surprising about this since Rubens' style was so markedly different to the prosaic 'factual' historical pieces commissioned from the talent then available in Spain.[11] Consequently something by Rubens would have looked quite out of place in the principal salon of that palace. That indeed seems to be a powerful argument. But it does not explain how Rubens was wholly absent elsewhere in the Buen Retiro; an absence which suggests that the accounts we read in Pacheco and Palomino of how much Rubens had been appreciated on his second visit to Spain, may have been exaggerated. Of course the whole point of the Buen Retiro was precisely that it was the brainchild of the Conde-Duque's, not of Philip IV: to that extent it reflected the tastes and priorities of Olivares and Olivares had no real affinity with pictures. Nevertheless the fact that no one thought of the world's greatest painter contributing properly to this pleasure dome, may suggest that Philip IV and his advisers had a distinctly limited vision as patrons of the visual arts – at least at this stage.[12]

So much then for the orthodox view of Rubens and the Spanish court; a location which all are agreed formed the most important source of patronage for the artist in the last decade of his life. However it is one thing to acknowledge the central, indeed the dominant importance of Spain and the Spanish monarchy for Rubens in the thirties, but it is quite another to believe that Philip IV was the most important figure in Rubens' dealings with Madrid. As it is there is some evidence to suggest that Philip may have been really rather less central than has been assumed hitherto.

To begin with there was a marked difference in character between Philip IV and his brother the Cardinal-Infante Ferdinand; a difference which made it much more likely that the younger brother set the pace of relations with Rubens. The Cardinal-Infante had a much more outgoing and confident character than Philip IV: ebullience and panache perhaps predisposed Ferdinand to think more boldly as an art patron than his altogether more reticent brother. Here it may be of value to remember that famous remark by Rubens in a letter to Gevaerts written on 29 December 1628:

> 'The King alone arouses my sympathy. He is endowed by nature with all the gifts of body and spirit, for in my daily intercourse with him I have learned to know him thoroughly. And he would surely be capable of governing under any conditions, were it not that he mistrusts himself and defers too much to others. But now he has to pay for his own credulity and others' folly, and feel the hatred that is not meant for him. Thus have the gods willed it.'[13]

All that Gerbier has to say in his close observation of the Cardinal-Infante's character, certainly anticipates the view of Brown and Elliott when they comment on the appointment of Ferdinand as a cardinal at the tender age of ten: 'a singularly inappropriate destiny for the liveliest of the three royal brothers, whose demeanour suggests that he would have been better with a baton in his hand than a biretta on his head'.[14] Cardinal at the age of ten, archbishop of Toledo at eleven, Ferdinand came to prefer the active to the spiritual life as he transformed himself into a huntsman of great audacity and a soldier of genuine ability. This was triumphantly demonstrated by Ferdinand's joint victory with his cousin, Ferdinand of Hungary, over the Swedes at Nördlingen on 6 September 1634. Consequently Ferdinand's eventual arrival in Brussels on 4 November 1634, was greeted with much joy. Thereafter Ferdinand seems to have ruled the Spanish Netherlands with: pragmatism towards his subjects, courage and skill as a military commander, temperance and flexibility over the perennially vexed question of religious difference.[15] Although it certainly cannot be claimed that Ferdinand was ever to be held with the same regard which his subjects had had for his predecessor, Ferdinand's aunt, the archduchess Isabella, he certainly created a very positive first impression; an impression which it seems he was able to sustain to judge by how crowds responded to a great feast held in his honour in Brussels in July 1638:

> 'The feast was on the 19th present the bonfires were never so great, several inscriptions and showes, the acclamations of the people great, one notable drunkard ventered to drinke a quart of wine to the Infanta Cardinal's health on the weather cocke of the market steeple.'[16]

Ferdinand was a man gifted with *sprezzatura*; perhaps better equipped than his morose elder brother to take on a painter who, in the words of the late Francis Haskell, had the 'broadest culture of any man in Europe'; a culture emanating from a personality as overpowering and energetic as the pictures he painted.

Early indications suggest that as soon as Ferdinand arrived in Flanders he took an active part in ensuring that painting would support Spain and the Spanish cause. What little we know of Ferdinand's dealings with Rubens over the former's state entry, the *Pompa Introitus Ferdinandi*, the more it seems that Ferdinand was qualifying himself to play a dominant role in that partnership in patronage which shortly thereafter would result in the Torre de la Parada: a partnership between Ferdinand and his brother Philip IV on one side, and Rubens on the other.

In so far as the Cardinal Infante has been considered as a patron this has been done by John Rupert Martin and Svetlana Alpers: Martin in the context of the Corpus Rubenianum volume on the *Introitus*, and Alpers in her companion text on the Torre de la Parada. What then do they say about Ferdinand? The answer in the case of Martin's monograph on the *Introitus*, is nothing in any pro-active sense. There is much by way of analysis of the preparations, and about Ferdinand as the object of the whole enterprise, but we get no sense from Martin's researches in Antwerp archives, that Ferdinand may have intervened to adjust the arrangements. However this is what is clearly suggested as a possibility in the Gerbier correspondence. Now once Gerbier puts such a thought into our minds, then surely it is indeed what we should expect? Ferdinand was bound to have a view as to how he was to be presented on stage for the *Introitus*. He was bound to have been interested if only because of the political significance of the Triumphal Entry in early modern Europe; and nowhere more spectacularly it might be added, than in the kingdom of Burgundy. As Ferdinand agreed to be the subject of the manifesto which Rubens and Gevaerts were evolving for him between January and April 1635, Ferdinand himself would have known very well how the Emperor Charles V had been received in Antwerp in 1520 – an entry incidentally witnessed by Dürer. That great spectacle had been succeeded by a series of others, studded throughout the sixteenth century and early seventeenth centuries.

Martin believed that the Antwerp archives give us no encouragement to see the Cardinal-Infante as having any views as to how he was to be packaged for the consumption of his subjects. So be it for Antwerp. But there is at least some grounds for a degree of reassessment of Ferdinand's rôle to be found in the Gerbier *Letter Books*. I am referring to two separate remarks which are suggestive. The first is a statement to the effect that it was acknowledged in court circles that Brussels had not had sufficient time to do justice to the first appearance of the Cardinal-Infante in their city. That event had taken place in the autumn of 1634, and it seems that a possible explanation as to why the *Introitus* into Antwerp was put back several times, was precisely because the feeling was that things had to be done better in this, the second city of the Spanish Netherlands. Accordingly there was a series of delays in order to ensure that a sufficient display was mustered on this second occasion.[17] This being the case, then an unpublished aside in a letter of Gerbier's of 17 November 1634 may be significant. Gerbier writes to the Secretary of State in London:

> 'The Infantas entry att Antwerp wilbe after the Christmas holydayes, ag$^{t}$ w$^{ch}$ time that towne prepares for his reception: Such showes as this towne minded for his Hignes entry here, for w$^{ch}$ wanted time, are now finishing, to the end his said Hignes may take a day to see what intended'.[18]

Now of course Gerbier is not telling us that Ferdinand summoned Rubens to talk about what he and Gevaerts intended, but clearly Gerbier had learned that he very well might. So it may be that he did. Now given that Ferdinand felt the need to stamp his authority on the principal cities of the Spanish Netherlands early in his governorship, I would simply suggest that the *Introitus* was not just put together by a group of Flemish bourgeois humanists. The project may have been invigorated by an infusion of Spanish royal blood. What could be a better or more intensive exposure to the genius of Rubens, than Ferdinand to have been locked in conclave with Rubens, Gevaerts, Rockox and other Flemish worthies as they worked out the complex allegories and the appearance of the arches for Ferdinand's imminent entry into Antwerp? Spanish governor and Flemish humanists together, may have negotiated the delicate business of reciprocity which lay at the heart of State Entries. The ruler wished to ordain, the subject to explain: state entries were a metronome swinging between the prince's demand for obedience, and the peoples' expression of their hopes and grievances. Even if after all, Ferdinand did not take that day to hear what Rubens had to say for himself, he certainly knew a great deal more about Rubens by the end of April 1635 than he had done on his arrival in Brussels six months earlier. With the exception of Marie de Médicis, no other patron was ever so elaborately framed by Rubens as Ferdinand during that Antwerp spring.

If we now move on to consider the Parada commission, what is the view here as to the relationship between the Cardinal-Infante and Philip IV? According to Alpers whose Corpus Rubenianum volume is one of the best, Philip used his younger brother to pass on orders and instructions for the paintings to Rubens. In other words, Alpers saw Ferdinand as the go-between or the ennabler of the project which she assumed, along with everyone else, had been initiated from Madrid and by Philip himself. The remainder of this essay is devoted to suggesting a role reversal: Ferdinand conceived the project and Philip responded to the written initiatives as they emerged from the court in Brussels.

The Torre de la Parada project is first mentioned in a letter from the Cardinal-Infante to Philip IV of 20 November 1636.[19] The enterprise then spanned a period of eighteen months: all the pictures had arrived in Madrid on or before 1 May 1638. What is clear from previously published sources is that Rubens was able to respond with some degree of independence to comments and correctives which Philip IV sent him. In another early published letter of 6 December 1636, Philip asked Rubens to make some changes to the landscapes in some of the pictures.[20] Having agreed, Rubens wished to add some figures to paintings that would otherwise have been without them. Although the Cardinal said he must wait for the King's permission, he tentatively gave Rubens his assent. That seems to be important for it suggests Rubens is able to modify the express wishes of the King. This being the case, I think the Cardinal-Infante would have intervened himself in more decisive ways than Alpers allows for in her chapter in her Corpus volume entitled 'The History of the Commission'.

Encouragement for believing that Ferdinand was altogether more pro-active as a patron than we have appreciated, may be forthcoming from an ambiguous reference in the Gerbier correspondence. In a letter of April 1637 to Sir John Coke, one of the two English secretaries of state, Gerbier refers to how Ferdinand is shortly to set out for Antwerp where he is to bargain for paintings destined for 'the king of Spaynes buen-retiro'. I take this to refer to the Torre de la Parada rather than to Olivares' palace: for the obvious reason that Olivares was still the dominant figure at the court in Madrid and it would have been somewhat perverse of Gerbier to reassign ownership five years before the fall of the favourite. At the risk of trying to tease too much from what Gerbier tells us here, I think it significant that Ferdinand seems to have wanted to deal direct with the Rubens 'team'. This suggests that here was a man who was firmly in control of the Torre de la Parada agenda: someone who was merely a passive agent for Philip IV would have contented himself with seeing to it that Rubens was quite clear what Madrid wanted and would then have left Rubens to get on with dealing with the host of artists to whom the work for the Torre had been parcelled out. But so far from that being the case, here Ferdinand proposed to step between Rubens and his surrogates. If indeed this was Ferdinand's intention, then it may be that he acted thus because he had a clear vision of what he wanted and what would be good for Philip's Torre. Whatever the truth, the full text of the letter reads as follows:

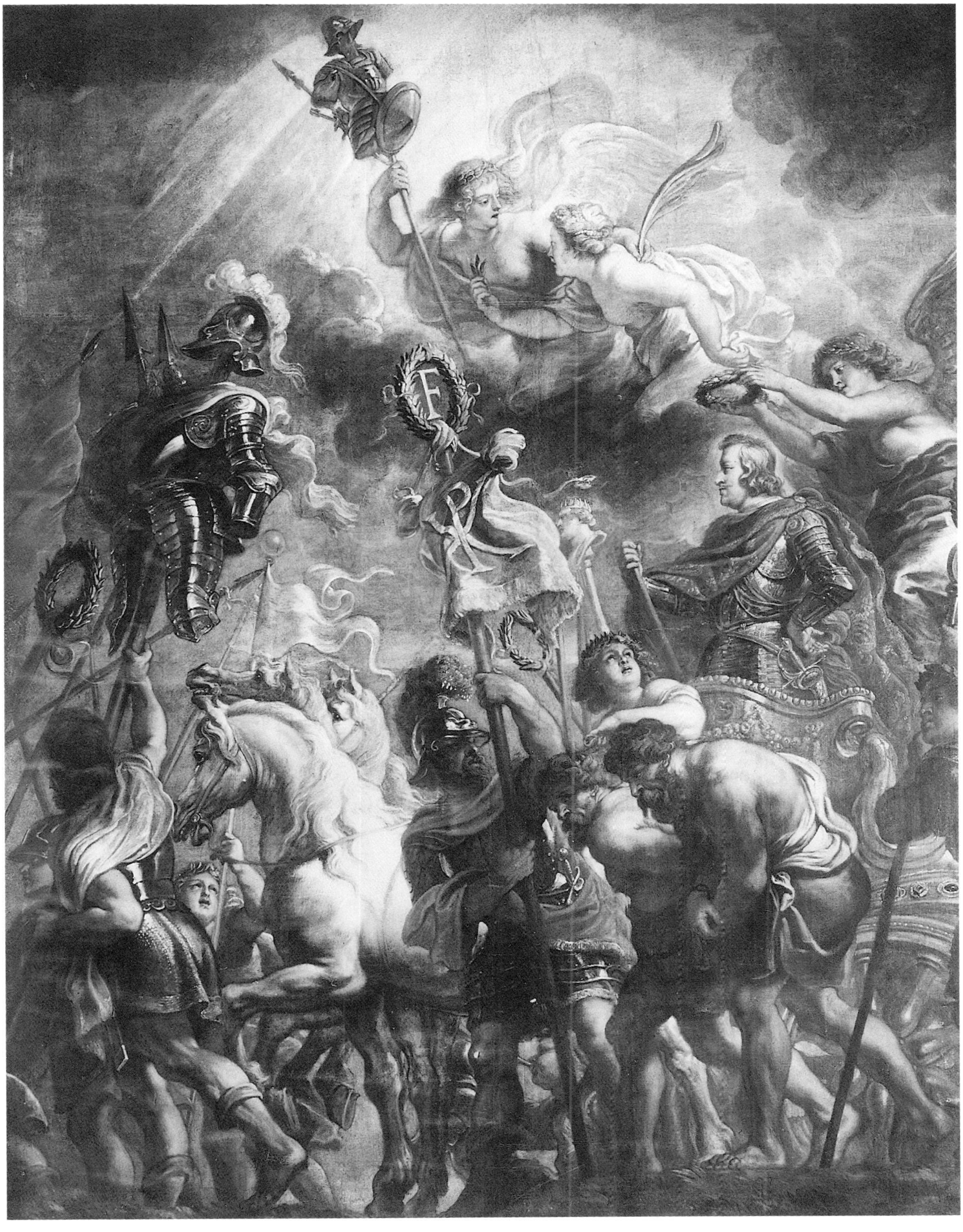

Fig. 2. Jan van den Hoecke after P.P. Rubens, retouched by Jacob Jordaens, *The Triumph of the Cardinal-Infante Ferdinand*. Florence, Galleria degli Uffizi

'The Infant Cardinal makes 21st prest for Antwerp, thence unto the land of Wars, and intends to retourne hither by the 29th. His journey said for recreation, to see at Antwerp many painters workes, bargained for m/ 8 Crownes to the ornament of the king of Spaynes buen-retiro, his passing through Flanders said to injoy a great chase appointed long since for him.'[21]

At this juncture it should be stated that any speculation as to the dynamics between Rubens

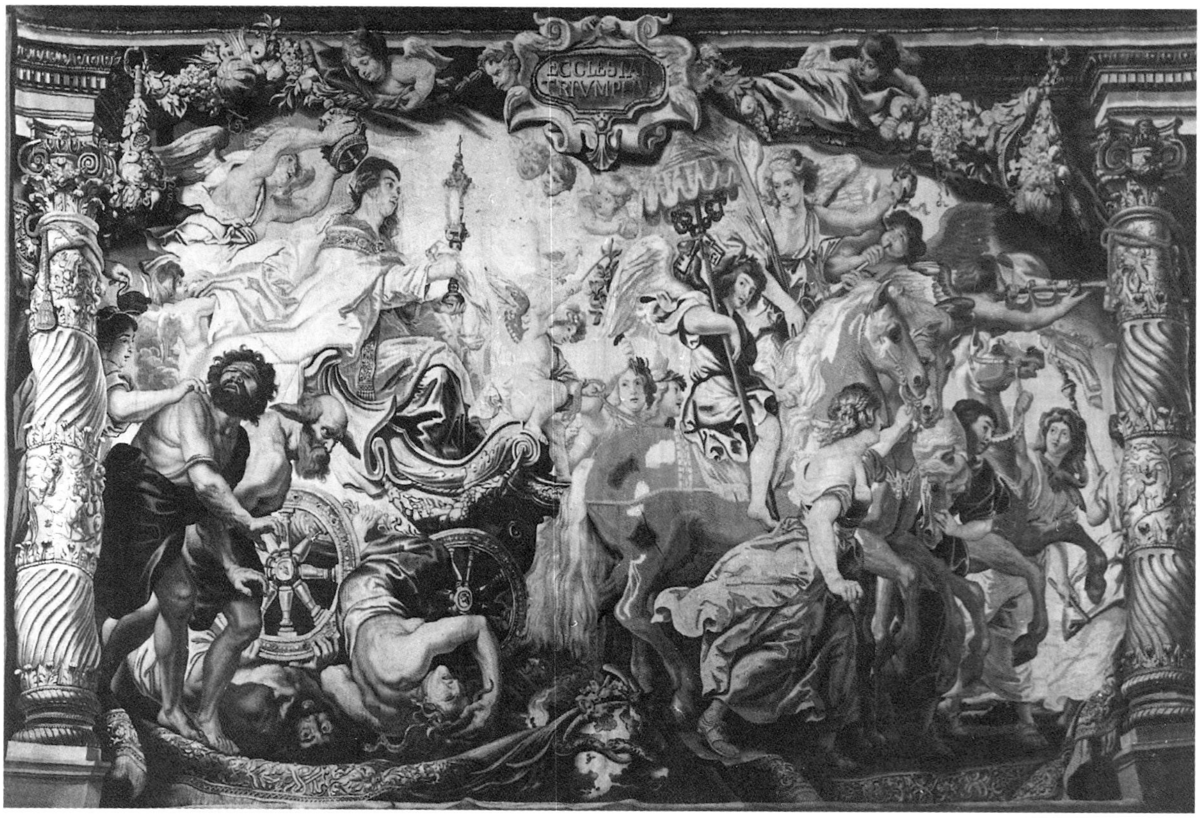

Fig. 3. Jan Raes after P.P. Rubens, *The Triumph of the Church*, tapestry. Madrid, Convent of the Descalzas Reales

and the two brothers would be brought into much sharper focus if we had the *memoria original* which Philip sent to Ferdinand. This in turn Ferdinand sent back to Spain with the names of the painters who executed the paintings designed by Rubens. If that document materialised then it might be possible to come to a clearer view as to which of them – Philip or Ferdinand – conceived of the whole project in the first place. In the meantime however, I wish to draw attention to a reference in Gerbier's correspondence which may suggest that it was actually Ferdinand who first dreamed up the commission of the Torre de la Parada.

Why is this so? The most important evidence comes in a statement by Gerbier, unknown to Alpers. It is a letter of 20 February 1638. Gerbier writes 'The Infanta Cardinal sends into Spain a present of [a] nomber of pictures drawne by severall famous painters in these parts'.[22] Now here we are surely on firmer ground, for I believe Gerbier would not have used the word 'present' if he did not mean what he said: it was a gift from one brother to another in celebration of their joint delight in the chase. Now although Gerbier may indeed have meant 'present' as we understand it, he could have been misinformed; or is it conceivable that by 'present' Gerbier actually meant what we would understand by the word 'presentation'? In that case, this semantic distinction would certainly allow for the commission to be wrested out of Ferdinand's hands and put back firmly into the grasp of Philip. However, vicarious evidence suggests that Ferdinand was the more likely of the two brothers to have initiated things with Rubens.

What appears to have happened is that Ferdinand carefully manipulated the situation so as to fit in with the elaborate protocol of gift-giving and gift-receiving as these gestures can be observed at the court in Madrid in the 1630s. Ferdinand may well have been acting on two levels in commissioning the Torre cycle as a gift. Privately he was giving his brother a present. That would have been tacitly acknowledged between them; provided that for public consumption, it appeared the initiative was the king's.[23] That scenario with its element of elaborate subterfuge fits perfectly with Spanish court etiquette at that time.

Furthermore, there are good reasons for believing that it would have been *politique* for

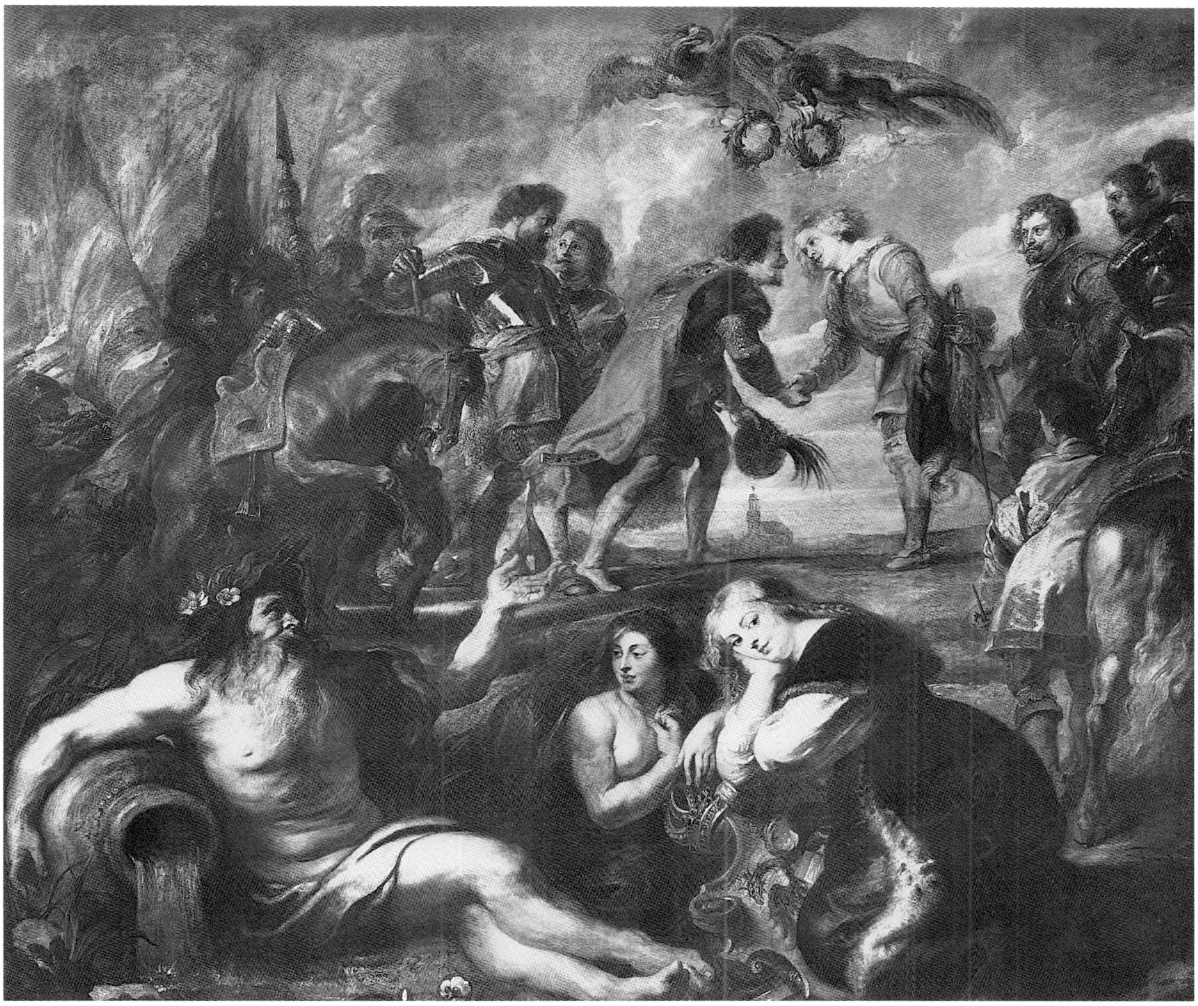

Fig. 4. P.P. Rubens and assistants, *The Meeting of the two Ferdinands at Nördlngen.* Vienna, Kunsthistorisches Museum

Ferdinand to flatter his brother in these ways. This Ferdinand may already have been careful to do if he had indeed had an in-put over the genesis of the *Introitus* designs. For that ensemble, there are at least two arches the designs of which depend to some degree on works of art by Rubens which had already been presented to Philip IV. I am referring to the *Triumph of Ferdinand* from the *Introitus* (fig. 2) which uses as its template *The Triumph of the Eucharist* tapestry (fig 3); commissioned as part of a series from Rubens in the mid twenties, by Philip IV's aunt, the archduchess Isabella for the Descalzas Reales in Madrid. The second scene from the *Introitus* which recalls previous Rubens triumphs in Spain is *The Meeting of the Two Ferdinands* (fig. 4). Here there is an obvious dependence on the *Jacob and Esau* (fig. 5); by 1636 a much admired Madrid Rubens and one incidentally, used by Velázquez in 1634 as his inspiration for the Hall of Realms *Surrender of Breda*. Now of course this may only be a case of Rubens' well known economy of invention. Rubens was never one to undersell a good idea; always alert to the fact that what had done for one commission would double up for another.[24] However the parallels between what Philip could admire by Rubens in Madrid, and what appeared in the *Introitus,* are at least noticeable even if their presence cannot be attributed to the diplomatic skills of Ferdinand who, like Janus, had to look both to his brother and his Flemish subjects.

Prior to his arrival as governor of the Spanish Netherlands, Ferdinand together with his namesake the Emperor, had won a famous victory over the Protestatnts at Nördlingen. However that victory was to create complications in the relationship between the two brothers. The point here is that Philip ached with frustration at being tethered by Olivares who sedu-

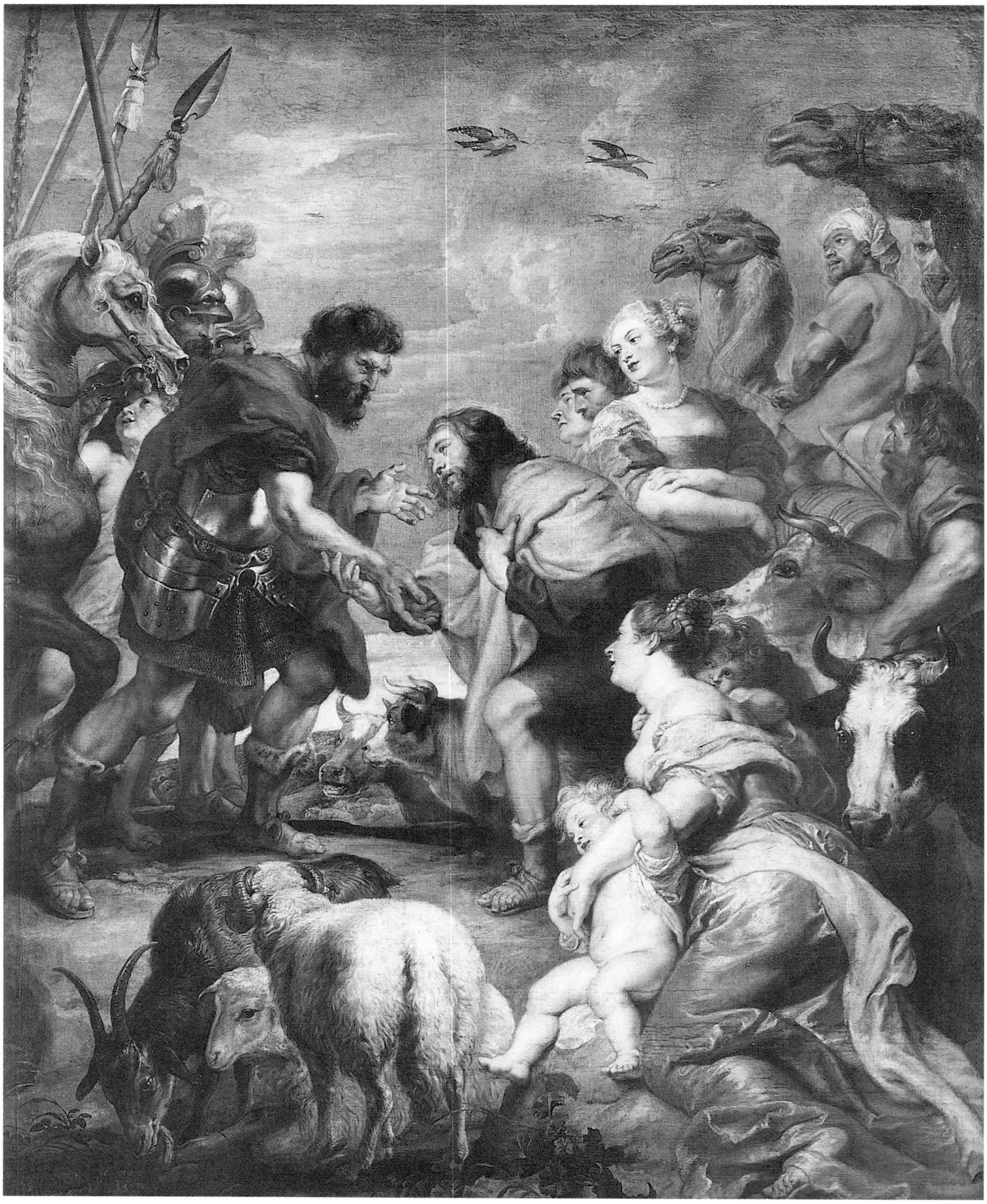

Fig. 5. P.P. Rubens, *The Reconciliation of Jacob and Esau*. Schleissheim, Schloss, Bayerische Staatsgemäldesammlungen

ously prevented Philip from leaving Madrid to head up a successful military campaign. The tension between Philip and his chief minister had become much more acute after Spain witnessed the successful intervention of Louis XIII in the affairs of Savoy. Now in order to divert Philip at this time, Olivares habitually directed the king towards the hunting field. A whole series of flattering poems appeared whenever Philip either shot a boar or disembowelled a stag. One of these, celebrating a moment when Philip dispatched a bull, inspired an allegorical account of how the animal represented Europa whilst the horns symbolised the victory of

Spain over the forces of Islam. Hunting then was absolutely central to the whole image of the Austrian Habsburgs and hunting was above all what brought Philip and Ferdinand together as it discharged some of the latent tensions between them. And tensions there were. Olivares' circle certainly saw Ferdinand as a potential focus of criticism of both himself and of the King. Tension too existed between Philip and Ferdinand whose victory at Nördlingen had been won with a double-edged sword. That triumph of Spanish and Austrian arms was of course the subject of much celebration when the news reached Madrid. However what is interesting is that it was celebrated as a Spanish victory and the role of Ferdinand was very much played down. How then was Ferdinand to cope with his brother who was still himself being led round the political ring on a leading rein by Olivares?

What better method could the real soldier Ferdinand devise than by flattering his brother through the presentation of a series of great hunting and mythological scenes for the Torre de la Parada; that favoured retreat dedicated to field sports. The implication of the gift was that Ferdinand was deferring to the more martial of the two huntsmen. Here there is an important further point to be made and it is this. Olivares and his scribblers worked hard to sell hunting as an adequate substitute for military campaigning because if Philip was adept at the one he need not practise the other; a sub-text in aristocratic image-making which Rubens had long acknowledged in work which had nothing to do with Spain. Here I am thinking of the great Munich *Lion Hunt* which Rubens had painted in 1621 for the Scottish Marquess of Hamilton. As for Spain itself, there it was often said that the courage, judgement and skill to be an accomplished huntsman, demonstrated to the satisfaction of Philip's subjects if to no one else, that he had all the qualities of a famous military victor. This reassured Spaniards that in the event of Spain having to go to war, Philip would discharge his duties on the battlefield with as great an effect as he had done in the hunting arena. Ferdinand himself loved hunting and he seems to have particularly relished the Flanders version of it. The day before his state entry into Antwerp, an enormous feast of killing had been laid on to put him in a good humour for parading up and down the streets. Hunting was clearly dear to the hearts of the two brothers. The third and last great commission for Philip IV, the hunting scenes for the *bovida de palacio* and the New Room in the Madrid Alcazar, would have been much to Ferdinand's taste too; although there is no encouragement to believe that Ferdinand commissioned that as well.

There is however some evidence in Gerbier's papers and elsewhere, which does make it clear that certainly there were occasions when Ferdinand had both the courage and the initiative to act as a patron in his own right. This was for the sake of making his own unsolicited and uninstructed contribution to the programme of the arts back in Madrid which Olivares was orchestrating. Brown and Elliott tell us that neither Philip nor Olivares cared for sculpture as an independent art form; such as there was at the Buen Retiro constituted what they describe as 'ornamental work': fountains, fireplaces etc. But the Cardinal-Infante certainly did appreciate sculpture for it was he who spotted a remarkable group of the Seven Planets which he snapped up for the Buen Retiro. These arrived in Madrid by 22 June 1637. Olivares was delighted and assured the Cardinal-Infante that his lavish present would always be honoured in the site of his magnificent gift.[25]

Whilst Ferdinand was negotiating hard with Rubens over the Torre de la Parada, he was patronising other artists as he promoted visual splendour in the cities of Flanders. He commissioned an expensive project for the church of St Gudula in Brussels. On 19 July 1637 Gerbier reports that the Cardinal Infante 'hath bestowed an ornament in the church of St Gudula of railes and balisters of beaten silver to stand about the high altar, which ornament cost about m/20 francs.'[26]

Of rather more interest is the relationship during this very time which Ferdinand seems to have developed with Van Dyck. It is clear from the Gerbier papers that Van Dyck returned to Antwerp a full six months earlier than we had previously thought: he was in Antwerp by 21 October 1633, not as previously believed the spring of 1634, and he returned to England in March 1635. As I have argued elsewhere, it is my belief that in returning to Antwerp in October 1633, Van Dyck considered that he had discharged himself from the service of the king of England; as far as Van Dyck was concerned he was coming home for good.[27] For this reason he probably made overtures to the Cardinal-Infante as soon as the new ruler arrived in Brussels almost exactly a year later; that is to say in the autumn of 1634. For his part the Cardinal-Infante seems to have moved fast to strike up a working relationship; at least to judge by what Gerbier has to tell us of Van Dyck's hurried and confused departure for England from Brussels at the beginning of March 1635; a mere five months after Ferdinand had begun his governorship. From this document I get the distinct impression that by the time Gerbier came to excuse Van Dyck for running off without the courtesy of a formal departure, the painter had a *servitú particolare* in relation to Ferdinand himself:

'I have received your letter dated 6/16 present bearing his Ma$^{ts}$ command to excuse S$^{r}$ Antony Van Dycks soudaine departure from hence w$^{th}$out taking leave of y$^{e}$ Infante Cardinall, I performed his said Maj$^{ts}$ commands last night and as I conceave soe att full as S$^{r}$ Athonis confessor freed to charge him w$^{th}$ pennance for that sinne. The Infante Cardinal laft and said to pardon S$^{r}$ Anthony since his retreat was to doe his Maj$^{tie}$ acceptable service asked whether would make long stay, on w$^{ch}$ proceeded to y$^{e}$ second part of my commission and obtayned convenient time for y$^{e}$ said Sr Anthony to performe such workes his Maj$^{tie}$ is graciously pleased to imploy him in, c'est done une affaire faiite, S$^{r}$ Anthony shall doe wel to looke to himselfe, for he hath enemis in this country who are suspected will strayne themselves for revenge uppon his person, Its w$^{ht}$ thought fitt to touch in this: Humbly take my leave.'[28]

It will have become clear to the reader that important claims made in this essay turn upon not even full sentences but mere phrases. All may therefore be a house of cards. However there is much contingent and vicarious evidence to support the promotion of Ferdinand in the life of Rubens. Philip as a client rather than in his capacity as political master, had almost no experience of dealing with Rubens prior to the winter of 1636. So Philip's sudden apparent engagement with the artist in the winter of 1636 makes no sense. By contrast there is much in the antecedents of Ferdinand which provide a *prima facie* case for believing him to have been the front man; he had the right temperament which his brother did not; he had arrived in Flanders after a year living in Milan, a sophisticated city the cosmopolitanism of which gave him an enhanced awareness of the arts. Soon after arriving in Brussels to take up his governorship, Ferdinand too had been exposed to the full power and range of Rubens' pictorial and intellectual gifts as the subject of one of the most complex of all Rubens' allegories.

So much then for what Ferdinand may have been doing in Brussels, but where does all this leave us in relation to Madrid, the Torre de la Parada and Philip IV? I finish by questioning a claim made twenty years ago by Brown and Elliott where in *A Palace for a King* they stated their belief that Philip's 'discernment and taste are nowadays underestimated'. Now in 2002 I would suggest there is a danger that Philip's discernment as a patron has become overestimated. Besides challenging the views of Brown and Elliott, I have tried to suggest that the Cardinal-Infante Ferdinand was a more important person than we have appreciated; altogether more central to the evening of Rubens' life than has been suspected. Finally, and this is an altogether broader point, implicit in this article is the belief that we need to be aware of how questions of patronage are perhaps more complex than we tend to assume. Just because a crowned head was the apex of a cultural system, this does not allow us to assume it was the Philip IV's and the Charles I's of that world who were necessarily responsible for these munificence acts of patronage like the Torre de la Parada mythologies. Careful dissection, subtle reconstruction of the dynamics of baroque courts, may offer a more sophisticated view of patrons and painters than perhaps we have allowed for. We have to look not just at the pediment but the whole temple of the arts.

# NOTES

* I would like to thank my colleague Jeremy Robbins of the Department of Hispanic Studies, Edinburgh University, for helpful insights into the workings of the court in Madrid in the 1630s. I am grateful too to Sir John Elliott who graciously listened to a revised version of this paper, first delivered at Louvain University, and which I repeated as a seminar at the Department of the History of Art, Oxford University. John responded with a number of illuminating criticisms; whilst also making it clear that he does not accept my revisionist view of his interpretation of the relationship between Rubens and Philip IV. I would also like to thank René Vermeir of the University of Ghent for an illuminating discussion of the political landscape of Flanders in the 1630s. Finally I am grateful to Frank Carroll for help in translating Dutch text.

1. Sainsbury published *Original Papers* in 1859. It appears that the *Letter Books* were accessioned only in 1863.

2. Most of the references to the artists listed above have appeared in my article '"The Entry Books" of Sir Balthazar Gerbier: Van Dyck, Charles I and the Cardinal-Infante Ferdinand', in H.Vlieghe (ed.), *Van Dyck 1599–1999, Conjectures and Refutations*, Turnhout, 2001, pp. 77–89. However it is of interest to note here the enthusiasm connoisseurs of the age of Rubens had for the work of Antonis Mor. Gerbier wrote to Edward Norgate on 5 September 1639: 'I pray represent also my good wishes and professions of true inclinations and respects unto my noble antient friend Mr Porter of whom I have not heard in an age and pray lett me know how he doth, and all his noble and sweet family. Also whether a picture I sent him of Antonio More (the best of that hand) hath pleased him, for I can assure you it was esteemed a jewell here and I paid a handfull of gold for the same; I shall be sorry the same shall not please.' (Public Record Office (hereafter P.R.O.), Letter Books, SP 105/16/ unfoliated). Gerbier wrote to Endymion Porter on 1 December 1639: 'I doe now trouble y$^{u}$ wth thease lines to answeare y$^{e}$ second l$^{re}$, in the first two lines whereof y$^{u}$ pay a great price for the shadow of ould Howard by saying y$^{t}$ y$^{u}$ like it, for y$^{t}$ satisfies me as much as Antony More would have esteemed the glory y$^{t}$ a good stroake of his hand had bin accepted by yours.' (P.R.O., Letter Books, SP 105/16/ unfoliated).

3. Jonathan Brown and J.H. Elliott, *A Palace for a King. The Buen Retiro and the Court of Philip IV*, New Haven–London, 1980, p. 42.

4. Ibidem, p. 46

5. A. Balis, *Rubens. Hunting Scenes* (*Corpus Rubenianum Ludwig Burchard*, XVIII, 2), London–Oxford–New York, 1986, p. 180.

6. L. Burchard and R.-A. d'Hulst, *Rubens Drawings*, 2 vols., Brussels, 1963, no. 80.

7. Alexander Vergara, *Rubens and his Spanish Patrons*, Cambridge, 1999, p. 99.

8. Ibidem, pp. 97–105.

9. Although Rubens does appear to have done other things besides portraits, according to Palomino these pictures were for members of the court and not for Philip IV. See Nina Ayala Mallory, *Lives of the Eminent Spanish Painters and Sculptors*, Cambridge, 1987, pp. 102–103.

10. It is surely significant in this context that Palomino should have had no hesitation in thinking of Rubens as a Spaniard. Accordingly he included a life of the Flemish artist in his biographical account of 224 Spanish painters and sculptors published in 1724.

11. With the shining exception of the contributions from Velázquez and Maino.

12. The one fully autograph Rubens known to have been destined for the Buen Retiro is the *Judgement of Paris*, now in the Prado. However this only appeared in 1638 and was ordered (perhaps at the behest of Philip IV) by the Cardinal-Infante. A large number of other Flemish pictures inspired by Rubens certainly did eventually find their way to the Buen Retiro. However the fact remains that there appears to have been nothing by Rubens as part of the first campaigns of interior decoration at the palace. See Brown and Elliott 1980 (as in note 3), pp. 130–131.

13. R.S. Magurn, *The Letters of Peter Paul Rubens*, Cambridge, Mass., 1955, p. 295.

14. See Brown and Elliott 1980 (as in note 3), p. 32.

15. Ferdinand was most consistent in his governorship in deferring to the commands of his brother Philip IV; sometimes it must be said, against his better judgement in military matters. In the context of the politics of the Spanish Netherlands, Ferdinand was controlled by two hardline advocates of Spanish intransigence: Aytona the field commander of the Spanish armies in Flanders, and Pieter Roose secretary of the Council of the Spanish Netherlands. Although Roose especially was able to manipulate Ferdinand, and indeed Philip IV secretly instructed Roose to obey his commands rather than Ferdinand's when differences of opinion arose between the two brothers, Ferdinand was perceived to be of real value by both Roose and Aytona. Ferdinand's exuberance, panache and charm made him an ideal gilded figure-head for the ship of state as it rolled in the swell of the Dutch rebellion. As someone whose value was in part his possession of undoubted military gifts but largely in the pyschological realm of affable exposure to his subjects, Ferdinand was well qualified to promote visual propaganda on behalf of Spain. For the most authoritative interpretation of the governorship of Ferdinand see: René Vermeir, *In Staat Van Oorlog: Filips IV en de Zuidelijke Nederlanden, 1629–1648*, Maastricht, 2001

16. P.R.O., State Papers Flanders, SP 77/28/ 386, Gerbier to Sir Francis Windebanke, 14/24 July 1638.

17. The citizens of Antwerp were conspicuous for their reluctance to make a positive contribution to the truimphal entry of Ferdinand into their city. Paradoxically this may have resulted in those who were involved in the production of the festive arches, including Ferdinand himself, redoubling their efforts so as to suppress this embarrassing note of dissension.

18. State Papers Flanders, SP 77/24/ 446, Gerbier to Sir John Coke, 7/17 November 1634.

19. Max Rooses and Charles Ruelens (ed.), *Correspondance de Rubens et documents épistolaires concernant sa vie et ses oeuvres* ..., VI, 1909, p. 170.

20. Ibidem, p. 171.

21. P.R.O., State Papers Flanders, SP 77/27/124 verso, Gerbier to Coke, 8/18 April 1637.

22. Ibidem, SP 77/28/71 recto, Gerbier to Coke, 10/20 February 1638.

23. Hence Ferdinand writing to Philip IV on 20 November 1636: 'Las pinturas que me manda V.M. para la Torre que se hagan, está ya Rubens encargada dellas y me avisa se han comenzado algunas.' (Rooses and Ruelens (as in note 19), p. 176.

24. A noticeable example of this 'recycling' is the reuse of the design of *Esther and Ahasuerus*. This Rubens had first evolved for the Jesuit ceiling in Antwerp in 1620. He used it again ten years later, for his *Union of the Two Crowns*, one of the three central canvases for the Whitehall ceiling.

25. Brown and Elliott 1980 (as in note 3), pp. 109–110.

26. P.R.O., State Papers Flanders, SP 77/27/285, Gerbier to Coke, 9/19 July 1637.

27. See Howarth 2001 (as in note 2), passim.

28. P.R.O., Letter Books, SP 105/11, 23 March 1635.

# 'Frayicheyt ende kunst daer syne inclinatie toe stryckt': beschouwingen over het mecenaat van aartshertog Leopold-Wilhelm tijdens zijn landvoogdij over de Zuidelijke Nederlanden (1647–1656)

*Hans Vlieghe*

In 1647 werd aartshertog Leopold-Wilhelm van Oostenrijk (1614–1662), zoon van keizer Ferdinand II, door zijn neef, koning Filips IV van Spanje, belast met de landvoogdij over de Zuidelijke Nederlanden. Hij volgde daarbij kardinaal-infant Ferdinand op, die in 1641 op jonge leeftijd was overleden. Na diens dood kon er niet meteen een geschikte opvolger gevonden worden, zodat de Zuidelijke Nederlanden gedurende de eerste zes daarop volgende jaren bestuurd werden door twee Spaanse militaire bevelhebbers, achtereenvolgens don Francisco de Melo en de markies van Castel Rodrigo.[1] De hoofdbron voor Leopold-Wilhelms levensbeschrijving is nog steeds de hagiografische biografie *Le prince dévôt et guerrier*, in 1667 geschreven door de jezuïet Nicolas Avancini. Uit dat relaas komt de aartshertog naar voor als een wat onwereldse *Miles Christianus*, die veel tijd besteedde aan gebed en meditatie, waaruit hij kracht putte voor zijn militaire exploten, gericht op de verdediging van het roomse geloof en het huis Habsburg tegen hun tegenstanders.[2] Deze bijzondere rol werd ook beklemtoond in de picturale voorstellingen die door Erasmus Quellin werden ontworpen ter gelegenheid van Leopold-Wilhelms Blijde Intrede in Antwerpen, in 1647 (afb. 1).[3]

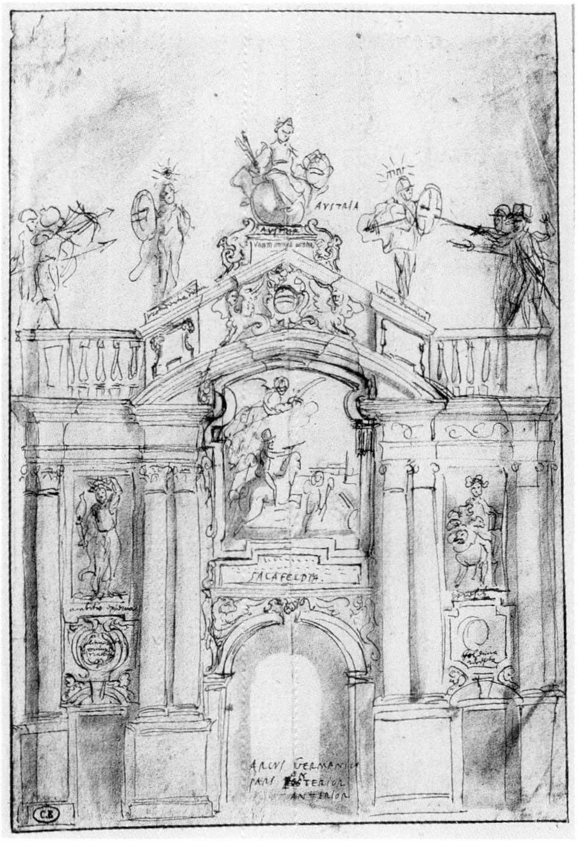


Afb. 1. Erasmus II Quellin, *Ontwerp voor de Arcus Germanicus*. Antwerpen, Koninklijk Museum voor Schone Kunsten

Leopold-Wilhelms onwrikbaar-dogmatisch contrareformatorische levenshouding moet natuurlijk mede gestuurd zijn geworden door de jezuïeten die hem tijdens zijn aan het Spaanse hof doorgebrachte jeugdjaren hebben gevormd en voorbereid op zijn latere loopbaan. Tijdens zijn bestuursperiode in de Zuidelijke Nederlanden zou hij zich trouwens nadrukkelijk door deze rigide godsdienstige opvattingen laten leiden, zoals vooral mag blijken uit zijn compromisloze veroordeling en vervolging van het Jansenisme.[4] Er is ongetwijfeld ook een samenhang tussen Leopold-Wilhelms opvatting van vroomheid en het indrukwekkend aantal van zijn geestelijke titels: hij werd achtereenvolgens bisschop van Passau, Straatsburg, Halberstadt, Olmütz en Breslau. En in dit verband moet natuurlijk ook melding worden gemaakt van Leopold-Wilhelms persoonlijke beleving van de *Pietas Austriaca* die traditioneel door het huis Habsburg werd gehuldigd en waarvoor vanuit de Contrareformatie nieuwe impulsen zijn uitgegaan.[5] Deze Habsburgse beleving van de vroomheid was meer dan een strenge levenshouding. Zij hield ook een zeer concrete gerichtheid in op de roomse geloofsmysteries. Centraal stonden de cultus van de Eucharistie, het H. Kruis en de Mariadevotie, vooral met betrekking tot de Onbevlekte Ontvangenis. Mede door het felle calvinistische verzet tegen Eucharistieverering en Mariacultus kregen deze aspecten van de *Pietas Austriaca* in Leopold-Wilhelms tijd een zeer actuele betekenis. Maar ook de verering van het H. Kruis werd opnieuw gestimuleerd door die andere geloofsstrijd waarin het huis Habsburg zich geëngageerd had, de verdediging van de christenheid en van het H. Roomse Rijk in het bijzonder tegen de oprukkende Turken. Hierbij aansluitend mag natuurlijk niet onvermeld blijven dat Leopold-Wilhelm ook grootmeester was van de Duitse Orde. Haar embleem werd, symbolisch genoeg, gevormd door het kruismotief en in deze overigens vooral honorifieke functie heeft de aartshertog nog een bescheiden poging gedaan om troepen op de been te brengen voor een militaire actie tegen de islam.[6] Evenzeer werd binnen het raam van de *Pietas Austriaca* de heiligencultus bevorderd, zij het met het accent op de bijzondere betekenis van de heiligen uit het huis Habsburg zelf. Behalve om hun rol als voorsprekers werden zij ook en vooral vereerd omwille van hun uitgesproken voorbeeldfunctie ten opzichte van hun nazaten.

Leopold-Wilhelms vroomheid wordt heel treffend geïllustreerd door de vele religieuze voorstellingen die zich bevinden tussen het werk van de door hem begunstigde en hierna nog te bespreken schilders. Hun aantal is inderdaad opvallend groot en de hoofdmomenten van de *Pietas Austriaca* worden er op treffende wijze door vertegenwoordigd.[7] Vooral de zeer vele Mariavoorstellingen vallen daarbij op. Uniek in dit verband was ook het merkwaardige ensemble van met contrareformatorische thematiek 'opgesmukte' bloemfestoenen van Daniël Seghers, Jan-Filips van Thielen, Jan Davidsz. de Heem en anderen. Na de dood van de aartshertog werd dit ensemble geïntegreerd in de keizerlijke verzamelingen te Wenen, waar het zelfs een hele zaal in beslag nam.[8]

Maar recenter onderzoek heeft tevens geleerd dat de persoonlijkheid van de aartshertog toch wel wat geschakeerder en rijker was. In de talrijke portretten die hij van zichzelf heeft laten maken door Vlaamse schilders die bedrijvig waren in de periode van zijn landvoogdij is hij nadrukkelijk uitgebeeld als krijgsheer, geharnast en klaar voor de strijd. Hier zien we vooral de 'prince guerrier' in beeld, die zijn militair ambt overigens uitoefende *ad maiorem Dei gloriam*. Hij was een gecultiveerde man met een uitgesproken goede smaak en een ruime artistieke belangstelling. Hij hield van muziek en dans en maakte aan het hof te Brussel o.m. de oudst bekende opvoering van een opera mogelijk.[9] Leopold-Wilhelms wereldse kant mag natuurlijk vooral blijken uit zijn grote voorliefde voor de schilderkunst. Hij slaagde erin 880 schilderijen van meesters uit de Nederlanden en Duitsland samen te brengen, en daarbovenop nog eens 517 Italiaanse werken. Behalve deze immense schilderijencollectie bezat de aartshertog verder nog 343 tekeningen en niet minder dan 542 stuks sculptuur. Dit gigantische ensemble is goed bekend dank zij de uiterst gedetailleerde beschrijving die Jan-Anton van der Baren, Leopold-Wilhelms hofkapelaan en ook schilder, ervan heeft gegeven in de in 1659 door hem opgestelde inventaris van de collectie. Dit is een voor zijn tijd uiterst zorgvuldige beschrijving van een kunstverzameling: niet alleen worden kunstenaarsnamen exact vermeld, ook de maten en de beschrijvingen van de schilderijlijsten vindt men er nauwkeurig in terug.[10]

In de kunstgeschiedenis is de aartshertog vooral beroemd geworden als gepassioneerd verzamelaar van Italiaanse Renaissancekunst. Tussen 1647 en 1656 heeft hij in zijn residentie op de Coudenberg te Brussel de belangrijkste verzameling van Italiaanse schilderkunst samengebracht, die er op dat ogenblik in Europa te vinden was. Deze schitterende collectie is grotendeels intact bewaard gebleven en vormt de kern van het schilderijenbezit van het Kunsthistorisches Museum te Wenen.[11] Als verzamelaar paste Leopold-Wilhelm trouwens helemaal in een specifiek Habsburgse traditie, met voorgangers als Karel V, Filips II, Rudolf II en Albrecht en Isabella.[12] In de veelzijdigheid en volledigheid van zijn schilderijenverzame-

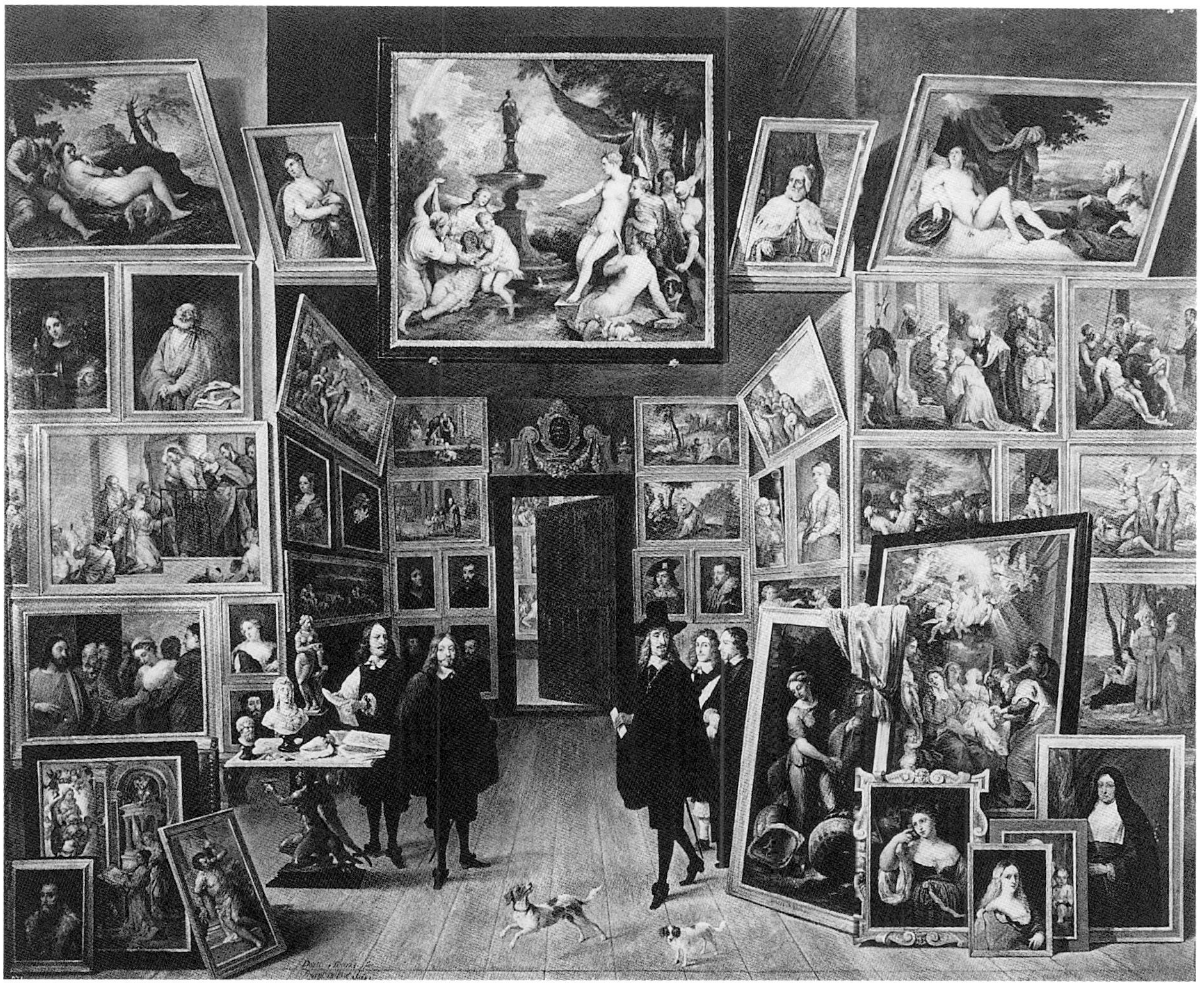

Afb. 2. David II Teniers, *Aartshertog Leopold-Wilhelm in zijn schilderijenverzameling*. Madrid, Museo del Prado

ling overtrof hij hen echter allemaal, ook de legendarische Rudolf II. Tezelfdertijd belichaamde hij in zijn verzamelaarschap ook ten volle het zeventiende-eeuwse connoisseurschap, dat volledig aan het loskomen was van de oude, encyclopedische 'Kunst-und Wunderkammer' met haar middeleeuwse wortels. Het model was de Italiaanse vorstelijke verzameling van de zestiende eeuw en de daarop geïnspireerde verzameldrift van zijn eigen tijdgenoten Filips IV en Karel I. Het is trouwens te danken aan het verwerven van belangrijke stukken uit de verzameling van deze laatste koning en ook uit andere door Cromwell geconfisqueerde en verkochte collecties van onfortuinlijke prominenten uit het eerste Stuarttijdvak, dat Leopold-Wilhelms verzameling zulke envergure heeft kunnen krijgen. Maar eerder al, nog voor zijn aankomst in Brussel, kocht Leopold-Wilhelm Italiaanse kunst a.h.w. in gros aan. Zo had hij de belangrijke Venetiaanse verzameling Della Nave weten te bemachtigen. Het beeld van de verzamelaar Leopold-Wilhelm is voor altijd vastgelegd in de vele en gevarieerde zichten op delen van de collectie door David Teniers de Jonge, met de aartshertog in het midden, uitgebeeld in een trotse en zelfbewuste pose (afb. 2). Deze uitbeeldingen verschillen in zoverre met de beroemde voorstellingen van kunstkamers uitgevoerd door schilders van vroegere generaties zoals Jan Brueghel, Frans II Francken of Willem van Haecht, dat zij voor het eerst het accent leggen op de visuele documentatie van de collectie en niet meer op het allegoriseren van het begrip 'Pictura'.[13]

Ofschoon het nog veel groter in aantal was dan het Italiaanse deel van de collectie, is het werk van Noord-Europese schilders in Leopold-Wilhelms bezit veel minder bestudeerd. Heel wat hiervan werd op de markt verworven. De landvoogd bezat een zeer uitgebreid ensemble van oudere Nederlandse schilderkunst uit de vijftiende en de zestiende eeuw, waarin zowat alle prominente kunstenaars vertegenwoordigd waren; deze verzameling werd door hem vervolledigd met belangrijk werk van Rubens en Van Dijck. Van Leopold-Wilhelms hofschilder Jan van den Hoecke, waarover verder meer, verneemt men dat zijn broodheer persoonlijk wenste te zien wat er in Antwerpen voorhanden en te koop was.[14] Ook laat hij zich, als hij in 1648 in Antwerpen zijn plechtige Blijde Intrede houdt, door het stadsbestuur het vorstelijke bedrag van 40.000 gulden schenken, om dit vervolgens naar eigen goeddunken te kunnen besteden aan de aankoop van kunstwerken.[15] De aartshertog wil zich daarbij door niemand iets laten opdringen: Van den Hoecke laat uitdrukkelijk weten dat Leopold-Wilhelm 'selfs liever verkiest de frayicheyt ende kunst, daer syne inclinatie toe stryckt'.[16] Van bij zijn aankomst in de Zuidelijke Nederlanden laat de aartshertog er ook zijn interesse blijken voor de actuele productie van levende schilders. In zijn verzameling treft men een vrij groot aantal schilderijen aan die hij tijdens zijn regeerperiode door bestelling of opdracht moet verworven hebben bij tal van Vlaamse schilders, die een rol speelden in het kunstleven op het ogenblik dat hij in Brussel zijn ambt uitoefende.

Het is op dit tot op heden ondermaats bestudeerd aspect van Leopold-Wilhelms kunstpolitiek[17] dat ik hier de aandacht wil richten. Daarbij spreekt het voor zich dat er binnen het bestek van deze bijdrage geen plaats is voor een exhaustieve studie over Leopold-Wilhelms beschermheerschap van de Vlaamse schilders van zijn tijd. Laat dit slechts een eerste bescheiden terreinverkenning zijn, mede gesteund op het tot heden bekende bronnenmateriaal. De hoofdbron die ons hierbij ter beschikking staat is de reeds genoemde, uiterst gedetailleerde en in 1659 opgestelde inventaris van de verzameling; daarnaast zijn er ook nog een aantal rekeningen uit de Brusselse hofhuishouding. Voor het overgrote deel zijn ook hier de relevante schilderijen nog te zien in het Kunsthistorisches Museum te Wenen. Ook de overvloed aan materiaal dwingt mij tot beperking van het te bespreken werk. In een eerste luik wil ik ingaan op de rol die werd gespeeld door de schilders die in vaste hofdienst werkten en uit hoofde daarvan met zeer specifieke taken werden belast. Daarna zal ik het hebben over de belangstelling die de aartshertog had voor het werk van de in Antwerpen en Brussel actieve schilders van monumentale historietaferelen en portretten. Op de betekenis van het in Leopold-Wilhelms verzameling eveneens zeer overvloedig aanwezige werk van de vele schilders van genrestukken, al dan niet met historietaferelen gestoffeerde landschappen, stillevens e.d. ga ik echter niet meer systematisch in.

## Hofschilders in vaste dienst

De eerste schilder die aldus een rol van betekenis heeft gespeeld, was Jan van den Hoecke (1611–51).[18] Na een opleiding bij Rubens vertrok hij in de latere jaren dertig naar Rome, waar hij zeker tot 1644 heeft gewoond. Zijn stijl, die aanvankelijk sterk verwant was met die van de late Rubens, oriënteerde hij in Rome op de strengere classicistische barokstijl, zoals die was geïntroduceerd door Annibale Carracci en diens leerlingen. Op een niet nader te bepalen ogenblik treft men Van den Hoecke aan in Wenen, waar hij in contact stond met het hof van keizer Ferdinand III en hij ook diens broer Leopold-Wilhelm moet hebben leren kennen. Toen deze in 1647 naar de Nederlanden kwam, bracht hij Van den Hoecke mee en die werd prompt zijn hofschilder. Tussen 1647 en 1652 wordt Van den Hoecke meerdere malen vermeld in de betalingsorders van Leopold-Wilhelms hof: behalve een vast loon ontvangt hij ook supplementair loon, vergoedingen voor schildermateriaal en geschenken ter gelegenheid van zijn huwelijk met Clara van Woonsel in 1648.[19]

Aanvankelijk ging Van den Hoecke terug naar Antwerpen, waar hij vandaan kwam en waar zijn familie woonde. Hij kon zich echter niet permitteren wat uitzonderlijkerwijze alleen aan Rubens was gegund: hofschilder te zijn en toch te blijven wonen in het als economisch en artistiek centrum belangrijkere Antwerpen. Ten laatste in 1649 moet hij zich in Brussel hebben gevestigd. De voornaamste beweegreden van de aartshertog om Van den Hoecke tot hofschilder aan te stellen was ongetwijfeld het feit dat hij hem al in Wenen had leren kennen. Het is daarbij ook goed mogelijk dat hij bij Van den Hoecke waardeerde, dat deze bij Rubens was opgeleid en door deze laatste ook betrokken

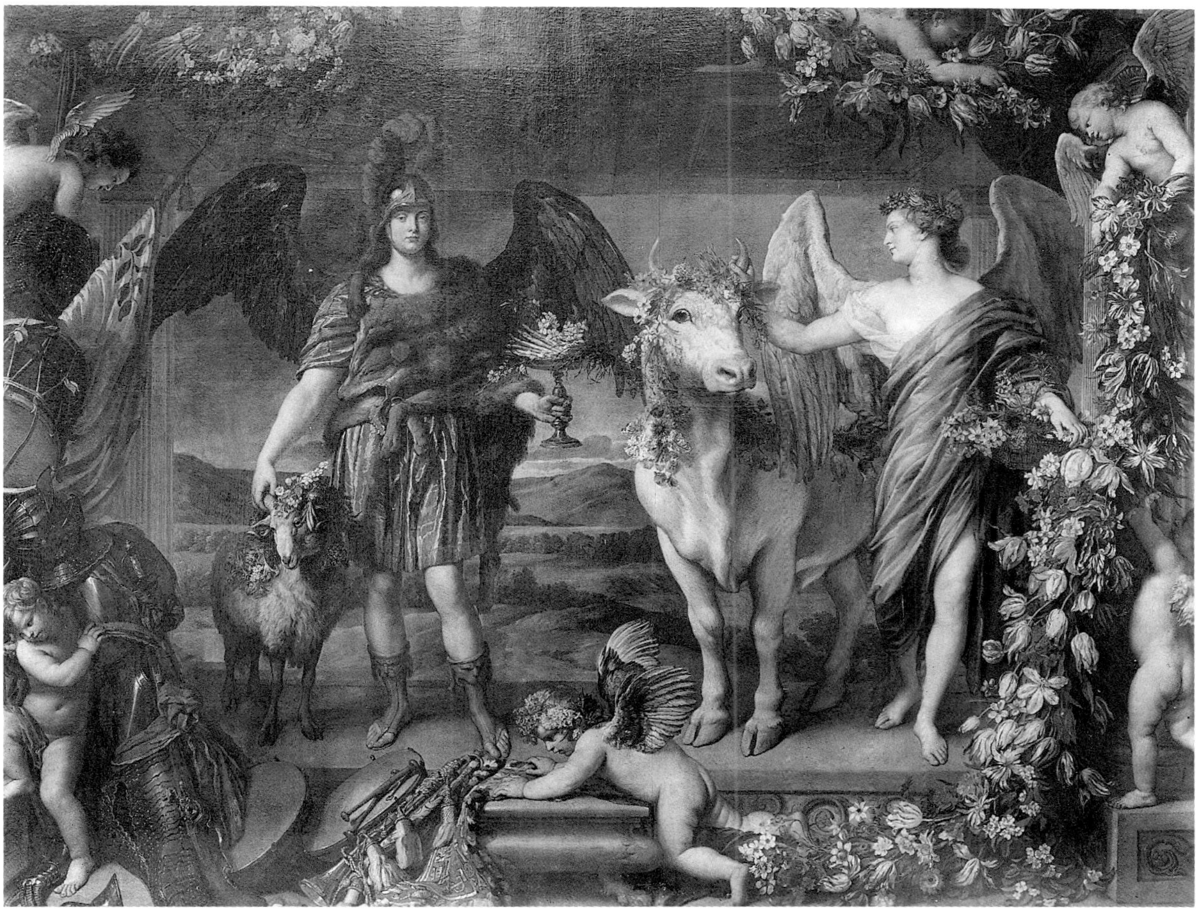

Afb. 3. Jan van den Hoecke, *De maanden maart en april.* Wenen, Kunsthistorisches Museum

was geworden bij de uitvoering van de ter ere van zijn voorganger geschilderde monumentale decoraties voor de *Pompa Introitus Ferdinandi.*[20] Wij zullen nog zien dat hij een niet te miskennen voorkeur had voor andere schilders die uit de 'Rubensstal' zijn gekomen, zodat men zich wellicht mag afvragen of hij niet op zoek was naar een plaatsvervangende Rubens of Van Dijck.

In ditzelfde verband is het zeker ook niet onbelangrijk vast te stellen dat Van den Hoecke, net als Rubens, een gecultiveerd schilder moet geweest zijn, met voor een hoveling geschikte kwaliteiten. Dat mag met name blijken uit het feit dat hij in 1644 in Rome vermeld staat onder de 'Virtuosi al Pantheon', een zeer elitair genootschap van historieschilders dat zich niet graag geassocieerd wenste te zien met de vaak nogal rumoerige groep van vooral Hollandse en Vlaamse genre- en landschapschilders.[21] Men stelt inderdaad vast hoe rond het midden van de eeuw ook andere vorsten op zoek waren naar *Ersatz* voor de twee corypheeën van de Antwerpse schilderkunst, beiden kort na elkaar, respectievelijk in 1640 en 1641, overleden op het absolute hoogtepunt van hun internationale roem. Een typisch voorbeeld wordt hier geboden door Leopold-Wilhelms tijdgenoten Frederik-Hendrik van Oranje-Nassau en zijn echtgenote Amalia van Solms, die beiden grote waardering voor Van Dijck hebben laten blijken en na diens dood de door Van Dijck opgeleide en sterk op diens stijl gerichte schilder Thomas Willeboirts Bosschaert – die overigens ook voor Leopold-Wilhelm zou werken – met tientallen opdrachten zijn blijven belasten.[22]

Maar ook een ander element kan voor Leopold-Wilhelms keuze medebepalend zijn geweest. De schilder was een neef van de toonaangevende Antwerpse kunsthandelaar Matthijs Musson, een omstandigheid waarvan de aartshertog met het oog op zijn verzamelaarsactiviteit zeker het belang moet hebben ingezien. En inderdaad zien wij hoe Van den Hoecke meteen na zijn aanstelling met zijn

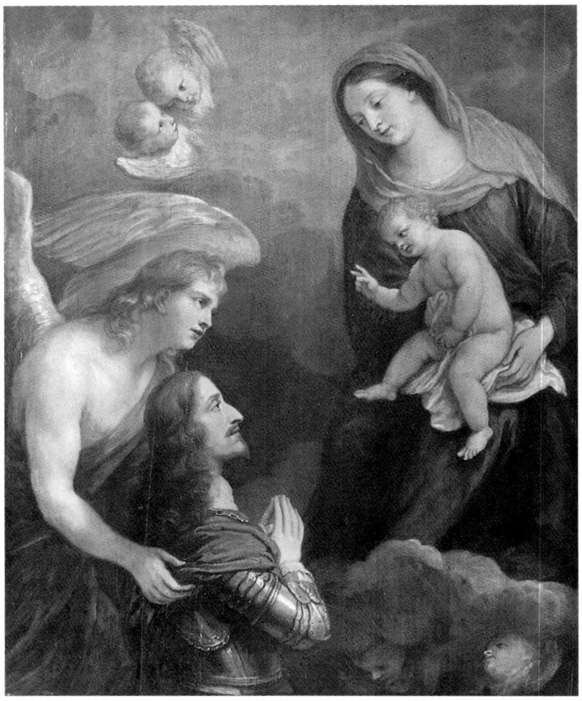

Afb. 4. Jan van den Hoecke, *Aartshertog Leopold-Wilhelm in gebed voor Maria en het Kind Jezus*. Wenen, Kunsthistorisches Museum

oom correspondeert over schilderijen en andere 'fray dingen' waarvoor de landvoogd belangstelling heeft.[23]

Te oordelen naar de inventaris van zijn verzameling, bezat Leopold-Wilhelm niet minder dan 43 schilderijen van Van den Hoecke, religieuze zowel als mythologisch-allegorische composities, maar ook portretten.[24] Een aantal van deze schilderijen kunnen overigens al ontstaan zijn in Wenen, nog voor de aartshertog tot landvoogd was aangesteld. Van den Hoeckes hoofdwerk zijn de in olieverf geschilderde cartons voor de tapijtenreeks met de allegorische uitbeelding van de tijd en de elementen (afb. 3). Uit de nog bewaarde stukken van deze reeks komt Van den Hoecke heel nadrukkelijk naar voor als een talentvol historieschilder, die zich in zijn vormgeving oriënteert op de Italiaans-classicistische barok van Guido Reni en andere gelijkgestemde schilders uit de zogenaamde Bolognese school die werkten in de traditie van Annibale Carracci; met deze stijl moet hijzelf tijdens zijn lang verblijf in Rome trouwens goed vertrouwd zijn geraakt.[25] Naar Reni heeft hij overigens gekopieerd.[26] Treffend is het groot aantal devotieschilderijen, met o. m. heel wat Mariale thematiek als onderwerp.[27] Opmerkelijk in deze laatste categorie schilderijen is vooral het tafereel waarin de knielende aartshertog door een engel wordt voorgesteld aan Maria en het Kind Jezus (afb. 4): als geen ander mag dit werk de betekenis van de *Pietas Austriaca* illustreren. Ook bezat Leopold-Wilhelm van Van den Hoecke kopieën naar Titiaan en Veronese, mogelijk met de bedoeling op die manier het ensemble van originele Venetiaanse schilderijen uit de eigen collectie te kunnen aanvullen met composities van deze meesters die hij niet (of nog niet) in zijn bezit had.[28] En ook als portretschilder werd hij door de aartshertog gebruikt. Zijn meest majestatische werk in dit opzicht is ongetwijfeld het grote staatsieportret van Leopold-Wilhelm, als veldheer te paard (afb. 5). Dit schilderij past in een typisch Habsburgse traditie van dergelijke monumentale ruiterportretten die alle uiteindelijk verwijzen naar het prototype in dit opzicht, het vermaarde ruiterportret van Karel V als overwinnaar op de Duitse vorsten, dat in 1548 was geschilderd door Titiaan. Ook dit werk treft door zijn rigide classicisme. De aartshertog zag zich blijkbaar het liefst martiaal uitgebeeld, in het vol ornaat van de Duitse Orde. Hierna zal nog blijken hoe ook andere schilders hem op een verwante manier vooral als 'prince guerrier' zouden uitbeelden.[29]

Wellicht in of rond 1651 kwam David II Teniers in vaste dienst van de aartshertog.[30] Hij kreeg de titel van *ayuda da camera* en ontving als zichtbare uitdrukking van dit ambt een gouden ketting met portretmedaillon van Leopold-Wilhelm (afb. 6).[31] Kennelijk volgde hij in deze functie Jan van den Hoecke op, die in datzelfde jaar 1651 zeer onverwacht gestorven was. Het kan enigszins verwonderen dat de aartshertog geen schilder van monumentale historietaferelen tot hofschilder aanstelde, maar wel een specialist op het gebied van de toch lager aangeslagen genreschilderkunst. Teniers' taken verschilden echter met die van Van den Hoecke in belangrijke mate. Meer nog dan zijn voorganger blijkt Teniers vooral omwille van practische overwegingen te zijn aangeworven. Naar alle waarschijnlijkheid heeft hij immers een hoofdrol gespeeld bij het aankopen van de Italiaanse schilderijen uit de Engelse collecties die door Cromwell publiek geveild zijn geworden.[32] En vermoedelijk kreeg hij ook de opdracht een catalogus te verzorgen van de hele verzameling, het beroemde *Theatrum Pictorium*.[33] Het is geweten dat ook Teniers al eerder

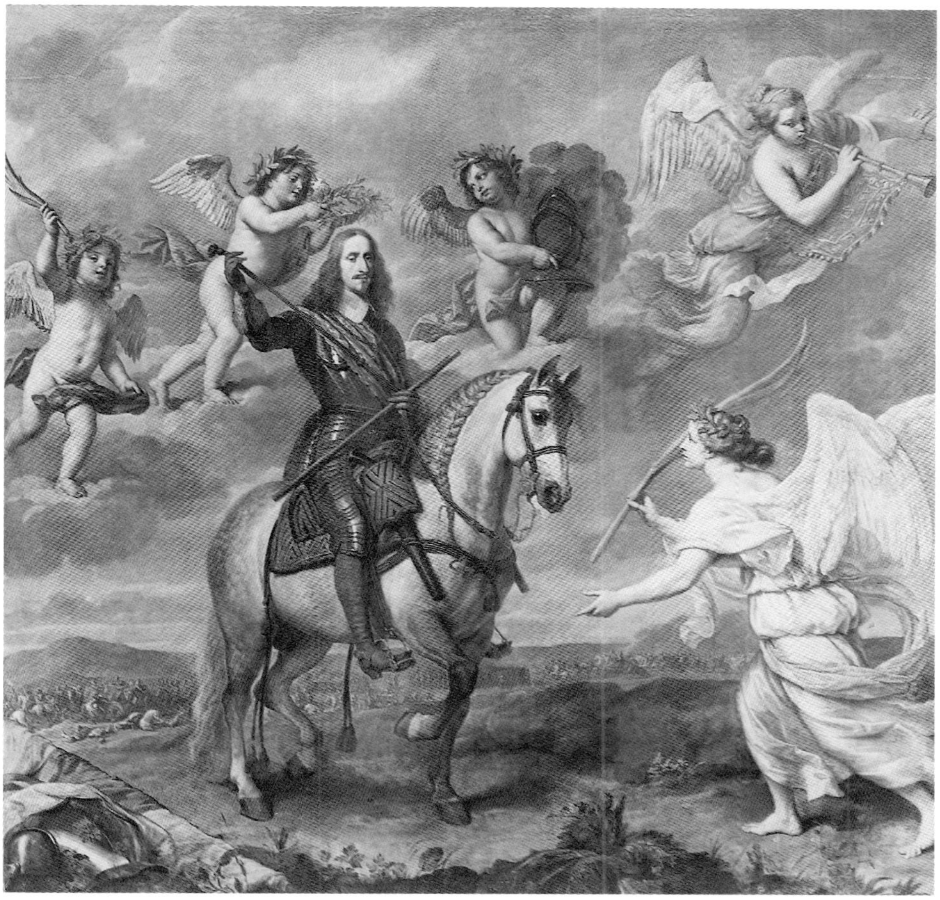

Afb. 5. Jan van den Hoecke, *Ruiterportret van aartshertog Leopold-Wilhelm*. Wenen, Kunsthistorisches Museum

uitstekende relaties onderhield met de Antwerpse kunsthandel, zoals de firma's van Van Immerseel en Musson. En inderdaad zien wij dat hij, net als Van den Hoecke, bij Musson op zoek gaat naar kunstwerken voor zijn broodheer. Ook laat hij zich door Musson voorlichten over werk dat te koop stond in belangrijke Antwerpse verzamelingen, zoals in deze van kanunnik de Tassis.[34] Teniers zelf was inmiddels ook een beroemd schilder geworden en was verwant aan enkele van de meest toonaangevende Antwerpse artistieke dynastieën, zoals de Brueghels en de Quellins. Het lijkt waarschijnlijk dat de aartshertog allereerst wenste te profiteren van de expertise van Teniers, met het oog op uitbouw en organisatie van zijn collectie, en slechts in tweede orde dacht aan diens oeuvre. Dat was overigens ook in zijn verzameling vertegenwoordigd.

Uiteraard waren Teniers' boerentaferelen in de aartshertogelijke verzameling aanwezig. Men vindt een vijftal van deze werken in de inventaris van 1659. Deze schilderijen zijn, op sti-

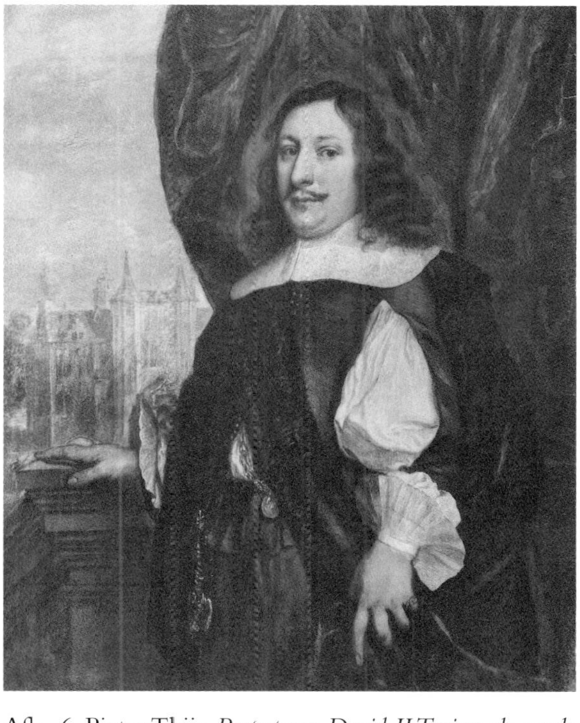

Afb. 6. Pieter Thijs, *Portret van David II Teniers als ayuda da camera van aartshertog Leopold-Wilhelm*. München, Alte Pinakothek

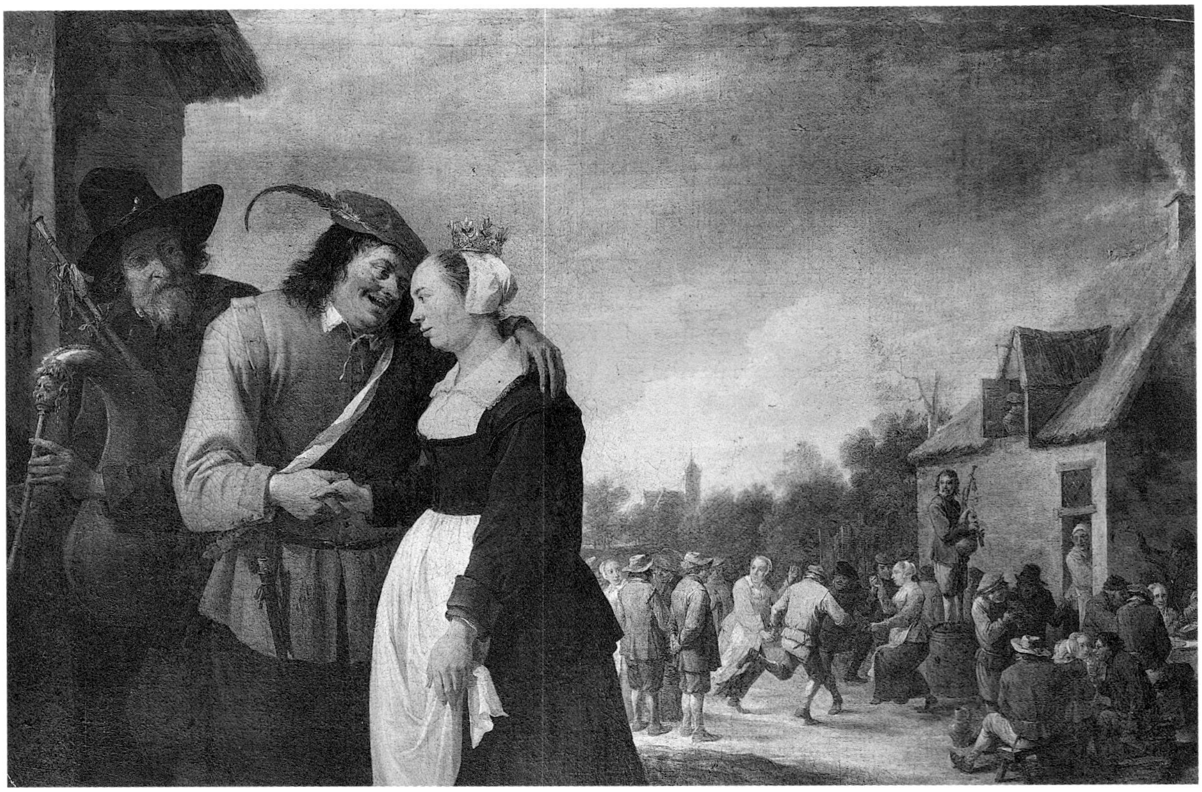

Afb. 7. David II Teniers, *Boerenbruiloft ('Boerenvreugd')*. Wenen, Kunsthistorisches Museum

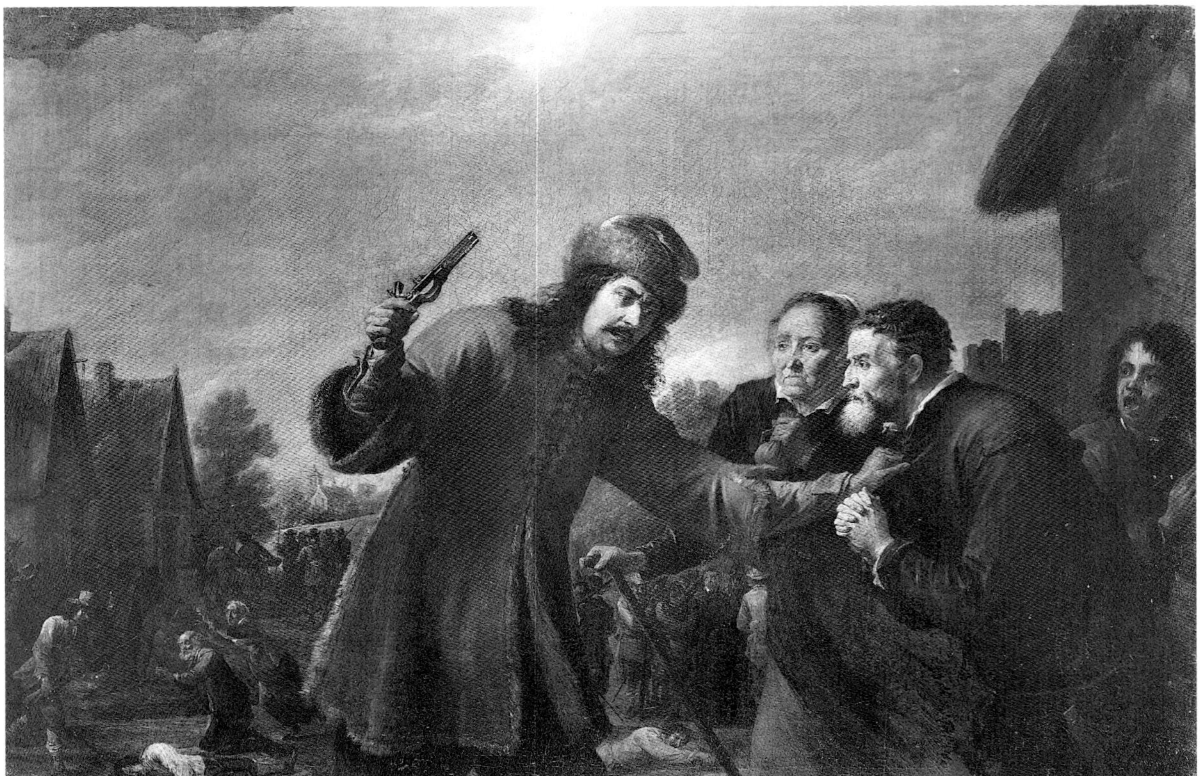

Afb. 8. David II Teniers, *Soldaten die een dorp plunderen ('Boerenverdriet')*. Wenen, Kunsthistorisches Museum

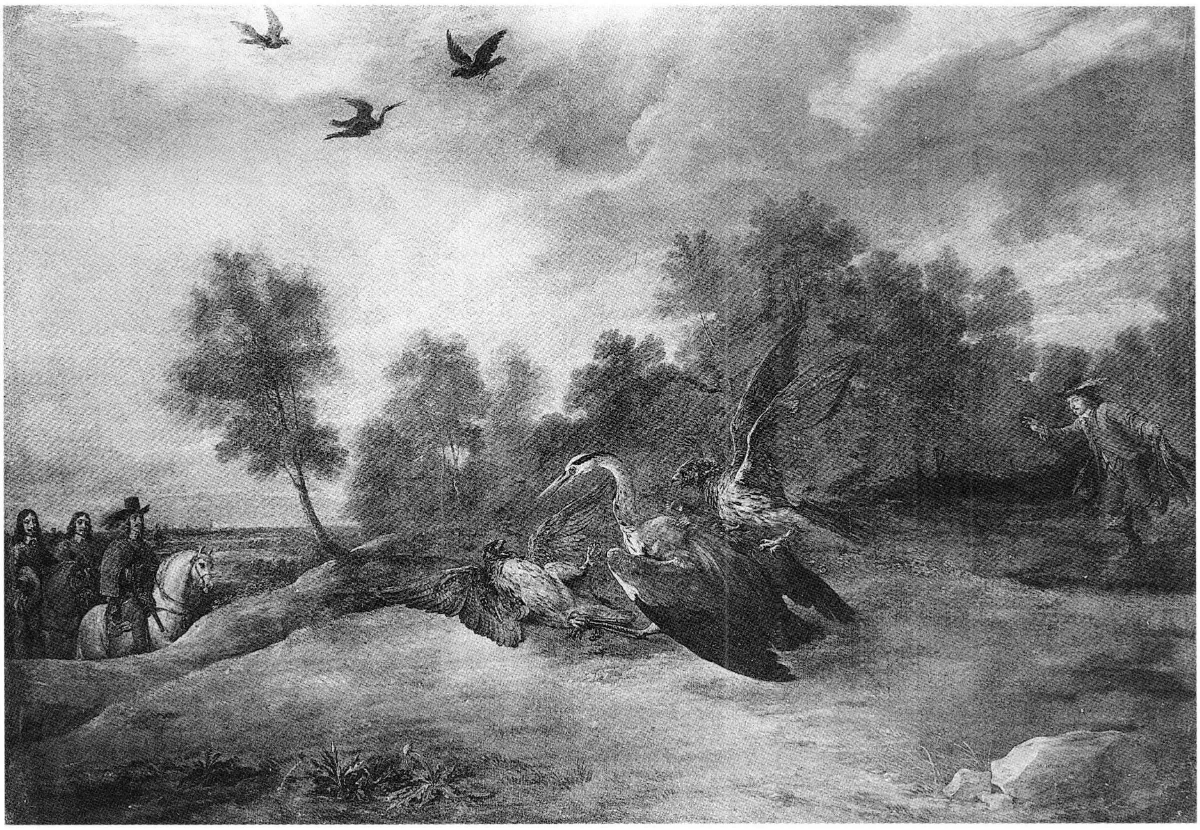

Afb. 9. David II Teniers, *Aartshertog Leopold-Wilhelm op reigerjacht*. Parijs, Musée du Louvre

listische gronden of op basis van hun datering, te situeren in de periode van Leopold-Wilhelms landvoogdij.[35] Opmerkelijk is wel dat deze taferelen nogal verstilde weergaven van het boerenleven zijn, anders dan de vooral in deze periode opmerkelijke kermistaferelen met hun drukke en vaak rumoerige stoffering. De twee als pendanten bedoelde stukken, *Boerenbruiloft* en *Soldaten die een dorp plunderen* zijn hierbij kenmerkend (afb. 7, 8). Deze taferelen hebben overigens een welbekende symbolische betekenis, als verzinnebeeldingen van resp. het *Boerenleed* en de *Boerenvreugde*.[36] Beide schilderijen zijn voorzien van het jaartal 1648, het jaar van de Vrede van Münster. Het is goed mogelijk dat Teniers hier bewust zinspeelde op het einde van de Dertig- en Tachtigjarige Oorlog. Het is alleszins bekend dat deze thematiek in de allegorisering van Oorlog en Vrede in de schilderkunst van de beide Nederlanden herhaaldelijk werd uitgebeeld sinds het einde van de zestiende eeuw.[37] Kennelijk was Leopold-Wilhelm in deze zeer specifiek genreachtige allegorisering van oorlog en vrede geïnteresseerd, want hij bezat nog soortgelijk werk dat hij bij andere Antwerpse specialisten van het kleinschalige kabinettafereel had verworven.[38] Ook *Leopold-Wilhelm op reigerjacht* kan worden gerekend tot de veeleer genreachtige taferelen van Teniers, die een allegoriserende verwijzing naar de oorlog inhouden. Dit schilderij, thans in het Louvre te Parijs (afb. 9), komt niet voor in de inventaris van 1659. De aartshertog is er voorgesteld terwijl hij samen met zijn gevolg gadeslaat hoe een reiger zich verweert tegen twee valken die hem hebben aangevallen. Mogelijk werd het schilderij door de landvoogd bestemd als diplomatiek geschenk en vervulde het werk in dat opzicht een enigszins analoge functie als de vele kunstkabinetten. Er is aangetoond dat het gevecht tussen de drie vogels verwijst naar een embleem van Camerarius uit 1596, waarbij een gevecht tussen een reiger en twee valken het wisselvallige verloop van de krijgskansen uitbeeldt. Meer bepaald zou de reiger Leopold-Wilhelm en Habsburg kunnen voorstellen, terwijl de beide valken hun twee belagers, resp. de Republiek en Frankrijk, zouden verzinnebeelden.[39]

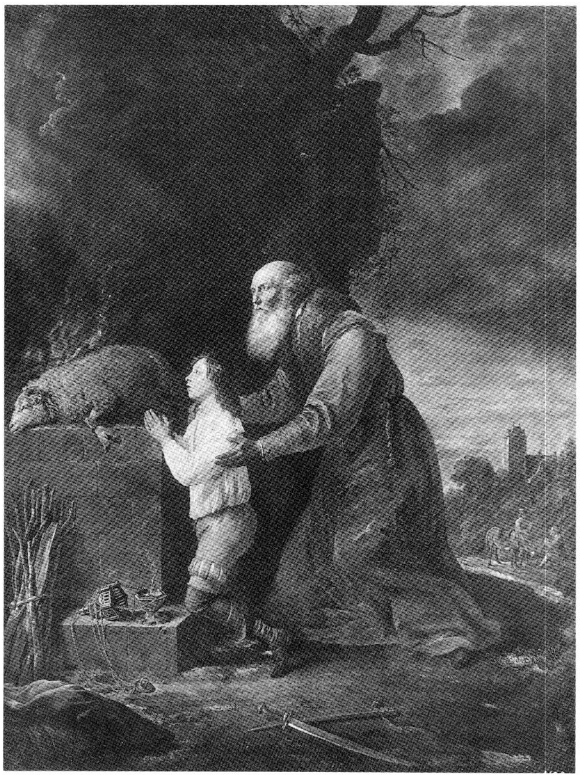

Afb. 10. David II Teniers, *Het brandoffer van Abraham.* Wenen, Kunsthistorisches Museum

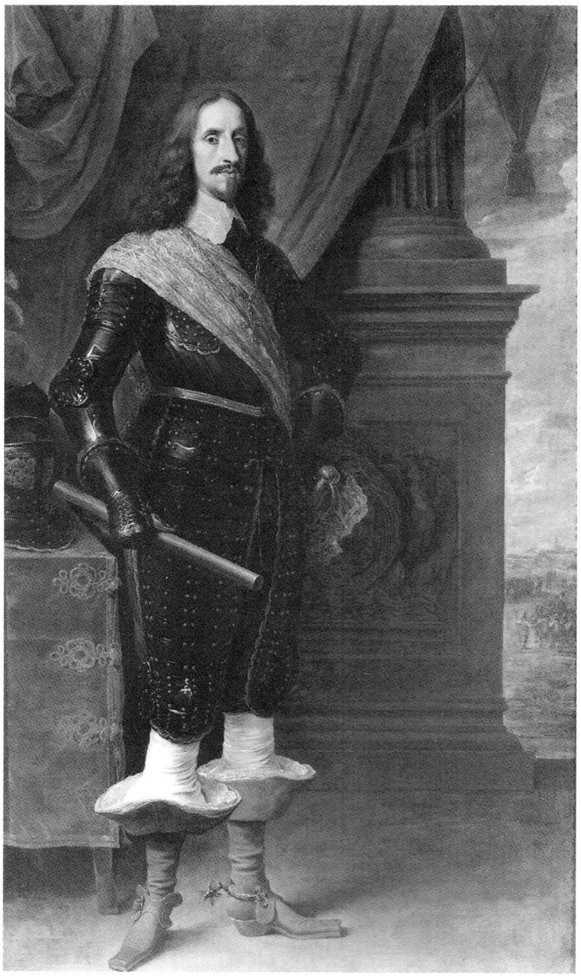

Afb. 11. David II Teniers, *Portret van aartshertog Leopold-Wilhelm als veldheer.* Wenen, Kunsthistorisches Museum

Maar de genreschilder die Teniers was diende ook tegemoet te komen aan Leopold-Wilhelms uitgesproken belangstelling voor religieuze thematiek. In dit opzicht zijn een aantal oudtestamentische taferelen van kabinetformaat te vermelden, meer bepaald *Het brandoffer van Abraham,*[40] nu in het Kunsthistorisches Museum te Wenen (afb. 10) en een thans verdwenen *Brand van Sodoma en Gomorrha.*[41] Het lijkt aannemelijk dat de aartshertog in het op stilistische gronden rond 1650 te dateren *Brandoffer van Abraham* niet alleen de decoratieve inbedding in een landschap wist te waarderen. De in beeld gebrachte thematiek wijst er mijns inziens ook op dat de keuze van het onderwerp beantwoordde aan een zeer specifieke wens vanwege de landvoogd. In de iconografie van het Oude Testament komt dit tafereel veel minder voor dan het in het boek Genesis eraan voorafgaande verhaal van het Offer van Izaäk. Het is geweten dat het onderwerp te interpreteren is als verzinnebeelding van de absolute gehoorzaamheid aan God. Die 'Vreze des Heren' was niet alleen geïntegreerd in de *Pietas Austriaca;* zij ligt ook ten grondslag aan Leopold-Wilhelms eigen devies *Timore Domini.*[42] Een nadrukkelijke uitbeelding van Leopold-Wilhelms *Pietas Austriaca* was het thans verloren schilderijtje op koper waarin is uitgebeeld hoe de aartshertog in volle wapenrusting knielt voor Maria en begeleid wordt door zijn patroonheilige uit het huis Habsburg, Sint-Leopold. Hij dankt Maria daarbij voor zijn in 1652 behaalde overwinningen bij Duinkerken en Grevelingen.[43]

Van een hofschilder werd ook verwacht dat hij het zelfbeeld van de vorst zou visualiseren. Van den Hoecke deed dat in een monumentaal en krijgshaftig ruiterportret. Het zegt iets over het belang dat de landvoogd aan dat welbepaalde imago hechtte dat hij ook door Teniers een levensgroot portret van zichzelf liet uitvoeren, waarin hij geheel geharnast en ten voeten uit verschijnt (afb. 11).[44] Wellicht is dit het enige monumentale schilderij dat Teniers ooit gemaakt heeft! Verder liet Leopold-Wilhelm Teniers ove-

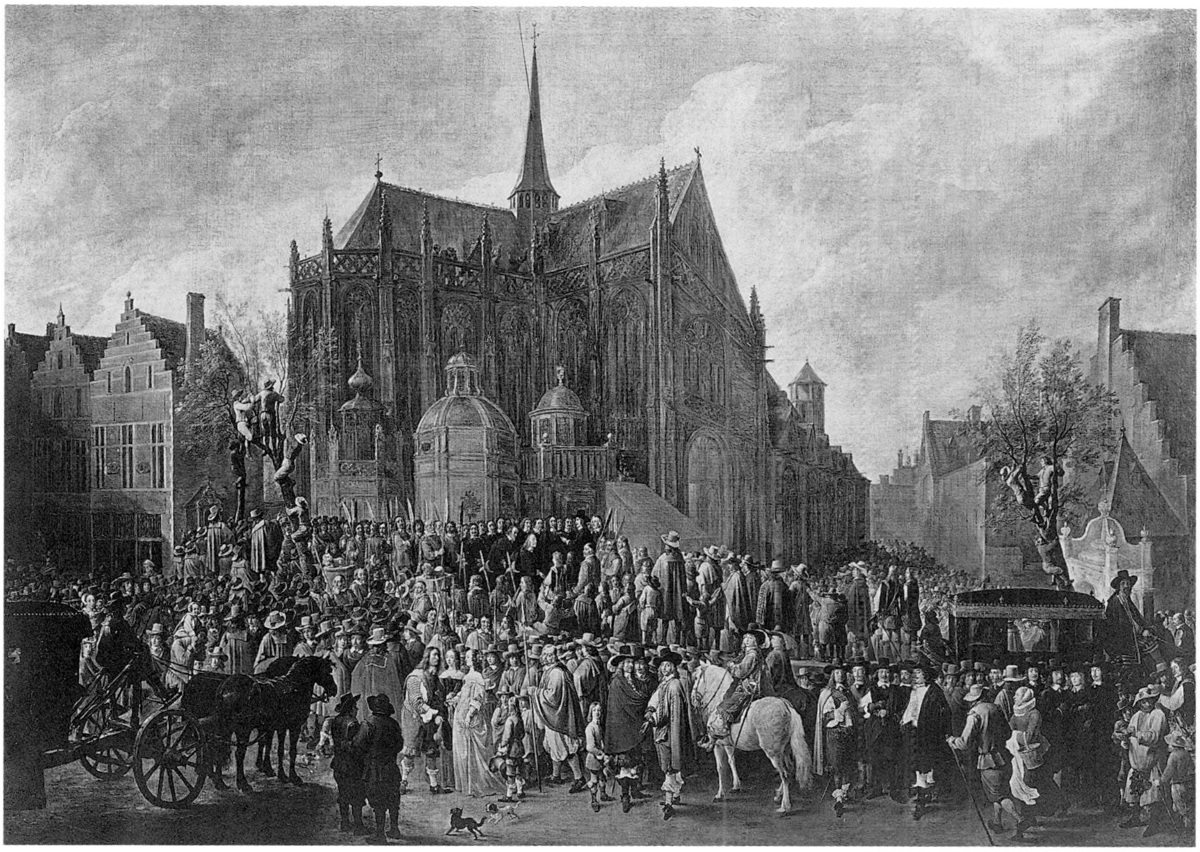

Afb. 12. David II Teniers, *Aartshertog Leopold-Wilhelm bij het feest van de Brusselse kruisboogschutters*. Wenen, Kunsthistorisches Museum

rigens aan zijn *image building* werken in diens eigen narratieve, genreachtige trant. Ik ging hoger reeds in op de vermoedelijke betekenis van het schilderij dat de aartshertog weergeeft op de reigerjacht. Maar het meest markante voorbeeld is ongetwijfeld Teniers' *Leopold-Wilhelm bij het feest van de Brusselse kruisboogschutters* (afb. 12), thans eveneens in het Kunsthistorisches Museum bewaard. En uiteraard zijn er de vele voorstellingen van de aartshertog als kunstkenner, in beeld gebracht te midden van zijn verzameling, schilderijen die bedoeld waren om door de aartshertog ten geschenke te worden gegeven aan andere vorsten of vorstelijke verzamelaars, of althans aan hun vertegenwoordigers.[45] Met het kruisboogschutterstafereel haakt Teniers overigens in op een karakteristieke traditie bij Brusselse hofschilders: dit werk ligt immers in de lijn van soortgelijke taferelen waarin Denijs van Alsloot en Anton Sallaert de infante Isabella betrokken bij de activiteiten van het Brusselse corporatiewezen.[46]

Maar, zoals ik al vermelde, verwachtte de aartshertog van Teniers vooral veel op het practische vlak, allereerst met betrekking tot zijn enorme verzameling die vooral in de Brusselse jaren tot stand moet zijn gekomen. Ik had het al over de zogenaamde 'Galeriebilder' en over het *Theatrum Pictorium*. Voor dit laatste, een folio-groot recueil met gravures naar de Italiaanse schilderijen in de verzameling, heeft Teniers ook enorm veel schilderwerk moeten uitvoeren. Om het voor de onder zijn leiding werkende graveurs mogelijk te maken de vaak monumentale schilderijen in het paleis convenabel te reproduceren, maakte Teniers er kleine kopieën naar, op exact hetzelfde formaat als de gravures dienden te hebben. Naar die kopieën konden de graveurs dan hun graveurstekeningen uitvoeren.[47]

## Historie- en portretschilders uit Antwerpen en Brussel

Het is niet gemakkelijk uit te maken wat rechtstreeks bij deze kunstenaars werd besteld of aangekocht, en wat los daarvan werd aan-

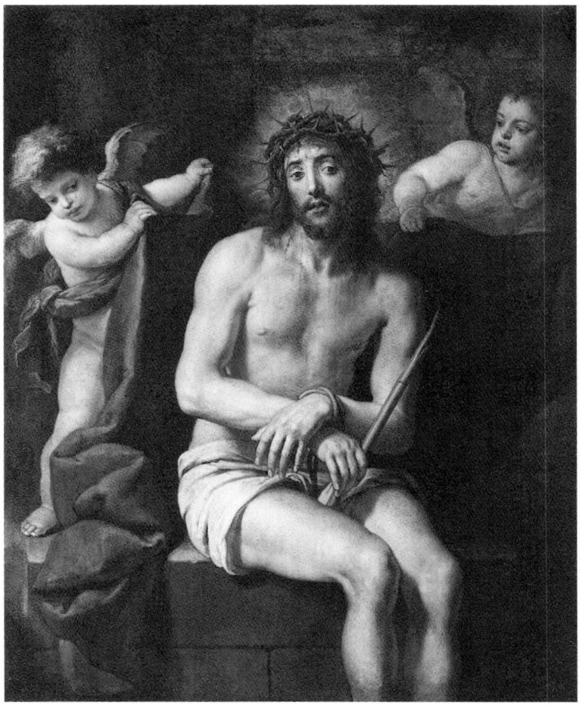

Afb. 13. Gaspar de Crayer, *Christus met de doornenkroon*. Wenen, Kunsthistorisches Museum

geschaft op de markt. In elk geval mag worden gesteld, dat de aartshertog een open oog had voor het werk van de toonaangevende historieschilders die in Antwerpen en Brussel bedrijvig waren meteen na de dood van Rubens en Van Dijck. Daarbij is het mijn mening dat ook deze artiesten fungeerden als *Ersatz* voor de niet meer in leven zijnde grootmeesters. Net als het geval was met Jan van den Hoecke gaat het immers allereerst om een aantal schilders die op Rubens' of op Van Dijcks atelier gevormd zijn geworden of daarvan zeer stimulerende impulsen ontvangen hebben. In het hierna volgende en chronologisch geordende overzicht zal ik van geval tot geval trachten na te gaan om welke specifieke redenen Leopold-Wilhelm belangstelling heeft geuit voor persoon en werk van deze stilistisch zeer verscheiden groep schilders.

Opmerkelijk is het oeuvre dat de aartshertog bezat van de hand van Gaspar de Crayer (1584–1669). Deze droeg overigens de titel van

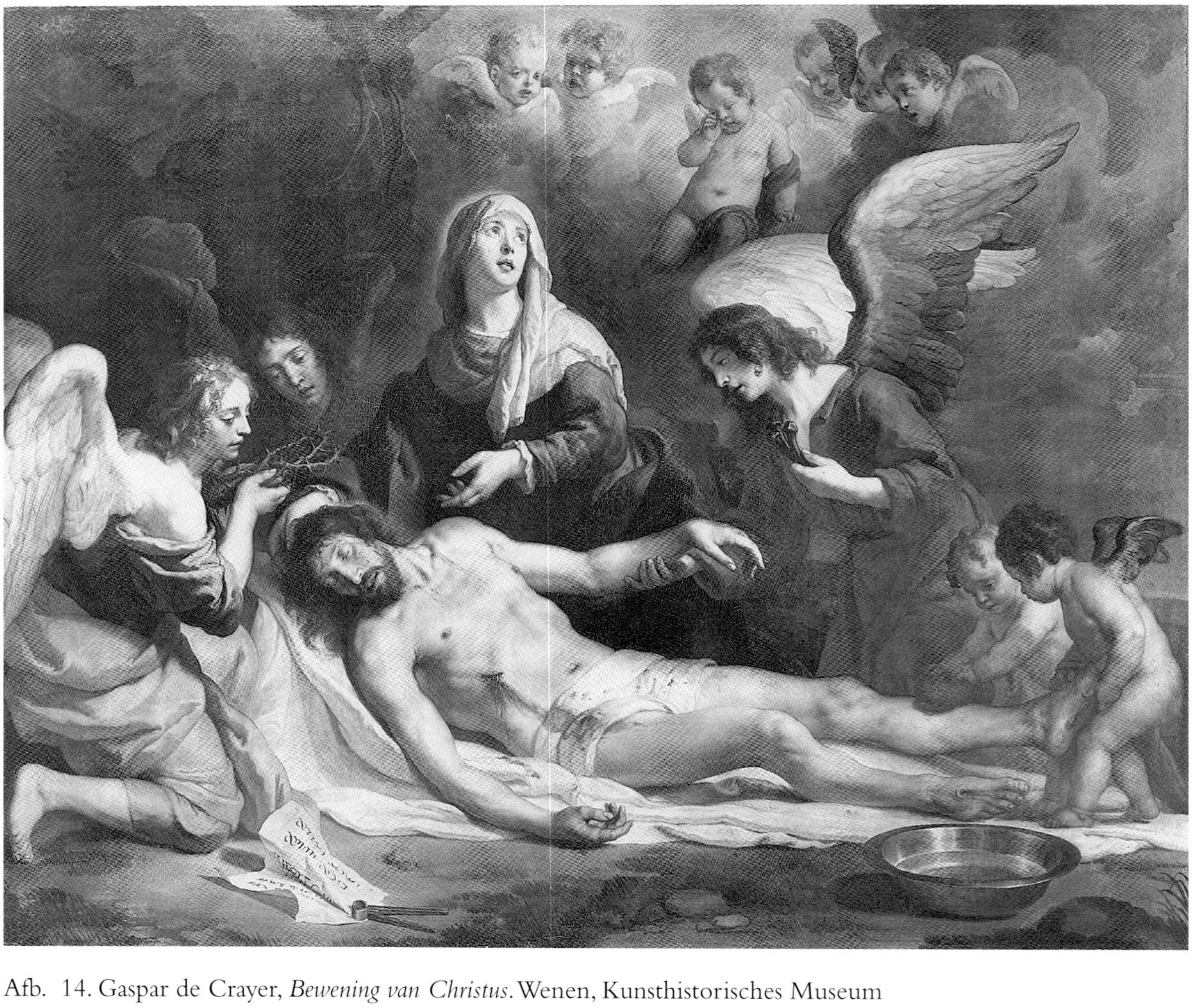

Afb. 14. Gaspar de Crayer, *Bewening van Christus*. Wenen, Kunsthistorisches Museum

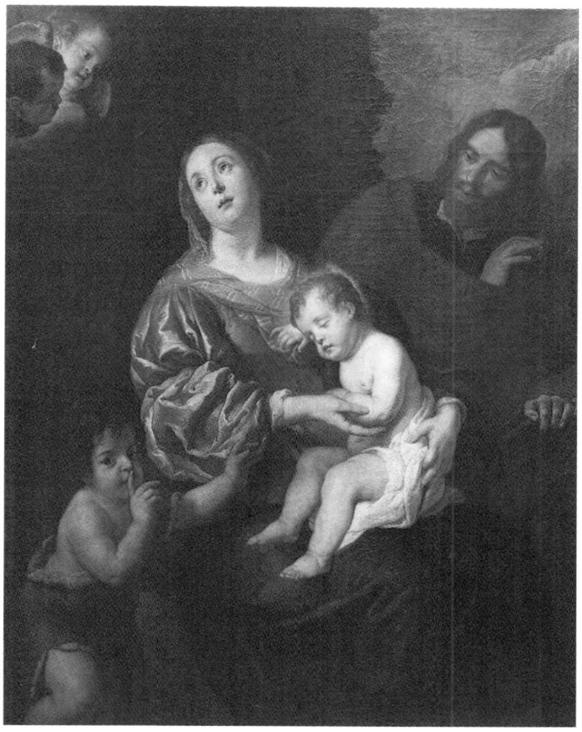

Afb. 15. Gaspar de Crayer, *De heilige Familie met Johannes de Doper.* Wenen, Kunsthistorisches Museum

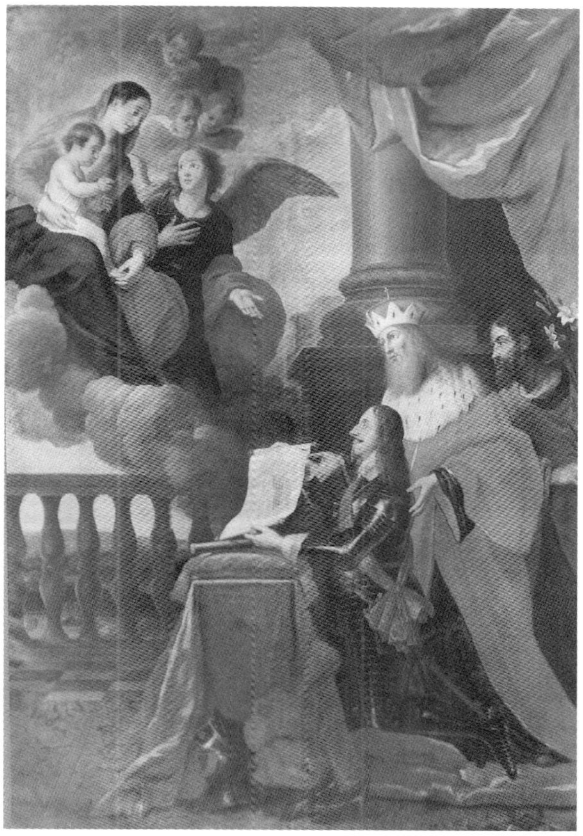

Afb. 16. Gaspar de Crayer, *Aartshertog Leopold-Wilhelm als stichter van de kerk van de ongeschoeide karmelieten te Gent.* Gent, Kerk van de ongeschoeide karmelieten

'domesticq' van Leopold-Wilhelms 'huys ende hoff', met de daaraan verbonden financiële privileges. Deze titel had hij reeds eerder gekregen van de voorganger van de landvoogd, kardinaal-infant Ferdinand, en hij mocht hem verder gewoon behouden. Kennelijk had De Crayer daarnaast geen vaste taken aan het hof te vervullen.[48] Ofschoon niet bij Rubens zelf opgeleid, heeft deze schilder zich als weinig andere van zijn tijdgenoten op Rubens' oeuvre gebaseerd om het in Brussel, waar hij leefde en werkte, tot zijn vast uitgangspunt te maken. Van De Crayer kan met recht gezegd worden dat hij in Brussel en omgeving al van voor 1620 een soort van plaatsvervangende Rubens is geweest. Buiten Antwerpen was Brussel immers de stad waar in kerken en openbare gebouwen Rubens' werk het best vertegenwoordigd was. En op die voorkeur heeft De Crayer handig weten in te spelen door zich als een der eerste schilders in te stellen op Rubens' stijl.[49] Vanaf de jaren veertig combineerde hij deze vormgeving met een duidelijk aan Van Dijck ontleende zin voor sentimentaliteit in de gemoedsexpressie.

De nog in het Kunsthistorisches Museum te Wenen bewaarde schilderijen uit Leopold-Wilhelms bezit, namelijk de *Christus met de doornenkroon* (afb. 13) en de *Bewening van Christus* (afb. 14) mogen dat goed illustreren. Dit geldt trouwens ook voor de *Heilige Familie*, nu in het Palazzo Pitti te Florence (afb. 15).[50] Twee andere in Leopold-Wilhelms inventaris vermelde schilderijen van De Crayer, een *Christus aan het Kruis* en een *Verrijzenis van Christus*, zijn verdwenen.[51] Stijlvergelijkend onderzoek maakt duidelijk dat althans de bewaard gebleven schilderijen in de jaren vijftig te dateren zijn, wat het aannemelijk maakt dat de aartshertog ze ook bij De Crayer besteld heeft. Net als de drie overige schilderijen van De Crayer die men aantreft in Leopold-Wilhelms inventaris, gaat het om werk met een uitgesproken devotioneel karakter. De Crayer heeft zijn vermaardheid dan ook hoofdzakelijk te danken aan zijn grootschalige religieuze composities die vormelijk en inhoudelijk perfect beantwoordden aan de idealen van de Contrareformatie. En daarbij valt het op dat de keuze van de aartshertog tevens goed de grondgedachten van de *Pietas Austriaca* verraadt: zowel de eucharistische gerichtheid op het H. Kruis als de devotie tot Maria komen er nadrukkelijk in tot uiting. De Crayer gaf overigens nog op een andere wijze gestalte aan de *Pietas Austriaca* van de aartshertog. In de beginjaren van diens landvoogdij maakte de schilder namelijk ook een altaarstuk voor de kerk van de ongeschoeide karmelieten te Gent, met een tronende Madonna en hemzelf als stichter van het klooster, vergezeld door zijn patroonheilige Leopold (afb. 16).

Gerard Seghers (1591–1651) was een van de meest uitgesproken italianisanten onder de Antwerpse schilders van zijn tijd. Hij maakte aanvankelijk naam met caravaggistische taferelen van groot formaat, zowel altaarstukken als verhalende bijbelse scènes. Vanaf zowat 1630 oriënteert hij zich coloristisch en compositorisch sterk op Rubens, met wie hij in de jaren dertig ook bij verschillende gelegenheden heeft samengewerkt, onder meer voor de decoraties van de Blijde Intrede van kardinaal-infant Ferdinand in 1635. De vehemente hoogbarokke expressiviteit die vooral in Rubens' latere oeuvre een bepalend stijlelement zou vormen temperde hij a.h.w. door haar in te passen in een strengere en meer statische vormgeving die haar uitgangspunt vindt in het classicisme van de zogenaamde Bolognezen. Seghers genoot grote vermaardheid om zijn talloze devotietaferelen, waarvan hij er opmerkelijk veel voor de jezuïeten schilderde.[52]

Mogelijk heeft ook deze laatste bijzonderheid er toe helpen bijdragen dat Leopold-Wilhelm zijn aandacht op Seghers richtte en deze laatste de opdracht gaf een enorm, meer dan vier meter hoog altaarstuk te laten schilderen, met een door engelen omkranste Madonna en Kind. Aan dit schilderij liggen de aartshertogelijke vroomheid en krijgshaftigheid beide ten grondslag. Het werk was bedoeld als votiefstuk en memoriseerde een van de door de aartshertog gewonnen veldslagen tegen de Franse troepen, kort na het sluiten van de Westfaalse Vrede: dit krijgstafereel ontwaart men in de verte, op de achtergrond. Het militair karakter van dit schilderij wordt verder vooral verduidelijkt door het grote harnas en andere krijgstrofeeën die werden uitgestald voor de voeten van de H. Maagd en haar Kind. Uit de gedetailleerde beschrijving in de inventaris van 1659 verneemt men dat andere schilders verantwoordelijk waren voor het zogenaamde 'bijwerk': Jan de Heem schilderde de

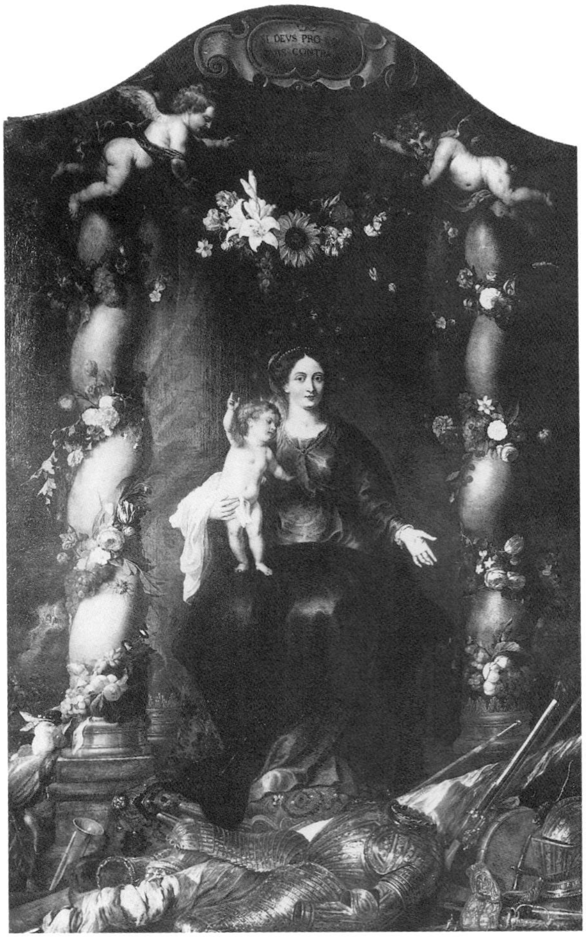


Afb. 17. Gerard Seghers e.a., *Tronende Madonna*. Laxenburg, Pfarrkirche (bruikleen Kunsthistorisches Museum, Wenen)

bloemenranken rond de omlijstende zuilen, David Teniers stond in voor het kleine veldslagtafereel en Paul de Vos werd ingehuurd voor de krijgstrofeeën op het voorplan. Er is ook sprake van Cornelis de Vos, maar diens aandeel is minder duidelijk omschreven: hij wordt eerder vaag vermeld in verband met de achtergrond. Bovenaan leest men in een cartouche het trotse devies 'Si Deus pro nobis, quis contra nos?', dat ook bij andere gelegenheden door Leopold-Wilhelm werd gebruikt. Na de terugkeer van de aartshertog in Wenen werd het schilderij geplaatst boven het altaar van de kerk te Laxenburg bij Wenen, waar het nog steeds te zien is (afb. 17).[53] Net zoals Gaspar de Crayer vertegenwoordigde Gerard Seghers in Leopold-Wilhelms verzameling vooral het contrareformatorisch-devotionele aspect van de Zuid-Nederlandse historieschilderkunst. Dat bewijzen ook de drie andere schilderijen van

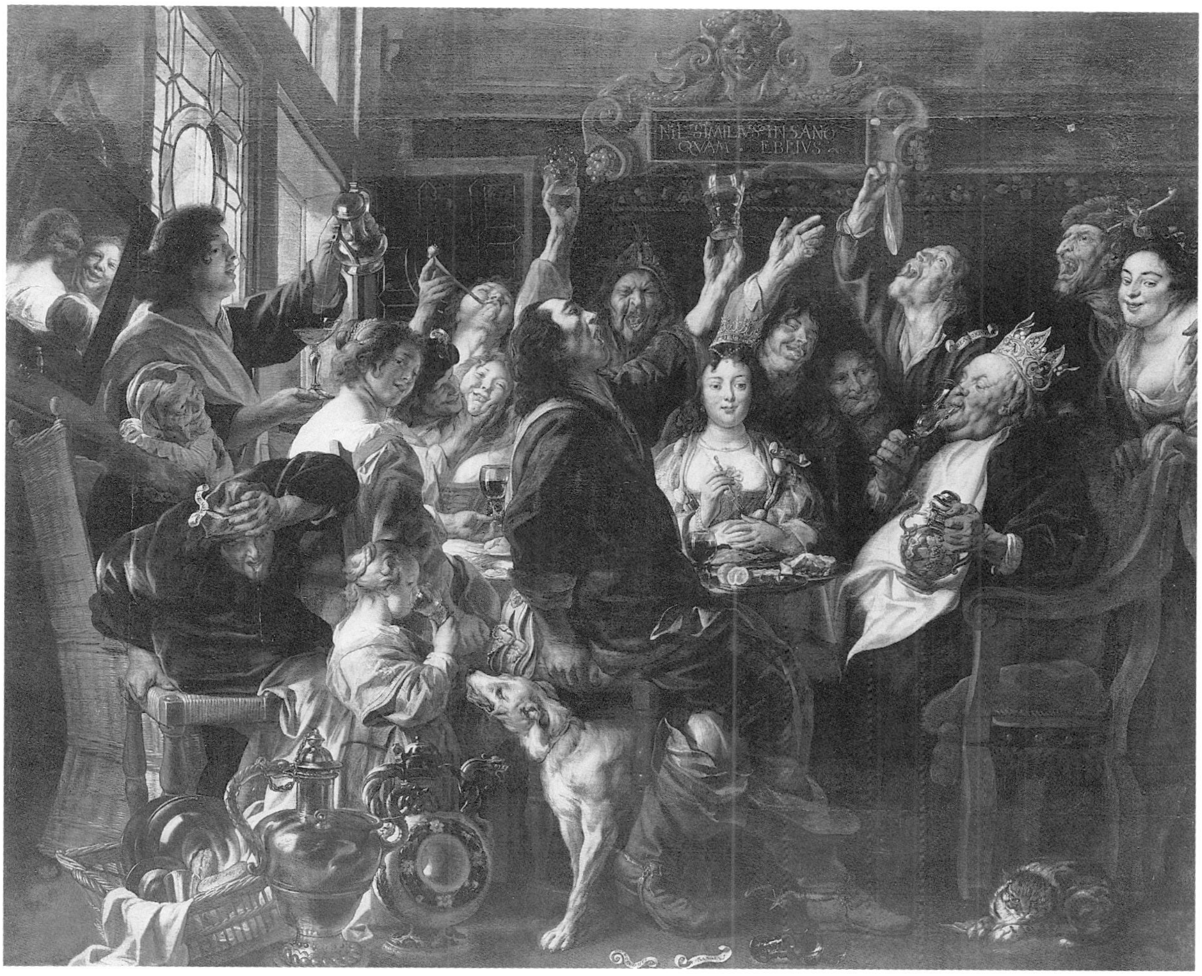

Afb. 18. Jacob Jordaens, *De koning drinkt*. Wenen, Kunsthistorisches Museum

zijn hand die in de inventaris worden vermeld: het gaat hierbij uitsluitend om Madonnavoorstellingen.[54] Slechts een van deze werken is bewaard in het Kunsthistorisches Museum te Wenen; het werk is in geen geval door de landvoogd in opdracht gegeven, aangezien zijn stijl verwijst naar de jaren rond 1630/35.

In 1661 noemt de kunstenaarsbiograaf Cornelis de Bie Jacob Jordaens (1593–1678) 'den derden gheest van dese eeuwe', na Rubens en Van Dijck.[55] Bij Jordaens had de aartshertog uitsluitend belangstelling voor de grootschalige moraliserende uitbeeldingen van land- en volksleven, zoals de *Koning Drinkt* (afb. 18)[56] en de door hem in 1647 bij de Brusselse tapijthandelaars Jan Cordijs en Boudewijn van Beveren gekochte tapijtenreeks met uitbeeldingen van *Spreekwoorden*, waarvoor de cartons evenwel reeds geruime tijd voor Leopold-Wilhelms aankomst in Brussel werden besteld, namelijk in 1644.[57] Hieruit lijkt vooral af te leiden dat de aartshertog een uitgesproken belangstelling had voor de meer genreachtige facetten van Jordaens' oeuvre: noch zijn profane, noch zijn religieuze historietaferelen waren in zijn verzameling vertegenwoordigd. Daar dergelijke schilderijen van de andere belangrijke contemporaine historieschilders in zijn collectie wél aanwezig waren, kan men zich afvragen hoe dat komt. Er is in dit verband al gesuggereerd dat Jordaens' protestantse geloofsovertuiging hierbij een rol zou kunnen gespeeld hebben. Het is inderdaad niet uitgesloten dat de voorvechter van de roomse zaak die Leopold-Wilhelm was het er moeilijk mee kan gehad hebben bij Jordaens religieuze taferelen te kopen of te bestellen; voor Jordaens als schilder van mythologische composities kan dat argument echter veel minder gespeeld hebben. Ook is geopperd dat Jordaens' zwierige barokstijl sterk verschilde van het strenge classicisme van zijn eerste hofschilder Jan van den Hoecke.

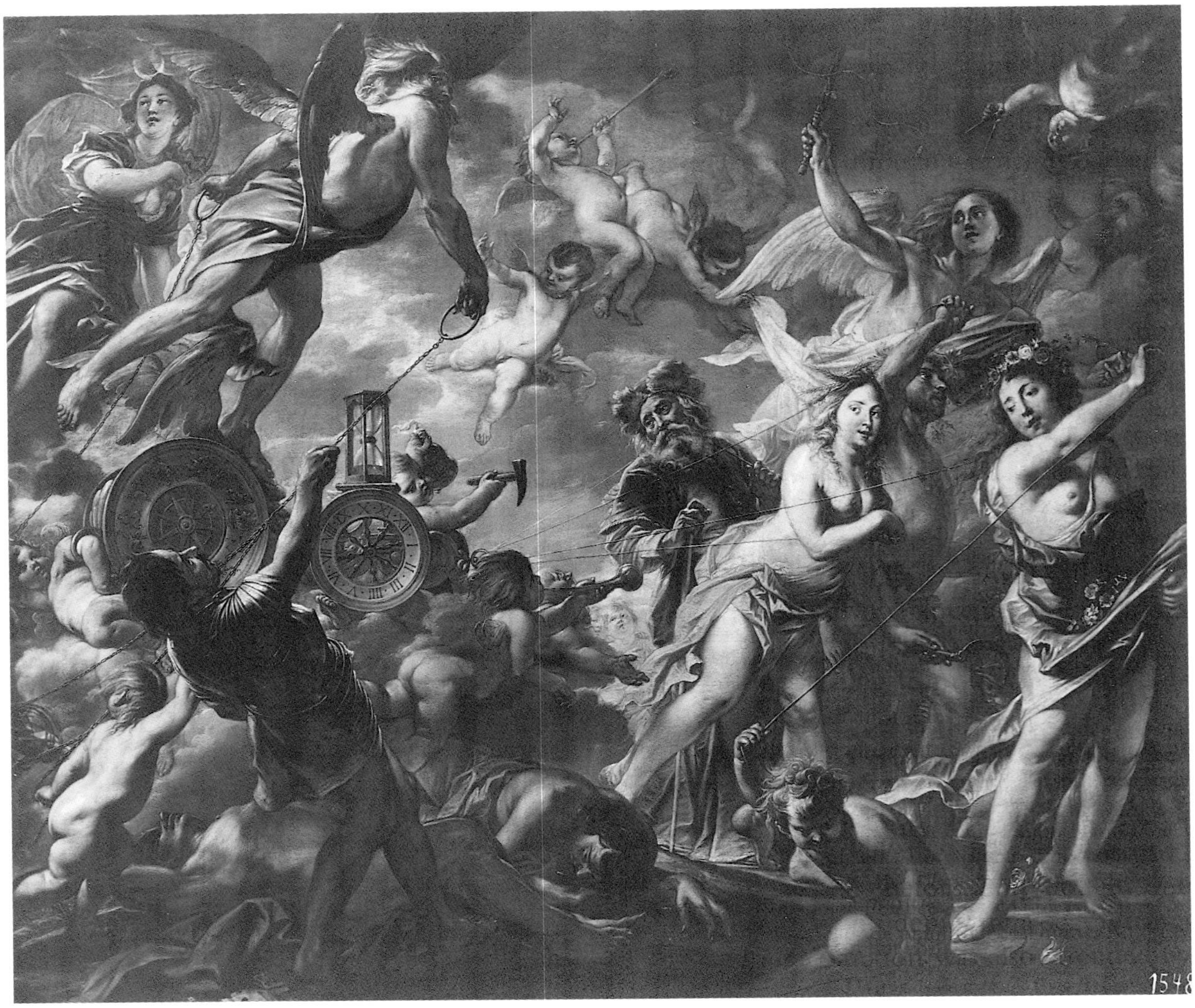

Afb. 19. Cornelis Schut, *Triomf van de tijd*. Wenen, Kunsthistorisches Museum

Hierna zal echter nog blijken dat de aartshertog zich bij zijn belangstelling voor de Vlaamse historieschilders van zijn tijd niet liet leiden door slechts één welbepaald stijlidioom.[58] Veeleer vraag ik mij af of hij in de monumentale genrethematiek niet het meest eigene en persoonlijke van Jordaens' kunst herkende.

Cornelis Schut (1597–1655) was een schilder met een zeer persoonlijke stijl. Zijn eigenlijke vorming had hij gekregen in Rome, waar hij in de loop van de jaren twintig beïnvloed werd door de dynamische hoogbarokke stijl in de trant van toen toonaangevende schilders als Pietro da Cortona, Guercino en anderen. Schuts werk vertoont daardoor een veel exuberantere vormgeving dan het oeuvre van zijn andere tijd- en vakgenoten in Vlaanderen. Het wordt met name gekenmerkt door een dramatisch bewogen expressiviteit in beweging, gebarenspel en lichteffecten. Zeer opvallend is daarbij zijn voorkeur voor sterk innerlijk en uiterlijk bewogen personages, vooral weergegeven in extreem perspectivische verkortingen en onder schril licht. Maar ook de bewogenheid van de latere Rubens wist Schut goed in zijn stijl te integreren. Zo is hij in zijn voorkeur voor raccourci-effecten schatplichtig aan de vernieuwende stijl van Rubens' plafondschilderijen uit 1620 voor de Antwerpse jezuïetenkerk. En ook andere schema's en motieven uit vooral Rubens' latere werk heeft Schut bij herhaling in zijn eigen oeuvre verwerkt. Hij behoorde trouwens tot de 'Rubensstal', zoals zijn betrokkenheid bij de uitvoering van de feestdecoraties voor de Blijde Intrede van Leopold-Wilhelms voorganger kardinaal-infant Ferdinand mag aantonen.[59]

Het werk dat Schut voor de aartshertog maakte, beantwoordt overigens in meer dan een opzicht aan diens specifieke belangstelling en voorkeur. Een *Triomf van de Tijd* (Wenen, Kunsthistorisches Museum) (afb. 19) schilderde hij ter aanvulling van Van den Hoeckes tapijtpatronen voor de maandenreeks en naar een modello van diens hand. Wellicht is hieruit af te leiden dat Schut dit werk uitvoerde rond 1651, het jaar van het onvoorzien vroege overlijden van Van den Hoecke. Overigens werd een tapijt naar deze *Triomf* niet meer geweven.[60] Schut was een virtuoos schilder van mythologische en allegorische composities en had, net als Van den Hoecke, langere tijd in Italië doorgebracht. Mogelijk hebben deze omstandigheden een rol gespeeld bij de keuze van de aartshertog. Toch had deze laatste al eerder werk van Schut gekocht. Op stilistische gronden is zijn *Bekering van Willem van Aquitanië* (Wenen, Kunsthistorisches Museum) (afb. 20) te dateren in de beginperiode van Leopold-Wilhelms landvoogdij, d. i. omstreeks 1647 of wat later.[61] Dit schilderij is ook omwille van zijn thematiek goed in verband te brengen met de aartshertog. De H. Willem van Aquitanië, de middeleeuwse edelman en militair die zich, dank zij de kracht van de eucharistie waarvan Sint-Bernardus van Clairvaux hem wist te overtuigen, bekeerde van een werelds leven, moet immers voor Leopold-Wilhelm een goed prototype hebben geleken. Bovendien was hij ook zijn tweede naamheilige. Zoals hij dat ook deed met de Habsburgse 'huisheilige' Leopold lijkt het aannemelijk dat de landvoogd zich tevens met Willem van Aquitanië kon identificeren. Leopold-Wilhelm bezat nog een derde werk van Schut, een *Aanbidding van de herders*.[62] Buiten zijn vermelding in de inventaris van 1659, is er over dit schilderij echter niets bekend.

Theodoor van Thulden (1606–69) vond zijn uitgangspunt bij Rubens' werk uit de jaren dertig. Precies in die jaren heeft hij ook een belangrijke rol gespeeld bij de uitvoering van de grote serieopdrachten die onder Rubens' leiding werden geschilderd voor de Blijde Inkomst van de kardinaal-infant Ferdinand in 1635 en voor de versiering van het jachtslot Torre de la Parada van Filips IV.[63] In aansluiting bij de vormgeving van Rubens' composities uit de jaren dertig schildert Van Thulden een groot aantal politiek-allegorische composities. Een karakteristiek voorbeeld is een doek uit 1654: de allegorie van de *Zuid-Nederlandse provincies die zich onderwerpen aan de H. Maagd* (afb. 21).

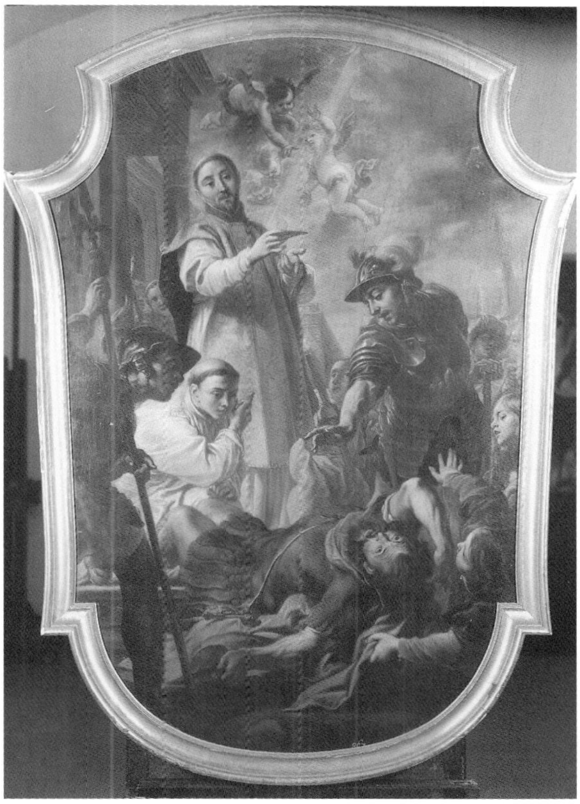

Afb. 20. Cornelis Schut, *Bekering van Willem van Aquitanië*. Wenen, Kunsthistorisches Museum

Andermaal gaat het hier om een religieuze compositie, waarin de band met de *Pietas Austriaca* heel opmerkelijk is. Vooral het vlezige, sensuele mensentype en het zachte, wat pastelachtige palet verraden grote vertrouwdheid met de vormgeving van de late Rubens. Dit schilderij wordt evenwel niet vermeld in de inventaris van Leopold-Wilhelms verzameling uit 1659. De datum én de zeer specifieke iconografie maken het anderzijds weinig waarschijnlijk dat deze politiek-religieuze allegorie zou zijn uitgevoerd zonder enig verband met de landvoogd en zijn opvattingen. Het is niet uitgesloten dat deze laatste het werk voor een bepaalde kerk of kapel heeft laten bestellen. Hoe en wanneer het schilderij uiteindelijk in Wenen terecht is gekomen, weet men niet.[64] Om het concipiëren van vernuftige, zij het vaak pedante allegorieën van vrede en oorlog, was Van Thulden bekend: met name mogen zijn vooral voor 's-Hertogenbosch geschilderde politieke allegorieën dat bewijzen. En dat ook de aartshertog voor dit facet van Van Thuldens kunst alleszins belangstelling had, wordt aangetoond door de *Terugkeer van de Vrede*, een reus-

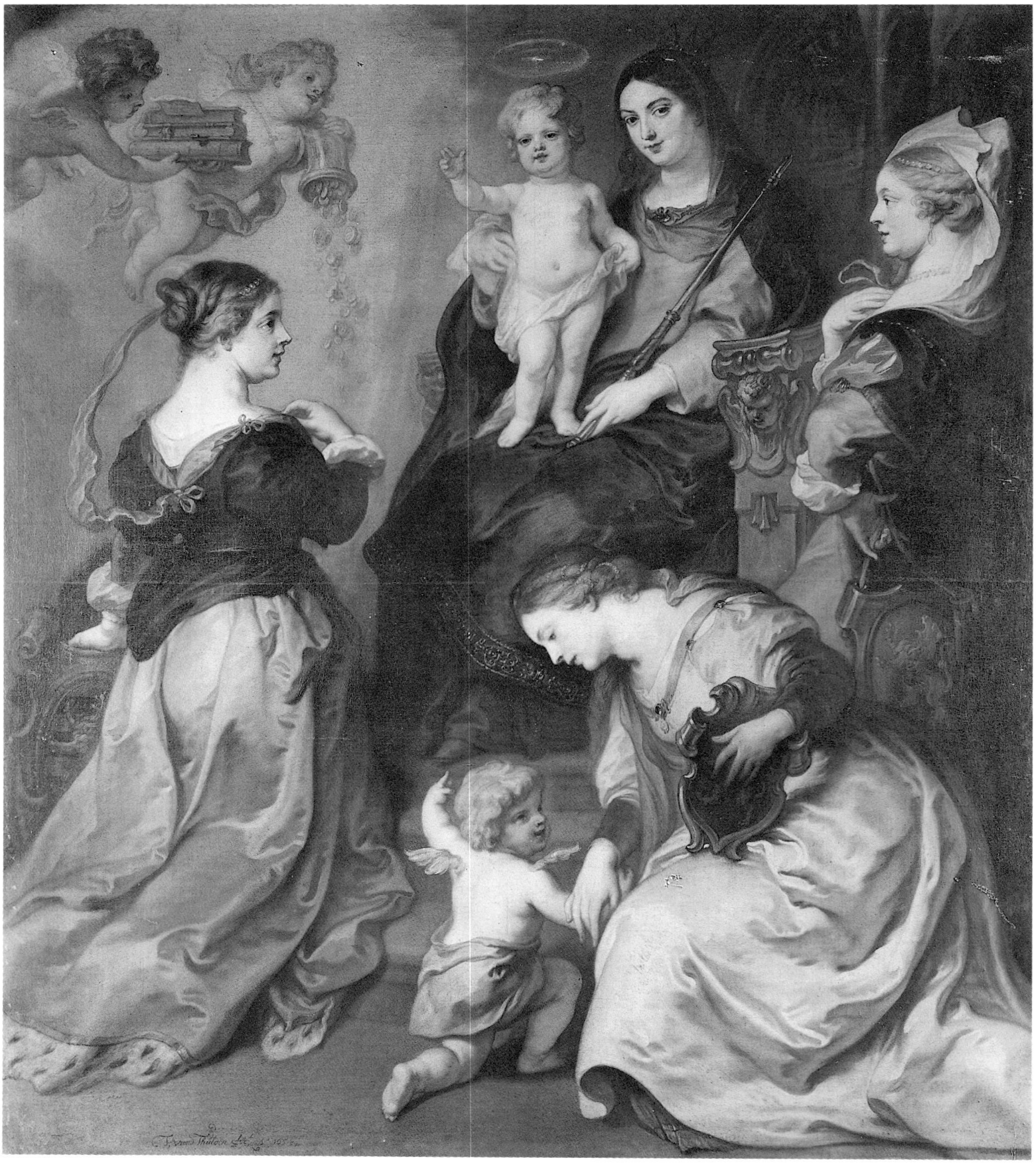

Afb. 21. Theodoor van Thulden, *De Zuidelijke Nederlanden onderwerpen zich aan de H. Maagd.* Wenen, Kunsthistorisches Museum

achtig doek uit 1655 (408 x 388 cm!), dat wél in de inventaris van 1659 wordt vermeld.[65]

Ook Jan Boeckhorst (1604–68) was gevormd bij de late Rubens. Na diens dood in 1640 retoucheerde en voltooide hij overigens werk uit zijn nalatenschap.[66] Vanaf de late jaren veertig echter, aansluitend bij een algemenere smaakverandering, oriënteerde Boeckhorst zich in zijn pathetische gelaatsuitdrukkingen en zijn weker gebarenspel meer op de emotioneel sterker geladen stijl van Van Dijck. Dat is ook het geval met zijn mythologisch tafereel *Mercurius en Herse* (afb. 22), een werk uit de jaren vijftig dat in Leopold-Wilhelms inventaris wordt vernoemd.[67] De klassieke mythologie en de profane allegorie zijn overigens dominant aanwezig in de door Boeckhorst behandelde thematiek.[68] Het is ook bekend dat deze erudiete schilder op het gebied van de profane historieschilderkunst een grote faam bezat: zo wordt hij in 1649

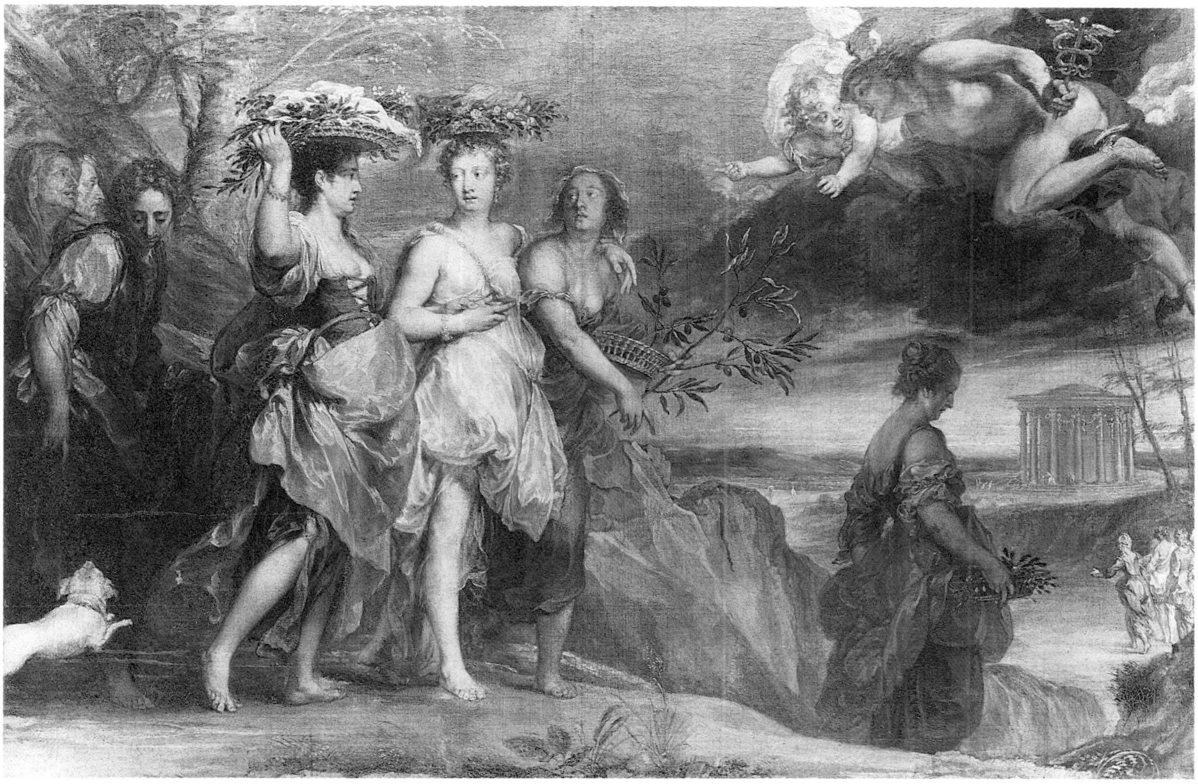

Afb. 22. Jan Boeckhorst, *Mercurius en Herse*. Wenen, Kunsthistorisches Museum

door de bekende kunsthandelaar Michel le Blon warm aanbevolen bij koningin Christina van Zweden als de meest gezochte schilder in Antwerpen, waarbij met name zijn profane historieschilderkunst en zijn op antieke voorbeelden geïnspireerd werk worden vernoemd.[69]

Toen Leopold-Wilhelm de landvoogdij over de Nederlanden aanvaardde, was Erasmus II Quellin of Quellinus (1607–78) een van de beroemdste schilders in Antwerpen.[70] Leopold-Wilhelms aandacht moet al meteen na zijn aankomst zijn uitgegaan naar Quellin, die immers de taferelen voor zijn Blijde Intrede in Antwerpen heeft ontworpen en uitgevoerd.[71] Ofschoon hij in de jaren dertig nauw samenwerkte met Rubens, werd Quellins stijl vanaf ca. 1640 uitgesproken classicistisch, in duidelijk aansluiten bij de Carraccitrant. Zelf is hij nooit in Italië geweest, maar deze italianisante variante van de barok kende hij langs zijn eigen broer, de beeldhouwer Artus Quellin. Deze was in 1640 naar Antwerpen teruggekeerd na een jarenlang verblijf in Rome, waar hij zich had geschoold bij François Duquesnoy, op dat ogenblik in Rome de belangrijkste beeldhouwer naast Bernini en diens antipode, als uitgesproken vertegenwoordiger van de classicistische richting in de barokstijl.[72] Van Erasmus II Quellin bezat de aartshertog o. m. een *Achilles onder de dochters van Lycomedes* (thans in de verzameling van de prins van Liechtenstein te Vaduz). Het schilderij is echter 1643 gedateerd en derhalve niet door de aartshertog in opdracht gegeven. Wel bij Quellin besteld is de in samenwerking met de bloemenschilder Jan-Filips van Thielen uitgevoerde *Madonna in een bloemenkrans*, een werk in het Kunsthistorisches Museum dat voorzien is van het jaartal 1648 (afb. 23).[73] Het schilderij is een van de talrijke en hoger reeds vermelde Mariavoorstellingen in het bezit van Leopold-Wilhelm en uiteraard andermaal uitdrukking van diens Habsburgse Mariacultus. Dat hij voor dit thema een beroep deed op Quellin mag niet verbazen, aangezien deze laatste bekend was om zijn illusionistisch geschilderde grisaillevoorstellingen, vooral van religieuze thematiek, ter versiering van bloemfestoenen door Daniël Seghers of zijn eigen zwager Jan-Filips van Thielen.[74]

Vanaf kort voor het midden van de eeuw werd het oeuvre van Anton van Dijck in groeiende mate het voorbeeld voor een jongere generatie van Antwerpse historieschilders. Het

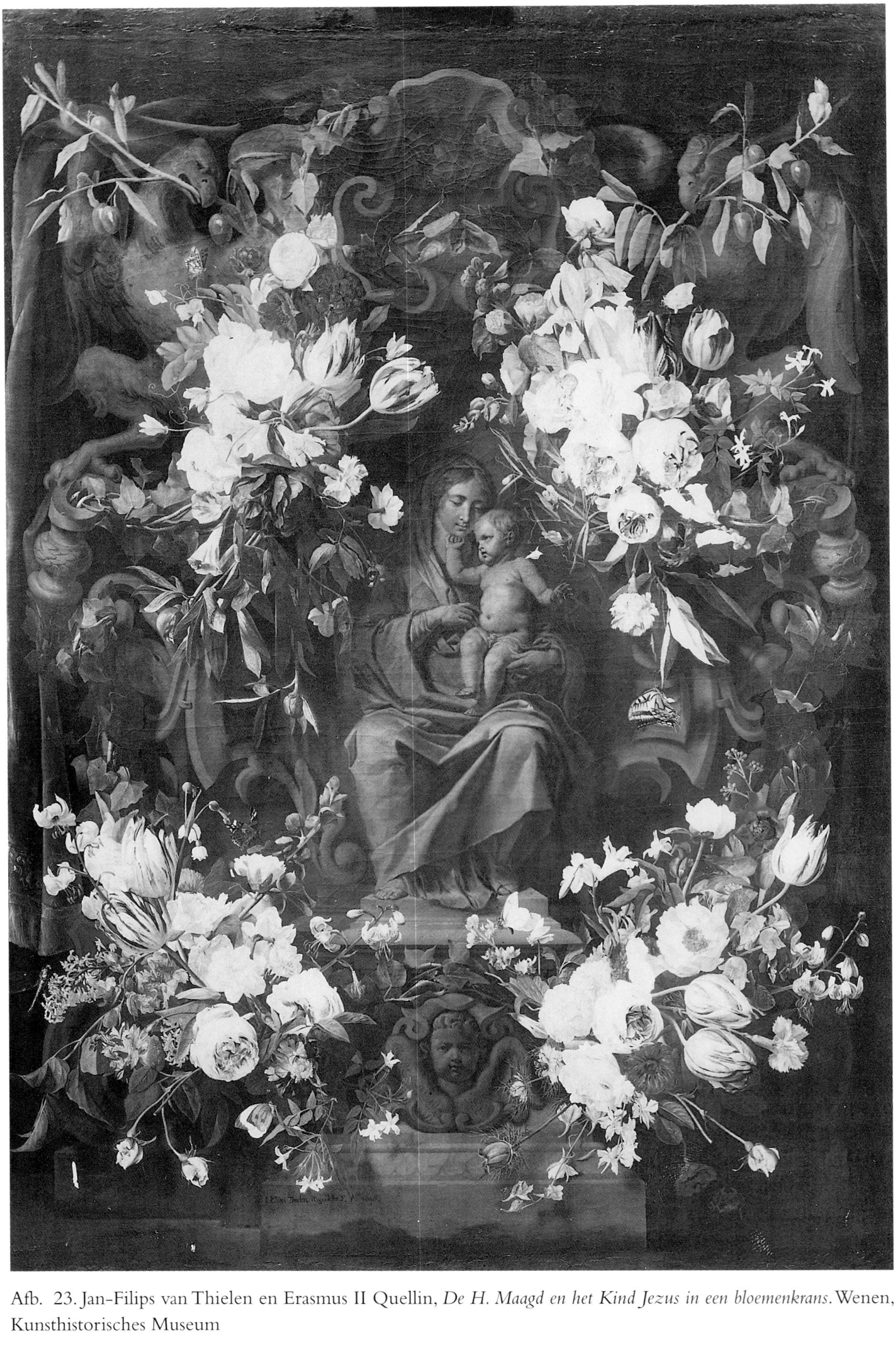

Afb. 23. Jan-Filips van Thielen en Erasmus II Quellin, *De H. Maagd en het Kind Jezus in een bloemenkrans*. Wenen, Kunsthistorisches Museum

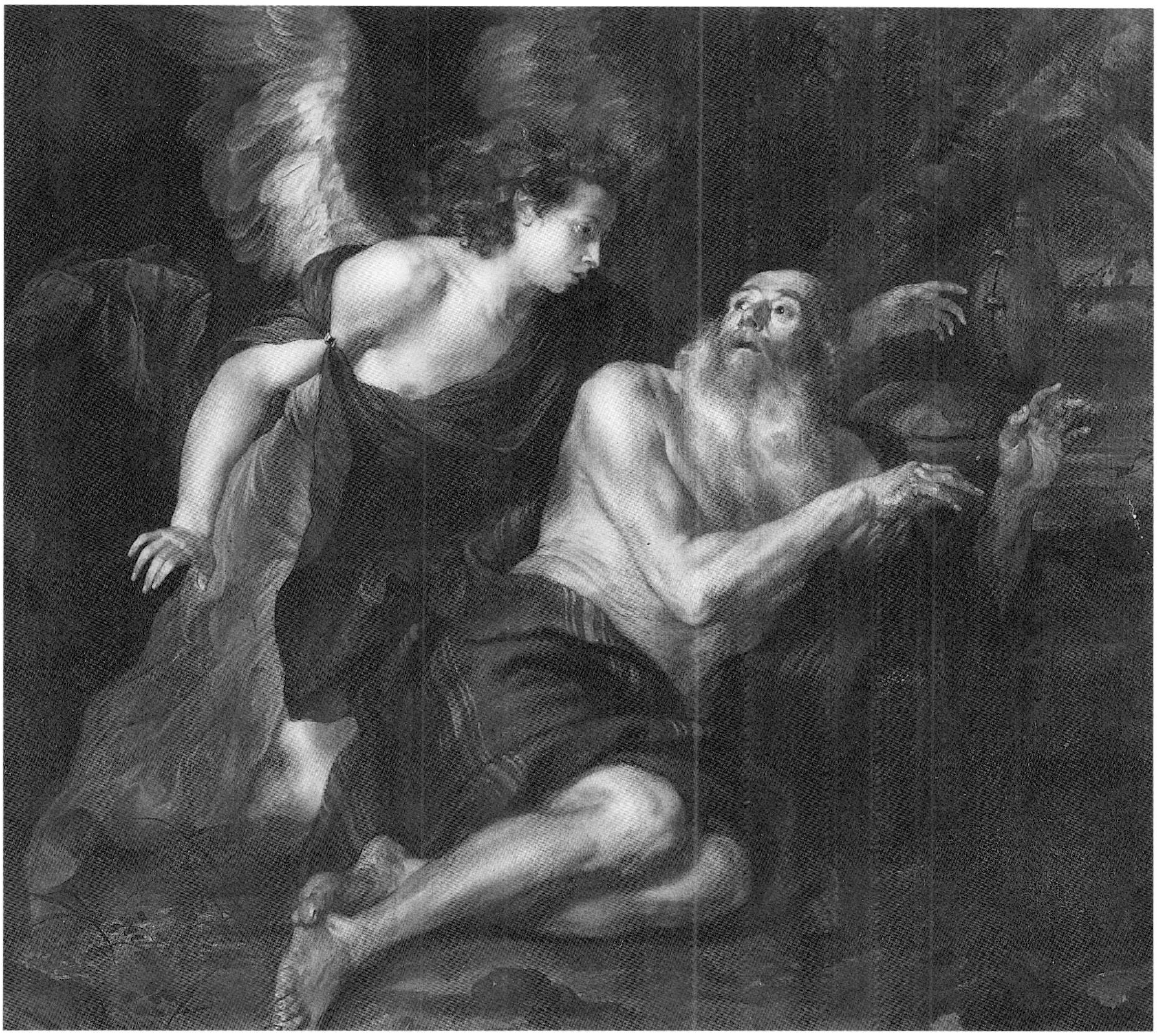

Afb. 24. Thomas Willeboirts Bosschaert, *Elias gevoed door een engel*. Wenen, Kunsthistorisches Museum

meest uitgesproken oriënteerden Thomas Willeboirts Bosschaert (1613/14–54) en Pieter Thijs (1624–78) zich met name op Van Dijcks late oeuvre. Van in den beginne was dit het uitgangspunt voor hun stijl, zodat men ze als echte Van Dijck-epigonen kan beschouwen.[75] Ook voor hun werk heeft Leopold-Wilhelm belangstelling betoond.

Van Willeboirts bezat de aartshertog een *Elias die door een engel wordt gevoed* (thans Wenen, Kunsthistorisches Museum) (afb. 24), een voorstelling die, zoals bekend, kan worden beschouwd als prefiguratie van de instelling van de eucharistie. In dit geval zou ook hier Leopold-Wilhelms keuze voor een oudtestamentisch thema in rechtstreeks verband kunnen worden gebracht met het belang van de cultus van de eucharistie binnen de beleving van de *Pietas Austriaca*.[76] Willeboirts Bosschaert was op dat ogenblik al een echte 'hoffähige' kunstenaar. Sinds 1641 werd hij door het Haagse hof van Frederik-Hendrik van Oranje-Nassau en diens echtgenote Amalia van Solms bij herhaling belast met belangrijke schilderopdrachten, vooral met een mythologisch en profaan-allegorisch karakter. Hoger wees ik er al op dat hij door dat hof, veruit zijn belangrijkste mecenas, kennelijk vooral werd beschouwd als een nieuwe Van Dijck.[77] En misschien heeft deze bijzondere omstandigheid op haar beurt Willeboirts dan weer gestimuleerd om zijn hele leven lang in een zeer sterk op Van Dijcks stijl gerichte vormgeving te blijven schilderen. Als schilder van grootschalige composities met profane onderwerpen voerde Willeboirts voor Leopold-Wilhelm evenwel

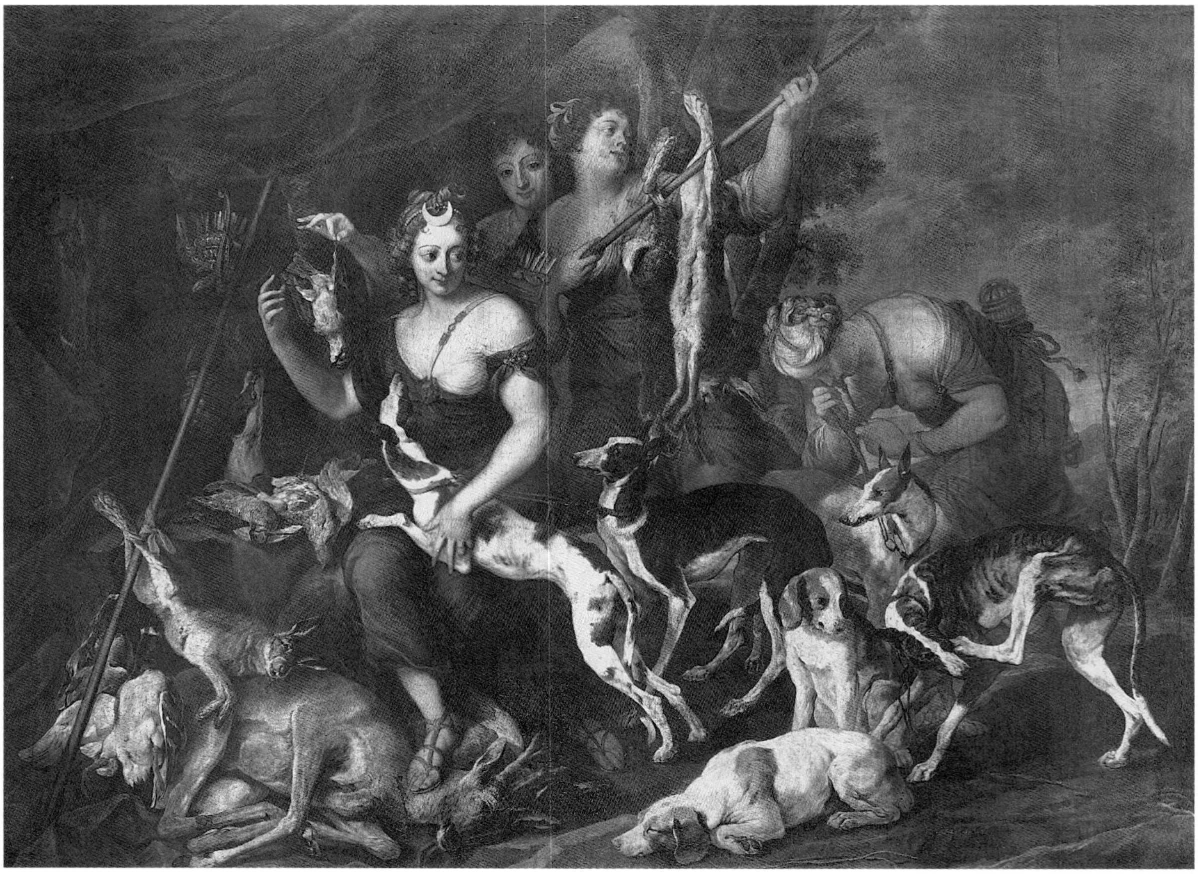

Afb. 25. Thomas Willeboirts Bosschaert en Jan Fijt, *Jacht van Diana*. Wenen, Kunsthistorisches Museum

een eveneens nog in het Kunsthistorisches Museum te Wenen bewaarde en in samenwerking met Jan Fyt geschilderde *Jacht van Diana* (afb. 25) uit.[78] Daarnaast is in dit zelfde opzicht verder nog melding te maken van zijn betrokkenheid, mede door de onverwacht vroege dood van Jan van den Hoecke, bij de voltooiing op groot formaat van de door deze laatste ontworpen patronen voor de tapijtenreeks over de allegorie van de tijd.[79]

Ook Pieter Thijs was met zijn oeuvre vertegenwoordigd in Leopold-Wilhelms verzameling. Hij moet al in een vroeg stadium de aandacht getrokken hebben, want ook hij heeft een actief aandeel gehad in de uitvoering van de door Van den Hoecke geconcipieerde tapijtenkartons. Zijn voornaamste bijdrage tot de uitvoering van deze suite zijn de nog bewaarde kartons met de voorstelling van de *Dag* en de *Nacht* (afb. 26); net als bij Schut en Willeboirts Bosschaert is op Thijs' talent een beroep gedaan om de door Van den Hoeckes onvoorzien overlijden onafgewerkt gebleven reeks voltooid te krijgen.[80] Verder blijkt de aartshertog ook de kwaliteiten van Thijs als portrettist te hebben gewaardeerd: in zijn portret van de landvoogd laat hij deze elegant poseren in een Van Dijckiaans contrapposto, zij het andermaal als 'prince guerrier', in volle wapenrusting (afb. 27).[81]

Opmerkelijk is dat de aartshertog ook een beroep heeft gedaan op een aantal schilders die tijdelijk in Brussel hebben verbleven. Hier is allereerst melding te maken van Justus van Egmont (1601–74) die o.m. tussen 1625 en 1628 op het atelier van Rubens heeft gewerkt. Hij vestigde zich daarna in Parijs, waar hij een vooraanstaande portretschilder werd in dienst van de familie Orléans en ook bekend werd als een van de stichtende leden van de Académie de Peinture et de Sculpture in 1648.[82] In 1649 echter duikt hij op in Brussel en schildert er in dat jaar op zijn beurt een staatsieportret van de aartshertog als geharnaste grootmeester van de Duitse Orde, thans nog in het Kunsthistorisches Museum te Wenen (afb. 28).[83] Evenals de andere van hem bekende vorstenportretten, zoals deze van Louis de Condé of Christina van Zweden is ook dit van de aartshertog uitge-

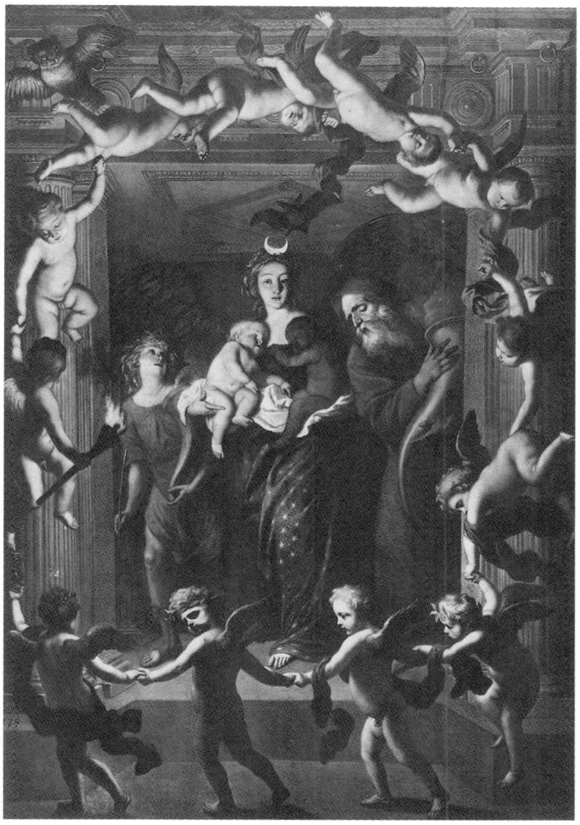

Afb. 26. Pieter Thijs, *Allegorie van de nacht.* Wenen, Kunsthistorisches Museum

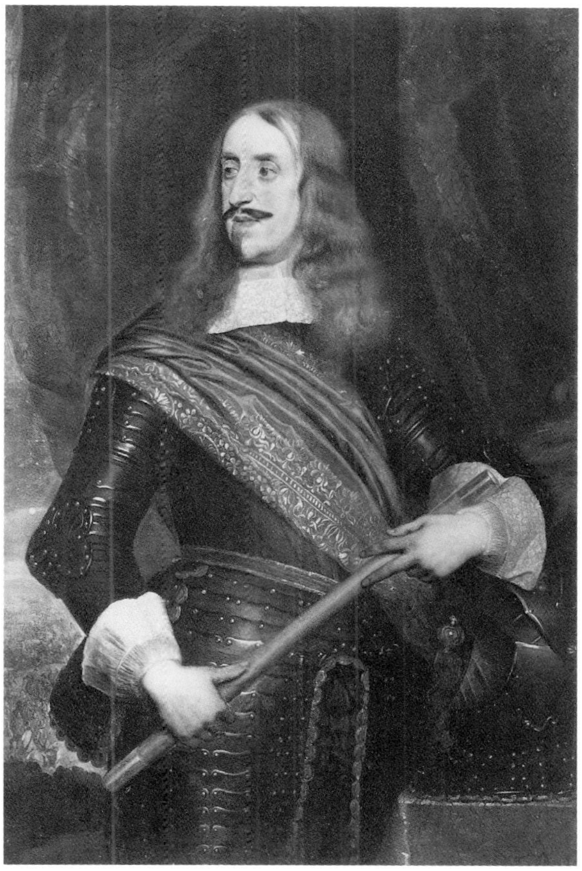

Afb. 27. Pieter Thijs, *Portret van aartshertog Leopold-Wilhelm als veldheer.* Wenen, Kunsthistorisches Museum

voerd in aansluiting bij de op dat ogenblik in Parijs modieuze, elegante maar licht sterotiepe stijl van toonaangevende portrettisten als de neven Henri en Charles Beaubrun.[84] Van Egmont bleef echter niet lang in de Nederlanden, want in 1652 en 1653 wordt hij weer in Parijs vermeld. Maar ook van daaruit bleef hij Leopold-Wilhelm bedienen. In 1651 of 1654 schilderde hij in Parijs voor hem de portretten van de jonge Lodewijk XIV, zijn moeder Anna van Oostenrijk en zijn broer Philippe d'Anjou; thans bevinden deze zich als bruikleen van het Kunsthistorisches Museum te Wenen in de portrettenverzameling van Schloss Ambras in Tirol.[85] In de loop van 1654 keert hij definitief terug naar de Nederlanden; hij verblijft hoofdzakelijk in Antwerpen maar werkt op bepaalde ogenblikken toch ook in Brussel. Ook na zijn definitieve terugkeer had Leopold-Wilhelm nog belangstelling voor Van Egmont als portretschilder. Zo weet men dat de aartshertog op 7 september 1654 in Antwerpen een portret van koningin Christina van Zweden had gezien.[86]

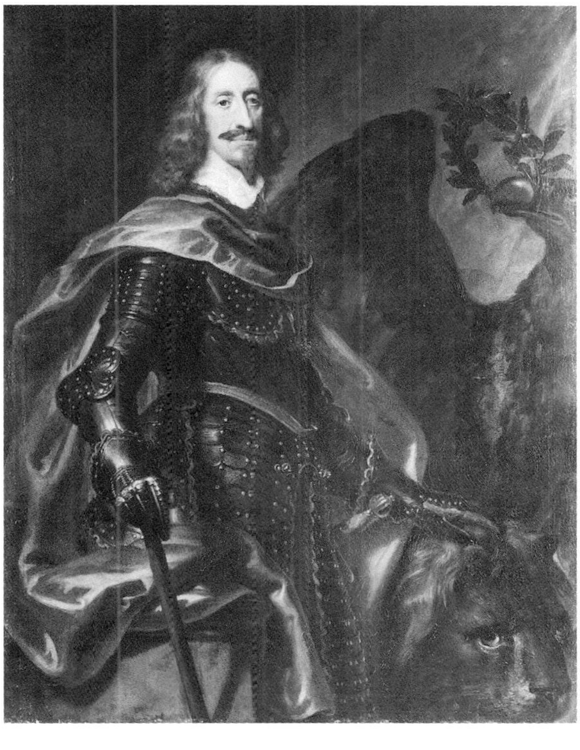

Afb. 28. Justus van Egmont, *Portret van aartshertog Leopold-Wilhelm als veldheer.* Wenen, Kunsthistorisches Museum

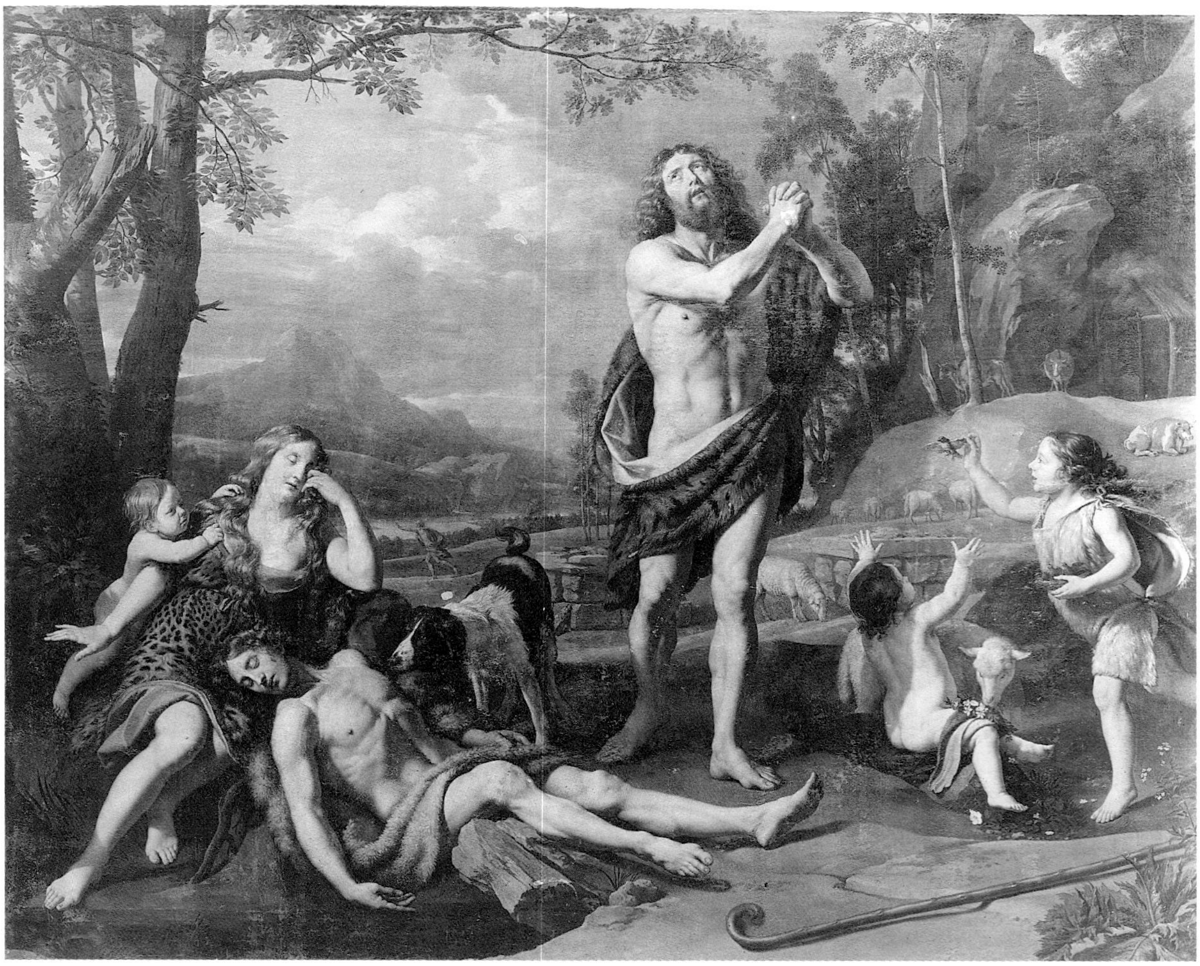

Afb. 29. Philippe de Champaigne, *Bewening van Abel*. Wenen, Kunsthistorisches Museum

Een aparte relatie tot Brussel had Philippe de Champaigne (1602–74). Deze schilder was weliswaar geboren in de hoofdstad van de Zuidelijke Nederlanden, maar had haar al in 1621 verlaten om daarna een van de meest prominente Franse schilders van religieuze historietaferelen en portretten te worden.[87] En ongetwijfeld had hij in Parijs ook zijn generatiegenoot Justus van Egmont leren kennen. Om niet meteen duidelijke redenen heeft hij zich in 1655–56 tijdelijk weer in Brussel gevestigd en bij die gelegenheid schilderde hij voor Leopold-Wilhelm de monumentale *Bewening van Abel* (afb. 29).[88] Dit grote schilderij, met zijn strenge beheersing van houdingen en bewegingen en zijn duidelijke oriëntatie op de antieke sculptuur, illustreert goed het classicisme zoals dit rond het midden van de eeuw typerend was voor de Franse schilderkunst. Net als andere oudtestamentische taferelen die de aartshertog bestelde of kocht, mag misschien ook dit schilderij worden beschouwd als uitdrukking van Leopold-Wilhelms bijzondere vroomheid. In de christelijke typologie is de *Dood van Abel* immers ook een van de voorafbeeldingen van Christus' kruisdood.[89] Bovendien lijkt de compositie een visuele parallel te trekken met de bewening van Christus: zou het dan al te ver gezocht zijn De Champaignes schilderij ook in verband te brengen met Leopold-Wilhelms bijzondere verering voor het H. Kruis?

*Venus beweent Adonis* (Wenen, Kunsthistorisches Museum) (afb. 30) werd geschilderd door Louis (of Luigi) Primo, bijgenaamd Gentile (1606?–ca.1667), wellicht in 1656, het jaar waarin hij na een lang verblijf in Rome terugkeerde naar Brussel. Ook dit schilderij maakt door zijn beheerste vormgeving een uiterst classicerende indruk, waarbij de Carracci-traditie het uitgangspunt was. Door zijn stijlverwantschap lijkt het wel een profane variante te zijn van het bijbelse beweningstafereel dat rond het-

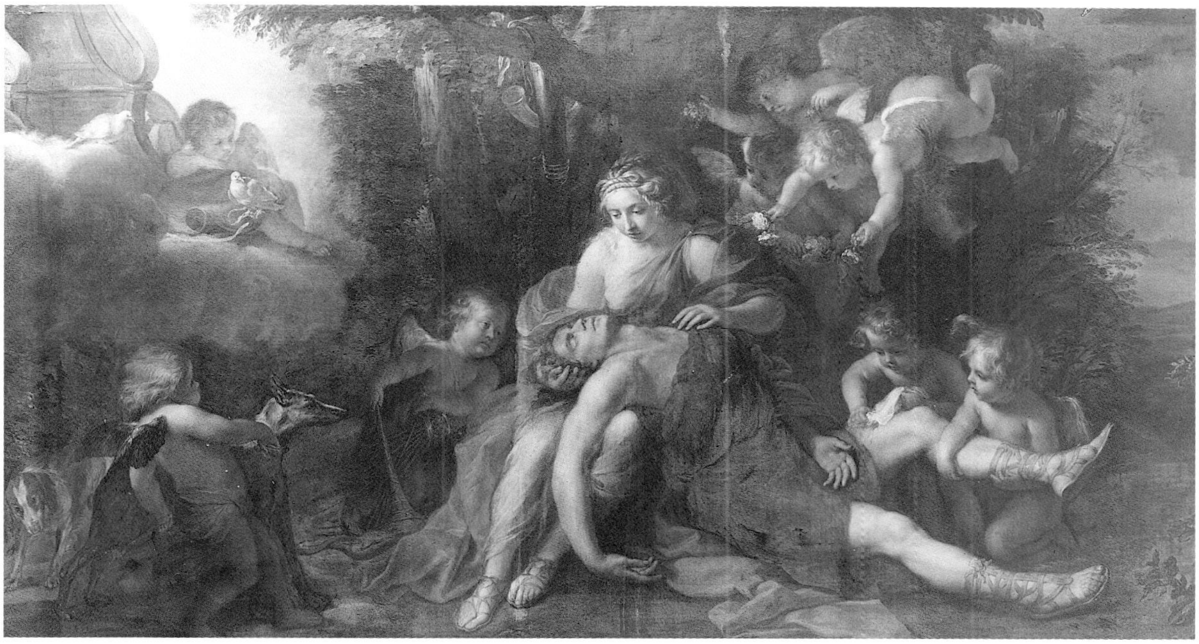

Afb. 30. Louis Primo, *Venus beweent de dood van Adonis.* Wenen, Kunsthistorisches Museum

zelfde ogenblik werd uitgevoerd door Philippe de Champaigne.[90]

Uitbeelding van mythologische thematiek was ook wat de aartshertog verwachtte van Jan van Dalem (voor 1610–na 1653) Deze schilder zou volgens recent onderzoek in Brussel zijn opgeleid bij Jacques Faydherbe, om daarna naar Rome te gaan.[91] De in de inventaris van 1659 beschreven[92] en in het Kunsthistorisches Museum te Wenen bewaarde *Bacchus* (afb. 31) is een gesigneerde en 1648 gedateerde voorstelling als buste. De realistische, ongeïdealiseerde typering van de wijngod laat vermoeden dat Van Dalem in zijn vroegere jaren contacten moet hebben gehad met het milieu van de caravaggisten zowel als dat van de bamboccianti.

Onze kennis van de Brusselse schilderkunst in de zeventiende eeuw is zeer fragmentair, in de eerste plaats als gevolg van de verwoesting van het centrum van de stad in 1695, waarbij het overgrote deel van het oude stadsarchief verbrand is. Onder meer door deze omstandigheid is het moeilijk hoogte te krijgen van de rol die in Brussel werd gespeeld door de uit Bergen afkomstige schilderes Michaelina Woutiers (ca. 1620–ca. 1705), waarvan werk is te situeren tussen 1642 en 1659.[93] Men kent van haar een beperkt oeuvre, hoofdzakelijk bestaande uit schilderijen met devotiefunctie, enkele portretten en ook genretaferelen en

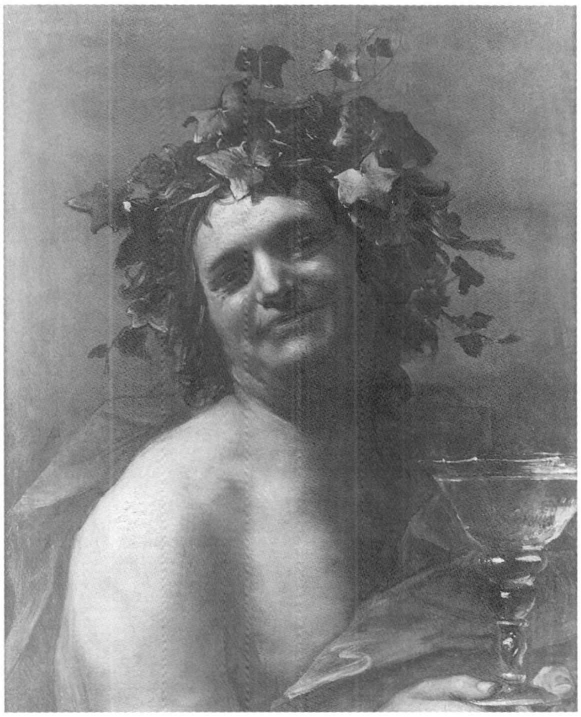

Afb. 31. Jan van Dalem, *Bacchus.* Wenen, Kunsthistorisches Museum

bloemstukken. Van haar hand bezat Leopold-Wilhelm niet minder dan vier schilderijen, alle nog bewaard in het Kunsthistorisches Museum te Wenen. Merkwaardig zijn twee pendanten, bustevoorstellingen van de H. Joachim en de H. Jozef.[94] Beide heiligen hadden met elkaar gemeen dat zij de kuise echtgenoten waren bij de 'onbevlekte' concepties van resp. de H. Anna en haar dochter Maria. Als symbool van zuiverheid moeten zij voor de streng-celibatair levende aartshertog een identificatiemodel zijn geweest. Overigens is het geweten dat Leopold-Wilhelms stiefmoeder, keizerin Eleonora, in de Habsburgse contreien zeer sterk de orde van de karmelietessen bevorderde en ipso facto ook de door hen zeer sterk gestimuleerde devotie tot de H. Jozef.[95] Uiteindelijk is wat Jozef en Joachim met elkaar verbindt de dubbele Onbevlekte Ontvangenis van de H. Maagd. Andermaal ziet men hierin dan ook Leopold-Wilhelms uitgesproken Mariadevotie tot uitdrukking gebracht. Zijn bijzondere belangstelling voor beide iconen van de mannelijke kuisheid krijgt binnen de hier besproken context verder bevestiging door de aanwezigheid in zijn verzameling van een tweede en eveneens door Michaelina Woutiers geschilderde voorstelling van de H. Joachim.[96] Met de teneur van deze drie devotiestukken in groot contrast staat het vierde werk dat Michaelina Woutiers voor de landvoogd schilderde, namelijk de zeer 'werelds' opgevatte *Optocht van Bacchus*, uitgevoerd in een veeleer Frans aandoende classicerende stijl. Het is niet onmogelijk dat deze stijleigenheid zou kunnen verklaard worden door Woutiers' contact met de tijdelijk ook in Brussel voor Leopold-Wilhelm werkende Philippe de Champaigne.[97]

## Tot besluit

Samenvattend kunnen wij stellen dat het moeilijk is in Leopold-Wilhelms voorkeur voor de eigentijdse Vlaamse kunst een duidelijk gemarkeerd smaakpatroon te onderscheiden. Het is zeker niet juist dat hij zich, zoals wel is gesuggereerd,[98] in de eerste plaats zou laten leiden hebben door een voorkeur voor classicistisch georiënteerde schilderkunst. Zijn smaak was eclectisch: hij koos gewoon uit het werk van de toonaangevende schilders. Vaak was dat speciaal voor hem gemaakt maar Leopold-Wilhelm kocht ook ouder werk van deze kunstenaars. En daarbij valt op dat het vooral gaat om de ganse pleiade van Antwerpse of uit Antwerpen afkomstige schilders die groot waren geworden in de directe schaduw van Rubens en Van Dijck. Dit bevestigt overigens alleen maar het contemporaine beeld van een op deze beide corypheeën gefundeerde Antwerpse kunsttraditie, zoals men dat eveneens uit andere bronnen kent.[99] Daarnaast is het ook zeer opvallend dat de aandacht van de landvoogd werd getrokken door kunstenaars van naam die in Brussel werkten, soms maar voor korte tijd, zoals Philippe de Champaigne. Dat zijn beide hofschilders Van den Hoecke en Teniers hem bij zijn keuze begeleid zouden hebben, kan men alleen maar veronderstellen.

Devotiestukken waren talrijk aanwezig in de aartshertogelijke verzameling en zijn in de regel vaak in verband te brengen met een typisch Habsburgse vroomheidsbeleving, die ook deze was van Leopold-Wilhelm zelf. Hij wist ze trouwens ook goed te verzoenen met het krijgshaftige zelfbeeld van *Miles Christianus* in zijn vele portretten. Maar behalve als uitbeelding en uitdrukking van de religieus-militaire taak die hij als zijn levensopdracht aanzag moet de aartshertog de vele Vlaamse schilderijen in zijn bezit toch ook en vooral hebben gewaardeerd vanuit een doorvoeld esthetisch beleven van hun artistieke kwaliteiten. Want terzelfdertijd completeerden de Vlaamse barokschilderijen immers het eveneens in zijn bezit zijnde *nec plus ultra* van de Italiaanse Renaissance. Zowel in de religieuze taferelen als in de composities met uitbeeldingen uit de Griekse mythologie moet de landvoogd de uiteindelijk in belangrijke mate op Rubens en Van Dijck teruggaande behandeling van expressie en pathos ook als emulatie met de Italiaanse kunst ten zeerste hebben weten te bewonderen. Leopold-Wilhelm had kennelijk ook een goed inzicht verworven in de individuele eigenheid en capaciteiten van de door hem begunstigde artiesten. Van schilders die nagenoeg uitsluitend contrareformatorische devotiethematiek in beeld brachten, bezat hij alleen maar werk van deze categorie. Maar van schilders die daarnaast ook naam hadden verworven met hun uitbeeldingen van mythologische en andere profane thematiek was ook dit bijzondere aspect van hun oeuvre meestal in zijn verzameling vertegenwoordigd. De kwaliteit en de naam van de kunstenaars lijken zijn voornaamste criterium te zijn geweest, net zoals dat het geval was bij het samenstellen van zijn beroemde collectie Italiaanse schilderijen.

# NOTEN

1. Zie in dit verband o. m. Henri Pirenne, *Histoire de Belgique*, IV, Brussel, 1927, pp. 280–283.

2. Nicolas Avancini, *Le prince dévôt et guerrier ou les vertus héroiques de Léopold Guillaume Archiduc d'Autriche*, vertaald uit het Latijn door H. Bex, Rijsel 1667 (oorspronkelijke titel: *Leopoldi Guglielmi Archiducis Austriae, principis bello et pace inclyti virtutes et gesta*, Antwerpen, 1665). Zie ook Franz Ritter von Krones, 'Leopold Wilhelm', in: *Allgemeine deutsche Biographie*, XVIII, Leipzig, 1883, pp. 402–404. Terwijl dit artikel in druk was verscheen Jozef Mertens & Franz Aumann (ed.), [cat. tent.] *Krijg en kunst. Leopold Willem (1614–1662), Habsburger, landvoogd en kunstverzamelaar*, Alden Biesen, 2003, veruit de meest gedetailleerde studie over de diverse facetten van Leopold - Wilhelms persoonlijkheid.

3. Zie hierover Hans Vlieghe, 'The decorations for Archduke Leopold Williams's state entry into Antwerp', *Journal of the Warburg and Courtauld Institutes*, XXXIX, 1976, pp. 190–198.

4.. Ten aanzien van het jansenisme voerde Leopold-Wilhelm een waarachtig schrikbewind: zie dienaangaande L. Ceyssens, 'Het theologisch denken en het Jansenisme', in: *Algemene geschiedenis der Nederlanden*, VIII, Haarlem, 1979, pp. 425–426.

5. Zie voor de zeventiende-eeuwse *Pietas Austriaca*: Anna Coreth, *Pietas Austriaca. Österreichische Frömmigkeit im Barock* (*Österreich Archiv. Schriftenreihe des Instituts für Österreichkunde,* 2de herziene editie, München, 1982); men raadplege in dit verband eveneens E. Kovacs, 'Die Österreichische Kirche im Zeitalter des Barock', in [cat. tent.] *Welt des Barock,* Wenen–Freiburg–Bazel, 1986, pp. 123–140.

6. Avancini 1667 (zie noot 2), pp. 129, 147.

7. Op de samenhang tussen Leopold-Wilhelms aankopen van eigentijdse Vlaamse religieuze schilderkunst en de *Pietas Austriaca* is overtuigend gewezen door Emmy Toonen in haar onder mijn leiding uitgevoerde licentiaatsverhandeling *'Timore Domini': Zuidnederlandse religieuze historieschilderkunst in het bezit van aartshertog Leopold-Wilhelm (1647–1656)*, Katholieke Universiteit, Leuven, 1990.

8. Zie dienaangaande de pertinente opmerkingen door Wolfgang Prohaska in zijn bijdrage 'Das geistliche Stillleben – Blumenkränze und Girlanden', in: [cat. tent.] *Das flämische Stillleben 1550–1680* (Wenen, Essen, 2002), Lingen 2002, pp. 324–325.

9. Hierop wordt o.m. gewezen door Karel Porteman in: *Emblematic exhibitions at the Brussels Jesuit College (1630–1685),* Turnhout–Brussel, 1976, p. 104. Het door Hiëronymus Janssens, bijgenaamd 'de danser' in 1658 uitgevoerde schilderij *Het bal* (Rijsel, Musée des Beaux-Arts) legt misschien iets vast van het hoofse amusement in de aristocratische kringen rond Leopold-Wilhelm (zie Francine Claire Legrand, *Les peintres flamands de genre au XVIIe siècle*, Brussel, 1963, p. 88, afb. 37). Op Leopold-Wilhelms betekenis voor de muziek van zijn tijd wordt uitvoerig ingegaan door Piet Stryckers, 'Het muziekmecenaat van Leopold Willem in Brussel', in Mertens & Aumann 2003 (zie noot 2), pp. 109–118, evenals in Sigrid T'Hooft, 'De opera "Ulisse all'Isola di Circe" in Brussel', in Mertens & Aumann 2003 (zie noot 2), pp. 119–128.

10. De inventaris werd pas voor het eerst uitgegeven in 1883; zie Adolph Berger, 'Inventar der Kunstsammlung des Erzherzogs Leopold Wilhelm von Österreich. Nach der Originalhandschrift im fürstlich Schwarzenberg'schen Centralarchive herausgegeben', *Jahrbuch der kunsthistorischen Sammlungen des Allerhöchsten Kaiserhauses*, I, 2, 1883, pp. 79–177.

11. Over de geschiedenis van deze collectie raadplege men vooral de doorwrochte bijdragen van Klara Garas: 'Die Entstehung der Galerie des Erzherzogs Leopold Wilhelm', *Jahrbuch der kunsthistorischen Sammlungen in Wien*, LXIII, 1967, pp. 31–80, en 'Das Schicksal der Sammlung des Erzherzogs Leopold Wilhelm', *Jahrbuch der kunsthistorischen Sammlungen in Wien*, LXIV, 1968, pp. 181–278.

12. Een zeer verhelderende samenvattende studie over het Habsburgse mecenaat is Hugh Trevor-Roper, *Princes and artists. Patronage at four Habsburg courts 1517–1633*, Londen, 1976.

13. Zie Hans Vlieghe, *Flemish art and architecture 1585–1700* (*Pelican History of Art*), New Haven–Londen, 1998, p. 205, met verwijzing naar oudere literatuur over het onderwerp.

14. '... want Syne Hoocheyt heeft my gesyt dat als hy t'Antwerpen comt dat hy wilt alle frayicheyt sin die t'Antwerpen te sin is van kunst van schildery, ende dat hy coopen wilt de fraiste dingen die hem het beste aenstaen, naer syn eygen goeste' (Jan Denucé, *Na Peter Pauwel Rubens. Documenten uit de kunsthandel te Antwerpen in de XVIIde eeuw van Matthijs Musson* (*Bronnen voor de geschiedenis van de Vlaamsche kunst*, V), Antwerpen–Den Haag, 1949, p. 67).

15. Denucé 1949 (zie noot 14), pp. 67, 68; zie ook Vlieghe 1976 (zie noot 3), p. 193 voor de beraadslagingen hierover in de Antwerpse stadsraad.

16. Denucé 1949 (zie noot 14), p. 67

17. Een basisstudie over Leopold-Wilhelms kunstpolitiek tijdens zijn landvoogdij te Brussel blijft Franz Mareš, 'Beiträge zur Kenntniss der Kunstbestrebungen des Erzherzogs Leopold Wilhelm', *Jahrbuch der kunsthistorischen Sammlungen des Allerhöchsten Kaiserhauses*, V, 1887, pp. 343–363; van recentere datum is er in dit verband slechts de beknopte maar verdienstelijke schets door Karl Schütz: 'Zeitgenössische niederländische Malerei in der Sammlung Erzherzog Leopold Wilhelms', *De Zeventiende Eeuw*, XIII, 1997, 1, pp. 371–378.

18. De hier samengevatte gegevens werden eerder reeds verwerkt in Günther Heinz, 'Studien über Jan van den Hoecke und die Malerei der Niederländer in Wien', *Jahrbuch der kunsthistorischen Sammlungen in Wien*, LXIII, 1967, pp. 109–164, en Hans Vlieghe, 'Nicht Jan Boeckhorst, sondern Jan van den Hoecke', *Westfalen*, LXVIII, 1990, pp. 166–183. Biografisch materiaal betreffende Van den Hoecke, inclusief zijn rol voor Leopold-Wilhelm, werd ook voortreffelijk samengevat in Marie-Louise Hairs, *Dans le sillage de Rubens. Les peintres d' histoire anversois au XVIIe siècle*, Luik, 1977, pp. 57–62.

19. Ongepubliceerde gegevens in het Algemeen Rijksarchief te Brussel (Manuscrits divers, 1374: Register der betalingsorders van Leopold-Wilhelms hofhouding (1647–52), fol. 4 °, 8v°, 13v°, 29r°, 47v°, 61r°, 73r°, 76v°, 78r°, 122v°, 142v°, 160r°); verzameld door Emmy Toonen en door haar verwerkt in haar hoger genoemde licentiaatsverhandeling Toonen 1990 (zie noot 7), p. 26.

20. De gegevens met betrekking tot zijn aandeel in deze feestdecoraties zijn vooral te vinden bij John Rupert Martin, *The decorations for the Pompa Introitus Ferdinandi* (*Corpus*

*Rubenianum Ludwig Burchard*, XVI), Brussel–Londen, 1972, pp. 142, 146, 148, 150n, 151, 153, 157–159, 161.

21. Zie dienaangaande J.A.F. Orbaan, 'Virtuosi al Pantheon. Archivalische Beiträge zur römischen Kunstgeschichte', *Repertorium für Kunstwissenschaft*, XXXVII, 1914–15, p. 43.

22. Zie aangaande Willeboirts Bosschaerts betekenis als 'nieuwe Van Dijck' in de ogen van Frederik-Hendrik en Amalia van Solms: Hans Vlieghe, 'Constantijn Huygens en de Vlaamse schilderkunst van zijn tijd', *De Zeventiende Eeuw*, III, 1987, 2, pp. 203–205; zie ook de monografie met catalogue raisonné door Axel Heinrich: *Thomas Willeboirts Bosschaert (1613/14–1654). Ein flämischer Nachfolger Van Dycks* (*Pictura Nova*, IX), Turnhout, 2003.

23. Gepubliceerd in Denucé 1949 (zie noot 14), p. 68.

24. Zie de gedetailleerde inventarisatie bij Heinz 1967 (zie noot 18), pp. 115–131.

25. Aangestipt door Heinz 1967 (zie noot 18), p. 114, en ook bij Vlieghe 1998 (zie noot 13), p. 87.

26. Hierover Heinz 1967 (zie noot 18), pp. 117 (afb. 105), 119–120.

27. Berger 1883 (zie noot 10), nr. 1, 3, 5, 16, 41, 80, 106, 138, 156, 192, 210, 221, 593, 598, 599.

28. Berger 1883 (zie noot 10), nr. 1 (naar Veronese), 3 (naar Titiaan), 9 (naar Titiaan), 16 (naar Titiaan); deze vier werken zijn helaas spoorloos.

29. In 1653 werd op verzoek van de stad Gent een reusachtige en door Erasmus II Quellin ontworpen gravure uitgegeven ter ere van Leopold-Wilhelm, om hem te huldigen als bevrijder van het graafschap Vlaanderen. Het opmerkelijke aan deze prent is dat het ruiterportret van de aartshertog, dat het centraal motief van de compositie vormt, letterlijk dat van Van den Hoecke herhaalt. Ten onrechte werd hieruit onlangs geconcludeerd dat het Weense ruiterportret na de prent zou zijn ontstaan (zie in dit verband Franz Aumann, ' "Flandria liberata" '. Een merkwaardige kunstprent in 1653 door de stad Gent opgedragen aan landvoogd Leopold Willem van Oostenrijk', *Bijdragen tot de geschiedenis van de Duitse orde in de Balije Biesen*, VI, 2000, pp. 265–310). In dat geval zou het schilderij dus niet van de hand van de in 1651 overleden Van den Hoecke kunnen zijn en eventueel zelfs door Quellin vervaardigd zijn geworden. Maar misschien is deze overeenkomst tussen beide ruiterportretten gewoon te verklaren door de tijdnood waarin Quellin kan verkeerd hebben en die hem er toe gebracht kan hebben een reeds bestaand 'officieel icoon' te integreren in zijn eigen compositie.

30. Het verzamelde bronnenmateriaal over Teniers' relatie tot de aartshertog is te vinden bij Hans Vlieghe, 'David II Teniers (1610–1690) en het hof van aartshertog Leopold-Wilhelm en Don Juan van Oostenrijk', *Gentse Bijdragen tot de Kunstgeschiedenis*, XIX, 1961–66, pp. 123–149. De beste monografie over Teniers is Margret Klinge, [cat. tent.] *David Teniers de jonge* (Antwerpen, 1991), Gent–Antwerpen, 1991.

31. Op de symboliek van de gouden ketting als veruiterlijking van bijzondere waardering voor kunstenaars in vorstendienst wordt diepgravend ingegaan door Jochen Becker, 'Aan een gouden keten: eerbewijzen voor kunstenaars', *De Zeventiende Eeuw*, XVIII, 2002, 1, pp. 51–64.

32. Een expliciet bewijs dat Teniers naar Engeland is gegaan om voor de aartshertog schilderijen te kopen uit de 'Commonwealth sale' is er niet. Anderzijds is het bekend dat hij dit tussen 1651 en 1655 wel heeft gedaan in opdracht van Leopold-Wilhelms 'aide de camp' in Brussel, de graaf van Fuensaldaña; het lijkt me derhalve weinig waarschijnlijk dat hij bij die gelegenheid ook niet van Leopold-Wilhelm opdracht zou hebben gekregen om met name uit de verzamelingen van de koning en de hertog van Hamilton werk aan te kopen (zie Alejandro Vergara, 'The court of Fuensaldaña and David Teniers: their purchases in London after the Civil War', *The Burlington Magazine*, CXXXI, 1989, pp. 127–132). Dat Teniers in opdracht van Fuensaldaña naar Engeland ging, vindt men overigens al vermeld in Cornelis de Bie, *Het Gulden Cabinet vande edel vry schilderconst*, Antwerpen, 1661, p. 338.

33. Ofschoon Teniers zijn *Theatrum Pictorium* in 1660 in eigen beheer heeft uitgegeven (het titelblad vermeldt in dit verband 'sumptibus auctoris', d.i. 'op eigen kosten'), kan het moeilijk anders dan dat hij met dit grootschalige werk heeft ingespeeld op de wensen van de landvoogd. Tekenend in dit verband is bij voorbeeld dat toen Leopold-Wilhelm in 1656 voortijdig Brussel verliet, de voor de publicatie bestemde schilderijen nog enige tijd op het paleis te Brussel zijn achtergebleven 'um dort copirt und in Kupfer gestochen zu werden', zoals Leopold-Wilhelms opperkamerheer, graaf Johann-Adolf zu Schwarzenberg, het uitdrukte. Zie de degelijke status quaestionis betreffende het *Theatrum Pictorium*, in Klinge 1991 (zie noot 30), pp. 278–279.

34. Denucé 1949 (zie noot 14), p. 93.

35. Meer bepaald *Boerenjongen met hond*, *Geitenstal*, *Koeienstal* en de twee pendanten als verzinnebeelding van 'Boerenleed' en 'Boerenvreugde'; behalve de *Koeienstal* die in 1922 door het Kunsthistorisches Museum van Wenen werd verkocht, zijn al deze stukken daar thans nog bewaard. Zie dienaangaande ook Vlieghe 1961–66 (zie noot 30), pp. 140–141, afb. 6–10.

36. Voor de duiding van deze schilderijen in de context van de typologie van 'Boerenverdriet' versus 'Boerenleed' in samenhang met de thematiek van oorlog en vrede, en in het bijzonder met de in 1648 gesloten Vrede van Münster, is vooral te verwijzen naar Klinge 1991 (zie noot 30), p. 180, nr. 60AB en K(arl) Schütz, in: K. Bussmann en H. Schilling (ed.), [cat. tent.] *1648. Krieg und Frieden in Europa* (Münster–Osnabrück, 1998–99), Münster, 1991, p. 132.

37. Zie dienaangaande Jane S. Fishman, *Boerenverdriet: Violence between Peasants ans Soldiers in Early Modern Netherlands Art*, Ann Arbor, 1982.

38. Zo bezat Leopold-Wilhelm – zij het met andersoortige stoffering – eveneens een 'diptiek' waarin het contrast tussen boerenleed en boerenvreugd wordt geïllustreerd, van de hand van David III Rijckaert (1612–61), Teniers' generatiegenoot en net als hijzelf gespecialiseerd in de boerenthematiek. Deze twee schilderijen zijn 1649 gedateerd en kunnen dus ook gemakkelijk met het einde van de dertigjarige oorlog in verband worden gezien (zie over deze twee pendants Bernadette Van Haute, *David III Ryckaert. A seventeenth-century Flemish painter of peasant scenes* (*Pictura Nova*, VI), Turnhout, 1999, pp. 44–45, 112–114, nr. A90–91). En het verwondert natuurlijk niet dat de veldheer Leopold-Wilhelm ook geïnteresseerd was in krijgsvoorstellingen op klein formaat. Dergelijke panoramische veldslagtaferelen, met o.m. de uitbeelding van zijn eigen campagnes, had hij laten bestellen bij Pieter Snayers (1592–na 1666), die op dit gebied trouwens al had gewerkt voor de infante Isabella en voor de kardinaal-infant, en vooral Robert van den Hoecke (1622–68), de broer van zijn hofschilder Jan (zie in dit verband *Die Gemäldegalerie des Kunsthistorischen Museums in Wien. Verzeichnis der Gemälde*, Wenen, 1991, pp. 69, 113, pl. 460–462).

39. Zie hierover Klinge 1991 (zie noot 30), p. 226, onder nr. 78, met verwijzing naar Joachim Camerarius, *Symbolorum et Emblematum ex volatilibus et insectis desumtorum centuria tertia collecta,* Neurenberg, 1596, onder het motto 'Exitus in dubio est'.

40. Vlieghe 1961–66 (zie noot 30), pp. 129 (afb. 5), 140.

41. Berger 1883 (zie noot 10), nr. 271.

42. Zie o.m. Louis Réau, *Iconographie de l'art chrétien, 3. Iconographie des saints*, Parijs, 1958, p. 135. De hier gesuggereerde duiding van Teniers' schilderij werd voor het eerst geponeerd in Toonen 1990 (zie noot 7), pp. 99–101.

43. Berger 1883 (zie noot 10), nr. 349.

44. Ook dit werk hangt in het Kunsthistorisches Museum te Wenen; hierover ook Vlieghe 1961–66 (zie noot 30), pp. 127 (afb. 3), 138, 140.

45. Zie over de voorstellingen van Leopold-Wilhelm in zijn verzameling: Matías Díaz Padrón & Mercedes Royo-Villanova, [cat. tent.] *David Teniers, Jan Brueghel y los gabinetes de pinturas*, Madrid, 1992; Barbara Welzel, 'Anmerkungen zu den Galeriebildern von David Teniers dem Jüngeren', *Marburger Jahrbuch der Kunstwissenschaft*, 1997, pp. 179–192.

46. Recent hierover vooral S(abine) v(an) S(prang), in Luc Duerloo & Werner Thomas (ed.), [cat. tent.] *Albrecht & Isabella 1598–1621* (Brussel, 1998–99), Turnhout, 1998, pp. 204–208.

47. Klinge 1991 (zie noot 30), pp. 278–297. Zie voor het *Theatrum Pictorium* eveneens Margret Klinge, 'David Teniers d.-J. – Theatrum Pictorium', in Mertens & Aumann 2003 (zie noot 2), pp. 101–108.

48. Gegevens over De Crayer in relatie tot Leopold-Wilhelm bij Hans Vlieghe, *Gaspar de Crayer. Sa vie et ses oeuvres*, Brussel, 1972, I, p. 48.

49. Op het rubeneske aspect van De Crayers werk en de specifieke betekenis daarvan in Brussel wordt ingegaan in Vlieghe 1998 (zie noot 13), p. 69.

50. Vlieghe 1972 (zie noot 48), pp. 48, 209–21, nr. A176–178.

51. Berger 1883 (zie noot 10), nr. 104, 379. De kleine *Christus aan het Kruis* blijkt overigens een ouder werk te zijn, door De Crayer 'in seiner Jugendt gemahlt'.

52. Zie vooral de monografie met oeuvrecatalogus door Dorothea Bieneck, *Gerard Seghers 1591–1651. Leben und Werk des Antwerpener Historienmalers* (*Flämische Maler im Umkreis der grossen Meister*), Lingen, 1992; op Seghers' relatie tot de aartshertog wordt daar ingegaan op p. 32. Zie voor Seghers' stijlontwikkeling ook Vlieghe 1998 (zie noot 13), pp. 77–79.

53. Bieneck 1992 (zie noot 52), nr. A139.

54. Bieneck 1992 (zie noot 52), nr. A97, A141, B65.

55. De Bie 1661 (zie noot 32), p. 238.

56. Berger 1883 (zie noot 10), nr. 117.

57. Hierover vooral Kristi Nelson, *Jacob Jordaens: design for tapestry* (*Pictura Nova*, V), Turnhout, 1998, pp. 33–36, 103–117.

58. Zowel het religieuze als het stilistische argument werden naar voor gebracht in Schütz 2002 (zie noot 17), p. 375. In dit verband mag er misschien ook even aan herinnerd worden dat Gaspar de Crayer in 1649 weigerde voor het Huis ten Bosch een groot ruiterportret van Maurits en Frederik-Hendrik van Nassau te schilderen, volgens Constantijn Huijgens omdat het 'subject est trop Huguenot et Orangeois pour estre exécuté dans Bruxelles' (Vlieghe 1972 (zie noot 48), pp. 56–57, 315, doc. 74).

59. Zie over Schut, zijn oeuvre en betekenis, de uitvoerige monografie met catalogue raisonné, samengesteld door Gertrude Wilmers: *Cornelis Schut (1597–1655): A Flemish painter of the High Baroque* (*Pictura Nova*, I), Turnhout, 1996.

60. Wilmers 1996 (zie noot 59), pp. 157–159, nr. A91.

61. Wilmers 1996 (zie noot 59), pp. 149–150, nr. A85.

62. Berger 1883 (zie noot 10), nr. 454.

63. Meer daarover bij resp. Martin 1972 (zie noot 20), passim, en Svetlana Alpers, *The decoration of the Torre de la Parada* (*Corpus Rubenianum Ludwig Burchard*, IX), Brussel–Londen–New York, 1971, p. 34; zie ook Alain Roy (ed.), [cat. tent.] *Theodoor van Thulden. Een Zuidnederlandse barokschilder/Un peintre baroque du cercle de Rubens* ('s-Hertogenbosch–Straatsburg, 1991–92), Zwolle, 1991, passim.

64. De oudste vermelding is deze in de uit 1783 daterende catalogus van de keizerlijke verzamelingen door Christian von Mechel (Die Gemäldegalerie 1991 (zie noot 38), p. 120).

65. Berger 1883 (zie noot 10), nr. 526. Dit voluit gesigneerde en gedateerde, maar nooit gefotografeerde schilderij bevindt zich als bruikleen van het Kunsthistorisches Museum in de universiteit te Innsbruck (Die Gemäldegalerie 1991 (zie noot 38), p. 120).

66. Hierover Hans Vlieghe, 'Jan Boeckhorst als medewerker/Jan Boeckhorst als Mitarbeiter', in [cat. tent.] *Jan Boeckhorst, 1604–1668, medewerker van Rubens/Jan Boeckhorst, 1604–1668, Maler der Rubenszeit* (Antwerpen–Münster, 1990), Freren, 1990, pp. 75–81.

67. Over dit werk en zijn plaats in Boeckhorsts oeuvre, zie Hans Vlieghe, 'De ontwikkeling van Boeckhorsts werk/Stilentwicklung in Boeckhorsts Oeuvre', in Jan Boeckhorst 1990 (zie noot 66), p. 71; zie ook Helmut Lahrkamp, 'Der "Lange Jan". Leben und Werk des Barockmalers Johann Bockhorst', *Westfalen*, LX, 1982, pp. 96–97, nr. 53.

68. Lahrkamp 1982 (zie noot 67), passim, en Jan Boeckhorst 1990 (zie noot 66), passim.

69. Hierover o.m. Lahrkamp 1982 (zie noot 67), p. 9.

70. Algemeen over Quellin de monografie met oeuvrecatalogus door Jean-Pierre De Bruyn: *Erasmus Quellinus (1607–1678). De schilderijen met catalogue raisonné* (*Vlaamse schilders uit de tijd van de grote meesters*, 4), Freren, 1988.

71. Vlieghe 1975 (zie noot 3).

72. Zie Hans Vlieghe, 'Erasmus Quellinus der Jüngere und Italien', in: Ekkehard Mai, Karl Schütz & Hans Vlieghe (ed.), *Die Malerei Antwerpens. Gattungen, Meister, Wirkungen. Studien zur flämischen Kunst des 16. und 17. Jahrhunderts. Internationales Kolloquium Wien 1993*, Keulen, 1994, pp. 217–218.

73. De Bruyn 1988 (zie noot 70), p. 178, nr. 112.

74. Zie Jean-Pierre De Bruyn, 'Erasmus Quellinus en Jan-Philips van Thielen. Een historieschilder werkt samen met een bloemenschilder', *Bulletin van de Koninklijke Musea voor Schone Kunsten van België*, 1974–80, pp. 207–244; Idem, 'De samenwerking van Daniël Seghers en Erasmus II Quellinus', *Jaarboek Koninklijk Museum voor Schone Kunsten Antwerpen*, 1980, pp. 261–329.

75. Hun rol onder de 'Van Dijck-epigonen' werd toegelicht in Hans Vlieghe, 'Thoughts on Van Dyck's early fame and influence in Flanders', in: Susan Barnes en Arthur K. Wheelock (ed.), *Van Dyck 350* (*Studies in the History of Art*, 46), Washington, 194, pp. 207–215.

76. Zie dienaangaande vooral Toonen 1990 (zie noot 7), p. 105, met verwijzing naar L. Hoffscholte, 'Elias', in: (E. Kirschbaum, ed.), *Lexikon der christlichen Ikonographie*, 1, Rome–Freiburg, 1968, col. 611.

77. Zie aangaande Willeboirts Bosschaerts betekenis als 'nieuwe Van Dijck' in de ogen van Frederik-Hendrik en Amalia van Solms: Vlieghe 1987 (zie noot 22), pp. 203–205; zie ook Heinrich 2003 (zie noot 22).

78. Heinrich 2003 (zie noot 22), nr. A59

79. Heinrich 2003 (zie noot 22), nr. A63–64; tevens Heinz 1967 (zie noot 18), pp. 140–142.

80. Heinz 1967 (zie noot 18), p. 142.

81. Berger 1883 (zie noot 10), nr. 283.

82. Een behoorlijke samenvatting van de biografische gegevens over Van Egmont vindt men bij Hairs 1977 (zie noot 18), pp. 44–46; die gegevens zijn aan te vullen met informatie van recentere datum die te vinden is in de twee uitvoerige bijdragen van Jacques Wilhelm: 'Le décor peint de la grand' salle du château de Balleroy', *Bulletin de la Société de l' Histoire de l'Art français*, 1985, pp. 61–84, en 'Portraits peints à Paris par Juste d'Egmont', *Bulletin de la Société de l'Histoire de l'Art français*, 1985, pp. 25–44. Het meest volledige overzicht van Van Egmonts leven en werk vindt men in de degelijke, maar onuitgegeven licentiaatsverhandeling geschreven door Steven Suykens, *Justus van Egmont (1602–1674): barokschilder tussen Vlaanderen en Parijs. Monografische studie en catalogus van de schilderijen*, Leuven, 2002.

83. Het portret wordt in de inventaris van 1659 beschreven met de vermelding 'Original, von Justo d'Egmont anno 1649. Bruxel'. (Berger 1883 (zie noot 10), nr. 287).

84. Zie over de Beaubruns en hun betekenis o.m. Anthony Blunt, *Art and architecture in France 1500–1700* (*Pelican History of Art*), 5de ed., New Haven–Londen, 1999, pp. 168.

85. Berger 1883 (zie noot 10), nr. 383–385; op de rugzijde van het portret van de jonge Lodewijk XIV is te lezen: *Justus van Egmont A. 165(.) 25 August Paris.*

86. Zie M. de Burenstam, *La reine Christine de Suède à Anvers et Bruxelles 1654–1655*, Brussel, 1891, p. 43; aangehaald door Suykens 2002 (zie noot 82), p. 27.

87. Zie Bernard Dorival, *Philippe de Champaigne 1602–1674*, Parijs, 1976, I, pp. 31 e. v.

88. Dorival 1976 (zie noot 87), p. 11, nr. 8.

89. Zie hierover o.m. Barbara Baert, *Een erfenis van heilig hout. De neerslag van het teruggevonden kruis in tekst en beeld tijdens de Middeleeuwen*, Leuven, 2001, p. 216.

90. Zie vooral Heinz 1967 (zie noot 18), pp. 153 (afb.), 154.

91. Zie in dit verband Didier Bodart, *Les peintres des Pays-Bas méridionaux et de la Principauté de Liège à Rome au XVIIe siècle*, II, Brussel–Rome, 1970, p. 22; voor de duiding van Van Dalems werk dient evenwel ook nog verwezen te worden naar de oudere bijdrage van Gustav Glück, in diens *Rubens, Van Dyck und ihr Kreis*, Wenen, 1933, pp. 251–255.

92. Berger 1883 (zie noot 10), nr. 61.

93. Zie recentelijk over haar vooral Katlijne Van der Stighelen, '"Une robustesse bien extraordinaire chez une femme": de schilderijen van Michaelina Woutiers', in *An unexpected journey. Vrouw en kunst. Woman and art*, Antwerpen, 1996, pp. 286–295; Idem & E(rwin) B(uijsen), 'Michaelina Woutiers', in (Katlijne Van der Stighelen & Mirjam Westen, ed.), [cat. tent.] *Elck zijn waerom. Vrouwelijke kunstenaars in België en Nederland 1500–1950* (Antwerpen–Arnhem, 1999–2000), Gent–Amsterdam, 1999, pp. 172–177.

94. Voor het eerst werden deze en de beide andere in Leopold-Wilhelms inventaris vermelde schilderijen van Michaelina Woutiers duidelijk als werk van haar hand herkend door Heinz 1967 (zie noot 18), pp. 149–150; hierover ook Van der Stighelen & Westen 1999 (zie noot 93), pp. 172, 174. Zie voor afbeeldingen het hiernavolgende artikel door Katlijne Van der Stighelen, '"Prima inter pares". Over de voorkeur van aartshertog Leopold-Wilhelm voor Michaelina Woutiers (ca 1620–na 1682)'.

95. Zie dienaangaande ook Toonen 1990 (zie noot 7); tevens Van der Stighelen–Westen 1999 (zie noot 93), p. 172.

96. Heinz 1967 (zie noot 18), pp. 150–151.

97. Dat Michaelina Woutiers veeleer belangstelling had voor de meer classicerende variante van de barokschilderkunst mag wellicht ook blijken uit het feit dat in haar *Opvoeding van Maria* (Den Haag, Kunsthandel Hoogsteder & Hoogsteder) stijlverwantschap met het oeuvre van haar oudere Brusselse stadsgenoot Theodoor van Loon kan worden vastgesteld: hierover Van der Stighelen & Westen 1999 (zie noot 93), pp. 175, 177 (afb.). Zie over de betekenis van Michaelina Woutiers en haar relatie tot Leopold-Wilhelm in het bijzonder ook het hoger onder noot 94 aangehaalde artikel van Katlijne Van der Stighelen, verder in deze bundel.

98. Aldus Heinz 1967 (zie noot 18), p. 153.

99. Reeds rond 1650 werden Rubens en Van Dijck in een door Paulus Pontius naar Erasmus Quellin uitgevoerde prent samen voorgesteld als de beide herauten van de Antwerpse schilderkunst. Deze tweepoligheid werd nog sterker gevisualiseerd in het slechts enkele jaren na Leopold-Wilhelms landvoogdij door Theodoor Boeyermans geschilderde programmatische schilderij *Antverpia Pictorum Nutrix*, waarin aan Rubens en Van Dijck een ereplaats werd toebedeeld als de stichtende vaderen van de Antwerpse schilderschool. Zie in dit verband ook Hans Vlieghe, 'Flemish Art, does it really exist?', *Simiolus*, XXVI, 1998, pp. 189, 190 (afb. 2, 3).

# 'Prima inter pares'. Over de voorkeur van aartshertog Leopold-Wilhelm voor Michaelina Woutiers (ca 1620–na 1682)

*Katlijne Van der Stighelen*

## Bronnen

'Als de neus van Cleopatra kleiner was geweest, zou het hele aangezicht van de wereld er anders uit hebben gezien', zei Blaise Pascal. In de in 1998 verschenen sociologische studie 'The face' beweert Daniel McNeill dat het uiterlijk van een vrouw belangrijker is dan dat van een man. Voor een vrouw is een mooi uiterlijk een snelweg naar maatschappelijk succes, aldus dezelfde auteur.[1]

Is het seksistisch een bijdrage over een markante vrouw uit het verleden op deze wijze in te leiden of draagt een dergelijke overdenking bij tot een juiste inschatting van de problematiek 'vanwaar de voorkeur van aartshertog Leopold-Wilhelm voor Michaelina Woutiers?'

Contemporaine bronnen over Michaelina Woutiers alias Wautier zijn schaars. Het mag een bijzonder gelukkig toeval heten dat aartshertog Leopold-Wilhelm belangstelling had voor haar werk. In de inventaris van zijn verzameling die in 1659 in Wenen werd opgesteld, brengt men vier werken met Woutiers in verband.[2] De Habsburger bevoorraadde zich, voor zover men weet, vooral in Antwerpen en Brussel. Het is dan ook niet verwonderlijk dat zowat alle belangrijke Zuid-Nederlandse barokschilders in zijn verzameling zijn vertegenwoordigd. De aanwezigheid van Woutiers wijkt af van de norm: zij is de enige vrouw onder de aanwezige artiesten.[3]

Om de één of andere reden bezat de aartshertog een uitgesproken voorkeur voor haar schilderijen. Een klein derde van haar nu nog bekende werk komt uit zijn collectie. De vier gerepertorieerde schilderijen zijn vandaag ondergebracht in het *Kunsthistorisches Museum* van Wenen, waar ze al eeuwen de reserveafdeling sieren.[4]

Michaelina Woutiers wordt al in het midden van de zeventiende eeuw anders dan andere collegae bekeken: *prima inter pares*. Haar schilderijen zijn in 1659 expliciet omschreven als werk van een *Jungfrau*. De inventaris vermeldt haar naam vier maal. De eerste identificatie is de meest uitvoerige. Een schilderij van een lezende Sint-Joachim wordt geregistreerd als inventarisnummer 75. *Ein Stuckh von öhlfarb auff Leinwath, warin der heyl. Joachim mit einem grossen weissen Barth, khalen Kopff, gelben Kläidt, rothen Mantl und eien offenen Buech in den Händten. In einer schwartz glatten Ramen, hoch 4 Span 3 Finger vnndt 3 Spann 6 Finger braith. Original von Jungfraw Magdalena Woutiers von Mons oder Berghen, Henegaw in Niderlandt.* De halflijfse voorstelling van Sint-Jozef wordt als nummer 87 – net na Rubens' schilderij van een heilige Theresia – geïnventariseerd: *Ein Brusststuckh von öhlfarb auf Leinwaeth, der heyl. Joseph mit einem braidten, weissen Barät, grawen Klaidt vnd feüglfarben Mantl mitt einem Büschel von weissen Lelien in der rechten Handt. In einer schwartz glatten Ramen, hoch 4 Spann 9 Finger vnndt 3 Spann 9 Finger braidt. Original von der Jungfrawen Magdalena Woutiers.* De beschrijving van het derde doek sluit aan bij het eerder genoemde schilderij: *88. Ein Brusststuckh von Öhlfarb auf Leinwath, warin der heyl. Joachim in einem feüglfarben Klaidt, gelben Mantl vndt mit einem grawen, braithen Bardt. In einer schwartz glatten Ramen, hoch 4 Span 3 Finger vnd 3 Span 8 Finger braidt. Original von Magdalena Woutiers.* Het grootste werk, een monumentale Bacchusstoet, is omschreven als inventarisnummer 365: *Ein grosses Stuckh von Öhlfarb auff Leinwath, warin desz Bacchi Triumph. In einer schwarzen Ramen, hoch 14 Span 4 Finger vnd 20 Span 4 Finger braidt. Original von N. Woutiers.*

De inventaris van 1659, een eigentijdse bron, introduceert Woutiers als ongehuwde vrouw[5] en stelt uitdrukkelijk dat zij afkomstig is van of werkzaam is in de Henegouwse stad: *'von Mons oder Berghen, Henegaw in Niderlandt'*. Opmerkelijk is dat ze *Magdalena* wordt genoemd en niet *Micheline*, hoewel die naam voorkomt op de rugzijde van de heilige Joachim uit dezelfde verzameling.

Mogelijk is de naam *Michaelina* eenvoudigweg onbekend. De drie eerste vermeldingen in de inventaris geven absoluut uitsluitsel over de toeschrijving van de werken.[6] Minder evident is de interpretatie van het auteurschap van de *Bacchusstoet*. Niettemin is de omschrijving van de identiteit van de maakster bij de opeenvolgende beschrijvingen systematisch ingekort en kan het bij de *N.* om een verschrijving of foutieve lezing van *M. Woutiers* gaan. Ofwel gebruikte men de 'N' als referentie aan 'nomen nescio'. In zijn bijdrage 'Studien über Jan van den Hoecke und die Malerei der Niederländer in Wien', in het *Jahrbuch der Kunsthistorischen Sammlungen in Wien* van 1967, benadrukte Günther Heinz voor de vier Weense schilderijen alvast *die unbedingte übereinstimmung der Handschrift*.[7]

De inventaris biedt ongetwijfeld een belangrijke getuigenis. Tot zover bekend, gaat het om de enige eigentijdse vermelding van schilderijen van *Jungfrau Michaelina Woutiers*. De inventaris is ook de enige bron die Woutiers associeert met de stad Mons. Archiefonderzoek in Bergen leverde totnogtoe echter weinig op. Hoewel vanaf de vroege zeventiende eeuw parochieregisters van de stad bewaard zijn gebleven, wordt nergens het doopsel van ene Michaelina, Micheline of Magdalena Woutiers vermeld. Wel blijkt Wautier of Wattier er een veel voorkomende familienaam te zijn. Op 6 juli 1661 wordt bij voorbeeld het overlijden geregistreerd van een zekere *Marguerite Wattier*. Dat het hierbij niet over de schilderes kan gaan, wordt verder duidelijk.[8]

Dankzij de vermelding in de inventaris van Leopold-Wilhelm kan haar werk en leven bij stukjes en beetjes worden gereconstrueerd. Naast de 'toeschrijvingen' van de schilderijen in de collectie van de aartshertog, is er één prent en zijn er twaalf schilderijen die de signatuur van 'Michaelina Wautier' dragen. Al deze werken zijn ontstaan tussen 1643 en 1659.

Dit weinig omvangrijke oeuvre is evenwel in menig opzicht uitzonderlijk. Op de eerste plaats is geen andere zeventiende-eeuwse Zuid-Nederlandse schilderes in staat geweest een dergelijk veelzijdige thematiek in beeld te brengen. In haar numeriek beperkte oeuvre komen portret, genretaferelen en historiestukken (zowel religieus als profaan) aan bod.[9] Geen andere vrouw is er bovendien in geslaagd in zeer diverse genres een zelfde opmerkelijke picturale kwaliteit te realiseren. Merkwaardig is voorts dat zij zich heeft toegelegd op schilderijen van monumentale afmetingen. De *Annunciatie* was aanvankelijk meer dan drie meter hoog; de *Bacchusstoet* meet in de oorspronkelijke toestand 215 bij 354 cm. Beide doeken worden verder uitvoeriger besproken.

Voor wie enigszins vertrouwd is met het schaarse aantal kunstwerken van vrouwelijke kunstenaars uit het verleden, zeggen voornoemde kenmerken al genoeg. De relatieve uniformiteit van schilderijen van vrouwen uit de westerse beeldtraditie leert meteen dat de kennismaking met het werk van Michaelina Woutiers een atypische confrontatie met vrouwelijk artistiek talent betekent. Haar oeuvre is veelzijdig in thematiek, technisch van een uitzonderlijk hoog niveau en monumentaal van formaat. Tussen 1783 en 1884 zijn de Weense schilderijen als werk van de Rubens-leerling Frans Wouters geïnventariseerd. *Leur ampleur, leur exécution large, leur coloris abondant* maakte associatie met een vrouwenhand onmogelijk.[10]

Doorgedreven specialisatie was in eerste instantie het gevolg van praktische omstandigheden. Vrouwen kregen, – enkele uitzonderingen niet te na gesproken, – geen brede intellectuele opvoeding en hadden evenmin de mogelijkheid zich technisch te vervolmaken in het atelier van een vooraanstaand meester. Wel kon een artieste een enkele keer terecht in de werkplaats van vader of broer, maar wellicht speelden morele codes hun rol tot binnen de muren van het atelier.[11] Studie naar levend model, in het bijzonder het naakt, was voor vrouwen zo goed als uitgesloten. We zijn hierover slecht ingelicht, maar de geringe anatomische kennis bij vrouwelijke kunstenaars uit het verleden zegt genoeg en bewijst dat de mogelijkheden nagenoeg ontbraken.

## 'a wonderfully gifted sister'

En wat nu met Michaelina Woutiers? Ongehuwd in de periode waarin de bekende werken te situeren zijn, veelzijdig en technisch gezien verbluffend knap. Het is aantrekkelijk dit *exquise* werk te zien als het resultaat van haar eigen ambitie en experimenteerlust, even uitzonderlijk als haar nagelaten werk zelf. Het maakt de vrouw boeiender en zelfs mysterieus omdat ze ook in contemporaine elogieën (waarin kunstenaressen als Johanna Vergouwen, Anna Maria van Schurman of de zusters van Thielen werden bewierookt) onvermeld is gebleven.[12] Zo was er tot dusver evenmin een spoor dat iets prijsgaf over eventuele leermeesters. Zij moet nochtans een uitvoerige opleiding hebben genoten om technisch de schilderijen te kunnen maken, die nu nog van haar hand bekend zijn. In het verleden werd meermaals gesuggereerd – terecht zoals verder zal blijken – dat zij verwant was aan Charles of Karel Wautier, een kunstenaar die veelal als leerling van Rubens wordt getypeerd.[13] Ook over deze man zijn we slechts schaars ingelicht. Hij schilderde portretten, religieuze composities en enkele profane historiestukken en was afkomstig uit Mons. De werken die vooral uit de jaren 1650–1660 dateren, signeerde hij steeds met *C. WAUTIER* of met *WAUTIER FECIT*.[14] Chronologisch gezien, is het weinig waarschijnlijk dat hij Michaelina's vader is geweest. Ze waren ongeveer tijdens dezelfde jaren actief wat waarschijnlijker maakt dat zij zijn zuster was. De naam *Charles Wautier* is bovendien wel in de parochieregisters van Mons terug te vinden. Zowel in 1609 als in 1610 werd er een jongen met deze naam gedoopt.[15]

Hoewel een samenwerking tussen broer en zus onder één atelierdak, voor zover bekend, een echte uitzondering zou zijn, is het evenmin onwaarschijnlijk. Kort voor 1620 werkt Magdalena van de Passe in het grafisch atelier van haar vader Crispijn I in Utrecht; haar broers Crispijn II, Willem en Simon verbleven er ook geregeld.[16] Hetzelfde geldt ook voor de Zwolse Gesina Terborch die heel wat opstak in het atelier waar ook haar broers Gerard, Harmen en Moses werkten.[17] In beide voorbeelden gaat het echter steeds om werkplaatsen van een vader-kunstenaar. Het artistieke werk, afgeleverd door de dochter wordt daarenboven veelal beduidend lager gewaardeerd dan dit van de zoons.[18] Dit laatste argument gaat niet op voor Michaelina Woutiers. In de aartshertogelijke collectie was geen plaats voor werk van Charles Wautier hoewel een door hem gesigneerd portret van aartshertog Leopold-Wilhelm bewaard bleef.[19]

Al is het *partnership* van de beide schilders Woutiers niet uitgesloten, de vraag blijft waar hun atelier dan wel gevestigd was. Omdat Rubens als hofschilder niet verplicht is zijn leerlingen te laten registreren, kan de band tussen Rubens en Charles Wautier niet 'historisch' worden bewezen. Dat er banden bestonden tussen Michaelina en Charles Woutiers enerzijds en Antwerpen anderzijds wordt bevestigd door hun contacten aldaar met verschillende graveurs. Zowel Paulus Pontius als Pieter de Jode II en Joannes Meyssens maakten gravures naar werk van Karel Wautier; een niet bewaard portret van de artilleriemeester Andreas Cantelmo door Michaelina – waaraan ik ook verder aandacht besteed – werd ook door Pontius in prent gebracht. De drie graveurs werken voornamelijk in Antwerpen. Maar in het bewaarde archief van diverse Antwerpse kunsthandelaars is nergens enige referentie te vinden aan Charles/Karel of Michaelina Woutiers.[20] Kortom vermoedens en onopgeloste vragen alom.

## 'Michaelina Woutiers fecit'

Misschien krijgen we meer vat op de artieste én vrouw na een grondige analyse van haar schilderijen. De stijltechnische kennis is vergelijkbaar met deze van vooraanstaande mannelijke tijdgenoten. De opvallende thematische variatie is in geen enkel opzicht technisch geconditioneerd. Michaelina heeft intense figuurstudie in haar vingers en kent zowel het mannelijke als het vrouwelijke naakt *de visu*. Stilistisch gezien is haar werk opmerkelijk eclectisch. Zij heeft ongetwijfeld de kans gehad om van verschillende artistieke stromingen kennis te nemen. Wellicht beschikte ze over de mogelijkheid om te reizen, wat alleen de rijkdom van haar inspiratiebronnen kan verklaren.

Günter Heinz, die in 1967 haar Weense schilderijen wat uitvoeriger bestudeerde, noemde het een 'merkwaardige combinatie van Vlaamse en Frans-classicistische invloed à la Philippe de Champaigne'. Ze was alleszins vertrouwd met het werk van de Venetianen, Poussin en Antwerpse barokschilders als Rubens en Van Dijck. De mate waarin zij zich door één van deze strekkingen liet beïnvloeden, was afhankelijk van het genre dat ze beoefende. Haar por-

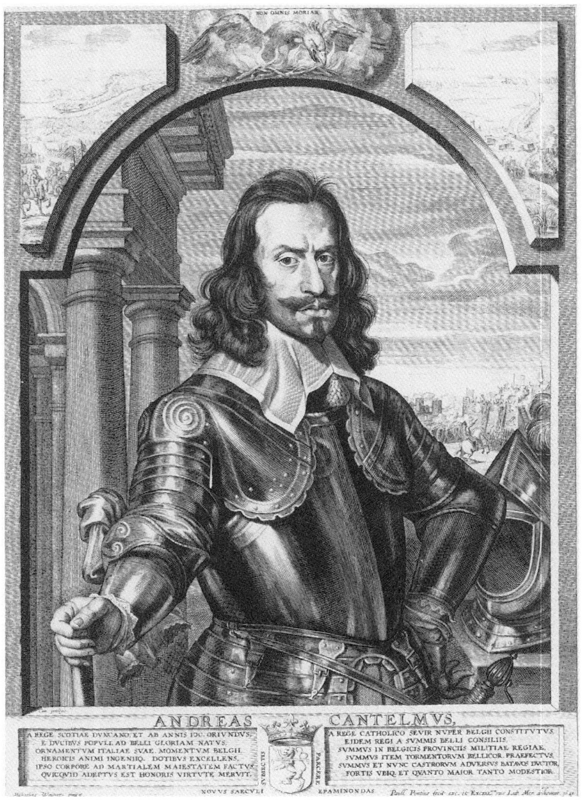


Afb. 1. *Portret van Andreas Cantelmus*, kopergravure, 1643

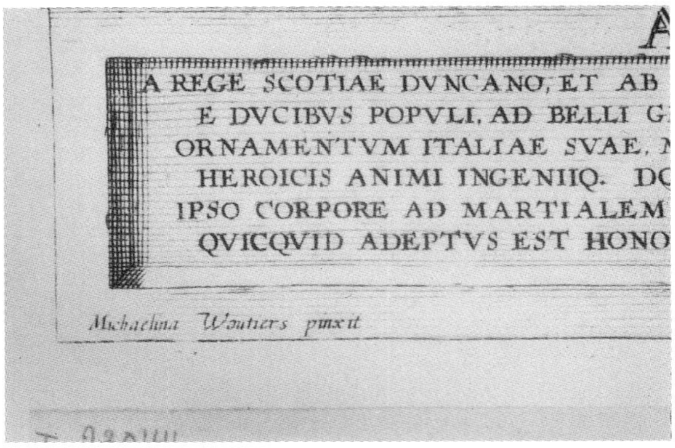


Afb. 2. Detail van afb. 1

tretten doen Frans aan; de bloemstukjes Vlaamser dan Daniel Seghers en haar historiestukken zijn expliciet 'italianisant'.

Het oudst bekende werk van Michaelina, de prent naar het geschilderde portret van Andreas Cantelmus, draagt als onderschrift: *Michaelina Woutiers pinxit, Paull. Pontius fecit exc. et Excell(entissi)me suae Lub. Mer. Dedicavit. 1643* (afb. 1–2). Allicht lag een levensgroot busteportret van de hand van Michaelina Woutiers aan de basis van de prent. De vraag stelt zich echter of zij ook de ontwerper was van het strijdtafereel op het achterplan van het portret evenals van de twee strijdtaferelen die de penanten in de bovenhoeken van de gravure sieren.[21] Op grond van het onderschrift van de kopergravure zou men geneigd zijn te vermoeden dat Paulus Pontius het initiatief nam om het portret te laten graveren.[22] Hij vermeldde immers dat hij de prent 'maakte, sneed en met onvervalst genoegen aan zijne excellentie heeft opgedragen'.[23] De edelman Cantelmo was in 1632 in de Nederlanden om aan het hoofd van een Italiaans regiment de stad Maastricht mee te helpen verdedigen. Nadien behaalde hij een aantal militaire successen waardoor hij het in 1642 tot artilleriemeester en in 1643 tot *maître de camp général* bracht.[24] Niet zonder reden staat onder zijn portret te lezen '*Novus saeculi Epaminondas*', een duidelijke referentie aan de Thebaanse veldheer die in 362 voor Christus sneuvelde. Cantelmo overleed in Spanje in 1644.[25] Het portret – een prestigieuze opdracht – ontstond wellicht in 1642 of 1643, een datering waarvoor de prent een *terminus ante quem* biedt. Cantelmo was geen slecht gekozen model om een portrettistenloopbaan mee aan te vangen. En ook hij had meerdere banden met Antwerpen omdat hij naar alle waarschijnlijkheid de opdrachtgever was van de tapijtenreeks met de voorstelling van de' Zeven vrije kunsten' waarvan de kartons in het begin van de jaren veertig in het atelier van Cornelis Schut werden besteld.[26] Mogelijk koos de humanistisch geïnspireerde mecenas zelf voor de jonge getalenteerde vrouw. Erycius Puteanus (1574–1646) die van 1606 tot 1646 in Leuven de leerstoel Latijn en welsprekendheid bezette als opvolger van Justus Lipsius, droeg één van zijn brievenbundels aan hem op (afb. 3): *Magno stratego D. Andreae Cantelmo, e regibus Scotiae, ducibus populi, et ad gloriam militiae nato, tormentorum bell. per alsatiam, et provinciae Flandriae praefecto, consiliis duci, manu militi, qui Germaniam pvgnando, Lvcemburgvm servando, Belgium defendendo, virtuti et fortunae suae obstrinxit, hostium victori et ante sui, Herculeo patronico musas, armis libros complexo, legionum ductori, epistolarum centuriam Erycivs Pvteanvs, stvdiis votisque consecratis, L.M. offert.*[27] De opdracht laat sterk vermoeden dat Cantelmo en Puteanus elkaar persoonlijk kenden. Dit vermoeden wordt trouwens bevestigd in de briefwisseling van de dichter-diplomaat Constantijn Huygens (1608–1687) die Puteanus reeds in 1632 tot zijn vrienden-

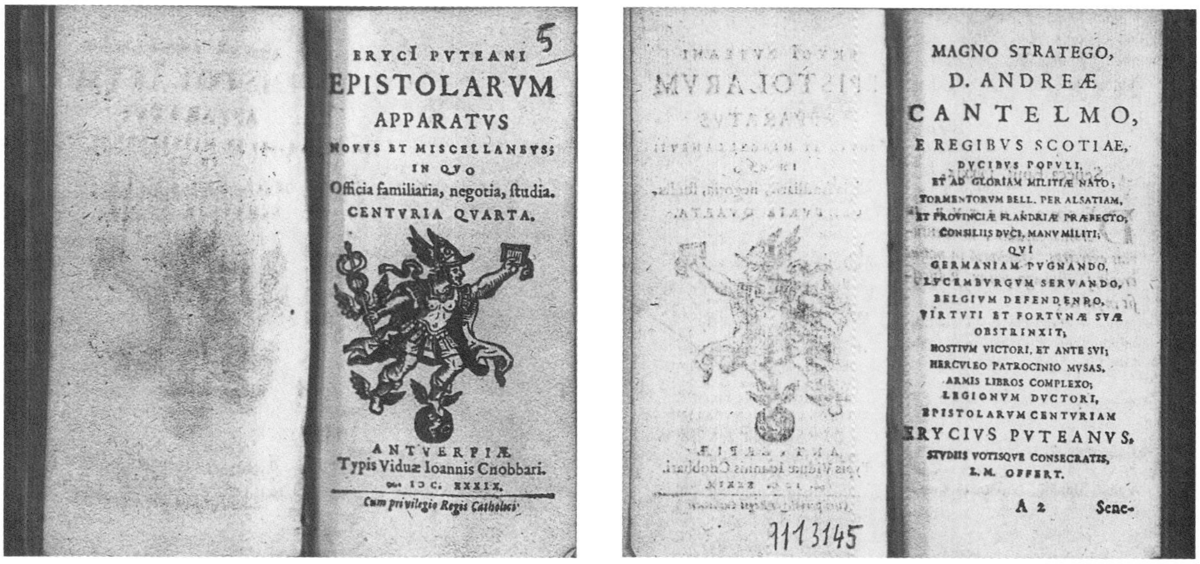
ERYCI PVTEANI
EPISTOLARVM
APPARATVS
NOVVS ET MISCELLANEVS;
IN QVO
Officia familiaria, negotia, studia.
CENTVRIA QVARTA.
ANTVERPIÆ,
Typis Viduæ Ioannis Cnobbari.
IↃ C. XXXIX.
Cum privilegio Regis Catholici.

MAGNO STRATEGO,
D. ANDREÆ
CANTELMO,
E REGIBVS SCOTIAE,
DVCIBVS POPVLI,
ET AD GLORIAM MILITIÆ NATO;
TORMENTORVM BELL. PER ALSATIAM,
ET PROVINCIÆ FLANDRIÆ PRÆFECTO,
CONSILIIS DVCI, MANV MILITI;
QVI
GERMANIAM PVGNANDO,
LVCEMBVRGVM SERVANDO,
BELGIVM DEFENDENDO,
VIRTVTI ET FORTVNÆ SVÆ
OBSTRINXIT;
HOSTIVM VICTORI, ET ANTE SVI;
HERCVLEO PATROCINIO MVSAS,
ARMIS LIBROS COMPLEXO;
LEGIONVM DVCTORI,
EPISTOLARVM CENTVRIAM
ERYCIVS PVTEANVS,
STVDIIS VOTISQVE CONSECRATIS,
L. M. OFFERT.
A 2 Scae-

Afb. 3. Erycius Puteanus, *Epistolarum apparatus novus et miscellaneus*, Antwerpen, 1639

kring kon rekenen.[28] Op 5 april 1644 schreef Erycius Puteanus een briefje aan Huygens waarin sprake was van Cantelmo. De Leuvense hoogleraar vertelt hierin dat zijn *'vriend Cantelmo'* hem uitnodigde om naar Mechelen te komen nog vóór hij naar Spanje terugkeerde. Bij die gelegenheid bood Puteanus hem zijn '*Stemma*' aan, een boek dat slechts op enkele exemplaren werd gedrukt en waarin naast de 'Stuarts' en de 'Oranje's' ook de 'Cantelmo's' worden geprezen.[29] Huygens zelf was minder gesteld op de aanvoerder van de vijandelijke troepen. Wanneer hij de naam van Cantelmo in brieven ter sprake bracht, had de mededeling steeds betrekking op zijn militaire acties. Zo omschreef hij '*Don Andrea Cantelmo'* op 25 september 1641 in een brief aan Amalia van Solms als iemand '*qui ne cesse de machiner des entreprinses*' [sic].[30] Vanuit het kamp van Assenede berichtte Constantijn Huygens haar twee jaar later over de onvoorspelbaarheid van Cantelmo's strategieën.[31] De Eindhovense predikant Johannes van der Hagen deed in hetzelfde jaar zijn beklag over de manier waarop Cantelmo na de opeising van Eindhoven feest had gevierd met de monniken. Het *in de kerck van Eyndoven* aangeheven triomfantelijke *Te Deum laudamus, en sall ick noyt anders noemen als de 'Cantica Cantelmi*.[32] Ook in een brief van 29 juli 1643 refereert Huygens nog aan het pochen van Cantelmo over de inname van Eindhoven: *Er zijn brieven in cijferschrift onderschept, waarin Cantelmo geweldig bluft op het innemen van Eindhoven en het kasteel van Heeswijk, die geen tegenstand hebben geboden, en ook hierop, dat hij is doorgedrongen tot Littoyen, waar in dertig jaar geene troepen van den Koning zijn geweest. En de inneming van den Bosch dan en de onderneming op Voorn! Cest homme là est estrangement fanfaron*.[33]

Er werd een poging gedaan om Cantelmo – de enige met zekerheid geïdentificeerde tijdgenoot die door Michaelina Woutiers werd geportretteerd, opnieuw in zijn culturele en militaire context te plaatsen. Van belang hierbij is dat ook de schilder Theodoor van Loon goede contacten onderhield met Erycius Puteanus. In een ander deeltje van dezelfde brievenbundel is een brief van Puteanus opgenomen: *Epistola XLV. Bruxellam. Theodoro Vanlonio, Amico intimo, ingenio & arte pingendi Celeberrimo*.[34] Puteanus was blijkbaar niet alleen bevriend met Cantelmo maar rekende ook Van Loon tot zijn Leuvense vriendenkring: *Vera amicitia quam rara est! sed nostra vera est, quam res nullae umquam humanae solvent*.[35] Het is zeer de vraag of Michaelina Wouters niet in contact kwam met het werk van de kunstenaar Theodoor van Loon via Andreas Cantelmo en/of Erycius Puteanus. Ontmoette Cantelmo de jonge Michaelina Woutiers in Brussel in de omgeving van de kardinaal-infant of had hij al eerder in het buitenland met haar kennisgemaakt?

Een tweede portret, ondertekend *Michaelina Woutier 1646*, bevindt zich in de Koninklijke Musea voor Schone Kunsten te Brussel (doek, 63 x 56,5 cm; inv. nr. 297) (afb. 4) waar ook

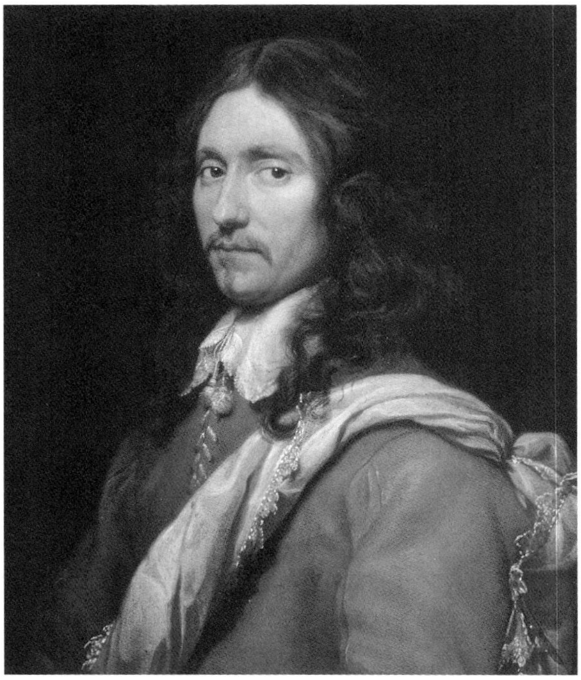

Afb. 4. Michaelina Woutiers, *Portret van een man*, 1646. Brussel, Koninklijke Musea voor Schone Kunsten van België

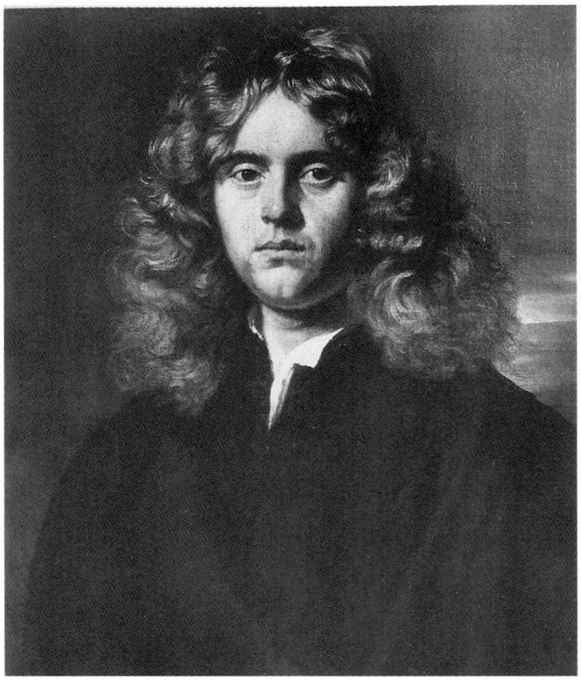

Afb. 5. Karel Woutiers, *Portret van een man* (zelfportret?), 1656. Brussel, Koninklijke Musea voor Schone Kunsten van België

twee mansportretten van Karel Woutiers uit 1656 en 1660 worden bewaard (afb. 5).[36] Het levensgrote busteportret van Michaelina maakt indruk. De man is niet geïdentificeerd maar zijn ambtelijke kledij met de dwars over de borst gedrapeerde roze sjaal doen vermoeden dat het om een man van aanzien gaat. Aangezien de kleur van dit attribuut nationaal was bepaald, is het niet uit te sluiten dat de geportretteerde van Spaanse origine was.[37] Het portret vult haast het hele beeldvlak en de driekwartwending van het gelaat met de uitdagende blik dwingt tot confrontatie. De fysionomische typering is meedogenloos realistisch of lijkt in elk geval zo te zijn. De suggestieve en wat impressionistische factuur van de los over de schouders vallende haren verraden een ervaren schildershand.

Genreachtige schilderijen maakte Michaelina Woutiers ook af en toe. In de collectie van '*M. de Malherbe*' in Valenciennes bevond zich in 1883 een reeks van vijf schilderijen met de voorstelling van de vijf zintuigen. Alle schilderijen waren voluit gesigneerd: '*Michaelina Wautier, 1650*'. Afmetingen: 68 x 58 cm. In 1898 veranderden ze nog een keer van eigenaar (*délaissé par feu Mr Jean-Baptiste Foucart, Valenciennes*)[38] en sindsdien is slechts één doek uit de serie nog opgedoken. Op 28 mei 1975 werd bij Drouot (Salle 6) in Parijs '*The Recorder Player*' geveild. Een door '*Michaelina Woutier*' gesigneerd doek van 70 bij 61 cm droeg de datum '1650' en werd omschreven als *One of a series of five canvases depicting young boys. A young lad in a cap plays a flared-bell recorder, the hole of the little finger of the lowermost (right) hand clearly shown*. Ongetwijfeld gaat het hier om de voorstelling van het Gehoor.[39]

In 1960 haalde een Stilleven van Michaelina Woutiers de tentoonstelling *Bloem en tuin in de Vlaamse kunst* (Museum voor Schone Kunsten, Gent).[40] De pendant van dit merkwaardige schilderij bevindt zich momenteel in Nederlands privé-bezit.[41] Het gaat om een descriptief bloemstuk op paneel (41,1 x 57,4 cm) in de Antwerpse stijl van rond het midden van de zeventiende eeuw (afb. 6). De guirlande is – uitzonderlijk voor haar – op paneel geschilderd én is gesigneerd '*Michaelina Woutiers fecit 1652*'. Het paneel draagt op de rugzijde bovendien een Antwerps merkteken. Dit laatste element bevestigt dat Woutiers inderdaad een band had met Antwerpen en er bij gelegenheid panelen aankocht.[42] De problematiek van het stilleven of bloemstuk intrigeerde haar. Dit blijkt uit de bijzonder inventieve wijze waarop deze compositie werd samengesteld. De evenwichtige

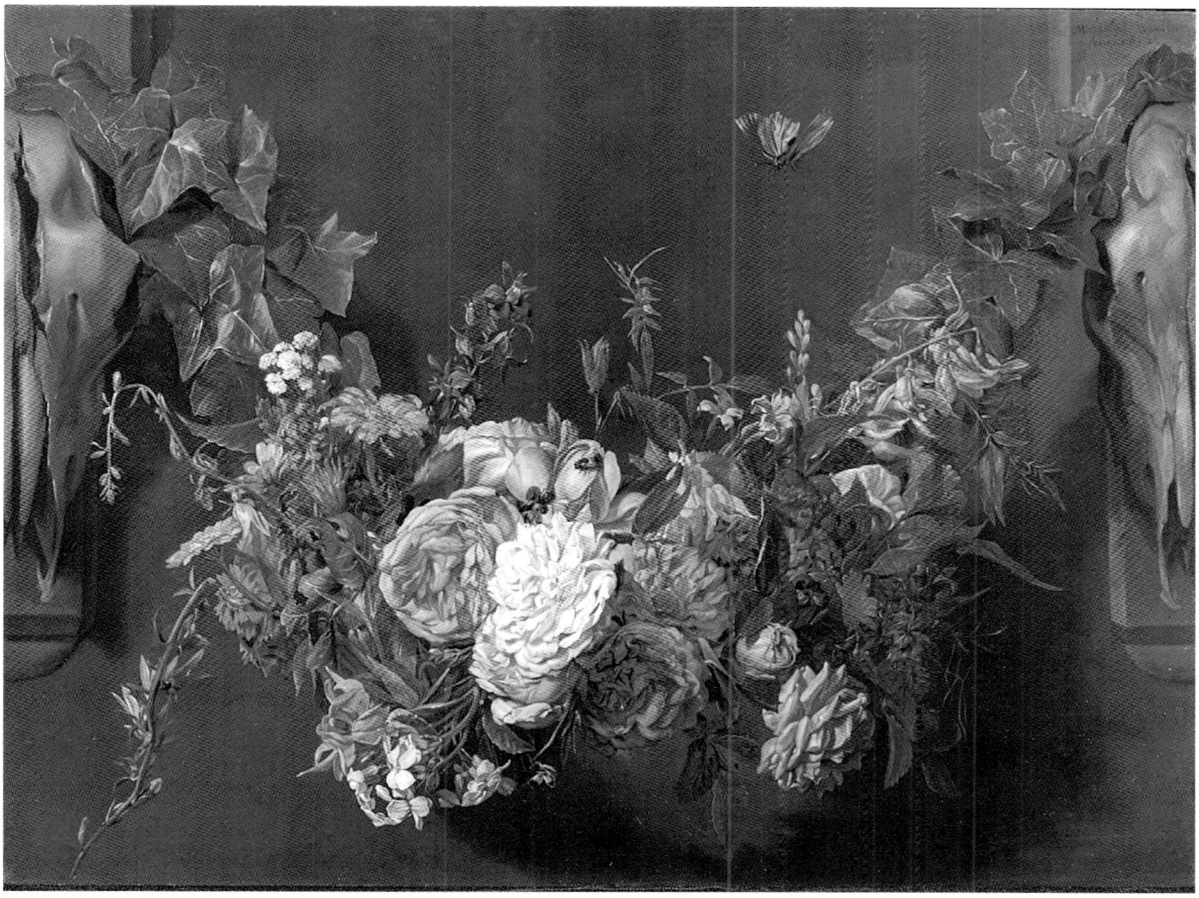

Afb. 6. Michaelina Woutiers, *Guirlande*, 1652. Privé-verzameling

schikking en de diversiteit van de bloemen met een enkele libel en een bijtje[43] tonen aan op welke indringende wijze ze dit genre meester is geweest. Uitgaande van prototypes van Daniël Seghers varieerde ze de ingrediënten van haar stillevens en initieerde ze een volledig nieuwe opbouw van het stilleven door een symmetrisch ontwikkelde raamcompositie te gebruiken. De aanwezigheid van de bucranieën – ook dit detail is vernieuwend op zich – verwijst ongetwijfeld naar antieke inspiratie en versterkt het vanitasgehalte van de voorstelling. De introductie van het motief van de 'ossenkop-console' illustreert Woutiers' artistieke ambitie.[44] Hans-Jörg Czech legde tevens het verband met de door Plinius de Oudere overgeleverde kunstenaarsanekdote van de Griekse schilder Pausias van Sikyon (vierde eeuw v.C.). Pausias wedijverde met zijn jeugdliefde, Glykera, om de mooiste bloemenkrans te maken. Hij gebruikte verf terwijl zij een echte krans samenstelde. Aldus konden 'cultuur' en 'natuur' de strijd met elkaar aangaan.[45] Dit thema was in Antwerpen niet onbekend aangezien ook Rubens de anekdote in beeld bracht (Sarasota, John and Mable Ringling Museum of Art, doek, 231 x 188 cm).[46] Door het uitvoeren in verf van de bloemenslinger steekt Michaelina Woutiers haar seksegenote Glykera naar de kroon en stelt ze zich concurrentieel op tegenover Pausias. De idee van 'emulatie' was haar in deze context zeker niet vreemd. De referenties aan de klassieke oudheid zijn inderdaad te interpreteren als kenmerkend voor *die humanistisch geprägte Kunstauffassung des 17. Jahrhunderts*.[47] Veel minder evident is het feit dat een vrouwelijke kunstenaar zich op dit terrein waagt en een innoverende vertolking van het thema introduceert. Een compositie als deze illustreert onomstotelijk de intellectuele ambitie van de maker en bewijst Woutiers' vertrouwdheid met de literaire traditie.[48]

Zoals al eerder werd gesuggereerd, fungeert Woutiers' compositie als het oudst bekende Zuid-Nederlandse exemplaar van dit type. Tussen 1631/32 en 1658 verbleef de in Utrecht geboren stillevenschilder Jan Davidsz. de Heem

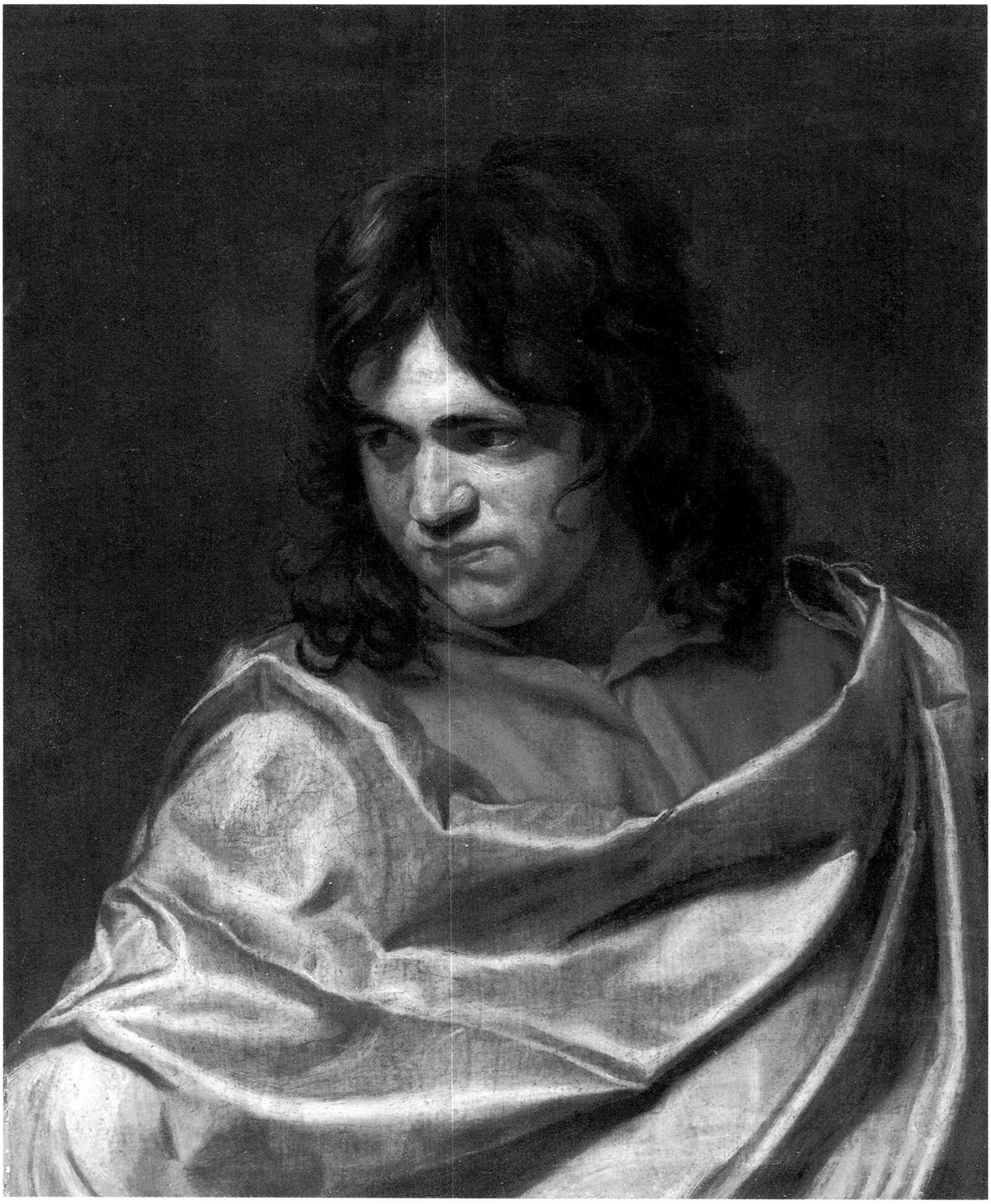

Afb. 7. Michaelina Woutiers, *Portret van een jonge man*. 1655. Antwerpen, Koninklijk Museum voor Schone Kunsten

(1606–1683/84) in Antwerpen. Zijn meest exuberante stillevens met een 'beeldvullende guirlande' schilderde hij pas in de loop van de jaren vijftig.[49] Een vergelijkbare opzet komt men in zijn oeuvre van vóór 1653 niet tegen. Het is dus goed mogelijk dat niet Jan Davidsz. de Heem maar wel Michaelina Woutiers als de 'uitvindster' van het bloemenstilleven met beeldvullende guirlande moet worden geboekstaafd.[50]

Op 28 maart 2003 werd bij Galerie Koller in Zürich een gesigneerd schilderij van Michaelina Woutiers geveild. Het Antwerpse Koninklijk Museum voor Schone Kunsten is de nieuwe eigenaar geworden (afb. 7–8) (inv. 5141). Op

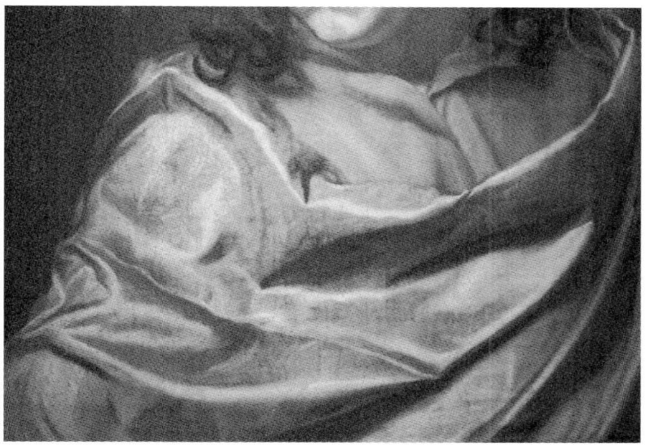

Afb. 8. Detail van afb. 7

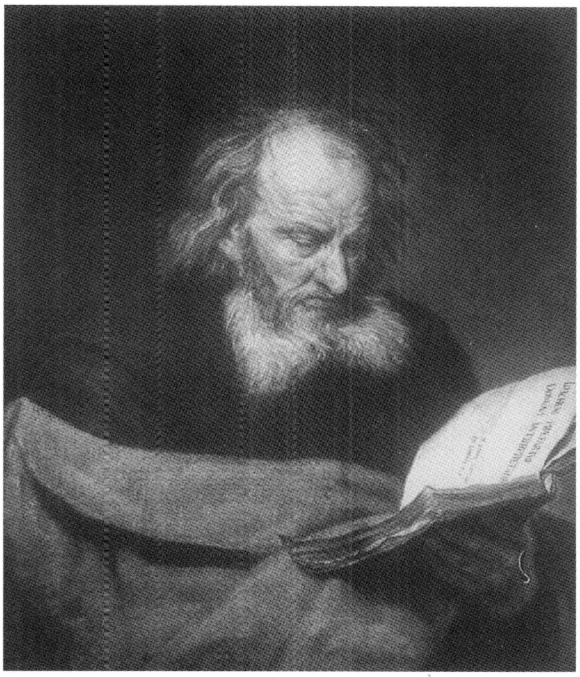

Afb. 9. Michaelina Woutiers, *H. Joachim*, vóór 1659. Wenen, Kunsthistorisches Museum

het doek (69 x 58 cm) is een halflijfse voorstelling te zien van een jongeman die in gedachten verzonken voor zich uitkijkt. Over de pedigree van het stuk is niets bekend; men weet alleen dat het afkomstig is uit een Zwitserse privé-verzameling. Het schilderij is rechts boven gesigneerd: '*Michaelina Wautier fecit 1655*'. Typologisch is het werk allicht verwant aan de hoger besproken voorstellingen van de Vijf Zintuigen waarbij steeds een jongeman met een attribuut aan één van de 'Zinnen' refereert. In het schilderij te Antwerpen ontbreekt elke vorm van anekdotiek. Het gaat niet om een formeel portret – de jongen lijkt nauwelijks te poseren – en het doek is evenmin tot het genre van de 'studiekop' te rekenen. De factuur is opmerkelijk vrij en vooral in het gelaat valt de brede, pasteuze werkwijze op. Dit laatste aspect is tevens opmerkelijk in de horizontaal voor de borst gedrapeerde mantel al is het kostuum gelikter van uitvoering. De kleurencombinatie van het oker met het roze brengt het in Brussel bewaarde portret in herinnering. Dat het schilderij ontstond in 1655 hoeft niet te verwonderen. De globale pose van de knaap, zijn lichaam is naar rechts gewend terwijl hij het hoofd heeft teruggedraaid, is erg verwant aan de manier waarop Michaël Sweerts zijn modellen liet poseren. In zijn *Diversae facies in usum iuvenum et aliorum delineatae per Michaelem Sweerts equit. Pict. Etc.*, een bundeltje prenten uitgegeven in Brussel in 1656, komen twaalf studiekoppen voor van wie er twee het hoofd 'terugdraaien'.[51] Ook in zijn schilderijen komen vergelijkbare halflijfse portretachtige taferelen voor. De jongen met hoed (Wadsworth Atheneum Museum of Art, Hartford, Connecticut) wordt rond 1655–1656 gedateerd terwijl het portret van een knaap in het Fine Arts Museum of San Francisco enkele jaren later wordt gesitueerd (ca. 1659–1661).[52] Het is verleidelijk te veronderstellen dat Michaelina Woutiers op een of andere manier in contact kwam met Sweerts en zijn werk via de door hem opgerichte Academie. Sweerts, in 1618 in Brussel geboren, verbleef tussen ca. 1646 en 1655 in Rome maar bevestigde in 1656 dat hij naar zijn vaderland was teruggekeerd en er een academie stichtte: (…) *heeft alhier in die selve met grooten kost opgericht ende nu langen tijt onderhouden d'accademie van die teeckeninge naer het leven, tot die welcke veele jongelingen dagelijcx sijn frequenterende.*[53] Ondanks de expliciete vermelding dat de tekenacademie werd opgericht ter scholing van 'vele jongelingen' is het niet geheel uit te sluiten dat Michaelina Woutiers er inspiratie opdeed.

Zoals eerder vermeld, bevatte de verzameling van aartshertog Leopold-Wilhelm volgens de inventaris van 1659 vier schilderijen die aan Michaelina Woutiers zijn toe te schrijven.[54] Wanneer ze er komen en door toedoen van wie, is evenwel niet duidelijk. Wel weten we dat David Teniers II vanaf 1651 hofschilder en *ayuda da camera* van Leopold-Wilhelm was geworden. Gezien zijn functie had Teniers onder andere als taak de aartshertogelijke verzameling uit te breiden. In mei 1656 verliet

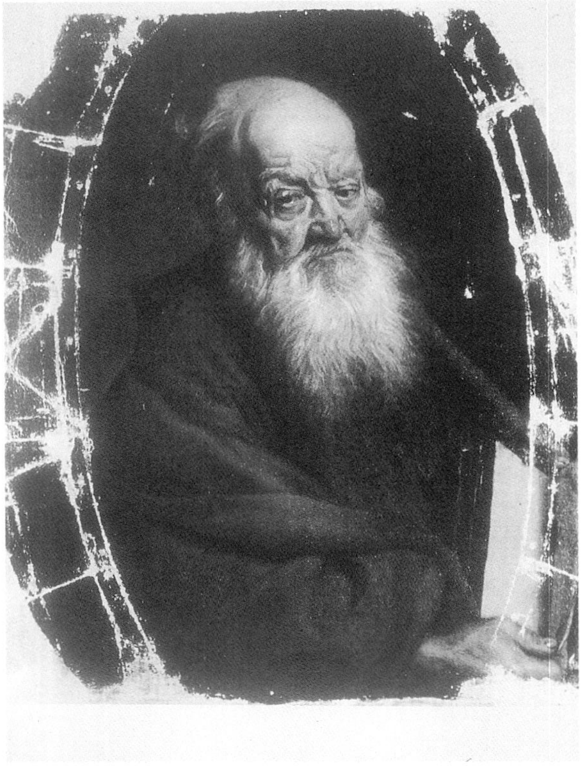

Afb. 10. Michaelina Woutiers, *H. Joachim*, vóór 1659. Wenen, Kunsthistorisches Museum

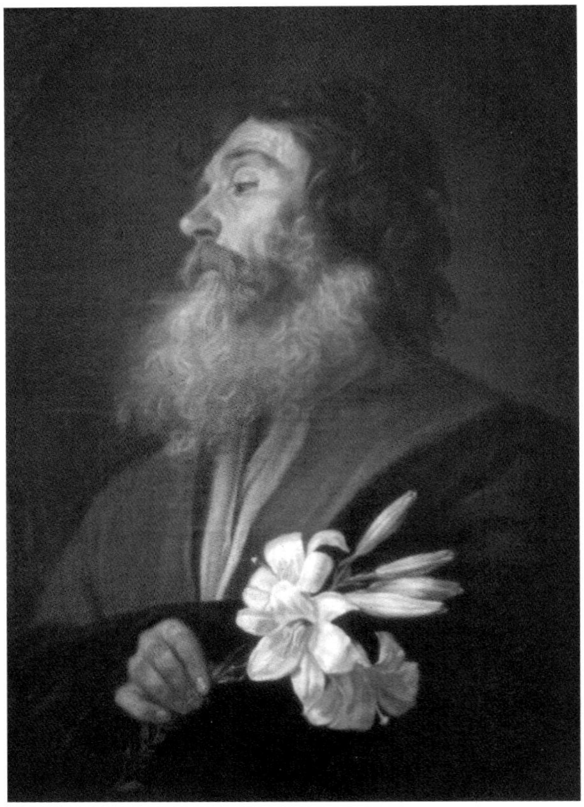

Afb. 11. Michaelina Woutiers, *H. Jozef*, vóór 1659. Wenen, Kunsthistorisches Museum

de aartshertog Brussel voor Wenen.[55] Vrijwel zeker arriveerden Woutiers' schilderijen tussen 1651 en 1656 in de collectie. Een datering kort na 1650 is bovendien te rijmen met haar overige werk.

Het gaat in de eerste plaats om drie halflijfse voorstellingen, twee maal de heilige Joachim, éénmaal Sint-Jozef voorstellend. In feite zijn deze doeken variaties op karakterportretten van een oudere man die overtuigend 'naar het leven' is weergegeven. Het haast naturalistische karakter wordt versterkt door de afwezigheid van aureolen. De eerste Sint-Joachim (afb. 9) is afgebeeld, verdiept in lectuur (doek, 75 x 64 cm).[56] De tweede versie van dit thema (afb. 10) (doek, 75 x 65 cm) toont een grijsaard die, het boek onder de arm, sceptisch de toevallige toeschouwer aankijkt.[57] Het derde doek (76 x 66 cm) is het meest aantrekkelijke door de ongewone invalshoek van het licht, dat erg 'caravaggesk' het naar achter gebogen profiel laat oplichten (afb. 11). In de hand houdt de heilige Jozef een tak met witte lelies: *gerade in diesem Detail erweist sich die Empfindsamkeit der Malerin gegenüber dem Sichtbaren*, aldus Günter Heinz.[58]

Beide mannelijke heiligen komen vaker voor in de barokiconografie omdat ze hun eigen rol vervulden in de controverse rond de onbevlekte ontvangenis van de Maagd en het maagdelijke moederschap van de heilige Anna. In deze context fungeert de witte lelie in het schilderij van de heilige Jozef als een gepast symbool van zuiverheid.[59]

Of deze werken in opdracht zijn ontstaan of op de vrije markt werden aangeboden, is niet uit te maken. Uit de biografie van de celibatair Leopold-Wilhelm door Avancini (1667) blijkt evenwel dat de aartshertog zich opwierp als een vurig verdediger van de *Immaculata Conceptio*.[60] Louter toeval is de aanwezigheid van Sint-Jozef en Joachim dus moeilijk te noemen. De twee doeken met de voorstelling van de heilige Joachim werden allicht op hetzelfde ogenblik aangeschaft.

Deze serie mannelijke heiligen illustreert Michaelina Woutiers' vaardigheid in het religieuze genre en ontlokte Günther Heinz de uitspraak dat Michaelina Woutiers door de kwaliteit van haar werk een niet te onderschatten vertegenwoordiger van het 'Nederlandse classicisme' kan worden genoemd. Uit stijltechnisch oogpunt

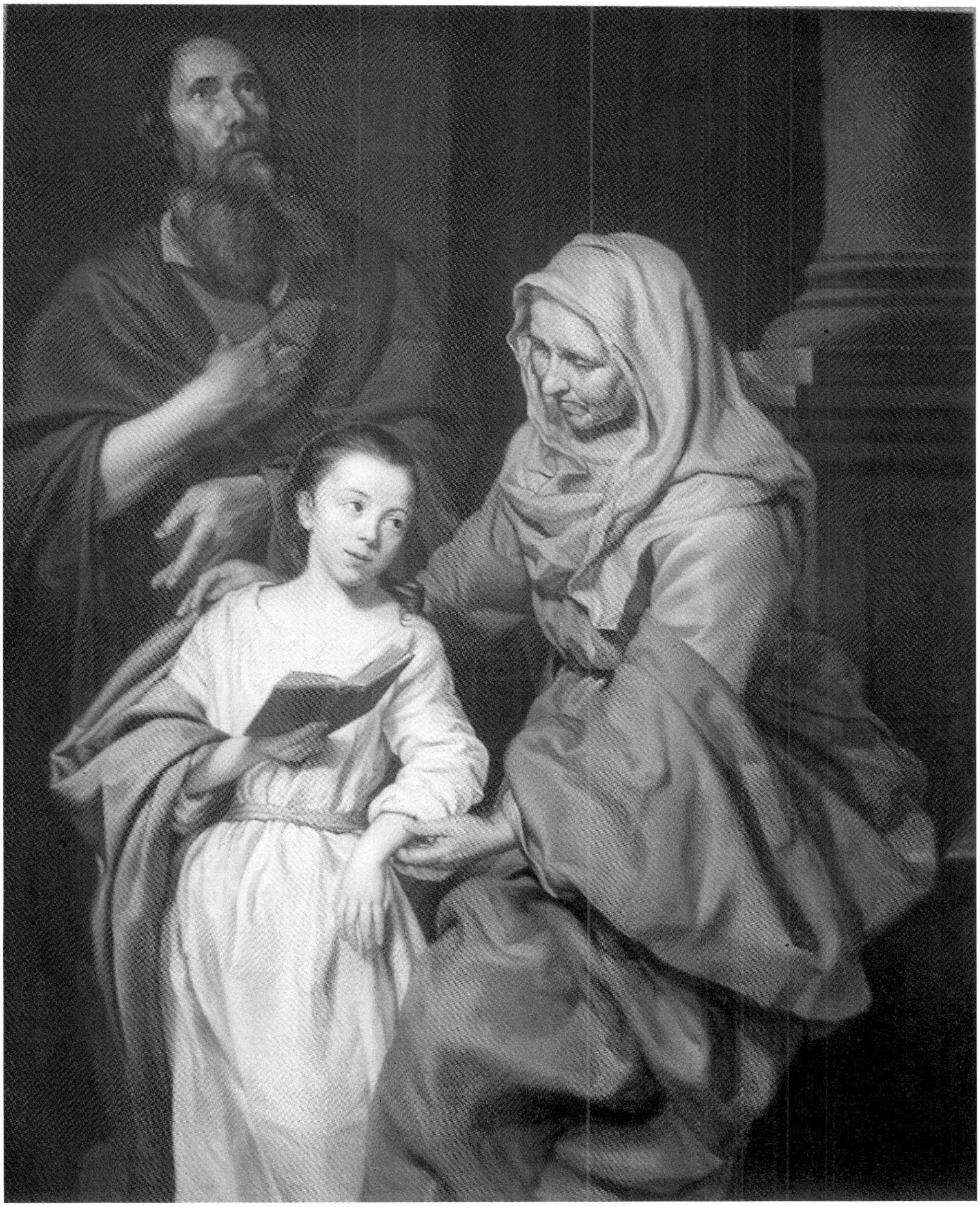

Afb. 12. Michaelina Woutiers, *De opvoeding van Maria*, 1656. Den Haag, Kunsthandel Hoogsteder en Hoogsteder

is het tafereel met de 'Opvoeding van Maria', daterend van 1656 (Den Haag, Kunsthandel Hoogsteder & Hoogsteder), nog veel indrukwekkender (afb. 12–13). Het doek (147 x 124 cm) is voluit *gesigneerd 'Michaelina Wautier invenit en fecit 1656'*, een statement om te benadrukken dat de compositie haar eigen vinding was. Zoals Edwin Buijsen reeds opmerkte sluit dit werk niet bepaald aan bij het Franse classicisme maar bij de internationale stroming van het Caravaggisme. De slagschaduwen kneden de gezichten en versterken de realistische typering van het oudere ouderpaar. Zowel Hans Vlieghe als Edwin Buijsen constateerden in dit werk een sterke invloed

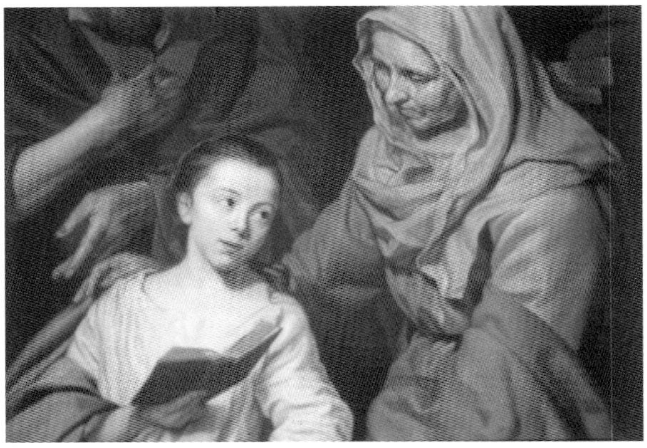

Afb. 13. Detail van afb. 12

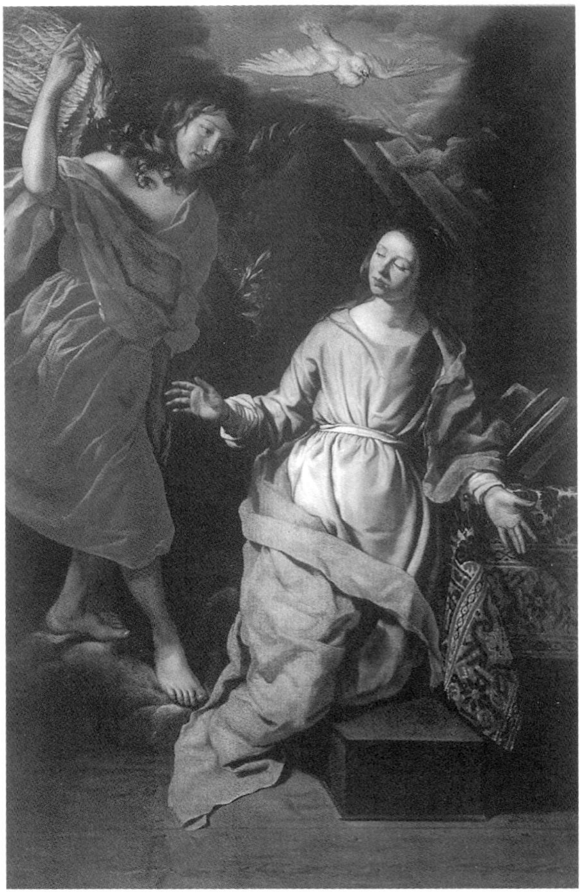

Afb. 14. Michaelina Woutiers, *De boodschap aan Maria*, 1659. Louveciennes, Musée Promenade de Marly-Le-Roi

van Theodoor van Loon (1585–1649).[61] Zo stelden beiden los van elkaar vast dat er tal van overeenkomsten aan te wijzen zijn tussen de protagonisten van deze *Opvoeding van Maria* en de figuren in de reeks van zeven schilderijen die Theodoor van Loon schilderde omstreeks 1625–1630 voor de basiliek van Onze-Lieve-Vrouw in Scherpenheuvel.[62] Hoewel niets bekend is over contacten tussen Van Loon en de schilderes, dient de vraag te worden gesteld of niet Puteanus een bemiddelende rol speelde.[63] Hoger bleek al dat Puteanus bevriend was met Van Loon en tevens met Don Andreas Cantelmo, de legeraanvoerder die ten laatste in 1643 door Michaelina Woutiers werd geportretteerd.[64] Verder onderzoek naar de activiteiten van Van Loon zal mogelijk meer klaarheid brengen.[65]

Stilistisch is het schilderij met de Opvoeding van Maria goed vergelijkbaar met het jongst bekende werk van Woutiers. De monumentale compositie (doek, 200 x 134 cm) met de Boodschap aan Maria draagt het opschrift '*Michaelina Wautier fecit* 1659' (afb. 14). Voor wie of voor waar het schilderij werd gemaakt, is niet bekend. De toeschrijving is trouwens van recente datum. Het wordt op dit moment bewaard in het *Musée Promenade de Marly-Le-Roi* in Louveciennes (Fr.). In 1977 werden enkele schilderijen weggehaald uit de kerk *Saint-Vigor* van Marly omwille van hun slechte bewaringstoestand. Eén van de werken, een *Boodschap*, werd tot op dat ogenblik toegeschreven aan de Franse barokschilder Pierre Bedeau. In 1686 had hij voor Lodewijk XIV een opdracht uitgevoerd in de kapel van het kasteel van Marly. Bij de restauratie in 1985 bleek de attributie aan Pierre Bedeau foutief. Rechts onderaan kwam de signatuur met de datum 1659 tevoorschijn.[66] Met een sterk gevoel voor ruimte lokaliseerde Woutiers het gebeuren in een binnenkamer. Maria is op de voorgrond haast frontaal afgebeeld, terwijl de aartsengel haar van op het achterplan benadert. De plasticiteit van de figuren is opmerkelijk, evenals de toepassing van het effectbeluste clair-obscur. Zuid-Nederlandse invloed ontbreekt hier totaal, het uitgangspunt is veeleer het sterk 'italianisante' Franse classicisme. Speelde deze stilistische accentverschuiving in op de smaak van de eventuele opdrachtgever of kwam Michaelina zelf tot andere inzichten? Het is opmerkelijk dat de twee laatst getoonde schilderijen technisch het meest verfijnd zijn en bovendien stilistisch het meeste verwantschap vertonen met het pronkstuk uit Michaelina Woutiers' nagelaten oeuvre, de Weense Bacchusstoet.

## Maagd of bacchante?

De Bacchusstoet wijkt af van het overige werk en maakt met de drie voormelde heiligenpor-

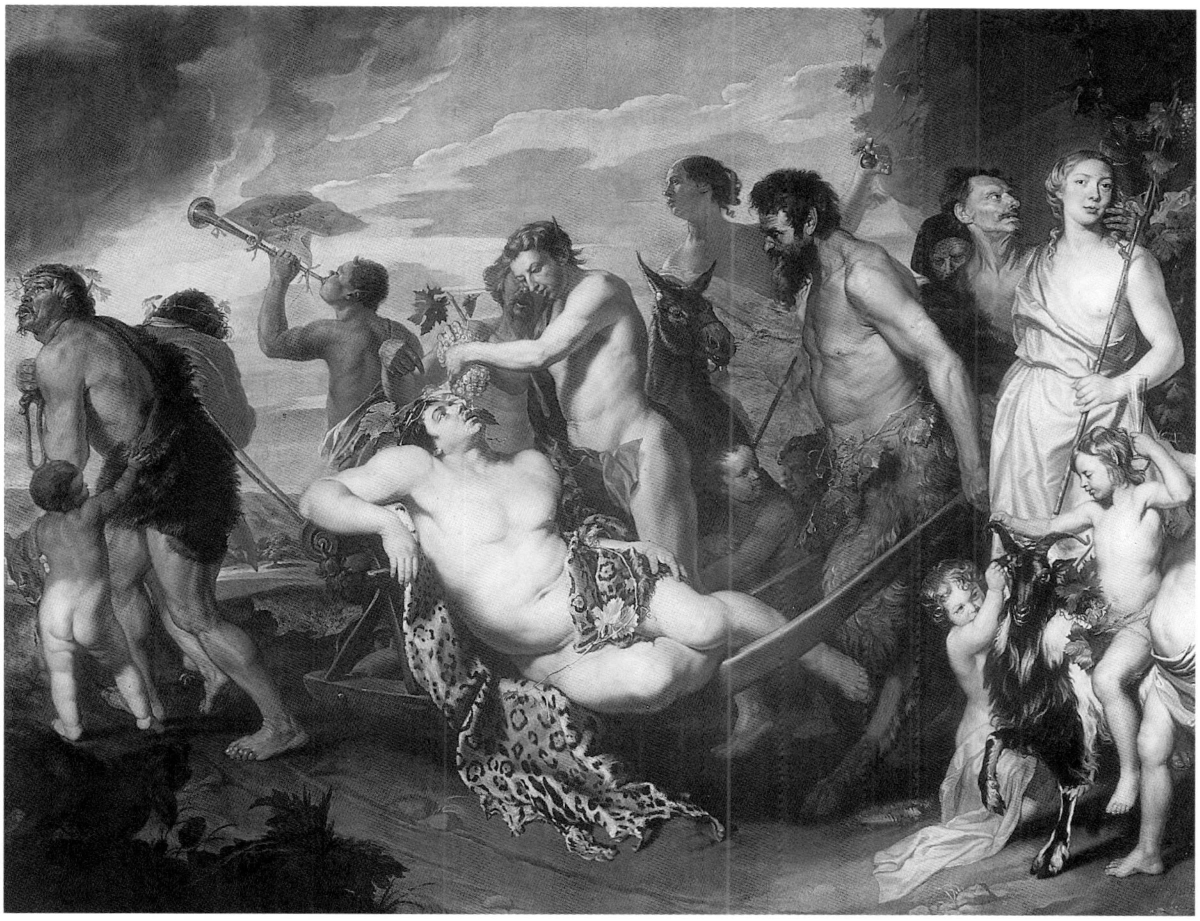

Afb. 15. Michaelina Woutiers, *Bacchusstoet*, vóór 1659. Wenen, Kunsthistorisches Museum

tretten deel uit van de Weense verzameling. Het onderwerp is mythologisch: een stoet mannen, vrouwen en kinderen vergezelt Bacchus. Een sater duwt de god van de wijn voort op een kruiwagen. Een jongeman perst hem het sap van zoete druiven in de mond. Het is een openluchttafereel met meer dan een dozijn grotendeels naakte protagonisten (afb. 15–18).

In de inventaris wordt het werk weliswaar aan *N. Woutiers* toegeschreven, toch lijdt het geen twijfel dat het van de hand van Michaelina is.[67] De stilistische gelijkenis met haar overige werk is opmerkelijk. Twijfel aan haar auteurschap is in het verleden vooral geuit door onderzoekers die thema en schaal van de Bacchusstoet niet conform het vrouwelijke palet achten. *Gustav Glück(...) glaubte ein Gemälde so grossen Formats der Hand einer Frau nicht zutrauen zu dürfen*, merkte Günther Heinz al in 1967 op hoewel ook Glück de stilistische verwantschap met het zekere werk moest toegeven.[68]

Het tafereel van Woutiers heeft als protagonisten vier ten voeten uit afgebeelde mannen. Ze worden gevolgd door een schaars geklede man en vrouw. De in profiel weergegeven man wendt zich tot de vrouw die uiterst rechts in het beeldvlak staat en nadrukkelijk uit het schilderij kijkt. Ze wil de toeschouwer viseren en treedt op als bacchante, de thyrsos in de hand.[69] Als enige in het tafereel poseert zij, zonder werkelijk deel te nemen aan de luidruchtige stoet. Zij is evenwel niet de enige vrouw in het gezelschap. Tegen de Venetiaanse lucht tekent zich het profiel van een tweede vrouw af die met castagnetten in de hand wat wezenloos aan de dans deelneemt. De vergelijking tussen het geïdealiseerde 'Venetiaanse' vrouwentype op het achterplan en de descriptieve karakterisering van de zich distantiërende vrouw rechts vooraan is bijzonder interessant. De *porträthafte* kenmerken van de bacchante zijn niet te ontkennen (afb. 18). Andere voorbeelden illustreren terdege Woutiers' vaardigheid in het portretteren. Tactisch gezien is de introductie van een zelfportret het meest zinvol. Dit vermoeden blijft vanzelfsprekend hypothetisch, maar wordt, naast het portretmatig karakter van de figuur, gedra-

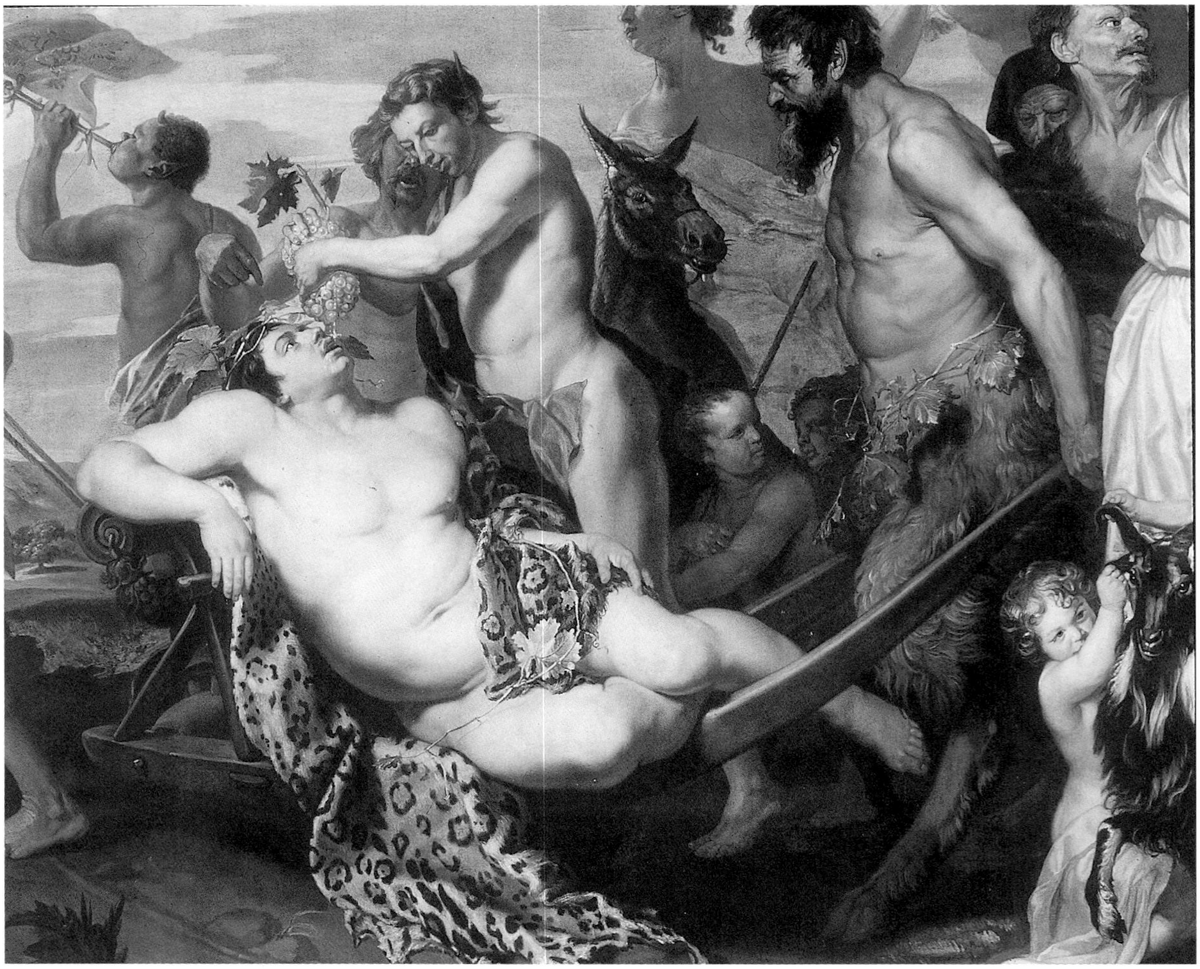

Afb. 16. Detail van afb. 15

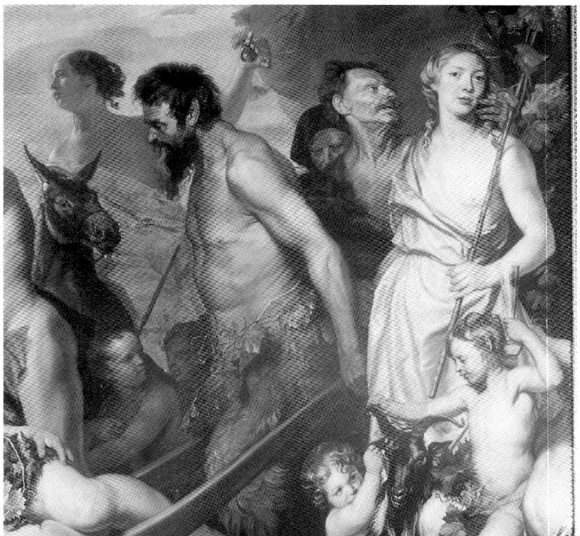

Afb. 17. Detail van afb. 15

gen door de blik uit het schilderij en vooral door het viseren van de kijker. De liederlijke context van het verhaal van Bacchus, de vrouw vervult de rol van menade of lenade,[70] rechtvaardigt de ontblote borst die er niet meteen 'Rubensiaans' uitziet en mogelijk daarom een 'autobiografisch' karakter heeft.[71] Bovendien kan de fysionomie van Michaelina Woutiers (afb. 18) worden vergeleken met een portret van een man dat eerder aan Charles of Karel Woutiers werd toegeschreven (afb. 19).[72] De attributie gebeurde naar analogie met een 'C.WAVTIER/ 1656' gesigneerd mansportret in het Koninklijk Museum voor Schone Kunsten van Brussel (afb. 5) (doek, 72 x 59 cm).[73] Beide portretten hebben dezelfde afmetingen en stellen allicht hetzelfde model voor. Opvallend zijn het hoge, bollende voorhoofd, de relatief ver uit elkaar staande ogen, de schouderlange krullende haren en de centrale plooi in de kin. Naar mijn mening is het in Londen geveilde portret niet het werk van Charles of Karel

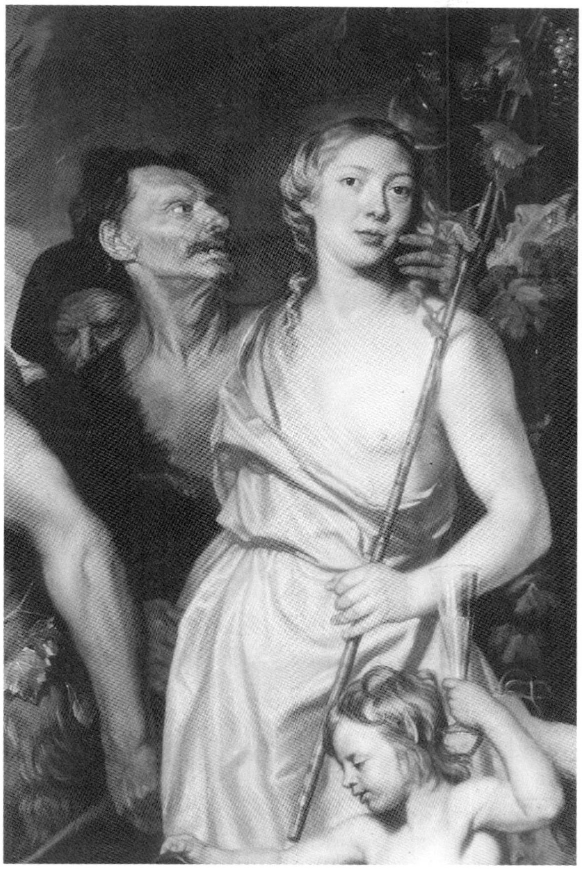

Afb. 18. Detail van afb. 15

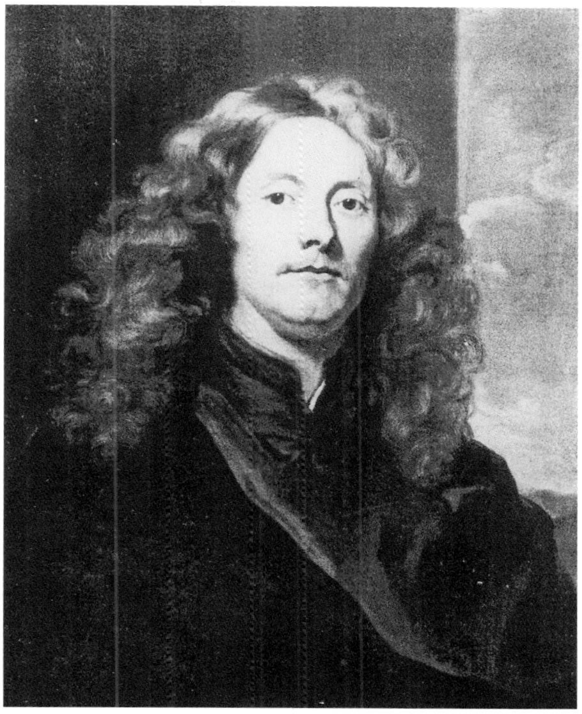

Afb. 19. Michaelina Woutiers (?), *Portret van Karel Woutiers*. Veiling Londen (Sotheby's), 16 november 1988, nr 25 (als P. Franchoys)

Woutiers maar wel van Michaelina Woutiers die, zoals verder zal blijken, effectief de zuster was van de in Brussel residerende schilder. Het schilderij in Brussel kan daarom als een zelfportret worden aangezien terwijl het Londense doek het portret is van de broer, van de hand van zijn zuster. Wanneer het in Londen geveilde werk wordt vergeleken met het hypothetische zelfportret van de schilderes op de Weense Bacchusstoet, is de gelijkenis treffend.

Terwijl systematisch zoeken naar relevante gegevens in het Algemeen Rijksarchief te Brussel – waarover verder meer – enkel een gefragmenteerd beeld oplevert, opent het intuïtief omgaan met haar werk onverwacht nieuwe perspectieven. Niet eerder is de menade als zelfportret geïnterpreteerd omdat men het portret van Michaelina Woutiers niet op deze wijze had verwacht. Rosi Braidotti meent dat de huidige feministische reflectie een breekpunt vormt in de intellectuele traditie van het Westen. Vrouwen introduceren, aldus Braidotti, een risico in de rationele activiteit omdat hun benadering van de discursieve praktijk vrijer en oneerbiediger is.[74] Het vrouwelijk naakt komt hoogst zelden voor in de schilderijen van vrouwelijke kunstenaars uit de 16de en de 17de eeuw. Indien er vergelijkingsmateriaal beschikbaar is, gaat het om voorbeelden van Italiaanse origine. Twee vroege voorbeelden zijn aanwezig in het oeuvre van Lavinia Fontana (1552–1614). Recent werden verscheidene mythologische scènes van haar hand ontdekt. Zowel in de voorstellingen van 'Minerva aan haar toilet' (afb. 20) als in 'Venus en Cupido' (afb. 21) maakt een erotiserend vrouwelijk naakt het hoofdthema uit.[75] Enkel in de schilderijen van Artemisia Gentileschi (1593–1652/53) verschijnen vrouwen geregeld halfnaakt tot naakt in hun vertolking van bijbelse taferelen (Susanna en de ouderlingen; David en Bethsabe of mythologisch/historisch geïnspireerde werken als Venus en Cupido, Danaë, Cleopatra, Lucretia).[76] De hoogst uitzonderlijke allegorie van 'Pictura' laat een op een stenen vloer liggend vrouwelijk naakt – met gesloten ogen – zien, van wie het onderlichaam schaars wordt bedekt door een damasten kleed. Een masker, een palet en ander alaam liggen naast haar.[77]

Michaelina Woutiers beeldt zichzelf af als halfnaakte bacchante in een heidens tafereel en verbindt daardoor conventie met inventie. Door

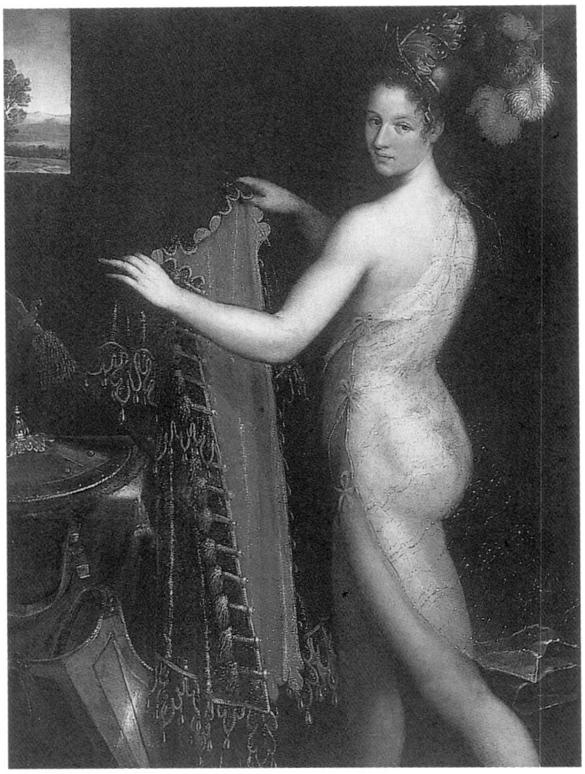

Afb. 20. Lavinia Fontana, *Minerva aan haar toilet*. Milaan, Galleria Marco Riccomini

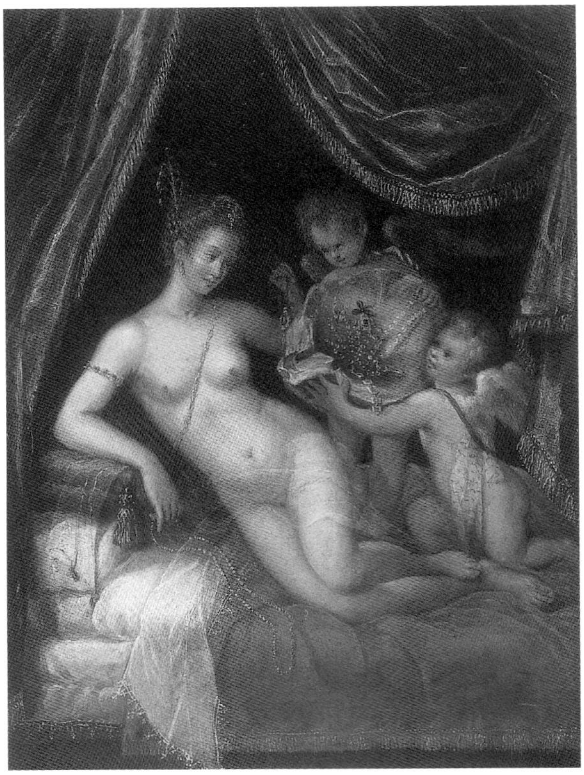

Afb. 21. Lavinia Fontana, *Venus en Cupido*. Milaan, Galleria Marco Riccomini

de op het eerste gezicht geijkte iconografie is men niet geneigd de invulling van het thema volgens een vernieuwende vrouwelijke strategie te lezen. Een bacchante verenigt in zich immers alles wat is tegengesteld aan het kuise vrouwbeeld dat mannen voor vrouwen formuleerden in de loop van de zeventiende eeuw.[78] Reeds Euripides verwees in een van de strofen van 'Bacchanten' naar een omkering van de norm: Dra danst het hele land en het is Bacchus die ons aanvoert: *Op naar de berg waar ons wacht Menigte vrouwen van Weefgetouw en de weefspoel weg, Opgejaagd door de Wijngod*. Waar Anna Maria van Schurman zich identificeerde met het ideaal van de *Pudicitia* (afb. 22),[79] opteert Michaelina Woutiers voor een zelfbeeld dat samenvalt met de *Impudicitia*. Aldus voegt het zelfportret een speelse ironie toe aan het schilderij. Het homogene, stereotiepe beeld van een vrouwelijke kunstenaar en van de vrouw-*an-sich* is verstoord geworden. Haar associatie met Bacchus wordt verder beklemtoond door de aanwezigheid van de bok naast haar. Ook in Ripa's Iconologia heeft de personificatie van de 'Libidine' of de Wellust een bok als attribuut (afb. 23).[80] Woutiers' belangstelling voor de Oudheid bleek reeds eerder uit de weergave van de bloemguirlande met de bucraniën. Ook in de Bacchusstoet heeft ze gebruik gemaakt van antieke bronnen.[81]

Ten slotte dienen er nog drie werken vermeld te worden die eveneens door Michaelina Woutiers zijn gesigneerd of aan haar kunnen worden toegeschreven. Bij het eerste gaat het om een portret, opnieuw een doek van 69 x 58,5 cm, dat op 18/19 oktober 1973 als nr. 665 bij Dobiaschofsky in Bern werd geveild (afb. 24).[82] Het portret is links boven gesigneerd en 1654 gedateerd. Rechts boven prijkt een drieregelig Latijns opschrift dat in de catalogus niet is getranscribeerd. Uit de identificatie van het portret als *Vermutliches Bildnis des Johannes Hus. Halbbildnis des bärtigen Reformators mit Pelzmütze, grauem Gewand und weissem Mantel nach rechts* is af te leiden dat de identiteit van de man in het opschrift wordt vermeld.[83] Dat Michaelina Woutiers een portret maakte van de Tsjechische kerkhervormer (1369–1415) is verwonderlijk. De omvang van het opschrift laat de mogelijkheid open dat het authentiek is en de kledij van de man is duidelijk historiserend van opzet. Dat Woutiers' portret gebaseerd is op een vijftiende- of zestiende-eeuwse

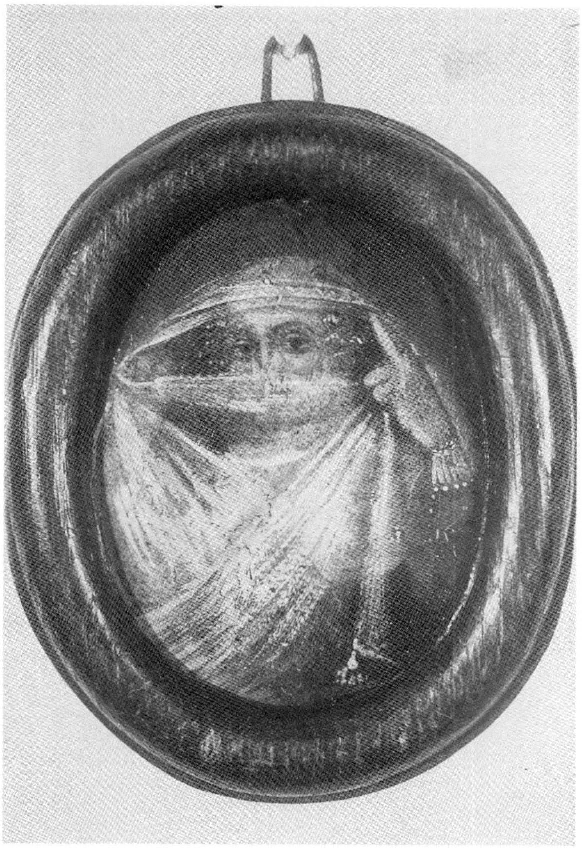

Afb. 22. Anna Maria van Schurman, *Zelfportret als Pudicitia*. Franeker, Museum 't Coopmanshûs

prent of op een geschilderd prototype ligt voor de hand.[84] Hus richtte zich in het spoor van John Wycliff (ca 1330–1384) tegen de verwereldlijking van de clerus, de aflaathandel en de kerkelijke hiërarchie. Hij was een voorstander van het prediken in de volkstaal en drong aan op de secularisatie van de kerkelijke goederen. In 1411 werd Hus in de ban gedaan en in 1415 stierf hij op de brandstapel. Door zijn dood groeide hij uit tot een symbool van verzet.

Waarom schilderde Michaelina Woutiers een portret van de Tsjechische hervormer? Ging het om een opdracht of voelde ze zelf enige affiniteit met zijn ideeëngoed? Aanzag ze Hus als een voorloper van de contemporaine hervormer Jansenius, voor wie de aartshertog in ieder geval weinig sympathie koesterde?[85] De veronderstelling dat Woutiers er hervormingsgezinde ideeën op nahield, blijft vanzelfsprekend hypothetisch. Op basis van haar overige werk is het in ieder geval duidelijk geworden dat haar intellectuele kwaliteiten niet onderschat mogen of kunnen worden.

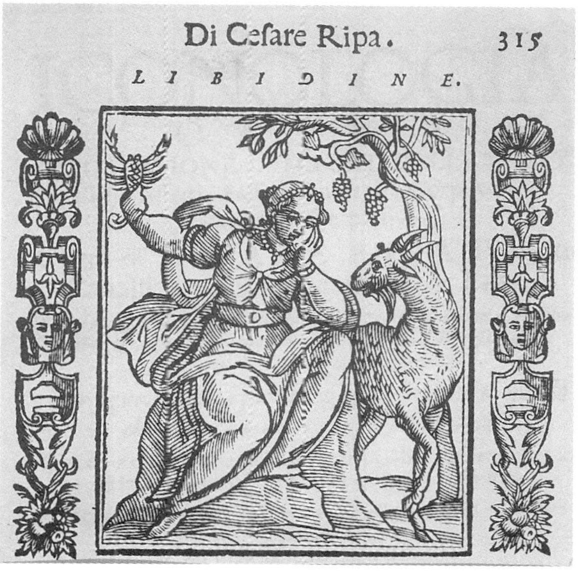


Afb. 23. *Libidine* (uit Cesare Ripa, *Iconologia*, 1611)

Een niet gesigneerd schilderij (paneel, 89 x 121 cm) uit het Koninklijk Museum voor Schone Kunsten van Antwerpen (inv.nr. 599) werd door verscheidene kunsthistorici reeds eerder met Michaelina Woutiers in verband gebracht. Hoewel het 'portrait historié' van twee meisjes afgebeeld als de heiligen Agnes en Dorothea recent nog werd gepubliceerd als een portret dat kon worden toegeschreven aan Thomas Willeboirts Bosschaert,[86] was Pierre-Yves Kairis de eerste om het doek effectief aan haar toe te schrijven (afb. 25). Na een vergelijking van de stijlkenmerken van de hoger genoemde 'Opvoeding van Maria' stelt hij het volgende voor: *A titre d'hypothèse de travail, je propose d'y adjoindre le panneau de Sainte Agnès et Sainte Dorothée conservé au Musée des Beaux-Arts d'Anvers comme oeuvre anonyme anversois du milieu du XVIIe siècle; s'y retrouvent les mêmes regards méditatifs et le même type de draperies bouffantes et à peine ciselée que dans l'Annonciation.*[87]

Dezelfde auteur publiceerde in de tentoonstellingscatalogus *Portrait en Namurois* van 2002 een volstrekt onbekend doek (156,5 x 218 cm) van haar hand dat voluit is gesigneerd en 1649 is gedateerd. De magistrale compositie brengt het Mystieke huwelijk van de heilige Catharina (afb. 26–29) in beeld en wordt bewaard in het *Séminaire de Namur*.[88] Hoewel de bewaringstoestand van het schilderij problematisch is, is ook hier haar brede toets en haar massieve typering van de figuren te herkennen. Zoals Pierre-Yves Kairis al opmerkte, is ook haar wij-

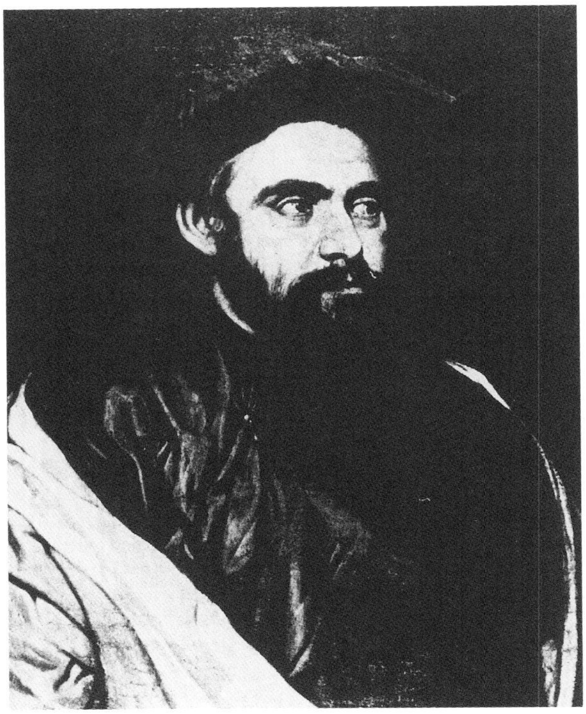

Afb. 24. Michaelina Woutiers, *Portret van een man* (Johannes Hus?). Veiling Bern (Dobiaschofsky), 18/19 oktober 1973, nr 665

ze van draperen hoogst karakteristiek. Het Naamse schilderij vormt een sleutelwerk in haar gehele oeuvre omdat er – met uitzondering van het gegraveerde portret van Cantelmo van 1643 – geen andere schilderijen uit de jaren veertig bekend zijn.

## De vrouw achter het werk

De levensloop retraceren van een vrouw die in staat was dit oeuvre te produceren, vormt een aparte uitdaging. Zoals eerder werd gezegd, bood de identificatie van haar schilderijen in de verzameling van Leopold-Wilhelm een uitstekend aanknopingspunt. Onderzoek in het Brusselse Rijks- en stadsarchief wierp enkele vruchten af. Op de eerste plaats kon er meer informatie worden opgedolven over Karel of Charles Wautier. De man bleef niet onopgemerkt in de Brusselse artistieke context omdat hij volgens het bestuur van het gilde van de schilders, goudslagers en glasblazers had nagelaten zich in het gilde te immatriculeren. Op 15 december 1642 werd genoteerd dat *ver-*

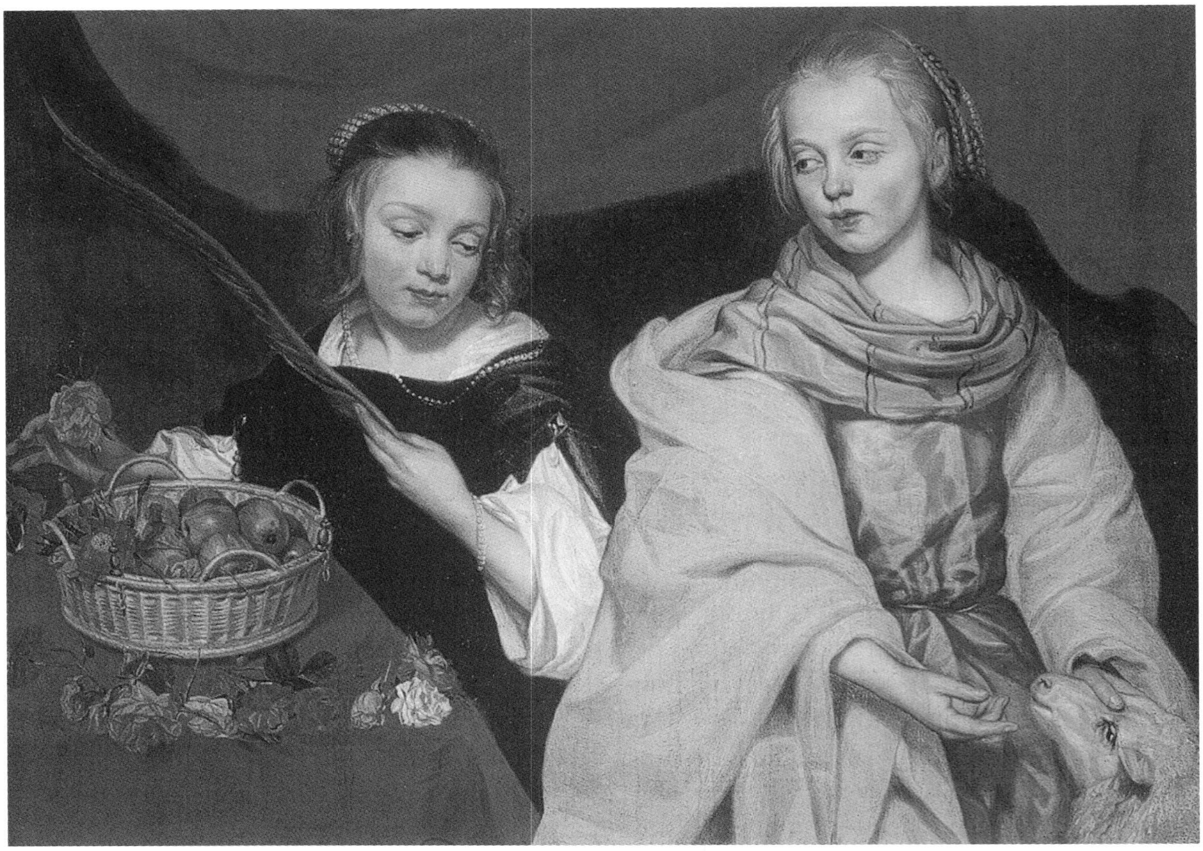

Afb. 25. Michaelina Woutiers, *Portret van twee meisjes als de H. Agnes en de H. Dorothea.* Antwerpen, Koninklijk Museum voor Schone Kunsten

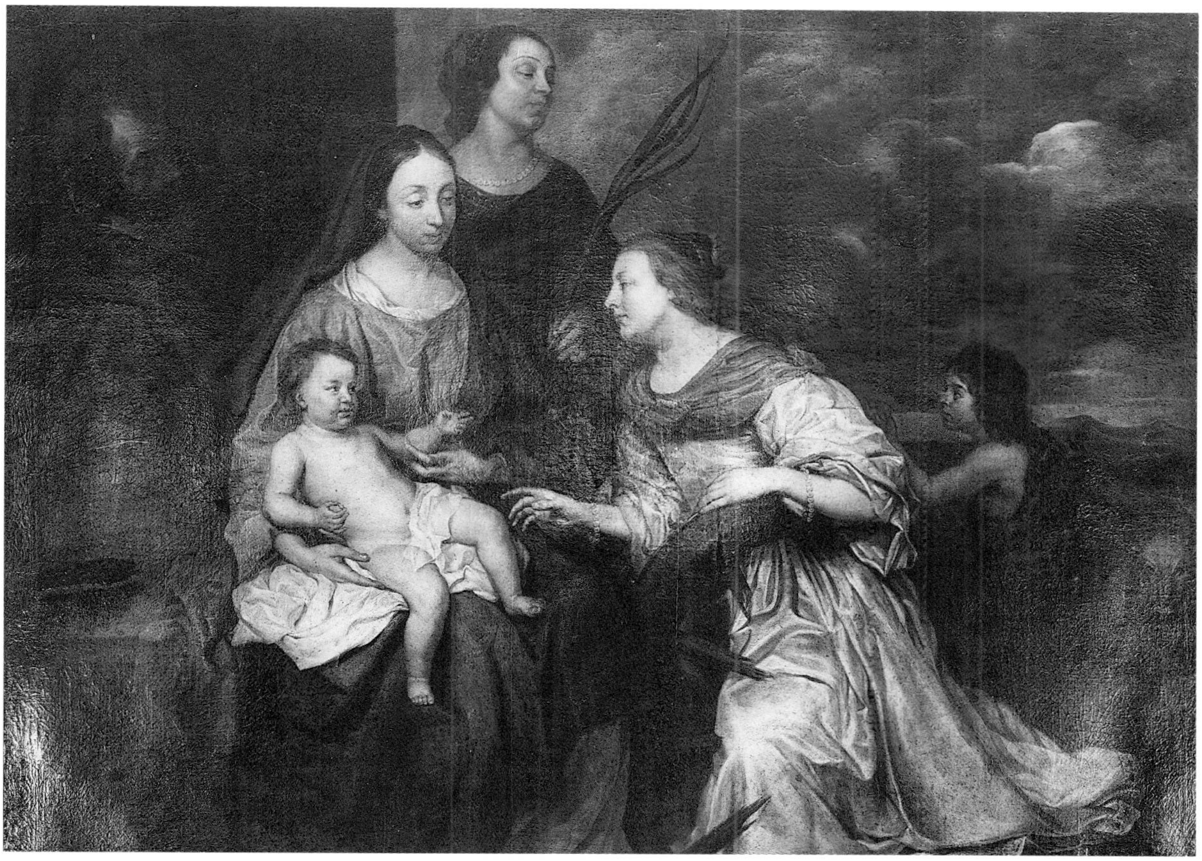

Afb. 26. Michaelina Woutiers, *Het mystieke huwelijk van de H. Catharina*, 1649. Namen, Séminaire

*scheyden vreemdelingen schilderen zonder te weesen poorteren oft meesters: eenen jonckman van Bergen in Henegouwen genoempt N. Woutier wonende in de Gasthuysstraete tegen over den Arent.*[89]

Het gilde was niet erg ingenomen met '*buytenlieden*' wat ook blijkt uit een contemporaine ordonnantie gericht tegen dit soort van 'profiteurs' die aldus het bestuur *quaemen alleenelyck 't gelt vuijtter stadt halen als t'hoff Inder stadt waere, ende gingen tselve buyten vertheiren, die welck oock ten tijde als sij in de stadt waeren heure spijse soo van buyten brochten, logerende op een camere oft twee ende en droncken nauwelyck eenen pot biers sdaeghs*; deze lieden worden aangespoord om *tvoorseyde ambacht binnen deser Stadt te vermeerderen ende in eeren te houden gelijck tselve een van de meeste ende oudste ambachten waere deser stadt.*[90] Woutiers woonde wel in Brussel zelf en was dus niet een van die tijdelijke residenten maar aarzelde toch om zich in het Brusselse gilde in te schrijven. Op 16 mei 1643 werd hij namelijk door '*den dienaar Verbiest*' tot de orde geroepen. In het gildenboek staat per 22 augustus 1643 opgetekend dat *opden sesthiensten maij lestleden hadden doen calengieren M: Wautier, Item Peeter Francois, Item Jacques Boesdonck ende Jaspar vanden Bemde die aen elcken van hen hadden gelaten een relaes om hen dijenvolgende te reguleren, met expres verboth van dat sy hen nyet meer en souden vervoorderen voorts te wercken aleer de selven souden wesen poirters deser stadt ende inder supplianten ambachte behoorelyck geadmitteert.*

De man was bovendien hardleers want het duurde nog tot 1651 vooraleer hij zich officieel in het gilde liet registreren. In het jaar 1651 (per 14 maart) staat genoteerd: *ontfanghen als meester Monsieur Wauti buytenslants gheleert ende heeft betaeylt de rechte van het ambacht over vyf jaer de welcke betaeylt het recht vande dekens, het recht van de knaep, het recht vande armbusse ende de vondelinghe(n) desen 14. Martij 1651.* In de marge werd aangevuld *gheboren tot Berghen Henegau.*[91]

In 1653 ontving hij een leerling in zijn *atelier Ontfanghen als leerjonghen Tomas Monnorino soene wylen Huybrecht Monnorino binnen geboeren leert by Carel Wautiers, schilder* en in 1657 wordt een tweede leerjongen geregistreerd: *Item ontfanghen als leerjongsen Pier Vyvier sone wylen Pier Vivier leert by ... Wautiers (sic).* Gillis Wauters vervoegde in

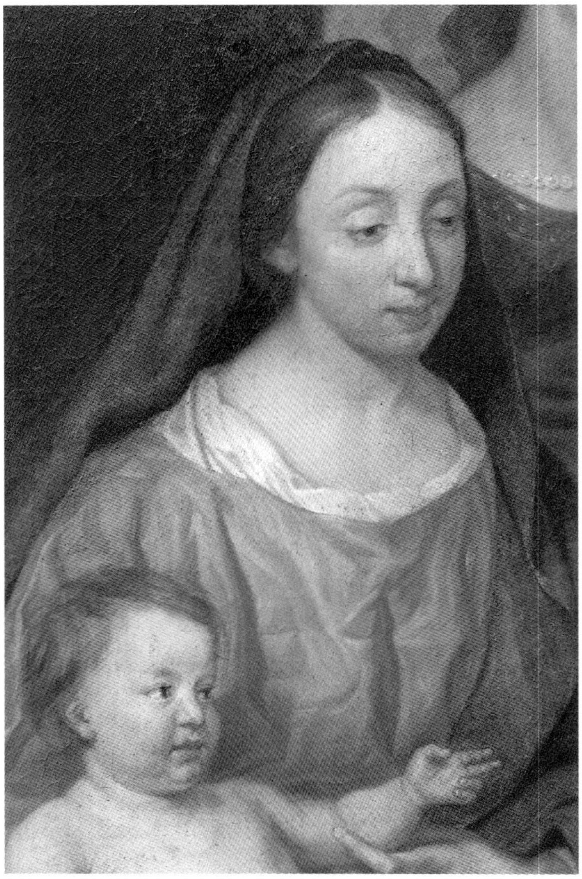

Afb. 27. Detail van afb. 26

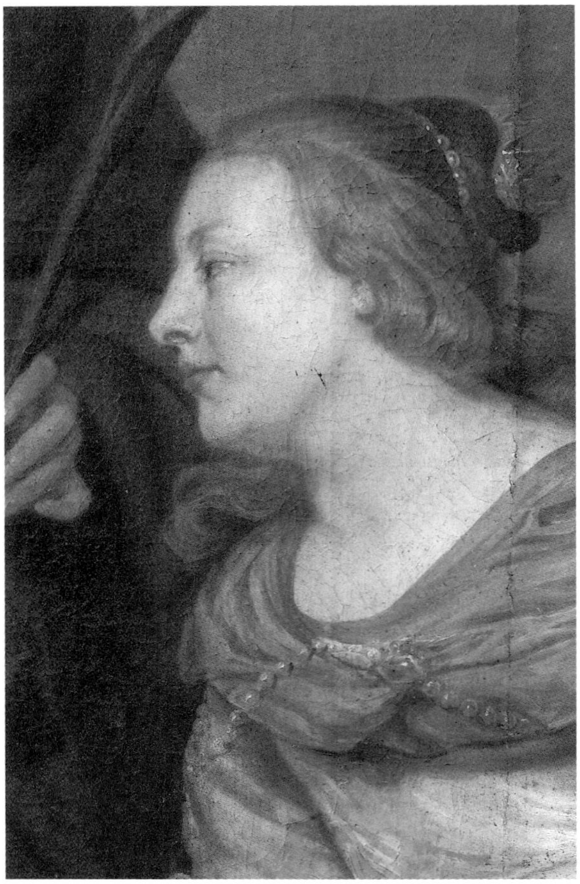

Afb. 28. Detail van afb. 26

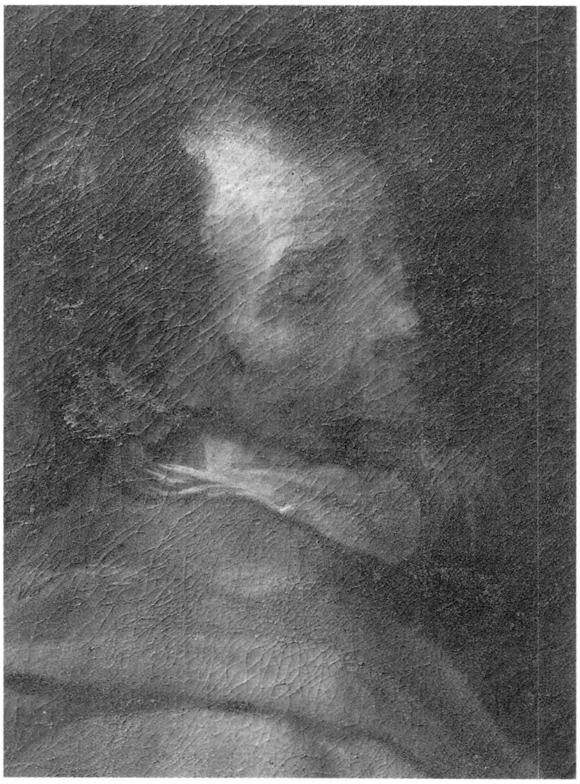

Afb. 29. Detail van afb. 26

1686 zijn atelier: *Ontfanghen als leerjongen Gillis Wauters leerende by S(enio)r Wautiers.*[92]

Volgens de parochieregisters van de Sinte-Goedelekathedraal werd 'Carolus Wautier' op 22 februari 1698 in de Brusselse kerk van Onze-Lieve-Vrouw ten Zavel begraven. Volgens deze aantekening woonde Karel Wautier of Woutiers op dat ogenblik 'omtrent de selve kercke'. Omdat de Zavelkerk geen parochiekerk was, noteerde men het overlijden van de gelovigen in het register van de nabijgelegen kathedraal. Carolus Wautier werd begraven met 16 priesters wat wijst op zijn welstand.[93]

Voor het onderzoek brengen deze vermeldingen heel wat aan. Allereerst kan worden bevestigd dat Karel Woutiers ten laatste vanaf 1642 in Brussel resideerde, een opleiding had genoten 'in het buitenland' en effectief afkomstig was uit de stad Mons of Bergen die ook met nadruk wordt vermeld in de aartshertogelijke inventaris om Michaelina te identificeren.

1. En er is meer: uit een akte opgesteld voor notaris Judocus Lemmens, daterend van 25

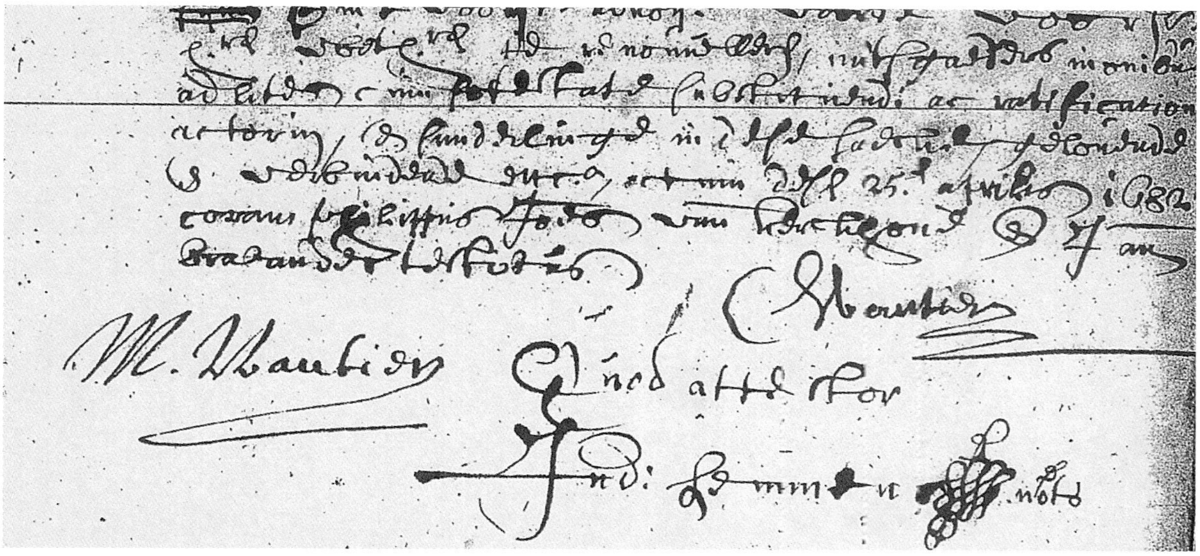

Afb. 30. Handtekeningen van Karel (Charles) en Michaelina (Michiele) Woutiers, 25 april 1682. Brussel, Algemeen Rijksarchief, 1754 A (zonder foliëring)

april 1682, blijkt dat *S(enio)r Charles ende Jo(ffrouw)e Michiele Woutier, innegesetene(n) deser stadt Brussel,* samen procederen tegen Guill(aum)e Lefebure 'cum suis'. Het betreft een verkoop van een stuk weiland *groot ontrent een bunder* waarvoor volgens Charles en Michiele Woutier nog niet de juiste taxatie gebeurde. Hun beider handtekeningen (afb. 30) prijken – naast deze van notaris Judocus Lemmens – onder het document. Op 29 mei 1682 beweerde Guillaume Lefebure 'cum uxore' voor dezelfde notaris dat zij *nijet en hebben connen overeencommen ten respecte van de weerde van(de) weyde die volgens de voors(eyden) app(licant)en inder vuegen voors(eyd) moeste worden getaxeert.* Even later, op 11 juni 1682, reclameren *Charles ende Michiele Woutier* een uitkering van een rente van 1500 Rijnsgulden met *den verloope derselven* bepand op een *huijse genoempt de Fontein ende seker cleyn wijcke gestaen ende gelegen op tsas van Vilvoorden.*[94] Deze documenten bevestigen de verwantschap tussen Karel en Michiele Woutiers en maken duidelijk dat ze beiden als inwoners van de stad Brussel er meerdere decennia verbleven.[95]

2. De naam Woutier of Wattier komt in het Brusselse niet al te vaak voor[96] en toch was er in het familie-archiefdossier een dubbele portefeuille te vinden die werd gelieerd aan de familie Gautier of Wautier. Bij het openen van deze bundel bleek meermaals de naam 'Mademoiselle de Vautier' of 'Joufffrou Woutie' te zijn genoteerd.[97] De bundel bevat tientallen kwijtingen die tussen 1693 en 1717 afgeleverd zijn aan eene juffrouw Woutier. De vrouw was op dat ogenblik bezig met de inrichting van een woning die rijkelijk werd gestoffeerd. Het pand was gelegen in de Brusselse Hoogstraat *aen Sinte Peetersclooster bij de Alle poorte.* Een andere rekening preciseert nog meer en situeert haar huis *vis à vis St Pier sur la Haut Rue* of nog *ghelevert in haer huys (het gaat om een partij kasseistenen) op de Hooghstrate recht teghen over het clooster van Ste Peeter.* Op basis van de talrijke rekeninguittreksels kunnen we vaststellen dat het huis een *haute chambre* had die aansloot bij *la Sael*, een *cleyn sael*, een *grande chambre*, een *cabinet*, een grote binnenplaats en een *balquon.*

Toegegeven, het zou om een kranige oude tante zijn gegaan. Men vermoedt dat Michaelina Woutiers geboren werd ca. 1620/25. Indien ze tussen 1693 en 1717 nog bestellingen deed, was ze op dat ogenblik tussen de 68 en de 92 jaar oud. Onwaarschijnlijk maar mogelijk, was mijn voorlopige hypothese. Ook Rachel Ruysch werd bijna negentig jaar oud en de renovaties van het huis kunnen gerelateerd worden aan het 'bombardement van Brussel' dat in 1695 over de hele stad voor zware schade zorgde. En bovendien bleek uit de stoffering dat deze dame niet alleen belangstelling had voor

mooi meubilair en tapijten maar ook heel wat schilderijen in huis had.
De schrijnwerker Jan Govaerts noteerde op 23 juli 1702 dat hij voor Mademoiselle Wautier had geleverd *Dito livré deux bordures pour des peintures l'une a quinze sols et l'autre a douze;* In dezelfde nota leest men ook: *Item livré sept rame pour des toiles à peindre copies des tapisseries.* En nog: *Item une bordure pour la peinture devant la cheminée de l'alcove, et agrandij la rame de laditte peinture* en *Item livré trois bordures pour des peintures les deux sur les portes de l'alcove en l'autre au dessus de la grande porte de la chambre de madamoiselle.* Vervolgens *Item livré 5 bordures ovales pour des portraits.*
Dezelfde Jan Govaerts is in de herfst van 1702 aan het werk in het huis tegenover het Sint-Pietershospitaal. Hij rekent *Madamoiselle Wautier'* volgende kosten aan: '*Item repare et nettoyé deux tables a fleurs; Item livré une grande bordure ovale pour le pourtrait du Roy d'Espagne.*

In 1713 werden door Jan Govaert naast lambriseringen een aantal lijsten geleverd: *Item de scrijen houten leste voer de scilderijen boven op de klijen sael.* Daarnaast wordt in dezelfde rekening genoemd: *Item eenen scrijen houten lest voor de groote scilderij staedt bij den trap* en *Item vijef scilderijlesten van wit houdt tot eenen gulden 8 stuyvers het stuck.* Een jaar later (30 november 1714) levert dezelfde schrijnwerker het volgende: *Item 2 oevalen schilderyramen ende schilderijen ghespannen opde ramen tot deselve ghelevert de lesten van lindenhout voer te snijden door den beltsnijder, bedracht samen 10 gulden.*

Om twijfel over de identiteit van Mademoiselle Wautier verder uit te sluiten werden vervolgens de Brusselse wijckboeken geverifieerd. Hierin zou sowieso een referentie moeten worden gevonden aan de eigenares van het huis gelegen bij de Hallepoort. Met betrekking tot de Brusselse Gasthuisstraat – waarin Karel Woutiers in 1642 woonde – werd dit eerder getoetst. Resultaten bleven in dit geval uit omdat de wijkboeken voor dit kwartier pas zijn gestart in 1656 en vanaf dat ogenblik werden geen aanknopingspunten meer teruggevonden.

De boeken van de Sint-Pieterswijck bestrijken de periode die ons aanbelangt. En hierin werd wel een referentiepunt ontdekt dat twee bevestigingen opleverde. Primo: Michiele Wautier wordt vernoemd als zuster van Charles Wautier en secundo: broer en zus accepteerden op die datum een rente bepand op een huis in de Hoogstraat. Op 7 augustus 1669 constitueerden *Don Pedro Consejo, Capiteyn ettc. (...) ende vr(ouw)e Isabelle Franchoise Marcelli, syne huysvrouwe, een rente van 31 Rijnsgulden, den penn(ingh) sesthiene, ten behoeve van Sr Charles Wautier en de Joffrouwe Michielle Wautier, syne [huysvr(ouw)e: gebarreerd]* sustere, *speciael(yck) op eenen huyse, metten gronde, hove ende alle synen anderen t(oe)behoirten, gelegen op de Hoochstraete gemey(n)lycken genoemt de Fortuyne.*[98]

Met de hoop aanvullende gegevens te vinden werd het hele wijkboek gefouilleerd. Zo bleek vervolgens dat op 21 maart 1710 in de namiddag een huis werd verkocht aan *Damoiselle Jenne Marie de Vautier: la maison et tous autres appendences scitué sur la haute rue vis à vis l'église de Saint-Pierre au malade venant d'une costé au biens des héritiers de Weathier Bijnens en les biens des héritiers Jacques Depayer d'autre.*[99] Meteen werd duidelijk dat de kwijtschriften die in het genealogisch fonds van de familie Gautier/ Wautier worden bewaard niet zijn verzameld door Michaelina maar wel door Jenne Marie Wautier. Was zij verwant aan Michaelina? Waren de schilderijen grotendeels geërfd en moesten ze daarom worden schoongemaakt en opnieuw ingelijst? Voorlopig is er geen zekerheid. Het lijkt alsof Michaelina Woutiers steeds terugwijkt wanneer men als onderzoeker denkt een tip van de sluier te kunnen oplichten.

De Brusselse Koninklijke Musea voor Schone Kunsten hebben enkele jaren geleden het mansportret van de hand van de enigmatische Michaelina Woutiers van de reserve naar de 'belle étage' verhuisd. Zo prijkt tenminste één van haar werken waar het thuishoort: op een ereplaats in het hart van de stad waar Michaelina samen met haar broer Charles/ Karel jarenlang productief is geweest. Haar virtuoos talent en uitzonderlijke veelzijdigheid verdient de aandacht die totnogtoe enkel aan Artemisia Gentileschi werd gegund. De voorkeur van aartshertog Leopold-Wilhelm voor de exquise schilderijen van Michaelina Woutiers bewijst onomstotelijk zijn onbevooroordeelde smaak en zijn oog voor kwaliteit. Florent du Rieu publiceerde in 1658 in zijn gedichtenbundel een kwatrijn met als titel *Pour Wautier Peintre en Portrait de la Ville de Bruxelle.*[100] Over het geslacht van de engel(en) had hij misschien nog niet nagedacht.

# NOTEN

1 Daniel McNeill, *Het gezicht. Evolutie, geheimen, betekenis, schoonheid*, vert. uit het Engels door Victor Verduin, Amsterdam, 1999, p. 261.

2. Adolph Berger, 'Inventar der Kunstsammlung des Erzherzogs Leopold Wilhelm von Österreich nach der Originalhandschrift im Fürstlich Schwarzenberg'schen Centralarchive herausgegeben', *Jahrbuch der Kunsthistorischen Sammlungen des allerhöchsten Kaiserhauses,* I, Wenen, 1883, pp. CXIX, CXXXIV.

3 Zie voor een overzicht van de verzameling van Leopold-Wilhelm de bijdrage van Hans Vlieghe, 'Frayicheyt ende kunst daer syne inclinatie toe stryckt': beschouwingen over het mecenaat van aartshertog Leopold-Wilhelm tijdens zijn landvoogdij over de Zuidelijke Nederlanden (1647–1656), in deze bundel.

4 Zie Arnout Balis, Frans Baudouin, Klaus Demus e.a., *De Vlaamse schilderkunst in het Kunsthistorisches Museum te Wenen* (*Flandria extra Muros*), Antwerpen, 1987, p. 298.

5 Hoewel Marie-Louise Hairs, *Les peintres flamands de fleurs au XVIIe siècle*, Brussel, 1985, pp. 404–405, betwistte dat de omschrijving 'Jungfrau' zou verwijzen naar een ongehuwde staat, heeft het verder besproken archiefonderzoek tot nog toe deze status bevestigd.

6 Voor referentie aan oudere catalogi van het Kunsthistorisches Museum, Wenen, zie noot 54. Ook het werk van Léopold Devillers, *Le passé artistique de Mons*, Bergen, 1880, p. 51, heeft het over 'Micheline Woutiers'.

7 Zie Günther Heinz, 'Studien über Jan van den Hoecke und die Malerei der Niederländer in Wien', *Jahrbuch der kunsthistorischen Sammlungen in Wien*, LXIII, 1967, p. 149: '*Dieser im Konzept der Kunst Champaignes verwandte Gedanke scheint den Erzherzog-Statthalter angesprochen zu haben, der vier Werke der Künstlerin erwarb. Das Inventar von 1659 erleichtert die Zuschreibung dieser Bilder, die alle noch erhalten sind; doch ist die charakteristische Handschrift ein so deutlich Gemeinsames, dass diese Werke auch ohne äussere Hilfsmittel als Schöpfungen einer Hand erkannt werden können*'. Voor het hoger aangehaalde citaat, zie Ibidem, p. 152.

8 Mons, Archives du Royaume, Régistres Paroissiaux, tables 326, p. 131.

9 Voor een overzicht van schilderessen uit de beide Nederlanden vóór 1800, zie Katlijne Van der Stighelen & Mirjam Westen (ed.), [cat. tent.] *Elck zijn waerom. Vrouwelijke kunstenaars in België en Nederland 1500–1950* (Antwerpen), Gent–Amsterdam, 1999, pp. 126–225 en zie ook: Idem, 'Ravissant of astrant, feminiem of 'onvraulic'? Vrouwelijke kunstenaars in de Zuidelijke Nederlanden tussen 1500 en 1800', in Van der Stighelen & Westen 1999 (zie hoger), pp. 26–41. Voor een theoretisch kader in verband met vrouwen en de door hen beoefende thematiek, zie Rozsika Parker & Griselda Pollock, *Old Mistresses. Women, Art and Ideology*, pp. 1–49; Elsa Honig Fine, *Women & Art. A History of Women Painters and Sculptors from the Renaissance to the 20th Century*, Montclair, 1978, pp. 24–38 (chapter two: 'Flemish and Dutch Artists: Still Life and Genre').

10 Zie onder noot 54 voor de bronvermelding.

11 Voor een overzicht van de positie van artistieke vrouwen in het verleden, zie Katlijne Van der Stighelen, 'De Craquelures van Lady Pictura. Over onbegrepen vrouwen en onderschatte modellen', in Bart Raymaekers en André van de Putte (ed.), *De mens en zijn wereld morgen. Lessen voor de eenentwintigste eeuw*, Leuven, 1999, pp. 222–246.

12 Voor een overzicht van historiografische bronnen waarin aan vrouwelijke kunstenaars aandacht wordt besteed, zie Esther Tobé, 'Parels en penseelprinsessen. Kunstenaressen in drie lexica (1550–1800)', in Van der Stighelen & Westen 1999 (zie noot 9), pp. 58–67 (naast Van Mander en De Bie worden Houbraken, Van Gool en Weyerman geciteerd).

13 Zie o.m. Leen Huet & Jan Grieten, *Oude meesteressen. Vrouwelijke kunstenaars in de Nederlanden*, Leuven, 1998, pp. 150–151 en Katlijne Van der Stighelen, '"Une robustesse extraordinaire chez une femme": de schilderijen van Michaelina Woutiers', in *An Unexpected Journey. Vrouw en Kunst. Woman and Art,* Antwerpen, 1996, pp. 286–295.

14 In de Koninklijke Musea voor Schone Kunsten van België in Brussel worden twee mansportretten van zijn hand bewaard, respectievelijk 1656 en 1660 gedateerd, naast een compositie met de voorstelling van de Opdracht in de tempel van 1661. Zie *Koninklijke Musea voor Schone Kunsten van België. Departement Oude Kunst. Inventariscatalogus van de oude schilderkunst*, Brussel, 1984, p. 323. In Antwerpen is het aan hem toegeschreven *Portret van een heraut van Karel II* te zien. Zie *Koninklijk Museum voor Schone Kunsten Antwerpen. Departement Oude Meesters. Catalogus Schilderkunst Oude Meesters,* Antwerpen, 1988, p. 420. Het museum van Bergen bezit het portret van abt Jacques Neutre (Bergen 1631–1679) met het opschrift 'C. WAUTIER FECIT 1663'. Zie Anne Herickx en Josée Mambour, *Catalogue du Musée des Beaux-Arts de Mons*, Brussel, 1988, p. 33. Tot het patrimonium van de kerk Saint-Servais in Gimnée behoort een doek met 'Het mirakel van Sint-Elooi'. Volgens de gegevens van het KIK draagt het schilderij de signatuur 'Wauthier' en is de voorstelling 1659 gedateerd.

15 Mons, Archives de Royaume, Régistres Paroissiaux, tables 351, 19 augustus 1609; 18 juni 1610.

16 Zie Ilja M. Veldman, 'Magdalena de Passe', in Van der Stighelen & Westen 1999 (zie noot 9), pp. 145–147; I.M. Veldman, *Crispijn de Passe and his Progenity (1564–1670). A Century of Print Production*, Rotterdam, 2000.

17 Cf. Alison McNeil Kettering, *Drawings from the Ter Borch Studio Estate, Catalogus van de Nederlandse Tekeningen in het Rijksprentenkabinet, Rijksmuseum, Amsterdam*, Deel V.1, 's Gravenhage, 1988, pp. XXIX–XXX.

18 Dit was evenmin het geval bij Magdalena de Passe als men zich voor deze bewering baseert op historiografische bronnen. Zie Veldman 1999 (zie noot 16), p. 145.

19 Huet & Grieten 1998 (zie noot 13), p. 155 (slot Hluboká nad Vltavou).

20 De bronnenpublicaties van Jan Denucé en Erik Duverger werden systematisch gefouilleerd. Omdat voor de publicatie van de inventarissen nog geen index beschikbaar is, wordt dit met enig voorbehoud meegedeeld.

21 In de linkerbovenhoek wordt verwezen naar een militaire slag nabij water; mogelijk gaat het om Kallo (1638). Rechts is strijdgewoel op het land in beeld gebracht terwijl in het portret zelf de belegering van een vesting is uitgebeeld.

22 Zie *Hollstein's Dutch and Flemish Etchings, Engravins and Woodcuts ca. 1450–1700*, XVII, Amsterdam, s.d., p. 167, nr. 61.

23 'Excellentie' kan hier niet verwijzen naar kardinaal-infant Ferdinand die in 1641 was overleden en evenmin naar zijn opvolger, aartshertog Leopold-Wilhelm, die pas in 1647 zijn Blijde Intrede maakt. Zie hiervoor de bijdrage van Hans Vlieghe, hoger in deze bundel.

24 In het onderschrift staat: 'A Rege catholico sevir nuper Belgii constitutus, eidem regi a summis belli consiliis, summus in belgicis provinciis militiae regiae, summus item tormentorum bellicor. praefectus, summus et nunc castrorum adversus batavos ductor, fortis ubiq. et quanto maior tanto modestior.'

25 A. Lauro, 'Cantelmo Andrea', in *Dizionario biografico degli Italiani*, XVIII, Rome, 1975, pp. 257–259 (referentie in het volgend artikel aanwezig). Zie ook Nora De Poorter, 'Cornelis Schut als tapijtontwerper: de reeks van 'De zeven Vrije Kunsten', in *Rubens and his World. Bijdragen-Etudes-Studies-Beiträge Opgedragen aan Prof. Dr. Ir. R.-A. d'Hulst*, Antwerpen, 1985, p. 255.

26 Gertrude Wilmers, *Cornelis Schut (1597–1655). A Flemish Painter of the High Baroque* (*Pictura Nova*, I), Turnhout, 1996, pp. 21, 47–48, 120–122, 287, noot 26.

27 Een exemplaar van dit boek is bewaard in de Bibliotheek Godgeleerdheid van de K.U.Leuven: *Eryci Puteani Epistolarum apparatvs Novvs et miscellanevs; in quo Officia familiaria, negotia, studia. Centuria Quarta*, Antwerpen, 1639 (940.226.1/160*/4).

28 J.A. Worp (ed.), *De briefwisseling van Constantijn Huygens (1608–1687), 1. 1608–1634* (*Rijks geschiedkundige Publicatieën*, 15), 's-Gravenhage, 1911, p. 354, brief nr. 686 aan G. Wendelinus: 'Puteanus is uw vriend en de mijne (...)'.

29 J.A. Worp (ed.), *De briefwisseling van Constantijn Huygens (1608–1687), 3. 1640–1644* (*Rijks geschiedkundige Publicatieën*, 21), 's-Gravenhage, 1914, p. 473, brief nr. 3491: '*Mijn vriend Cantelmo, die naar Spanje terugkeert, riep mij naar Mechelen en ik heb hem een Stemma aangeboden, dat slechts in enkele exemplaren gedrukt is. Zeg mij uw oordeel er over. Niet alleen de Cantelmo's, maar ook de Stuart's en de Oranje's worden er in geprezen*' (Leuven, 5 april 1644).

30 Worp 1914 (zie noot 29), pp. 237–238, brief nr. 2874.

31 Ibidem, p. 402, brief nr. 3305: '*Er is geen nieuws. 'D. Andrea Cantelmo aussi faict la mine de ne vouloir bouger du poldre de Namur, ou il entrecouppe les digues, et se barricade contre l'approche de l'infanterie, que jusques ores on n'a pas daigné d'y envoyer, se pouvant bien juger que ce n'est qu'une fanfaronnerie qu'il faict, et que ces Messieurs qui ont assez de peine à se défendre veulent tirer vanité de faire comme les assaillans (...)*" (8 juli 1643). Zie ook Ibidem, p. 407, brief nr. 3316 (eveneens een brief van C. Huygens aan Amalia van Solms): '*Wij hooren nu, dat Cantelmo naar Gent is gegaan; anderen zeggen, dat hij gelegerd is bij St. Jans Steen. Ook is er bericht, dat hij met al zijne troepen de brug bij Antwerpen is overgetrokken*' (16 juli 1643).

32 Ibidem, p. 408, brief, nr. 3319 (s.d.); pp. 410–411, brief nr. 3324 van D. van Cassiopijn aan C. Huygens (21 juli 1643): '*Het singen van Te Deum laudamus in de kerck van Euyndoven en sall ick noyt anders noemen als cantica Cantelmi; het vermaek, dat hy des Vrydachs nam in het clooster te Eyndoven by de monincken, heeft de predicant eensdeels aengeroert. Dan dit wordt my noch gesegt, dat hy vandaer het huys te Heesich wilde neemen, daernaer Crevecoeur, oock St. Andries, vmdat hhet syn naem hadde. Hadde ock noch een matresse, die Geertruyda heeten, meynden G. Berge, ende so voort. Ick can nyet syen, dat syn desseynen so bijster groot syn. Hoewel my gesegt wordt naer het toesluyten van syn Hts. Bryeff, dat hy noch meerder volck soude gecregen hebben*'.

33 Ibidem, p. 416, brief nr. 3336 (brief van C. Huygens aan Amalia van Solms, 29 juli 1643).

34 Zie hoger onder noot 27 voor de volledige referentie, *Centuria tertia*, pp. 98–101.

35 Ibidem, p. 100.

36 *Koninklijke Musea voor Schone Kunsten van België ... 1984* (zie noot 14), p. 323, inv.nrs. 4419 (gesigneerd links boven 'C. WAVTIER/1656) en 4394 (gesigneerd links boven WAVTIER FECIT/ 1660).

37 Zie hiervoor: Rüdiger Klessmann en Bernhard Roosens, 'Le grand Condé. Ein Reiterbildnis von Gonzales Coques in Braunschweig', *Niederdeutsche Beiträge zur Kunstgeschichte*, XL, 2001, pp. 55–58. In Velázquez' *Overgave van Breda* (Madrid, Prado), draagt ook Spinola over het harnas een roze sjaal gedrapeerd evenals Gaspar de Guzman, hertog van Olivares, op het ruiterportret van de hand van Velázquez (Madrid, Prado). Een vergelijkbare roze sjaal treft men ook aan in Velázquez' portretten van Filips IV en Baltasar Carlos (beide Madrid, Prado).

38 Deze bron is ook reeds vermeld door Czech (zie noot 41), pp. 155–156, 216.

39 De informatie werd ontleend aan de website van 'The Research Center for Music Iconography'.

40 *Bloem en tuin in de Vlaamse kunst*, Brussel, 1960, nr. 77; cat.nr. 167; Op dat ogenblik was het Bloemstilleven in het bezit van de Galerie Benito Pardo in Parijs. Zie ook de afbeelding in *The Burlington Magazine*, september 1960. Zie ook Hairs 1985 (zie noot 5), pp. 404–405 (met afbeelding).

41 Van deze gelegenheid maak ik graag gebruik om Prof. Dr. Hans-Joachim Raupp (Bonn) te danken voor zijn collegiale medewerking. Hij bezorgde me een kleurendia van het bloemstuk in de Duitse privé-verzameling en gaf inzage in de bijdrage die Drs. Hans-Jörg Czech schreef over het schilderij in de catalogus 'Stilleben in der Kollektion Sør'. Zie: Hans-Joachim Raupp, *Stilleben und Tierstücke. Niederländische Malerei des 17. Jahrhunderts der Sør Rusche Sammlung*, Münster, 2004, pp. 278-281. De ter illustratie van dit artikel gebruikte foto werd vriendelijk bezorgd door R. Noortman die het schilderij onlangs heeft verworven en het opnieuw verkocht. Met zeer oprechte dank aan Noortman Master Paintings Maastricht voor de welwillende bemiddeling.

42 Op zich is dit feit niet uitermate verwonderlijk. Hetzelfde geldt ook voor een kunstenaar als de 'Pseudo-Vande Venne' die eveneens als Brussels meester panelen aanschafte in Antwerpen. Dit verschijnsel had allicht te maken met de beschikbaarheid van betere paneelmakers in de havenstad. Zo trof men ook op een door Jan Asselyn gesigneerd paneel het merkteken aan van paneelmaker Nicolaes Vrient. Voor zover bekend, verbleef Asselyn niet in Antwerpen. Zie Jan Van Damme, 'De Antwerpse tafereelmakers en hun merken. Identificatie en betekenis', *Jaarboek van het Koninklijk Museum voor Schone Kunsten Antwerpen*, 1990, pp. 227–228.

43 Op het schilderij in de verzameling Benito Pardo komt een vlinder voor. Ook in stillevens van Daniël Seghers uit de jaren dertig komt dit motief reeds voor. Zie bij voorbeeld: Claus Grimm, *Stilleben . Die niederländischen und deutschen Meister*, Stuttgart–Zürich, 1988, p. 43, afb. 11.

44 Het motief kwam o.m. voor op de architraven van de tempel van Vespasianus. Cornelis Galle graveerde dit architectonisch onderdeel naar Rubens (Cf. Ph. Rubens, *Electorum Libri II*, Antwerpen, 1608). Voor afb., zie Marjon van der Meulen, *Rubens Copies after the Antique* (*Corpus Rubenianum Ludwig Burchard*, XXIII, 1), Londen, 1994, tekst ill. 59.

45 Cf. Antoon Erftemeijer, *De aap van Rembrandt. Kunstenaarsanekdotes van de klassieke oudheid tot heden*, Bloemendaal, 2000, p. 15.

46 Michael Jaffé, *Rubens. Catalogo completo*, Milaan, 1989, p. 185, nr. 199.

47 Czech (ter perse) (zie noot 41).

48 Dat zeventiende-eeuwse vrouwelijke kunstenaars uit de Nederlanden manifest uiting geven aan hun vertrouwdheid met de antieke traditie is uitzonderlijk. Een voorbeeld biedt het Zelfportret van Catharina van Hemessen uit 1548 (verwijzend naar *Plinius-Boccaccio-Christine de Pisan*; zie hiervoor Van der

Stighelen 1999 (zie noot 11), pp. 224-226). Een ander voorbeeld biedt een zelfportretje door Anna Maria van Schurman als 'Pudicitia' (Zie Katlijne Van der Stighelen, *Anna Maria van Schurman (1607–1678) of 'Hoe hooge dat een maeght kan in de konsten stijgen'* (*Symbolae Facultatis Litterarum et Philosophiae Lovaniensis. Series B/*, 4), Leuven, 1987, pp. 74–75, afb. 5.

49 Czech (ter perse) (zie noot 41): 'De Heem hängt seine Girlanden jedoch vor dunkle Wanföffnungen, welche die farbige Leuchtkraft und die plastische Fülle verstärken (...)'.

50 Deze hypothese werd reeds eerder gelanceerd door Czech (zie noot 41) enerzijds en door Huet & Grieten 1998 (zie noot 13), p. 156, anderzijds.

51 Guido Jansen & Peter C. Sutton, [cat. tent.] *Michaël Sweerts (1618–1664)* (Rijksmuseum Amsterdam / Fine Arts Museums of San Francisco), Zwolle, 2002, cat. P. 9–21.

52 Jansen & Sutton 2002 (zie noot 51), cat.nr. XXIV–XXV. Ook een aan Sweerts toegeschreven schilderij met de voorstelling van één van de Vijf Zintuigen, met name het Gehoor (Stuttgart, Würtembergische Staatsgalerie, doek, 53,7 x 41 cm) vormt een uitstekend referentiepunt.

53 Jansen & Sutton 2002, pp. 31–34 (met volledige transcriptie van het document).

54 In oudere museumcatalogi staan de schilderijen van de heiligen vermeld als werken van 'F[rans] Wouters' of van 'Magdalena Woutiers' (zoals ze ook in de inventaris van A. Berger (zie noot 2). Cf. Erasmus von Engert, *Kurzgefasstes Verzeichniss der Kaiserl. Königl. Gemälde-Gallerie*, Wenen, 1869, p. 27, nr. 6–7 (als F. Wouters, *Der heil. Joachim; Der h. Joseph*); Eduard r.v. Engerth, *Kunsthistorischen Sammlungen des allerhöchsten Kaiserhauses. Gemälde beschreibendes Verzeichniss, II. Band. Niederländische Schulen*, Wenen, 1884, pp. 560–561, nr. 1401–1402 (als Woutiers, Michelina [sic] oder Magdalena Woutiers, auch Wouters, *Der heil. Joachim, der heil. Joseph*); *Kunsthistorischen Sammlungen des allerhöchsten Kaiserhauses. Die Gemäldegalerie Alte Meister*, Wenen, 1907, p. 246, nr. 1091–1092 (als Magdalena Woutiers, *Der heil. Joachim; Der heil. Josef*).

55 Zie in verband met de functie van David Teniers, de bijdrage van Hans Vlieghe, hoger in deze bundel (p. 66-71).

56 Volgens Heinz 1967 (zie noot 7), p. 150, is 'Das Bild des hl. Joachim in rotem Mantel ist auf der Rückseite signiert: 'MICHELINE WOVTEERS.F.'

57 Deze laatstgenoemde voorstelling werd, evenals het schilderij met Sint-Jozef, in de achttiende eeuw tot een ovaal herleid. Zie Heinz 1967 (zie noot 7), p. 150.

58 Voor referentie, zie Heinz 1967 (zie noot 7), p. 150.

59 Aangaande deze controverse, zie Emmy Toonen, *'Timore Domini': Zuidnederlandse religieuze historieschilderkunst in het bezit van aarsthertog Leopold-Wilhelm (1647–1656)*, onuitg. licentiaatsverhand., Leuven, 1990, passim.

60 Zie in dit verband, de bijdrage van Hans Vlieghe, hoger in deze bundel, p. 62, 66, 73-74.

61 Voor de visie van Hans Vlieghe, vergelijk met zijn bijdrage in deze bundel en zie Hans Vlieghe, *Flemish Art and Architecture, 1585–1700, Pelican History of Art*, New Haven–Londen, 1998, pp. 82–84; zie voor de mening van Edwin Buijsen in: Katlijne van der Stighelen & Edwin Buijsen, 'Michaelina Woutiers' in Van der Stighelen & Westen 1999 (zie noot 9), p. 175.

62 Ibidem. Een vergelijking met Van Loons schilderij 'De vier evangelisten' in Toulouse is eveneens opportuun. Zie [cat. tent.] *Le siècle de Rubens dans les collections publiques françaises* (Grand Palais, Parijs), Parijs, 1977, p. 285 (met afb.). Zie verder: Marcel De Maeyer, *Albrecht en Isabella en de schilderkunst. Bijdrage tot de geschiedenis van de XVIIe-eeuwse schilderkunst in de Zuidelijke Nederlanden* (*Verhandelingen van de Koninklijke Vlaamse Academie voor Wetenschappen, Letteren en Schone Kunsten van België*, 9), Brussel, 1955, pp. 209–210.

63 Het is ook opmerkelijk dat aan Charles/ Karel Woutiers in 1685 werd gevraagd om een schilderij te maken voor het hoogaltaar van de Leuvense Sint-Pieterskerk. Het doek met als thema 'Saint-Pierre se prosternant devant Jésus' bleef niet bewaard. Zie E. Van Even, *Louvain dans le passé & dans le présent*, Leuven, 2001 (anast. herdr. van de uitgave uit 1895), pp. 352, 367.

64 Reeds op 26 april 1625 wou Puteanus Van Loons schilderij van de 'Geboorte van Christus' met het geld van de aartshertogen aankopen voor de kerk van het kasteel van Leuven. Zie De Maeyer 1955 (zie noot 61), pp. 211–212, en cf. doc. 196.; A. Castan, 'Les relations du peintre Théodore Van Loon avec la citadelle de Pallas à Louvain', *Bulletin de l'Académie Royale des sciences, des lettres et des arts de Belgique*, 3e s., t. 7, 1884, pp. 204–208.

65 Sandra Janssens bereidt aan de K.U.Leuven momenteel een proefschrift voor over deze meester.

66 Inv.nr. 77.30.1. Cf. M.-A. Denis, *Le Musée Promenade de Marly-Le-Roi-Louveciennes: Histoire et analyse d'un tableau. L'annonciation de Michaelina Wautier-1659. Petite exposition réalisée autour de la restauration d'un tableau des Collections du Musée*, Louveciennes, 1985; Van der Stighelen & Buijsen 1999 (zie noot 61), pp. 174–175.

67 Heinz, 1967 (zie noot 7), pp. 150–152: 'Das erstaunlichste Werk von Micheline Woutiers ist die grosse Komposition des Bacchuszuges mit mehr als einem Dutzend lebensgrosser Figuren. Die ausmasse und der kräftige Vortrag dieser Malerei haben begreiflicherweise Zweifel an der Zuschreibung, die durch die Inventarnotiz nahegelegt war, aufkommen lassen. Auch Gustav Glück, der die Verwantschaft der Ausführung des Bacchuszuges mit derjenigen der gesicherten Werke erkannte, glaubte ein Gemälde so grossen Formats der Hand einer Frau nicht zutrauen zu dürfen. Doch müssen diese Bedenken bei der Beobachtung der unbedingten Übereinstimmung der Handschrift zurückgestellt werden. Gerade die bärtigen Männerköpfe bieten bis ins letzte Detail gute Vergleichsmöglichkeiten; Zeichnung der Gesichter, Ausarbeitung der Haare, die charakteristische Art und Weise der akzentuierenden Höhungen, alles stimmt so eindeutig mit den Eigenheiten der signierten und gesicherten Werke überein, dass das eindrucksvolle Werk doch als Arbeit der Malerin gelten muss, die somit als eine ebenso begabte wie kraftvolle Künstlerpersönlichkeit erscheint.'

68 Heinz 1967 (zie noot 7), p. 152.

69 Zie in dit verband de bemerkingen die Arnold Houbraken maakte over het belang van de literatuur ter inspiratie van de schilders: Arnold Houbraken, *De groote schouburgh der Nederlantsche konstschilders en schilderessen*, 3 2e dr., Den Haag, 1753, pp. 145–146: 'En wyl zy[=Ariadne] nog haar klachte, en klaachelyke reden, Uyt storte op 't droeve strant, komt Bacchus aangetreden. Met zynen dronken hoop, die afgekeert van tucht Vast schreeuden dat de galm zig spreide tot de lucht, In't naad'ren van de strand. Tien breissende Menaden, Omringden zyne Koets, en evenveel Lenaden, Elk had een lange Spies, bewoelt aan allen kant, Met klimmerbladeren, in hare rechte handt. De satyrs sprongen: en Silenus vol gezopen Kwam met zyn Ezel, traag van agter aangedropen. (...)'. In voetnoot voegt Houbraken ter verklaring toe: 'Lange spies, Thyrsus genaamt, bekleed met wyngerdbladen of klim (...)'.

70 De onder noot 69 aangehaalde Houbraken identificeert de gezellinnen van Bacchus enerzijds als 'menaden' (p. 146: 'Dus worden de vrouwen die Bachus feest hielpen vieren genoemt, naar het Griekse woord, dat dol en razende beteekent'), anderzijds als 'lenaden' (ibidem: 'Dus worden ook de Priesteressen van Bachus genoemt, naar het Griekse woord dat zo veel te kennen geeft, als *van de Pers*, daar men 't sap meê uit de druiven perst'.

71 Een andere mogelijkheid is dat M. Woutiers zich eerder liet inspireren door het esthetische ideaal van de Italiaanse

Renaissance dat kleine, ronde borsten impliceerde. Cf. Marilyn Yalom, *A History of the Breast*, New York, 1997, pp. 49–76.

72 Het verkeerdelijk als Pieter Franchoys geveilde portret ('Portrait of a gentleman said to be Philip Herbert, 5th Earl of Pembroke', doek, 72 x 58,5 cm) werd aangeboden in Londen, Sotheby's, 16 november 1988, als lot nr. 25 (het doek werd geschat op 4000£ maar werd verkocht voor het bedrag van 7280£). Een afbeelding van het bewuste portret bevindt zich in het RKD te Den Haag (dossier Wautier/ Woutiers) met annotatie 'Ch. Wautier (J. de Maere, augustus 1997)'. Hetzelfde portret werd volgens dezelfde bron eerder gesignaleerd op een veiling in Amsterdam, 30 april 1907, als lot nr. 78.

73 *Koninklijke Musea voor Schone Kunsten van België ... 1984* (zie noot 36), p. 323, inv.nr. 4419.

74 Rosi Braidotti, *Beelden van de leegte. Vrouwen in de hedendaagse filosofie*, vert. uit het Engels, Kampen, 1990, pp. 275–282.

75 Zie Vera Fortunati, [cat. tent.] *Lavinia Fontana of Bologna, 1552–1614*, The National Museum of Women in the Arts, Milaan, 1998, cat.nrs. 16, 20 en 30; zie ook: Daniele Benati, *Amor è vivo. Due dipinti erotici di Lavinia Fontana*, Milaan, 2002 (Galeria Marco Riccomini).

76 Zie Keith Christiansen en Judith W. Mann, [cat. tent.] *Orazio and Artemisia Gentileschi*, The Metropolitan Museum of Art, New Haven–Londen, 2001, cat.nrs. 51, 53, 54, 65, 67, 70, 76, 80, 82, 83.

77 Ibidem, cat.nr. 64.

78 Cf. Wayne E. Franits, *Paragons of Virtue. Women and Domesticity in Seventeenth-Century Dutch Art,* Cambridge, 1993, pp. 18–194. Een vrouw diende te behoren tot de eerbare categorieën van 'Maeght en 'Vryster', 'Bruyt' en 'Vrouwe', 'Moeder' of 'Weduwe'.

79 Zie hoger onder noot 48 voor referentie.

80 Cf. Cesare Ripa, *Iconologia*, anast. herdr. van de uitgave in Padua, 1611, New York–Londen, 1976, pp. 314–315. 'Libidine' houdt bovendien een schorpioen in de rechterhand.

81 Op basis van het overzicht bij A. Pigler, *Barockthemen. Eine Auswahl von Verzeichnissen zur Ikonographie des 17. Und 18. Jahrhunderts*, 2, 2e verb. uitg., Boedapest, 1974, pp. 44–46, wordt duidelijk dat het in de schilderkunst van de Zuidelijke Nederlanden geen 'hot topic' was

82 De informatie werd ontleend aan de gegevens in het dossier 'Woutiers/ Wautier' van het RKD te Den Haag. In de catalogus is een afbeelding aanwezig die hier wordt gereproduceerd. Deze gegevens zijn reeds gebruikt in de bijdrage van Pierre-Yves Kairis, 'Foisonnement et diversité: les peintres du XVIIe siècle' in *Un double regard sur 2000 ans d'art wallon*, Doornik, 2000, pp. 321–341.

83 De omschrijving in de veilingscatalogus spreekt verder van een 'Seltenes, Künstlerisch und historisch interessantes Werk' en vermeldt dat het portret 'mit altem, geschnitztem und echtvergoldetem Eichenrahmen' wordt aangeboden. Ook Huet & Grieten 1998 (zie noot 13), pp. 156–157, vermeldden dit werk reeds (zonder afb.).

84 Huet & Grieten 1998 (zie noot 13), p. 157, merkten op: 'De forse Hus wijkt af van de traditie, waarin hij sinds de eerste decennia van de zestiende eeuw voorgesteld werd als een ascetische, graatmagere man met een puntbaardje – daarop gaat ook zijn standbeeld uit Praag terug'. De iconografie van Johannes Hus is vrij beperkt. Het standbeeld van Ladislav Saloun op de Praagse *Staromestske námesti* dateert uit de periode 1903–1915 en levert dus evenmin een referentiepunt. Vergelijk o.m. met het portret van Hus in Jean-Jacques Boissard en Theodor de Bry, *Bibliotheca chalcographia, hoc est Virtute et eruditione clarorum Virorum Imagines,* Heidelberg, 1669 (cf. http://www.unimannheim.de/mateo/desbillons/aport/seite10.htmlte d.d. 20 januari 2003), waarop hij in profiel is te zien.

85 In verband met het anti-Jansenisme van aartshertog Leopold-Wilhelm, zie Toonen 1999 (zie noot 59), pp. 2–3.

86 Zie Katlijne Van der Stighelen, in Jan Baptist Bedaux & Rudi Ekkart (eds.), [cat. tent.] *Kinderen op hun mooist. Het kinderportret in de Nederlanden 1500–1700* (Frans Halsmuseum Haarlem; Koninklijk Museum voor Schone Kunsten Antwerpen), Gent–Amsterdam, pp. 204–205, nr. 51. Ook in Axel Heinrich, *Thomas Willeboirts Bosschaert (1613/14–1654). Ein flämischer Nachfolger Van Dycks* (*Pictura Nova*, IX), Turnhout, 2003, p. 363, nr E70, afb. 177, staat het portret vermeld onder de 'foutief toegeschreven portretten'.

87 Kairis 2000 (zie noot 82), pp. 321–341.

88 Pierre-Yves Kairis, *Le portrait dans le Namurois au XVIIe siècle*, Namen, 2002, pp. 40–41 (met afb.).

89 Brussel, Stadsarchief, nr. 1293, 810v°–811r°. Met oprechte dank aan Dr. Koen Brosens die me deze referentie bezorgde.

90 Brussel, Algemeen Rijksarchief, inv. Nr. T 082, nr. 818, f.° 190.

91 Brussel, Algemeen Rijksarchief, inv. nr. T 082, nr. 818, f.° 194.

92 Brussel, Algemeen Rijksarchief, inv. nr. T 082, 818, f.° 203, 214, 271.

93 Brussel, Stadsarchief, Ste-Goedele, PR 159 (film 59), sub dato: 'Een sinck met 16 ad sab. Carolus Wautier ontrent de selve kercke pal. 6-13'. Voor wat de aanwezigheid van de 16 pbrs [presbyteres] betreft, is een vergelijking mogelijk met de begrafenis van de barones van Poederlee in de Sinte-Goedelekathedraal op 16 september 1698, waar eenzelfde aantal priesters assisteerde.

94 Brussel, Algemeen Rijksarchief, NGB, Notaris Judocus Lemmens, volume 1754 A (microfilm 759272) (niet gefolieerd).

95 Helaas kon er geen registratie worden teruggevonden van het overlijden van Michaelina Woutiers. Voor wat de Sinte-Goedelekathedraal betreft, is er een lacune in de parochieregisters (overlijdens) voor de periode tussen 10 april 1683 en 28 december 1694. Het is zeker niet uit te sluiten dat Michaelina Woutiers dus overleed tussen het voorjaar van 1683 en de winter van 1694. In 1682 was ze immers nog in leven zoals blijkt uit het hoger aangehaalde document (zie hoger onder voetnoot 93).

96 Zo is er allicht geen verwantschap tussen Charles/ Karel en Michaelina Woutiers enerzijds en Hendrik Wauthier anderzijds. In het testament van 'Henricus Wauthier, priester en de canonick van de tweede fondatie der collegiale kercke van S(in)te Gudula alhier' van 2 juni 1722 wordt nergens een vermelding gemaakt die deze hypothese zou kunnen ondersteunen. Zie Brussel, Algemeen Rijksarchief, NGB, Notaris Joannes van der Elst, volume 1414A (microfilm 758687).

97 Brussel, Rijksarchief, Familiearchief, Portefeuille nr. 74 (documenten van 1693 tot 1705); nr. 102 (documenten van 1708 tot 1717), passim (niet gefolieerd).

98 Brussel, Algemeen Rijksarchief, Wijckboeken, T 128/ 2305/7, nr. 169 (zie ook nr. 258–259, 357, 450, 498).

99 Ibidem, nr. 498, 510. In de herfst van 1711 verwierf dezelfde dame nog meerdere panden in dezelfde straat '*une heritage avec ses deux maisons (...) avec leurs appendences et dependences cy devant redigez en rue neufve et apresent nouvellement baptie scituee sur la haute rue vis à vis le cloistrer de S(aint)t Pierre aboutisant du cote des peres capuciens (...)*'. Uit de eerder vermelde rekeningen blijkt wel dat er reeds werken werden uitgevoerd vanaf 1693 toen Jenne Marie nog geen eigenares was.

100 Deze informatie dank ik aan Pierre-Yves Kairis. Voor referentie, zie hoger onder noot ( 82 ). Het is hoogst verwonderlijk dat tot nog toe geen enkele literaire bron kon worden achterhaald waarin over Michaelina of haar werk wordt gesproken. Vergelijk ook hoger onder noot (12).

# Institution and Framework: the New Chapter of Canons and its Choir Space in the St. Jacob's Church, Antwerp*

*Jeffrey M. Muller*

On 21 May 1657, the second day of Pentecost, Ambrosius Capello, Bishop of Antwerp, installed a new chapter of canons in St. Jacob's, the most important parish church in his city (fig. 1).[1] Capello had approved foundation of the new chapter the previous year, after a long process of negotiation.[2] This in itself was highly unusual because most chapters active then were vestiges of the middle ages.[3] By the seventeenth century there grew a weighty body of opinion that attacked canons as an entrenched, conservative elite who tenaciously defended ancient privileges against administrative and liturgical reforms.[4] No wonder, as Marie Juliette Marinus has observed, that they have been ignored by historians who dismiss the chapters as peripheral to the Counter Reformation.[5] If the institution itself has been neglected, this holds even more for the actual spaces – the choirs – which chapters claimed as their exclusive inner sanctums. Yet I will argue that the foundation of the new chapter at St. Jacob's marked an important aspect of the Counter Reformation in Antwerp and that the institution emerged with and defined the character of its choir space in the church. My argument is based on evidence drawn from what is the first attempt to integrate the actual space of the choir with the institutional and social history of a Counter Reformation chapter. It is a history that depends above all on the survival of the choir in St. Jacob's, when most other choir spaces in the South Netherlands have been either destroyed or radically changed by a succession of ideological opponents starting in the seventeenth century. Equally important is the archive of St. Jacob's which exists intact, making it possible to question through different kinds of sources the deeper motives for foundation of the chapter, the social profiles of its canons and benefactors, and the symbolic meanings of the space they shaped for themselves.

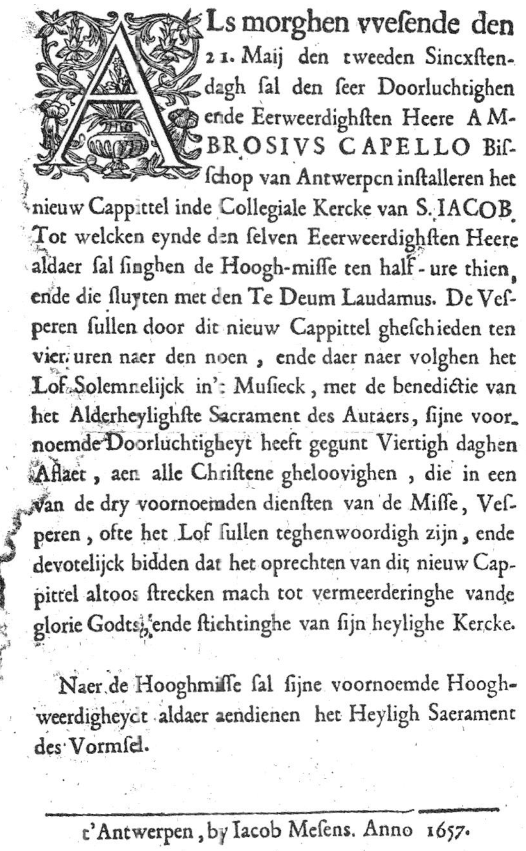
ALs morghen vveſende den 21. Maij den tweeden Sincxſten-dagh ſal den ſeer Doorluchtighen ende Eerweerdighſten Heere AMBROSIVS CAPELLO Biſſchop van Antwerpen inſtalleren het nieuw Cappittel inde Collegiale Kercke van S. IACOB. Tot welcken eynde den ſelven Eerweerdighſten Heere aldaer ſal ſinghen de Hoogh-miſſe ten half-ure thien, ende die ſluyten met den Te Deum Laudamus. De Veſperen ſullen door dit nieuw Cappittel gheſchieden ten vier uren naer den noen, ende daer naer volghen het Lof Solemnelijck in't Muſieck, met de benedictie van het Alderheylighſte Sacrament des Autaers, ſijne voornoemde Doorluchtigheyt heeft gegunt Viertigh daghen Aflaet, aen alle Chriſtene gheloovighen, die in een van de dry voornoemden dienſten van de Miſſe, Veſperen, ofte het Lof ſullen teghenwoordigh zijn, ende devotelijck bidden dat het oprechten van dit nieuw Cappittel altoos ſtrecken mach tot vermeerderinghe vande glorie Godts, ende ſtichtinghe van ſijn heylighe Kercke.

Naer de Hooghmiſſe ſal ſijne voornoemde Hoogh-weerdigheydt aldaer aendienen het Heyligh Sacrament des Vormſel.

t'Antwerpen, by Iacob Meſens. Anno 1657.

Fig. 1. Archive St. Jacob's Church Antwerp, Oud Nr.181/17: placard posted 20 May, 1657

Canons formed colleges of the clergy whose defining purpose was to chant each day the canonical offices of the hours. The principal reason stated for founding the chapter at St. Jacob's was to assure that divine offices would be celebrated there in a fitting manner.[6] Devoting themselves to the praise of God, they were like angels on earth, at least if they fulfilled the requirement to verse themselves in plainchant.[7] David singing psalms and the twenty-four

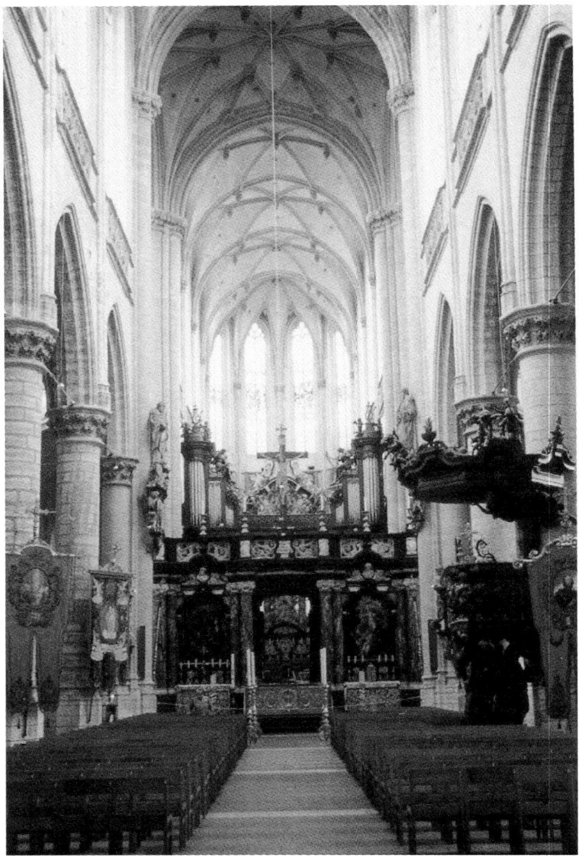

Fig. 2. St. Jacob's Church, Antwerp: view of the nave from the West

elders of *Revelation* (5: 8–10) worshipping the lamb were their biblical counterparts.[8] Priests among the canons also celebrated mass at the high altar. And they were charged as well with the protection of holy relics.[9]

Cold drafts in high vaulted churches and need for good acoustics constrained the canons to meet in the choir which they closed off, with stalls, a rood screen, and an encircling fence that separated them from the rest of the faithful.[10] Chapters also were exclusive social institutions, because each canon was supported for life by a prebend often donated by the noble or wealthy family to which he belonged.[11]

So, I return to the question: why did the bishop of Antwerp approve a new chapter at St. Jacob's in 1656, a branch of the conservative Cathedral Chapter that had opposed the bishop's power ever since the establishment of the episcopacy at Antwerp in 1559?[12] Paradoxically, economic crisis, plague, and poverty were the immediate stimuli to found an institution based on wealth and a conspicuous display of magnificence.

The crisis at St. Jacob's was rooted in the construction of the building and the distinct status the church occupied in its neighborhood and in the city (fig. 2). In 1585, after Catholics regained control of St. Jacob's from the Calvinist regime, the church was still incomplete. In fact, only a wooden roof, at an elevation below the clerestory as it now stands, covered the nave and transept. The choir was a small, makeshift enclosure. Parishioners faced the challenge of vaulting the whole church and building the whole east end including choir, ambulatory, and radiating chapels. This was accomplished in a succession of campaigns met by fervent support from the community. In 1596 the churchwardens who controlled finances and construction, convinced a group of merchants from the parish with whom they chose a new plan for the high choir.[13] Dedicated in 1604, the choir rose only to the height of the piers.[14] Vaults, ambulatory, and chapels followed, until the last of the radiating chapels was completed in 1656. But this also is the year when St. Jacob's was plunged into crisis and the chapter was founded.

In 1647 the churchwardens attached for the first time to their annual account submitted to the city an appendix of outstanding debt they could not pay with the regular income of the church. Most of this debt was incurred from construction of the Rubens and Vincque chapels in the east end of the ambulatory.[15] As the debt increased, income declined. By 1654 plague infested Antwerp. An annual grant awarded by the city to support construction of St. Jacob's had been diverted to care for the sick and dying.[16] In their request for permission to found the new chapter, the churchwardens also maintained that gifts from the parish community had declined under the pressure of Antwerp's weakened economy.[17] Actual figures contradict this claim, because Sunday and feast day contributions to the collection plate, along with total church revenue, remained steady from 1647 through 1655, inside a narrow and predictable range.[18] Nevertheless, by 1656 St. Jacob's did not have enough income to maintain regular services and the church partly suspended operations.[19]

Indeed, in the next year, 1657, St. Jacob's felt its very existence threatened when the Jesuits proposed to build a second church in Antwerp, close by on the site of their college, now the

University of Antwerp. In answer to the churchwardens of St. Jacob's, who tried to block the new Jesuit Church by pleading poverty, the Jesuits countered that the crisis in St. Jacob's actually was the result of excessive construction costs into which foundations for masses had been poured, certainly an extreme measure guaranteed to discourage any further bequests. [20] The Jesuits, who had found a donor willing to pay for their new church, could afford to be self-righteous.[21] But it truly was the pot, just polished, calling the kettle black, because to build their first Antwerp church the Jesuits had piled up an enormous debt that dwarfed what St. Jacob's had to pay.[22] Both cases actually exemplify the ingrained practice of deficit spending, investing in magnificence to attract new wealth, and in both cases, it worked,[23] To solve its problems, St. Jacob's in 1656 needed to find donors who would pay the debt, support construction of the finishing touches on the church, and fund perpetual masses. To thrive, this church had to consolidate its position as the parish church for Antwerp's elite.

The most fitting means to this end, and what would contribute most to the lustre and advantage of the church, would be the erection of a new canonical college, in which the canons could enjoy the distributions of their income only if they participated in the daily services of the choir.[24] Donors already had given three benefices to support three canons, and several other devout people were prepared to follow their example when the authorities granted approval. The first intention and principal end of the foundation was to assure that divine services would be celebrated.[25]

But to found their chapter, the churchwardens of St. Jacob's had first to obtain permission from the dean and chapter of the Cathedral whose most avid interest was to protect their own privileges.[26] Before 1559 when Philip II gave Antwerp its own bishop, the chapter of the Church of Our Lady, the future Cathedral, had ruled the secular clergy of the city, and was still a powerful force in the seventeenth century.[27] The Cathedral Chapter agreed to the founding of a new, subordinate chapter in 1656 for several reasons. St. Jacob's, as they put it, was in respect to the magnificence and size of the building, as well as the number of its parishioners, the leading church of the city after the Cathedral, and divine services had been celebrated there from time immemorial. Recently, however, because gifts dwindled while debt increased, services had begun to slack off, cancelled in part, and consequently stood on the brink of complete abandonment, unless a remedy was found quickly.[28]

The new chapter of canons was the best guarantee that this never would happen again, although in fact St. Jacob's was forced to shut down completely in 1659.[29] Nevertheless, the chapter flourished and grew, with eleven prebends founded by the end of 1662, and twenty-two by 1702, each supported through an endowment of 8,000 or more guilders as well as other sources of income.[30] Nor did shortage of money prevent the completion of major new projects. As I will show, the choir stalls, rood screen, and most of the marble balustrade that fenced the choir off from the ambulatory all were built at great expense, before 1671.

I think Armand Boni, the author of a popular book on St. Jacob's, was mistaken to take the churchwardens at their word and consequently to accuse them of trying to hide poverty with a veneer of luxury.[31] Boni's argument depends on the tenacious historiographical tradition that contrasts the misery of Antwerp in decline with the superficial splendor of the Counter Reformation Church – a brilliantly deceptive façade that masked the actual decay of South Netherlands society.[32] But there was plenty of wealth. Those who had it wanted to spend on founding the chapter and creating its space. At least twice during these years of crisis the churchwardens of St. Jacob's had applied strong pressure to divert money from care for the sick and poor to support for their building.[33] St. Jacob's, according to the Jesuits, did not adequately deal with the real poverty that blighted the Ox Market and Cauwenbergh quarters of the parish.[34] At this stage in my research on the church, I have not yet figured how much of their wealth the merchants and nobles of St. Jacob's Parish gave to the poor. It is certain, however, that by founding the chapter they turned instead to making something exclusively for themselves.

It was the positive will of a clearly defined group in the parish who used the financial need of the church to push through in 1656 a plan already proposed in 1628. St. Jacob's after all was the parish church of Antwerp's wealthiest community where nobles, urban patricians, foreign merchants, and famous artists from Rubens to Artus Quellinus the Younger made their homes.[35] Nicolas Rockox, who stood at the center of this interlocking group of Antwerp's elite, was the driving force behind the campaign to found a collegiate chapter of canons that would ensure eternal prayer and remembrance for his ancestors buried in the St. Dymphna Chapel of St. Jacob's.[36]

In 1628 Rockox, along with dean of the Cathedral Chapter Aubertus Miraeus, treasurer of the Cathedral Chapter Frans Dinghens, city pensionary Jan de Gaverelles, merchants Martin van Ginderdeuren and Jacob Vekemans proposed foundation of the chapter at St. Jacob's. Each pledged to donate a prebend and together they won backing from the Archduchess Isabella who wrote on their behalf to the bishop of Antwerp.[37] Nevertheless, the Cathedral Chapter, jealous of its rights, blocked the plan in 1628 and again, ten years later in 1638.[38] New donors came forward, bringing the number of prebends to eleven, including the Spanish merchant Alonso Carillo, magistrate and merchant Hendrik de Clerck, and Portuguese banker Francisco Lopes Franco. They very accurately represent the interests at play.[39] All three had made important separate contributions to building the east end of St. Jacob's and were at the center of a group of businessmen in the parish who kept a guiding hand on the plans to complete their church. I suggest that they always conceived the choir of St. Jacob's as the fitting inner sanctum for a chapter of canons, and that the east end of the church was shaped to receive the new institution. The expansive size and unified Gothic construction furnished a magnificent ceremonial space for this purpose.

Why then did the plan bear fruit in 1656? The east end of the church had been completed, and claimed a special status that called for perfection, luxury, and embellishment. But this same construction had plunged St. Jacob's into debt. Magnificence of the church and debt were the two major reasons the churchwardens gave in their request for the chapter, almost as if this was a long-term strategy that fell into place. Franciscus van den Bossche, pastor of St. Jacob's since 1640, also was an effective politician constantly active in promoting the interests of his church.[40] Indeed, he occupied the first prebend, and was appointed as first dean of the new chapter.

A new group formed in 1656 to found prebends. The bishop himself, Ambrosius Capello, donated the first which was reserved for the current pastor of St. Jacob's. True to the commitment made in 1628, the estate of Nicolaas Rockox supported a canon through the foundation of the Chapel of St. Dymphna where Rockox's ancestors were entombed. The churchwardens of St. Jacob's funded a third, Anna van Gemert a fourth, Michiel de Backer and his wife Catherina Hazaert a fifth.[41]

I want to point out two features shared among the founders who by 1703 had donated twenty-two prebends, features that defined the character of the new institution. First, at least ten founders belonged to the nobility, and the rest were part of the wealthy merchant class who aspired to that status.[42] Second, twelve of the prebends were occupied at some point by either the donor or a member of the family.[43] This went hand in hand with the so-called lay patronage, according to which the founders and their heirs kept the legal right to present a suitable candidate to fill the prebend whenever it fell vacant.[44] It was thus a long-term family investment. The chapter was therefore the closed preserve of the Antwerp elite and played a dynamic role in the accelerated process of ennoblement that occurred in the city during the late-seventeenth and eighteenth-century.[45] It was precisely the group of merchants living around St. Jacob's in particular who were drawn into this process, because so many of them depended on the trade with the Iberian Peninsula that now dried up. Land and bonds became the new means of investment that brought with it the trappings of nobility.[46] Poverty was not hidden so much as ignored. Nobles and merchants wanted to assure perpetual prayer for themselves and theirs, prestigious sinecures for their younger or less talented sons, and the magnificence of their communal temple.[47]

Once founded by this group, the chapter quickly made its presence fell in the choir. In 1656 the new vaults and ambulatory created an expansive monumental space in the choir. At this point the choir was defined by elements designed more than fifty years earlier for a much smaller space. Inside it was furnished in 1594 with two cantors' chairs and benches for the priests who were supposed to chant the divine offices.[48] It was bordered on the front by a rood screen in place at least since 1604, the entrance from the nave through a pair of wooden doors, each ornamented by five weighty brass columns.[49] At least one altar stood against the rood screen in the nave, on the south side, dedicated to the Three Kings and decorated in 1607 with a triptych painted by Jan Snellincx.[50] As for the high altar, Marten De Vos's *Martyrdom of St. James* and the wings by Ambrosius Francken were set in an elaborate wooden framework carved by Hans Haecht.[51]

When the vaults of the choir were erected in 1641 the whole structure below also was rebuilt to include new crypts and a new foundation for the high altar.[52] During the 1640s and early 1650s generous donors were granted burial under the new choir space. After 1656 the chapter imposed its own presence on the choir, completely transforming the space over a period of thirty years.[53]

In 1658 the canons addressed themselves first to the irregular extrusion of gravestones and cenotaphs which had cropped up over the previous decades. In order to remove any impediment from the divine offices these monuments were banned from the choir. Unifying their corporate sacred space of the choir by pushing out intrusive funerary monuments, the chapter conformed to a general principle of church decoration decreed by Pius V, who, in his Bull of 1566, called for elimination of tombs projecting above ground.[54]

The canons also forbade use of white or black liturgical cloths to 'preserve the congruous variety of colors' in the weekly services at the high altar.[55] Luxury of variety was granted through a lavish gift of liturgical vestments and cloths made by Henrica Duivenvoorde of Wassenaar who died on 4 May 1658. Now they could use a red silk antependium for weekdays, in addition to the altar frontals of white and green damask with gold fringe, and red velvet, along with altar cloths and priestly vestments of many colors, all reserved for use of the chapter.[56] However, the decisions to impose unity of space and to ornament services with a congruous variety of color also put into practice the principles of decoration already applied in the nave of the church, and this suggests a deeper foundation of judgment based on a shared standard of what is beautiful and fitting.

The canons were proudly aware that the magnificence of St. Jacob's made il their fitting home. When fire threatened the church on the night of celebrations that followed the inauguration of the chapter, 'merciful God indulgently averted harm from so excellent a structure' which easily could stand comparison with the illustrious amplitude, furnishing, and construction of the Cathedral, and with the splendor of the Jesuit Church made precious by its gold, pictures, and marble. To be preferred over these, especially the choir of St. Jacob's was admired, by strangers and Antwerpenaars alike, for its 'most exquisite, rare, and illustrious elegance, with so lucid and spacious an ambulatory, and surrounded on all sides, as it were, by marble chapels.'[57] Although the canons could describe their church in terms suitable to a Vitruvian temple, it was still the churchwardens who were explicitly responsible for providing the chapter with all its material needs and for any new decoration and construction in the building.[58] Canons and churchwardens saw eye to eye because they shared the perspective of Antwerp's elite for which St. Jacob's was the most representative sign of community. Nor should the genuine religious character of this view be ignored in our rush to seek signs of power and status, because it was God, after all, who spared the church on account of its elegance, which was addressed, to Him.

In the nave the churchwardens, in 1661, requested that the executors of the estate of Nicolaas Rockox pay for the marble balustrade enclosure – the 'tuin' – still missing from the Rockox Chapel, but an important element in the decoration of the other chapels flanking the north aisle (figs. 3–4). If the executors neglected to do so, said the churchwardens, they would inflict a terrible deformity or disfigurement [misstand] especially on so beautiful and well-proportioned a church, and in the principal line of sight, and thus they would betray the memory of Rockox who had been so solicitous of the ornament of God's house.[59] Good proportions, perfection, symmetry, rich materials, calculated lines of sight, lack of clutter, uniformity tempered by congruous variety of color, all served as guiding principles for the churchwardens and also for the canons in the decoration of St. Jacob's. They aimed at a golden mean of sober, magnificent elegance between the conspicuous splendor of the Jesuit

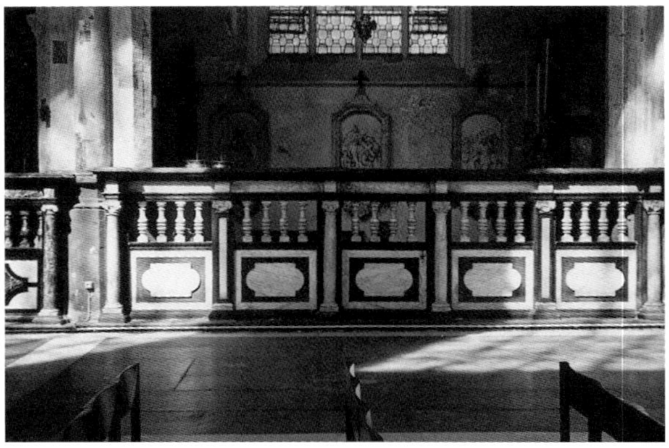

Fig. 3. Balustrade of the Rockox-St. Dymphna Chapel, North aisle, St. Jacob's Church, Antwerp

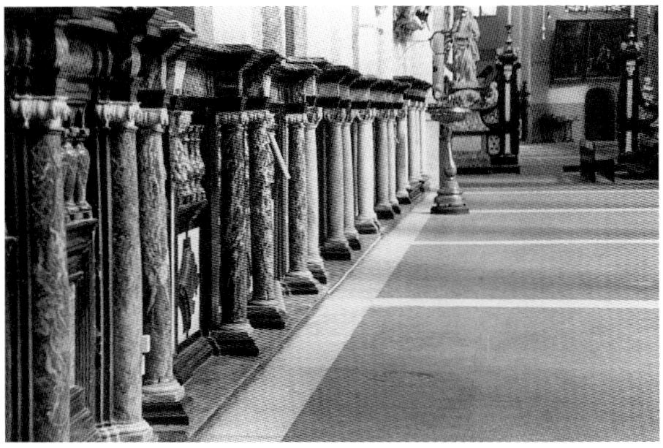

Fig. 4. View from West to East, North aisle, St. Jacob's Church, Antwerp

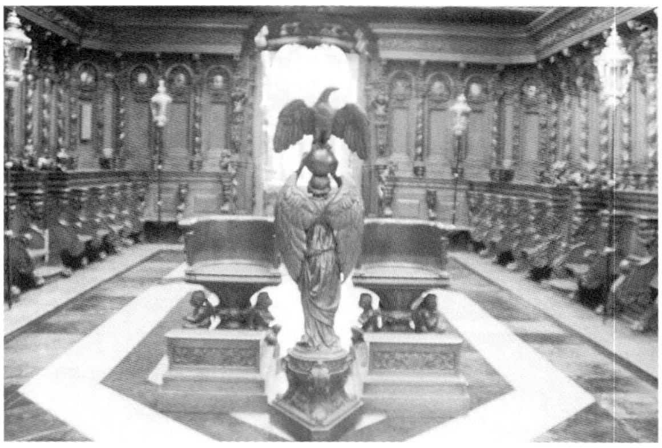

Fig. 5. Choir stalls, from East to West, St. Jacob's Church, Antwerp

Church and the conspicuous poverty of the Discalced Carmelites.[60]

Through this noble ideal of sober magnificence the Antwerp elite symbolised its collective social identity in the parish church. The balustrades in the aisles marked a border between communal parish space and the private domains of the chapels. In the choir the chapter applied the same principles to enclose a separate and exclusive space reserved for a clerical college of nobility. Nevertheless, the churchwardens also paid for and regulated the decoration of the choir. It is evident that everything in the choir depended upon a consensus maintained among the canons, the churchwardens, wealthy donors, and also the pastor who was instrumental in selecting the churchwardens and was himself a canon of the chapter. By extension and law, the bishop of Antwerp and the Magistrate of the city, the heads of the sacred and worldly powers, also had to grant their approval for any significant new decoration.

All these groups cooperated first to build the choir stalls – the decoration that pertained most distinctively to the chapter of canons, framing their space with architecture animated by sculpture in a manner fittingly traditional and innovative at the same time (fig. 5). But it was Joannes Baptista Batkin, Treasurer of Antwerp, who first decided that the two plain benches in the choir were 'undignified' and supplied momentum-generating money and impetus for the project. He donated one stall, the Magistrates of Antwerp the second and third, followed by nobles and merchants of the parish.[61] Pastor, canons, and churchwardens signed a contract on 22 November 1658 with the cabinet maker Octavio Henry for choir stalls al the price of 24 Flemish Pounds or 144 guilders each (six guilders to the Pound), the number of stalls open-ended and dependent on the number of donations that were made mostly in the uniform amount of 150 guilders, enough for one unit. Each stall was to comprise an upper and lower seat, two rows in the long run, that fixed an obvious hierarchy separating the canons above from the assisting chaplains and singers below. Henry also was responsible for having 'curiously' painted the donors' coats of arms on the cartouches carved over the upper seats, thus displaying the noble status of the institution and its founders (fig. 6). A special tablet was carved to identify as well the canon elected cantor of the choir.[62]

Twelve stalls had been build by 1660, and twelve more by 1664. In that last year symmetry was restored with the plan, completed in

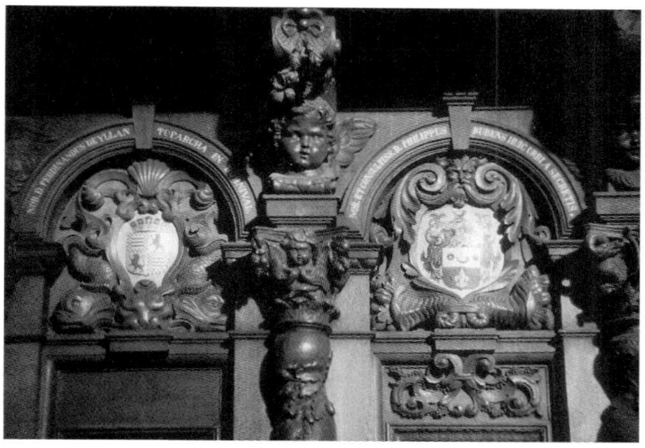

Fig. 6. Coats of arms of Ferdinandus d'Ÿllan, Lord of Bornewal and Philip Rubens, Secretary of Antwerp, repainted by J. van Halle during 1842-1844, choir stalls, St. Jacob's Church, Antwerp

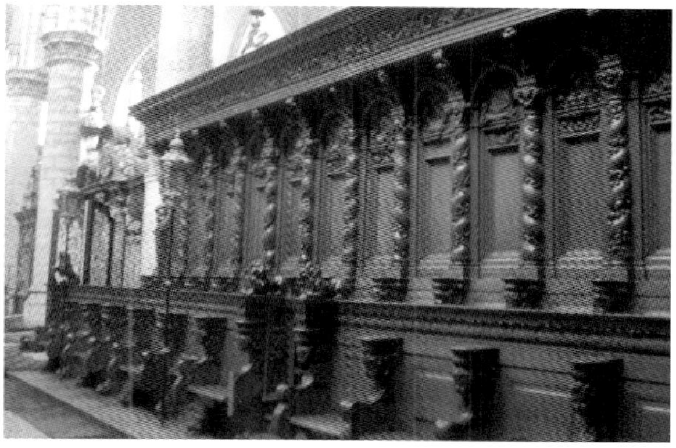

Fig. 7. Choir stalls, South side, St. Jacob's Church, Antwerp

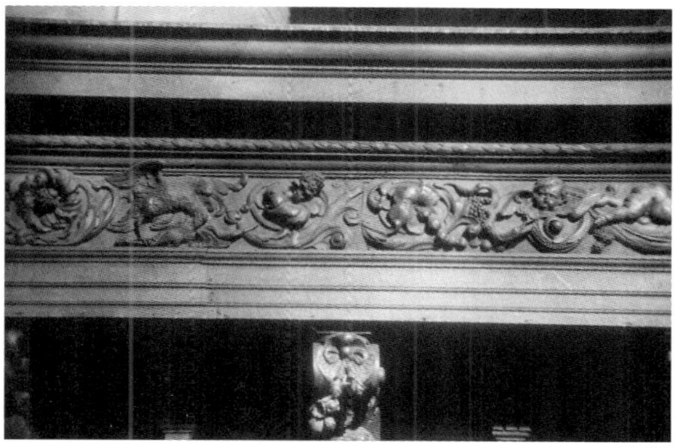

Fig. 8. Frieze, choir stalls, St. Jacob's Church, Antwerp

1670, to add twelve stalls on the north side of the choir, since the previous twenty-four had closed off the cast end bordering on the rood screen, where Henry also had carved the new portal into the nave, and the south side. Altogether, twenty-eight institutional and private benefactors paid for thirty-six choir stalls. Among these donors were several of the Portuguese and other foreign merchants so prominent in the parish, two successive abbots of St. Michael's Abbey, the Confraternity of the Holy Trinity housed in St. Jacob's since its foundation in 1642 and privileged to share the high altar with the chapter, the city of Antwerp, and Philip Rubens, nephew of the painter, and secretary of the city. Most important, Henricus Hillewerve also contributed, marking the start of his influential support for the chapter and decoration of the choir.[63]

The cabinetmaker Henry also contracted to build and install two chairs for the cantors of the choir and between them a beautiful lectern of cabinetmaker's wood in which he could take pride (fig. 5). These pieces define a border between the area of the choir stalls and the high altar and, after the high altar, mark the second ritual center for the canons when they sang the offices of the hours. He who during the Office will sing the reading of the Gospel, 'when he has come to read it in the middle of the choir, where it is usual to read, having genuflected towards the altar, next the canons should make a profound reverence, first from the part of the choir, where the canon performing the office sits, then from the other part.'[64] The cantors' chairs are ornamented appropriately with music making angels, and the lectern is figured as an angel who lifts a globe surmounted by an eagle, a traditional iconography for lecterns, referring to the eagle of St. John Evangelist who stands here for all the Gospels read.[65] When the stalls had been built to the middle pier, Henry promised to remove two fish already standing in the passage from portal to altar, and replace them with beautiful lions – eight of them – one at each corner of the mouldings above the lower stalls (fig. 7). These evoke the lions on the throne of Solomon [l Kings, 10: 19].

The choir stalls in St. Jacob's are innovative first as a strongly unified architectural frame for the space.[66] Here for the first time, the sharply angled, overhanging cornice, the ornamental frieze, and heavy architrave are uninterrupted and trace an emphatic visual enclosure (fig. 8). Spirals and curves in the deeply carved architectural elements infuse the weighty volumes with organic animation. The sculptural deco-

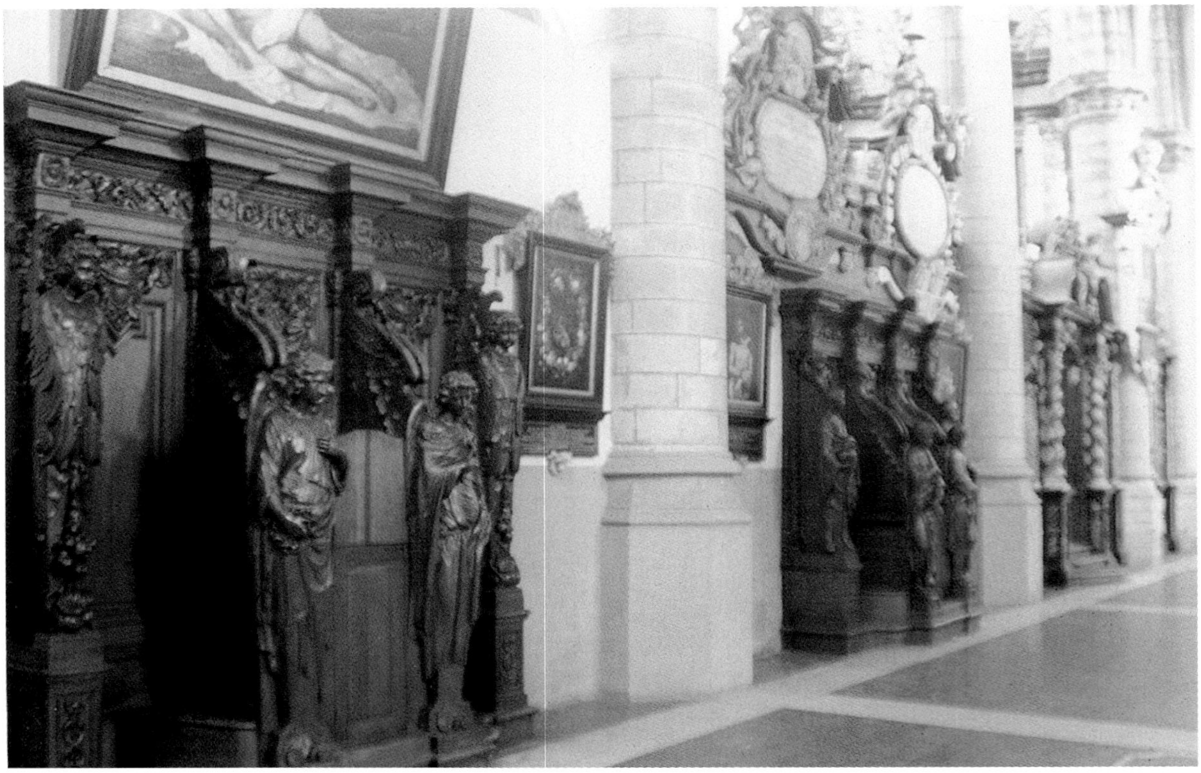

Fig. 9. Confessionals of Canons De Succa and De Wolf, North ambulatory, St. Jacob's Church, Antwerp

ration also is innovative through the profuse variety of motifs that revives late-medieval fantasy in the decoration of choir stalls.[67] In many cases the animals and angels winding around the Solomonic columns contain symbolic meaning as well. Putti angels hold garlands of Eucharistic wheat and grapes, a death's head capital proclaims the vanity of human life, the pelican bleeding to feed her young becomes the type of Christ, and at several places the divine eagle swoops down to destroy an infernal serpent.[68] The result is unified, sober, and magnificent taken as a whole, varied, playful, and graceful in detail. Nobility is served through the coats of arms and through the grave and lustrous richness of the decoration.

In 1664, the same year that the contract was signed to complete the choir stalls, the canons also turned their attention to decorating the exterior of the choir facing south to the ambulatory and the Holy Sacrament Chapel. Behind the choir stalls, on either side, a wall rises just above the canopy of the choir stalls, extending from the rood screen to the middle piers of the choir. These partitions serve an obvious practical function in relation to the choir stalls, offering the canons privacy and protection from cold drafts, and masking the backs of the stalls. Nevertheless, they make an awkward transition, perhaps the least elegant passage in the architecture of the church, It may be that they date from around 1550 when the piers of the choir were built and the Eucharist Chapel was located in the place it since has occupied under a succession of different configurations. Windows into underlying layers of paint on the wall – opened by Lode De Clerck – demonstrate that the heavy mass of the wall was lightened by decorative patterns – appropriately of grapes and ciboria – until white washing became the norm later in the seventeenth century.[69]

In 1664 two canons, Franciscus de Wolf and Bartholomeo de Succa donated to the chapter two confessionals placed against the wall facing the Eucharist Chapel (fig. 9). The date is crucial because the Chapel had been expanded to its present size only in 1664, by incorporating the first private chapel – the Carrillo Chapel – built in the south ambulatory. The canons paid close attention and expressed fervent admiration in particular for the chapel master and silversmith Joannes Moermans whose zeal was instrumental to finishing the project in less than a year's time. Indeed, Canon

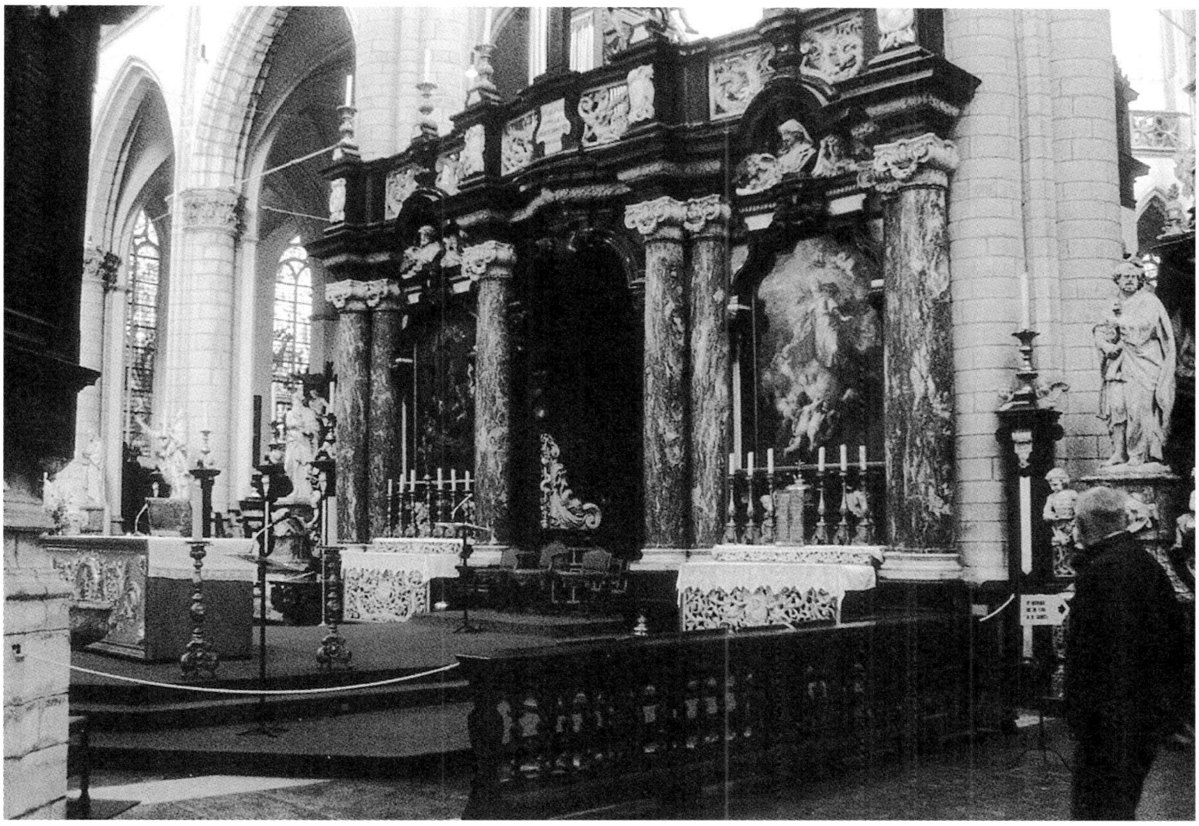

Fig. 10. Rood screen, St. Jacob's Church, Antwerp

Franciscus de Wolf celebrated the first mass at the newly constructed Eucharist Chapel altar, and this close personal involvement suggests to me that the confessionals were a reciprocal gesture of devotion in dialogue with the grand space of the Eucharist Chapel created by the faith of silversmith Moermans.[70] These two confessionals also introduced significant innovation by adapting the figured decorations of confessionals built 1659 into the aisles of the Dominican Church – now St. Paul's – to confessionals that stand as independent structures.[71] In St. Jacob's they belonged to the chapter and were reserved for the donor canons and their successors who heard confession in them, thus extending the space and religious function of the canons out into the more public part of the church. The two confessionals also add decoration that breaks up the Spartan severity of the wall and allows for a more graceful transition.

If these confessionals make a gesture outward, then the next major undertaking, the new rood screen built 1664 to 1671, closed the door on the rest of the parish (fig. 10). The enclosed choir cut off by the rood screen conveyed a strong symbolic message of exclusion that gained greater force through the sustained opposition it rejected. Tearing down rood screens and opening the august ceremony of mass at the high altar to the whole community of faithful was an eloquent gesture of Catholic reform made first – as Marcia Hall has shown – in the great regular churches of Florence – Santa Croce and Santa Maria Novella – and then built into the ritual structure of Jesuit architecture, who were contemptuous of canons sitting like silent statues in their sheltered stalls.[72] In their church at Antwerp the Jesuits substituted a low communion rail that made concrete the vital ritual of the mass and communion at the high altar. Erecting a new rood screen in the Cathedral of Antwerp around 1600 asserted the continued power of the Cathedral Chapter.[73] With the exception of St. Jacob's, Antwerp's parish churches by contrast were for the pastor's flock and the high altars were open in St. Walburgis, St. Andries, and St. Joris.

The act of exclusion at St. Jacob's gains even greater force when seen as a counter move

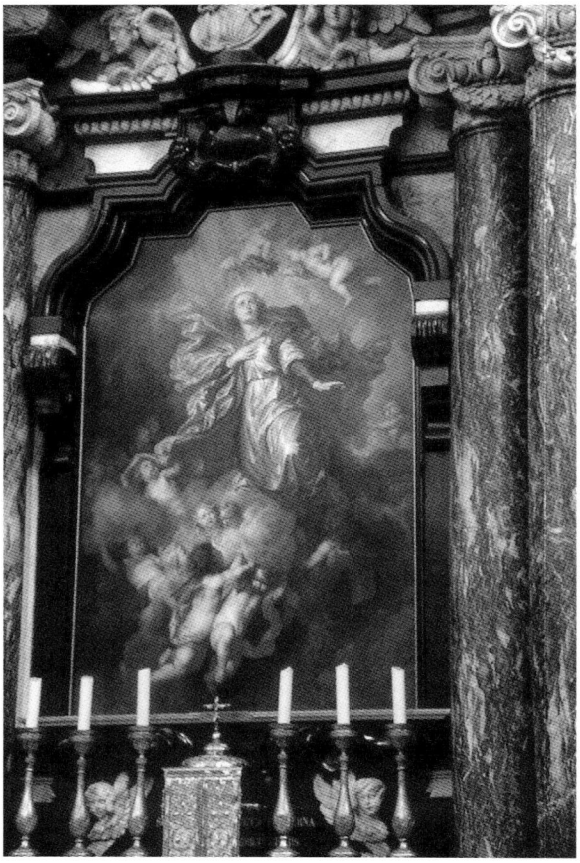

Fig. 11. Theodoor Boeyermans, *Assumption of the Virgin*. Antwerp, St. Jacob's Church, Antwerp

against the Jesuit-driven opposition to rood screens that climaxed at just this time in the controversy fought over the new rood screen for St. Rombout's Mechelen, the seat of the archbishop. During completion of the new high altar for St. Rombout's designed by Lucas Fayd'herbe, the Cathedral Chapter also commissioned a new rood screen. Unexpectedly, sharp opposition was expressed by the city of Mechelen which objected to the cost, by Fayd'herbe who resented anything that would block the view of his work, and by the Jesuit architect Willem Hesius who wanted the make the high altar accessible to the faithful. Despite these objections the canons at Mechelen insisted on a rood screen that would give them complete privacy to hold their services, and they rejected as well a series of ingenious compromises proposed by Hesius in 1664 and 1665,[74] Chapters throughout the South Netherlands fought against elimination or change in design of the rood screens, thus making these enclosures a symbol of conservative tradition.[75]

No similar protests were made against the rood screen at St Jacob's, even though all those involved must have been well aware of the controversy in Mechelen. One of the last in a centuries-long series, the St. Jacob's rood screen is nevertheless a great work of art that anchors the whole church – the center of gravity that brings nave, transept, and choir together through a dynamic union of architecture, sculpture, and painting.[76] It completes the principal view down the nave in a triumphal arch of three bays. As originally planned, the two altarpieces painted by Theodoor Boeyermans in 1670 made the triumph explicit through *The Resurrection of Christ* on the North altar and *The Assumption of the Virgin* on the South.[77] In *The Assumption* that still remains in situ one can see the congruous variety of colors that provides a key to the tenor of taste which represented nobility in Antwerp around 1670 (fig. 11). The dark blue ground picks up the black Dinant stone of the frame, so carefully chosen in 1664 by the churchwardens and the sculptor Sebastian de Neve who directed the project. The shimmering red of the virgin's mantel and the silver white of her gown reverberate with the red and white speekled marble columns. Dark, sober, a little bruised and luxurious, these are the colors that dominate elite Antwerp painting and decoration al this time. If I fall into the lyrical mode of art history to describe this work, it only proves the effectiveness of the strategy, to make the church into a work of art that would insure its own elite status and survival.

In 1669 when the churchwardens of St. Jacob's requested official permission from the bishop to build the rood screen they were instructed to consult Franciscus Hillewerve, canon of the Cathedral and provisor of St. Jacob's.[78] Hillewerve would have approved the project that involved above all the interests of St. Jacob's Chapter not only because he was himself a canon of the Cathedral Chapter, but even more because by that time his brother Henricus had become an active and important supporter of the St. Jacob's Chapter, having contributed to the new choir stalls in 1664.[79] Eventually, Henricus Hillewerve bought himself and his family all the privileges of the choir in St. Jacob's by founding the fourteenth prebend of the chapter in 1683, paying for the magnificent new high altar erected in 1685, and donating a rich treasure of liturgical vestments and ornaments to the service of the high altar at his death in 1694. Wealthy, lord of Heyns and Weert, he was ordained a priest after the death of his wife Margareta Catharina Goos in 1657, and lived in the St. Jacob's Parish, having purchased Rubens's house which he had engraved with his portrait and coat of arms by Jacobus Harrewijn in 1684, the same year he agreed with the canons and churchwardens of St. Jacob's to pay for their new high altar.[80]

What they got is well-known as one of the masterpieces of seventeenth-century Flemish art: St. James in Glory and the Trinity above in the pediment were carved by Artus Quellinus the Younger, the spiral columns by Ludovicus Willemsen, Willem Kerricx, and Norbert Herryn (fig. 12).[81] In return Hillewerve received a daily mass celebrated by the canon of the chapter whose prebend he founded, a key to enter the choir whenever he liked where he could celebrate mass using the ornaments belonging to the high altar, and the crypt directly under the high altar that would be reserved for him and his family.[82]

I will point out only how exclusive the agreement was, and that if Hillewerve was given a key to the inner sanctum, most parishioners could have glimpsed James in glory only as a partly revealed mystery from the side or through the doors of the rood screen that rise to half the height of the portal doors and therefore frame the figure of the saint for anyone looking from a close distance. Chapter, churchwardens, wealthy donor, and the Brotherhood of the Trinity all collaborated in agreement.

By 1685 the choir was mostly complete as it exists today. In less than thirty years choir stalls, rood screen, and high altar had been build to enclose and transform the character of the space. How did the choreography of ritual direct actions of the canons in their sacred offices? A ceremonial printed for the canons of Antwerp Cathedral in 1644, also forms part of the archive of the chapter in St. Jacob's and set the standard that the canons of St. Jacob's were expected to meet.[83] Canons were first required to dress properly in tunic, baretta in hand. Each canon, entering the choir, had to bow deeply to the cross on the high altar, and genuflect if the consecrated host was present. Whenever they passed in front of the high altar, canons were supposed to bow head and shoulders. Canons were warned, once inside the

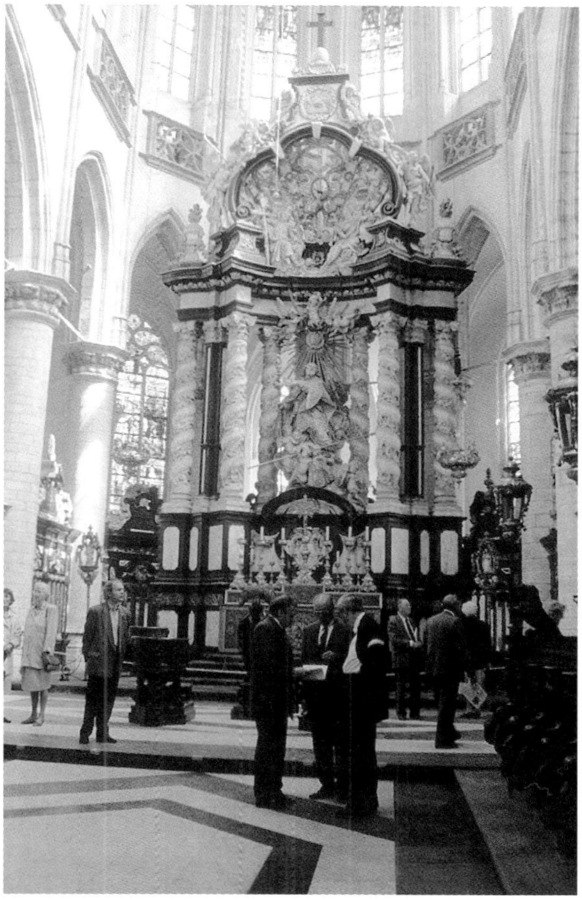

Fig. 12. High altar retable, St. Jacob's Church, Antwerp

choir, to avoid all the time-tested methods for breaking the tedium of what should ideally have been a taste of paradise; what must have seemed to them the eternal singing of praise to God. They were forbidden to talk, laugh, sleep, or read anything not connected to the divine office; exhortations that repeated church-wide and archdiocesan attempts to reform a corrupt practice.[84] It was instead everyone's duty to chant ad alta voce in unison with the choir. No random gestures were allowed, no backs were to be turned, and attention was to be paid in silent contemplative admiration to the divine mysteries. More detailed instructions told the canons when to stand, genuflect, and make the sign of the cross, for each of the liturgical hours.

The new chapter of canons at St. Jacob's was a conservative institution, founded by and for Antwerp's noble, patrician, and merchant elite. Yet it also was part of a dynamic social process through which the institutions of the Catholic Church continually integrated different social groups into the communal body of the Church.

With this prestigious new college of canons celebrating the divine offices in their splendid choir, the status of St. Jacob's as the church of Antwerp's elite was confirmed, and this strategy then made St. Jacob's the most attractive home for the new journeymen's confraternities that Alfons Thijs has shown to be a phenomenon particular to late-seventeenth and eighteenth-century Antwerp; one result of the city's radically changing economy.[85] The workers, who sought status through association, expanded the range of constituencies affiliated with St. Jacob's.

In 1746, eighty years after its erection, one of the canons assembled a manuscript history of the chapter, extracted mostly from the official Acts.[86] At the start, in an introduction, he established St. Jacob's as a place of illustrious beauty, the fitting home for a great institution.[87] Old texts were, as the canon put it, usurped to accomplish this purpose. First he embellished upon the encomium of 1657, which I already have cited. Next, he adapted Carolus Scribani's famous poem in praise of Antwerp, setting St. Jacob's as the most precious jewel in a glorious crown.[88] The history proper of the chapter is, by contrast, a chronicle of lists. It deepens into descriptions of events and place mostly when it touches on the choir. One learns that the choir always was intended for chanting the canonical hours, was rebuilt more beautiful and splendid in 1602, perfected in 1637, graced in 1685 with the new high altar of finest marble, invented, drawn, and constructed by the famous master-sculptor Artus Quellinus the Younger.[89] The choir, in this retrospective view, formed the character of the chapter.

I have shown that this view was not only retrospective. It was accurate. The chapter at St. Jacob's inhabited and decorated the exclusive space of the choir that had been designed in 1596 and then built during the first half of the century, always with the intention to accommodate a large chorus who would chant the divine offices, and with the plan in the works by 1628 at the latest to found a chapter. The attempts made in 1628 and 1638 foundered against the resistance of the powerful Cathedral Chapter. An elite coalition of nobles, patrician magistrates, and merchants succeeded only in 1656. They turned into opportunity the general crisis in which the church's strategy of deficit spending had enmeshed it. The new chapter at St. Jacob's was a unique institution that could emerge only from these circumstances and through the demand created by the ennoblement of Antwerp's elite during the second half of the seventeenth century. After 1656 the canons of the chapter, the churchwardens of St. Jacob's, the patrons of the chapter, and the artists of Antwerp collaborated to build a distinctive and exclusive choir space. It was a place that evolved over a period of thirty years, where innovative and paradigmatic works of art were unified through a dialogue of successive generations who applied the same principles that had guided decoration of the church during the earlier years of the seventeenth century.

# NOTES

* This paper was researched and written during my tenure as fellow in residence at the Netherlands Institute for Advanced Study and I am very grateful for the opportunity. Dr. J. van den Nieuwenhuizen generously made available documents from the Archive of the St. Jacob's Church in Antwerp.

1. Archive St. Jacob's Church Antwerp, Oud Nr. 181/17: placard posted 20 May, 1657.

2. For the official account sec Capello's letter of approval, 12 December 1656, published in *Erectio Subalternæ Ecclesiæ S. Jacobi Antverpiæ in Collegiatuam nec non Capituli in ea Institutio Anno 1656. Eijusdemque Erectionis & Institutionis Confirmatio Pontificia Anno 1705,* Antwerp, 1705, pp. 3–11: Archive St. Jacob's Church Antwerp, Oud Nr. 181/4.

3. In L'abbé A. Pasture, 'La réforme des chapitres séculiers pendant le règne des archiducs (1596–1633)', *Bulletin de l'institut historique belge de Rome,* V, 1925, pp. 5–50, and VI, 1926, pp. 5–69, all chapters extant in the Spanish Netherlands during the reign of the Archdukes had been founded earlier.

4. P. Loupès, *Chapitres & chanoines de Guyenne aux XVIIe et XVIIIe siècles,* Paris, 1985, pp. 15, 34; G. Rauch, 'Das Mainzner Domkapitel in der Neuzeit. Zu Verfassung und Selbstverständnis einer adeligen geistlichen Gemeinschaft (Mit einer Liste der Domprelaten seit 1500). II. Teil', *Zeitschrift der Savigny-Stiftung für Rechtsgeschichte,* XCIII, kanonistische Abteilung, LXII, 1976, pp. 271, 275–278.

5. M.J. Marinus, *De Contrareformatie te Antwerpen (1585–1676)* (*Verhandelingen van de Koninklijke Academie voor Wetenschappen, Letteren en Schone Kunsten van België, Klasse der Letteren.* LVII, 1995, Nr. 155), Brussels, 1995, p. 103. This view is represented, for example, in A. Lottin, *Lille citadelle de la Contre-Réforme? (1598–1668),* Dunkirk, 1984, p. 75, and runs as a leitmotif through C. Hairline and E. Put, *A Bishop's Tale: Mathias Hovius Among His Flock in Seventeenth Century Flanders,* New Haven–London, 2000. For the official efforts to reform chapters by insisting that canons be in residence, properly celebrate the cult, and wear correct ecclesiastical garments, see Pasture 1925 (as in note 3), pp. 5–50.

6. *Erectio* 1705 (as in note 2), p. 5: 'het eerste insicht ende Principaelste eynde van dese fundatie ende oprechtinge is, dat voortaen de Godts diensten, betamelyck souden geschieden.'

7. *Erectio* 1705 (as in note 2), p. 5: holders of prebends in the chapter are to live an honorable life, be of good fame, dress appropriately in religious habit, and gain experience in church song – 'Kerkelycken sanck' – during their first year of residence. We learn what kind of song was meant when we read that only a priest capable of plainchant could substitute for one of the canons in the divine offices: p.10: 'eenen eerlycken Priester die synen simpelen sanck sal connen'. Indeed, each canon was assigned an adjutant chaplain expert in music, with sonorous voice, to keep harmony in the choir on Sundays and feast days, and the anniversary mass for J. de Weerden, celebrated on 1 December 1665, was sung in 'cantu gregoriano'. Archive St. Jacob's Church Antwerp, Oud Nr. 160: Actorum Capituli Liber I, 1656–1675, p. 34 for chaplains, p. 257 for Gregorian chant.

8. Loupès 1985 (as in note 4), pp. 57, 263.

9. Loupès 1985 (as in note 4), p. 61.

10. Loupès 1985 (as in note 4), p. 302.

11. Loupès 1985 (as in note 4), pp. 232–242, comments that collegiate chapters of large cities were dominated by the nobility, but that membership in smaller chapters was more diverse.

12. Marinus 1995 (as in note 5), p. 110, on the Cathedral Chapter.

13. J. van den Nieuwenhuizen, 'Extracten uit de kerkrekeningen van de Sint-Jacobskerk te Antwerpen in verband met de bouw en de stoffering van de kerk', p. 156.

14. Théodore van Lerius, *Notice des œuvres d'art de l'église paroissiale et ci-devant insigne collégiale de St. Jacques à Anvers, précédé d'une introduction historique et rédigée d'après des documents authentiques,* Borgerhout, 1855, pp. 183–184.

15. Archive St. Jacob's church Antwerp, Oud Nr. 52: Kerkrekening 1647–1648, fol. 28r.: February 1647: appended to this account is a: 'Staet vande schulden staenden tot laste vande prochie van St Jacob alhier geprocedeert voorden meestendeel over het maecken van twee cappellen, een sacrastyne met een stuck vanden ommeganck'.

16. Stadsarchief, Antwerpen, K318: 1661 appeal by the churchwardens of St. Jacob's to the Antwerp Magistrate for restoration of the subvention.

17. *Erectio* 1705 (as in note 2), p. 12, Philip IV, King of Castile, etc., consent to erection of the chapter, 5 June, 1657, acknowledges the request: 'inhoudende hoe dat over eenige Jaeren, door het weynigh innecomen vande selve Kercke, ende principalyck door het cesseren van den gewoonelycken offer der gemeynte, om de quaede tyden de selve Kercke in sulcken ellende ende armoede gevallen is, dat by gebreke van betaelinge, den gewoonelycken en dagelyckschen dienst der Priesters heeft moeten geschorst worden tot groot ongerief vande Gemeynten.'

18. Archive St. Jacob's church Antwerp, Oud Nr. 52: Kerkrekeningen 1635–1653; Oud Nr. 58: Kerkrekening 1654–1668 (in guilders and stuivers: 1 guilder = 20 stuivers).

| kerk-rekening | income Sundays and feast days | total income | total expenditures |
|---|---|---|---|
| 1647–48 (n.b. 2 years) | f.1v.: 2,250–13 | f.13r.: 12,313–17 | f.27r.: 12,090–14 |
| 1649 | f.1v.: 1,159–1 | f.15r.: 6,822–9 | f.29v.: 6,591–2 |
| 1650 | f.1v.: 1,222–16 | f.13r.: 6,715–15 | f.26r.: 6,778–8 |
| 1651 | f..lv. 1,329–17 | f.14r.: 9,369 | f.26r.: ,373–12 |
| 1652 | f..lv. 1.016–17 | f.11r.: 13,462–10 | f.26r.: 13,057–18 |
| 1653 | f..lv. 890–19 | f.7v.: 8,460–8 | f.17r.: 7,755–10 |
| 1654 | f..lv. 1,085–7 | f.7v.: 7,466–17 | f.16r.: 7,400–17 |
| 1655 | f.lv.: 1,432–19 | f.8r.: 5,943–8 | f.15v.: 5,901–13 |

See however M.J. Marinus, 'Financiering van de contrareformatie te Antwerpen (1585–1790)', in E. Put, M.J. Marinus and H. Storme ed., *Geloven in het Verleden. Studies over het godsdienstig leven in de vroegmoderne tijd, aangeboden aan Michel Cloet,* Leuven, 1996, p. 249, who charts Sunday and feast day collections for the Cathedral decade by decade from 1586–1675, and observes a significant decline in gifts after 1645 which she correlates with economic conditions – the 'conjuncture'. It also is possible that the decline marked the end of large-scale building projects that previously attracted enthusiastic community support.

19. It is remarkable that the church suspended operations to the extent that it submitted no annual account for 1656: see Archive St. Jacob's Church Antwerp, Oud Nr. 58, Kerkrekeningen 1654–1668. Also see below, note 29.

20. The sore points of this conflict are layed bare in an exchange of charges between the Antwerp Jesuits on the one side, and the pastor and churchwardens on the other, in a series of letters written to the Antwerp Magistrate, recorded in the acts of the St. Jacob's chapter: Archive St. Jacob's Church Antwerp, Oud Nr. 160: 1656–1675: Actorum Capituli Liber I, pp. 38–43. The Jesuits argued that the crisis in St. Jacob's was caused by construction costs 'waer inne gesmolten syn fundatien der missen' and should not count against their plan to build a new church.

21. L. Brouwers, *De Jezuïeten te Mechelen in de 17e en 18e eeuw en hun Xaveriuskerk, de huidige Parochiekerk S.S. Petrus en Paulus,* Mechelen, 1977, pp. 52–53.

22. A. Poncelet, *Histoire de la compagnie de Jésus dans les anciens Pays-Bas. Établissement de la compagnie de Jésus en Belgique et ses développements jusqu'à la fin du régne d'Albert et d'Isabelle* (*Académie Royale de Belgique, classe des lettres et des sciences morales et politiques, mémoires, deuxième série,* XXI), Brussels, 1926, I, pp. 458–483.

23. See O. Hufton, '"Every Tub on its Own Bottom": Funding a Jesuit College in Early Modern Europe', in *The Jesuits II: Cultures, Sciences, and the Arts, 1540–1773,* June 5–9, 2002, Boston College, Chestnut Hill, Massachusetts, pp. 29–30. In her paper Hufton observed that the Jesuits operated in a debt culture where spectacular building attracted donations, that deficit funding was vulnerable in times of crisis, and that subsequent maintenance of what had become less glamorous always presented a problem.

24. *Erectio* 1705 (as in note 2), pp. 3–4: Ambrosius Capello, bishop of Antwerp, 15 December 1656, citing a report from the dean of the Cathedral Chapter.

25. *Erectio* 1705 (as in note 2), p. 4: Ambrosius Capello, bishop of Antwerp, 15 December 1656, citing a report from the dean of the Cathedral Chapter.

26. *Erectio* 1705 (as in note 2), p. 3: Ambrosius Capello, bishop of Antwerp, 15 December 1656, citing a report from the dean of the Cathedral Chapter that is most concerned to assert precedence of the Cathedral Chapter in rank, seating, order in processions, right to wear distinctive habits, and collection of different sources of income.

27. Marinus 1995 (as in note 5), pp. 103–115.

28. *Erectio* 1705 (as in note 2), p. 3, Ambrosius Capello, bishop of Antwerp, 15 December 1656, citing a report from the dean of the Cathedral Chapter: the churchwardens of St. Jacob's have demonstrated: 'hoe inde selve Kercke (wesende ten opsicht van Magnificentie ende groote des Bouws, als oock vande menighte der Parochianten de eerste ende principaelste naer de Cathedrale:) de Goddelycke ende ander dinsten aldaer van immemoriale lyden gewoon synde te doen, nu onlanckx door het verminderen vanden offer ende beswaerenisse der Fabrique, midts des bouws, soodanighlyck hebben begginen te verslappen, dat de selve van nu af ten deele syn geschorst, ende vervolgens staen om geheelyck naergelaeten te moeten worden, ten sy daer tegens behulp middelen worden bedacht, ende cortelinckx de remedie in 't werck gestelt, suggererende tot dien eynde alle de bequaemste middelen ende meest streckende tot luyster ende voordeel vande voorsz. Parochiale kercke, het operechten van een nieuw Canonicael Collegie inde selve.'

29. Archive St. Jacob's Church Antwerp, Oud Nr. 58, Kerkrekeningen 1654–1668.

30. Stadsarchief Antwerp, K316: *Breviarium Capituli Insignis Collegiale ac Parochialis Ecclesiae Sancti Jacobi Apostoli Antverpiae. Decerptum ex libro principali ejusdem Actuaris Anni 1746:* pp. 24–71: de 22. præbendis canonicalibus, quæ hactenus fundatæ et dotatæ sunt.

31. A. Boni, *Antwerpens Roem St. Jacobskerk,* Antwerp, n.d., pp. 146–147.

32. For example, G. Bekaert, '"Che del vero più bella è la menzogna". Facade, Architectural and Moral', in J. Van der Stock ed., *Antwerp Story of a Metropolis 16th-17th Century,* Antwerp, 1993, p. 329.

33. Appeal in 1661 for restoration of the city subvention as discussed above (see note 17); appeal ca. 1660 to the executors of the estate of Nicolaas Rockox for release of funds to pay for a marble balustrade to enclose the Rockox Chapel in St. Jacob's, the cost of which the heirs of the estate, the almoners of the city, would not support at the expense of the poor: Archive St. Jacob's Church Antwerp, Oud Nr. 560, pp. 599–601, transcription by Theodoor van Lerius of a document, no longer traceable, in the Rijksarchief Antwerp, retranscribed by J. van den Nieuwenhuizen, 'Transcriptions of Documents Pertaining to the Chapels in the St. Jacob's Church, Antwerp' (unpublished manuscript), p. 88; see further, below.

34. Archive St. Jacob's Church Antwerp, Oud Nr. 160: 1656–1675: Actorum Capituli Liber I, p. 43: Jesuits testify that they assist the pastor of St. Jacob's in hearing confessions and caring for the sick 'int quartier vande osse merckt, Cauwenberghe, etc waer veel arme gemeynte is'.

35. R. Baetens, *De Nazomer van Antwerpens Welvaart. De Diaspora en het handelshuis De Groote tijdens de eerste helft der 17de eeuw* (*Historische Uitgaven Pro Civitate,* reeks in-8°, nr. 45), Brussels, 1976, I, pp. 279–280, and map, inside II, with color-coded indications of poor and wealthy streets; B. Timmermans, 'Een elite in het zeventiende-eeuwse Antwerpen: Het milieu van de wethouders (1585–1699) en de stedelijke samenleving in een periode van transformatie', licentiaatsverhandeling KU Leuven, Leuven, 1998, p. 162, reproduction of Baetens' map showing in addition concentrations of high rent houses belonging to 60 'wethouders', based on documents from 1659, 1667, 1689.

36. The link between Rockox's involvement in foundation of the St. Jacob's chapter and his family's chapel of St. Dymphna in the church is stated in *Erectio* 1705 (as in note 2), p. 11, referring to the foundation of the prebend 'ter eeren van S. Dympna by wylen Heere Nicolaus Roccocx Riddere'.

37. Archive St. Jacob's Church Antwerp, Oud Nr. 224: title page: Poogingen aengewend in 1628, tot opregting van een Kapittel binnen gezegde kerk. Kopy van een Handschrift voortkomende van de Kapittel Cathedrael deser Stad. fol. 1r: Anno Domini 1628, adspirante Deo, Venerabilis admodum Dominus Aubertus Miraeus, Bruxellensis, Decanus ecclesiae Cathedralis S. Mariae Antverpiae, nec non Vicarius generalis, R.D. Dingens, eiusdem ecclesiae thesaurarius, Illustrus et Amplissimus Dominus Gaverelles, D. Roccox Consul olim Antverpiae, D. Martinus a Ginderdeuren mercator, d. Vekemans, unanimi concordia et resolutione ad maiorem Dei gloriam, S. Jacobi honorem et eiusdem ecclesiae exaltationem, conceperunt singuli singuluas fundare praebendas, quibus collegium erigeretur canonicorum in ecclesia Sti Jacobi Antverpiae. post itaque annos decem per D. Ant. Piperem Pastorem S. Jacobi qui judicabat pias voluntates praeclarorum et fundationes sanctas ad Dei cultum [fol. lv.] tendentes, et ecclesiae elevationem emori non debere, rursum RR. DD. fundatores ad consummandum opus conceptum animos provocavit.'

38. Archive St. Jacob's Church Antwerp, Oud Nr. 224, fol. 1r.: 'Interim intercidit remora eo quod conditiones aliquae proponerentur capitulo cathedralis ecclesiae cuius erat in hanc

capituli erectionem condescendere et consentire quibus se gravatem sentiret.'

39. Archive St. Jacob's Church Antwerp, Oud Nr. 224, fol. 5r., for a list of prospective founders. Also, Archive St. Jacob's Church Antwerp, Oud Nr. 160: 1656–1675: Actorum Capituli Liber I, p. 3, where Abrahamus Meys Presbyter and Joannes Appels are included in the list of willing founders. Alonso Carillo was donor of the first ambulatory chapel in St. Jacob's, built 1626 on the south side and dedicated to St. Alfonso. In 1664 it was torn down and the space was incorporated into that of the adjacent Eucharist Chapel. Hendrik de Clerck (see Baetens 1976 (as in note 35), p. 290) was instrumental in financing construction of St. Jacob's and made large personal contributions to completion of the Chapel of Our Dear Lady (Onze-Lieve-Vrouw). Benito Rodriguez, executor of the estate of Lopes Franco (see Baetens 1976 (as in note 35), I, pp. 226–227, for Lopes Franco) offered the benefice on behalf of Lopes Franco's heirs who also paid for the Lopes Franco Chapel of the Visitation built on the north side of the ambulatory of St. Jacob's.

40. See T. Van Lerius, 'Naemlyst der eerweerde heeren kapellanen of geestelyke opperbestuerders der Kapel van den H. Jacobus, in Het Kipdorp, alsook der eerw. heeren parochianen of pastoors der gemelde kapel, opgerigt tot parochiekerk ten jare 1477. Getrokken uit de archieven der kerk en der oude pastory, de aenteekeningen van wylen den Heer J.-B. van der Straelen en van den Eerw. Heer Carolus de Ridder, onder-pastoor der kerk van de HH. Joannes en Stephanus, voormalige Minimenkerk). tot Brussel, enz.', in *Verzameling der Grafen Gedenkschriften van de Provincie Antwerpen. Arrondissement Antwerpen,* II, *Antwerpen. – Parochiekerken.* 1e Afdeeling / *Inscriptions funéraires et monumentales de la Province d'Anvers. Arrondissement d'Anvers,* II, *Anvers. Eglises paroissiales,* le partie, Antwerp, 1863, pp. XLVII–XLVIII.

41. *Erectio* 1705 (as in note 2. above), p. 11.

42. Stadsarchief Antwerp, K316: *Breviarium* (as in note 30), pp. 24–72: 'de 22. præbendis canonicalibus, quæ hactenus fundatæ et dotatæ sunt'. In the order given, the following prebends were donated by nobles: 2. Rockox; 7. Carenna; 10. Bollaert; 12. Van Horenbeeck; 13. Lopez Franco y Feo; 14. Hillewerve; 17. Vequemans; 20, Della Faille; 21. De Clerck; 22. De Clerck.

43. Stadsarchief Antwerp, K316: *Breviarium* as in note 30), pp. 24–72: 'de 22. præbendis canonicalibus, quæ hactenus fundatæ et dotatæ sunt'. In the order given, the following prebends were occupied by the founder or a member of the family: 4. Ter Linden; 6. Van Tichelt; 7. Carenna; 8. Huart; 9. Mendez; 11. De Lannoy; 12. Van Horenbeeck; 16. De Backer-Vinck; 17. Vequemans; 18. Brughmans-Janssens; 19. Borrekens-Chretien; 20. Della Faille.

44. *Erectio* 1705 (as in note 2), p. 7: ''t Patronaetschap Laicum, ofte recht van te presenteren een bequaem persoon soo dickmaels soodanige prebenden sullen comen te vaceren'.

45. K. Degryse, 'The Aristocratization of the Antwerp Mercantile Elite (17th–18th Century), in C. Lesger and L. Noordegraaf ed., *Entrepreneurs and Entrepreneurship in Early Modern Times: Merchants and Industrialists within the Orbit of the Dutch Staple Market* (*Hollandse Historische Reeks,* 24), The Hague, 1995, pp. 35–34 (many thanks to Bert Timmermans for this reference).

46. The thesis of Degryse 1995 (as in note 45), pp. 36–37.

47. Stadsarchief Antwerp, K316: *Breviarium* (as in note 30), pp. 24–72: 'de 22. præbendis canonicalibus, quæ hactenus fundatæ et dotatæ sunt'. In the order given, the following five prebends were connected to a family chapel or tomb in St. Jacob's: 2. Rockox (St. Dymphna); 7. Carenna (Carlo Borromeo); 10. Bollaert (Peter and Paul); 13. Lopez Franco y Feo (Visitation); 14. Hillewerve (High Altar).

48. Archive St. Jacob's Church Antwerp, Oud Nr. 36, Kerkrekening 1593–1594, transcribed by J. van den Nieuwenhuizen, 'Extracten uit de kerkrekeningen van de Sint-Jacobskerk te Antwerpen in verband met de bouw en de stoffering van de kerk', p. 155, paid to Mr. Otto (Otmar van Ommen), on 3 April 1594, 'voor twee pilaren aen den hogen choor ende twee canterstoelen achtentseventich gulden'. These chairs were altered in 1601 and four long benches for sitting and kneeling were added to the choir in 1605 (Archief St. Jacob's Church, Oud Nr. 41, Kerkrekening 1601–1602, fol. 56v.: 18 March 1601 to Pieter Butkens 'schrynwercker voort vermacken vande Canters stoelen inde hooghen choor': 2 guldens 8 stuyvers; Kerkrekening 1605–1606, fol. 46r.: 28 November 1605, to Hans de Clercq, carpenter, for four long 'sitte ende kniel bancken' for the high choir: 9 guilders.

49. Van den Nieuwenhuizen, 'Kerkrekeningen' (as in note 47), pp. 166–168; Archive St. Jacob's Church Antwerp, Oud Nr. 41, Kerkrekening 1607–1608. Peter Vermeren coppersmith was paid 258 guilders on 16 November 1608 for the eight whole and four half brass columns he set into the choirs doors, with cumulative weight of 470 pounds.

50. Van den Nieuwenhuizen, 'Kerkrekeningen' (as in note 47), p. 165; Archive St. Jacob's Church Antwerp, Oud Nr. 41, Kerkrekening 1605–1606, p. 166; Kerkrekening 1607–1608.

51. Van den Nieuwenhuizen, 'Kerkrekeningen' (as in note 47), pp. 155–156 for De Vos (Archive St. Jacob's Church Antwerp, Oud Nr. 36, Kerkrekening 1593–1594), p. 169 for Francken (Archive St. Jacob's Church Antwerp, Oud Nr. 44, Kerkrekening 1609–1610); for Haecht see Ph. Rombouts and Th. van Lerius, *De Liggeren en andere historische archieven der Antwerpsche Sint Lucasgilde onder zinspreuk: 'Wt lonsten Versaemt',* 2 vols., 1864–1876, reprint, H. Gerson ed., Amsterdam, 1961, I, p. 332.

52. Van den Nieuwenhuizen, 'Kerkrekeningen' (as in note 47), p. 195.

53. At first glance its seems as if Josse Lambrecht van Gemert's *View of the Eucharist Chapel in St. Jacob's Church, Antwerp,* still hanging in the church, offers a tantalizing glimpse of the state of the high altar before it was rebuilt in 1684. However, Van Gemert was active in the mid-eighteenth century, and although his picture is reliable in all its verifiable details, I do not know what visual source he used to reconstruct the long-vanished early-seventeenth-century retable.

54. Archive St. Jacob's Church Antwerp, Oud Nr. 160: 1656–1675: Actorum Capituli Liber I, p. 118: In 1658: 'Ut removerentur a choro divini officii impedimenta, et Altarie congrui coloris varietati serviret, resolverant Capitulares non ultra admittere per hebdomadas Altare summum atro aut candido velamine tegi, nec sandapilas aut cenotaphia in choro subsistere' (So that impediments to the divine offices might be removed from the choir, and to protect the congruous variety of colors of the altar, the chapter has resolved not to admit any longer to the weekly service that the high altar be covered with either a white or black altar cloth, and that biers and cenotaphs no longer remain in the choir). On the elimination of obtrusive funerary monuments, see A. Petrucci, *Writing the Dead: Death and Writing Strategies in the Western Tradition,* trans. Michael Sullivan, Stanford, 1998, p. 86.

55. See the text in note 35 above.

56. Archive St. Jacob's Church Antwerp, Oud Nr. 112/16: fol. 1r: 'Inventaris van alle het silverwerck, ende ornamenten ende iegelycks voordere mobiliere effecten, ende misgewaedt bevonden ende berustence in de sacristye, van het Capittel van de Vermaerde Collegiale ende Parochiale kercke van St. Jacobs binnen dese stadt van Antwerpen, wesende ter dispositie van de Heer Eerw H H: Dken en Canonnicken der selve kercke tot het doen van de Goddelycke diensten in de hooge Choor...

de date 23 marchi 1709 synde den [fol. lv:] bovenschreven Inventaris begonnen ende voltrocken in april 1709 door den eerw H Anthonius Aegidius Chrestien Canonnck ende Actuaris vant Capittel.' fol. 5v.: 'Tweede Classe rackende de Ornamenten van den hoogen autaer. l eene roodt frauweelen (oft caffa) antependium voor onder, oock een voor boven, met gaude canten en fremien... vereerdt door de Edele Joffrouw Henrica van Duvenvoordc gelyck alle de volgende tot nr 50 inclues... 3 een roodt gare damaste antependium... 5 een roodt saeyette antependium om op wercken dagen te gebruycken.' Duivenvoorde's gift was also recorded and inventoried in Archive St. Jacob's Church Antwerp, Oud Nr. 160: 1656–1675: Actorum Capituli Liber I, pp. 106–112; p. 113: she declares to notary Jacques le Rousseau the nature and content of her gift of vestments and cloths: 'begheerende dat allen de selve naer de veranderlyckheyt der feest daghen tot dienst van den voorschreven hooghen choor behoorlyck ende pertinentelyck geimployeert sauden woorden ten eeuwighen daghen.'

57. Archive St. Jacob's Church Antwerp, Oud Nr. 160: 1656–1675: Actorum Capituli Liber I, p. 81, on the danger of fire: 'quod misericors Deus malum clementer avertit, a tam praecellenti structura, Amplitudinem quippe, et praeclarum domus Marianeæ suppelectilem ac fabricam, multi suspiciunt, Ignatianæ vero fabricæ depredicant rarum ab auro, a picturis, a marmore pretium et splendorem, verum tamen exquisitissimam Ecclesiæ Jacobeæ elegantiam, tam spatioso ac lucido ambitu raram ac præolaram [sic, for præclaram?], ac sacellis marmoreis pene [?pæne] undique cinctam, urbis incolæ, et advene pariter admirantur'. My reading of 'ambitus' as ambulatory depends on the unequivocal use of the word to describe this part of the church in Archive St. Jacob's Church Antwerp, Oud Nr. 103: 'Monumenta Epitaphia et Inscriptiones sepulchrales insignis collegiatae parochialis Ecclesiae Divi Jacobi Apostoli Antverpiae,' p. 21: 'Redeamus ad ambitum, ubi Sacellos. S. Trinitatis versus orientem contiguum est aliud Do Ivoni ...sacrum.'

58. *Erectio* 1705 (as in note 2), p. 8: establishment of the chapter, with its obligation to celebrate the divine services: *'sal geensints de fabrique der Kercke ontlasten van te moeten fournieren alle dingen die noodigh sullen wesen, soo van buyten tot de reparatie ende conservatie vande Kercke selfs, als van binnen tot het wel ende hehoorelyck doen der Godts Diensten besonder van den choor: te weten alle behoorelycke Ornamenten, Boecken, Licht, Broodt, Wyn, Sacristaen, Coraelen met hunnen Meester, Organist ende andere oncosten van 't Musieck,* alle welcke gelyck oock alle andere voordere noodige dingen de Fabrique sal moeten leveren ende becostigen' (italics given in original text).

59. J. van den Nieuwenhuizen, 'Transcriptions from the Archive St. Jacobs Church, Antwerp: Chapels and Brotherhoods', pp. 88–89: from the transcription by Theodoor van Lerius in Archive St. Jacob's Church Antwerp, Oud Nr. 560, pp. 599–601, of a document that is no longer traceable, and dated by him without supporting evidence to ca. 1660. The three signatory churchwardens, however, were in office together only in 1661: see Archive St. Jacob's Church Antwerp, Oud Nr. 630, Voortsganck van St. Jacobs Parochie ofte Derde Eeuwe, p. 115 (1659, Wils elected, 1660, Colyns elected), p. 117 (Van Coevoorden elected). It must in any case postdate 1656 because it refers to St. Jacob's as a 'collegiale' church. From the churchwardens of St. Jacob's to the executors of the foundations of Nicolaas Rockox: 'Verthoonen reverentelyck de kerckmeesters der collegiale ende parochiale kercke van S. Jacobs hoe dat de selve schoone kercke nu volmaeckt synde in den bouw, boven andere cieraten, soo verre is geavanceert dat voor alle de capellen der selve, tot seventhien in getal, marmore thuynen syn opgerecht, ende dat onder de seer weynige resterende capellen, die diergelyckx cieract noch vereyschende syn, eene is op den naeme ende onder de heerschappye van den seer edelen heere Nicolaes Rockox, ridder ende oudt borgemeester deser stadt, van salige ende seer loffelycke gedachtenisse, gestaen int principaelste bynaer van de kerck tegens over den preeckstoel, van een schoon autaerstuck en andere ciraeten tamelyck voorsien.' The churchwardens ask the executors to commandeer money from the heirs of the estate, the almoners of the city who do not want to pay for a balustrade at the expense of the poor. In this they are concerned as well for the honor of Rockox, who, if he were alive, 'nu d'andere capellen soo verre geavanceert syn, tot dusdanich goet werck ongetwijfel soude inclineren, als eenen sonderlingen ieveraer voor t'cieraet van t'huys Godts, gelyck hy in vele andere kercken ende capellen menichmael heeft bethoont, oock soude het wesen een groot afsien oft mistant voor eene soo schoone ende geproportioneerde kercke, dat alle andere capellen versien synde van dusdanich cieraet int' principaelste gesicht van de kercke, aen de capelle alleen van eenen persoon van soo groote meriten, t'selve soude comen te ontbreken.'

60. C. Göttler, *Die Kunst des Fegefeuers nach der Reformation. Kirchliche Schenkungen, Ablaß und Almosen in Antwerpen und Bologna um 1600,* Mainz, 1996, pp. 230–231, citing the rules of the Discalced Carmelites, notes as well that they were observed mostly in the breach.

61. Archive St. Jacob's Church Antwerp, Oud Nr. 160: 1656–1675: Actorum Capituli Liber l, p. 96: 1658: 'huc usque canonicorum in choro sedilia, schamna fuerunt, quod indignum ratus dominus Joannes Baptista Batkin urbis Thesaurarius, vir æque religionis ac probitatus amans, novarum sedium Canonicalium fundamenta jecit, primam gratis nec rogatus offerando. Secundum ac tertiam superaddidit senatorum urbis, munificentia'. Other donors: Maria van der Goes, widow of Jacob Roelants, knight, and prefect of the Royal Post; Alexander Balthasar Roelants, Lord of Eenthaut and Royal Postmaster; Ferdinand D'Ÿllan, Lord of Bornewal; Francisco Barraca; Ambrosius Aynescom.

62. Archive St. Jacob's Church Antwerp, Oud Nr. 111/21: Contract over het maeken van de Canonicaele gestoelten in de choor di Anno 1658, 22 9ber. The coats of arms presumably were destroyed during the occupation of the French Republic which banned all signs of nobility, and then repainted by J. van Halle during 1842–1844: Archive St. Jacob's Church Antwerp, Oud Nr. 111/92.

63. Archive St. Jacob's Church Antwerp, Oud Nr. 111/21: extension of contract from 1658, signed and dated 11 December 1664. List of contributors with gifts of 150 guilders unless another figure is given: city of Antwerp, 330; Ambrosius Aynscombe, merchant; Ferdinandus d'Ÿllan, Lord of Bornewal; Joannes Baptista Batkin, treasurer of the city; Petrus and Philippus Helman, brothers; Lord Henricus Hillewerven, Priest; Lord Franciscus Barrola Portuguese; The Worthy Lord, My Lord Norbertus Couweren, abbot of S. Michiels Abbey; Maria Anna Vandergoes, widow of Jacobus Roelants, postmaster, 300; Joannes Butteler, Englishman and merchant; Miss Margarita vanden Bergen, widow of late Jacobus van Hulst; Jacobus van Eyck, former alderman (schepen) of the city; Confraternity of the Holy Trinity, 300; Philippus Rubens, secretary of the city; Marcarius Simeomo, abbot of St. Michiels and successor of Norbertus van Couweren; Joannes Losson, merchant; Joannes Benedictus Engels and Miss Catharina Losson in the week they married; Miss Susanna Wellens; Georgius Shaw Englishman and merchant; Antonius de Gastro Lopez, Portuguese merchant; Sr. Guilielmus Tielemans secretary of Hoboken; Miss Blois, widow of the late Sr. Carolus Batkin, 48; Franciscus van den Bossche, pastor of St. Jacob's and dean of the chapter; Pedro Andrea Martini; Elisabeth Collaert, spiritual daughter; Gabriel Dyck, canon of the church; anonymous married couple.

H. Pohl, *Die Portugiesen in Antwerpen (1567–1648),* Wiesbaden, 1977, p. 356, notes in particular the important contribution made by Portuguese merchants to the project.

64. *Cæremoniæ spectantes ad Officivm Chori: Desumptæ ex Rubricis Breuiarij & Missalis Romani, ac Cæremoniali Episcoporum per Ven. d. Michaelem Baert Presbyterum, Magistrum Cærimonium*

*Ecclesiæ Cathedralis B. Mariæ Antuerpiæ,* Antwerp, 1644, p. 9, under Capvt II. De ordine standi, sedendi, & genuflectendi ab omnibus sub Officiis Horarum, p. 9: 'Cantaturus Lectionem, cum peruenerit ad legile in medio Chori, vbi Lectiones legi solent, genuflectit versus Altare, deinde profundè facit reuerentiam Canonicis, primùm a parte Chori, vbi est Canonicus faciens Officium; deinde ab alter parte'. The Chapter of St. Jacob's was bound to follow the ceremonies observed by the Cathedral Chapter: *Erectio* 1705 (as in note 2), p. 7, under conditions for erection of the new chapter: 'Wat aengaet de Getyden, Loff ende andere Godts-Dinsten sullen hun (soo veel als 't gevoegelyck is) trachten te conformeren met d'observatie ende manieren der Cathedrale Kercke.'

65. See Heinrich G. Lempertz, 'Adlerpult', in *Reallexikon zur deutschen Kunstgeschichte,* ed. Otto Schmitt, Stuttgart, 1937, I, pp. 187–195.

66. C. van Herck, 'Antwerpse Gestoelten uit de Baroktijd', *Jaarboek Koninklijke Oudheidkundige Kring van Antwerpen,* XXVI-II, 1955–1957, pp. 28–29, on the unified composition of the St. Jacob's choir stalls.

67. Without, however, the barbed wit analysed by L. Maeterlinck, *Le Genre satirique fantastique et licencieux dans la sculpture flamande et wallonne: les miséricords de stalles (art et folklore),* Paris, 1940. Maeterlinck, pp. 329–330, describes the St. Jacob's choir stalls.

68. The *Physiologus* was decisive in equating the pelican with Christ (thanks to Fiona Healy for the reference: see *Physiologus,* trans. Michael J. Curley, Austin and London, 1979); see R. Wittkower, 'Eagle and Serpent', in *Allegory and the Migration of Symbols, The Collected Essays of Rudolf Wittkower,* London, 1977, pp. 31–44, on this motif in Christian symbolism.

69. Stadsarchief Antwerp, PK 3198: E. Dilis, MS history of the Holy Sacrament Chapel, p. 10, summarizing the 1598–1599 accounts, notes that among other changes, 'deed men de Kapel opnieuw schilderen: met loofwerck en vergulde ciborie(n).'

70. Archive St. Jacob's Church Antwerp, Oud Nr. 160: 1656–1675: Actorum Capituli Liber I, p. 256: An agreement was signed by the dean of the chapter on 4 November 1664, reserving to Franciscus de Wolf the 'sedem confessionalem ornatam sculptis imaginibus duorum Angelorum Mariæ magdalenæ atque Apostoli Petri positam iuxta confessionalem R.D. Canonici Bartholemei de Succa e regioni sacelli Dm. Carillio ad usam pænitentinum atque in ecclesias ornamentum, datam a R D Canonico Francisco de Wolff' (the confessional seat decorated with sculpted images of two angels, Mary Magdalene, and the Apostle Peter, placed next to the confessional of Canon Bartholomeus de Succa and in the vicinity of the Carrillo Chapel, for use of penitence and ornament of the church, given by Canon Franciscus de Wolff); pp. 257–258, on expansion of the Eucharist Chapel, praise for Joannes Moermans, and celebration of the first mass by De Wolff.

71. S. Zajadacz-Hastenrath, *Das Beichtgestühl der Antwerpener St. Pauluskirche und der Barockbeichtstuhl in den südlichen Niederlanden (Monographien des 'Nationaal Centrum voor de Plastische Kunsten van de XVIde en XVIIde Eeuw',* III), Brussels, 1970, pp. 103–104, 108.

72. M.B. Hall, *Renovation and Counter-Reformation: Vasari and Duke Cosimo in Sta Maria Novella and Sta Croce 1565–1577,* Oxford, 1979, pp. 1–9; Marinus 1995 (as in note 5), p. 103, on Jesuit contempt for canons; J. Steppe, *Het Koordoksaal in de Nederlanden* (*Verhandelingen van de Koninklijke Vlaamse Academie voor Wetenschappen, Letteren en Schone Kunsten van België, Klasse der Schone Kunsten*), Brussels, 1952, p. 44, on Jesuit elimination of rood screens.

73. On the rood screen in the Cathedral see C. van de Velde, 'Art Heritage, The Sixteenth Century', in W. Aerts ed., *The Cathedral of Our Lady in Antwerp,* Antwerp, 1993, p. 192.

74. Steppe 1952 (as in note 70), p. 414, extracts from report by Gulielmus Hesius over the dispute between the Chapter of St. Rombouts and the Magistrate of Mechelen concerning the erection of the new choir enclosure in the church, September 1664; K. De Jonge, et al., 'Lucas Faydherbe als architect', in H. De Nijn, H. Vlieghe, H. Devisscher ed., (cat. exh.) *Lucas Faydherbe 1617–1697. Mechels beeldhouwer & architect,* Mechelen, 1997, pp. 111–113.

75. Steppe 1952 (as in note 70), pp. 383–384.

76. See Steppe 1952 (as in note 70), pp. 376–378, for the genealogy of the St. Jacob's rood screen in the new type introduced at St. Michiel's Antwerp and then developed further in the Dominican Church, Antwerp.

77. Van den Nieuwenhuizen, 'Kerkrekeningen' (as in note 47), p. 211, Archive St. Jacob's Church Antwerp, Oud.Nr. 61, 1670: 'betaelt aen Theodor Boijermans over twee schilderyen onder het oxsael by hem gemaect als per quitantie 100 gl.' The *Resurrection* was replaced in 1693 by Jan-Erasmus Quellinus's *Agony of Death* altarpiece, still in situ. An inventory of the altar's property in Archief St. Jacob's Church Antwerp, Oud Nr. 112/13: fol. 1r. 'Inventarisatie ende aenteeckeninge geschiet op den 29en: november 1700 & naer volgende daegen van alle & Igelycke de naervolgende kerckelycke ornamenten, Ciraten & goederen raeckende de Collegiale & Parochiale kercke van St: Iacob binnen deser stadt van Antwerpen'; fol. 9r.–9v.: Under the rubric: 'De volgende ornamenten worden gebruyckt aenden autaer van den doodtstryt gestaen onder het ocksael' is listed 'Item een autaer stuck wesende de Veryssenisse ons heeren hangende in St. Ians cappelle'. Boeyermans' picture has disappeared.

78. Archive St. Jacob's Church Antwerp, Oud Nr. 111/24: 17 April 1669, request to bishop from churchwardens for permission to build the rood screen is answered with instructions to consult Canon Hillewerve 'van onse cathedrale ende proviseur van de collegiale kercke van S. Jacobs'. Franciscus Hillewerve as actuary of the Cathedral Chapter was instrumental in gaining approval for the erection of the St. Jacob's Chapter: *Erectio* 1705 (as in note 2), p. 9: letter of consent from the Cathedral Chapter 'onderteeckent Franciscus Hillewerven Actuarius'.

79. See note 63.

80. Stadsarchief Antwerp, K316: *Breviarium* (as in note 5), p. 54: the fourteenth prebend was founded and given 'per R. ac Prænobilem D. Henricum Hillewerve viduum Dnæ Margaretæ Catharinæ Goos Toparcham in Heÿns et Weert, deinde Presbÿterum et Prænotarium Apostolicum 19. Augusti 1683. obiit 20. Febr. 1694. / sepultus est in choro ante pedem summi altari, quod ab ipso privato ære munificentia et singulari pietate constructum, fundatum, atque erectum est opera Famosi illius Magistri – artificis Arnoldi Quelini, qui invenit, delineavit, et ex pario lapides sive marmore elegantisime...extruxit Anno 1685.'

81. Archive St. Jacob's Church Antwerp, Oud Nr. 111/32: 'Uyttreksels uyt den Reken Boeck van den Eerweerden en Edelen Heer Henricus Hillewerve nu ter tyd (1846) berustende onder Jonker Ludovicus Le Candele te Antwerpen' [in the hand of Theodoor van Lerius]: 1684–1687 payments of 6,273 guilders 3 stuyvers for materials and work on the altar, including: 26 January 1686 'Noch betaelt aen N.Ikens, voor de tekening van den Autaer 50 guldens'. On the basis of this document it has been asserted by Van Lerius, *Notice des œuvres d'art* (as in note 14), p. 186, that the mysterious Ikens made his drawing as the design for the altar, but I consider this unlikely. It is more probable that he was paid in 1686 to make an

elaborate drawing of the altar which already had been erected by that date.

82. Archive St. Jacob's Church Antwerp, Oud Nr. 385/1: contract between Hillewerve, churchwardens, and Chapter of St. Jacob's, 19 August 1684, also approved by the bishop and Magistrate of Antwerp.

83. *Cæremoniæ spectantes ad Officivm Chori* (as in note 64).

84. P.F.X. de Ram, ed., *Synodicon belgicum, sive acta omnium ecclesiarum Belgii a celebrato concilio Tridentino usque ad concordatum anni 1801,* Leuven-Mechelen, 1828–1858, I, p. 381: decrees and statutes of Provincial Council, Mechelen, 1607: 'Titulus XII. De Officio divino, ac Cærimoniis. Caput I. Cum in Officio divino negotium nobis sit cum Deo ipso, qui Rex regum est et Dominus dominantium, meritò non modò statis semper horis ad chorum conveniatur, sed in eo etiam à fabulis risibus, et aliis insolentiis omninò abstineatur. sub pœna amittendæ distributionis.'

85. A.K.L. Thijs, 'Religieuze rituelen in het emancipatieproces van Vlaamse en Brabantse handwerksgezellen (zestiende-negentiende eeuw)', in *Werken volgens de regels: Ambachten in Brabant en Vlaanderen 1500-1800,* Brussels, 1994, p.240.

86. Stadsarchief Antwerp, K316: *Breviarium* (as in note 5).

87. Stadsarchief Antwerp, K316: *Breviarium* (as in note 5), pp. 1-4.

88. Stadsarchief Antwerp, K316: *Breviarium* (as in note 5), p. 2: the distinctive features of St. Jacob's attract so much attention 'ut non immerito, sed et verissime usurpari liceat vetus illud Antverpiæ eloquium, quod sic sese habet'. See Carolus Scribani, *Antverpia,* Antwerp, 1610, p. 136.

89. Stadsarchief Antwerp, K316: *Breviarium* (as in note 5), pp. 4-6, 54.

# Saintly Patronage: Peter Paul Rubens and Bishop Maximilian Villain de Gand in the Cathedral of Tournai

*Christine Göttler*

Visitors to the cathedral of Tournai may be surprised at seeing, in the first chapel of the south ambulatory, a large altarpiece by Peter Paul Rubens representing the liberation of souls from purgatory (figs. 1, 2). Removed from its original location, disconnected from any altar, and no longer the focus of liturgical actions, special prayers and masses, the 'curious' content of the altarpiece seems to make little sense. Up to the French Revolution, however, Rubens's painting served as a visible marker of a monument that, since the late Middle Ages, had been closely associated with liturgical services for the dead: the 'autel des trépassés', or 'de requiem' or 'de la férie', as this altar at the very end of the choir of the cathedral was alternately called (fig. 3).[2]

Along with the other furnishings and decorations the 'altar of the departed' was destroyed when Tournai cathedral was seized by iconoclasts on 23 August 1566.[3] In the 1630s, however, it was rebuilt and refurnished by Bishop Maximilian Villain de Gand as part of his burial chapel – the bishop thus choosing to be buried at a location associated both with the late medieval rites of commemoration of the dead and the recent Calvinist polemic against this 'false belief'. He decorated the altar with two paintings by Peter Paul Rubens that were, in accordance with his will, displayed back to back. This rather unusual altar type was designed by Bishop Maximilian himself who thus distinguished between a more public and a more private view. The image representing the ascent of souls faced the main altar and advertised the particular services the 'altar of the departed' offered in liberating souls. The painting facing the back wall of the choir chapel illustrated the rarely depicted scène of Judas Maccabaeus's prayer for the dead (2 Maccabees 12, 12–46) (fig. 4).[4] Positioned directly above Bishop Maximilian's tomb it referred to his own hope of attaining salvation while at the same time underscoring his anti-Calvinist stance. The first two books of the Maccabees had been made part of the biblical canon only in 1546, by the Tridentine decree on sacred books. Conversely, Luther viewed these books as apocryphal and the Calvinist Church disregarded them completely.[5]

In this essay, I discuss the tomb monument of Maximilian Villain de Gand in the context of this reform-minded bishop's other donations. His efforts to reinstall and refashion this late medieval altar of the dead appear to have been aimed at the following goals: to reaffirm and maintain the traditional communal practices of suffrages for the dead, and connected with this, to promote the doctrine of purgatory – a doctrine that was at the very center of Catholic practices and beliefs; to strengthen episcopal authority within the church as it was redefined by the Council of Trent; and to establish the bishop's Austrian Habsburg identity at Tournai's most prominent sacred site. I argue that the visual imagery developed for the decoration of this burial chapel both opposed the Protestant doctrine of justification and demonstrated Maximilian's right to exercise control over the cult of the dead in 'his' cathedral. Specifically, he attempted to extend episcopal discipline to the other world, a right that, strictly speaking, was granted only to the pope. By making a formerly communal altar part of his own scrupulous preparations for death, Maximilian Villain also mediated between his episcopal duties to serve the 'common good' and his private interests in achieving salvation.

As we shall see, a complex interaction of motives informed Bishop Villain's vigorous campaign to reconstruct a late medieval altar for the dead: a campaign linking Counter-Reformation propaganda with an ostentatious family cult as well as reflecting the bishop's more

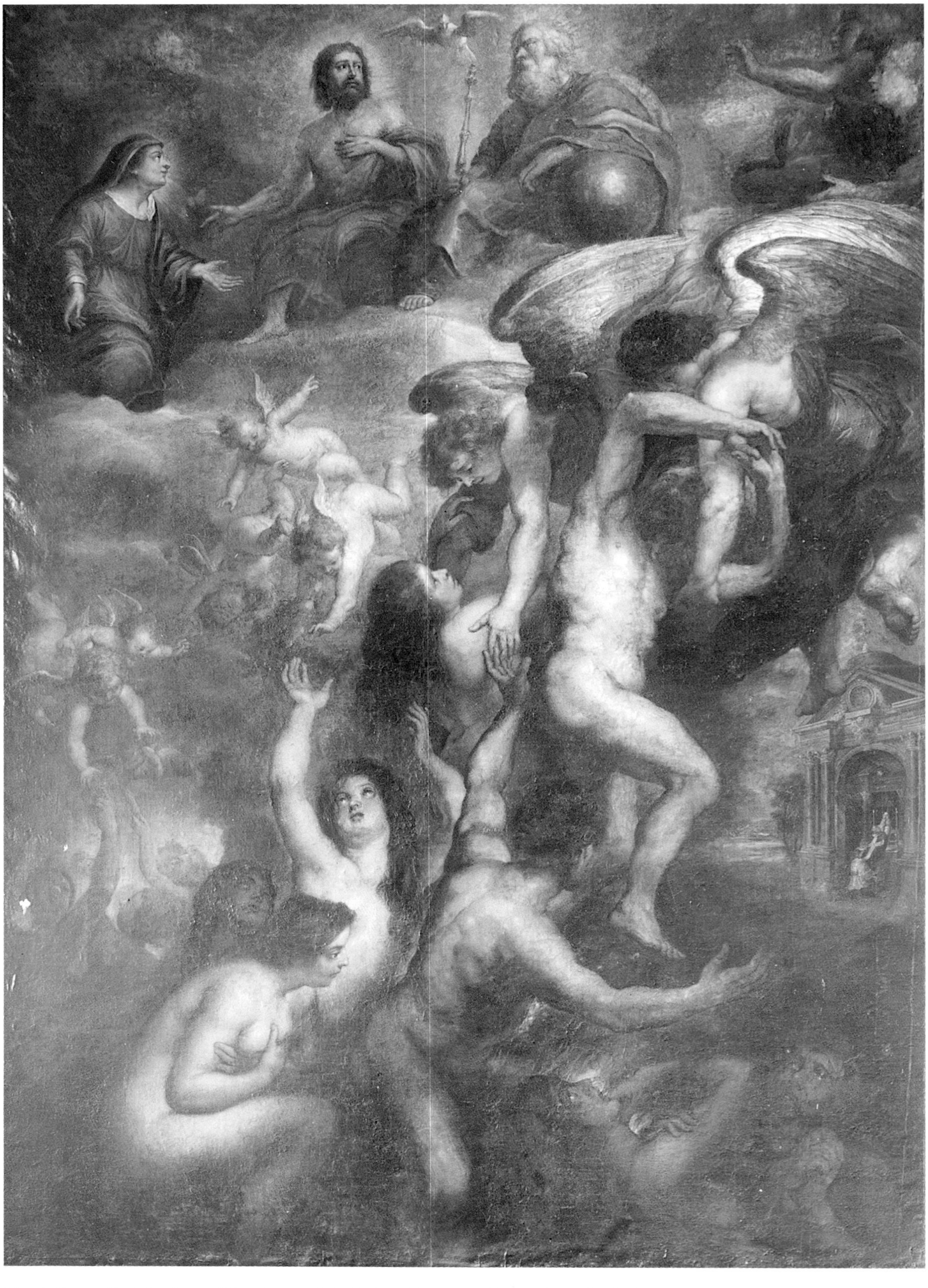

Fig. 1. Peter Paul Rubens, *The Ascent of Souls from Purgatory*. Tournai, Cathedral

personal concerns about a life after death. The various functions and uses of the images Maximilian Villain purchased and commissioned are here of primary concern. With visibility generally being understood as a central feature of Baroque culture and art, scholarly literature has tended to focus on works on a large scale; small art objects that were often deliberately kept out of sight have not yet received much attention. Maximilian Villain's preparation for death included grand and small, magnificent and humble images. The study of his testament is in this context particularly revealing. On the one hand, the bishop planned Rubens's imposing altar decoration with painstaking care; on the other hand, he asked that a cherished 'devotional toy' – a carved prayer-nut (which he describes in detail) – be buried with him.[6] While Rubens's altarpiece is closely connected with the official liturgical services read at this altar for Maximilian's soul, the prayer-nut displays a belief in the magical power of an image not regulated by the official church. The small carved object – often worn as a charm against evil – thus suggests a sense of intimacy and corporeal connectedness that expands and complicates our notion of Baroque religious art as mainly serving didactic and propagandistic aims.

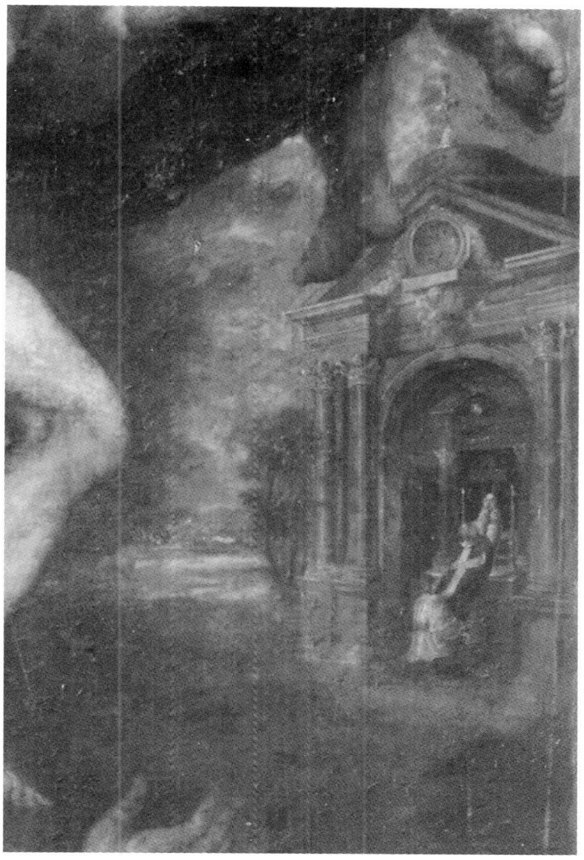

Fig. 2. Peter Paul Rubens, *The Ascent of Souls from Purgatory*, detail of fig. 1

## Iconography of Hope

Down to virtually the smallest detail, the iconography of Rubens's altarpiece was requested by Bishop Maximilian himself. Depicting the passage of the souls from purgatory to paradise, from a dark to a lofty place, the painting expresses eschatological hope. Because the ascending men and women are cleansed from sins, Rubens rendered them as physically beautiful and in their prime. Placing their nearly life-size bodies close to the picture plane, he further enhances the rhetorical effects of the scène. Doubtless some viewers would have also derived aesthetic pleasure from the display of twists and contortions characterizing these figures in upward motion. At the time, with nudity in sacred images being treated with suspicion, Rubens avoided giving offence to religious authorities by shielding all intimate parts from the beholder's sight. Some of the figural motifs are quoted from his own earlier *Large Last Judgment* (c. 1616). The crouching woman holding her arms across her breasts in the foreground, for example, is borrowed from the *Large Last Judgment* but originates, in fact, in an antique prototype.[7] Rubens differentiated the soft and translucent female from compact and muscular male flesh, and, perhaps even more importantly, distinguished between the subtle bodies of the saved souls and the heavy corporeality of those still suffering in the flames. Whereas a number of putto-like angels hasten to deliver souls from the fiery pool at the left, no escape is yet provided for the man and woman in the lower right corner of the painting. Although closest to the beholder's space, their shadowy contours can hardly be perceived against the dark, smoky background. By exhibiting both the proximity and the remoteness of the other world, they seem to function as figures who, according to art criticism of the time, should in some way communicate with the viewer in order to draw attention to the main action of the painting.[8] The imploring gestures of the two figures intensify the emotional engagement of the spectator, while their upward gaze conveys the overall meaning of the representation – hope.

Heavenly forces give reason for such hope: Above, in the sky, the Virgin appeals to Christ who in turn pleads with his father on behalf of the suffering souls; between Christ and God the Father, the Holy Spirit hovers in the form of a dove – a well known motif from depictions of the Last Judgment, used here to demonstrate the efficacy of the intercessory prayer immediately after death. However, the principal agency for the upward movement of the souls seems to be the action taking place at the altar, visible in the background to the right and separated from the main scene (fig. 2). Here, a priest, accompanied by an acolyte, raises the consecrated host, Christ's body. His emphatic gesture marks the climactic moment of consecration from which powerful rewards for the living and their dead kinsmen can be reaped. The moment the elevated host could be seen was, for the faithful, the moment to petition the sacramental Christ for salvation and deliverance from all manner of spiritual and physical disease.[9] Rubens's altarpiece made the salvific potency of this altar, the site of requiem masses, visually explicit. Contemporary viewers would have concretized the ascent of the souls in Rubens's painting in the context of the physical altar it decorated – also referred to by the painted altar in the background of Rubens's composition. Seen from a distance and across a dimly lit room, it would have seemed as though the souls had entered the pictorial space from the actual space of the altar – a sensation which must have had a spectacular effect.

In the present setting, this effect seems to be lost. Although recently restored, there is hardly a trace remaining of Rubens's original brushwork; the work has been repeatedly cleaned, repaired and excessively repainted. The lamentable condition of the canvas was recorded by Jean Baptiste Descamps who, in his *Voyage pittoresque de la Flandre et du Brabant,* published in Paris in 1769, states that 'a bold hand had spoiled this painting, which is washed and repainted everywhere'. Descamps was also told about a letter by Rubens kept in the chapter-house in which the artist described this painting 'as one of the most cherished of all his works'.[10] Further damage to the painting occurred when the work was sent to Paris by the French in 1794, and in its long and wearisome journey back to Tournai cathedral in 1816.[11]

Reflecting the previous age's conflicting views on sacred images, the history of the altar is particularly interesting. The 'altar of the departed' was used, as indicated by its name, for the celebration of requiem masses; it also occasionally served as a kind of communal altar on feast days when the Eucharist had to be celebrated twice.[12] The altar was, thus, almost as prestigious as the high altar, and its image was often honored with gifts. Before Tournai cathedral was seized by the iconoclasts in 1566 and its furnishings and decorations destroyed, a silver statue of the Virgin, donated by Bishop Jean de Thoisy in 1433, was located on the altar.[13] An account of the cathedral, drawn up before the iconoclastic destruction but edited after the events, describes the Virgin as seated on a chair with the Christ child stretching out one hand and holding a rosary of corals 'as if he would incite the faithful to pray for the deceased'.[14]

The monument's original appearance can be reconstructed from Bishop Maximilian's charter of donations (1636),[15] his last will and testament (1639),[16] the travel literature up to the French Revolution, and a handwritten description of the cathedral by Denis-Dominique Waucquier, canon of the cathedral from 1737 to 1761.[17] Waucquier places much emphasis on the highly precious marbles Maximilian Villain chose for the construction of this altar, its tabernacle, and his magnificent tomb behind the altar, He also mentions that the niche above the altar was crowned by a statue of the resurrected Christ, thus underscoring the theme of eschatological hope.[18] The subject matter of Rubens's two paintings is described by Bishop Maximilian in considerable detail:

> 'We took care to decorate this altar with two paintings. The one in front of this altar depicts, in a lifelike manner, the liberation of the faithful souls from the pains of purgatory in a way similar to the meaning of the offertory said in Requiem masses *Lord Jesus Christ, King of Glory etc.;* the one on the reverse side of this altar illustrates the story of Judas Maccabaeus who, according to 2 Maccabees 12, collected twelve thousand drachms to be sent to Jerusalem for a sin offering on behalf of his dead soldiers.'[19]

Maximilian also donated a golden crucifix with his coat of arms for the decoration of this altar.[20]

It becomes clear from the date of his charter of donation that Rubens's works were completed by September 1636. Later, a full-size monument to Bishop Maximilian was added, commissioned perhaps by his nephew François, Maximilian's successor and one of the executors of his last will.[21] Sir Joshua Reynolds briefly described Rubens's paintings and the monument in the notes he took on his second visit to Flanders and Holland in 1785, supplementing his notes with a sketch of the tomb figure.[22] The reclining posture of the deceased, draped in pontifical habits with his mitered head supported by one hand, follows a figural type quite often used in local episcopal tombs.[23]

In early seventeenth-century Flanders the repair and refurbishment of the damaged churches was one of the bishops' main tasks. Work generally started in the choir of the cathedral, the most representative and also the most visible sacred space. Customarily set up in proximity to the high altar, tombs of high ecclesiastics were thus often related to extensive building and restoration programs.[24] In this regard, Maximilian Villain's ecclesiastical donations were no exceptions. His choice of 'this most famous painter Rubens', as Villain calls the artist in his last will, might have been inspired by the high altarpiece that Bishop Antoon Triest had commissioned from him for the cathedral of Saint Bavo in nearby Ghent. Rubens completed that altarpiece, the *Conversion of Saint Bavo,* in 1624.[25]

## Picturing the Mass for the Dead

In Tournai cathedral, however, both the type of altar and its iconographic program are very unusual. Maximilian's source was the revised *Missale Romanum,* standardized by Pope Pius V and first published in 1570. While *The Ascension of Souls from Purgatory* is based on the offertory prayer within a requiem mass (as mentioned by the bishop himself),[26] the subject of the painting facing the bishop's tomb was chosen from the concluding verses of the second book of Maccabees; this passage was read as an Epistle during the commemorative mass on the anniversary of someone's death:

> 'At that time. The most valiant Judas, making a gathering, sent twelve thousand drachms of silver to Jerusalem for sacrifice to be offered for the sins of the dead, thinking well and religiously concerning the resurrection. (For if he had not hoped that they that were slain should rise again, it would have seemed superfluous and vain to pray for the dead.) And because he considered that they who had fallen asleep with godliness, had great grace laid up for men. It is therefore a holy and wholesome thought to pray for the dead, that they may be freed from sins'[27] (2 Maccabees, 12, 43-46).

Judas Maccabaeus's donation to the temple of Jerusalem takes place after his spectacular victory over Gorgias, in which a number of his soldiers are killed. When he and his men arrive to recover the bodies of the dead in order to bury them in their ancestral tombs, they find objects consecrated to the idols of Jamnia under their coats: The possession of idolatrous objects being forbidden by Jewish law, the sin of the soldiers, who plundered the shrines in the battle of Jamnia, is understood as the cause of their death:

> 'Then they all blessed the just judgment of the Lord, who had discovered the things that were hidden. And so betaking themselves to prayers, they besought him, that the sin which had been committed might be forgotten. But the most valiant Judas exhorted the people to keep themselves from sin, forasmuch as they saw before their eyes what had happened, because of the sins of those that were slain' (2 Maccabees, 12, 41-42).

According to the Catholic exegesis, Judas's donation served to redeem the sins of the slain soldiers, thus demonstrating his faith in both the resurrection and the possibility of securing expiation for the dead. As a very recent addition to the canon of the Catholic Bible, the books of the Maccabees gained considerable importance during the later sixteenth-century, particularly in Jesuit exegesis. Chapter 12 served as proof that belief in purgatory was already expressed in the Old Testament. The renowned Jesuit Cornelius a Lapide (1567-1637), for example, concludes from Judas's donation to the temple that the king and high priest of Judea -whom he calls 'pope' or 'quasi pope' -'believed in purgatory, in which the souls after this life are cleansed of guilt'.[28] Defining the 'theft *(furtum)*' of the soldiers as a 'venial sin *(peccatum veniale)*' caused by their greed, Cornelius a Lapide interprets Judas Maccabaeus's prayer and sacrifice within the framework of the Catholic doctrine of sacramental confession, especially emphasizing the dead soldiers' 'sorrow of mind (*contrition*) and the works of penance and satisfaction on their behalf performed by the living:

> 'They (Judas Maccabaeus and his soldiers) thus assumed that the slain soldiers had repented of their theft before death; and that they wiped away the theft's principal part, namely the guilt, through contrition; for this reason only the other part remained, namely the debt of punishment that had to be paid off in purgatory after this life, but that could be atoned for through sacrifice, in order to wipe away the sin completely; and that in this way their souls, spared from the punishments of purgatory, were carried over to the limbo of the fathers or to the bosom of Abraham.'[29]

In the later Middle Ages, intense remorse – contrition – often expressed by tears, became the essential step in the penitential process, which would absolve a sinner from guilt ('peccatum');[30] at one's death, outstanding debts of punishment ('poena peccatorum') had to be paid off in purgatory, but could be drastically reduced through 'suffrages of the faithful', in particular through the Sacrifice of the mass, prayers, alms and other works of piety'. The Council of Trent confirmed these late medieval teachings,[31] which, on the one hand, must have had a soothing effect on the conscience of an anxious sinner; although, on the other hand, it remained undecided whether the suffrages undertaken by the living would indeed suffice to redeem one's sins after death. Exchanging the word 'peccatis' with 'a poenis peccatorum'), Cornelius a Lapide manipulates 2 Maccabees 12, 46, using the biblical text for his own argumentative ends:

> 'SANCTA ERGO ET SALUBRIS (Graece, εὐσεβής, id est pia) est cogitatio pro defunctis exorare ut a peccatis (id est a poenis peccatorum) solvantur – It is therefore a holy and wholesome (Greek, εὐσεβής, that is to say pious) thought to pray for the dead, that they may be freed from sins (that is to say from punishment for their sins).'[32]

Consequently, Cornelius views this verse as the 'epiphonema of canonical Scripture that affirms the belief of the ancient Synagogue in purgatory and the suffrages for the souls detained there'[33] for further reading, he directs the reader to *The State of the Souls in Purgatory* by the Spanish Jesuit Martin de Roa (1561-1637) – translated into several languages, that treatise would soon became a bestseller;[34] Cornelius also draws on Saint Augustine in support of his argument.[35]

In planning the iconography of the altar decoration, Maximilian Villain must have consulted, alongside Cornelius a Lapide's writings, the commentary on the Old and New Testament by the Antwerp Jesuit Jacob Tirinus (1580-1636); published in Antwerp by Martinus Nutius in 1632, this was a book that he owned.[36] Tirinus, a student of Cornelius a Lapide, was the first superior of the Professed House in Antwerp and played an important role in the construction of the new Jesuit church. In his commentary on verse 43 of this chapter ('And making a garnering, he sent twelve thousand drachms of silver to Jerusalem for sacrifice to be offered for the sins of the dead, thinking well and religiously concerning the resurrection'), following his teacher's views, Tirinus speaks of the 'very clear evidence of the Scripture concerning the suffrages for the dead. And the truly noble deed and example of the Pope and the Church of that time was not only related, but also praised and approved by the Holy Author, that is to say by the Holy Spirit, as Serarius, Bellarminus and other doctors extensively explain.' Tirinus goes on to defend the canonicity of the books of the Maccabees against Sebastian Munster and other 'heretics' such as Paulus Fagius.[37] In addition, Bishop Maximilian must have known the biblical commentary by the German Jesuit Nicolas Serarius (1555-1609),[38] which Tirinus mentions, as well as the highly influential treatise on purgatory by the Jesuit Cardinal Roberto Bellarmini (1542-1621) who taught at the University of Louvain from 1569 to 1576. Bellarmini's *De Ecclesia, quae est in Purgatorio* is located in the third volume of his *Disputationes de Controversiis Christianae Fidei adversus huius temporis haereticos,* first published between 1586 and 1593. Also for Bellarmini, 2 Maccabees, 12 demonstrates 'that purgatory exists' ('Purgatorium esse probatur ex Scripturis Testamenti Veteris'). He concludes as follows:

> 'FIRST, the dead can be freed from sins after this life, and therefore purgatory exists. SECOND, the offerings and prayers of the living benefit the dead. THIRD, the burden

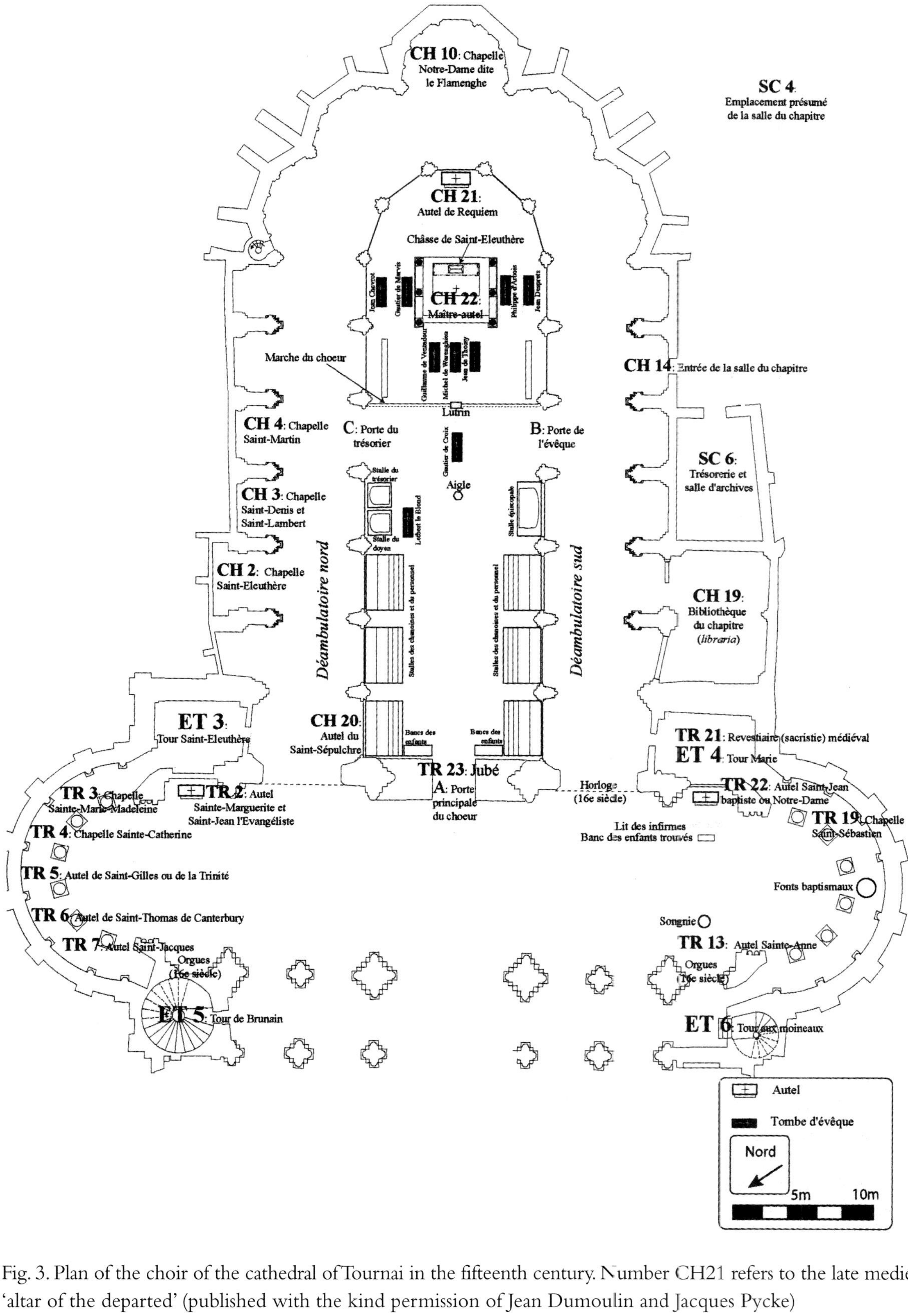


Fig. 3. Plan of the choir of the cathedral of Tournai in the fifteenth century. Number CH21 refers to the late medieval 'altar of the departed' (published with the kind permission of Jean Dumoulin and Jacques Pycke)

of remaining sins is not always extinguished, as Luther claims; for those for whom he (Judas) asked to pray, died from a violent death and for the religion, and yet Judas still believed that they were not fully purged. FOURTH, a man can die virtuously and faithfully, and nonetheless have a certain debt to pay, either because of venial sins that were not absolved in life or because the satisfaction for deadly sins that were absolved was not yet fully completed; now the Scripture says to this point that those for whose sins Judas demanded to pray had respectfully accepted death. FIFTH, this is in accordance with faith.'[39]

Although the words 'sancta ergo et salubris cogitatio pro defunctis exorare ut a peccato solverentur' (2 Maccabees, 12, 46) figure quite often as inscriptions below engraved representations of purgatory,[40] Rubens's composition is the only known altarpiece that illustrates the scene. He depicts Judas Maccabaeus in full armor, with his eyes raised toward heaven and his right arm outstretched in a rhetorical gesture. In the foreground, soldiers remove the stolen votive offerings from the bodies of the dead (fig. 3). According to the biblical text Judas and his soldiers prayed to God that the sin be expunged, while Judas exhorted the people to keep themselves from sin 'forasmuch as they saw before their eyes what had happened, because of the sins of those that were slain' (2 Maccabees, 12, 42). By representing the removal of the consecrated objects in the foreground, Rubens makes evident the consequences of the soldiers' sin, puts them 'before our eyes'. Expressing the Jewish hero's belief in the resurrection of the dead, the upward glance of Rubens's Judas Maccabaeus follows traditional tomb iconography while giving it a personal, biographical note.

Originally placed above the bishop's tomb, the 'pious' and 'noble' hero and 'first pope' who had introduced suffrages for the dead must have provided a model for the zealous Maximilian Villain, who equally strived at exercising discipline over the faithful and at leading their souls to a better life. The Jesuit Matthaeus Rader, in his precious three volume work *Bavaria Sancta* (published between 1615 and 1624 on behalf of Maximilian I, duke elector of Bavaria), compares Saint Maximilian to Judas Maccabaeus (Bishop Maximilian owned a copy of this work):

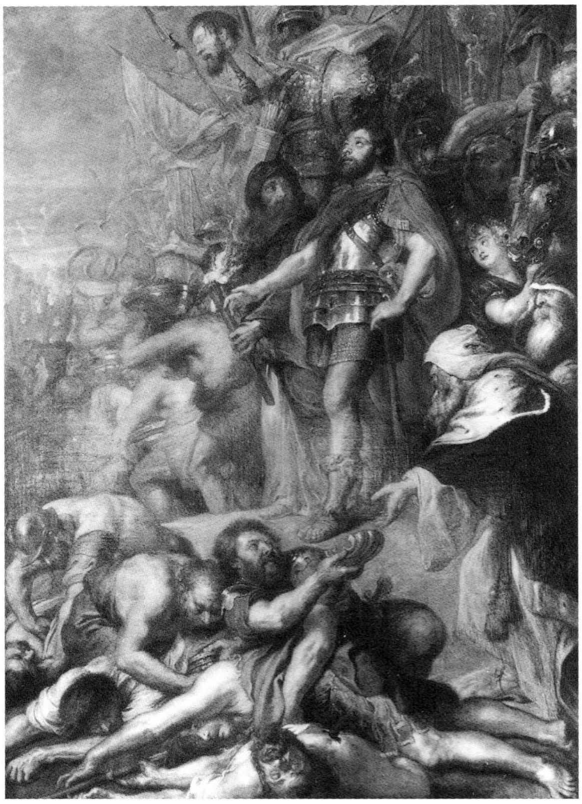

Fig. 4. Peter Paul Rubens, *Judas Maccabeus's Prayer for the Dead*. Nantes, Musée des Beaux-Arts

'Maximilian's virtue shone forth in the worst times of the Christian Republic. Like (Judas) Maccabaeus, he opposed impious idolatry and through his steadfastness encouraged others who hesitated out of fear of execution to approach death without trembling.'[41]

Saint Maximilian, missionary in Bavaria and Archbishop of Lorch, had suffered martyrdom in Rome in 284 because he refused to offer sacrifices to the war-god Mars. Promoting prayers for the dead and relentlessly battling against immoral conduct and superstitious beliefs, Bishop Maximilian might well have been inspired by the lives of both, the Jewish and early Christian martyrs.

### Purgatory after the Council of Trent

The text of the offertory of the mass for the dead – the subject of the painting which faces the high altar – describes the difficult passage of the souls from death to life and the deliverance of the departed 'from the pains of hell and from the deep pit, [...] from the lion's mouth, that hell may not swallow them up, and they may not fall into darkness'.[42] Because of this offertory's ancient and ambivalent language (partially taken from Psalm 21, 22) it had provoked much discussion since the Middle Ages. Interestingly, in his story of the usurer of Liège in the *Dialogue on Miracles* (written between 1219 and 1223), the German Cistercian monk Caesarius of Heisterbach felt obliged to explain that redemption from 'the depths of the abyss' would here mean 'from the harshness of purgatory'.[43] Apart from Rubens's painting for Bishop Maximilian I know of only one other altarpiece that explicitly refers to this offertory: Cerano's altarpiece for the chapel of the newly instituted *Confraternità del Suffragio dei Morti* in the Basilica San Vittore in Varese (the first mass was said in the chapel in 1617) (fig. 5).[44] In the left middle distance of this altarpiece, Saint Gregory, who can be recognized by his attribute, the dove, is celebrating at an altar. Above his head, a banner spirals up into heaven with the words 'at vitam transire de morte - to pass from death to life'. What is here being depicted is the release of souls from purgatory through masses said at this altar.

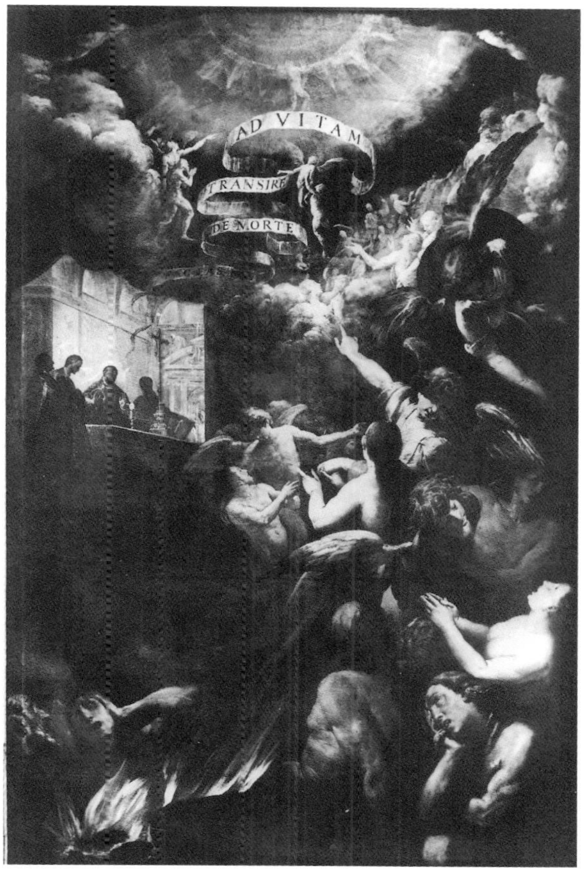

Fig. 5. Il Cerano, *Mass of Saint Gregory the Great.* Varese, San Vittore

While the central focus in Cerano's altarpiece is the mass, Rubens literally backed up the salvific effects of indulgenced masses with the same effects imparted by a collection of twelve thousand silver drachms, serving as atonement for sins. This iconography again seems to gloss and paraphrase late medieval purgatorial imagery, furnishing it with a new meaning. The interior wings of an altarpiece for a cemetery chapel in Niederolang (Austria), painted around 1525, provide an example of the earlier iconography of the theme (fig. 6).[45] Divided into two registers, the upper scenes depict the distribution of alms at the left and the celebration of a mass at the right. The priest has broken the host in three parts – representing the saints in heaven, the souls in purgatory and the living – and is now prepared to receive the host. The affluent figure kneeling in the foreground may represent the benefactor who initiated the construction of the chapel. The two lower scenes document the effects pious and charitable works have on the other world. Testifying to the benefits both of masses and of alms given to the poor in this world, some of the souls in purgatory are carried by angels to heaven. Here masses and alms appear nearly equal in their redemptive power. In contrast, Rubens lends more weight to the celebration of the mass, while at the same time dispensing with an ostentatious donor portrait – although the question remains whether the celebrant at the altar in the background does not in fact allude to Maximilian Villain, who certainly said masses and liberated souls at this altar.

In order to better understand Maximilian Villain's 'altar of the departed', it is helpful to review some of the changes that had taken place since the Reformation concerning ideas of the other world. As is well known, Protestants dismissed the doctrine of purgatory as non-biblical, claiming that a place of penance for souls who in their lives had been neither entirely evil nor entirely good, was a fantastic invention by the Pope. The Swiss reformer Huldrych Zwingli mocked purgatory as 'the Pope's milk-cow',[46] underlining the prominent role of purgatory in the economy of salvation as designed by the Roman church. Luther ridiculed it as 'the fire of dishonesty and unholy commerce'

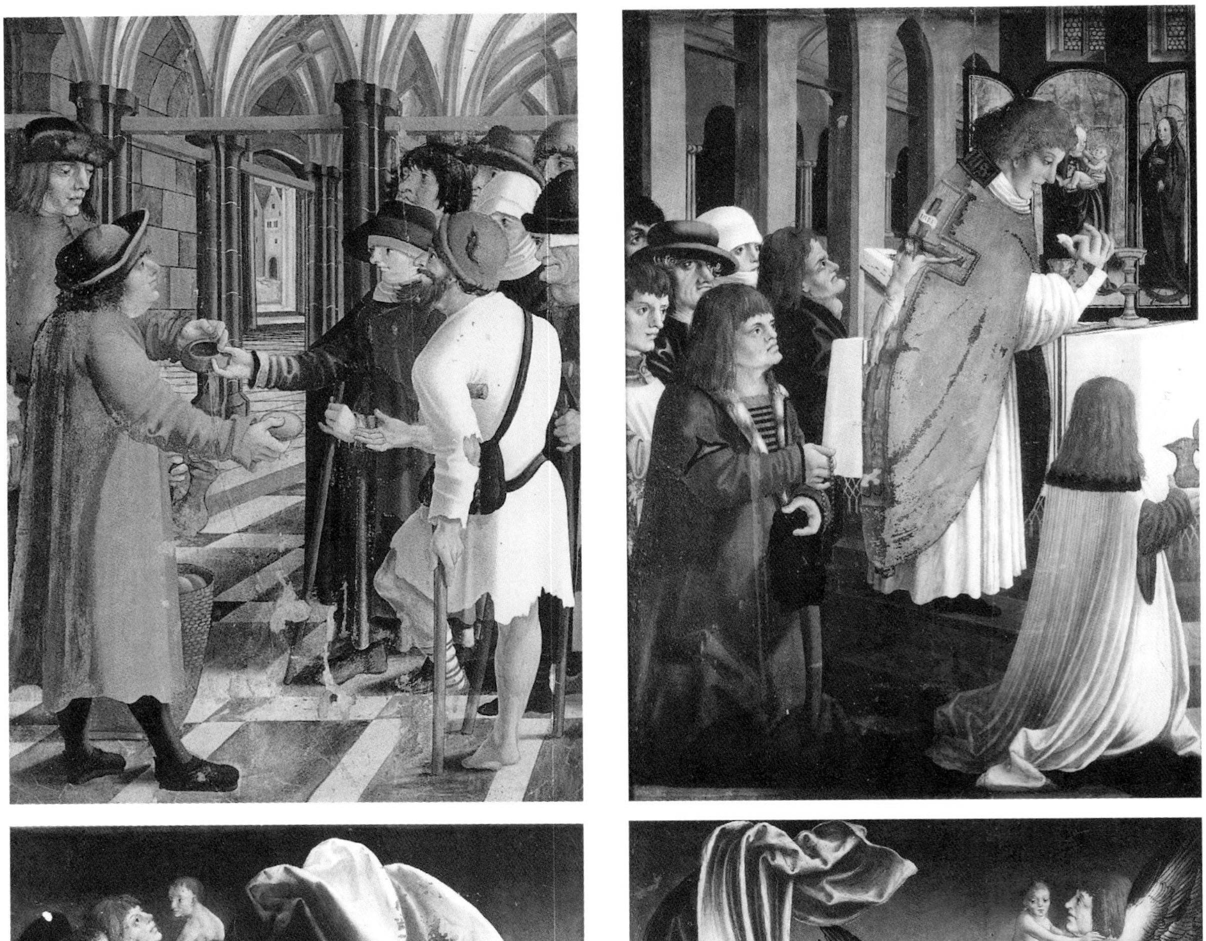

Fig. 6. Anonymous, *Masses and Alms Benefit of the Souls in Purgatory*, c. 1525, wings of a retable from Saint Michael's chapel in Niederolang (Austria). Innsbruck, Tiroler Landesmuseum (*Mass* and *Suffering Souls*); Brixen, Kloster Neustift (*Alms*)

and – referring to the vast amount of money garnered from anxious sinners willing to pay for a shortcut to heaven – the 'greatest mint in the world'.[47] Luther's rejection of purgatory was closely connected to his critique of the mass, the most powerful rite effecting salvation. On the eve of the Reformation, the demand for private masses had dramatically increased; this required a costly apparatus, including chapels and altars with their decorations, and the services of priests. According to Luther, the mass was 'the monopoly of the clergy, the hope that wastes the whole world. What shall I say about the increase of vestments, vessels, candles, garments, organs, music, and pictures? There was scarcely an art on earth that, to a great part, did not profit from the commerce of the mass and did not feed on the mass.'[48] Moreover, if purgatory did not exist, then saying masses for the needs of the dead was meaningless.

As a response to the challenge posed by the Reformation, the Council of Trent confirmed the special sanctity of the mass, and, albeit at one of its very last sessions on 3 December 1563, decreed that 'there is a purgatory, and that the souls there detained are aided by the suffrages of the faithful and chiefly by the acceptable sacrifice of the altar'.[49] By the end of the sixteenth century, the concept of purgatory and its modes of expression had undergone radical transformation within the Roman Catholic church as well. An important factor seems to have been an invention by Pope Gregory XIII: a new altar-privilege in honor of his famous predecessor Saint Gregory the Great, apart from the Virgin perhaps the most successful intercessor for suffering souls. At these so called 'privileged altars for the dead', an individual soul of the benefactor's own choosing, most commonly the soul of the benefactor himself or herself, could be released from purgatory through a mere mass. Around 1600, privileged or indulgenced altars for the dead were widespread all over the Christian world. Purgatory was thus established as a 'through station' that nobody could really escape, but that led with certainty to paradise. The Catholic clergy propagated this idea – an opportunity, standing in contrast to Protestant doctrine, for the average sinner to have a second chance.

After the turn of the century, images of souls in purgatory frequently decorated public altars, either the high altar or (more often) one of the large side altars in the transept. These altars and chapels were generally established by members of the high-ranking clergy or by the new confraternities founded specifically to pray for the suffering souls. While late medieval altarpieces displayed, at times crudely, the most efficacious ways of helping the souls (prayers, works of penance, alms-deeds, and masses), purgatorial imagery for Baroque altars of the dead no longer depicted the meritorious acts of laymen. Instead, images of the souls' journey to heaven focused on what is brought about – invisibly – during mass, as well as on the intercession of various saints, and especially on the intercession of Mary and Christ.

Bishop Maximilian's decoration of the 'altar of the departed' was inspired by altarpieces created for privileged altars of the dead. With a painter such as Rubens having been accustomed to drawing in his own pictorial inventions for various occasions, the fact that he received such precise iconographic instructions from the bishop underscores the high degree to which the theme preoccupied the latter's mind.

### A Counter-Reformation Bishop

Born in 1569, Maximilian came from a distinguished noble Catholic lineage. He was the eldest son of a high government official, Maximilian Villain de Gand, Baron of Rasseghem, Count of Isenghien, governor of Lille, Douai and Orchies; during the religious troubles Bishop Maximilian's father was imprisoned by the Calvinists in Ghent and consequently rewarded for his loyalty by Philip II with a personal letter.[50] His mother, still alive when Maximilian was appointed Bishop of Tournai by the archdukes in 1614, was equally renowned for her Catholicism. She had a household chapel in her palace with chaplains for the celebration of mass. Two of Maximilian's brothers joined the Society of Jesus and his younger sister entered a convent in Lille. Once bishop, Maximilian Villain made at least two of his nephews, Adrien-Lamorald Villain de Gand and Maximilian de Hem, canons of Tournai, while his nephew Francois followed him on the see. Some of the witnesses heard by the nuncio during Maximilian's nomination process testified that he had attended courses in rhetoric and philosophy at the universities of Douai and Pont-à-Mousson in Lorraine and written essays on Thomas Aquinas and Saint Jerome; whether Maximilian actually acquired an academic degree is nevertheless unknown. In 1597 he was ordained priest by Michel d'Esnes, Bishop of Tournai, whom he would later succeed in office. That same year he became a canon of the chapter of Tournai, then gaining a particular reputation among his colleagues for his charitable acts on behalf of orphans and foreign refugees, especially the expatriate Irish and Swiss. During the 1600 jubilee, he traveled to Rome, purchasing, among others, 'four images of silk set in wood' in the city; he would later bequeath the images to his nephew and godson Maximilian de Hem whom he had made a canon of Tournai.[51]

When Maximilian was consecrated as Bishop of Tournai in 1616, there were according to several witnesses, still 'many heretics concealed in the diocese';[52] in particular, the 'foreign merchants from Holland and Zeeland' were seen as 'a threat for the faith'.[53] The cathedral still suffered from the damage caused by the iconoclastic attacks in 1566, and it was expected that the future bishop would devote large sums to the reparation of churches.[54]

In connection with two arrests ordered by Maximilian Villain between 1639 and 1641 (on the respective charges of 'carnal excesses' and 'sorcery'), the papal nuncio Pauli-Stravius complained bitterly about the bishop who, he felt, excused all his 'injustices and usurpations' on the pretext of 'correction of morals'. For Pauli-Stravius, Maximilian Villain's actions were not motivated by 'the zeal of this bishop for justice', but rather by his 'innate pride and his ambition to dominate in his diocese'; he thus recognized 'neither the authority of the Holy See, nor of the nunciature or of the archbishop of Cambrai, his metropolitan'.[55] In his concerns for public morality. Bishop Maximilian resembled Milan's model Archbishop Carlo Borromeo (canonized in 1610), whose ambitious program to reform his diocese had gained him the reputation of 'Pope of Lombardy'[56] and had led to bitter disputes with the secular authorities and Rome. It is consequently not all that surprising that Maximilian owned a portrait of Carlo Borromeo, which he bequeathed to his nephew and godson Maximilian. We will see that the Milanese bishop also had strong influence on Maximilian Villain's preparations for death.

### Bishop Maximilian Villain and Saint Maximilian of Lorch

Bishop Maximilian's claims to rule over his diocese are reflected in his ecclesiastical donations, particularly in his reconstruction and redecoration of the 'altar of the departed' in Tournai cathedral, to which we will now return. What, now, was the role of the visual arts in this campaign? The 'altar of the departed' was, in fact, part of a larger project, described in detail in Maximilian's foundation charter. At the charter's start, immediately after identifying himself and his familial relationships, Maximilian confirms his spiritual union with the Tournai cathedral, which was dedicated to the Virgin; because of this union, he feels an obligation to embellish the church as his spiritual spouse and the mother of the other churches.

The sort of marriage imagery upon which Maximilian's description of his donations to the cathedral is based was widespread in seventeenth-century catechisms and religious literature. As an example, we may refer to a manual on married life by the Jesuit Claude Maillard (1586-1606), *Le Bon Mariage ou Ie moyen d'estre heureux. estat et faire son salut en mariage,* published in Douai in 1643 (fig. 7). The title engraving depicts the marriage between the Church (as the bride) and Christ (as the spouse). Standing in ceremonial habits on a pedestal, the personification of the Church is surrounded by male and female saints and framed by Moses and Saint Paul. Represented above in the sky are God the Father, the Holy Ghost and Christ in the form of a lamb. The symbolism of the frontispiece is further explained at the beginning of the text: The two angels blowing their trumpets represent 'the preachers who invite the people to the wedding'; the spouse is the lamb that signifies Christ; the bride is the Church; Moses and Saint Paul are the bride's men'; and so forth.[57] Claude Maillard, rector of the Jesuit colleges in Charleville and Nancy, is also the author of a successful *Traite du Iubilé et autres indulgences, et des conditions pour les gagner, Tant pour soy, que pour les Ames de Purgatoire.*[58]

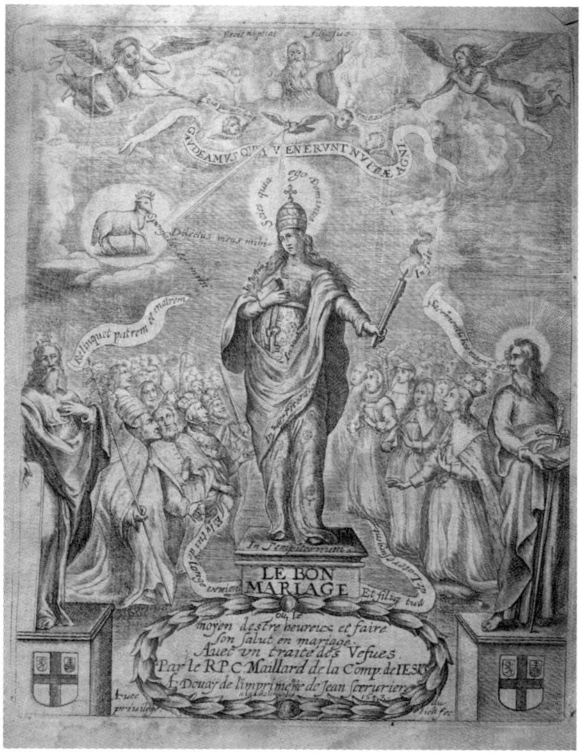


Fig. 7. Du Fielt, *The Church as Christ's Bride*, engraving. Frontispiece in C. Maillard, *Le Bon Mariage* (Douai, 1643)

Maximilian's patronage focused on the choir's two most prestigious altars. In 1616, when the bishop assumed office, he arranged for an image in honor of the Virgin to be fashioned and set up in the choir behind the high altar – in fact his last such gesture toward the Virgin for the next fifteen years. In 1631, however, 'eager to promote further the veneration of the image of his spouse, the Virgin', he ordered a silver chandelier with three columns to be hung before the image he had previously donated. In addition, he established a foundation for purchasing white candles weighing one pound each, to be lit during various types of masses and liturgical prayers – except during Lent when the image would be covered.[59] Two years later Maximilian paid for the costs of surrounding the Saint Martha chapel in the left hand (evangelical) corner of the ambulatory with a marble fence.

At this time he seems to have been recovering from a serious illness. Reminded of his own mortality, he 'applied his mind to higher things' directly concerning his future life. It was then that he chose his burial place, located below the altar of the dead at the end of the choir of the cathedral, and arranged for its decoration. 'God, in his divine clemency', he concludes, 'mercifully granted us to pursue and bring to perfection these plans with the necessary delay while still alive.' Maximilian also donated a 'subtly embroidered' antependium for the high altar, with the Assumption depicted in the antependium's center, and his patron saint Maximilian along with the saints Piat, Eleutherius, and Eloy, especially venerated in Tournai at the time, located at its sides.[60]

Bishop Maximilian's further efforts to embellish the cathedral and secure powerful intercessors for the fearful moment of death were mainly devoted to promoting the cult of Saint Maximilian, 'the martyr and archbishop of Lorch who has always been the patron and protector of Germany and particularly the Austrian house and after whom, by miraculous intuition, a number of emperors were called'.[61] Writing in the middle of the Thirty Years' War, in the year after the Peace of Prague (30 May 1635),[62] he emphasizes the saint's powerful intercession on behalf of the Austrian monarchy and the 'peculiar devotion' his own family had toward him: in addition to Bishop Maximilian, other family members were honored with this name. He describes how after several years of tiresome negotiations and only with the help of influential men, he recently obtained two small bones from the body of Saint Maximilian 'which is highly venerated in the cathedral of Passau'- he had to compete with the emperor's mother for these saintly bones. To celebrate the newly acquired relics Bishop Maximilian spent 4000 florins for a silver statue of Saint Maximilian, made 'at great expense, and with equal art and labor'. Shortly after the statue's creation, he commissioned Jean-Jacques Courvoisier, provincial of the Minorites in Belgium, to write a *Life of Saint Maximilian,* the 'apostle and patron of Austria', dedicating the volume to himself.[64] The statue is here described as 'large, beautiful and costly, partially gilded, partially enriched with precious stones, though even more adorned and embellished with saintly relics'.[65] These precious remains of the body of Bishop Maximilian's patron were displayed behind a crystal affixed to the chest of the statue, together with letters of authentication and other relics Bishop Maximilian had collected over the years: a particle of the veil of the Virgin (which he received as a present when he traveled to Aachen in 1615), a bone of the body of Saint Bartholomew, another bone from the skull of Saint Apollinaris of Ravenna (a gift from the Archbishop of Cambrai), and a relic of Saint Augustine. An inscription on the base of the silver statue commemorated the donation of this reliquary in honor of Saint Maximilian of Lorch, the bishop and martyr who 'died by the sword for the Christian faith in the persecution of emperor Decius under Gelasius in 284', and in remembrance of Bishop Maximilian Villain and his parents. The dedication occurred, appropriately, on the Feast of the Assumption of the Virgin in 1636.[66]

In his charter, Bishop Maximilian dedicates 'this elaborately worked silver statue' together with the other ornaments and art works created upon his request 'forevermore' to the greater glory of God, the Virgin and the saints Piat, Eleutherius, Eloy, and Maximilian. As in the embroidered antependium Bishop Maximilian donated for the decoration of the high altar, the Virgin and the local saints Piat (the third-century missionary of Tournai), Eleutherius (the first bishop of this city whose saintly body is preserved in a precious thirteenth-century shrine in the treasury of Tournai cathedral), and Eloy (mintmaster at the Frankish court and later bishop of Tournai), are joined by Saint Maximilian, Bishop Maximilian's patron saint, the patron saint of his father and other members of his family and the protector of the Austrian Habsburg house. Maximilian Villain further writes that the silver statue was set up for the first time when the feast of the Elevation of the Cross, held on September 14, was near. This was the main feast of Tournai, 'during which the solemn annual procession is celebrated', with the explicit intent of carrying the new image in the procession.[67]

Interestingly, Bishop Maximilian's charter of donation is dated 12 September, 1636, two days before the 'grand procession' actually took place. Therefore we do not really know if this new reliquary with the remnants of a Bavarian bishop was carried together with the shrines of the Virgin and Saint Eleutherius, the reliquary of the True Cross, the silver statues of Saint Barbara and Saint Nicolas, and the arm reliquary of Saint Eleutherius.[68] If, however, the wish of Bishop Maximilian Villain did come true, the see of Tournai was associated visibly and in a most powerful manner with the Austrian Habsburg house.

By replacing the destroyed silver statue of the Virgin with a silver reliquary of Saint Maximilian, Bishop Maximilian transformed the formerly communal 'altar of the departed' into a monument for his own salvation, and for that of his family, the Habsburg dynasty. But Maximilian Villain's 'altar of the departed' did not serve solely personal concerns: The embellishment of an old and outmoded altar with a new decorative and iconographic program resulted in a kind of 'assemblage' corresponding to the ambivalent status associated with tombs, which were partially considered as private, partially as public monuments in early modern writings on art. The reconstructed medieval altar with its curious retrospective character reflects Bishop Maximilian's efforts to reassess the sacred space, which had been violated during the iconoclastic past, and to buttress his own claims to rule. Likewise, his donations to the cathedral advertised Austrian Habsburg piety closely associated with the devotions to the Eucharist and to the Virgin Mary — in Rubens's painting the most powerful agents of salvation.

The donation of a silver reliquary was not the only means through which the bishop promoted the cult of Saint Maximilian. He endowed an annual mass in the saint's honor that had to be celebrated in the manner as in Passau on the saint's feast day, 12 October.[69] In the foreword and the conclusions of *L'Austriche saincte,* Courvoisier praises the bishop's donations to the Tournai cathedral at length, comparing his silver reliquary with the two-foot high silver reliquary of Saint Maximilian that Maximilian I had given to the Virgin of Halle after his marriage with Mary of Burgundy. In his last will and testament, Maximilian Villain bequeathed several copies of this book to his relatives and ecclesiastical friends. In short, Bishop Maximilian practised a 'saintly patronage' expecting that Saint Maximilian (his patron) would intercede with the Virgin (his spouse) and aid himself and his family in entering the kingdom of heaven.

## Anxieties about Approaching Death: a Prayer Nut and a Pamphlet taken to the Grave

Maximilian Villain died on 29 November 1644, after having governed his diocese for nearly thirty years.[70] He had secured the most favorable grave-site possible close to the high altar where the sacrifice of the mass was offered regularly. As his last will reveals, he did not expect to be spared passage through purgatory and thus took precautions, ensuring that his soul would not be 'detained there for long'.[71] For this reason, he requested that 2000 requiem masses be said at the indulgenced altars of his diocese immediately after his death – a request that, while not exaggerated for a high ecclesiastical official, needed considerable clerical resources. The bishop had previously acquired the privilege of an 'indulgenced altar' for the altar in the Saint Andrew chapel in the transept of the Tournai cathedral.[72] He also requested that orphans, foundlings and widows attend his funeral, providing each with a double loaf of bread and some ells of cloth. He bequeathed money and wheat to the 'poor exiled Irish students', and wheat to the 'truly poor and sordid households of the city'.[73] Along with leaving money for all of Tournai's religious houses, with special attention paid to the Jesuits, he initiated a perpetual fund for burning an oil lamp in front of the image of Notre Dame des Samedis in the town's house for orphaned girls.[74] In addition, he donated a set of tapestries in eight pieces to the cathedral, depicting the conversion of Saint Paul.[75] Finally, Maximilian Villain stipulated that the enameled golden crucifix he had worn through much of his life be placed around the neck of Saint Maximilian's silver statue.[76]

His library and art works were to be distributed among his relatives. His eldest nephew Don Philippe Balthazar, count of Isenghien and at that time 'maistre de camp' in Spain, received a 'beautiful set of tapestries in eight pieces with the story of Gideon', a book with the genealogy of his family printed on vellum, the *Revelations* by Saint Bridget of Sweden annotated by Consalvus Durantus, Saint Augustin's works in eight volumes, the above mentioned commentaries by the Antwerp Jesuit Tirinus, three copies of a life of Saint Maximilian (clearly Courvoisier's *L'Austrice saincte)* and Matthaeus Rader's *Bavaria Sancta* with the beautiful engravings by Raphael Sadeler.[77] Perhaps his most intimate objects were given to his nephew and godson, Maximilian de Hem: three images of Our Savior, one of them showing him with the crown of thorns, another in the act of pressing wine, and the third, woven with golden thread, depicting him praying in the Garden of Olives. Apart from the portrait of Carlo Borromeo, his godson received another portrait of the blessed Loys de Blois (1506-1565) – in the bishop's words, a 'saintly person as demonstrated by his writings' – previously displayed above the bishop's fireplace, as well as the hung bed on which he slept.[78]

There were in any event two objects that the bishop wished to keep with his body, even as it decayed in the grave. The first was a 'small book' by Carlo Borromeo that Maximilian kept in a 'purse of velvet': *La Dernière Volonté de l'Ame, en forme de Testament,* translated into French by the Carmelite Daniel van Audenaerde (Daniel de la Vierge Marie). The 24 page pamphlet – at that time immensely popular, today virtually forgotten – promises to 'assure the soul against the temptations of devils in the hour of death'.[79] According to the notice to readers, this 'testament of the soul [...] can be made by everybody sound in body and mind through writing his or her name or having it written at the beginning' of the text. On page 13, there are further blank spaces for the names of the devout readers' favorite saints; on page 17, the same readers are told to 'assert and formally declare that they agree to all above'. Those not able to read or write are encouraged to ask someone to read the text aloud to them while they are kneeling; this person is also meant to enter their names and the names of their patron saints in the blank spaces. On page 17, they are allowed to sign with a cross.

The booklet, one reads, is meant to be kept with other cherished objects, taken along while traveling and, after confession, held in the hour of death. The devout are then to 'once more solemnly declare what is written herein' and ask their next of kin to always keep the booklet with them.[80] The book is divided into fourteen small chapters that address the following themes: the possible temptations of the devil threatening one's faith (sections I-IV); hope (V-VI); love for God and for one's neighbor (VII-VIII); the soul thanking God for received benefices (IX); the soul appointing advocates and attorneys concerning its will (X); the soul appointing the executors of its last will (XI); the soul asking friends for help (XII); the soul choosing a grave (XIII); and finally, the soul submitting its will (XIV); the treatise concludes with three prayers (to Christ, the Virgin, and the Guardian Angel) and a short exercise for preparing oneself for a good death. The faithful are advised to read the pages weekly after having confessed and received communion, or if this is not possible, monthly or at least once a year.

The Carmelite monk's French translation of Carlo Borromeo's treatise on the soul's last will and testament was approved by the head of the inspection of books in Lille in 1628; it was not the only publication of that sort circulating at that time and onward in the Spanish Netherlands. Even before Borromeo's *Dernière Volonté de l'Ame* was put on the market, the renowned Jesuit Antoine Sucquet, provincial of Flandro-Belgica in Malines, published a voluminous book in both Latin and French versions that had similar aims: the *Testamentum Christiani hominis, et salutis aeternae* or *Fais ton testament et monument.*[81] According to the preface to the French version, two copies of the booklet are meant to be bought by one person: a medium size is to be kept in either the oratory or a room reserved for private prayers, a small pocket edition is to be carried on one's person at all times, held in the hour of death, placed next to one's body in the grave. In the preface, Sucquet explains that he has drafted the booklet in order to offer ordinary people a more accessible preparation for death than the instructions in his earlier large volume, the *Via Vitae Aeternae* (1620). Sucquet's book, too, had to be personalized by the individual readers or users. Aware of the lure of visual imagery, Sucquet designed an epitaph – an illustration that itself needed completion by the reader (fig. 8): The recumbent figure of death, holding a sickle, is placed on an altar-like monument. At the feet of this figure, one finds an hour glass and the symbol of eternity (a snake biting its tail with a palm tree and a scourge). On the front side of the monument, below three running figures, the following words invite the reader to enter his or her name and date of birth:

IE COURS A
L'ETERNITE
DEPUIS L'AN / MOIS / IOUR

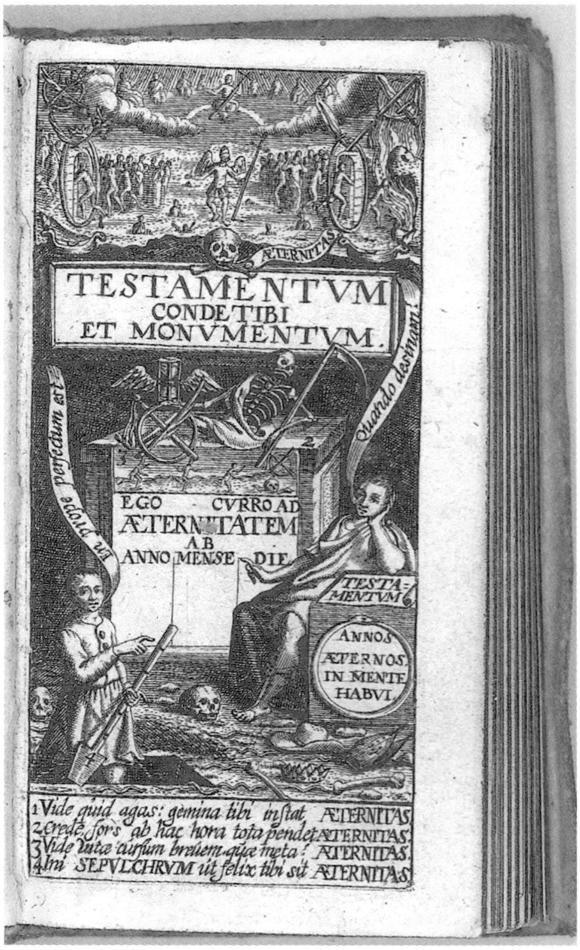


Fig. 8. Epitaph to be completed by the individual user, engraving, in Antoine Sucquet, *Testamentum Christiani hominis*, Antwerp, after p. 14

Next to the epitaph, a figure resting his head on his left hand points toward the inscription and utters the words 'When will I end'?, while a gravedigger declares 'It is nearly achieved'. At the very beginning, under the title 'A true epitaph for all Christians, which is good to read often and to meditate upon seriously -VRAY EPITAPHE de tout Chrestien, qu'il est bon de lire souvent, et de le mediter serieusement' – the reader, addressed as a 'pilgrim', is offered space to fill in his or her name, date of birth, and profession, as well as possessions.

Neither Borromeo's *Dernière Volonté,* disseminated by the Carmelites, nor the Jesuit elaborations on this treatise, have been mentioned in scholarly literature. But once brought to light through the entry in Maximilian Villain's unpublished testament, the few remaining copies of the *Volonté* do attest to the great success of this type of literature. While Borromeo's or Sucquet's books reflect the religious orders' prescriptions concerning an anxious soul's attitude toward death, the second object to be buried with Bishop Maximilian was his personal choice alone: 'a carved walnut in which the Savior on the cross with the Virgin and Saint John the Evangelist on one side and Saint Mary Magdalene and Saint Barbara on the other side are represented, the former associated with penitence, the latter with confession (fig. 9).[82] The production of such small sculptures had flourished in the first half of the sixteenth-century, particularly in Antwerp, but had long died out by the 1640s. Maximilian may have received the carved object from an older family member; it certainly had sentimental value for him. Like the popular *Volunté,* this small religious curiosity was intended to bring the dying man luck, helping him approach the end of earthly being and impending judgment with confidence and hope.

In his attempts to refurbish the cathedral in Tournai, Bishop Maximilian Villain followed the Council of Trent's demands of reform almost to the letter: his patronage of the visual arts reflects his efforts to establish a Catholic society in his diocese, to convert the souls of Tournai's citizens to the Catholic faith. Following the instructions laid down by Carlo Borromeo, he built his tomb at one of the cathedral's prominent sites, associated with a central devotion, a charitable service abolished by the Protestant Reformation. The iconographic program of the altar visualized a prayer and a letter read during the requiem mass, in the form it now took in all Catholic churches. By privatizing a once communal space, Maximilian Villain strengthened his position as Bishop of Tournai and, in fact, appropriated a role that challenged papal rights. The question of who was in charge of the souls of the dead regularly led to conflicts between bishops, eager to achieve local reforms, and the pope as the head of the universal Church.[83] The geographical distance from Rome may have given Maximilian Villain some freedom to pursue his goals. In the end, he would make use of public media – a reliquary statue carried along during the most important Tournai procession, a commemorative mass, and a written biography- to promote the cult of Saint Maximilian of Bavaria, hence the fame of his own Habsburg house.

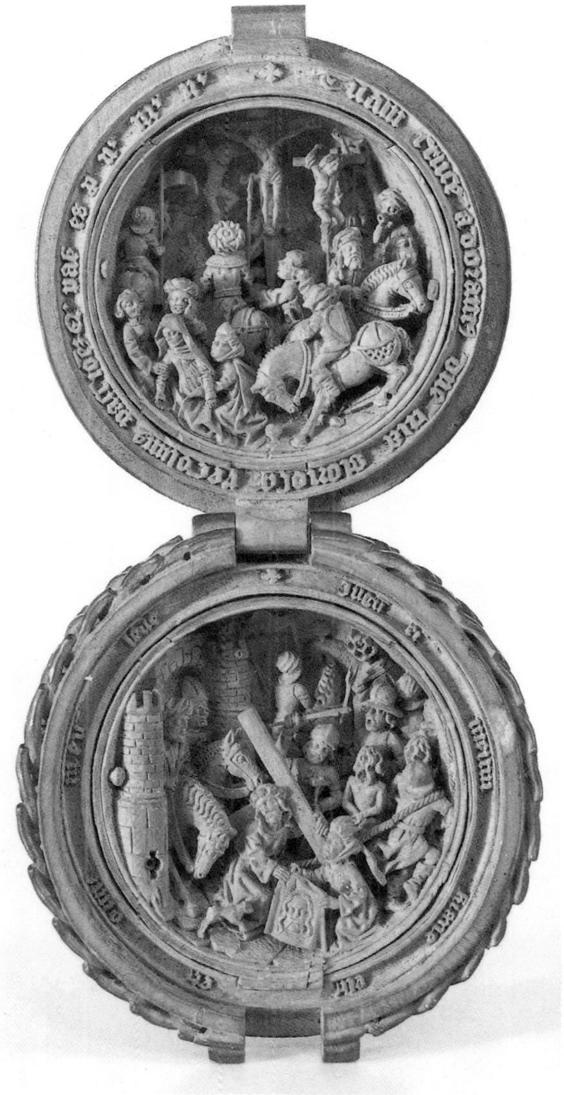

Fig. 9. Prayer-nut, boxwood, c. 1515, Flemish. Amsterdam, Rijksmuseum

Maximilian Villain shared his eagerness for reform with other Flemish bishops.[84] But claims to status, honor, and episcopal dignity do not explain all aspects of his patronage. Although he openly displayed his trust in the means of salvation offered by the institutional Church, some doubts clearly remained whether his precautions would suffice to liberate his soul from purgatorial pain. Despite the intensified propaganda for purgatory as a means to avoid hell, publications such as those by Carlo Borromeo and Antoine Sucquet demonstrate that there was, in general, an increasing demand for reassurance in the hour of death. Even Carlo Borromeo's pamphlet, although written by a canonized bishop, apparently failed to remove

Maximilian's personal doubts, since he insisted on being buried with the prayer-nut, an old-fashioned devotional image, as well.

The case of Maximilian Villain increases our awareness of the fragmentary character of the imagery that has survived, as well as of the difficulties in studying possible functions and meanings of both public art and private devotional objects. The persistence of late medieval traditions in an age obsessed with salvation – the most central problem of the Christian faith – points to an aspect of religious art after the Council of Trent that requires further research: both the (re-)invention of new types of images, objects, and texts in light of the overall presence of death and a growing scepticism about the efficacy of visual media as a means of salvation. If one takes Maximilian's last will and testament seriously, then Borromeo's pamphlet and the prayer-nut (which vanished with his body in the grave), the silver statue with the treasure of relics and the 'altar of the departed' (which, apart from Rubens's triumphant decoration, was most probably destroyed during the French Revolution) were distinct types of images that served the same aim: to ward off demonic forces when Maximilian's soul separated from its body, shorten its stay in purgatory, and help it enter the eternal abode of heaven.

# NOTES

1. Peter Paul Rubens, *The Ascent of Souls from Purgatory,* oil on canvas, 350 x 258 cm, Tournai cathedral. Cf. David Freedberg, *Rubens. The Life of Christ after the Passion* (*Corpus Rubenianum Ludwig Burchard,* VII), New York, 1984, pp. 241–245, cat. 54 (with previous literature); Jean Dumoulin et al., *Les tableaux de Pierre Paul Rubens à la Cathédrale de Tournai,* Tournai, 1993. I would like to thank the participants of the symposium *Commissioned Art. Flemish Art and Patronage, 1550–1700* (Leuven, 2001) for their stimulating comments. My study would not have been possible without the kind assistance of Jean Dumoulin, Jacques Pycke and Anne Dupont. Warmest thanks go to Barbara Budnick who read previous versions of this essay and to Irene Mannheimer who helped me with the translations from the Latin. I am grateful to Joel Golb who edited the final text.

2. See, for example, 'Description d'aucunes particularitéz concernants l'estat de l'église cathédrale de Tournay avant les saccagemens de l'an 1566', in Jean Dumoulin and Jacques Pycke, 'Mobilier et vêtements liturgiques à la cathédrale de Tournai avant les iconoclastes (1566)', *Mémoires de la Société Royale d'Histoire et d'Archéologie de Tournai,* I, 1980, p. 96. *Testamentum defuncti Reverendissimi Domini Maximiliani Villani a Gandavo* (April 19, 1639). Archives de la Cathédrale de Tournai, Registrum testamentum, vol. 2, fol. 192 r.

3. The violent iconoclasm in Tournai cathedral is described by Paquier de le Barre, royal procurator-fiscal in the balliage of Tournai. Cf. *Mémoires de Pasquier de le Barre et de Nicolas Soldoyer pour servir à l'histoire de Tournai,* 1565–1570, ed. Alexandre Pinchart, vol. 1, Brussels, 1865, p. 135: '[...] Le lendemain, jour de vendredy, xxiije jour dudict mois d'aoust, on commencha a abattre et sacager les ymages [...] et [...] en l'église catédralle Nostre-Dame, y faisant un merveilleux dégast, car sans respecter excellence de tableaux, orghes, ricesse des autelz ny aultre chose quelconcque, sacaigèrent entièrement ce quy estoit dédié et aproprуé pour l'agensissement de ladicte église, y délaissans seulement entiers les pilliers et principaulx bastimens de la machonnerie [...]'.

4. Peter Paul Rubens, *Judas Maccabaeus's Prayer for the Dead,* oil on canvas, 310 x 228 cm, Nantes, Musée des Beaux-Arts. Cf. R.-A. d'Hulst and M. Vandenven, *Rubens. The Old Testament* (*Corpus Rubenianum Ludwig Burchard,* III), New York, 1989, pp. 222–227, cat. 6; Dumoulin 1993 (as in note 1). For the iconography of the rare theme, see J. Paul, 'Judas Makkabäus', in *Lexikon der christlichen Ikonographie,* II, Rome et al., 1970, cols 448–449; A. Pigler, *Barockthemen,* I, Budapest, 1956, p. 233; Louis Réau, *Iconographie de l'art chrétien,* II, 1, Paris, 1956, p. 303; Emile Mâle, *L'art religieux de la fin du XVIe siècle, du XVIIe siècle et du XVIIe siècle. Etude sur l'iconographie après le concile de Trente,* Paris, 1951, pp. 59–60; B. Knipping, *De iconografie van de contra-reformatie in de Nederlanden,* II, Hilversum, 1940, p. 133.

5. For the Tridentine decree, see *Enchiridion Symbolorum. Definitionum et declarationum de rebus fidei et morum,* ed. Henricus Denzinger and Adolfus Schönmetzer S.J., 34th enlarged edition Barcelona et al., 1967, pp. 364–365, 1501: 'Decretum de libris sacris et de traditionibus recipiendis'. For the canonicity of the books of the Maccabees, see Georg Schmuttermayr, 'Makkabäer, Makkabäerbücher', in *Lexikon für Theologie und Kirche,* VI, 1997, col. 1228; Werner Dommershausen, *1 und 2 Makkabäer,* Die Neue Echter Bibel: Kommentar zum Alten Testament mit der Einheitsübersetzung, XII, Würzburg, 1985, pp. 5 ff.

6. I borrow this expression from Reindert Falkenburg, 'Toys for the Soul: Prayer-Nuts and Pomanders in Late Medieval Devotion', in [cat. exh.] *A Sense of Heaven: 16th-century Boxwood Carvings for Private Devotion,* Henry Moore Institute, Leeds, 1999, pp. 32–47. Cf. also the essay by Frits Scholten, 'Prayer-Nuts and Other Boxwood Micro-Carvings', ibid.

7. Cf. Freedberg 1984 (as in note 1), p. 204.

8. Alberti was the first who advised artists to include figures in their compositions who would mediate between the viewer's and the pictorial space. See Leon Battista Alberti, *Della Pittura* [1436], ed. L. Mallé, Florence, 1950, p. 94: 'Et piacemi sia nella storia chi admonisca et insegni ad noi quello che ivi si facci: o chiami con la mano a vedere o, con viso cruccioso e con li occhi turbati, minacci che nuino verso loro vada; o dimostri qualche pericolo o cosa ivi maravigliosa o te inviti a piagnere con loro insieme o a ridere' ('In a narrative I like to see someone who advises us or points out to us what is going on, or draws us near to look with a gesture or, with worried expression or wild eyes, warns us not to approach, or draws attention to something dangerous or marvelous in it, or invites you to weep with them or laugh'). For the influence this passage exerted on subsequent treatises on art, cf. John Shearman, *Only Connect: Art and the Spectator in the Italian Renaissance,* The A.W. Mellon Lectures in the Fine Arts, 1988; Bollingen series, XXXV, 37, Princeton, 1992, 33, note 36.

9. Joseph A. Jungmann, *The Mass of the Roman Rite: Its Origins and Development* (*Missarum Sollemnia*), trans. Francis A. Brunner, I, New York et al. 1950, p. 121; Miri Rubin, *Corpus Christi: The Eucharist in Late Medieval Culture,* Cambridge, 1991, p. 58 and passim.

10. Jean Baptiste Descamps, *Voyage pittoresque de la Flandre et du Brabant,* Paris, 1769, p. 24: 'une main hardie a gaté ce Tableau, lavé et repeint par-tout'. Cf. also Descamps's earlier work, *La vie des peintres flamands, allemands et hollandais,* I, Paris, 1753, p. 325: 'A Tournai, dans l'Eglise Cathédrale, on admire un Purgatoire et des Anges qui en retirent les ames: Ce morceau est placé au retable du grand Autel: Il est presque perdu par la negligence de ceux qui auroient dû veiller à sa conservation. Le Tableau d'Autel dans la Chapelle derrière le Choeur, représente le Martyre des Machabées: Ces Tableaux sont admirables.' According to this source, in the mid eighteenth-century, Rubens's purgatory painting had been placed on the main altar, while the image representing the prayer of Judas Maccabaeus for the dead still decorated the altar of the dead or the axial chapel behind the choir.

11. Freedberg 1984 (as in note 1), p. 243; Adolph Hocquet, 'L'Art et la Révolution française à Tournai', *Revue Tournaisienne,* I, 1905, pp. 78–86.

12. Dumoulin and Pycke 1980 (as in note 2), p. 82, no. 55: 'altare de Requiem in choro'.

13. Ibidem, p. 86, no. 78.

14. Ibidem, p. 96: 'A l'autel des trépassés il y avait une Notre-Dame d'argent, assise en une chaise, et le petit Jésus estendant son bras, tenant un chapelet de corail, comme voulant induire les chrétiens présents de prier pour les trépassés.'

15. *Donations of Bishop Maximilian Villain de Gand* (September 12, 1636). Archives de la Cathédrale de Tournai, fonds des évêques, FE. 84: Dossier Maximilien Villain de Gand.

16. Maximilian, *Testamentum* (as in note 2), fol. 192 r–198 v.

17. Denis-Dominique Waucquier, *La Basilique des Nerviens, ou Description de l'Eglise cathédrale de Tournay* ('acheté en 1763'), Bibliothèque de la Cathédrale de Tournai, MS B 10 (a. c. 494).

18. Waucquier, *Basilique* (as in note 17), pp. 59, 113, 117, 123.

19. Maximilian, *Testamentum* (as in note 2): 'Altare ergo pro defunctis situm in fine chori dictae nostrae ecclesiae cathedralis retro summum altare de diversis marmoribus exstrui curavimus, locumque sepulturae nostrae sub eodem elegimus nec non idem altare duabus picturis ornari curavimus, una in facie ipsius altaris repraesentante ad vivum liberationem animarum fidelium defunctorum de poenis purgatorii conformiter ad sensum offertorii quod legitur in missa pro defunctis "Domine Jesu Rex gloriae etc." Altera vero a retro exprimente historiam Judae Machabaei qui collatione facta mittit duodecim millia dragmas Jerosolimam ut pro defunctis militibus sacrificium offeratur, Machab. 2 cap. 12.'

20. Waucquier, *Basilique* (as in note 17), p. 154.

21. Cf. J. Warichez, *La Cathédrale de Tournai et son Chapitre,* Wetteren, 1934, p. 51.

22. Joshua Reynolds, *A Journey to Flanders and Holland,* ed. Harry Mount, Cambridge, 1996, pp. 204–205 (*A journey to the Netherlands in the year 1785,* MS Reynolds 39, Yale Center for British Art, fol. 7 v–8 v): 'In the same abbey of St. Mart. [Reynolds meant in fact Tournai cathedral, as is confirmed by the inscriptions on his sketches] are two Pictures said to be Rubens but more probably by [...] one of them represents the Victory over the Maccabees. There is something well in the Composition of this Picture [...] The Principal is well distinguished from the rest [...] a Monument of Maximilian Bishop of Tourney. He is lying along leaning on his hand a fine air of head great dignity in the expression of the countenance [...] his head is thrown a little back & looking up.' The pencil sketches are also on fol. 7 v and 8 v.

23. An earlier example is the sepulchral monument of Bishop Joannes Miraeus (died 1611) in Antwerp cathedral, created by Robrecht and Jan de Nole in 1613. The monument is illustrated in Jacobus Le Roy, *Notitia Marchionatus Sacri Imperii Romani,* Amsterdam, 1678, p. 70.

24. Hans Vlieghe, *Flemish Art and Architecture, 1585–1700,* New Haven–London, 1999), p. 242; S. Durian-Ress, 'Das barocke Grabmal in den südlichen Niederlanden. Studien zur Ikonologie und Typologie', *Aachener Kunstblätter,* XLV, 1974, pp. 235–330; C.J.H.M. Tax and A.C.M. Tax-Koolen, 'Het verdwenen grafmonument van Franciscus Sonnius in de Onze-Lieve-Vrouwekathedraal te Antwerpen', *Jaarboek Koninklijk Museum voor Schone Kunsten Antwerpen,* 1993, pp. 203–225.

25. For the history of the decoration of the high altar in Ghent cathedral, see Hans Vlieghe, *Rubens. Saints* (*Corpus Rubenianum Ludwig Burchard,* VIII), I, Brussels, 1972, pp. 107–109, cat. 72.

26. See *Missale Romanum,* Editio Princeps (1570), ed. Manlio Soldi and Achille Maria Triacca, Citta del Vaticano, 1998, fol. 42v [p. 650/4188]. For the text, see below, note 42.

27. *Missale Romanum,* fol. 43r [p. 653/4209]: 'In diebus illis. Vir fortissimus Judas, collatione facta, duodecim millia drachmas argenti misit Hierosolymam offerri pro peccatis mortuorum sacrificium, iuste et religiose de resurrectione cogitans. (Nisi enim eos qui ceciderant, resurrecturos speraret, superfluum videret et vanus orare pro mortuis.) Et quia considerabat quod hi qui cum pietate dormitiones acceperant, optimam haberent re positam gratiam. Sancta ergo et salubris est cogitatio pro defunctis exorare: ut a peccatis solvantur.' For an English translation of the relevant version of 2 Maccabees, 12, see *Douay-Rheims English translation of the Latin Vulgata:* http://www.scriptours.com/bibl.bible. For an interpretation of the Hebrew text, see Jonathan A. Goldstein, *II Maccabees,* A New Translation with Introduction and Commentary, Garden City, New York, 1964, pp. 429–451.

28. Cornelius a Lapide, *Commentarius in Esdra, Nehemiam, Tobiam, Iudith, Esther, et Machabaeos,* Antwerp: Iacobus Meursius, 1669, p. 301: 'Hinc ergo liquet Iudam Pontificem credidisse Purgatorium, in quo animae post hanc vitam a culpis expientur.' Cornelius a Lapide (Cornelius van den Steen) first taught exegesis in Leuven (1598–1616), then at the Collegio Romano. See Carlos Sommervogel, *Bibliothèque de la Compagnie de Jésus,* IV, Brussels–Paris, 1893, cols 1511–1526.

29. Cornelius a Lapide, *Commentarius* (as in note 28), p. 301. 'Supponebant ergo caesos ante mortem de furto poenituisse, eiusque partem praecipuam scilicet culpam per contritionem delevisse: quare alteram partem scilicet reatum poenae post hanc vitam in purgatorio luendae tantum restare, qui per sacrificia expiandus erat, ut peccatum perfecte deleretur, itaque ipsorum animae a poenis purgatorii exemptae ad limbum patrum sive ad sinum Abrahae transferrentur.'

30. The parts of the sacrament of penance are contrition, confession, satisfaction. The sacrament of penance was discussed in the fourteenth session of the Council of Trent on 25 November 1551. See *Canons and Decrees of the Council of Trent,* trans. H.J. Schroeder, Rockford, III, 1978, pp. 88–105. The foundational study of late medieval contritional theory is Thomas N. Tentier, *Sin and Confession on the Eve of the Reformation,* Princeton, 1977. For Tridentine views on penance, see Wietse de Boer, *The Conquest of the Soul: Confession, Discipline, and Public Order in Counter-Reformation Milan,* Leiden–Boston–Cologne, 2001, pp. 48–53.

31. Cf. the Tridentine 'decree concerning purgatory [...] begun on the third and closed on the fourth day of December, 1563'. In *Canons and Decrees* (as in note 30), p. 214.

32. Lapide, *Commentarius* (as in note 28), p. 301.

33. Ibidem: 'Hoc est Epiphonema Scriptoris Canonici, quod fidem Synagogae priscae de purgatorio, et suffragiis pro animabus in ea detentis clare astruit.'

34. Martin de Roa, *Estado de las Almas de Purgatorio. Correspondencia que hazen a sus Bienhechores: Meditationes, i varios Exemplos a este proposito,* Seville: Matias Clauijo, 1619. I have consulted the following edition, located in Antwerp's Ruusbroecgenootschap, 3047 i 22: Martin de Roa, *Den staet der Sielen des Vageviers. Met schoone Devote Meditatien ende vergeldingen aen haere weldoenders,* Leuven: Henrick van Hastens, 1625. (The printer dedicated this edition to Gertrudis van den Heet-Velde, mother of the archbishop of Mechelen, Jacobus Boonen.) The eleventh chapter of the treatise is about the advantages of requiem masses for the living and the dead: Roa 1625 (see above), p. 118: 'Hoe seer profijtich dat is voor levende, ende dooden het Sacrificie der Missen, ende welcke meer, van REQUIEM, oft vande Heyligen.' For Martin de Roa, see Sommervogel, *Bibliothèque* (as in note 28), VI, 1895, cols 1887–1896. For the overwhelming success of Roa's treatise on purgatory, see Peter Burke's essay in *The Jesuits: Cultures, Sciences, and the Arts, 1540–1773,* II, ed. John W. O'Malley, Gauvin Alexander Bailey, Steven J. Harris, and T. Frank Kennedy, Toronto, 2003.

35. Lapide, *Commentarius* (as in note 28), p. 302.

36. Cf. Maximilian, *Testamentum* (as in note 2), fol. 194 b–195 a.

37. *Iacobi Tirini Antverpiani e Societate Iesu Commentariorum in S. Scripturam tomus secundus,* Antwerp: Martinus Nutius, 1632, p. 928: 'En clarissimum Scripturae testimonium pro suffragiis defunctorum: en factum & exemplum nobilissimum pon-

tificis & Ecclesiae illius temporis, ab auctore sacro, id est, a Spiritu sancto, non modo narratum, sed & laudatum atque approbatum, ut Serarius, Bellarminus [Bellarm. liber 1. de Purgatorio c. 3] & alii Doctores fuse explicant.' Tirinus mentions, among other titles, the commentaries of Sebastian Munster and Paulus Fagius on Deuteronomy, 14, 1 ('Be ye children of the Lord your God: you shall not cut yourselves, nor make any baldness for the dead'). I have consulted: *Critici Sacri sive Doctissimorum Virorum in SS. Biblia Annotationes et Tractatus,* London: Jacobus Flesher, 1660, cols. 1226–1234 ('Annotata ad Deuteronomium, cap. XIV): 'Munsterus: Nullas Judaei fundunt preces pro mortuis suis, nec opera aliqua pietatis pro salute eorum faciunt [...]'; for Tirinus, see Sommervogel, *Bibliothèque* (as in note 28), VIII, 1898, cols 49–52.

38. See Nicolas Serarius, *In sacros divinorum bibliorum libros, Tobiam, Iudith, Esther, Machabaeos, commentarius,* Mainz: Balthasarus Lippius, 1610, pp. 454–461. On 2 Maccabees, 12, 38–46). On Nicolas Serarius, see Sommervogel, *Bibliothèque* (as in note 28), VII, 1896, cols 1134–1145).

39. I cite here from the following edition: *Disputationum Roberti Bellarmini [...] de controversis christianae fidei,* Venice, 1603, cols 512–18, here cols 512–513: 'PRIMO, posse mortuos post hanc vitam a peccatis solvi, et proinde esse Purgatorium. SECUNDO, sacrificia, et orationes vivorum prodesse defunctis. TERTIO, non expiari semper in morte ones peccatorum reliquias, ut Lutherus dicit; nam isti pro quibus orari iussit, mortui erant morte violenta, et pro religione, tamen credebat Iudas adhuc illos non plene esse purgatos. QUARTO, posse hominem sancta et pie mori, et tamen habere debitum aliquod solvendum, vel propter venialia peccata non remista in vita, vel propter satisfactionem pro mortalibus remissis non plene expletam; nam Scriptura hoc loco dicit eos, pro quorum peccatis iussit orari Iudas, cum pietate dormitionem accepisse. QUINTO, hoc esse de fide.' For Bellarmini, see Gustavo Galeota, 'Bellarmini, Roberto (1542–1621)', in *Theologische Realenzyklopädie,* V, 1980, pp. 525–531.

40. See, for instance, Schelte a Bolswert, after Peter Paul Rubens, *Saint Teresa of Avila Interceding for the Soul of Bernardino de Mendoza and other Souls in Purgatory,* engraving, 468 x 347 mm. F.W.H. Hollstein, *Dutch and Flemish Etchings, Engravings and Woodcuts ca. 1450–1700,* III, Amsterdam, 1951, p. 85, cat. 277. For a discussion of this print see my *Die Kunst des Fegefeuers nach der Reformation. Kirchliche Schenkungen, Ablass und Almosen in Antwerpen und Bologna um 1600,* Mainz, 1996, pp. 186–194.

41. Matthaeus Raderus, *Bavaria Sancta,* Munich: Raphael Sadeler, 1615: 'Maxima virtus huius Maximiliani iniquissimis Reip. Christianae temporibus enituit, cum veluti Machabaeus impiis Idolorum sacris se obiecit, aliosque metu suppliciorum dubios sua constantia ad mortem intrepide subeundam firmavit.'

42. See *Missale Romanum* (as in note 26), fol. 42 v [p. 650/4188]: 'Domine Jesu Christe rex gloriae, libera animas omnium fidelium defunctorum de poenis inferni, et de profundo lacu: libera eas de ore leonis, ne absorbeat eas tartarus, ne cadant in obscurum.'

43. I cite after Jacques Le Goff, *The Birth of Purgatory,* trans. Arthur Goldhammer, London, 1984, pp. 303–304.

44. Marco Rosci, *Il Cerano,* Milano, 2000, pp. 198–202, cat. 129.

45. Peter Jezler, [cat. exh.] *Himmel. Hölle, Fegefeuer. Das Jenseits im Mittelalter,* Schweizerisches Landesmuseum, Zürich, 2nd ed. Zürich, 1994, pp. 290–291.

46. I cite after Christine Göttler, Peter Jezler, 'Das Erlöschen des Fegefeuers und der Zusammenbruch der Auftraggeberschaft für sakrale Kunst', in '*... kein Bildnis machen'. Kunst und Theologie im Gespräch,* Würzburg, 1987, p. 130.

47. Martin Luther, 'Widerruf vom Fegefeuer' (1530), in *D. Martin Luthers Werke* (=WA), XXX, 2, Weimar, 1909, pp. 369–370.

48. Luther, 'Formula Missae et Communionis' (1523), *WA,* I, 1891, pp. 207–208: 'Tum cepit Missa esse monopolium sacerdotale, totius mundi spes exhauriens [...] Nam additamenta externa vestium, vasorum, cereorum, pallarum, deinde organorum et totius musice, imaginum quid dicam? Nihil pene fuit in toto orbe artificiorum, quod non magna ex parte sua negocia ac suum quaestum haberet et e missa aleretur.'

49. Cf. *Canons and Decrees* (as in note 30), p. 214. For the following see Göttler 1996 (as in note 40), pp. 54 ff.

50. For the following, see L. Jadin, 'Proces d'information pour la nomination des évêques et abbés des Pays Bas, 1ère partie, 1564–1637', *Bulletin de l'Institut historique belge de Rome,* VIII, Rome, 1928, pp. 106–111; Marie-Sylvie Dupont-Bouchat, 'Le procès d'Henri Sanctorum, magicien et sorcier. Tournai, 1639–1641', *Mémoires de la Société Royale d'Histoire et d'Archéologie de Tournai,* III, 1982, pp. 37–52. On Bishop Maximilian's father, see also Jean-Jacques Courvoisier, *L'Austriche saincte on l'idee du vray prelat, tirée de la vie parfaite et innocente, de S. Maximilian, apostre et patron de l'Austriche,* Brussels: Godefroy Schoevaerts, 1638, fol. a 3 r.

51. Maximilian, *Testamentum* (as in note 2), fol. 195 r.

52. Jadin 1928 (as in note 50), p. 108.

53. Ibidem, p. 107.

54. Ibidem.

55. W. Brulez, 'Correspondance de Richard Pauli-Stravius (1634–1642)', *Analecta Vaticano-Belgica,* 2e série, Nonciature de Flandre, X, Brussels–Rome, 1955, pp. 516–517.

56. De Boer 2001 (as in note 30), p. xiv.

57. Claude Maillard, *Le Bon Mariage ou le moyen d'estre heureux, et faire son salut en estat de mariage,* Douai: Jean Serrurier, 1643, fol. e 2 v–e 3 v ('Explication de la peincture du frontispice'). For Claude Maillard, see Paul Bergmans, 'Maillard (Claude)', in *Biographie Nationale de Belgique,* XIII, Brussels, 1854–95, pp. 169–170. Sommervogel, *Bibliothèque* (as in note 28), V, 1894, cols 334–336.

58. Claude Maillard, *Traité du Jubilé et autres indulgences, et des conditions pour les gagner. Tant pour soy, que pour les Ames de Purgatoire,* 2nd ed., Brussels: Guillaume Scheybels, 1645.

59. *Donations of Bishop Maximilian Villain de Gand* (as in note 15).

60. Ibidem.

61. Ibidem.

62. Charles W. Ingrao, *The Habsburg Monarchy 1618–1815,* 2nd ed. Cambridge, 2000, p. 46.

63. *Donations of Bishop Maximilian Villain* (as in note 15).

64. Courvoisier 1638 (as in note 50).

65. Ibidem, p. 265–266. For the relics venerated in the cathedral of Tournai before 1628, see Arnoldus Rayssius, *Hierogazophylacium Belgicum sive Thesaurus Sacrarum Reliquiarum Belgii,* Douai: Gerardus Pinchon, 1628, pp. 311–317 ('S. Mariae cathedralis ecclesia, Tornaci').

66. *Donations of Bishop Maximilian Villain* (as in note 15). See also Courvoisier 1638 (as in note 50), p. 266.

67. *Donations of Bishop Maximilian Villain* (as in note 15).

68. For the annual procession in Tournai, see Jean Dumoulin and Jacques Pycke, *La Cathédrale Notre-Dame de Tournai. Le guide du visiteur,* Tournai–Louvain-la-Neuve, 1994, p. 41; Jean

Dumoulin and Jacques Pycke, eds, *La Grande Procession de Tournai (1090–1992),* Tournai–Louvain-la-Neuve, 1992, especially pp. 77–78 (Catherine Dambroise and Ana Maria Jorge).

69. The text of the 'office of Saint Maximilian, bishop and martyr, according to the breviary of the Cathedral of Passau' is included in Courvoisier 1638 (as in note 50), pp. 278–284.

70. R. Chalon, 'De la mort et enterrement de Maximilien de Gand et Villain', *Bulletin de la société historique et littéraire de Tournai,* III, 1853, pp. 220–222.

71. Maximilian, *Testamentum* (as in note 2), fol. 193 r.

72. Courvoiser 1638 (as in note 50), fol. a l v.

73. Maximilian, *Testamentum* (as in note 2), fol. 193 v.

74. Ibidem, fol. 196 r.

75. Ibidem, fol. 194 r.

76. Ibidem.

77. Ibidem, fol. 194 v–195 r. For Tirinus's commentaries and Rader's *Bavaria Sancta,* see above, notes 37, 41. Maximilian Villain could have owned the following edition of the *Revelations of Saint Bridget: Revelationes S. Birgittae,* ed. Consalvus Durantus, Cologne: Bernardus Gualtherius, 1628.

78. Maximilian, *Testamentum* (as in note 2), fol. 195 r–195 v. Ludovicus Blosius (Loys de Blois) was abbot of the Benedictine Abbey of Liessies near Avesnes in Northern France. A compilation of his writings with the commentaries by Abbot Antonius van Winghe and the Benedictine fathers of Liessies was published by Balthasar Moretus in 1632. The title page was designed by Rubens and engraved by Cornelis Galle. See J. Richard Judson and Carl Van de Velde, *Rubens. Book Illustrations and Title-Pages* (*Corpus Rubenianum Ludwig Burchard,* XXII), Brussels, 1978, pp. 260–265, cat. 61.

79. Maximilian, *Testamentum* (as in note 2), fol. 192 r. In the following, I cite from Carlo Borromeo, *La Dernière Volonté de l'Ame, en forme de Testament: Que l'on doit faire Durant la vie, afin d'asseurrer l'Ame contre les tentations des diables à l'heure de la mort,* trans. Daniel van Audenaerde (Daniel de la Vierge Marie), Brussels: Jean Mommart, 1648. Bibliothèque Royale Albert Ier, Brussels, III 77.968 A 2.

80. Borromeo 1648 (as in note 79), pp. 3–4.

81. I have consulted the following copies: Antoine Sucquet, *Testamentum Christiani hominis, et salutis aeternae, quoad licet, Assecuratio Christo Iesu et Deiparae Virgini,* Antwerp: Ioannes Cnobbarus, 1625 (Antwerp, Stadsbibliotheek, 501317); Antoine Sucquet, *Fais ton testament et monument,* s.l., 1625. (Antwerp, Ruusbroecgenootschap, 3041 E 2). I will publish a more detailed discussion of this genre of literature elsewhere.

82. Maximilian, *Testamentum* (as in note 2), fol. 192 v. Saint Barbara was frequently invoked to assist the dying.

83. For comparable tensions between Gabriele Paleotti, archbishop of Bologna, and pope Gregory XIII, see Göttler, *Kunst* (as in note 40), pp. 89–92. Conflicts between popes and bishops concerning the bishops' jurisdiction have recently been analyzed by Craig Harline and Eddy Put, *A Bishop's Tale* (New Haven, London, 2000), pp. 61–62.

84. A comprehensive study of art patronage by Netherlandish bishops has still to be written. See, however, the literature mentioned in note 24.

# Abbot Van der Sterre and St. Michael's Abbey: the Restoration of its Church, its Image, and its Place in Antwerp

*Barbara Haeger*

## Introduction

The no longer extant Premonstratensian or Norbertine Abbey of St. Michael's was one of the key churches and most significant monuments in Antwerp from its foundation in the 12th century to its destruction in the nineteenth.[1] Although, like many other religious institutions in Antwerp, it suffered considerable damage during the period between the iconoclasm of 1566 and the return of the city to the Catholic fold in 1585, its difficulties did not stop then. Indeed, in 1590, St. Michael's was in such a terrible state that Bishop Torrentius recommended its dissolution Not only was the abbey impoverished and its buildings badly damaged but the reputation of the resident canons was in tatters.[2] By 1660, however, when Lucas Vorsterman made this engraving (fig. 1), St. Michael's had returned to its former splendor and once again enjoyed an important and respected position in Antwerp. The person most responsible for restoring the canons' reputation and their church was Johannes Chrysostomus van der Sterre, during whose abbacy (1629–1652) St. Michael's experienced a Golden Age. It was a period of unprecedented growth and a highpoint in the learning and discipline of the resident canons.[3] It was also a period of reconstruction and of acquisition of works of painting and sculpture for the abbey.[4]

While the majority of the buildings required attention, the church was in particular need of restoration. A serious fire in 1620 contributed to the extensive damages inflicted by iconoclasts and occupying forces in sixteenth century,[5] and although restoration began under his predecessor Abbot Yrsselius (1614–29), much still remained to be done in 1629 when Van der Sterre was made abbot. It is my belief that, in addition to commissioning works of art that propagated key Counter-Reformation doctrines, Van der Sterre considered the need to restore the abbey's church as an unparalleled opportunity to influence the perception of the Norbertines in Antwerp and to create a lasting monument to his order's beneficial presence in the city. I will discuss the iconography of the church's key monuments – the high altar and the choir screen – and argue that the orthodox, universal, Counter-Reformation program would have been understood as having a Premonstratensian inflection as well as local and historical significance.[6] Without question the dominant feature of the program is the demonstration that the benefits of Christ's sacrifice are made available through the Eucharist which is administered to the faithful by the True Church. However, when viewed in the context of time and place, these monuments, I believe, also were understood as presenting the Norbertines as supporters of papal authority, heroic foes of heresy, and promoters of a unified Catholic Antwerp. This can be demonstrated by examining the altar and choir screen not only in light of related images, especially other paintings and sculptures in the abbey acquired by Van der Sterre, but in conjunction with St. Michael's place in the city and it's role during significant periods in both Antwerp's recent and more distant past.

## The History of St. Michael's Abbey and the Norbertines in Antwerp

The history of St. Michael's is linked to one of the most significant events in the history of the Premonstratensian order – the victory of its founder, St. Norbert, over the Tanchelmian heresy. In 1122, St. Norbert was asked by the Bishop of Cambrai to go to Antwerp to combat the pernicious heresy which denigrated the power of both the Eucharist and the clergy.

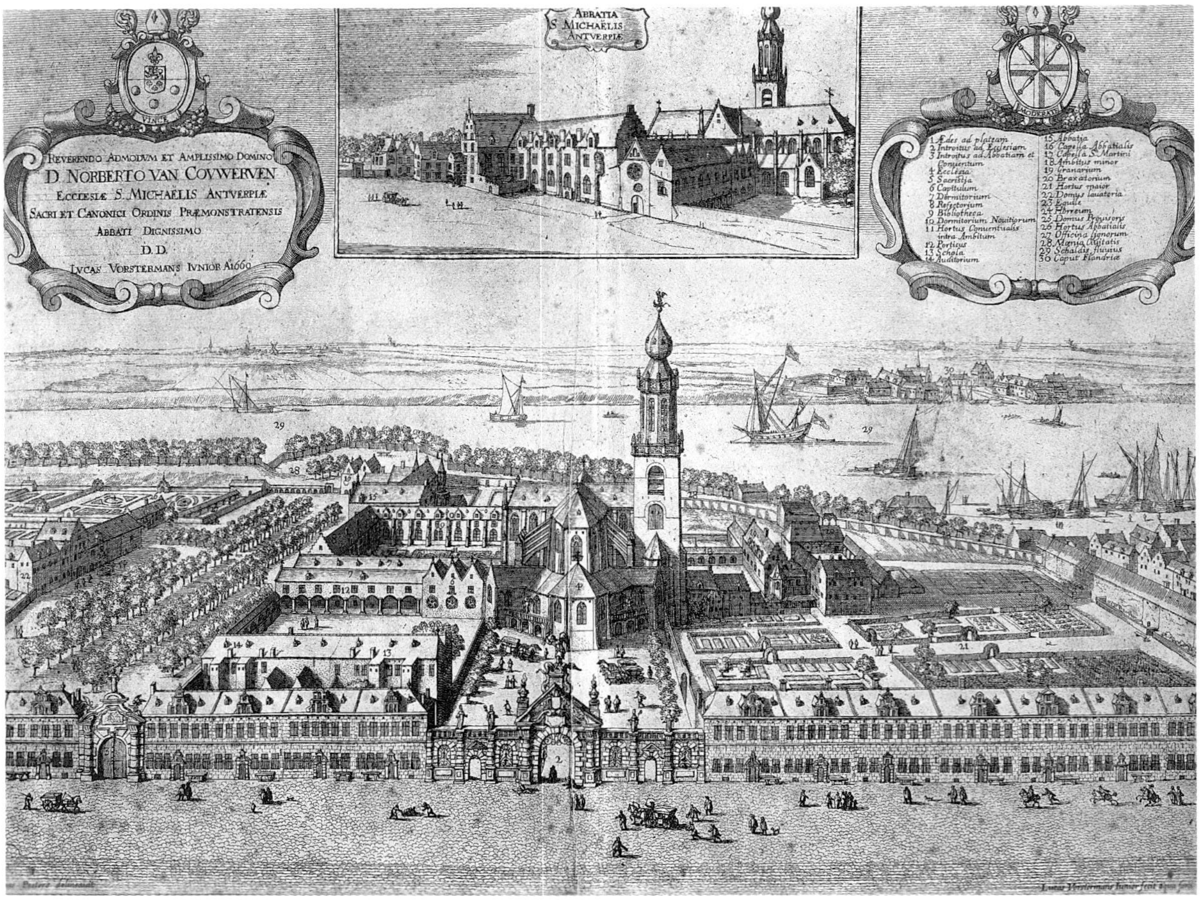


Fig. 1. Lucas Vorsterman, *St. Michael's Abbey, aerial view*, engraving

Norbert achieved the goal and successfully eradicated the heresy in 1123 after which he departed, leaving the Blessed Waltmann and his eleven companions to help minister to the needs of the citizens of Antwerp. The latter were given the church of St. Michael's in 1124 and there they founded their abbey.[7] From then on the abbey occupied a significant place in Antwerp's civic as well as its religious life. The abbot of St. Michael's, who until 1570 when the bishopric of Antwerp was definitely established, was the most prominent religious personage in the city,[8] served as host to visiting royalty, dignitaries, and rulers in residence. From time immemorial the abbey was the residence of the Dukes of Brabant when they were in the city.[9] Moreover, it was the endpoint of the *blijde inkomst* (joyous entry), the ceremonies and procession through the streets which accompanied their assumption of authority. It was presumably this association with authority as well as the existence of the Prinsenhof[10] that made St. Michael's during the revolt the headquarters of both the Spanish and the States General under William of Orange when each had control of the city.[11]

During roughly the first half sixteenth century St. Michael's prospered materially but not spiritually. It's numbers diminished and the life of its religious was ill regulated. By the time Willem Greve became abbot in 1562, the religious at St. Michael's were known for their ignorance and lack of discipline.[12] Greve did not improve matters. Moreover, his failure to institute the Tridentine reforms and his adherence to the rebellion brought the abbey into direct conflict both with the Abbot General of the Premonstratensian order and with the pope. While other abbots, provoked by the New Bishoprics Plan, had initially opposed Philip II, they gradually abandoned this position in the face of the rebels' increasing hostility to Catholicism, a hostility that by 1578 was undeniable. Greve, however, persisted.[13] In 1578 when the Jesuits left Antwerp rather than denounce Don Juan and take the required oath of loyalty to

William of Orange's puppet ruler, the Archduke Mathias of Austria, Greve and all but three Norbertines stayed on at St. Michael's.[14] By June of 1579 all public displays of Catholicism were outlawed and Catholic services mostly impossible; the Norbertines were practically the only remaining regular clergy in the city, which says a good deal about their accommodating attitude.[15] By 1581 all the canons, excepting Greve, had been expelled. In addition, most of the abbey's goods had been sold, its buildings adapted to the needs of the government of the States General, and the nave of its church given to the Lutherans; the latter, however, was reopened for restricted Catholic worship in 1582 when the Duke of Anjou took up residence.[16] In 1585 when Alessandro Farnese took Antwerp back into the Catholic fold, the canons at St. Michael's were impoverished and their buildings were badly damaged. In addition, their ability to command respect, already badly damaged, was further impaired by a bitter dispute about who should succeed Greve.[17] Consequently, they were in no position to lead the campaign to transform heterodox Antwerp into a unified Catholic city. It appeared that the Jesuits, who returned in triumph with Alessandro Farnese, were to take this role.

Initially this was the case. It was a Jesuit sodality that replaced the statue of Brabo on the Town Hall with one of the Virgin Mary and managed the accompanying celebrations.[18] Such events were a key part of transforming Antwerp into a Catholic stronghold,[19] and the Jesuits were masters of the art. They orchestrated similar festivities in 1622 to mark the successful conclusion of their campaign for the canonization of their founder Ignatius Loyola and his early follower Francis Xavier.[20] This campaign was especially conspicuous in Antwerp where it included two large pictures of the men painted by Rubens in 1617–18 which the Jesuits audaciously placed over the high altar of their recently completed church.[21] By this time, however, the canons at St. Michael's were beginning to recover[22] and they, too, employed Rubens to create the high altar for their church. While their church would not rival that of the Jesuits until Van der Sterre effected its restoration, the splendid new high altar created by Rubens and Hans van Mildert in 1622–24[23] signaled the re-emergence of St. Michael's as a respected and important religious institution in the city.

The erection of the new high altar coincided with the 500th anniversary of St. Norbert's eradication of the Tanchelmian heresy in Antwerp in 1123 and the subsequent founding of St. Michael's by his companions in the following year.[24] Norbert's victory over the heresy signified the restoration of the True Faith in Antwerp, and, consequently, its anniversary was tailor made for reinforcing the Catholic identity of the city. Marking such anniversaries with processions and works of art formed part of the Archdukes' strategy for fostering unity by establishing Catholic identity for the Southern Netherlands. It was no doubt for this reason that the Archduchess Isabella contributed to the costs of the high altar of St. Michael's by paying for two of its statues – the sculptures of St. Norbert trampling Tanchelm and St. Michael vanquishing Lucifer that adorned the ends of the pediment.[25]

Underscoring the connection between the founder of their order and the restoration of the True Faith in Antwerp clearly served the Norbertines' need to improve their image, and they took advantage of the anniversary for this purpose. This is clearly indicated in the dedication Van der Sterre wrote to the Dutch version of his life of St. Norbert which was printed the previous year in Latin. He states that he produced *Het Leven vanden H. Norbertus* in 1623 in commemoration of the 500th anniversary of the saint's victory over heresy with the explicit aim of acquainting the citizens of Antwerp with the great deeds of Norbert and his companions of the white order, as the Norbertines were known because of their white habits. The book thus is a celebration not only of the life of St. Norbert but of the order he established.[26] As a result, the book also serves as a means of rehabilitating the reputation of the Premonstratensian order and re-establishing the prominence of St. Michael's within the city. As Van der Sterre writes in his preface, *Het Leven vanden H. Norbertus* teaches the people of Antwerp what they owe this order and should motivate them to express their gratitude.[27]

Van der Sterre's account of Norbert's restoration of the True Faith in Antwerp and of his particular devotions is invaluable in understanding the significance not only of the choir screen but of the high altar at St. Michael's, and I believe that he played a role in devising the programs for both. Although the high altar was commissioned by Yrsselius, perhaps in tandem with his portrait,[28] this does not preclude Van der Sterre's involvement in the conception of its program. What could have been more reasonable than that the aged abbot (already 82 years old in 1623) – laboring to bring his house in order and engaged in a campaign to acquire the relics of St. Norbert[29] – should have entrusted his energetic and learned prior with collaborating with Rubens on devising the particulars of the high altar's program? This seems all the more credible when one considers that Yrsselius's respect for Van der Sterre's learning caused him to encourage the latter to write the life of St. Norbert, as a consequence of which Van der Sterre must have become the leading authority on the subject and on the history of the order. Who could have been better suited to assist Rubens? Moreover, Yrsselius was, in the words of Floris Prims, a man of the old tradition who was overtaken by the spirit of the Counter Reformation. Van der Sterre on the other hand was a man of the times,[30] and this is reflected not only in the works that he commissioned but in the high altar. Finally, the triumphant mode and metaphorical imagery of the altar find their counterpart in Van der Sterre's life of St. Norbert and correspond to the works acquired during Van der Sterre's abbacy.

## The Program of Johannes Chrysostomus van der Sterre

Van der Sterre was the most learned of the canons at St. Michael's. He was educated at the Jesuit school and spent four years in Leuven at the Premonstratensian college from which he received a degree in theology (bachelier formé en théologie). He became prior and master of the novices at St. Michael's in 1621, seven years after being ordained (which required a special dispensation due to his youth). In 1629 he succeeded Yrsselius as abbot of St. Michael's and in 1634 was made vicar general for Brabant and Friesland. The following year changes in the order's structure led to his being granted the authority to make apostolic visits.[31] In 1639, he established a confraternity at St. Michael's dedicated to St. Norbert, thereby contributing to the active veneration of the saint.[32] He was apparently an exemplary abbot and is described as being virtuous, hard-working and learned.[33] Already, as prior and master of the novices, Van der Sterre was rigorous in establishing discipline in St. Michael's and consequently improving the abbey's reputation.[34] By the time he died in 1652, he was renowned as one who not only returned St. Michael's to its former respected position but who promoted knowledge of his order and of its saints through numerous publications.[35] His restoration of the church of St. Michael's contributed to both achievements.

If St. Michael's was to recover its position in Antwerp, the memory of Greve's alliance with the forces of heresy and rebellion had to be obliterated and the canons' religious orthodoxy and commitment to the aims of the Counter Reformation recognized. The choir screen and high altar between them glorify the Virgin as co-redeemer, celebrate the Church's victory over heresy, attest to the power of the clergy, affirm the authority of the Pope, and, above all, reveal the redeeming power of the Eucharist. The other works Van der Sterre acquired for the abbey represent St. Norbert or the Blessed Waltmann; these demonstrate the order's special veneration of the Eucharist and the Virgin[36] and attest to its service to Antwerp particularly in the eradication of heresy. That the Tanchelmian heresy that Norbert vanquished denigrated the clergy and denied the efficacy of the Eucharist in contributing to salvation[37] made it comparable to the Protestant heresies that denied the Real Presence, and consequently, as Knipping points out, the saint's deeds were invested with a Counter-Reformation flavor.[38] Thus, Norbert's victory and subsequent restoration of the True Faith could be seen as analogous to the Church's recent triumph in Antwerp. It would appear that Van der Sterre's strategy was to exploit these parallels as a means of linking his order with the restoration of the Counter Reformation devotions in the city in 1585 and thus simultaneously demonstrating the orthodox beliefs of the canons of St. Michael's and restoring their image.

## Images of St. Norbert and the Blessed Waltmann

Two of the works that Van der Sterre commissioned for St. Michael's attest to this strat-

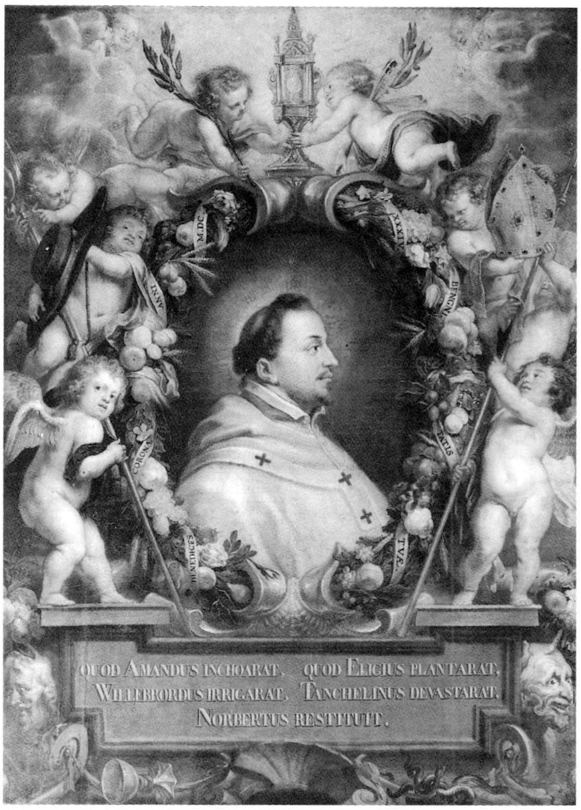


Fig. 2. Abraham van Diepenbeeck, *St. Norbert*. Antwerp, Cathedral

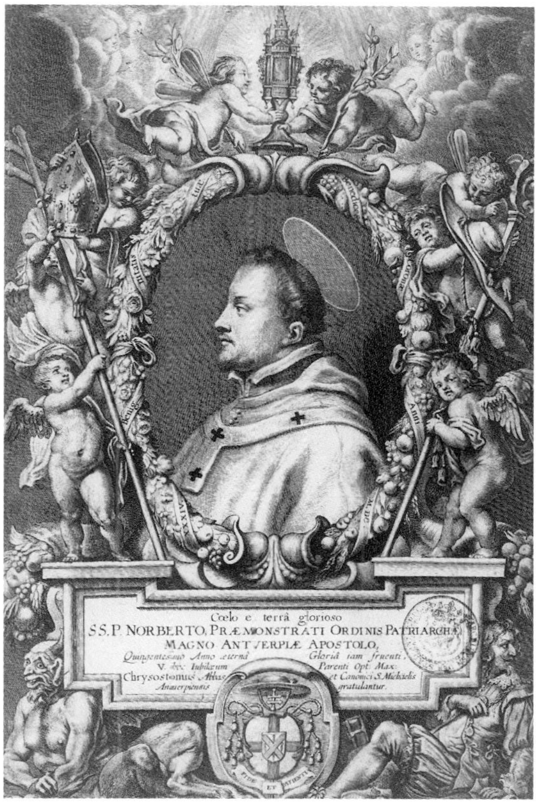


Fig. 3. Lucas Vorsterman, after Abraham van Diepenbeeck, *St. Norbert*, engraving

egy by linking the Eucharist, the favored Counter-Reformation devotion, to St. Norbert's restoration of the True Faith in Antwerp. These are depictions of the saint that were intended to increase St. Norbert's visibility in the city. One is a no longer extant statue of the saint on the facade of the chapel that faced the river and was thus visible to those passing the abbey;[39] the other is Abraham van Diepenbeeck's 1634 painting, currently in the Antwerp Cathedral (fig. 2), an image which was disseminated in modified form by Lucas Vorsterman's engraving executed the same year (fig. 3).[40] Sculpture and painting include Latin verses that portray Norbert as an apostle by likening him to others who brought Christianity to the region. These verses, attributed to Van der Sterre, state: 'Quod Amandus inchoarat/ Quod Eligius plantarat/ Willebrordus irrigarat/ Tanchelinus devastarat/ Norbertus restituit' (What Amand began, what Eligius planted, Willebrord watered, Tanchelm destroyed and Norbert re-established). [41] While both works include the monstrance, Norbert's attribute that attests to his special veneration of the Eucharist and championship of the Real Presence,[42] it is the painting that makes visibly explicit the connection between the Sacrament and the restoration of the Holy Roman Church in Antwerp. The picture emphasizes the theme of victory. Tanchelm and the devil, his ally in leading souls to hell, are crushed by the plaque that proclaims the re-institution of the true religion, while the monstrance, placed atop the wreath that encompasses St. Norbert, is flanked by putti holding palms of victory. Moreover, the latter appears as a radiant object that dispels the clouds of darkness. The light that drives away darkness attests to the Real Presence and thus clearly signifies not only the defeat of heresy but Christ's victory over death and the promise of eternal life inherent in the sacrament. It is worth noting that Van der Sterre employs the same metaphorical language in describing the Sacrament, Norbert's victory over heresy, and the triumph of the Church.[43] Furthermore, he writes that St. Norbert re-established the true faith in Antwerp by celebrating the Eucharistic rite.[44] Clearly, the painting makes

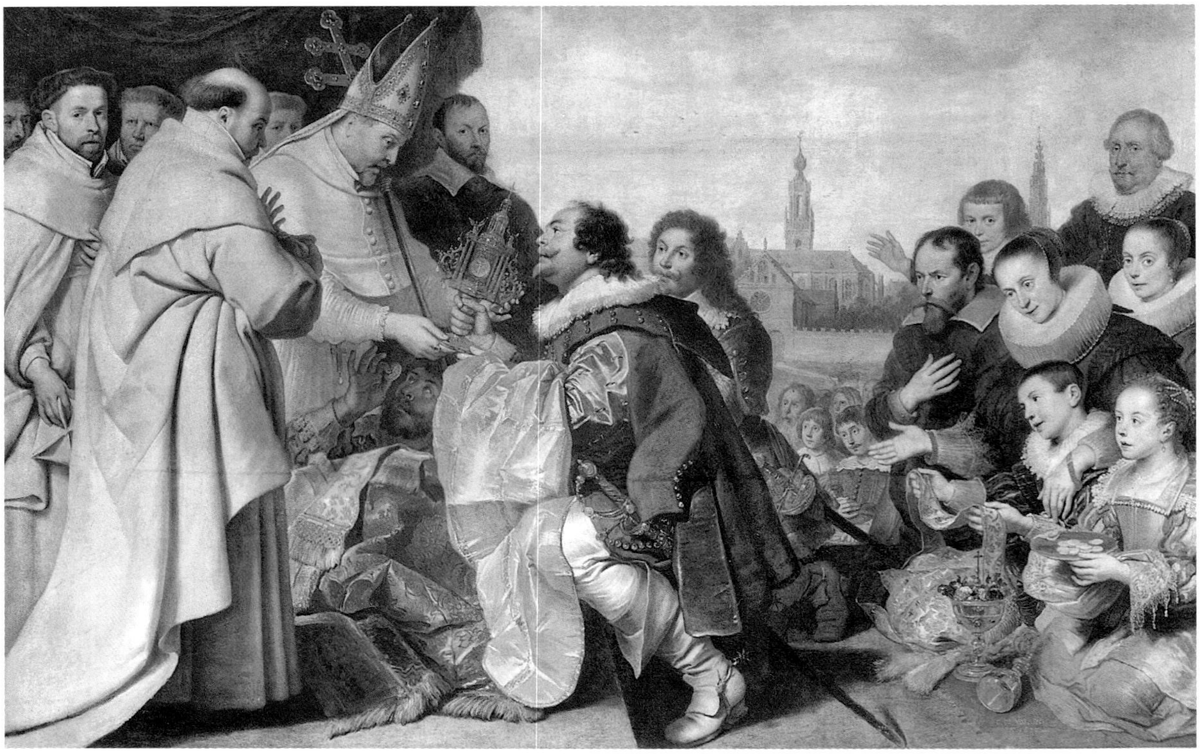

Fig. 4. Cornelis de Vos, *Restitution of Church Treasures to St. Norbert after the Defeat of the Tanchelmian Heresy.* Antwerp, Koninklijk Museum voor Schone Kunsten

visible Van der Sterre's conception of the Holy Sacrament as both the instrument of victory and the emblem of the restoration of the Holy Church.

Despite the elimination of the verses, the same message is conveyed by the print. The reestablishment of the True Faith is referred to in the new inscription that proclaims Norbert as Antwerp's great apostle, while his restoration of what Tanchelm destroyed is here made clear by changes in the portrayal of those he crushes beneath the plaque on which his image rests. Vorsterman develops these representations from the mere heads depicted in the painting into full figures and displays both host and chalice to demonstrate Tanchelm's denigration of the Eucharist. Thus, the print, which commemorates the 500th anniversary of Norbert's death (his enjoyment of eternal glory), conveys the same meaning as the painting in a more accessible way and hence to a broader audience. Significantly, it also underscores St.Norbert's connection with St. Michael's. The inscription names him not only as a great apostle but as the founder of the Premonstratensian order, and it states that Abbot Van der Sterre and canons of St. Michael's rejoice in the saint's eternal glory.[45]

While Vorsterman's print verbally identifies the saint as a Norbertine and refers to the canons of St. Michael's, Cornelis de Vos's *Restitution of the Church Treasures to St. Norbert after the Defeat of the Tanchelmian Heresy* (Antwerp, Koninklijk Museum voor Schone Kunsten), painted in 1630 for the Chapel of the Holy Sacrament to the north of the choir, makes visibly manifest Norbert's connection with the abbey and portrays the current canons as participants in the victory over Tanchelm (fig. 4).[46] The picture is somewhat curious in that the figure of Tanchelm is rather awkwardly introduced at Norbert's feet as he receives the monstrance; the result is a work which combines the iconic image of the saint with a narrative scene.[47] This curious combination may be the consequence of De Vos's fulfilling Van der Sterre's demands as well as those of his patrons. The painting, an epitaph for Nicolaes Snoeck and Catherina van Uytrecht, was commissioned by the couple's children and heirs, one of whom was Johannes Snoeck. The latter was a canon at St. Michael's who in 1630 held the position of sacristan and treasurer, and Katlijne van der Stighelen plausibly suggests that he devised the iconography for the epitaph.[48] He may well have proposed the return of the church vessels as the subject; indeed his position lends credence to the notion. However, I would argue that at the very least Van der Sterre played a role in the picture's conception. The combination of the iconic image of the saint with the narrative scene supports such a conclusion, as it recalls the section in *Het Leven vanden H. Norbertus* in which Van der Sterre explains what one should think of when seeing Norbert standing on Tanchelm and holding the monstrance, an explanation that includes an account of De Vos's narrative scene. Van der Sterre describes how the sacrament was the instrument of the saint's victory over heresy and the devil and the object of his devotions. He relates how the great veneration Norbert both displayed toward the Sacrament and expressed in his sermons moved the people of Antwerp to return the sacred vessels and the hosts that they had hidden when the heretics desecrated the churches. After reiterating these points, Van der Sterre adds that Norbert is shown holding the monstrance because he took the host to so many to whom he brought to penance and because he used the sacrament in purifying the churches of Antwerp where he restored Christ to his throne.[49] De Vos depicts the monstrance as the focus of attention and shows it being handed to Norbert above the head of Tanchelm. Thus, in the painting, as in Van der Sterre's text, the Holy Sacrament is presented as the instrument of victory and the emblem of the restoration of the True Faith.

De Vos's painting was ideally suited to both its location in the Chapel of the Holy Sacrament and Van der Sterre's aims discussed above. Moreover, the inclusion of the Norbertines along with the abbey of St. Michael's in the background reminds that Norbert was assisted in the eradication of the anti-sacramentarian heresy by his twelve companions, who remained in Antwerp to minister to the needs of its citizens, and consequently that the founding of the abbey coincides with the restoration of the Holy Roman Church. Finally, the painting not only celebrates the twelfth-century canons and the role they played in Antwerp's Catholic identity but links them to the abbey's current occupants. This is explicitly achieved by the seventeenth-century costumes and equally anachronistically rendered buildings, as well as by the inclusion of portraits, identified by Van der Stighelen. Van der Sterre is portrayed to the right of St. Norbert and Johannes Snoeck likely appears behind him. Nicholas Rockox is represented on Norbert's left and members of the Snoeck family are shown among the citizens of Antwerp who return the liturgical vessels which they had protected from Tanchelm's followers.[50] The anachronistic features surely prompted viewers to perceive parallels between the subject of the painting and the return of Antwerp to the Catholic fold in 1585 and the on-going restoration of the city's churches necessitated by the desecration and destruction of the Calvinists. Such connections present the canons in a positive light and create an image of the renewed importance of St. Michael's in Counter Reformation Antwerp.

By 1630, St. Michael's recovery was a reality; moreover, three years earlier it had been the focus of the city's attention. In 1627 the canons of St. Michael's finally succeeded in acquiring relics of St. Norbert. The acquisition of the relics was the occasion for city-wide processions, ceremonies, and celebrations involving not only the Norbertines but the Jesuits and, among others, members of the Confraternity of the Holy Sacrament of the Cathedral.[51] In other words, it was precisely the kind of occasion that could be effectively employed to unite the city and reinforce its Catholic identity. It seems likely then that, as Van der Stighelen proposes, De Vos's picture, which shows the citizens and representatives of Antwerp's government, such as Nicholas Rockox, united in expressing their devotion to their apostle, recalls the occasion, an occasion commemorated by Van der Sterre in his book *Echo S. Norberti triumphantis* printed the previous year.[52] However, it should be noted that while the citizens' Catholic identity is expressed in their veneration of the Eucharist, emblematic of the Counter-Reformation Church, the religious establishment, as the subject's narrative requires, is presented as Norbertine.[53] Thus, the incorporation of anachronistic elements and allusions into the depiction of a twelfth-century event enables the shaping of the positive perception of the abbey's current canons in Antwerp.

In De Vos's painting, Van der Sterre is portrayed on Norbert's right and this, combined

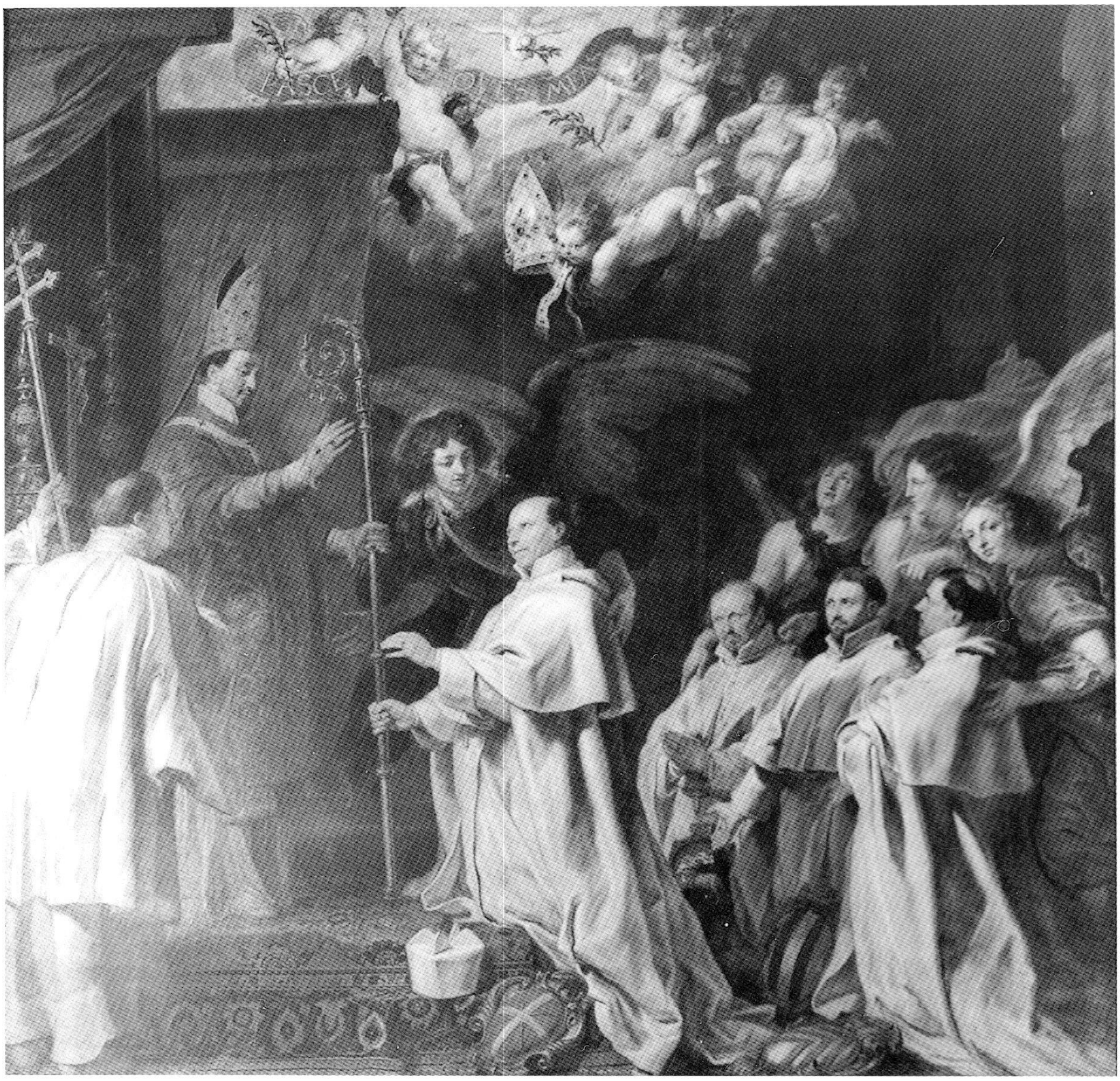

Fig. 5. Abraham van Diepenbeeck, *Consecration of the Blessed Waltmann*. Deurne, Sint-Fredeganduskerk

with his prominence, suggests that he may represent the Blessed Waltmann, the first abbot of St. Michael's, who can be described literally as Norbert's right-hand man in Antwerp. Support for this thesis can be found in a painting that Van der Sterre commissioned for the main hall of the abbey. This is Abraham van Diepenbeeck's *Consecration of the Blessed Waltmann by St. Norbert* (Deurne, St. Fredegundus) in which the abbot appears in the guise of the Blessed Waltmann as he is being invested as abbot by St. Norbert (fig. 5). Painted in the 1640's, likely to commemorate either the fifteenth or twentieth anniversary of his own investiture,[54] the work represents St. Norbert extending his blessing to the Blessed Waltmann beneath the dove of the Holy Spirit, putti bearing the abbot's mitre, and a banderole displaying the command that Christ gave Peter: 'Pasce oves meas' (Feed my Sheep). The archangel Michael stands at Waltmann's right, while other angels accompany the abbots of Middelburg, Tongerloo, and Averbode, all identified by their shields. The anachronistic presence of the last two makes reference to the role of St. Michael's in spreading the true faith in the southern Netherlands.[55] That Van der Sterre should have identified with Waltmann is not surprising considering the similarity of their programs; Cynthia Lawrence notes that the Blessed Waltmann labored tirelessly to develop St. Michael's as a center for religious unity and orthodoxy in Antwerp.[56]

Van der Sterre's particular attachment to the Blessed Waltmann is also attested to in the Waltmann Memorial which he had erected in 1631 to mark the tomb of the founder of the abbey on the north wall of the nave.[57] As depicted in P. Bouttats's engraving (fig. 6) and on the left wall of Henri Causé's engraving after Jan van Croes's 1694 drawing of the interior of St. Michael's (fig. 7),[58] the monument depicts the Blessed Waltmann in adoration of the Virgin and Child. Consequently, as Lawrence points out, the Waltmann Memorial is unique for a tomb monument in Antwerp between 1570 and 1650. Although the representation of the kneeling figure before the Virgin and Child was common in fifteenth-century tombs, by 1570, in response to Tridentine recommendations concerning art, the suffering Christ of the Passion or the triumphant Christ of the Resurrection had replaced the Mother of God as the object of the deceased's devotion.[59] As already noted, the Premonstratensians had two special devotions, one to the Holy Sacrament and the other to the Virgin Mary, the patroness of their order and of all of their houses.[60] In addition to demonstrating the order's and Norbert's particular devotion to her, Waltmann's adoration of the Virgin and Child ties that devotion, and consequently the canons of St. Michael's, to the most visible sign of Antwerp's Catholic identity–the Virgin Mary. It was the Virgin's statue that was installed on the facade of the Town Hall in 1587 as the means of marking the city's return to the Catholic fold. Moreover, she was the patroness of the city. She achieved this status in the twelfth century, at least according to Van der Sterre who connects the event with his order. He writes that the citizens of Antwerp were so impressed by the intensity of Norbert's veneration of the Virgin and his sermons in her honor that they made her the principal patroness of their city.[61] While the sculpture shows Waltmann's resemblance to the founder of the order in his devotion to the Virgin, the inscription likens his apostolic zeal to Norbert's, noting his activity in converting the citizens of Antwerp. It also celebrates his saintliness and his role as the first abbot of St. Michael's. Thus, like the images of St. Norbert commissioned by Van der Sterre, that of the Blessed Waltmann – which makes visible the canon's devotion to the Virgin and to the Holy Church that she personifies – connects St. Michael's and Norbertine devotions with the propagation of the True Faith and the Catholic identity of Antwerp.

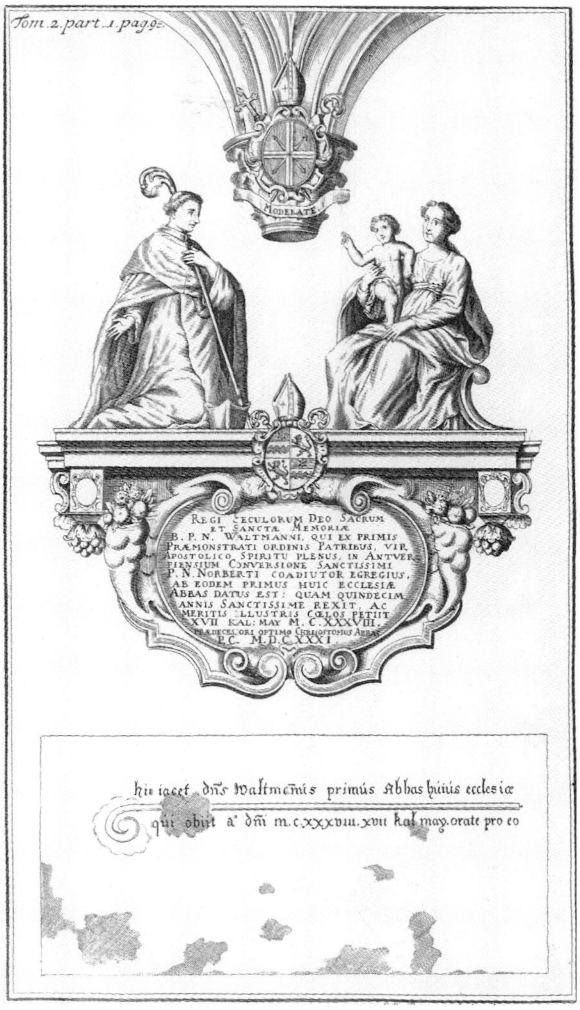


Fig. 6. P. Bouttats, *Waltmann Memorial*, from J. Le Roy, *Le Grand Théâtre Sacré du Duché de Brabant*, engraving

## The Choir Screen and the High Altar

This connection is also made in the programs for the choir screen and the high altar. The former, like the Blessed Waltmann's tomb, was irreparably damaged by iconoclasts in 1566,[62] and it seems likely that rebuilding the choir screen was one of Van der Sterre's first acts as abbot. As Frans Baudouin has convincingly argued, the sculptures for the monument by Hans van Mildert most likely were executed between 1629 and 1633, dates based on Van Mildert's other activities. Moreover, noting the close personal and professional relationship between Van Mildert and Rubens and the resemblance between the

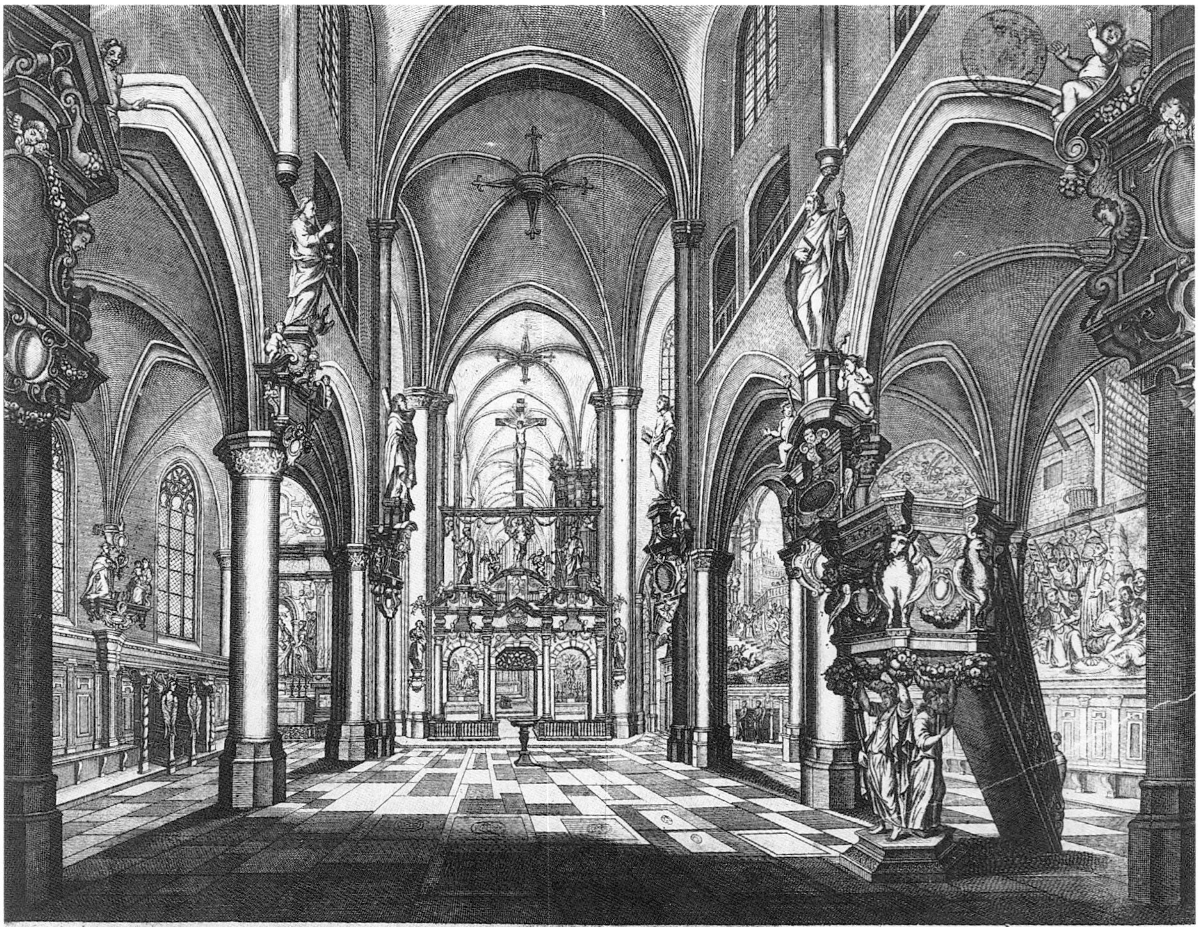


Fig. 7. Henri Causé, after Jan van Croes, *St. Michael's Abbey, interior*, engraving

structure and the portico in Rubens's courtyard, he raises the distinct possibility that, like the high altar, the choir screen was designed by the latter.[63] Considering that the entrance portico to the abbey, also erected by Van der Sterre and attributed to Rubens in the seventeenth century, shows similar features, and recalling Rubens, numerous connections with the abbey, this seems more than likely.[64] All that remains of the monument today are the statues of Peter and Paul, now in the Cathedral. However, the appearance of the structure is recorded in written descriptions and in paintings by Pieter Neeffs, Hubert Quellinus, and most clearly in Causeé's engraving (fig. 7).[65] Beneath the huge triumphal cross which, as Jan Steppe notes, traditionally marked the entrance to the choir,[66] is Christ as the Good Shepherd. This image is combined with the depiction of Christ as the Fountain of Life, a unique conflation to the best of my knowledge. A stream of blood spurts from Christ's side and flows into the chalice held by one of two flanking angels. This group is, in turn, flanked by Saints Peter and Paul. The placement as well as the configuration of statues, like the conflation of the Fountain of Life and Good Shepherd images, is unusual. Most choir screens, like that at 's Hertogenbosch, place the sculptures – most often the Virgin or Salvator Mundi flanked by Evangelists or Apostles[67] – along the face of the structure. Only the triumphal cross alone or forming a Calvary group along with the Virgin and St. John generally appears above the architectural structure.[68] At St. Michael's the figures are placed on top of the choir screen and consequently are given greater prominence.

Obviously, the placement of Peter and Paul on either side of the image of Christ as the Fountain of Life, which is directly beneath the huge triumphal cross, is intended to represent the Church that administers the sacrament that is the vehicle by which the benefits of Christ's redeem-

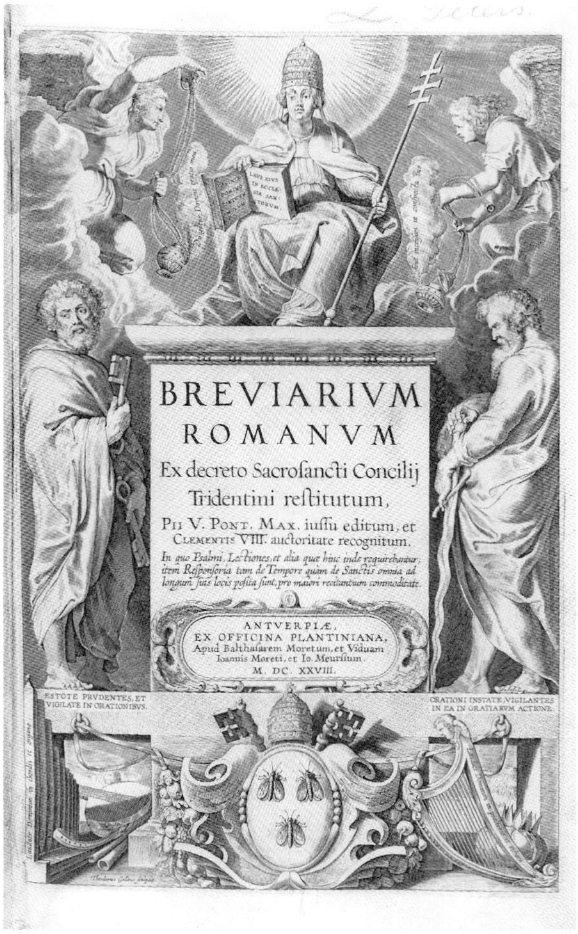


Fig. 8. Theodoor Galle, after Peter Paul Rubens, *Title-page for Breviarium Romanum*

ing sacrifice are made available to the faithful. These apostles – one to the East and the Jews, the other to the West and the Gentiles – also represent the unity of the Church and its foundation, a significance to which I shall return. Thus, they are emblematic of orthodoxy.[69] Consequently, they appear on official Church publications such as the *Brevarium Romanum*. It is perhaps not irrelevant to point out the resemblance between Rubens's title page for this work (fig. 8) and the design for the choir screen. Both include similar portrayals of Peter and Paul on either side of a central figure flanked by angels.[70] The publication of the *Brevarium Romanum* itself signifies Church unity, as it represents part of a campaign to standardize Catholic liturgy and ceremonial practices. That the Premonstratensian order adopted most Roman liturgical practices in 1628 is worth noting.[71] As mentioned above, under Abbot Greve St. Michael's had failed to adopt the Tridentine reforms and had added rebellion and disunity to unorthodox rule. Thus, Van der Sterre may have intended the prominent placement of Peter and Paul to attest to the obedience and orthodoxy of the Norbertines and their place within the universal Holy Roman Church.

Depictions of Peter and Paul flanking Christ also refer to the apostolic succession and are thus emblematic of the power and authority of both pope and clergy, as is evident in this print by Hieronymous Wierix (fig. 9). It bears an inscription that refers to Peter and Paul respectively which in translation reads: 'On this stone I shall build my church and I shall give you the keys of the kingdom of heaven. This man is my chosen vessel so that he may carry my name among the Gentiles.'[72] The transmission of authority and power from Christ to his apostles and from them to their successors was essential to the Church's claims of orthodoxy and the power of priests. Franciscus Costerus, whose numerous writings defending Catholic doctrines and beliefs were printed in Antwerp, makes this point when he states that Christ told the apostles, the founders

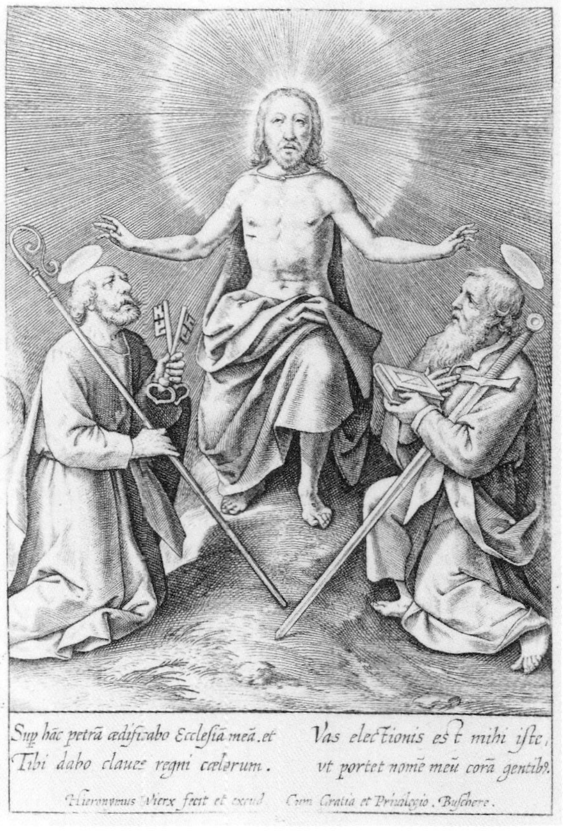


Fig. 9. Hieronymus Wierix, *Christ between Saints Peter and Paul*, engraving

of the Church, that those who heard them heard him, and he connects the apostles with the pastors and those who follow the same faith. The Roman Church, he asserts, is completely the same as that founded and governed by Peter.[73] According to both Van der Sterre and Costerus among others, this continuity, something that heretics cannot claim, attests to the validity of Catholic doctrine.[74] At St. Michael's, Peter, displaying the keys to the kingdom of heaven, appears on Christ's right to demonstrate that he is Christ's successor on earth, and he and Paul are linked with the apostles that adorn the columns of the nave. The Church is repeatedly described as a column of truth and the apostles are seen as representing the foundation of the Church and are also described as columns that support it [75] Consequently, the connection between the apostles on the choir screen and those on the nave columns serves to make visible the apostolic succession and emphasizes that the Church is not only an invisible community of saints, as Calvin would have it, but a visible church ruled by Christ's successor on earth.[76] That salvation is to be found in the visible Church governed by Peter's successor is conveyed by incorporating the image of the Good Shepherd.

The placement of Christ as the Good Shepherd directly over the entrance into the choir suggests that Van der Sterre intended a reference specifically to the Parable of the Good Shepherd as recounted in John 10. It is here, rather than in Luke, that the metaphor of the door is employed. In John 10: 1–18, Christ compares himself to the Good Shepherd who lays down his life for his sheep, and in verse 9 he states: 'I am the door, by me if any man enter in, he shall be saved.' Christ also says that those who try to enter another way, break in; they are thieves and murderers. In his commentary on the parable printed in 1604, Costerus explains that the door is Christ; the sheep stall is the Church, and the gatekeeper is the Holy Spirit who lets the pastors in who govern the sheep and who are sheep themselves. All the sheep must enter in through faith in Christ. The Holy Ghost lets them in and forgives their sins and gives the pastors the authority to perform their service. Those who break in are the murderers who kill souls; they are heretics. Costerus continues with an explication of verse 14 in which Christ states: 'I am the Good Shepherd; and I know mine and mine know me.' He notes that Christ says that he gives his soul for his sheep and that He dies willingly to rescue them from eternal death. He adds that Christ states that all his sheep shall live in one stall, that is the Holy Church, and under one shepherd that is not only under Christ who reigns invisibly but under one leader who unifies the visible Church. This ruler, Costerus concludes, is Peter whom Christ chose and to whom he gave the command: 'Feed my sheep'.[77]

In light of Costerus's commentary, it is clear that the Good Shepherd flanked by Peter and Paul would have been understood as a representation of the visible Church, papal authority, and of the power and duties of the clergy. The incorporation of Christ as the Fountain of Life reinforces this meaning, reminding that from the side of Christ sprang the Holy Church and its power to forgive sins, as Costerus states.[78] In this context, the image, which attests to the Real Presence and makes explicit the means by which the access to the redeeming benefits of Christ's sacrifice are made available, presents the Holy Sacrament as emblematic of the Church and its foundation. This significance is pertinent to my thesis that Van der Sterre gives the universal Counter-Reformation program a local connection and a Premonstratensian inflection. This can be demonstrated by considering the inscription that was placed beneath the cross and which connects the choir screen to events in Antwerp. In translation it states: 'Those who threw me down in 1566, Restored me in 1585.'[79] The 'me' likely refers literally to the cross as well as figuratively to the Church. The former was literally thrown down by the iconoclasts in St. Michael's in 1566[80] and presumably was raised again when Catholicism was restored in Antwerp following Alessandro Farnese's victory in 1585. But how are we to interpret the statement that those who threw me down raised me? As good Catholics wouldn't desecrate the cross, nor committed iconoclasts raise one, this must be a reference to the people of Antwerp in a broad, general sense. In other words, the people of Antwerp, led astray by the Calvinist heretics in 1566, returned to the fold in 1585. Heresy is defeated and the Church is triumphant. Who is responsible? Farnese defeated the military forces but it was the Church, the clergy, who were responsible for bringing the lost sheep back to the fold, and

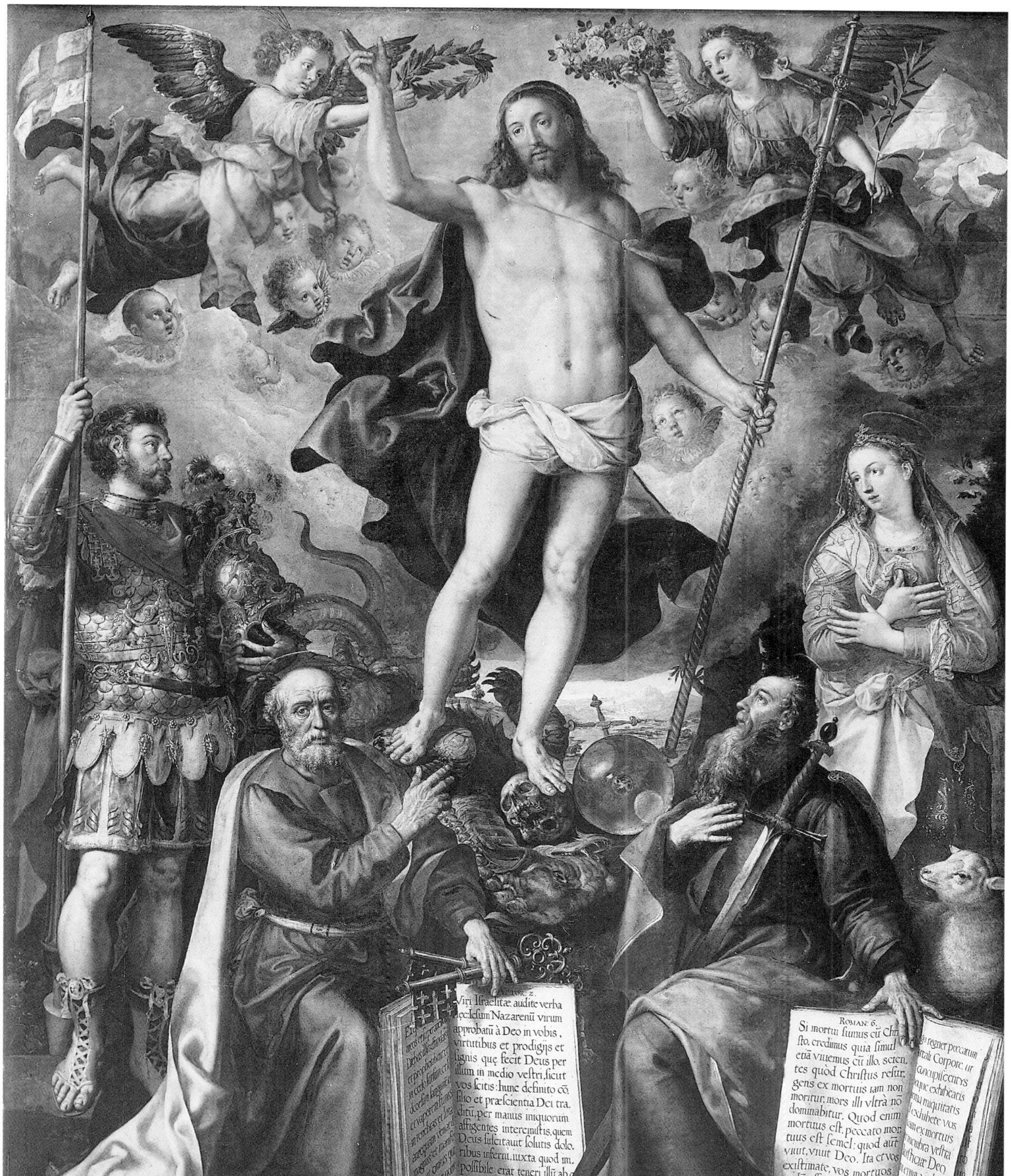


Fig. 10. Marten de Vos, *St. Georg Triptych for the Old Crossbowmen*. Antwerp, Koninklijk Museum voor Schone Kunsten

thus the presence of the Good Shepherd is also meaningful in this context.

Peter and Paul are placed atop the triumphal arch that constitutes the choir screen to represent the triumph of the Holy Roman Church in Antwerp. The apostles appear in the central panel of Marten de Vos's 1590 triptych (fig. 10) for the altar of the Old Crossbowman in the Antwerp Cathedral. As Leo Wuyts has demonstrated, the program of the triptych (Antwerp,

Koninklijk Museum voor Schone Kunsten) refers to Farnese's victory and the triumphant restoration of the True Faith in Antwerp.[81] Between the two apostles in De Vos's work, Christ appears as victor over sin and death and effectively makes visible the triumphant mood associated with the Church's victory. The figure of Christ in St. Michael's resonates with no such sense of triumph. If Van der Sterre and Rubens, as it would appear, wished to allude to the same event, why did they combine Christ as the Fountain of Life rather than Christ Triumphant with the image of the Good Shepherd? The reasons are various and relate both to the already existing high altar and to Van der Sterre's desire to foreground his order's special veneration of the Holy Sacrament and to link his canons to the restoration of 1585, in which they did not distinguish themselves, by connecting that event to Norbert's restoration of the True Faith in Antwerp in 1123.

The Fountain of Life must be considered in relation to the crucifix beneath which it appears, the cross of triumph that symbolizes Christ's victory over death and the devil. Placed as it is, the image attests to the Sacrifice of the Mass and the Real Presence. Moreover, it demonstrates that the blood, in St. Augustine's words, is the sign of Christ's cross that gives all the sacraments their power, a statement reiterated by Franciscus Costerus in his sermon on the Eucharist printed in Antwerp in 1616.[82] It thus makes visible the means of salvation by which believers are freed from sin and death. As noted above, the Holy Sacrament was central to both the identity of the Counter-Reformation Church and Norbertine devotions. Moreover, in 1623, St. Michael's became a particular site for the veneration of the Sacrament. Because, as Van der Sterre records, St. Norbert was such an excellent champion of the Holy Sacrament, Pope Gregory XV granted a special indulgence to those who visited the abbey and venerated the Eucharist on the Sunday after Octave.[83] The presence of Christ as the Fountain of Life makes visible the Norbertines' special devotion, championed by their founder and acknowledged by the papacy, and thus demonstrates the central position of St. Michael's in forming the Catholic identity of Antwerp.

The Holy Sacrament was not only the object of St. Norbert's devotion but, as already mentioned, the instrument of his defeat of heresy, and it would appear that the choir screen was intended to evoke both. While the inscription explicitly refers to the defeat of heresy, the architecture by its rusticated surface and triumphal form alludes respectively to battle and victory. The fortress-like effect of the surface relates to the image Van der Sterre wished to convey of his order as soldiers in the battle against heresy. This is evident in his life of St. Norbert and in the face that the abbey presented to the city, an entrance commissioned by Van der Sterre and attributed to Rubens and one that displays a similar rusticated surface.[84] This entrance portal of the abbey, as seen in Vorsterman's engraving (fig. 1), is crowned by a sculpture of St. Michael victorious over a demonic Lucifer. The image of St. Michael, the protector of the Church, crushing the monstrous Lucifer atop a fortress-like gateway was surely intended to charcterize St. Michael's as a bulwark against heresy.[85] Indeed, this is how Van der Sterre describes it. He writes that the abbey was erected as a 'Fort royael' and a strong fortress where day and night watch is kept for the well being of the city.[86] Moreover, he repeatedly connects the founding of St. Michael's with the defeat of heresy and the restoration of the Eucharistic rite and the True Faith, which he characterizes as raising up again the bloody banner of the cross of Christ.[87] This resemblance between Van der Sterre's text and the form as well as the central figures and inscription on the choir screen suggests that the abbot may have intended to connect the events of 1123 with those of 1585. Whether or not this is the case, the choir screen signifies the Holy Roman Church and testifies to its power to forgive sins transmitted through the apostolic succession, while a reference to it as a bulwark evokes a militaristic image and hence the battle with heresy. It is thus particularly fitting to a monument that refers to the restoration of the True Faith in Antwerp in 1585. Here it should be recalled that Peter, in particular, was renowned as committed foe of heresy, and De Vos's triptych is only one of a number of images that employ the two apostles in connection with the return of Antwerp to the Catholic fold.[88] While the choir screen refers to the triumph of the Holy Roman Church in Antwerp, the high altar makes that triumph visible and gives it a markedly Premonstratensian character. Moreover, because the two monuments are

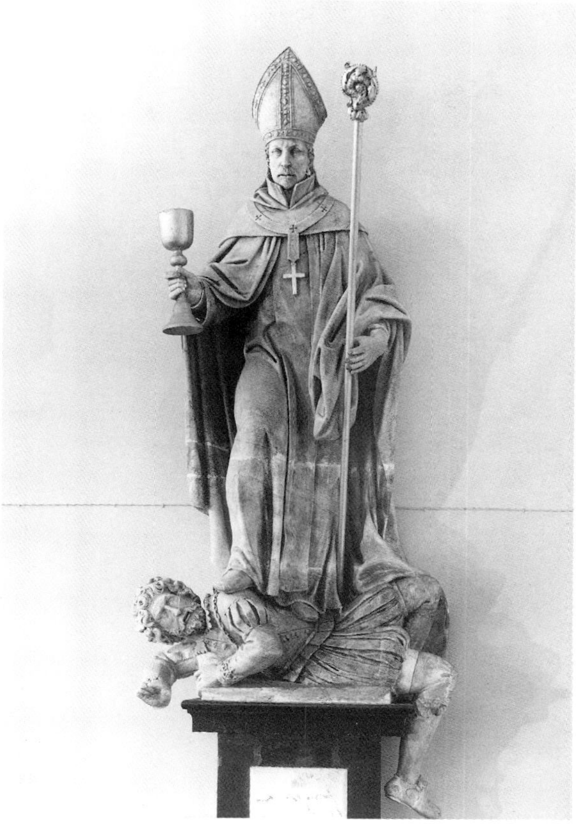

Fig. 11. Hans van Mildert, *St. Norbert*. Zundert, Sint-Trudokerk

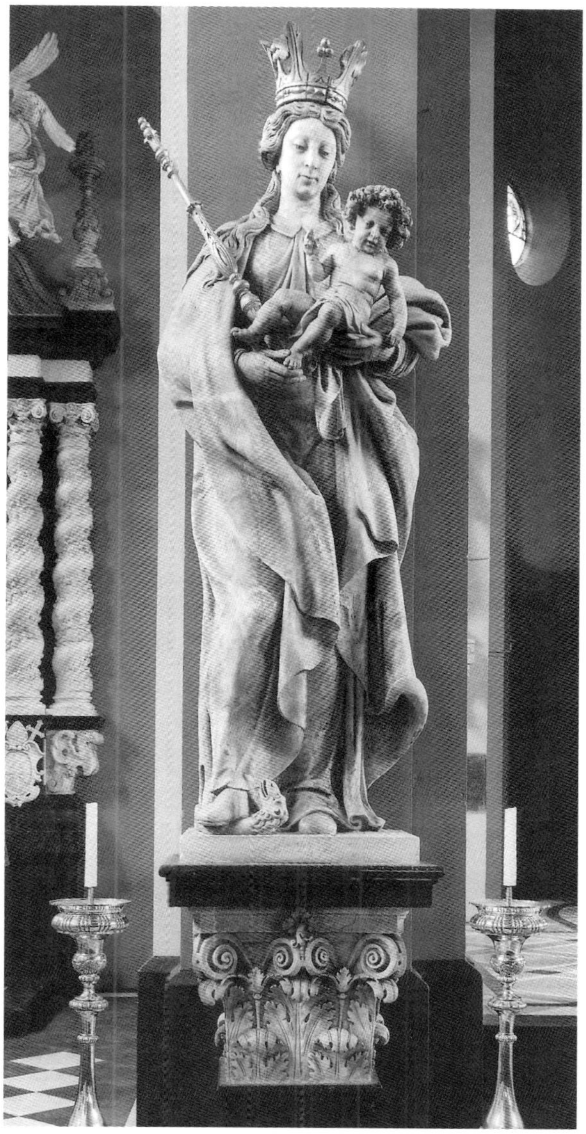

Fig. 12. Hans van Mildert, *Virgin and Child*. Zundert, Sint-Trudokerk

linked, the parallels between the restoration of the True Faith in 1123 and in 1585 are clearly drawn.

The triumph of the Church is presented in three pairs of figures that crown the pediment of the high altar which, as noted above, was erected in 1622–24, in conjunction with the 500th anniversary of Norbert's victory over Tanchelm and the foundation of St. Michael's Abbey.[89] These victorious figures all signify the Church's triumph over heresy, and all three are connected with St. Michael's and described by Van der Sterre as being patrons of the city of Antwerp: St. Norbert trampling Tanchelm (fig. 11), the Virgin and Child crushing the serpent (fig. 12), and St. Michael vanquishing Lucifer (fig. 13).[90] They are shown here (fig. 14) in a pastiche of Rubens's painting and a 1910 photograph of the altar as it was re-assembled in St. Trudo in Zundert after the abbey's dissolution.[91] The altar obviously was broken apart when it was removed from St. Michael's; the statues were damaged and, as I will argue below, mistakenly re-installed. It was presumably at this time that the chalice was substituted for the monstrance in Norbert's right hand. Rubens's sketch portrays Norbert with the monstrance and Van der Sterre's account of the statues' appearance accords with the sketch. He describes Norbert as a glorious apostle of the city of Antwerp and leader of the bright white army of Jesus and notes that he tramples on the arch-heretic Tanchelm and holds forth in triumph the sacred monstrance of the venerable sacrament in his right hand and the crozier in his left.[92] As I have argued elsewhere, the program devised by Rubens and Van der Sterre connects the defeat of heresy with Christ's victory over sin, death, and the devil and the foundation of the Church. I can only summarize

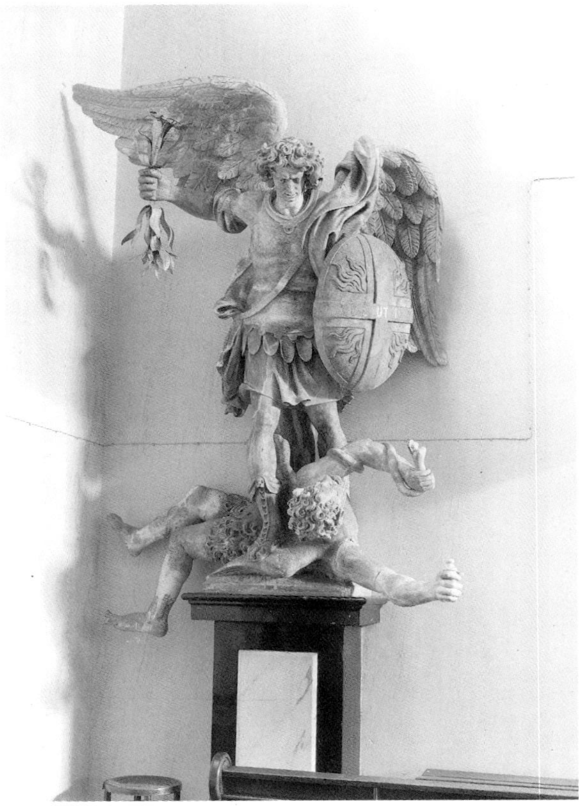

Fig. 13. Hans van Mildert, *St. Michael*. Zundert, Sint-Trudokerk

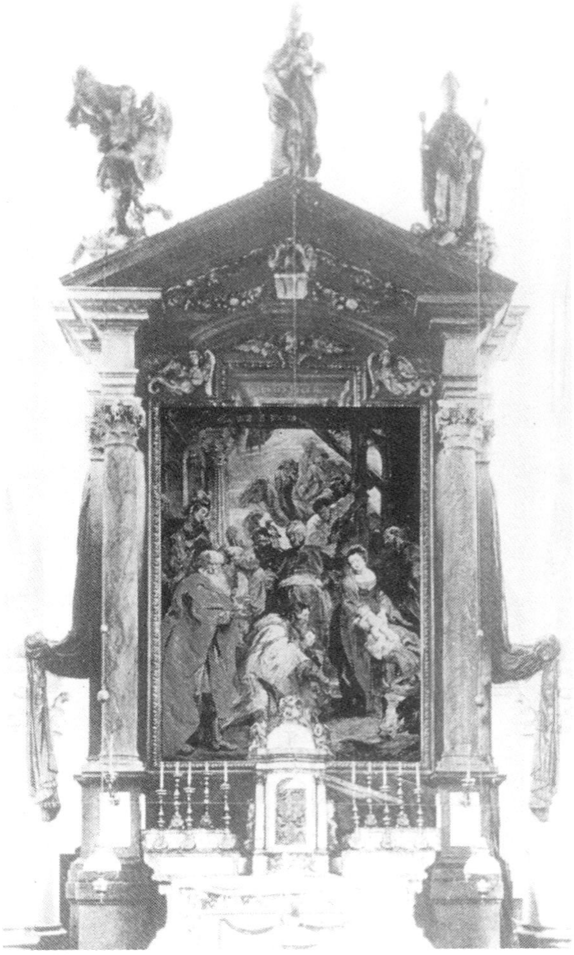

Fig. 14. Reconstruction of the high altar of St. Michael's Abbey, reproduced from S. Beele et al., *P.P. Rubens, Catalogue: paintings - oil sketches, Antwerp, Koninklijk Museum voor Schone Kunsten*, Antwerp, 1990, p. 64

the most relevant aspects of my argument with minimal evidence here.

Within the triumphal arch of the altar's framework[93] is Rubens's splendid *Adoration of the Magi*, whose dazzling light and brilliant color add to the celebratory tone of the high altar. As others have noted, Rubens invests the *Adoration of the Magi* (fig. 15) with a ceremonial character, thus emphasizing its Eucharistic significance. The Child is placed on the sheaf of wheat on the altar-cum-manger thereby prompting the viewer to recall that the Virgin's presentation of the Child to the Magi is to be understood as the Church's making available to the faithful the body and blood of Christ, in other words the Eucharist.[94] That Christ willingly sacrifices himself is indicated by the elimination of the ass and the prominence of the ox beneath the altar; the ox is emblematic of sacrifice, and Gregory the Great writes that Christ agreed to die as an ox in the sacrifice that brought about our redemption. As stated in the Decrees and Canons of the Council of Trent, the sacrifice of the mass represents the moment of Christ's offering of himself, 'when by shedding his blood he redeemed and delivered us from the power of darkness and translated us into his kingdom.'[95] That deliverance from the powers of darkness is referred to in the unravelling spider's web, a motif Rubens employed elsewhere for the same purpose. The spider was then a common symbol for both the devil and heretics and the web signified his works. The unravelling web reminds the viewer that it is through Christ's Incarnation and sacrifice that the devil is defeated.[96] Furthermore, the deliverance from the power of darkness achieved by Christ's sacrifice is made visible by the light that floods the scene.

The light that floods the scene, distinguishing this from most of Rubens's other depictions of the subject, such as the Brussels

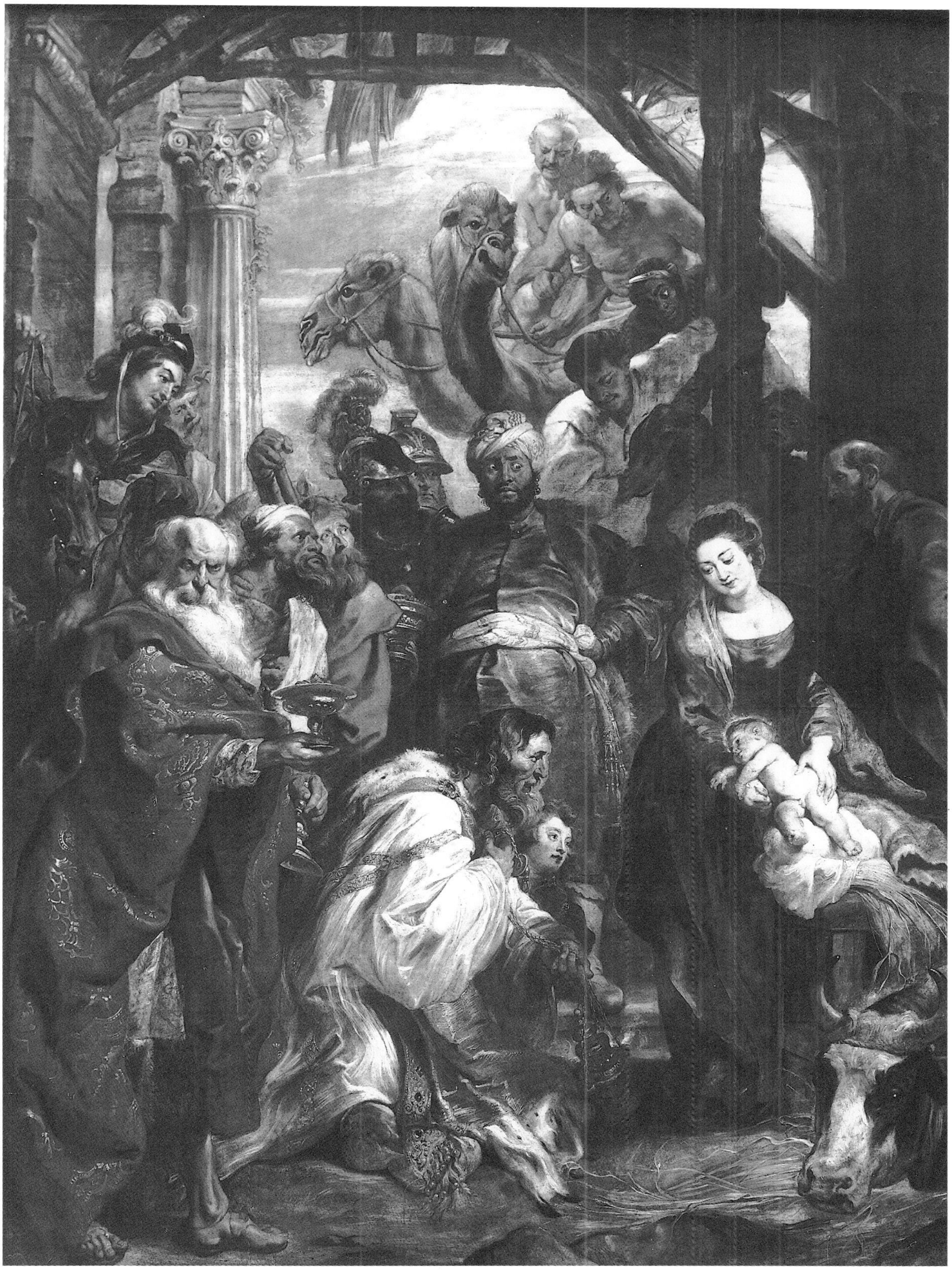

Fig. 15. Peter Paul Rubens, *Adoration of the Magi*. Antwerp, Koninklijk Museum voor Schone Kunsten

*Adoration* (Musées Royaux des Beaux-Arts),[97] represents deliverance; it is the dawn of the era of grace. Like Roger van der Weyden, whose Bladelin Triptych (Berlin, Staatliche Museen Preußischer Kulturbesitz) he knew, Rubens connects the infancy scene with the start of a

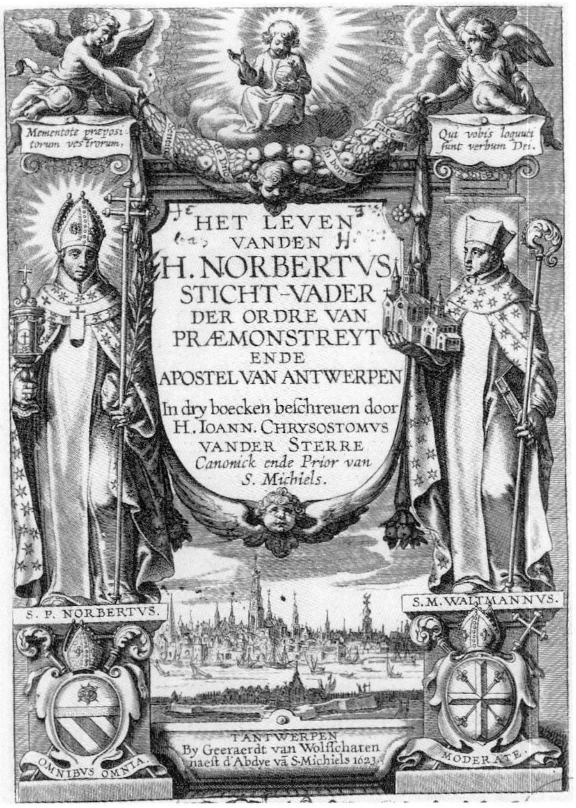


Fig. 16. Title-page for J.C. Van der Sterre's *Het Leven vanden H. Norbertus*

new day, the dawn of the era of grace. Moreover, he, too, reinforces this association by employing a single prominent column rising midst the crumbling structure to refer to the New Testament replacing the Old, the Church established on the foundations of the ruined Synagogue. The column appears as a metaphor for the Church in the Bible, the theological writings of Rubens's contemporaries, and in Netherlandish art.[98] Rubens transforms Roger's simple pillar into a splendid, glowing Corinthian column whose visual splendor combines with the dawn light and the rich colors of the work to give the scene a celebratory character, a character fitting to a scene of triumph. Additional reasons affected his decision to show the column as a glowing white form.

While the column or pillar was repeatedly used to as a metaphor for the Church, it was also employed as a metaphor for the apostles, and Cardinal Baronius referred to Norbert, the apostle of Antwerp, as a pillar of the Holy Church.[99] Moreover, Van der Sterre states that all who conquer shall be clothed in white, and he explains that white is the color of the habit of the Premonstratensian Order because the function of the order is to preach faith in the resurrection and eternal life. On the title page of Van der Sterre's book, Norbert and Waltmann appear as those who show the way to everlasting life (fig. 16). They are clothed in white and presented as radiant columns, reminding that Van der Sterre speaks of Norbert and others in his order as towers of light who guide us; they bring the light of true faith that drives out the darkness of heresy.[100] Norbert's chosen instrument in the eradication of heresy is the Holy Sacrament, and it is this that drives away the darkness, as is portrayed in Van Diepenbeeck's painting of St. Norbert (fig. 2). Moreover, it is the monstrance that Norbert raises up as he tramples the heretic Tanchelm. Surely, Norbert was originally placed above the radiant column that signifies both the Church and Antwerp's own apostle. Thus, the connection between his victory over Tanchelm and the return of the true faith to Antwerp would have been visually underscored as the column was read metaphorically as the Church in tandem with the dawn of a new day, the light of salvation.[101]

This arrangement places Norbert raising up the monstrance on Christ's and the Virgin's right side with its associations of salvation, while St. Michael striking down Lucifer appears on Christ's sinister side associated with damnation. Thus, Norbert appears above the column with all its positive associations, while Michael is placed above the spindly beam bearing the symbol of the defeat of the devil and heresy, the spider in its unravelling web.[102] That this arrangement is correct can be verified by viewing the high altar in the context of the choir screen. If the statues were placed as I contend, Michael striking down Lucifer appears on Christ's left in both monuments– in sculptural form on the high altar and in a painting above the altar dedicated to the Archangel on the choir screen. It also would mean that the altar of the Holy Cross displaying the Veneration of the Cross and St. Norbert would be linked;[103] thus, in each case the defeat of the devil on Christ's sinister side would have been contrasted with the source of salvation on his right – in the choir screen, the cross, on the high altar, the monstrance.

In conclusion, both monuments present the Holy Sacrament as the source of the redeeming benefits of Christ's sacrifice, and both reveal that those benefits are available to the faithful only through the Church, personified by the Virgin Mary as co-redeemer at the apex of the high altar and by Peter and Paul on the choir screen. While Peter and Paul – signifying the unity of the universal Church and the apostolic succession – remind of Rome, the figures on the high altar, the three patrons of the city of Antwerp, define the Church's local identity and underscore St. Michael's centrality in that context. The connections between the two allow Van der Sterre to celebrate his order while attesting to its orthodoxy and obedience to papal authority. Moreover, by creating a program that ties the two monuments together, Van der Sterre links his order's defeat of heresy and the restoration of the True Faith in Antwerp in 1123 with the city's return to the Catholic fold in 1585. Finally, the emphasis placed on the Holy Sacrament in sculpture and in painting foregrounds its central place in both the Norbertine devotions and the Counter-Reformation Church. Thus, like the other works that Van der Sterre commissioned – works that celebrate his order's special devotion to the Virgin and the Holy Sacrament, portray Norbert's victory over heresy, and link the current canons to their illustrious predecessors – these structures testify to the key role that St. Michael's and its canons played in Antwerp's history and in shaping the city's Catholic identity. Consequently, until the nineteenth century, the church of St. Michael's stood as a visible monument to the beneficial presence of the Premonstratensian order and testified to its (restored) position in the religious life of the city.

# NOTES

1. After St. Michael's was deconsecrated in 1796, the contents of the abbey were disbursed. The abbey was used as an arsenal and was destroyed by fire in 1830 after being shelled by the French. K.J. Vander Eyken, [cat. exh.] *De Sint-Michielsabdij Antwerpen: Iconografische Tentoonstelling 1124–1830*, Antwerp, 1988, p. 8; Martin Konrad, 'Antwerpener Binnenräume in Zeitalter des Rubens', in Paul Clemen. ed., *Belgische Kunstdenkmäler*, Munich, 1923, p. 194.

2. M.J. Marinus, *De Contrareformatie te Antwerpen (1585–1676)*, Brussels, 1995, p. 181; J. Corthouts, *De Witheren van de Sint-Michielsabdij te Antwerpen in de 17de en 18de eeuw: Een bijdrage tot de studie van de kloosterdemographie* (onuit. lic. verh.), Leuven, 1982, pp. 79–81.

3. Corthouts 1982 (as cited in note 2), pp. 81–83. N.J. Weyns, 'Jean-Chrysostôme vander Sterre abbé de Saint-Michel d'Anvers', *Analecta Praemonstratensia*, XLVIII, 1972, p. 94. E. Valvekens, *De Zuid-Nederlandsche Norbertijner Abdijen en de Opstand tegen Spanje (Maart 1576–1585)*, Leuven, 1929, p. 248. It should be noted that Van der Sterre's accomplishments were enabled by those of his predecessor, Mathias Yrsselius (Mathias van Iersel), who was responsible for returning St. Michael's to a stable financial footing; F. Prims, *Geschiedenis van Antwerpen: met Spanje 1555–1715*, Brussels, 1982, pp. 529–530.

4. Van der Sterre is credited with commissioning numerous works of art and erecting various structures both within the church and elsewhere in the abbey and on its grounds. These works include: on the grounds of the abbey, the entrance portico attributed to Rubens and a chapel bearing a statue of St. Norbert with accompanying verses; within the church, the choir screen and the monument to the Blessed Waltmann; within the abbot's quarters, portraits of Van der Sterre and of his predecessors, a painting by Abraham van Diepenbeeck of the consecration of the Blessed Waltmann (the first abbot of St. Michael's) in which the latter bears Van der Sterre's features, and a painting also by Van Diepenbeeck of St. Norbert with the same verses that were inscribed beneath the statue; Weyns 1972 (as in note 3), pp. 101–102.

5. For description of the sixteenth-century damage and of the fire, see: E. Valvekens, 'De Sint Michielsabdij te Antwerpen vanaf 1564 tot 1596', *Analecta Praemonstratensia*, I, 1925, pp. 170–171; P. Genard, *Verzameling der Graf- en Gedenkschriften van de Provincie Antwerpen*, IV, Antwerp, 1859, p. liii; J. Van den Niewenhuizen. *Monasticon Belge: Tome VII Province d'Anvers, premier volume: Abbaye de Saint-Michel à Anvers*, 1992, p. 241.

6. I would like to stress that in order to present the most salient features of Van der Sterre's program, I have had to sacrifice consideration of artistic and iconographic issues that enrich our understanding of the paintings and monuments. While I already have published a more complete discussion of the high altar, I am currently preparing an article on the choir screen. How these monuments functioned in the liturgical space is part of my on-going and still far from complete research on St. Michael's and its place in Antwerp's past.

7. Genard 1859 (as cited in note 5), pp. xxiv–xxix; J.C. van der Sterre, *Het Leven vanden H. Norbertus*, Antwerp, 1623, pp. 202–226. Although Van der Sterre notes that St. Michael's was officially given to the order in 1124 (p. 218), the date that all others give to the founding of the abbey, he states that the Blessed Waltmann, the first abbot of St. Michael's, was made abbot in 1123 (p. 219). Moreover, in his discussion of the events commemorated in the 500th anniversary year of 1623, he states that Norbert drove out the heresy and raising again the bloody banner of Christ founded the abbey (3 *verso* – '...1623. het thiende Iubileeum, dat Norbertus de Kettereije Tanchelini hier t'Antwerpen uytgheroeyt hebbenende en de bloedighe Baniere van het Cruys Christi wederom opgerecht hebbende, sijn Antwerpsch Clooster begonst heeft, aldaer stellende voor eerste Praelaet den Godt-saligen Waltmannus.'

8. Valvekens 1925 (as cited in note 5), p. 250.

9. Valvekens 1925 (as cited in note 5), pp. 155–156.

10. The Prinsenhof was erected by Abbot van der Hagen (d. 1562) after the abbey had had difficulty housing the particularly large and splendid party of Charles V and Philip II following the latter's *Blijde Inkomst* in 1549; E. Valvekens 1925 (as cited in note 5), pp. 155–156.

11. Valvekens 1925 (as cited in note 5), p. 250; E. Valvekens, 'De Sint Michielsabdij te Antwerpen vanaf 1564 tot 1596', *Analecta Praemonstratensia*, II, 1926, p. 347. On the relations between the States General and Abbot Greve, see: Valvekens 1929 (as in note 3), pp. 89–102 and 130–133.

12. Valvekens 1929 (as cited in note 3), p. 5; Corthouts (as cited in note 2), pp. 77–80.

13. Valvekens 1929 (as cited in note 3), pp. 198–202; for a detailed discussion, see: E. Valvekens 1926 (as cited in note 11), pp. 337–356.

14. Valvekens 1929 (as cited in note 3), p. 119; Greve remained an ally of the rebels and submitted to all the reformers' demands (p. 129).

15. Valvekens 1926, (as cited in note 11), pp. 353–356.

16. Valvekens 1929 (as cited in note 3), pp. 130–132.

17. Valvekens 1929 (as cited in note 3), pp. 244–248; Corthouts 1982 (as in note 2), pp. 80–82.

18. A. Thijs, [cat. exh.] *De Jezuieten en het Katholieke Hestel te Antwerpen na 1585*, Antwerp, 1985, pp. 1, 33; A. Thyssen, *Antwerpen vermaard door den Eeredienst van Maria: Geschiedkundige aanmerkingen over de 500 Heiligen beelden in de straten van Antwerpen*, Antwerp, 1902, pp. 151–153.

19. Given Antwerp's history, it was a key city for such demonstrations. For example, a procession took place annually from 1586 on that expressed gratitude for the city's reconciliation with the sovereign and served to recall the conflict between Catholics and Protestants, thus keeping alive hostility toward heresy; A.K.L. Thijs, *Van Geuzenstad tot katholiek bolwerk: Maatschappelijke betekenis van de Kerk in contrareformatorische Antwerpen*, Brepols, 1990, p. 172.

20. On the campaign for canonization, see: Christine Göttler, '"Actio" in Peter Paul Rubens' Hochaltarbildern für die Jesuitenkirche in Antwerpen', in *Barocke Inszenierung*, Zürich, 1999, pp. 11–21; on the celebrations, see Thijs 1990 (as in note 19), p. 174.

21. Göttler 1999 (as cited in note 20), pp. 11–31.

22. In 1614, Mathias Yrsselius, a highly respected Norbertine from the Middelburg abbey from which the canons had been ousted, was made abbot and immediately set about reviving

the abbey's fortunes; Prims 1982 (as cited in note 3), pp. 529–530, Corthouts 1982 (as cited in note 2), p. 81; Nieuwenhuizen 1992 (as cited in note 5), pp. 241–242.

23. B. Haeger, 'Rubens's *Adoration of the Magi* and the program for the high altar of St. Michael's Abbey in Antwerp', *Simiolus*, 25, 1997, pp. 45, note 1 and 47, note 4.

24. Although the founding of St. Michael's is usually dated to the deeding of the church to the canons in 1124, Van der Sterre, presumably desirous of connecting the founding of the abbey with the defeat of heresy, gives a date of 1123 for both events. See note 7 above.

25. Werner Thomas refers to this strategy and points to the donation of the two statues at St. Michael's as a perfect example of it; 'Andromeda Unbound: The Reign of Albert and Isabella in the Southern Netherlands, 1598–1621', in Werner Thomas and Luc Duerloo, eds., *Albert & Isabella 1598–1621: Essays*, Brepols, 1998, pp. 9–10. For a discussion of this strategy see Luc Duerloo's 'Archducal Piety and Habsburg Power' in the same volume (pp. 267–284).

26. His keen interest in spreading knowledge of these great deeds in Antwerp is expressed in both the dedication (separate pagination) and preface; Van der Sterre 1623 (as cited in note 7), pp. 2 *recto*- 3 *verso* and 4. In addition, to praising the illustrious men and other worthies of the order, which Van der Sterre states that he was prompted to do by perceiving how industriously others celebrated the members of their orders (2 *verso*), no doubt an allusion to the Jesuits, Van der Sterre extolls recent deeds and current Norbertines; Van der Sterre 1623 (as cited in note 7), pp. 167, 224.

27. Van der Sterre 1623 (as cited in note 7), p. 6.

28. Hans Vlieghe, *Rubens Portraits of Identified Sitters Painted in Antwerp* (*Corpus Rubenianum Ludwig Burchard,* XIX ), II, London–New York, 1987, pp. 204–206.

29. The abbey's affairs were still not in a satisfactory state as is indicated by the negative report of the order's vicar general in 1625; N.J. Weyns, 'De geestelijke geschiedenis van de Premonstratenzers in de Lage Landen', in [cat. exh.] *De glans van Prémontré: Oude Kunst uit Witherenabdijen der Lage Landen,* Park-Heverlee, 1973, p. 30. On the attempts to acquire Norbert's relics, see: P. Lefèvre, 'Une Tentative de Transferer en Belgique le Corps de Saint Norbert (1613–1626)', *Analecta Praemonstratensia*, 26, 1950, pp. 115–116.

30. Prims 1982 (as cited in note 3), pp. 529–531.

31. On Van der Sterre, see Leon Goovaerts, *Ecrivains, Artistes et Savants de l'ordre de Prémontré*, II, Brussels, 1911, pp. 287–295; especially pp. 287–288 and Weyns 1972 (as cited in note 3) pp. 94–123.

32. A. Sanderus, *Chorographia sacra Coenobii S. Michaelis Antverpiae*, Brussels, [1659], p. 26. I am very grateful to Bernie Autsema for her translation of Sanderus's text.

33. Goovaerts 1911 (as cited in note 31), pp. 287–288.

34. On Van der Sterre's restoration of orderly religious life at St. Michael's, see Weyns 1972 (as cited in note 3), pp. 98–99.

35. The recognition that Van der Sterre's achievements received is attested to by his princely funeral and the attendance of all who counted in Antwerp ('Heel kerkelijk en civiel Antwerpen'); A. Erens, 'Relaas over de Begrafenisplechtigheid van Prelaat vander Sterre, der St.-Michielsabdij te Antwerpen', *Analecta Praemonstratensia*, 5, 1928, p. 382. For a discussion of Van der Sterre's publications, see: Weyns 1972 (as cited in note 3), pp. 108–116.

36. As noted below, Van der Sterre repeatedly cites Norbert's devotion to both. Moreover, the Premonstratensian order had five particular ends; two of these are a special devotion to the Holy Eucharist and a special devotion to the Virgin Mary who is the patroness of the order; *The Catholic Encyclopedia,* 12, New York, 1911, p. 387. In addition, the first chapter of the order's *Statua* indicates that a devotion to the Holy Eucharist should occupy a particular place in the heart of a Premonstratensian, while the third notes the valued place of the Virgin as the order's singular patron (p. 388).

37. This is how the heresy was described in the seventeenth century; Cesar Baronius and Henricus Spondanus, *Generale kerckelycke historie van de Geboorte onses H. Jesu Christ tot het jaer 1624,* Antwerp, 1625, p. 119; J. Stalpart van der Wielen, *Gulden-jaers feestdagen,* Antwerp, 1635, p. 547; Van der Sterre (as cited in note 7), pp. 206–207.

38. J.B. Knipping, *Iconography of the Counter Reformation in the Netherlands*, II, Nieuwkoop–Leiden, 1974, p. 303.

39. An engraving of the statue appears in J. Le Roy, *Le Grand Théâtre Sacré du Duché de Brabant,* The Hague, 1729, pp. 92–93. The statue may have been executed by Hans van Mildert; I. Leyssens, 'Hans van Mildert 158?–1638', *Gentsche Bijdragen tot de Kunstgeschiedenis*, 7, 1941, pp. 112–113.

40. The original site of the painting is not known. In the eighteenth century it was hung in the abbot's quarters; David Steadman, *Abraham van Diepenbeeck: Seventeenth-Century Flemish Painter,* Ann Arbor, 1982, pp. 8, 85.

41. W. Aerts ed., *The Cathedral of Antwerp,* Antwerp, 1993, p. 254. Steadman gives no specific source for asserting that Van der Sterre composed the verses; (as cited in note 40), p. 8. However, the attribution is plausible. In *Het Leven vanden H. Norbertus,* Van der Sterre implies a connection between Norbert and his illustrious predecessors when he states that Tanchelm's followers broke into the garden of flowers planted by Amandus, Eligius, and Willibrordus; Van der Sterre (as cited in note 7), p. 207.

42. That his particular veneration of the Eucharist was central to his importance as controversy raged about the Real Presence is attested to in representations of the saint and perhaps contributed to the decision to canonize him. Norbert was canonized in 1582 and given a feast day of June 6th. In the sixteenth-century, the monstrance became his attribute and he appears holding it, rather than the chalice which he held in earlier depictions, as he tramples Tanchelm and the devil underfoot; T.J. Gerits, [cat. exh.] *Sint Norbertus in de Brabantse Kunst,* Averbode, 1971, pp. 14 and 16.

43. For example, in the chapter on Tanchelm he says that he will relate the victory over the darkness of heresy which along with the devil brings souls to hell and describes how Norbert brought the light of the Holy Roman faith to Antwerp when because of heresy her soul was dead; moreover, he links radiance with the Real Presence; (as in note 7), pp. 202–203, 225–227. In addition, Van der Sterre describes the Holy Sacrament as the instrument of Norbert's victory over not only Tanchelm (p. 213) but the devil (p. 198) who is also crushed beneath the plaque in Van Diepenbeeck's painting.

44. Van der Sterre 1623 (as cited in note 7), p. 220.

45. 'Cœlo et terrâ glorioso, SS. P. Norberto; Præmonstrati Ordinis Patriarcæ, Magno Antverpiæ Apostolo, Quingentesimo Anno æternâ Gloriâ iam fruenti, V. hoc Iubilæum Parenti Opt: Max: Chrysostomus Abbas et Canonici S. Michaëlis Antuerpiensis gratulantur.' My paraphrase is based on Professor Harry Vredeveld's translation. I am indebted to him for this and all other translations of Latin texts in this article, unless otherwise indicated. It is worth noting that the identification of Norbet as an apostle and the reference to St. Michael's would have been understood by all literate persons.

46. For a discussion of the picture and complete bibliography, see: K. van der Stighelen, *De Portretten van Cornelis de Vos (1584/5–1651): een kritische catalogus*, Brussels, 1990, pp. 144–150. On the location of the painting in Chapel of the Holy Sacrament, see: J. de Bosschere, ed., *De kerken van Antwerpen (Schilderijen, Beeldhouwwerken, Geschilderde Glasramen, enz. in de XVIIIe beschreven door Jacobus de Wit)*, Antwerp–The Hague, 1910, pp. 153–154.

47. Van der Stighelen notes that Norbert is shown as he usually is and as Van der Sterre describes him with Tanchelm underfoot and holding the monstrance, and she remarks on the unusual combination of this image of the saint with a family portrait; 1990 (as cited in note 46), p. 149, note 366.

48. Van der Stighelen 1990 (as cited in note 46), p. 145–147, note 358.

49. Van der Sterre (as cited in note 7), pp. 212–213.

50. Van der Stighelen 1990 (as cited in note 46), p. 148.

51. Van der Stighelen 1990 (as cited in note 46), p. 147; see also: C. D. Muir, 'Art and religion in seventeenth-century Antwerp: Van Dyck's *Mystic marriage of the Blessed Hermann-Joseph*', *Simiolus*, 28, 2000–2001, pp. 58–59.

52. Van der Stighelen 1990 (as cited in note 46), pp. 147–148; Weyns 1972 (as cited in note 3), p. 114.

53. The inclusion of the Cathedral represents the larger clerical community and the site of the Chapel of the Confraternity of the Holy Sacrament. Nonetheless it is definitely overshadowed by St. Michael's and the only religious portrayed are Norbertines.

54. For a discussion of the painting, oil sketch, and the literature see Steadman 1982 (as cited in note 40), pp. 18–19, 89–90. David Steadman dates the picture to the 1640's and suggests that Van der Sterre may have commissioned the painting in 1644 on the fifteenth anniversary of his own investiture. A date of 1649 coinciding with the twentieth anniversary of that event has also been proposed; E. Mai and H. Vlieghe, eds., [cat. exh.] *Von Bruegel bis Rubens: das goldene Jahrhundert der flämischen Malerei*, Wallraf-Richartz-Museum, Cologne / Koninklijk Museum voor Schone Kunsten, Antwerp / Kunsthistorisches Museum, Vienna, 1993, pp. 316–137. Steadman also reproduces a portrait of Van der Sterre (fig. 24) and notes that its location is unknown (p. 91).

55. St. Michael's was the mother house of the order in the Netherlands. For it's role in establishing these abbeys, see: Van der Sterre 1623 (as cited in note 7), p. 224.

56. Cynthia Lawrence, 'Het Waltmann Memoriaal: Een verloren werk uit de Sint-Michielsabdij van Antwerpen', *Antwerpen: Tijdschrift der stad Antwerpen*, 33, 1987, p. 146.

57. Inscribed on the plaque that forms part of the monument is Van der Sterre's dedication to his excellent predecessor in 1631. Lawrence, while stressing that the lack of visual evidence makes it impossible to determine, considers the Waltmann Memorial in the context of related works by Rubens and Hans van Mildert and speculates that it may have been the result of another collaboration between the two artists; (as cited in note 56), pp. 148–150.

58. J.C. van Herck and A. Jansen, 'Archief in Beeld. Het meubilair van onze abdijen en kloosterkerken (naar oude tekeningen)', *Tijdschrift voor Geschiedenis en Folklore*, 21, 1958, p. 29. Bouttats's engraving appears in J. Le Roy, *Le Grand Théâtre Sacré du Duché de Brabant* [1734] as noted in Lawrence 1987 (as cited in note 56), p. 150.

59. Lawrence 1987 (as cited in note 56), pp. 146–148.

60. See above, note 36. All of the Norbertine abbeys, whomever else they were dedicated to, were dedicated to the Virgin; Van der Sterre 1623 (as cited in note 7), p. 131. On Van der Sterre's discussion of the special favor the Virgin showed the Premonstratensian order, see: Haeger 1997 (as cited in note 23), p. 68.

61. Van der Sterre 1623 (as cited in note 7), p. 216.

62. Valvekens 1925 (as cited in note 5), pp. 170–171; Sanderus 1659 (as cited in note 32), p. 31.

63. Frans Baudouin, 'De beelden van de H. Petrus en de H. Paulus door Hans van Mildert', *Antwerpen: Tijdschrift der stad Antwerpen*, 1983, pp. 173–180 (especially p. 180). On the choir screen see also: Leyssens 1941 (as cited in note 39), p. 91; Jan Steppe, *Het koordoksaal in de Nederlanden*, Brussels, 1952, pp. 375–377.

64. The structure, listed among the other works of art commissioned by Van der Sterre, is given as being by Rubens; D. Papebrochius, *Acta Sanctorum, Junii*, I, Antwerp, 1695, p. 957. The portico is illustrated by Konrad who cites it as being the work of Hans van Mildert perhaps after a drawing by Rubens; Konrad 1923 (as cited in note1), p. 195. Rubens's mother and brother Philip were buried in the Chapel of the Holy Sacrament and over the tomb of his mother he placed the first panel he painted for the altarpiece for Sta. Maria in Vallicella in Rome; Bosschere 1910 (as cited in note 46), pp. 151, 154. Part of the picture, now in Grenoble, is visible to the left of the choir screen in Causé's engraving. In addition, Rubens married his first wife, Isabella Brant, in the abbey church; C. White, *Peter Paul Rubens: Man and Artist*, New Haven–London, 1987, pp. 58–59.

65. For reproductions of the statues, see: Baudouin 1983 (as cited in note 63), pp. 176–177. The locations of the paintings are not known; photographs of both are in the photo archive of the Rijksbureau voor Kunsthistorische Documentatie in The Hague. The information accompanying the photograph of the picture which may be by Pieter Neeffs the Younger states that it is a panel (38 x 52.5 cm) and is signed Pieter Neeffs 16(5?)5. In 1953 it appeared in an exhibition in Utrecht (architectuurtentoonstelling Utrecht 1953 no. 70) as the work of Pieter Neeffs the Elder. I am grateful to Anna Knaap for bringing this to my attention. The choir screen in the painting by Hubertus Quellinus is far more visible than in the Neefs painting and corresponds in all respects with Causé's engraving. The picture, a canvas (74 x 68 cm) that is signed and dated, was last listed in the collection of the Reichsgräfin von Sparr when it was sold in Munich on October 17, 1933. Written descriptions include: Sanderus 1659 (as cited in note 32), p.31; Papebrochius 1695 (as cited in note 64), p. 957; Le Roy 1729 (as cited in note 39), p. 93.

66. Steppe 1952 (as cited in note 63), p. 35.

67. M. Westermann, 'A monument for Roma Belgica: Functions of the oxaal at 's Hertogenbosch', *Nederlands Kunsthistorisch Jaarboek*, 1994, p. 417; Steppe 1952 (as cited in note 63), pp. 41–43.

68. Steppe 1952 (as cited in note 63), pp. 35–36 and 364.

69. R.W. Sullivan, 'Saints Peter and Paul: some ironic aspects of their imaging', *Art History*, 17, 1994, pp. 63–64; Knipping 1974 (as cited in note 38), pp. 481–482; Westermann 1994 (as cited in note 67), p. 417.

70. Rubens designed the title page in 1614; the engraving by Theodor Galle was modified in 1628 to replace Paul V's coat of arms with those of Urban VIII; J.R. Judson and C. Van de Velde, *Book Illustrations and Title Pages* (*Corpus Rubenianum Ludwig Burchard*, XXI), I, Brussels, 1977, pp. 118, 121. It is worth noting that other title pages produced in Antwerp during the late 16th and early 17th centuries also bear a structural resemblance. This is particularly true of those, such as Johannes David's *Christelijcken Waerseggher* of 1603, that include architectural frameworks; for this and other examples, see: Judson

and Van de Velde, II, plates 7, 9, and 11. An especially pertinent example is Thomas Stapleton's *Antidota Apostolica contra nostri temporis haereses* of 1595 which includes Peter and Paul beneath angels on segmental pediments. For an illustration, see: M. Mauquoy-Hendrickx, *Les Estampes des Wierix*, III, Brussels, 1982, no. 1, p.305 (#1984).

71. The liturgical code established in 1128–31 was strictly adhered to by the order; it was considered a source of unity and uniformity. Although a concerted effort was made to preserve the rite in the face of the demands of the Congregation of Rites, many in the order wished to adopt the Roman Rite. The Roman Mass Ordinary and Missal were almost completely adopted and a hybrid liturgy emerged in 1628, which much impoverished the Premonstratensian Breviary; *New Catholic Encyclopedia*, 11, Washington, D.C., 1967, p.740.

72. Sup hanc petram aedificabo Ecclesiam meam et/ Tibi dabo claves regni caelorum. Vas electionis est mihi iste, / ut portet nomem meum corem gentib. See: Mauquoy-Hendrix (as cited in note 70), (#563).

73. F. Costerus, *Het Boecken der Broederschap; Dat is 5 Boecken der Christelijcker leeringhen / Voor de Broederschap der H. Maghet Maria*, Antwerp, 1603, pp. 452–453, 460. In addition, he notes that the Holy Church is a pillar of truth meaning that not only does the Church have the truth but that, like a column, it supports the truth and he adds that there is no truth outside the Church, only error (p. 132). He repeatedly stresses the importance of continuity of belief and the apostolic succession. For example, he asserts that as we believe now so our ancestors believed since the time of the apostles, and he notes that only in the Holy Roman Church will you find an unbroken succession from the time of the apostles (p. 136).

74. Costerus 1603 (as cited in note 73), p. 136; Van der Sterre 1623 (as cited in note 7), p. 227.

75. See note 73; Johannes David, *Den Bloem-hof der keckelicker cerimonien*, Antwerp, 1622, p. 11; Franciscus Costerus, *Het Nieu Testament onses Heeren Jesu Christi met korte uytlegginge door Franciscum Costerum*, Antwerp, 1614, p. 762.

76. It is worth noting that in his commentary on I Timothy 3:15 Costerus underscores that, as the scripture states, the Church as a pillar of truth and asserts that it is visible and not invisible as heretics claim; Costerus 1614 (as cited in note 75), p. 760.

77. 'Voedt mijne schapen'; F. Costerus, *Het Nieu Testament onses Heeren Jesu Christi met korte uytlegginge door Franciscum Costerum*, Antwerp, 1604, pp. 316–317.

78. Costerus 1603 (as cited in note 73), p .92.

79. 'Qui me dejecit anno MDLXI / Me fecit anno MDLXXXV'; Sanderus 1659 (as cited in note 32), p. 31. The location which is not clearly fixed by Sanderus is explicitly indicated by Le Roy; (as cited in note 39), p. 93. Le Roy erroneously gives the first date as 1568; Genard gives the correct date but quotes the second line as 'Me refecit A[nn]o 1585'; (as cited in note 5), p. 6. In the *Acta Sanctorum* of 1695 (p. 946), Papebrochias gives the inscription as: 'Qui me dejecit anno MDLXVI, me refecit anno MDLXXXV,' according to Valvekens 1925 (as cited in note 5), p. 171.

80. Valvekens 1925 (as cited in note 5), pp. 171; Sanderus 1659 (as cited in 32) p. 31.

81. L. Wuyts, 'Het St.-Jorisretabel van de Oude Voetboog door Maarten De Vos: Een ikonologisch onderzoek', *Jaarboek Koninklijk Museum voor Schone Kunsten Antwerpen*, 1971, pp. 107–135 (especially pp. 124–134). Wuyts explains the Princess who is rescued by St. George as signifying the Church saved by Farnese, and, noting the texts displayed by Peter and Paul and previous representations of Christ between the two apostles, he defines the apostles as witnesses to Christ's divinity who testify to the Catholic doctrine of redemption (p. 127). Thus, their presence can be seen as making clear that the Church that is rescued and restored is the Holy Roman Church.

82. F. Costerus. *Sermoonen op alle de Epistelen van de Sondaghen van den geheelen Iare met twee Sermoon-Octaven d'eerste van 't H. Sacrament des Autaers...* Antwerp, 1616, p. 5.

83. Van der Sterre 1623 (as cited in note 7), p. 213.

84. See above, note 64. On Van der Sterre's discussion of his order's militancy, see: Haeger 1997 (as cited in note 23), p. 69. On the rusticated style and its connection to Rubens, see: Ulrich Becker, *Studien zum flämischen Altarbau im 17. und 18. Jahrhundert*, Brussels, 1990, pp. 47–48.

85. For the significance of Michael in the Counter Reformation, see: Haeger 1997 (as cited in note 23), p. 62.

86. Van der Sterre 1623 (as cited in note 7), p. 220.

87. Van der Sterre 1623 (as cited in note 7), pp. 2 *verso*, 3 *verso*, 4, 5, 6, and 220.

88. Knipping 1974 (as cited in note 38), II, p. 482. As indicated above (note 70), Thomas Stapleton displays their images, like statues on the choir screen, on the title page of his text which employs the writings of Peter and Paul to defeat the arguments of heresies current in 1595. Moreover, as Mariët Westermann points out, the inclusion of statues of the two apostles on the choir screen in the Antwerp Cathedral may be intended to mark the city's return to the Catholic fold; Westermann date (as cited in note 67), p. 417.

89. Haeger 1997 (as cited in note 23), p. 68; K. vander Eyken also connects the erection of the altar with the 500th anniversary of foundation of the abbey for which he gives the usual date of 1124; 'Mijmeren bij het hoogaltaar van de oude St.-Michielsabdij te Antwerpen', *Averbode*, 1987, pp. 15-17.

90. Haeger 1997 (as cited in note 23), p. 61.

91. Leyssens 1941 (as cited in note 39), p. 119; Royal Museum of the Fine Arts Antwerp, *P.P. Rubens. Catalogue: Paintings - Oil Sketches*, Antwerp, 1990, p. 64.

92. Rubens's sketch (Private Collection) is reproduced and discussed in P. Sutton et al, [cat. exh.] *The Age of Rubens*, Museum of Fine Arts, Boston / Toledo Museum of Art, 1993, no. 25, pp. 285-287 (entry by Marjorie E. Wiesemen: with bibliographic references). J.C. van der Sterre, *Echo S. Norberti triumphantis*, Antwerp, 1629, pp. 59-60. The text is also transcribed with some errors in Leyssens 1941 (as cited in note 39), pp. 120-121

93. Leyssens 1941 (as cited in note 39), p. 120.

94. Haeger 1997 (as cited in note 23 ), pp. 48–50.

95. Haeger 1997 (as cited in note 23), pp. 55–58, note 62.

96. Haeger 1997 (as cited in note 23 ), pp. 58–60.

97. Haeger 1997 (as cited in note 23), p. 48.

98. Haeger 1997 (as cited in note 23), pp. 50–56.

99. Haeger 1997 (as cited in note 23), p. 70.

100. Haeger 1997 (as cited in note 23), pp. 68–70.

101. Haeger 1997 (as cited in note 23), pp. 66–71.

102. Haeger 1997 (as cited in note 23), pp. 59–60 and 64–67.

103. Van der Sterre erected the altars dedicated to the Holy Cross and St. Michael on the choir screen; Sanderus 1659 (as cited in note 32), p. 31.

# Vroomheid verbeeld. Iconografie van de zeventiende-eeuwse Zuid-Nederlandse retabelsculptuur: de rol van de opdrachtgevers

*Valérie Herremans*

*[...] Tusschen twee engelen te midden komt ten toon*
*Den vader, die onthaeld syn dogter in de ermen;*
*Den Zoon, die 't hemels Croon aen syne Moeder geeft*
*In haere hemelvaert, die Rubens edel heeft*
*Op 't autaerstuk verbeld, en de apostels samen*
*Met maegden en een schaer van engelen, die quamen*
*Tot dienst der koningin van hemel en aerdrijk.*
*Den bouw en 't pinceel dus glanst tot Gods eer gelijk*

Toen Jacobus Van der Sanden in zijn *Oud Konst-Toneel*[1] deze lovende verzen neerpende, had hij het indrukwekkende hoogaltaar van de Antwerpse hoofdkerk voor ogen (afb. ).[2] Het ruim veertien meter hoge kunstwerk werd tussen 1621 en 1632 door de meest vooraanstaande kunstenaars uitgevoerd.[3] Kostbare materialen als Italiaans marmer en albast, werden voor de gelegenheid via de haven van Amsterdam uit Genua ingevoerd.[4] Robrecht Colyns de Nole († na 9 juli 1636), die samen met zijn broer Hans en na diens overlijden in 1624 met zijn neef Andries (1598–1638) de architectuur en het beeldhouwwerk voor zijn rekening nam, bekleedde sinds 1604 de functie van meester-beeldhouwer van aartshertogelijk hof.[5] Het prijskaartje van het geheel bedroeg meer dan 17000 gulden, een duizelingwekkend bedrag.[6] Hier bovenop kwamen nog de vijftienhonderd gulden voor het altaarstuk van Peter Paul Rubens. Deze *Tenhemelopneming*[7] van de patrones van de kathedraal siert heden ten dage het huidige, negentiende-eeuwse hoofdaltaar.[8] Jacobus Van der Sanden was wellicht niet de enige bewonderaar op wie dit imposante geheel een diepe indruk naliet.

Zoals Katherine Fremantle en Frans Baudouin maar ook reeds Van der Sanden in zijn achttiende-eeuwse lofdicht terecht opmerkten, was het bijzondere aan de hele constructie de relatie tussen de gebeeldhouwde Christusfiguur en de afbeelding van de H. Maagd op het schilderij van Rubens.[9] De meer dan levensgrote Zoon reikte vanuit de nis boven op de portiek zijn op het centrale altaarstuk weergegeven, door een schare engelen ten hemel gevoerde Moeder een kroon aan. Gelukkigerwijs vereeuwigde Adriaan Lommelin in 1631 het hoogaltaar in een gravure zodat het oorspronkelijke uitzicht van het geheel bekend bleef, want de altaarportiek en de sculptuur zouden de sloophamers van de Franse revolutie niet overleven (afb. 1).[10]

Precies omwille van deze thematische eenheid over de grenzen van de verschillende artistieke media heen, deed dit retabel reeds heel wat inkt vloeien.[11] Aan het geheel zou een initieel totaalconcept – wellicht van Rubens' hand – ten grondslag hebben gelegen, waardoor het bouwwerk door verschillende auteurs een voortrekkersrol toegewezen krijgt bij de introductie van de multimediale barokke vormentaal in de retalbelbouwkunst van onze gewesten. Dit uitgangspunt en het feit dat zowel de formele kwaliteiten als de complexe wordingsgeschiedenis van deze opdracht hierover vragen oproepen, maakt haar tot een interessant vertrekpunt voor deze bijdrage.

Carl Van de Velde wijdde in 1975 een zeer verhelderend artikel aan de complexe ontstaansgeschiedenis van het werk.[12] Deze verliep *grosso modo* in twee fasen. Rubens legde op twee verschillende tijdstippen, op 22 april 1611 en 16 februari 1618, twee ontwerpen aan het kapittel voor die beiden, zoals uit de *Acta Capitula* van 1611 blijkt, '*de geschiedenis van de Tenhemelopneming*' voorstelden.[13] Deze procedure, waarbij de kandidaat-uitvoerder de opdracht-

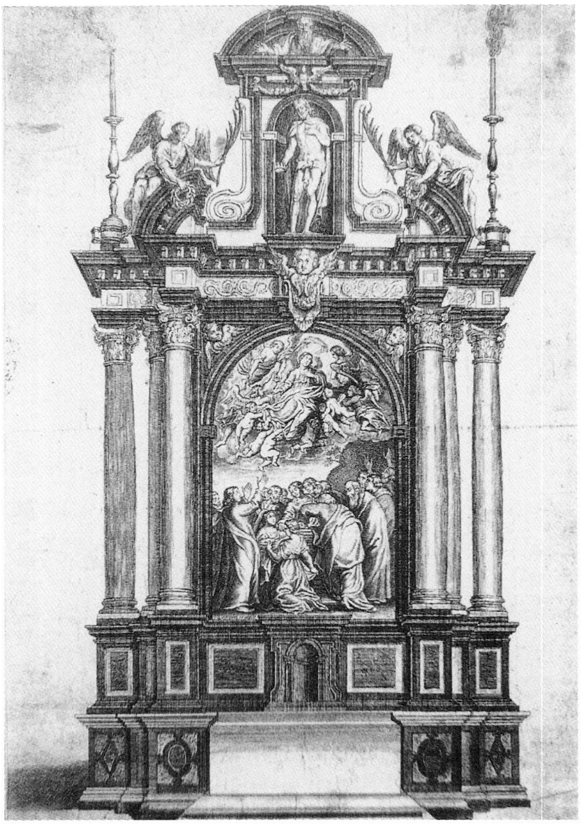

Afb. 1. Adriaan Lommelin, *Hoogaltaar van de Antwerpse kathedraal*, 1631, prent

gever twee varianten presenteerde, wijst er mogelijk op dat minstens één van beide modellen het volledige retabel, inclusief omlijsting, inhield.[14]

Zoals Van de Velde terecht argumenteert, was de grond voor deze werkwijze – de veeleer uitzonderlijke twee verschillende *modelli* – niet zozeer de creativiteit van Rubens op zich, en hiermee bedoel ik het aanbieden van twee 'inventies' als variaties op hetzelfde thema, dan wel het ingenieuze antwoord dat de schilder kon bieden op de specifieke en complexe eis van de opdrachtgevers. Uit een archiefstuk anno 1611 met betrekking tot het afgewezen voorstel van een andere kandidaat, 'Octavio' (Otto Van Veen), blijkt dat het iconografische programma inderdaad zeer karakteristiek was. Het werd omschreven als *Christus roept zijn Bruid uit Libanon op tot de Kroon*.[15] Kijken we naar het uiteindelijke resultaat op de gravure van Adriaan Lommelin (afb. 1), dan is dit ook precies het onderwerp van het ganse project, inclusief schilderwerk én beeldhouwwerk. Het geheel beeldt de *geschiedenis* uit, waarin de H. Maagd ten Hemel wordt opgenomen én de Kroon van haar Zoon ontvangt. Deze complexe iconografie, bestaande uit twee episodes, kon natuurlijk voorgesteld worden op één enkel altaarstuk. Dit was wellicht het geval bij Van Veens ontwerp en bij één van de twee Rubensmodellen uit 1611. Er stelde zich echter een probleem: vermits de geschiedenis twee scènes bevatte, diende een oplossing gevonden te worden voor de herhaling van de Madonna-voorstelling bij de *Tenhemelopneming* en bij de *Kroning*. Het model van Van Veen lijkt verloren te zijn gegaan, maar dankzij het onderzoek van Frans Baudouin kon het Rubens-ontwerp uit 1611 mogelijk geïdentificeerd worden met het schilderij *De Tenhemelopneming* uit de Hermitage te Sint-Petersburg.[16] Rubens balt hier beide episodes samen tot één tafereel, waarbij de *Tenhemelopneming* slechts gesuggereerd wordt en de H. Maagd enkel bij de *Kroning* door haar Zoon wordt weergegeven.

Maar, zoals blijkt uit het eindresultaat, voorzag Rubens echter nog een vernuftig alternatief waarbij de uitbeelding van de geschiedenis werd opgedeeld in twee taferelen, verspreid over twee zones in de altaarportiek, boven en onder de kroonlijst (afb. 1).[17] Hierbij stelt het altaarstuk enkel de *Tenhemelopneming* voor, terwijl het bovenste deel voorbehouden wordt voor een uitbeelding van Christus, deel uitmakend van de H. Drievuldigheid, die de kroon klaarhoudt. Door de opsplitsing in twee scènes én het creëren van een visueel verband – de Moeder Gods richt te blik reeds op haar Zoon –, beantwoordde dit voorstel perfect aan de complexe gegevenheid van de twee episodes en werd de herhaling van het hoofdpersonage overbodig. Dat het centrale retabelgedeelte – het visuele middelpunt van de constructie – in deze optiek volledig kon aangewend worden voor het voorstellen van *Onze-Lieve-Vrouw-Tenhemelopneming*, de titularis van de kathedraal, moet de opdrachtgevers zeker over de streep getrokken hebben bij de uiteindelijk keuze voor deze oplossing.

Komen we tot het aandeel van de sculptuur in de complexe genese van deze opdracht. Vermits van het bovenste retabelgedeelte of van het gehele retabel geen ontwerp van Rubens' hand werd bewaard, rijst de vraag of de schilder voor het zogenaamde *opperwerck* een geschilderde dan wel gebeeldhouwde Christusvoorstelling voor ogen had. Mogelijk werd in het eerste stadium van de ontstaangeschiedenis, rond 1611, door de schilder nog een gepenseeld tafereel voorzien. Een gelijkaardige volledig geschilderde ensceneringstechniek paste hij immers rond dezelfde periode toe bij het hoogaltaar van de Antwerpse Sint-Walburgiskerk, waar een geschilderde God de Vader het centrale altaarstuk aanvulde.[18] Hierbij inspireerde hij zich op een zestiende-eeuwse formeel-iconografische traditie.[19]

Tijdens de decisieve fase van het ontstaansproces, rond 1618, koos men echter voor een volledig gebeeldhouwde bovenbouw: naast twee liggende engelen op de beide bogen van het gebroken segmentfronton, ook een reusachtige, 2,30 meter grote Christusvoorstelling die samen met een halflijfse God de Vader boven op de nis en een duif de H. Drievuldigheid vormde. Dit alles diende vervaardigd te worden uit kostbaar wit marmer.[20] Misschien stelde de schilder in een van beide modellen, voorgelegd op 16 februari 1618, zelf die mogelijkheid voor. Het staat vast dat Rubens interesse betoonde voor de architecturale omlijsting van zijn altaarstukken.[21] Mogelijkerwijs stelde hij dus een totaalontwerp aan zijn opdrachtgevers voor: schilderij en omlijsting. Maar welke plaats voorzag hij hierin zelf voor de sculptuur, die zijn eigen, geschilderde aandeel in de opdracht kon vervangen?

Hier past het te verwijzen naar het hoogaltaar van de Brusselse Onze-Lieve-Vrouw-ter-Kapellekerk (1617–18).[22] Hans Van Mildert (1588–1638) voerde hier een retabelontwerp (contract 19 mei 1617)[23] van Rubens uit (afb. 2).[24] In dit retabel beantwoordt het aandeel van sculptuur geheel aan de geplogenheden van het eigentijdse Italiaanse portico-retabel. Bij sommige van deze realisaties rusten twee (liggende) engelen op de zijgedeelten van een – al dan niet gebroken – segment of driehoekig fronton. Eveneens conform de Italiaanse altaarbouwkunst wordt het centrale gedeelte van een gebroken fronton niet opgevuld door een nis met een volplastisch beeld, zoals in de Zuidelijke Nederlanden reeds een tijd bij portiekaltaren de gewoonte was. In Italië bevindt zich hier meestal een plat vlak, een soort mini-attiek die in sommige gevallen een reliëf vertoont, zoals ook in Brussel met de reliëfbuste van de God de Vader het geval is. Rubens gebruikt hier dus duidelijk de overheersende, contemporaine Italiaanse retabelbouw-canon waarin het

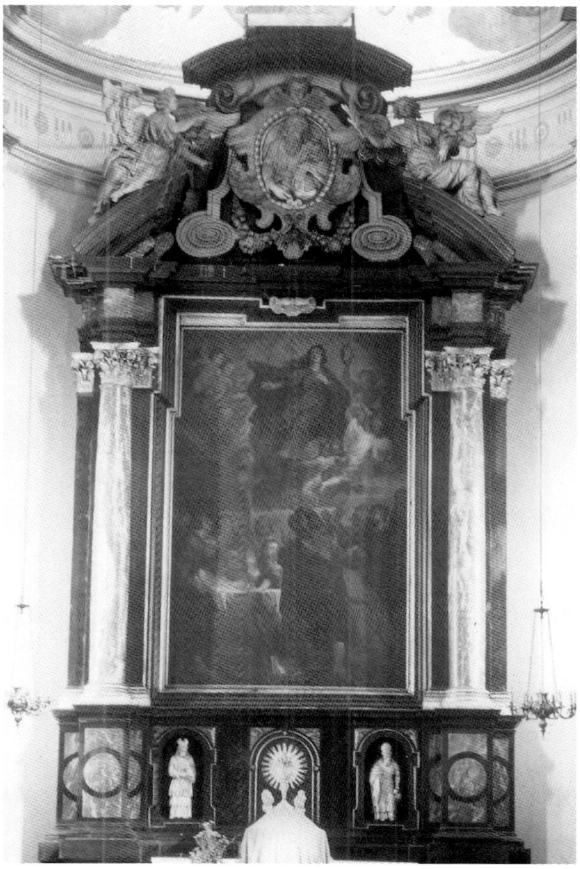

Afb. 2. Hans van Mildert, *Hoogaltaar*, 1617–18 (afkomstig van de Onze-Lieve-Vrouw-ter-Kapellekerk, Brussel). Sint-Joost-ten-Node, Sint-Joostkerk

altaarstuk centraal staat en de *ronde-bosse* sculptuur beperkt wordt tot enkele aanbiddende engelen in de bekroning. Het Brusselse voorbeeld toont aan dat de schilder in 1617 aansloot bij de overheersende vormprincipes uit de Italiaanse retabelbouwkunst – weliswaar vormgegeven met meer *grandissimo splendore et ornamento*[25] – en hier behoorde zeker niet de combinatie van een altaarstuk met een meer dan levensgrote figuur in een bekronende nis.[26]

Er is echter nog een andere mogelijkheid. Misschien ontstond het Antwerpse eindresultaat in samenspraak met de uitvoerende beeldhouwers-architecten, de broers Hans en Robrecht Colyns de Nole. Zij leverden immers op 29 mei 1618, enkele weken nadat Rubens zijn tweede paar ontwerpen had voorgelegd, op hun beurt een *modello*. Vermeldenswaard in dit opzicht is de weliswaar summiere passus uit Akten van het kapittel die vermelden dat '*Exhibita fuit in capitulo modellum Summi Altaris ex lapide factum per Schulptores Hollandes [...].*' Zoals

Carl Van de Velde met recht opmerkt, slaat de uitdrukking uit steen (*ex lapide*) wellicht op de altaarportiek en niet op het ontwerp zelf dat de beeldhouwers voorstelden. Stenen *modelli* waren, in tegenstelling tot houten of terracotta exemplaren inderdaad niet gebruikelijk.[27]

Maar deze uitdrukking doet nog een andere belangrijke vraag rijzen: was dit *modello* een ontwerp waarin de ideeën van Rubens geïntegreerd waren, bijvoorbeeld een driedimensionale maquette van het uitverkozen Rubens-ontwerp, of dienden de De Noles een eigen voorstel in? In het laatste geval slaan de uitdrukkelijke woorden *ex lapide* mogelijk op een model dat een volledige uitvoering in steen, inclusief afbeeldingen, voorstelde.[28] Deze laatste mogelijkheid mag zeker niet uitgesloten worden, vermits zich een gelijkaardig scenario afspeelde bij een quasi gelijktijdige opdracht, namelijk het hoogaltaar van de Gentse kathedraal.

In de loop van de niet minder ingewikkelde ontstaansgeschiedenis (1612–1623) van deze opdracht wedijverden de De Noles met Rubens om de gunst van de opeenvolgende bisschoppen-opdrachtgevers.[29] Er ontstond een soort artistieke krachtmeting (of moeten we het een gezonde concurrentie om den brode noemen?[30]) waarbij de respectieve kandidaten hun eigen artistieke medium op het voorplan schoven. Bekend is de brief van Rubens aan aartshertog Albrecht uit 1614 waarin de schilder vraagt om een tussenkomst met betrekking tot deze kwestie.[31] Hij herinnert de vorst aan zijn eigen ontwerp dat hij twee jaar tevoren aan hem had gepresenteerd en laat zich zeer laatdunkend uit over het ontwerp van de beeldhouwers, hetgeen op dat ogenblik de voorkeur van bisschop Franciscus Henricus van der Burch (1567–1644) wegdroeg. Hij schrijft verontwaardigd dat zijn concurrenten voorstellen het hoogaltaar te maken '*op buitengewoon dwaze wijze zonder een schilderwerk van welke soort ook, maar enkel met een beeld van de H. Bavo tegen een achtergrond van marmer en enkele kolommen*'.[32]

Uiteindelijk, pas in 1623, trok Rubens aan het langste eind. Een nieuw contract werd opgesteld en de beeldhouwers dienden het retabel te wijzigen zodat het altaarstuk van de schilder in het midden kon prijken.[33] Het eindresultaat werd een compromis tussen een – reeds door de opdrachtgevers gewijzigd – volledig uit architectuur en sculptuur bestaand ontwerp dat door de beeldhouwers-architecten was voorgesteld en Rubens' altaarstuk, evenwel zonder de inhoudelijke coherentie die we bij het Antwerpse hoogaltaar terugvinden. Het iconografische programma van dit retabel onderging trouwens evenveel wijzigingen als het aantal opeenvolgende opdrachtgevers!

Of het zo geroemde multimediale karakter van het iconografische geheel – de inhoudelijke coherentie tussen de gebeeldhouwde Christusfiguur en het schilderij – op het Antwerpse hoogaltaar voorzien werd door Rubens, voorgesteld werd door de broers Colyns de Nole of het resultaat was van een door de opdrachtgevers verkozen compromis, zoals ook te Gent het geval was, is tot op heden niet duidelijk. Wat vaststaat is dat enkel de opdrachtgever het laatste woord had. Ons lijkt daarom de laatste optie de meest overtuigende, want in beide gevallen bleek het eindresultaat op het formele vlak niet echt een voltreffer te zijn. Het Gentse retabel dat trouwens reeds op het eind van de zeventiende eeuw werd vervangen, bezat een van de vreemdste opstanden uit onze streken, waarbij de proporties niet bijster geslaagd kunnen genoemd worden.[34] Hetzelfde kan gesteld worden over het Antwerpse retabel waarvan de opstand reeds in 1624 volgens de richtlijnen van een architect, aangesteld door de aartshertogin, werd gewijzigd.[35] Volgens een nieuw contract van 30 juli 1626, moest de constructie met twee extra zuilen verbreed worden.[36] De verticale disproportie werd veroorzaakt door de hoogte van het altaarstuk in verhouding tot de breedte van de portiek,[37] een element dat bij de eenduidige uitvoering van een ontwerp, zij het van Rubens' hand of van deze van de De Noles, waarschijnlijk vermeden was geweest. De formele ongerijmdheden tussen de verschillende componenten van het ganse retabel, beeldhouwkunst, architectuur en schilderkunst, wijzen eerder in de richting van een tijdens de praktische uitvoering moeizaam tot stand gekomen compromis, dan naar de coherente uitvoering van een eenduidig multimediaal concept.

Uit deze beide *high-end* voorbeelden blijkt de complexe interactie in het veld van de altaarbouwkunst, waar verschillende media en hun respectieve uitvoerders hun plaats opeisen. Een waaier aan factoren, waaronder niet in het minst de opdrachtgevers, beïnvloedden de totstandkoming van het uniek eindresultaat dat hier-

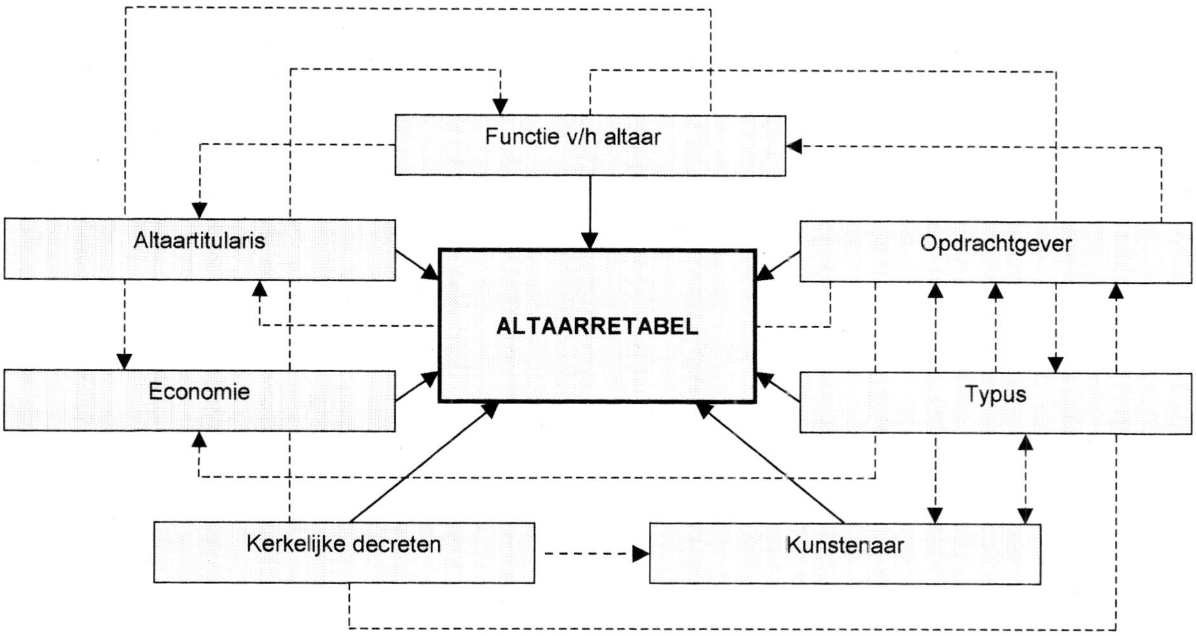

Afb. 3. Contextueel model

door ook op het artistieke vlak hun – niet altijd even geslaagde – stempel droeg. Bij deze relatief goed gedocumenteerde toplaagrealisaties kan het aandeel van de opdrachtgever in het eindresultaat en bijgevolg in het iconografische programma betrekkelijk duidelijk omschreven worden. Hoe bepalen we echter de relatie van de opdrachtgevers tot de algemene iconografie van de Zuid-Nederlandse retabelbouwkunst die een massa aan bescheiden, *lower-art* realisaties beslaat?

## De relatie opdrachtgever-iconografie in de zeventiende-eeuwse retabelbouwkunst

De verdwenen hoogaltaren van Gentse en Antwerpse kathedralen confronteren ons met het belangrijkste probleem dat het onderzoek naar de iconografie van het zeventiende-eeuwse retabel in de weg staat: de teloorgang of verandering van zijn componenten, altaarstuk of beeldhouwwerk, of de afbraak van het gans retabel *tout court*. Om aan dit probleem tegemoet te komen, maar vooral om een zo representatief mogelijk beeld te verkrijgen, dient in de eerste plaats een breed kwantitatief onderzoek plaats te grijpen. Ter aanvulling kan een identificatie en definiëring van alle factoren in het veld van de altaarbouwkunst door uitsluiting de ruimte afbakenen waarin de relatie opdrachtgever-iconografie zich situeert (afb. 3).

De meest voor de hand liggende gegevenheid die de iconografie van het retabel bepaalt, is de *titularis* die aan het altaar wordt toegekend, de goddelijke persoon, de heilige(n) of de devotie waaraan het altaar is gewijd. Deze canonieke patroon valt noodzakelijk samen met de relieken die tijdens de altaarwijding, meestal in de altaarbasis, in een speciaal daartoe aangebrachte ruimte (*sepulchrum* of *fenestella*) worden opgeborgen.[38] Om een altaar aan een zalige te kunnen toewijden is er een apostolische indulgentie nodig.[39] Vermits sommige altaren een hele reeks canonieke patronen bezitten, is het in de praktijk gebruikelijk om de altaren te identificeren met één of soms twee van de dedicaties die zijn ganse titularis uitmaakten. Bij het hoogaltaar is deze primaire titularis gelijk aan de dedicatie van de kerk.[40] De altaarpatroon moet in de vorm van een opschrift of een afbeelding duidelijk op het altaarretabel geafficheerd worden.[41]

Een tweede gegeven is de functie van het altaar. Eerst en vooral dient het onderscheid gemaakt tussen de twee liturgisch-hiërarchische categorieën: de hoofd- en de neven- of zijaltaren. Beiden omvatten verschillende soorten. Het hoogaltaar (*altare majus*) vormt het liturgische brandpunt van het kerkgebouw, het is het belangrijkste onderdeel van het kerkmeubilair. In de parochiekerk dient het hoogaltaar tot het opdragen van de hoogmis en het vieren van het parochiale officie. In de kathedraal daarentegen, staat het essentieel in dienst van de bisschoppelijke liturgie. Die bezit in principe een publiek karakter en kan bijgewoond worden door alle diocesanen. Het *altare conventuale* treffen we aan in kloosterkerken met een publiek karakter en kapittelkerken. Deze hoogaltaren zijn bestemd voor de – evenzeer publieke – liturgische activiteiten van reguliere en seculiere kanunniken en niet-contemplatieve orden, maar zij vinden meestal plaats in een (grotendeels) afgesloten koor.[42] Binnen deze categorie vormen de hoogaltaren van de Zuid-Nederlandse jezuïetenkerken de illustere uitzondering. Zij bevinden zich in de apsis van een basilikale kerkruimte en worden niet door een afsluiting, tenzij een lage communiebank, aan het oog van de gelovigen onttrokken.[43] Hoogaltaren in gesloten kloosterkerken, waar de liturgie niet door leken mag bijgewoond worden, behoren eveneens tot deze categorie.

Buiten het hoogaltaar bezit een kerk in de regel verschillende zijaltaren (*altare minor*). Belangrijke kerken, zoals de hoofdkerk van Antwerpen, beschikken meestal over tientallen exemplaren. Het patronaatschap *(jus patronatus)*, de zorg *voor* en de inkomsten verbonden *aan* een nevenaltaar, kan – behalve aan de kerkpatroon – toebehoren aan allerlei verenigingen. Dit kunnen religieuze genootschappen of beroepsverenigingen zijn. We noemen ze de gilde- of ambachtsaltaren. Het *jus patronatus* van een zijaltaar kan ook in het bezit komen van een familie of privé-persoon. Kerken met enerzijds een hoogaltaar waaraan een publiek officie plaatsvindt en met anderzijds een secundaire parochiale functie (kathedralen, kapittelkerken en sommige kloosterkerken), kunnen hun parochiale liturgie laten plaatsvinden in een aparte kapel of aan een apart zijaltaar: het *parochiealtaar.* Dit altaar was dikwijls gesitueerd aan het doksaal.[44]

Naast deze functies, verbonden met de liturgische categorieën, zijn er echter nog andere die in verband staan met devotionele objectieven, zoals de eucharistische vroomheid, het hiernamaals en de heiligenverering. Alle drie deze geloofspunten, vormden cruciale twistpunten met de hervormingsgezinden. De

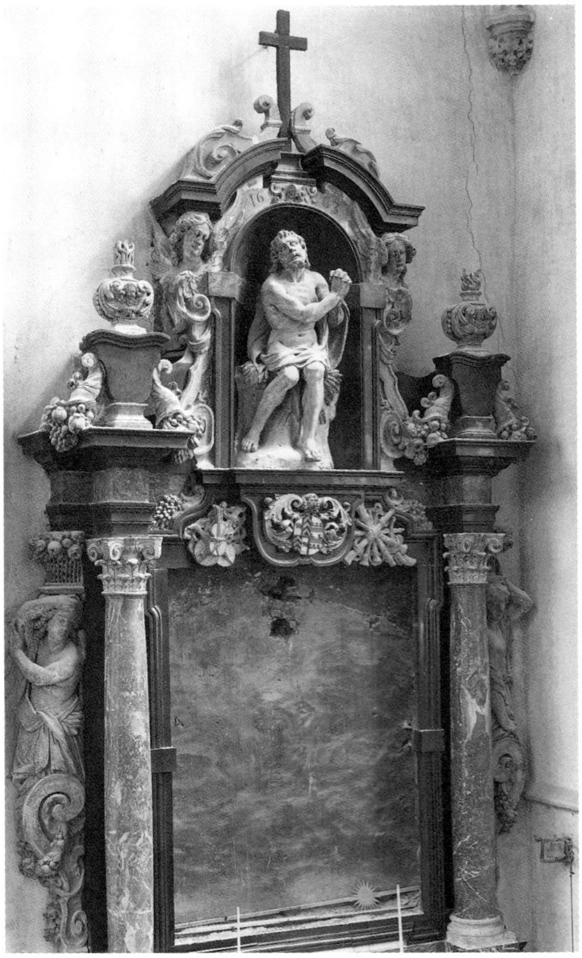

Afb. 4. Sebastiaan de Neve (?), *Altaar van de Gilde van de Speellieden*, 1663. Antwerpen, Sint-Jacobskerk

katholieke hervormingen spraken hun voorkeur uit voor de bewaring van de Eucharistische Reserve op het altaar.[45] Volgend uit de dogma's van de waarachtige en de permanente Aanwezigheid van Christus in de geconsacreerde Hostie, dient deze bewaard te worden op de meest waardige plaats van het kerkgebouw. Hoewel wandtabernakels en sacramentstorens nog tot een eind in de zeventiende eeuw in gebruik bleven, kende de plaatsing van het tabernakel op het altaar in de zeventiende eeuw een steeds grotere verspreiding. De katholieke leer over het hiernamaals gaf naast de privé-altaren ook het ontstaan aan de zogenaamde geprivilegieerde altaren (*altare privilegiatum pro mortuis*).[46] Deze altaren bezaten het voorrecht van een volledige aflaat, bestemd voor de ziel voor wie aan deze altaren een mis werd opgedragen. Een specifiek aspect van de heiligendevotie, de reliekenverering, weerspiegelt zich in de zogenaamde reliekaltaren, waarbij het altaarretabel geheel of gedeeltelijk wordt ingenomen door een reliekschrijn. Het meest illustere voorbeeld hiervan in onze contreien vinden we in de Mechelse kathedraal, waar de portiek van het hoogaltaar in beslag genomen wordt door de kast waarin zich het reliekschrijn met de resten van de kerkpatroon bevindt.[47]

Vele altaren combineren verschillende functies omdat hun patronaatsrecht door verschillende instanties gedeeld wordt. Het altaar van het gilde van de Speellieden in de Antwerpse Sint-Jacobskerk (toegeschreven aan Sebastiaan de Neve, 1663)[48] bijvoorbeeld, was niet alleen een gildealtaar, in de kapel bevindt zich ook de laatste rustplaats van de familie van de Werve-van Cuyct (afb. 4).[49] Hendrik Van de Werve (†1540) en Heylwick (Hedwig) Van Cuyct (†1571) liggen begraven voor het altaar. Onder de voorstelling van Sint-Job, samen met Sint-Cecilia, de patrones van de muzikanten, en Maria Magdalena ziet men in het midden van de kroonlijst het wapen van de stichters.

Hoe staat het met de kerkelijke richtlijnen en het uitzicht van de altaardecoratie? De verordeningen in verband met het altaar situeren zich op twee vlakken. Enerzijds, in het licht van het iconoclasme, de verdediging van het gebruik in het algemeen van afbeeldingen op het altaarretabel, anderzijds de formele en materiële vereisten van het altaar zelf. Deze laatste zijn voornamelijk gericht op de altaartafel en het altaargerei en niet zozeer op de decoratie. Buiten de vereiste van duidelijkheid omtrent de titularis, zijn er geen concrete richtlijnen met betrekking tot de aard van de afbeeldingen op het retabel. De Contrareformatie brengt hierin geen fundamentele verandering, ze bevestigt enkel de traditionele roomse doctrine die de heiligenafbeelding in het kerkinterieur, en dus op het altaar, verdedigt. Ze omvat drie pijlers: de juistheid (dogma), de gepastheid (decorum) en de plaats van de afbeelding in de heiligenverering (verantwoording). Heidense of wulpse taferelen en naaktheid zijn uit den boze.[50] Voorstellingen van wereldlijke of levende personen dienden vermeden te worden.[51] In de lijn van de Leuvense theoloog Joannes Molanus verdedigde men de heiligenvoorstelling (schilderij of beeldhouwwerk), weliswaar binnen het hierboven geschetste kader. Molanus stelde dat '*het groter zijn van een verering voor de ene afbeelding van een heilige dan voor een andere voorstelling van dezelfde heilige niet wijst op afgoderij en dat men de ketterse opvattingen hierover niet moet geloven.*'[52]

De beeldhouwer-architect op zijn beurt speelt een essentiële rol in de overdracht van elementen die de ontwikkeling van de stijl én de iconografie van het barokretabel wederzijds beïnvloedden en ontwikkelden. Zo kunnen in oorsprong formele artistieke keuzen, dragers worden van betekenis. Omgekeerd kunnen iconografische formules de stijlontwikkeling beïnvloeden. Een eerste voorbeeld uit de retabeliconografie zijn de vruchtenkorf dragende kariatiden (afb. 4). Het eerste retabel waarop deze personages figureren is – voor zover bekend – het verdwenen hoogaltaar van de Antwerpse Geschoeide Karmelieten uit 1637–38 (Hans van Mildert). Frans Baudouin kon hiervan aantonen dat dit retabel werd opgetrokken naar het ontwerp van Peter Paul Rubens.[53] Deze decoratieve figuren die reeds tot het decoratieve vocabularium en tot het repertorium van de prentkunst behoorden, sluiten door het attribuut van de vruchtenmand aan bij de eucharistische dimensie van het altaar.[54]

In dit verband kan ook het volgende voorbeeld aangehaald worden. Het gaat om een medaillon met de voorstelling van de buste in profiel van een heilig persoon, meestal geplaatst op de basissen van de zuilen van de altaarportiek. Dit motief blijkt herhaaldelijk voor te komen bij opdrachten uitgevoerd door een zelfde atelier namelijk dat van Andries Colyns de Nole en zijn leerlingen annex atelier-overnemers Sebastiaan de Neve (1612–1676) en Jacques Couplet (†1657/58).[55] Het gaat dus om een element met weliswaar iconografische kwaliteiten, maar dat tevens als een soort stijlkenmerk van dat atelier fungeert. Het atelier was werkzaam in de Houtappelkapel van de Antwerpse jezuïetenkerk, waar we gelijkaardige bustes in de wanddecoratie kunnen terugvinden. Sebastiaan de Neve paste het motief ook toe bij een andere belangrijke Antwerpse opdracht: het altaar van de Onze-Lieve-Vrouw-van-de-Rozenkrans in de dominicanenkerk (1650) (afb. 5–6).[56] Hier stellen de bustes de 'ware afbeeldingen' van Christus en Maria voor. Zij vertonen overeenkomsten met gelijkaardige werken uit de zeventiende-eeuwse schilder- en graveerkunst die het ware gelaat van de Verlosser en zijn Moeder uitbeeldden.[57] De

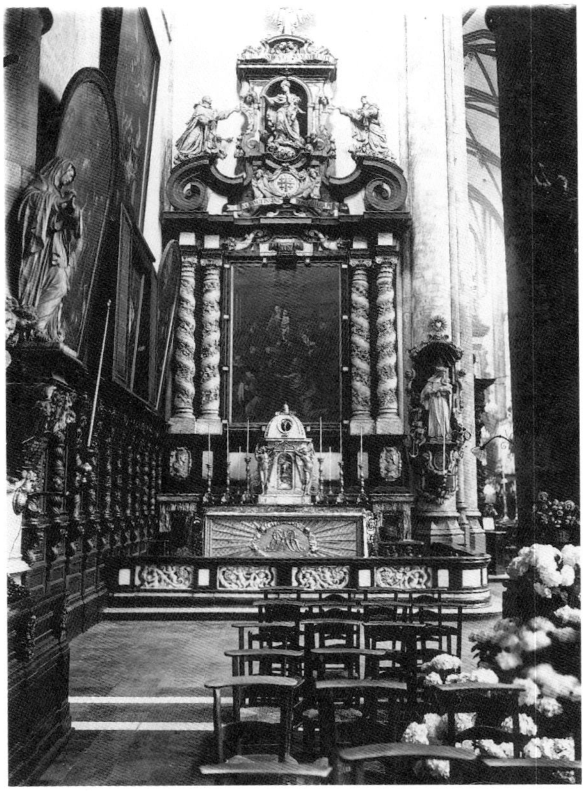

Afb. 5. Sebastiaan de Neve, *Altaar van Onze-Lieve-Vrouw-van de Rozenkrans*, 1650. Antwerpen, Sint-Pauluskerk

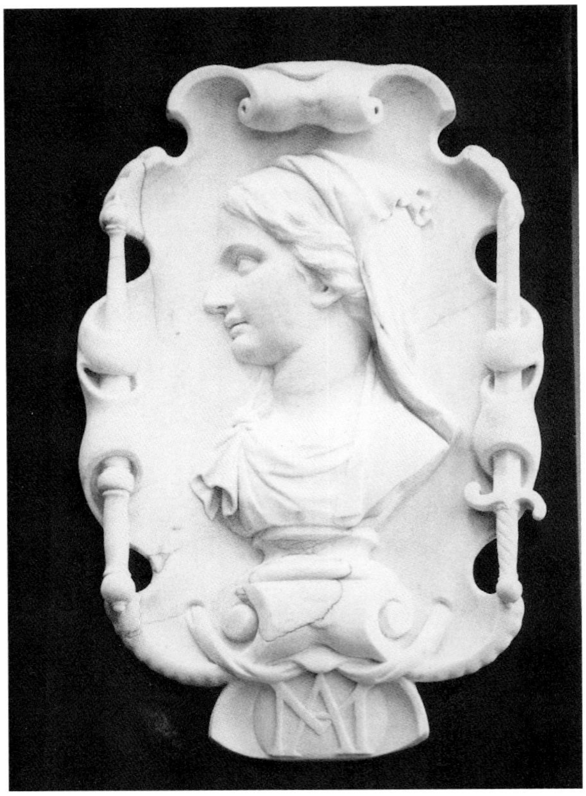

Afb. 6. Sebastiaan de Neve, *Ware afbeelding van de H. Maagd* (detail van het *Altaar van Onze-Lieve-Vrouw-van de Rozenkrans*, 1650). Antwerpen, Sint-Pauluskerk

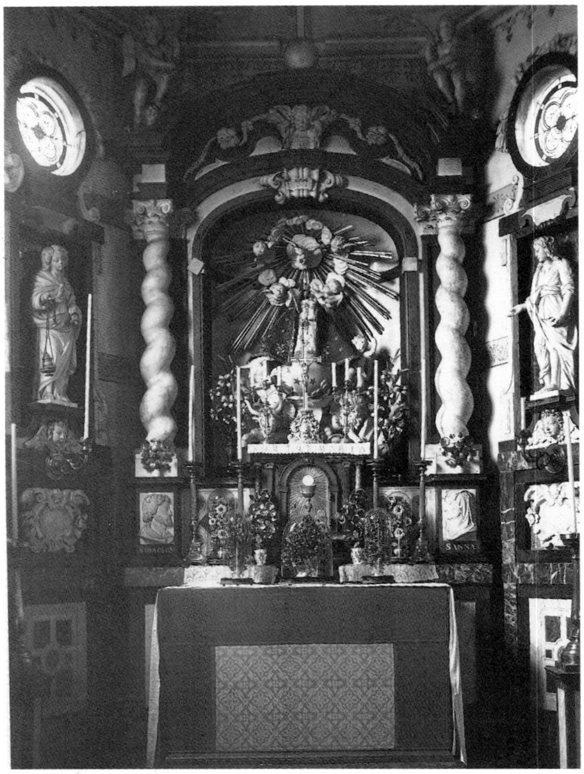

Afb. 7. Sebastiaan de Neve (?), *Altaar van Onze-Lieve-Vrouw-van-Zeven-Weeën*, 1661? (afkomstig uit het Antwerpse Victorinnenklooster). Minderhout, Kapel Onze-Lieve-Vrouw-van-Zeven-Weeën

voorstelling op deze medaillons wordt soms aangepast aan de omstandigheden. Dit is bijvoorbeeld het geval bij het altaar van de Minderhoutse kapel van Onze-Lieve-Vrouw van Zeven Weeën, een op basis van stijlovereenkomsten aan het de Neve-atelier toe te schrijven altaar, afkomstig uit het Antwerpse Victorinnenklooster (1661?) (afb. 7).[58] Hier stellen de bustes de ouders van Maria voor: Anna en Joachim.

Resten er naast de opdrachtgever nog twee andere factoren die de realisatie van een retabel bepaalden. Een eerste kunnen we omschrijven als de typus: de iconografisch-formele tradities en de interne iconografische logica. Met iconografische en formele tradities bedoelen we op de eerste plaats de gewoonte die reeds in de eerste decennia van de zestiende eeuw ontstaat om boven op geschilderde of gebeeldhouwde retabels gebeeldhouwde heiligenfiguren te plaatsen. Naast de titularis van het altaar worden er hier ook andere heiligen geplaatst met wie de opdrachtgever een of andere devotionele band bezat. De gewoonte om zeven-

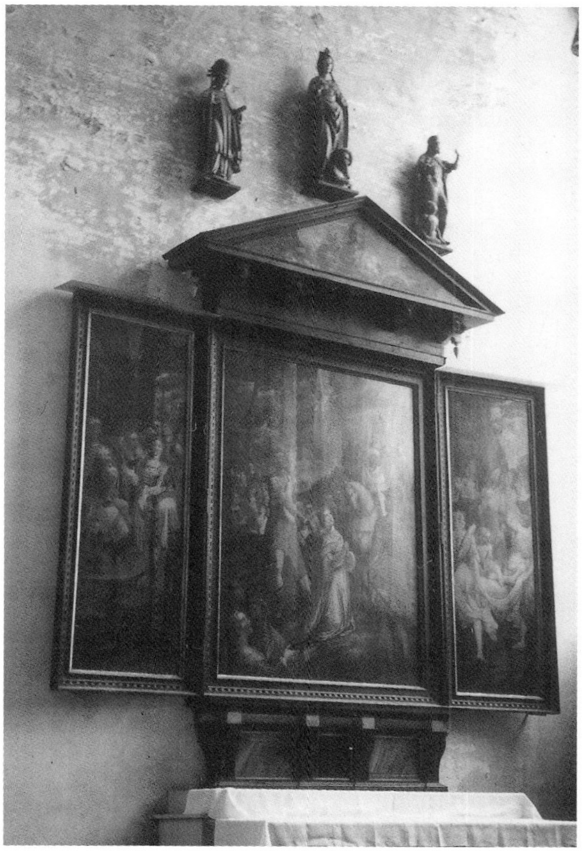

Afb. 8. Jan Baptist Saive, *Drieluik van de H. Catharina van Alexandrië*, 1600(?). Mechelen, Onze-Lieve-Vrouw-over-de-Dijlekerk

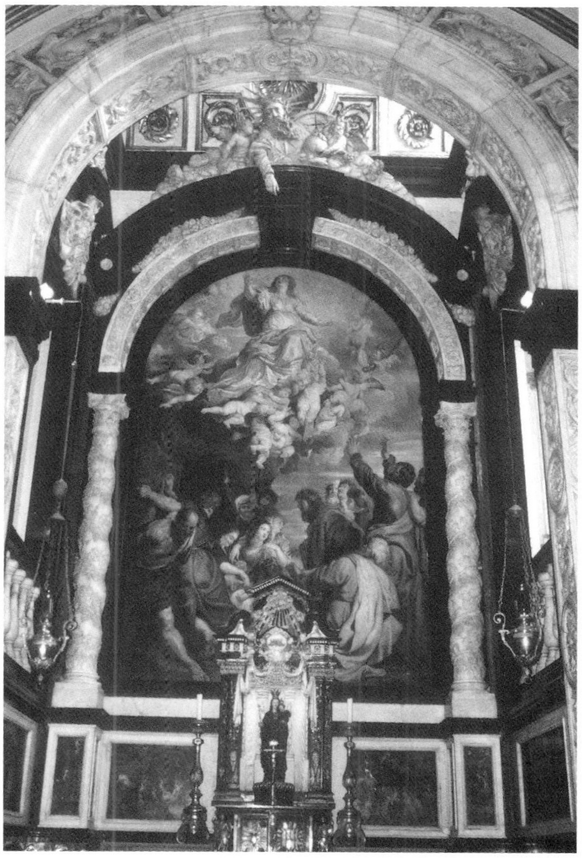

Afb. 9. Andries Colyns de Nole (?), *Altaar van de Houtappelkapel*, ca. 1635(?). Antwerpen Sint-Carolus Borromeuskerk

tiende-eeuwse altaren met beeldhouwwerk te bekronen ontstond dus niet uit het niets. Bovendien leefde de gewoonte om andere afbeeldingen dan deze van de titularis op het retabel te plaatsen ook in de zeventiende eeuw door. In de Aalsterse Sint-Maartenskerk bijvoorbeeld, pronken op het H. Rochus-altaar van het gilde van de Hophandelaars naast de patroon nog vier andere heiligen: de HH. Christoffel, Sebastiaan, Antonius en Arnout.[59]

Een andere iconografisch-formele traditie leefde eveneens voort in de zeventiende eeuw. In de tweede helft van de zestiende eeuw komen reeds geschilderde triptieken voor met boven op het drieluik een aparte geschilderde voorstelling van God de Vader. Te Mechelen, in de Onze-Lieve-Vrouw-over-de-Dijlekerk, wordt nog een zeldzaam volledig exemplaar bewaard, het *Drieluik van de H. Catharina van Alexandrië* van de hand van Jan Baptist Saive (1571–1624) (paneel, ca. 1600?)[60] (afb. 8). In Italië kwam dit compositieschema, zowel in geschilderde als gebeeldhouwde vorm nog veel vroeger voor.[61] Het ligt aan de basis van de gelijkaardige zeventiende-eeuwse interne iconografische logica, die weliswaar dikwijls multimediaal van aard was. In de Houtappelkapel van de Antwerpse jezuïetenkerk komt het tot een bijna fysieke interactie (afb. 9). Oorspronkelijk hield de uitermate dynamisch weergegeven God de Vader-figuur een kroon in de hand die hij de op het altaarstuk weergegeven Madonna aanreikt.[62] Hoogstwaarschijnlijk ontstond deze werkelijk 'barok' te noemen sculptuur rond 1635 toen Andries Colyns de Nole begon met de sculpturale inrichting van de kapel.[63]

Dit is echter niet de enige wijze waarop door middel van de gebeeldhouwde decoratie van de altaarportiek aan iconografische uitdieping wordt gedaan van het centrale, meestal geschilderde, tafereel. De basis van de portiek, waar zich volgens de traditie ook geschilderde predellataferelen kunnen bevinden (afb. 9), wordt

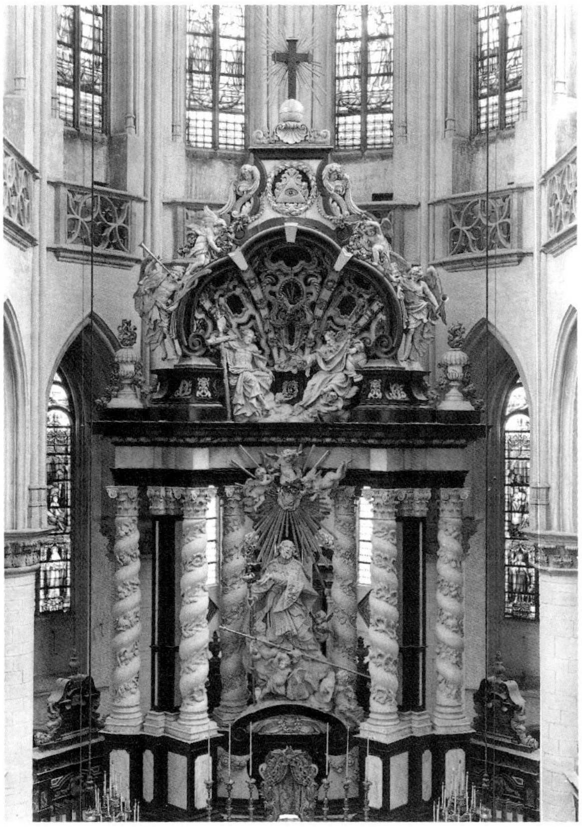

Afb. 10. Artus II Quellinus, Guillelmus Kerrickx, Ludovicus Willemsens en Norbert Herry, *Hoogaltaar*. Antwerpen, Sint-Jacobskerk

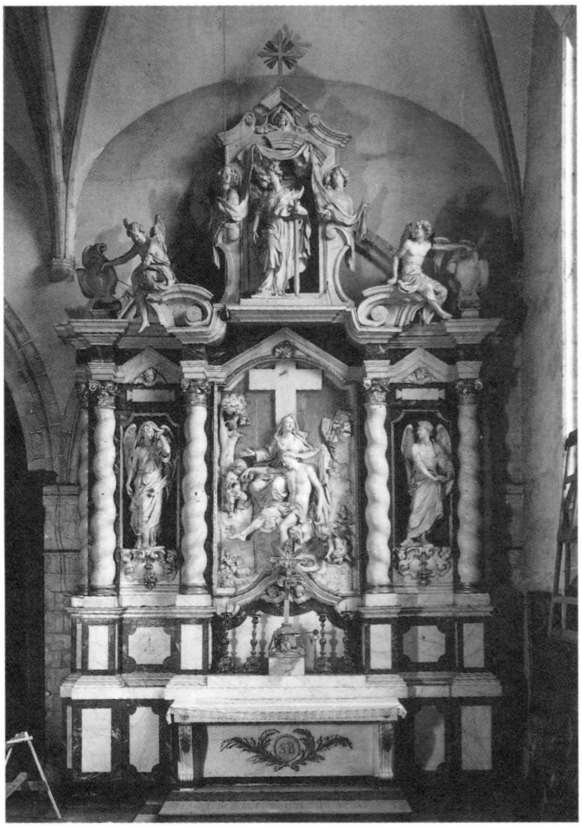

Afb. 11. Mattheus van Beveren, *Altaar van Onze-Lieve-Vrouw-van-Zeven-Weeën*, 1668. Dendermonde, Onze-Lieve-Vrouwkerk

bij sommige altaren ingenomen door gesneden voorstellingen die het centrale tafereel begeleiden (afb. 23). Ook op de zuilbasissen prijkten, zoals vermeld, soms reliëfs (afb. 5, 7, 17 en 24). De onderwerpen variëren van taferelen uit het leven van de heiligen tot hun attributen of de kentekenen van de opdrachtgever. Een andere mogelijkheid voor dit soort iconografische verrijking is de decoratie van de zuil of pijler. Daar waar salomonische zuilen in eerste instantie bijdroegen tot de eucharistische dimensie van het altaar, door ze te omzwachtelen met door druivenranken bevolkte puttini die met vruchten en planten spelen (afb. 5), werden er ook aangepaste variaties bedacht, zoals op het hoogaltaar van de Antwerpse Sint-Jacobskerk [64] (1685) (afb. 10). Hier krijgen ze schelpen en ander maritiem speelgoed, als toepasselijke begeleiding bij de centrale voorstelling van de H. Jacob de Meerdere.

Het medium beeldhouwkunst bezit een aantal eigenheden die het gebruik ervan in een heel ander economisch perspectief plaatsen dan de schilderkunst. Deze factor wordt in het contextuele model omschreven als de economie van de gebeeldhouwde voorstelling. De economische en materiële realiteit van sculptuur veroorzaakt op het artistieke vlak – en bijgevolg ook op het iconografische vlak – een inherente tendens naar de meest spaarzame of *economische* manier van voorstellen. Een complexe voorstelling, bijvoorbeeld een tafereel, heeft een verregaand effect op het gebruik van het materiaal, het aantal werkuren en bijgevolg de prijs van het kunstwerk. De wijze waarop en de mate waarin beeldhouwwerk wordt aangewend in een opdracht, zijn *linea recta* verbonden met het budget en de materiële context van de opdrachtgever.

Eén van de weinige Zuid-Nederlandse voorbeelden van zeventiende-eeuwse retabels met een centraal reliëf in de plaats van een altaarstuk, bevindt zich in de Dendermondse Onze-Lieve-Vrouwkerk. Het werd in 1668 ten behoeve van het broederschap van Onze-Lie-

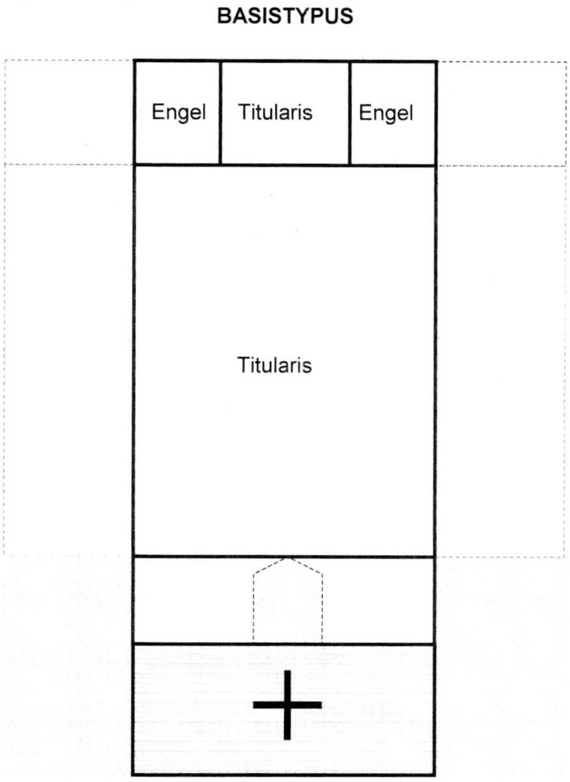


Afb. 12. Basistypus

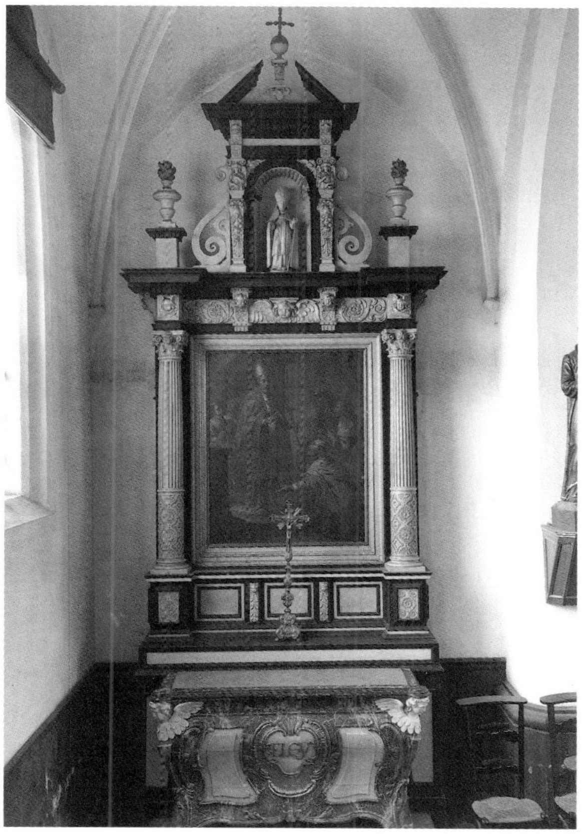

Afb. 13. Anoniem, *Altaar van de H. Eligius*, 1642. Wezemaal, Sint-Martinuskerk

ve-Vrouw-van-Zeven-Weeën uitgevoerd door Mattheus van Beveren (1630–1690) in opdracht van een particuliere opdrachtgever, de wellicht begoede kanunnik Van der Meersche, (afb. 11).[65] Het centrale reliëf dat de *Pietà* voorstelt, is duidelijk geïnspireerd op het altaarstuk dat Antoon van Dyck rond 1629 schilderde voor de Antwerpse Begijnhofkerk.[66] In 1670 sluit het Antwerpse Schermersgilde met Artus II Quellinus (1625–1700) en Norbertus van den Eynde (1628–1704) een contract af voor haar nieuwe retabel én tuin in de kathedraal ten bedrage van 8400 gulden.[67] In dezelfde periode werden doorsnee stenen zijaltaren gebouwd voor prijzen tussen de 1000 en de 3000 gulden. Het verdwenen retabel werd geflankeerd door twee meer dan levensgrote, marmeren voorstellingen van oudtestamentische krijgers.[68] Twee jaar vroeger levert Norbertus van den Eynde twee marmeren retabelbeelden voor de prijs van 1500 gulden te Sint-Niklaas.[69] Hierbij moet men voor ogen houden dat de prijzen van de altaren buiten Antwerpen, ongeveer de helft bedragen van wat men in de Scheldestad voor een gelijkaardig werk vraagt. De beide krijgersbeelden moeten de prijs van het Schermersaltaar dus aanzienlijk de hoogte in gedreven hebben. Beide voorbeelden illustreren het verband tussen het materieel-economische perspectief van de opdrachtgever en de complexiteit van het iconografische programma van het bestelde altaarretabel.

Ten slotte zijn er de opdrachtgevers zelf. Hun spectrum is bijzonder ruim, en wordt bepaald door het beschikbare budget, de context waarin zij functioneren en aanwezigheid van persoonlijke motieven. Zijn hun iconografische keuzen even uiteenlopend of komen er een aantal patronen bovendrijven? Wat leert deze kwantitatieve analyse van de gedateerde zeventiende-eeuwse retabels ons over de iconografische smaak van de opdrachtgever? Het levert een brede horizont op met aan de ene einder de doorsnee-iconografie, aan de andere einder de uitzonderlijke themata. Centraal een interessant middenveld.

Uit het kwantitatieve onderzoek trad een veel voorkomend iconografisch schema naar voren

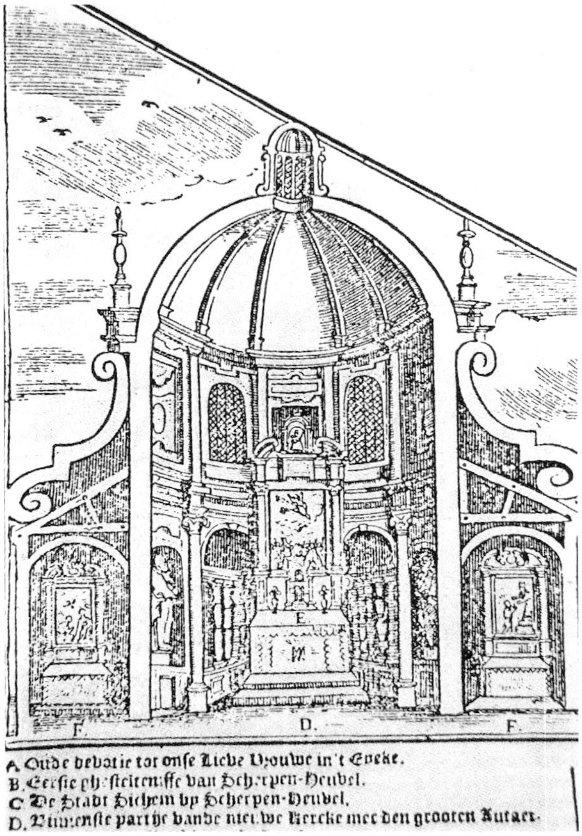


Afb. 14. Jan Jeghers, *Bedevaartvaan van Onze-Lieve-Vrouw-van-Scherpenheuvel*, detail

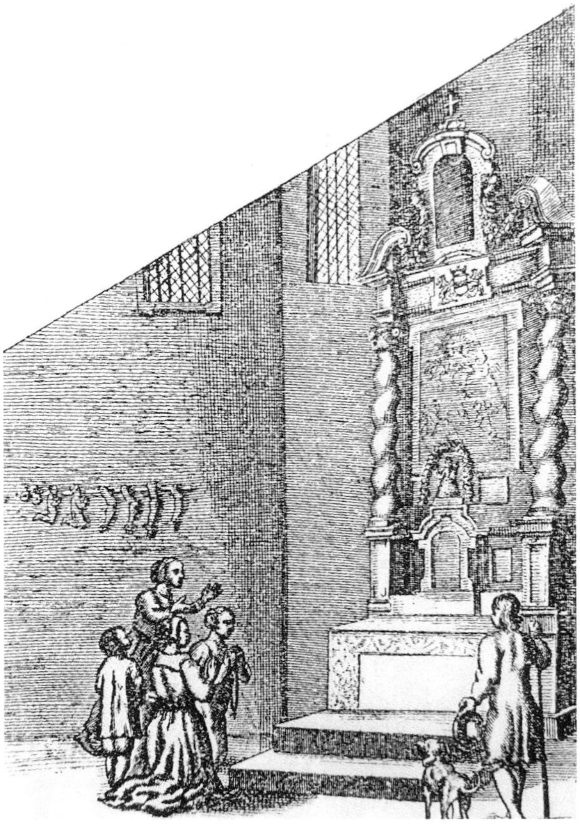

Afb. 15. Anoniem, *Bedevaartvaan van Onze-Lieve-Vrouw-van-Argenteau* (Luik), detail

dat de beide media, schilderkunst en beeldhouwkunst bevat, verspreid over de twee zones van de altaarportiek, boven en onder de kroonlijst. Dit retabeltype beschouwen we als de basistypus (afb. 12, weergegeven in vet).[70] Boven op de portiek bevindt zich een nis waarin een gebeeldhouwde voorstelling van de titularis wordt geplaatst. Onder het lijstwerk kiest men voor een altaarstuk, waarop eveneens de titularis wordt afgebeeld (afb. 13). In vele gevallen bevinden zich links en rechts naast de bekronende nis nog twee gebeeldhouwde engelen. Ze worden weergegeven als lichtdragers, zwaaien met palmen of lauwerkransen, blazen de loftrompet of knielen in aanbidding.

Het opvallendste kenmerk van deze basistypus is het feit dat de titularis twee keer voorkomt. Een keer geschilderd en een keer gebeeldhouwd. De vraag die zich hierbij onmiddellijk opdringt is: waarom twee keer dezelfde voorstelling? Willen we de motivatie van bepaalde opdrachtgevers voor het maken van een hiervan afwijkende keuze doorgronden, moeten we eerst de drijfveren voor deze dubbele voorstelling achterhalen. Zou de door de Contrareformatie zo geprezen aanschouwelijkheid, hier benadrukt door een herhaling, voor de ongeletterde gelovige de enige reden zijn? Ons inziens niet.

Deze herhaling van de heiligenvoorstelling in de basistypus is er in wezen geen. Dit wordt duidelijk aan de hand van de voorstellingen op eigentijdse bedevaartvanen, waarop de essenties van de devotionele handelingen zijn vastgelegd. In talloze kerken bestond een bloeiende verering voor een specifieke heilige en kwam men van heinde en verre op bedevaart om zijn hulp af te smeken. Het materiële brandpunt van deze devotie zijn de relieken of de wonderdadige beelden. De devotiebeelden worden tijdens hoogdagen beneden op de altaartafel uitgestald of in processies meegedragen, maar hun eigenlijke plaats bevindt zich boven op het retabel (afb. 14–15). In de Brusselse SS. Michiel- en Goedelekathedraal koopt men in 1592 een Onze-Lieve-Vrouwbeeld voor het Maria-altaar. Een jaar later koopt men echter een tweede exemplaar aan *dwelck men omme-*

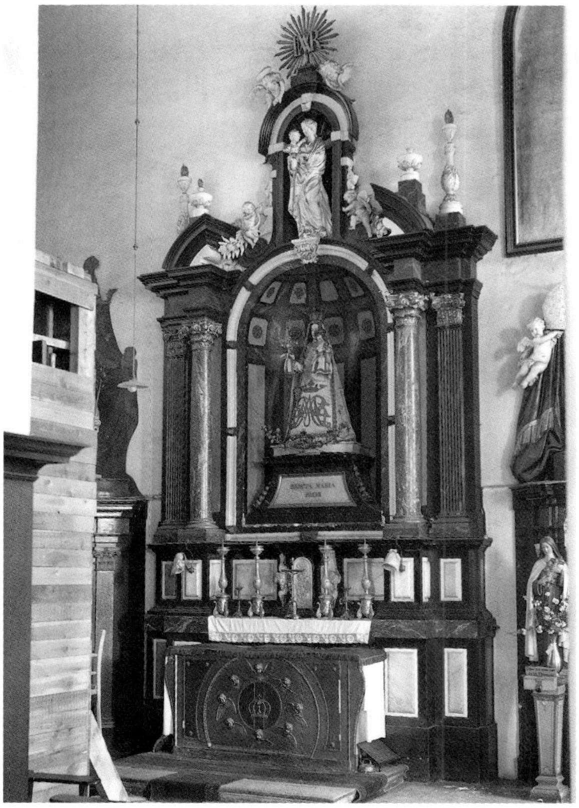

Afb. 16. Jan vanden Cruyce, *Altaar van Onze-Lieve-Vrouw*, 1641. Deurne, Sint-Fredeganduskerk

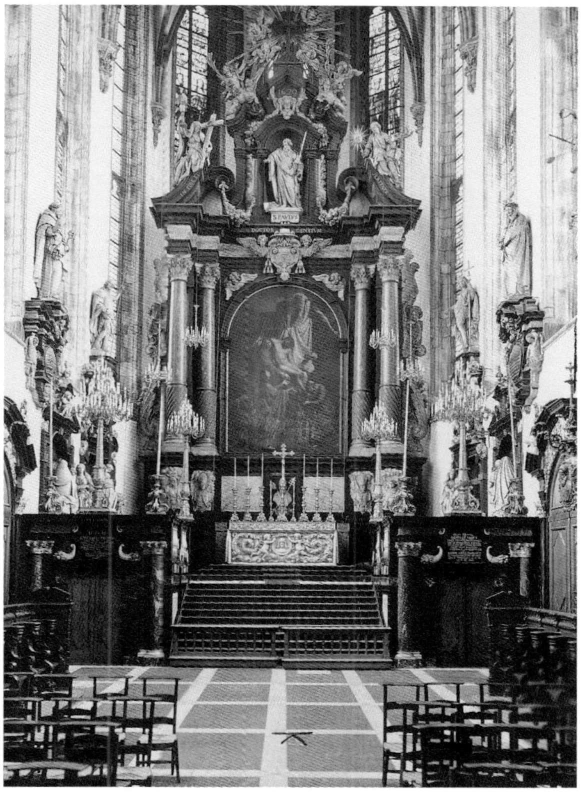

Afb. 17. Peter II Verbrugghen, *Hoogaltaar*, 1670. Antwerpen, Sint-Pauluskerk

*draeght in de processie van O.L.V halfoighst, want t'beelt staande boven O.L.V autaer niet is bequaem om te paleren, ende oick niet sonder perijkel int affneemen ende opsetten.*[71]

Het is natuurlijk zo dat lang niet al de afbeeldingen die boven op het retabel geplaatst worden, ook functioneren in devotionele handelingen. Dit blijkt mooi uit een retabel uit de Sint-Fredeganduskerk te Deurne uit 1641 van de hand van Jan vanden Cruyce (afb. 16).[72] Ook hier wordt twee keer de H. Maagd uitgebeeld, maar hun functie is duidelijk verschillend. In de loop van de zeventiende eeuw groeit trouwens de tendens om het devotionele beeld centraal in het retabel uit te stallen in plaats van er bovenop. De grens tussen de gewone beelden en de wonderdadige beelden is lang niet altijd duidelijk. En artistieke kwaliteit is hierin geen scheidsrechter. Belangrijk is te onthouden dat, zeker tijdens de eerste decennia van de zeventiende eeuw, de gewoonte bestond om deze beelden in de nis boven op de portiek te zetten. De plaats van deze beelden beklemde hun intermediaire functie als voorsprekers van de gelovigen bij de hemelse heiligen. Hun driedimensionale karakter sloot aan bij hun vermogen om – in letterlijke zin – het heilige te *belichamen*. Slechts zelden worden in onze streken aan een tweedimensionaal schilderij wonderdadige of heilige kwaliteiten toegeschreven. Dit alles bepaalt het collectieve geheugen van de zeventiende-eeuwse gelovige en de blik waarmee hij het altaar tegemoet trad. In dit licht, de driedimensionale afbeelding als brandpunt van devotie, moeten we dus ook de keuze van bepaalde opdrachtgevers benaderen voor het plaatsen van afwijkende, specifieke onderwerpen op deze locatie.

Aan de andere einder van de iconografische horizont vinden we de uitzonderlijke, of moeten we zeggen gepersonaliseerde onderwerpen, waaronder de absolute opdrachticonografie: het portret. Als gevolg van de kerkelijke richtlijnen, maakten privé-opdrachtgevers doorgaans hun rol als stichter kenbaar door het plaatsen van hun wapen of van een schenkingsopschrift.[73] Soms lieten ze evenwel hun beeltenis in de voorstelling integreren. In de zeventiende-eeuwse retabelsculptuur gebeurt dit echter hoogst uitzonderlijk en dan nog op

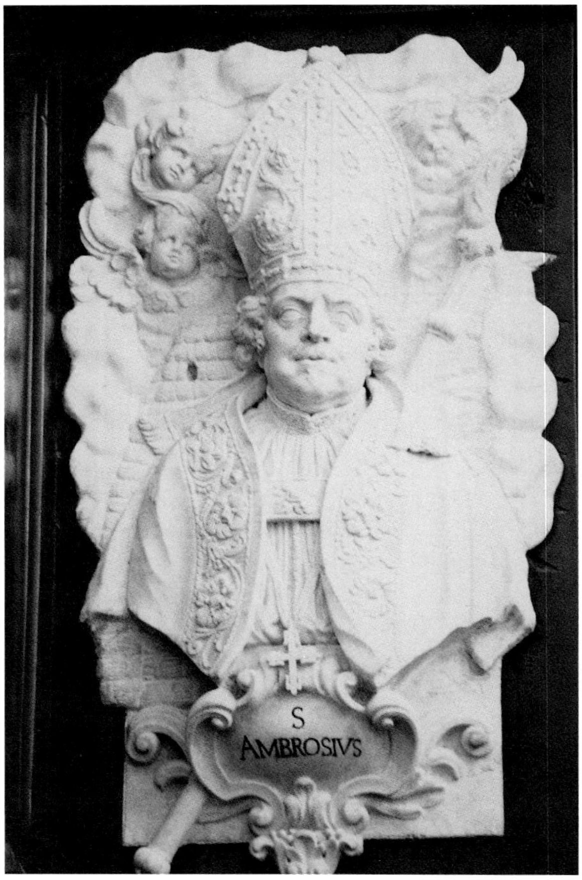


Afb. 18. Peter II Verbrugghen, *Buste van de H. Ambrosius, met de gelaatstrekken van Bisschop Ambrosius Capello*, detail van het hoogaltaar, 1670. Antwerpen, Sint-Pauluskerk

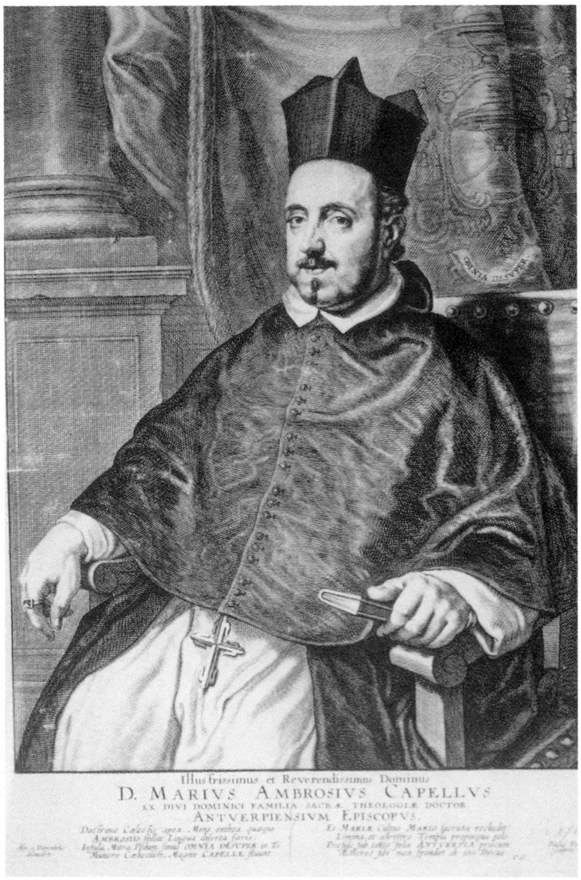


Afb. 19. Paulus Pontius naar Abraham van Diepenbeeck, *Ambrosius Capello*, prent

'verdekte' wijze. Eigenlijk kan er slechts een voorbeeld aangehaald worden: het portret van bisschop Ambrosius Capello (1597–1676)[74] op het hoogaltaar van de Antwerpse Sint-Pauluskerk (1670), uitgevoerd door Peter II Verbruggen (1648–1691) naar het ontwerp van Franciscus van Sterbeeck (1631–1693), rector van het begijnhof, mycoloog en architect (afb. 17–19).[75] De schenker liet zijn trekken vereeuwigen in het reliëfmedaillon dat de westerse kerkvader en zijn naampatroon Ambrosius voorstelt.

In dit verband wordt er door sommigen ook gewezen op de uitermate realistische trekken van de Sint-Norbertusfiguur afkomstig van het hoogaltaar van de voormalige Antwerpse Sint-Michielsabdij (ca. 1624) (afb. 20–21). Dat deze met de fysionomie van de officiële opdrachtgever, abt Mattheus Yrsselius (1614–1629) zouden overeenkomen is twijfelachtig, want de man was op dat ogenblik ongeveer zeventig jaar (vgl. met het portret van Rubens uit het Statens Museum Kopenhagen, afb. 22).[76] De levensechte weergave lijkt mij, ondanks oppervlakkige overeenkomsten met het portret, eerder verbonden met het fenomeen van het zogenaamde *vera effigies*. Net als bij de jezuïeten kende de premonstratenzerorde in de zeventiende eeuw de verspreiding van de zogenaamde waarachtige afbeelding van hun ordestichter.[77] Bovendien zou het nogal aanmatigend geweest zijn van deze abt om zijn eigen trekken te verlenen aan zijn ordestichter die bovendien niet eens zijn patroon was.

Andere vormen van opdrachticonografie treffen we bijvoorbeeld aan bij ambachts- en gildealtaren, waar we – weliswaar sporadisch – als verwijzing naar hun patronaatschap niet alleen een afbeelding van hun patroon maar ook de attributen van hun nering aantreffen. De Antwerpse gilde van Speellieden onder andere, liet haar retabel met gebeeldhouwde instrumenten decoreren (afb. 4). Naast het heraldische wapen van privé-stichters, waren deze attributen de enige vorm van profane iconografie die

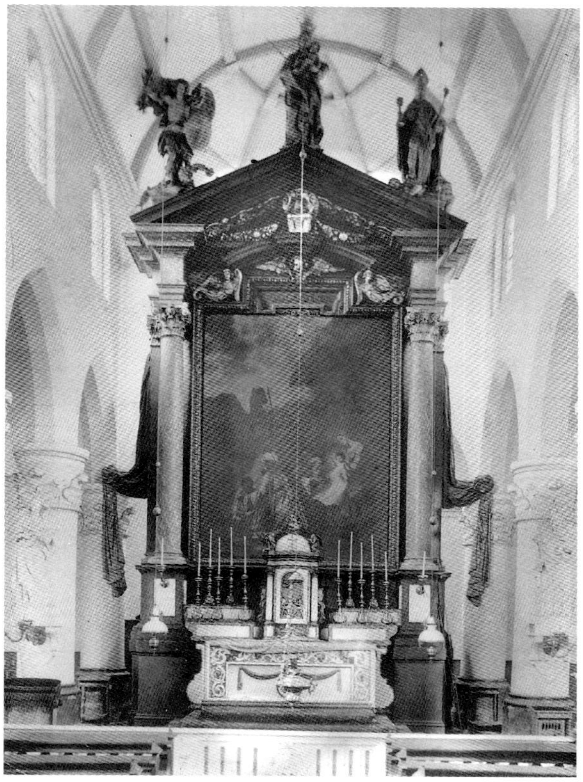

Afb. 20. Anoniem, *Hoogaltaar van de Antwerpse Sint-Michielsabdij*, ca. 1624. Zundert, Sint-Trudokerk (situatie vóór 1926), ca. 1624

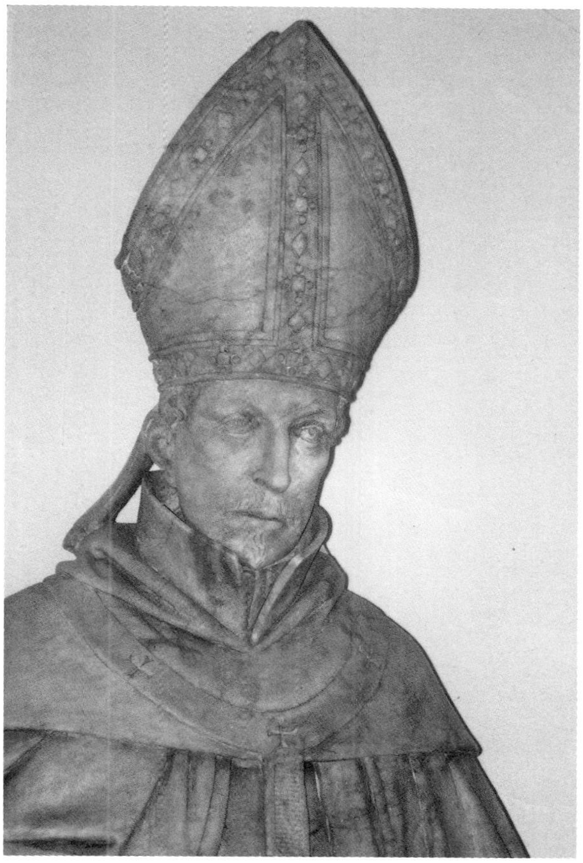

Afb. 21. Anoniem, *Sint-Norbertus*, ca. 1624 (afkomstig van het hoogaltaar van de Antwerpse Sint-Michielsabdij). Zundert, Sint-Trudokerk

door toedoen van de opdrachtgevers op het retabel terechtkwamen.

Een laatste, duidelijk aan de opdrachtgever gerelateerde categorie iconografische themata vormen de ordeheiligen. In de meeste gevallen krijgen gebeeldhouwde voorstellingen van ordeheiligen een plaats op een aan hen gewijd zijaltaar in de kloosterkerk. In dit geval kunnen ze ondergebracht worden in de categorie van de basistypus. Het zegt natuurlijk meer over de opdrachtgevers wanneer ze deze voorstellingen op hun hoogaltaar plaatsen, zonder dat het aan de betrokken heilige gewijd is. In tegenstelling tot wat men zou vermoeden blijven de voorbeelden hiervan uiterst beperkt. Slechts op vier altaren worden ordestichters, regelgevers of ordeheiligen ten voeten uit afgebeeld. Het meest nadrukkelijk is de ordestichter op het vroegste voorbeeld aanwezig, het vermelde hoogaltaar van de Antwerpse Sint-Michielsabdij (afb. 20). Het is ook de enige keer dat de gebeeldhouwde voorstelling van de ordestichter boven op het retabel wordt geplaatst. Nog een andere oplossing bestond erin om de gebeeldhouwde voorstellingen van ordefiguren niet *op* het retabel maar in de onmiddellijke omgeving ervan te plaatsen. De Antwerpse jezuïeten plaatsen de beelden naar Italiaans voorbeeld in nissen aan weerszijden van het retabel.[78] Een andere mogelijkheid was het plaatsen van afbeeldingen op de portieken aan weerszijden van het retabel die toegang verlenen tot de ruimte achter het bouwwerk (afb. 23).

Ten slotte komen we tot het middenveld van de iconografische horizont. Dit bestaat uit een aantal onderwerpen die op een relatief kleine schaal vertegenwoordigd zijn, maar zeker niet uitzonderlijk kunnen genoemd worden. We vinden ze terug op altaren waar hun aanwezigheid op het eerste gezicht noch met de titularis, noch met de functie van het altaar in verband staat. Het best vertegenwoordigde onderwerp in dit middenveld is Maria. In een aantal gevallen kan haar tegenwoordigheid verklaard worden doordat zij – weliswaar de eerste maar weinig bekende – patrones is van de

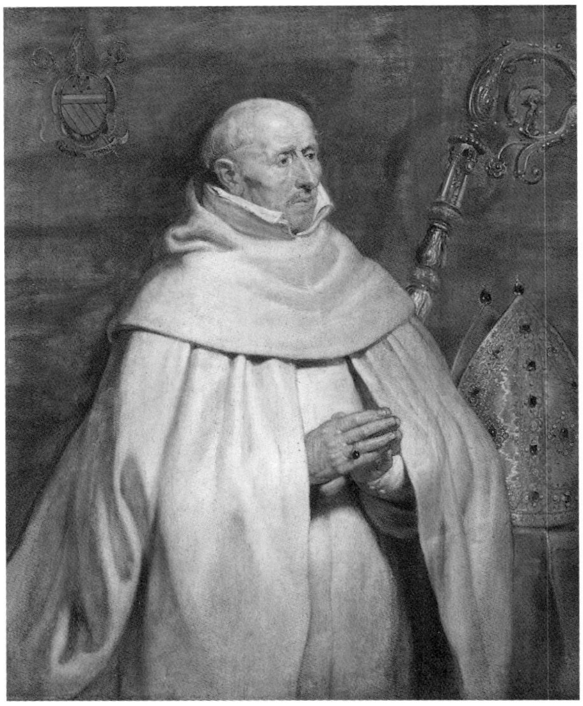

Afb. 22. P.P. Rubens, *Abt Mattheus Irsselius*. Kopenhagen, Statens Museum for Kunst

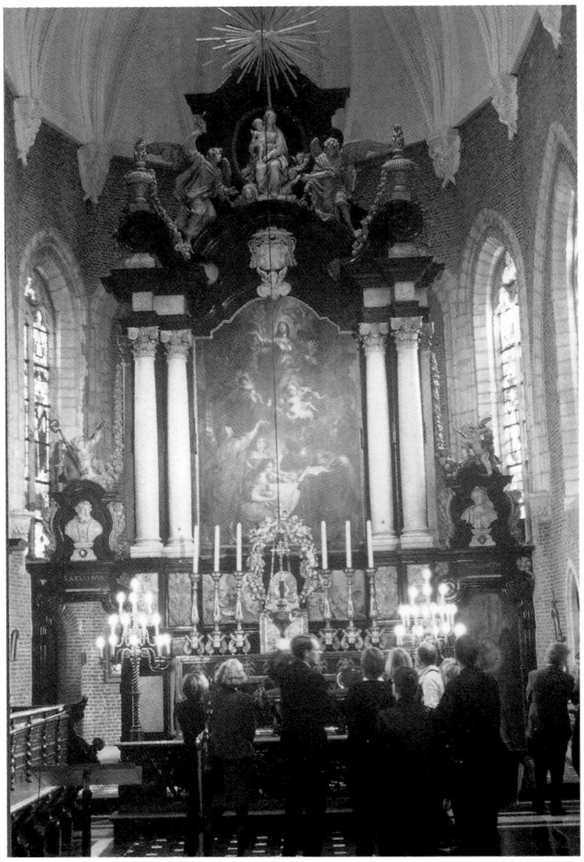

Afb. 23. Artus II Quellinus(?), *Hoogaltaar*, ca. 1682. Antwerpen, Kapel Sint-Elisabethgasthuis

kerk. Om deze reden vinden we haar bijvoorbeeld terug op het hoogaltaar van de Antwerpse jezuïetenkerk, oorspronkelijk gewijd aan de H. Ignatius én de Moeder Gods, in de Sint-Janskathedraal te 's-Hertogenbosch[79] en in de kapel van het Antwerpse Sint-Elisabethgasthuis (Artus II Quellinus (?), ca. 1682) (afb. 23)[80]. Bij enkele altaren kan haar aanwezigheid verklaard worden vanuit een interne iconografische logica, bijvoorbeeld wanneer het altaar in kwestie gewijd is aan de moeder van de H. Maagd. Centraal wordt dan de titularis uitgebeeld, boven op het retabel de H. Maagd. Elders, bij hoogaltaren van religieuze orden zoals de premonstratenzers, is de Madonna aanwezig als bijzondere ordepatrones (afb. 20). Slechts enkele stichters van privé-altaren drukken hun bijzondere toewijding tot de Madonna uit, door haar naast de gewone titularis ook met een plaats op het retabel te vereren. In de meeste gevallen kunnen er voor de bijzondere aanwezigheid van de H. Maagd op retabels redenen achterhaald worden die buiten het kader van de persoonlijke vroomheid van de opdrachtgever vallen.[81]

De vermelde hoogaltaren van de Antwerpse kathedraal (afb. 1) en de Brusselse Onze-Lieve-Vrouw-ter-Kapellekerk (afb 2) zijn slechts twee voorbeelden van de gebeeldhouwde aanwezigheid van God de Vader in de bekroning van een altaarportiek. In het zog van de zestiende-eeuwse traditie, blijft hij op het zeventiende-eeuwse retabel de trouwe begeleider van de Moeder Gods. Doorgaans wacht hij Haar op, terwijl het geschilderde altaarstuk haar *Tenhemelopneming* uitbeeldt, terwijl in andere gevallen in het midden van de portiek een wonderdadige beeltenis van Haar staat uitgestald.

Maar ook Christus zelf vinden we volplastisch op het retabel voorgesteld. Hij wordt enerzijds in de gedaante van *Verrezen Christus*, anderzijds als de *Goede Herder* uitgebeeld. Het is opmerkelijk dat Hij op al deze altaren steeds deel uitmaakt van een geheel van gebeeldhouwde figuren. Meestal wordt Hij begeleid door de HH. Petrus en Paulus (afb. 24). Met andere woorden, Christus en het apostelpaar behoorden doorgaans tot een iconografisch ensemble. Maar in welk licht moeten we dit samengaan interpreteren? De aanwezigheid van Christus op het retabel zowel als *Salvator Mun-*

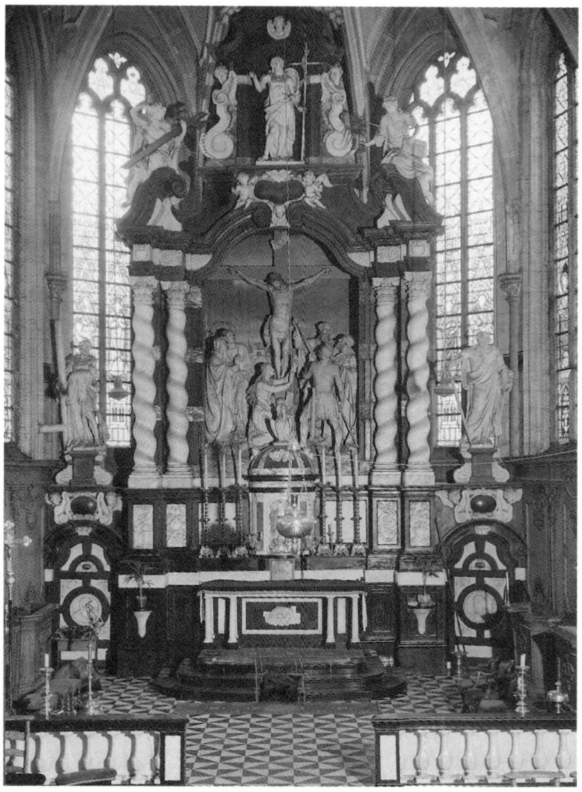

Afb. 24. Peter I of Peter II Verbrugghen, *Hoogaltaar*, 1679. Lebbeke, Onze-Lieve-Vrouwkerk

*di* als in de gedaante van de *Pastor Bonus* staat in rechtstreeks verband met het essentiële altaargebeuren: het H. Sacrament van de Eucharistie en de hierbij – door de gereformeerden betwiste – waarachtige Aanwezigheid. Door de driedimensionale weergave van de mensgeworden Christus op het retabel, wordt de tegenwoordigheid van het lichaam van Christus in de geconsacreerde hostie, als een soort visuele catechese, op zeer aanschouwelijke wijze zichtbaar gesteld. De *Salvator Mundi*-voorstelling vertolkt niet alleen de met het sacrament verbonden Verrijzenisgedachte, maar verwijst bij altaren die tevens als bewaarplaats van de eucharistische reserve fungeren naar het tabernakel als het nieuwe graf voor het Lichaam van Christus. Bij altaren opgetrokken door privé-stichters, staat de uitbeelding van de Verrezene duidelijk in relatie tot het funeraire aspect van het altaar: de bijdrage tot het zielenheil van de opdrachtgevers in het hiernamaals door hun bekostiging van het bouwwerk of de stichting van missen aan het altaar. Een voorbeeld hiervan vinden we in de Gentse kathedraal, in de zogenaamde Triest-kapel bij het retabel opgetrokken door Hans van Mildert in de privé-kapel van de bisschop.[82]

Het gezelschap van de apostelprinsen bouwt verder op een voorstellingstraditie die tegen de achtergrond van de kerkelijke hervormingen in de tweede helft van de zestiende eeuw tot bloei komt.[83] Het iconografische thema van de beide apostelen dat vroeg-christelijke wortels heeft, wordt verbonden met het fundament van het katholieke geloof: het H. Sacrament. Hiervan getuigen de talrijke voorstellingen van het apostelpaar op zeventiende-eeuwse monstransen, meermaals ter aanvulling van gelijkaardige Christusvoorstellingen.[84] In de vroeg-christelijke periode werden de beide apostelen beschouwd als de *duces in militia Christi*: de aanvoerders in de strijd voor het christendom.[85] In deze hoedanigheid vergezelden zij Christus dikwijls in Majesteitsvoorstellingen op sarcofagen. Met ditzelfde aura van strijdbaarheid, stonden zij symbool voor de zestiende en zeventiende-eeuwse verdediging van essentiële geloofspunten tegen de aanvallen van de hervormingsgezinden. We vinden hen daarom terug op frontispices van post-tridentijnse uitgaven van onder andere het *Missale Romanum*[86] maar ook bijvoorbeeld op Heribertus Rosweydus' (S.J.) *Generale kerckelycke historie [...]*, (Antwerpen, 1623).

Ten slotte zijn er nog enkele marginale themata die hun toekomstige bloei in de achttiende eeuw aankondigen. De gebeeldhouwde H. Drievuldigheid komt in de zeventiende-eeuwse retabelbekroning slechts zelden voor. Meestal dankt zij haar aanwezigheid op het retabel aan het inhoudelijke verband met de centrale voorgestelde *Apotheose van Maria*, zoals op het hoogaltaar van de Antwerpse kathedraal (afb. 1).[87] Op een gelijkaardige wijze vinden we ze ook terug in het kader van een eucharistische thematiek, met name als begeleider van een altaarstuk met uitbeelding van *Christus aan het Kruis*.[88] In de Antwerpse Sint-Jacobskerk,[89] waar zich het imposantste voorbeeld bevindt, lijkt de aanwezigheid van de H. Drievuldigheid, ondanks de relatie tot de voorstelling van de apotheose van de H. Jacob in het centrum van de portiek, voornamelijk te danken aan de rechten die het broederschap van de *H. Drievuldigheid ter Bevrijding der Christenslaven* op het hoogaltaar bezat (afb. 10).[90] In de achttiende eeuw zal een groot deel van de talrijke Drievuldigheidsvoorstellingen op altaren te danken zijn aan de groei van het aantal broederschappen, gewijd aan deze devotie.[91]

Evenzeer in tegenstelling tot de achttiende eeuw, komen we in de zeventiende eeuw slechts zelden gesculpteerde personificaties tegen op het retabel. Slechts een enkele keer zitten zij op het gebroken fronton, aan weerszijden van de centrale nis. In alle drie de gevallen kan moeilijk gesproken worden van doorsnee opdrachten. Op het verloren gegane hoogaltaar van de kathedraal van 's-Hertogenbosch (Hans Van Mildert, 1616–17) stelden zij de *Gerechtigheid*, en aan de linkerzijde waarschijnlijk de *Vrede* voor.[92] Het altaar werd in het strategisch gelegen 's-Hertogenbosch tijdens het Twaalfjarig Bestand (cf. iconografie?) opgetrokken, met de hulp van de aartshertogen. Op het reeds aangehaalde hoogaltaar van de Antwerpse Dominicanenkerk, volledig door bisschop Capello bekostigd, vinden we het *Geloof* en de *Waarheid* terug (afb. 17). In Lebbeke, een belangrijk mariaal bedevaartsoord, wordt in 1679 een retabel met identieke personages opgetrokken, door dezelfde kunstenaar of door zijn vader Peter I Verbrugghen (afb.24). Net als bij het vorige bouwwerk, dient de kunstenaar te werken naar het ontwerp van een geestelijke, in dit geval een zekere '*broeder Beernaerts, architect*.'[93] Het Lebbeekse altaar werd voorzien van een van de meest complexe, gesculpteerde iconografische programma's uit de zeventiende eeuw, bestaande uit de *Verrezen Christus* met begeleidende apostelprinsen, samen met twee volplastische uitbeeldingen van het *Geloof* en de *Waarheid*. Op de zuilbasissen prijken nogmaals vier reliëfs met attributen die verwijzen naar de drie theologische deugden *Spes*, *Caritas* en *Fides* en een vierde met een voorstelling van de *Iustitia* (?).

## Besluit

Tot besluit kan worden gesteld dat voor de zeventiende-eeuwse opdrachtgevers van retabels, in de lijn van de kerkelijke verordeningen, de heiligenverering centraal stond. De concrete keuzemogelijkheden die zij bezitten bij de materialisering van hun devotionele doeleinden, zijn nauw verbonden met hun economische draagkracht. Degenen met de meest beperkte mogelijkheden, bijvoorbeeld rurale parochiekerken of de meer bescheiden zijaltaren uit de stedelijke context, kozen doorgaans voor de basistypus, met een iconografisch programma conform de titularis van het altaar. Centraal hierin staat het altaarstuk, het beeldhouwwerk is meestal zeer eenvoudig van aard. Zij die over ruimere financiële mogelijkheden beschikten, bisschoppen en kapittels, vermogende privépersonen, verenigingen, religieuze orden of altaren uit kerken van belangrijke bedevaartsoorden, konden deze basistypus iconografisch aanvullen door de altaarportiek aan te kleden met extra beeldhouwwerk. Meestal beperkt dit zich tot een uitdieping van het centrale thema, bijvoorbeeld door attributen, of inhoudelijk gerelateerde themata, zoals God de Vader. Een minderheid drukt een eigen stempel op het iconografische programma door te kiezen voor de uitbeelding van een specifieke devotie, of – in het geval van een kloosterkerk – hun ordestichter. Ten slotte geeft de eucharistische devotie van de zeventiende-eeuwse opdrachtgevers het leven aan een volplastisch iconografisch retabelprogramma: Christus begeleid door zijn *duces in militia christi:* de HH. Petrus en Paulus.

# NOTEN

1. J.Van der Sanden, *Oud Konst-Tooneel van Antwerpen* (autograaf), Antwerpen, [1771], deel II, vol 2, p. 421.

2. P. Baudouin, J. Bungeneers, e.a., *Onze-Lieve-Vrouwekathedraal van Antwerpen. Kunstpatrimonium van het ancien régime* (*Inventaris van het kunstpatrimonium van de provincie Antwerpen*, 3), S. Grieten en J. Bungeneers eds., [Turnhout], 1996, p. 16, met overzicht van alle betrokken archivalische documenten en literatuur.

3. '*[...] wesende hooch van deerde tot boven ontrent de vyftich voeten [...]*', vijftig Antwerpse voet komt overeen met ca. 14,3 m. M. Casteels, *De beeldhouwers de Nole te Kamerijk, te Utrecht en te Antwerpen* (*Verhandelingen van de Koninklijke Academie voor Wetenschappen, Letteren en Schone Kunsten van België. Klasse der Schone Kunsten*, 16), Brussel, 1961, p. 367, doc. 203.

4. '*[...] den witten ende gecoleurden italiaenschen marmer die by de kercke alreede tot het maeken van den voors. aultaer gecocht ende hier van Amsterdam gebrocht is [...]*' en '*[...] de twee gepolysterde grote albaste pileernen, die van Genua ontboden sijn [...]*': Casteels 1961 (zie noot 3), p. 369, doc. 203 en p. 391, doc. 225.

5. Casteels 1961 (zie noot 3), p. 279–280, doc. 102.

6. De toenmalige gemiddelde kost van een stenen hoofdaltaar schommelde tussen de zevenduizend en achtduizend gulden. De uiteindelijke kostprijs van het hoogaltaar van de Gentse kathedraal (atelier Colyns de Nole, 1615–1623) bijvoorbeeld, bedroeg 7825 gulden. Die van het hoofdaltaar van de basiliek van Scherpenheuvel (atelier Colyns de Nole, 1622) 7220 gulden. Casteels 1961 (zie noot 3), doc. 158, 196, 198 & 207.

7. Deze uitgave werd bekostigd door kanunnik Joannes del Rio (1555–1624), deken van de kerk. In ruil voor deze schenking verkreeg del Rio een graf aan de noordelijke kooringang en het recht tot het plaatsen van een epitaaf die zijn milddadigheid herdacht: D. Freedberg, *Rubens. The Life of Christ after the Passion* (*Corpus Rubenianum Ludwig Burchard*, VII), Londen, 1984, p. 175, nr. 43; C.Van de Velde, 'Rubens' Hemelvaart van Maria in de Kathedraal te Antwerpen', *Jaarboek Koninklijk Museum voor Schone Kunsten Antwerpen*, 1975, p. 246.

8. De nieuwe altaaromlijsting werd in 1824–26 opgetrokken door architect Jan Blom; zie Freedberg 1984 (zie noot 7), p. 177; Van de Velde 1975 (zie noot 7), p. 245.

9. F. Baudouin, 'Altars and Altarpieces before 1620', in J.R. Martin ed., *Rubens before 1620*, Princeton, 1972, p. 82 e.v.; K. Fremantle, *The baroque Townhall of Amsterdam* (*Utrechtse Kunsthistorische Studiën*, 4), Utrecht, 1959, pp. 127–128.

10. De altaarportiek werd ontmanteld en de onderdelen ervan verkocht op de veiling van de inboedel van de kathedraal in 1798: Baudouin en Bungeneers 1996 (zie noot 2), p.16.

11. Baudouin 1972 (zie noot 9), p. 64 e.v., p. 82 e.v.; U. Becker, *Studien zum flämischen Altarbau im 17. und 18. Jahrhundert* (*Verhandelingen van de Koninklijke Academie voor Wetenschappen, Letteren en Schone Kunsten van België. Klasse der Schone Kunsten*, 49), Brussel, 1990, p. 68 e.v.; W. Bergé, 'Het voormalige hoogaltaar in de Sint-Jan', in A. Koldeweij ed., [tent. cat.] *In Buscoducis. Kunst uit de Bourgondische tijd te 's-Hertogenbosch. De cultuur van de late middeleeuwen en de renaissance*, Maarssen–Den Haag, 1990, pp. 455, 463; Fremantle 1959 (zie noot 9).

12. Van de Velde 1975 (zie noot 7), pp. 245–277.

13. '*[...] duo modella continentia historiam Assumptionis B. Mariae Virginis [...]*': Van de Velde 1975 (zie noot 7), p. 252, noot 13.

14. Freedberg 1984 (zie noot 7), p. 175; Van de Velde 1975 (zie noot 7), p. 258. In de altaarbouwkunst daarentegen, was het wel gebruikelijk de opdrachtgever verschillende oplossingen voor te stellen. In de loop van de zeventiende eeuw werd het zelfs gangbaar twee verschillende varianten in twee altaarhelften op één enkele ontwerptekening weer te geven.

15. '*[...] Dominum nostrum sponsam suam de Libano provocantem ad coronam [..]*': Van de Velde 1975 (zie noot 7), p. 252 noot 11.

16. Baudouin 1972 (zie noot 9), p. 65; F. Baudouin, *Rubens en zijn eeuw*, Antwerpen, 1972, p. 55–57; Van de Velde 1975 (zie noot 7), p. 252, afb. 4.

17. Ook een schets in de Albertina te Wenen (J. Held, *Rubens. Selected Drawings*, Londen, 1958, 2 vols., pp. 108–109, nr. 35, pl. 38) en een schilderij de *Tenhemelopneming* uit het Kunsthistorisches Museum te Wenen (inv. 518, paneel, 458 x 297 cm; cf. Freedberg 1984 (zie noot 7), p. 147, nr. 37) die mogelijk met deze opdracht in verband kunnen gebracht worden, tonen een gelijkaardige oplossing. Van de Velde 1975 (zie noot 7), p. 254 e.v., afb. 5, 6.

18. Baudouin 1972 (zie noot 9), pp. 73–74; U. Heinen, *Rubens zwischen Predigt und Kunst: der Hochaltar für die Walburgenkirche in Antwerpen*, Weimar, 1996; C. Lawrence, 'Before The Raising of the Cross: The Origins of Rubens's Earliest Antwerp Altarpieces', *The Art Bulletin*, LXXXI, 1999, 2, pp. 267–295.

19. Op deze traditie komen we verderop in de bijdrage terug. Zie ook afb. 8.

20. '*[...] item in de voors. nitse eenen Christus, hooch acht voeten, ende boven den selven eenen heyligen gheest met de festoenen ter syen uythangende, den hemelschen Vaeder daerboven naer syne behoorlycke groote, int hoochste het cruysken met syn cartoesen aen het pedestal ende twee cartoesen ter sye, aende voors. nitse ende op elck van de voors. timpanen eenen sittende off halff liggenden engel ront om gevrocht al vuytwysende selve model; alle welcke figueren ende cieraeten sullen wesen van witten marmer [...]*': Casteels 1961 (zie noot 3), pp. 368–369, doc. 203.

21. Baudouin 1972 (zie noot 9), p. 73. In de welbekende brief van Rubens aan aartshertog Albrecht (1614) met betrekking tot het hoogaltaar van de Gentse kathedraal, schrijft Rubens dat hij zich de moeite getroost heeft om een ontwerp te maken voor het volledige altaar, ook de omlijsting: *'io havendomi affaticato molto nel fare el apparato di tutta l'opera tanto per l'ornamento di marmo quanto per la pittura'*. Merk op dat de schilder het heeft over het *'marmeren ornament'*. Er is geen sprake van sculptuur als evenwaardig element in een totaalconcept. Het marmeren beeldhouwwerk fungeert 'slechts' als decoratieve omlijsting van zijn altaarstuk. Zie ook noot 31.

22. Dit altaar bevindt zich sinds 1870 in de Sint-Joostkerk van Sint-Joost-ten-Node. I. Leyssens, 'Hans van Mildert 158?–1638 levensbeschrijving, in *Gentse Bijdragen tot de Kunstgeschiedenis*, 1941, p. 118.

23. Brussel, Koninklijke Bibliotheek, Handschriftenkabinet, 16574, *Copie d'une sentence étendue au profit du prévot de la*

*Chapelle contre le curé et mambours de l'église de la Chapelle ou tous les droits honneurs et privilèges de la Prévoté sont repris*, 1632: '*[...]contract fait par le curé et les marguelliers de (la) d.e Eglise de la Chapelle de 19. may 1617 avec M.re Hans Van Meldert (sic) concernant le grand autel [...]*', (ongepubliceerd).

24. Van dit altaar kan met relatieve zekerheid gesteld worden dat het in zijn geheel ontworpen werd door Rubens dankzij de passus uit de akten van het kapittel die door Max Rooses gepubliceerd werden: '*Anno 1618. Ergitur in choro, altare marmorum juxta prototypam Rubeniam, in que exponitur Assumpta Virgo depicta a praefato famoso pictore*'. Het feit dat de kunstenaar expliciet twee keer vermeld wordt lijkt er inderdaad op te wijzen dat '*prototypam*' wel degelijk op het altaar en niet op het altaarstuk slaat. M. Rooses, *L'oeuvre de P.P. Rubens. Histoire et description de ses tableaux et dessins*, II, Antwerpen, 1888, p. 171. De toeschrijving wordt bevestigd in een negentiende-eeuwse kroniek van de kerk: '*[...] un autel magnifique y avait été élévé dans le choeur de l'eglise en l'année 1500, par les soins du curé Jacques Oliviers; les sectiares l'ayant détruit, on lui substitua, en 1617. Le maître autel actuel qui fut élévé d'après les dessins de Rubens. Il est de pierre de touche et en marbre, et a couté 6.600 florins, non compris ses accessoires.*'; Brussel, Stadsarchief, Oud archief, 2930, *Histoire de l'église paroissiale de Notre-Dame de la Chapelle à Bruxelles, depuis son origine jusqu'à l'époque actuelle par J.F. Commun, prêtre-assistant de la dite paroisse depuis l'an 1825. Bruxelles, 1844* (handschrift), p. 213 (ongepubliceerd).

25. P.P. Rubens, Inleiding tot de *Palazzi di Genova*, Antwerpen, 1622. Zie ook K. Ottenheym, 'De correspondentie tussen Rubens en Huygens over architectuur (1635–'40)', *Bulletijn van de Koninklijke Nederlandse Oudheidkundige Bond*, 1997, 1, pp. 1–11.

26. Staande figuren bovenop het fronton van een altaarportiek komen, weliswaar eerder uitzonderlijk, voor in de Italiaanse altaarbouwkunst (bv. het hoogaltaar van de Madonna dei Monti-kerk te Rome door Giacomo della Porta, ca. 1588). Zij bereiken echter nooit de monumentale schaal van de Christusfiguur in dit geval. Het enige mij bekende Italiaanse voorbeeld van een (onuitgevoerd) altaar, bekroond door een gebroken fronton, waartusssen zich een nis met een volplastisch beeld bevindt, is de ontwerptekening voor de inrichting van de Rusticucci-kapel in de Romeinse Gesù-kerk door de beeldhouwer-architect Carlo Maderno (Wenen, Albertina, inv. It. AZ Rom 854). H. Hibbard, *Carlo Maderno and Roman Architecture 1580–1630* (*Studies in Architecture*, 10), Londen, 1971, afb. 3. Anthony Blunt acht het mogelijk dat Rubens dit ontwerp tijdens zijn verblijf te Rome gezien heeft. Over de relatie van Rubens tot Maderno: A. Blunt, 'Rubens and Architecture', in *The Burlington Magazine*, 1977, p. 613.

27. F. Baudouin, 'Van concept tot beeldhouwwerk. Het arbeidsproces van de beeldhouwer in de Zuidelijke Nederlanden tijdens de 17de en de 18 de eeuw', in [cat. tent.] *Tekeningen uit de 17de en de 18de eeuw. De verzameling Van Herck*, Museum Plantin-Moretus-Koninklijk Museum voor Schone Kunsten, Antwerpen, 2000, p. 32.

28. Een argument dat hiertegen spreekt is het feit dat beeldhouwers een tafereel dienden uit te beelden, hetgeen het gebruik van een reliëf zou opgedrongen hebben. Reliëfs ter opvulling van portieken waren op dat ogenblik in de Zuidelijke Nederlanden zeker niet gebruikelijk. Maar, in deze context dienen wel twee weinig bekende altaren uit de basiliek van Scherpenheuvel vermeld die volledig uit een hoogreliëf bestaan en die wellicht tijdens de inrichtingscampagne door het atelier van de De Noles ontstonden (ca. 1622).

29. Voor een volledige chronologie van deze opdracht, zie Casteels 1961 (zie noot 3), p. 113 e.v.; H. Vlieghe, *Saints* (*Corpus Rubenianum Ludwig Burchard*, VIII), I, p. 107, nr. 72, afb. 123.

30. Volgens het contract van 9 april 1620 met bisschop Jacob Boonen aangaande het hoogaltaar van de Gentse kathedraal, kregen de De Noles enkel voor een wit marmeren Christusfiguur van slechts zes voet hoog 1000 gulden! Casteels 1961 (zie noot 3), p. 362, doc. 198.

31. *Pietro Paulo Rubens. Lettere italiane*, (*Bibliotheca biografica*), Rome 1987, p. 78–79. Zie ook noot 21.

32. *[...] far l'altar maggiore di una maniera sciocissima senza pittura di sorte alcuna, ma solo con una statua di S. Bavone et recinto de marmo con alcune colonne [...]*

33. Casteels 1961 (zie noot 3), pp. 381–384, doc. 214 & 215

34. Casteels 1961 (zie noot 3), afb. 42.

35. Baudouin en Bungeneers 1996 (zie noot 1), p. 16.

36. Casteels 1961 (zie noot 3), p. 390 e.v. doc. 225.

37. De bestelling van het altaarstuk door deken del Rio had reeds plaatsgevonden in 1619 en had bepaald dat het paneel *'sal wesen hooch ontrent sesthien voeten ende breet advenant onbegrepen der maten als naerden eyssche vanden nyeuwen aultaer'*, Freedberg 1984 (zie noot 7), p. 175 In april 1626 werd het paneel dat 490 x 305 cm (17 voet x 11,5 voet) mat, met twintig centimeter verbreed omdat het te smal bleek te zijn voor de altaarportiek. Vertrekkend van de gegevenheid van de hoogte van Rubens' altaarstuk en rekening houdend met de Maderniaanse verhoudingen (zie noot 26), had het schilderij volgens Italiaanse normen idealiter 430 cm (ca. 15 voet) breed moeten zijn en de altaarportiek 10,86 m breed of ca. 38 voet i.p.v. de 22 voet! De Christusfiguur had de nog reusachtigere afmetingen van 306 cm moeten bereiken of 10,5 voet i.p.v. de voorziene 8 voet. Het spreekt voor zich dat deze proporties een wellicht onoverkoombare meerkost voor het kapittel betekende. Het lijkt dus zeer onwaarschijnlijk dat Rubens zulk ambitieus totaalconcept aan het kapittel had voorgelegd en dat het uiteindelijke resultaat een 'ongelukkige' reductie van dit model was.

Volgens het *Pontificale Romanum* dienen twee van deze relieken aan heilige martelaren toe te horen. Deze kunnen eventueel aangevuld worden met de relieken van andere heiligen, bij voorkeur diegene aan wie het altaar toegewijd is. Zonder de relieken van de martelaren kan het altaar niet gewijd worden. De andere relieken zijn facultatief. Ze zijn niet strikt noodzakelijk. Dat een altaar aan een bepaalde heilige toegewijd is hoeft dus niet te betekenen dat er zich ook in het altaar relieken van deze heilige bevinden. A.J. Schulte, art. 'Altar Cavity', in *The Catholic Encyclopedia*, vol. I, online editie 2003.

39. Normaliter kon geen enkel altaar noch kerk aan een zalige gewijd worden. De verering en voorstelling van zaligen was aan strikte regels gebonden. *Codex iuris canonici Pii X pontificis maximi iussu digestus Benedicti Papae XV auctoritate promulgatus [...]*, Rome, 1919, Can. 1168. § 3.: '*Ecclesiae dedicari Beatis nequeunt sine Sedis Apostolicae indullo.*' & Can. 1201. § 4.: '*Altaria Beatis etiam in ecclesiis et oratoriis quibus eorum officium et Missa concessa sunt, dedicari nequeunt sine Sedis Apostolicae indulto.*' C. Baccari, 'The Blessed', in *The Catholic Encyclopedia*, vol. II, online editie 2002.

40. *Codex iuris canonici Pii Xpontificis maximi iussu digestus Benedicti Papae XV auctoritate promulgatus f...}, Rome*, 1919, Can. 1201. §2.: '*Titulus primarius altaris maioris idem debet esse ac titulus ecclesiae.*'

41. In het begin van de veertiende eeuw werd deze officiële richtlijn uitgevaardigd tijdens de synode van Trier. P. Humfrey, *The Altarpiece in Renaissance Venice*, New Haven–Londen, 1993, p. 57.

42. In kerken van reguliere (bv. reguliere kanunniken van Sint-Augustinus, Premonstratenzers) en seculiere kanunniken en van niet-contemplatieve orden wordt het liturgische koor meestal afgesloten door een doksaal. Doorgaans bestaat dit uit drie geledingen: een centrale poort, geflankeerd door twee altaren, zogenaamde doksaal-altaren. Cf. J. Steppe, *Het koor-*

*doksaal in de Nederlanden* (*Verhandelingen van de Koninklijke Vlaamse Academie voor Wetenschappen, Letteren en Schone Kunsten van België. Klasse der Schone Kunsten*, 7), Brussel, 1952; J.S. Witsen Elias, *De Nederlandse koordoksalen tijdens de gotiek en de renaissance*, Amsterdam, 1937.

43. De beste overzichten met betrekking tot de architectuur van de Belgische jezuïetenkerken vindt men nog steeds in de standaardwerken van J. Braun, *Die belgischen Jesuitenkirchen*, Freiburg, 1907 en J.H. Plantegna, *L'architecture religieuse dans l'ancien duché de Brabant depuis le règne des archiducs jusqu'au gouvernement autrichien (1598–1713)*, Den Haag, 1926.

44. In de abdijkerk van Grimbergen bijvoorbeeld, was dit echter niet het geval. Hier bevond het altaar zich, bij gebrek aan doksaal, in het transept van de abdijkerk. J. Snaet, *De Norbertijnenabdijkerk van Grimbergen: een architectuur-historisch onderzoek*, lic. verh. K.U.Leuven, 1997, p. 38.

45. E. Maffei, *La réservation eucharistique jusqu'à la renaissance*, Brussel, 1942.

46. C. Goettler, *Die Kunst des Fegefeuers nach der Reformation. Kirchliche Schenkungen, Ablass und Almosen in Antwerpen und Bologna um 1600* (*Berliner Schriften zur Kunst*, 7), Mainz am Rhein, 1996.

47. H. Vlieghe, H. De Nijn & H. Devisscher eds., [cat. tent.] *Lucas Faydherbe 1617–1697. Mechels beeldhouwer en architect*, s.l., 1997, p. 168, nr. 43.

48. A. Jansen, 'Documentatie over Antwerpsche beeldhouwers (2de deel)', *Jaarboek Koninklijke Oudheidkundige Kring van Antwerpen*, 1940, pp. 12–13 (overdruk).

49. T. Van Lerius, *Notice des oeuvres d'art de l'église paroissiale et ci-devant insigne collégiale de St. Jacques à Anvers*, Borgerhout, 1855, p. 69.

50. E. Van Autenboer, 'Het Concilie van Trente en de kunst in het Mechelse', in *Studia Mechliniensia*, Mechelen, 1976, pp. 220–229. In dit artikel worden talrijke voorbeelden aangehaald van 'disciplinaire' interventies van de kerkelijke overheid met betrekking tot deze problematiek.

51. Portretten mochten niet op het middenpaneel van altaarstukken prijken. A. Monballieu, 'Het probleem van het 'portret' bij Rubens' altaarstukken', in *Gentse Bijdragen tot de Kunstgeschiedenis*, 1976–78, pp. 159–168.

52. J. Molanus, *De historia SS. Imaginum et picturarum*, Leuven, 1570, boek II, hoofdstuk XXXVI: *'Citra superstitionem unam Sancti Imaginem prae alia eiusdem celebriore esse: neque hic audiendos esse haereticos'*

53. F. Baudouin, 'Het door Rubens ontworpen hoogaltaar in de kerk der Geschoeide Karmelieten te Antwerpen', *Mededelingen van de Koninklijke Academie voor Wetenschappen, Letteren en Schone Kunsten van België. Klasse der Schone Kunsten*, 1991, 1, pp. 27–32.

54. Frontispice van F. Aguillonius, *Opticorum libri sex*, Antwerpen, 1613., door T. Galle naar een ontwerp van P.P. Rubens cf. J. Judson en C. Van de Velde, *Book Illustrations and Title-Pages* (*Corpus Rubenianum Ludwig Burchard*, XXI), Brussel, 1971, nr. 10 en 10a, afb. 55 en 56. J. Vreedman Vriese, *Caryatidum (vulgus termas vocat)[...]*, Antwerpen, [1560]. Cf. *Vredeman de Vries Part I 1555–1571* (*Hollstein's Dutch & Flemish Etchings, Engravings and Woodcuts 1450–1700*, XLVII), G. Luijten ed., Rotterdam, 1997, pp. 206–214. Zie ook hiervoor A. Blunt, 'Rubens and Architecture', *The Burlington Magazine*, 1977, p. 613.

55. A. Jansen, ' De beelden van de O.L.Vrouwkapel in de Sint-Caroluskerk te Antwerpen', *Antwerpen's Oudheidkundige Kring, Jaarboek*, 1938, pp. 50–55.

56. V. Herremans, 'Sebastiaan de Neve, het Rozenkransaltaar en hun plaats in de vormgeschiedenis van de Zuid-Nederlandse altaarbouwkunst', *Sint-Paulus-Info*, 2001, pp. 1686–1698; A. Jansen, 'Het O.L.Vrouwaltaar in de Sint-Pauluskerk te Antwerpen', *Tijdschrift voor geschiedenis en folklore*, 1941, pp. 137–145.

57. Deze afbeeldingswijze van Christus' ware gelaat ging terug op medaillons die in Italië een grote verspreiding kenden. H. Vlieghe, *Saints I* (*Corpus Rubenianum Ludwig Burchard*, VIII), Brussel, 1972, p.28, nr. 2, afb. 4, 5.

58. Pastoor De Croes kocht het altaar in 1784 voor 80 gulden van de Antwerpse Victorinnen (het klooster Ter Nonnen of Sinte-Margaritendael). Het gaat wellicht niet om het hoogaltaar, maar om het altaar uit de kapel van Onze-Lieve-Vrouw-Boodschap, gesticht door Cornelis Van Wyck (†1669) en Isabella Charle (†1661). [P. Genard], *Verzameling der graf- en gedenkschriften van de provincie Antwerpen. Arrondissement Antwerpen. Vierde deel. Antwerpen. Abdyen en kloosters. 1e afdeeling*, Antwerpen, 1859, p. 398; J. Lauwerys, *Minderhout: de kleine Sint-Michiel*, Hoogstraten, 1981, pp. 164–165.

59. L. Robijns, *De Sint-Martinuskerk te Aalst. 2. Kunstwerken (Band 1)*, (*Inventaris van het Kunstpatrimonium van Oost-Vlaanderen*, 14–15), Gent, 1983, pp. 52–53, afb. 30.

60. Datering en toeschrijving: Koninklijk Instituut voor het Kunstpatrimonium.

61. Talrijke voorbeelden zijn te vinden in P. Humphrey, *The Altarpiece in Renaissance Venice*, New Haven–Londen, 1993, afb. 81, 107, 147, 257 en 266.

62 Freedberg 1984 (zie noot 7), p. 151, nr. 37.

63. Freedberg 1984 (zie noot 7), p. 153 noot 21, nr. 37; P. Visschers, 'Iets over de gebroeders de Nole vermaerde beeldhouwers der XVIe eeuw', in *Iets over Jacob Jonghelinck, metaelgieter en penningsnyder, Octavio van Veen, schilder in de XVIe eeuw en de gebroeders Collyns de Nole, beeldhouwers in de XVe, XVIe en XVIIe eeuw*, Antwerpen, 1853, p. 95 e.v.

64. Het indrukwekkende, volledig gesculpteerde altaar (17874 gulden!) werd uitgevoerd door Artus II Quellinus, Guillelmus Kerrickx, Ludovicus Willemsens en Norbert Herry. Van Lerius, 1855 (zie noot 46), p. 185 e.v.

65. E. Dhanens, *Dendermonde* (*Inventaris van het Kunstpatrimonium van Oost-Vlaanderen*, 4), Gent, 1961, pp. 86–87.

66. *Koninklijk Museum voor Schone Kunsten – Antwerpen. Departement Oude Meesters. Catalogus Schilderkunst oude Meesters*, Antwerpen, 1988, p. 116, nr. 403.

67. Baudouin en Bungeneers 1996 (zie noot 2), p. 3.

68. Volgens A. Jansen en C. Van Herck ('Archief in beeld. De nog bestaande kerken van Antwerpen', *Tijdschrift voor geschiedenis en folklore*, 1949, p. 71), gaat het om voorstellingen van Josua en Gideon. Deze beelden overleefden de teloorgang van het altaar en worden nog steeds in de Antwerpse kathedraal bewaard.

69. H. Nauts, 'Beeldhouwwerk van Huybrecht en Norbertus van den Eynde en van Lucas Faydherbe in de hoofdkerk te Sint-Niklaas', *Annalen van de Oudheidkundige Kring van het Land van Waas*, 1969, pp. 42 en 44.

70. Van de zijaltaren waarvan de volledige opstelling als oorspronkelijk kan beschouwd worden, ziet ongeveer zestig procent er zo uit.

71. J. Caudron, *De beeldhouwkunst*, in *De kathedraal van Sint-Michiel en Sint-Goedele*, Tielt, 2000, p. 221; J. Jansen, 'Mechelse rondsculptuur in hout tijdens de Renaissance: de studie van twee modellen', in [cat. tent.] *Mechels houtsnijwerk in de eeuw van Keizer Karel. Het Mechelse meubel 1500–2000 van houtsnijwerk tot design*, Gent, 2000, p. 36; *La Cathédrale*

*Saint-Michel. Trésors d'art et d'histoire* [tent. cat], Brussel, 1975, pp. 171–173.

72. J. Van Damme, 'Documenten betreffende de Antwerpse beeldhouwers Jan en Jan-Anthoni Van den Cruys', in *Cornelis Floris*, 1989, p. 44; F. Nooyens, *Geschiedenis van Deurne*, Deurne, 1981, dl. 1, p. 909 en 914; J. Proost, 'De St.-Fredeganduskerk te Deurne. Verwoesting en heropbouw', *Heemkundig handboekje voor de Antwerpse randgemeenten*, 1962, p. 22; J.B. Stockmans, *Deurne en Borgerhout sedert de vroegste tijden tot heden*, Brussel, 1975 (herdruk 1895–99), dl. 2, p. 38 en dl. 3, p. 130.

73. Een van de privilegies verbonden aan het *ius patronatus* was het aanbrengen van insignes. *Codex iuris canonici Pu X pontiflcis maximi iussu digesttis Benedicti Papae XV auctoritate promulgatus [...]*, Rome, 1919: Can. 1455: *'Privilegia patronorum sunt: [...] 3° Habendi, si ita ferant legitimae locorum consuetudines, in mi patronatus ecclesia stemma gentis velfamiliae, praecedentiam ante ceteros laicos in processionibus vel similibus functionibus, digniorem sedem in ecclesia, sed extra presbyterium et sine baldachino.'*

74. De bisschop bekostigde volledig het reusachtige altaar dat volgens zijn testament '*veele duysenden*' had gekost. S. Landuyt en M. Buonocore, 'Het funerair oeuvre van Artus Quellinus de Jonge', *Monumenten & Landschappen*, jan.–feb. 2001, p. 15; L. Theunissens, 'Testaments des premiers évêques d'Anvers', in *Analectes pour servir à l'histoire ecclésiastique de la Belgique*, 1878, p. 127.

75. Op de inscriptie van een portretgravure door Franciscus Ertinger uit 1680 wordt Van Sterbeeck zelfs met Vitruvius vergeleken! L. Philippen, *Franciscus van Sterbeeck, Antwerpsche mycoloog, bouwkundige en historicus*, Antwerpen, 1930, p. 34.

76. Olieverf op paneel, 104 x 120 cm, inv. nr. 613: H. Vlieghe, *Portraits II, Antwerp~Identified Sitters* (*Corpus Rubenianum Ludwig Burchard*, XIX), p. 204 e.v., nr. 161. Een ander portret van de abt uit 1616, bevindt zich in het Groot Seminarie van Brugge (door een anoniem schilder): K. Vander Eycken (O.Praem.), *De St.-Michielsabdij Antwerpen. Iconografische tentoonstelling 1124–1830. St. Michielskerk Antwerpen 17 september– 2 oktober 1988*, s.l., [1988], p. 70.

77. In tegenstelling tot het portret van de H. Ignatius bestond er geen historische grond voor dat van de reeds in 1134 overleden Nobertus. De Norbertus-*vera effigies* ontstond tegen de achtergrond van de verspreiding van zijn verering, verbonden met zijn canonisatie in 1582 door paus Gregorius XIII: *Sint-Norbertus in de Brabantse Kunst. Tentoonstelling in de abdij van Averbode 26 juni–28 augustus 1971*, Averbode, 1971, p. 17; L.C. Van Dyck (O. Praem.), 'De vernieuwde aandacht voor de norbertijner heiligen en hun iconografie in de zeventiende eeuw: over het ontstaan van de barokke Sint-Norbertusafbeelding in Antwerpen', in *Omgang met nobertijner heiligen. Achtergronden en vormgeving van de heiligenverering in de orde van Prémontré* (*Werkgroep Norbertijner Geschiedenis in de Nederlanden. Bijdragen van de contactdag*, 8), Brussel, 1998, p. 73. Voorbeelden: schilderij op doek; 140 x 184 cm door Abraham Van Diepenbeeck in de Antwerpse kathedraal en de gravure van Lucas Vorsterman de Oude naar Abraham Van Diepenbeeck (31,2 x 21 cm), 1634 Cf. *Lucas Vorsterman I. Volume XLIII*, (*Hollstein's Dutch & Flemish Etchings, Engravings and Woodcuts 1450–1700*) D. De Hoop Scheffer ed., Amsterdam, 1993, p. 90, nr. 93.

78. C. Van de Velde, 'Rubens, de gebroeders Quellin en de beelden van Sint-Ignatius en Sint-Franciscus in het koor van de Jezuïetenkerk te Antwerpen', in *Rubens and his World*, Antwerpen, 1985, pp. 297–306.

79. Boven op de nis van dit grotendeels verloren altaar, bevond zich de beeltenis van de H. Maagd. W. Bergé 1990 (zie noot 11), p. 461.

80. E. Pais-Minne, 'Het Kunstpatrimonium, in *750 jaar St.-Elisabethgasthuis Antwerpen* 1238–1988, [Gent], 1988, p. 352.

81. De evolutie van de mariale devotie dient dus eerder gemeten te worden aan het optrekken van nieuwe altaren die aan de H. Maagd werden gewijd, dan wel aan een wijziging in de gangbare iconografie.

82. H. Vlieghe, 'Hans van Mildert en de chronologie van de bisschopskapel in de Sint-Baafskathedraal te Gent', in *Miscellanea Jozef Duverger. Bijdragen tot de kunstgeschiedenis der Nederlanden*, Gent, 1968, pp. 625–632.

83. In de Zuid-Nederlandse schilderkunst vinden we voorbeelden bij Michiel Cocxie (ca. 1561) op het middenpaneel van de triptiek van de familie Morillon-de Mil (159 x 295 cm), Leuven, Stedelijk Museum Vanderkelen-Mertens of op het middenpaneel van de triptiek van het Gilde van de Oude Voetboog (1590), 397 x 200 cm, afkomstig uit de Antwerpse kathedraal, nu in het Koninklijk Museum voor Schone Kunsten Antwerpen.

84. Duffel, Sint-Martinuskerk, anoniem, ca. 1615, *Verrezen Christus met kruis*; Langdorp, Sint-Pieterskerk, Jan Wynants, 1643 (ca), zilver, hoogte 63,5 cm, *Verrezen Christus met kruis*; Hamme, Sint-Pietersbandenkerk, Guilliam Vander Mont, 1625–26, zilver, hoogte 81 cm, *Verrezen Christus met kruis*; Leuven, Sint-Pieterskerk, Guilliam Vander Mont, 1613–14, verguld zilver, hoogte 71,5 cm, *Verrezen Christus*; Roeselare, Sint-Michielskerk, Frans Ghuens, 1636 verguld zilver, hoogte 80 cm, *Christus Goede Herder draagt het schaap*; Veurne, Sint-Niklaaskerk, Jacques Van Nieukerke, 1616, zilver, verguld, hoogte 73 cm. *Bloed van Christus aan het kruis vloeit in kelk*; Diest, Stedelijk Museum, Egidius Goetsbloets, 1671, zilver, hoogte 74,5 cm, *Verrezen Christus met kruis*; Sint-Truiden, Museum Vlaamse Minderbroeders, anoniem, 1601–1650, zilver en koper, hoogte 76,5 cm, *Christus aan het kruis*.

85. F. Gerke, 'Duces in militia christi. Die Anfänge der Petrus-Paulus-Ikonographie', *Kunstchronik*, 1954, pp. 95–101.

86. Onder andere bij Keulse uitgave door Cornelis van Egmont uit 1629. De beide apostelen worden weergegeven aan weerszijden van een tafereel dat het H. Misoffer uitbeeldt (exemplaar uit de Antwerpse Sint-Jacobskerk).

87. Een ander, laat-zeventiende-eeuws voorbeeld bevond zich te Pulderbos, Onze-Lieve-Vrouwkerk, noordelijk zijaltaar, Guillielmus Kerrickx, 1691 (verdwenen): A. Jansen en C. Van Herck, 'Guillielmus Kerrickx, Antwerpsch beeldhouwer, 1652–1719', in *Antwerpen's Oudheidkundige Kring, Jaarboek*, 1941, p. 59 (met afb.)

88. Voorbeelden: Tongeren, Begijnhofkerk, hoogaltaar, anoniem, 1664 en Antwerpen, Sint-Andrieskerk, H. Kruisaltaar, 1664–65, Cornelis Van Mildert.

89. Van Lerius 1855 (zie noot 46), p. 185 e.v.

90. Op deze feiten wordt nader ingegaan in de bijdrage van Prof. Dr. J. Muller in deze publicatie. De broederschap werd opgericht in 1643: J.C. Diericxsens, *Antverpia christo nascens et crescens*, deel VII, Antwerpen, 1773, p. 271.

91. V. Herremans, 'De Mechelse beeldhouwer Petrus Valckx (1734–1785). Nieuwe gegevens en documenten', *Handelingen van de Koninklijke Kring voor Oudheidkunde, Letteren en Kunst van Mechelen*, 1998 [1999], p. 193.

92. Bergé 1990 (zie noot 11), p. 461.

93. J. Broeckaert, *Geschiedenis van O.L. Vrouw van Lebbeke*, Gent, 1908, p. 54.

# Een elite als actor binnen een zeventiende-eeuwse kunstwereld. Uitbouw en patronen van patronage(netwerken) in de Antwerpse Nazomer*

*Bert Timmermans*

## Inleiding

Kunstpatronage wordt in deze bijdrage niet zozeer als proces,[1] wel als sociale constructie bestudeerd.[2] Staat bij de eerste benadering de relatie kunstenaar-opdrachtgever centraal, dan komt in de tweede het zwaartepunt te liggen op de organisatorische inbedding. Op de patronen die het kunstpatronage – i.c. dat van de elite – aannam binnen de lokale kunstwereld (een netwerk van actoren wier coöperatieve activiteit noodzakelijk is om de productie, distributie en receptie van kunstproducten tot stand te brengen).[3] De vraagstelling die hiermee samenhangt, komt bondig geformuleerd op het volgende neer: hoe zag dit patronage eruit, welke patronen vallen erin te onderkennen? En, welke netwerken en dwarsverbanden speelden er?[4]

Vat men de patronen die een patronagemodel aanneemt op als een resultante van de interactie tussen de sferen van cultuur, politiek en economie, dan hoeft het geen verwondering te wekken dat het Antwerpse patronagemodel verschilde van dat in Rome onder Urbanus VIII,[5] Londen ten tijde van Karel I Stuart[6] of andere steden met een toonaangevend hof. In Rome fungeerden de paus en zijn *nepoti* als brandpunt binnen het kunstpatronage, in Londen de hofkringen rond de Stuarts. Door de afwezigheid van een dergelijke, duidelijk afgebakende nucleus ontbrak het het Antwerpse patronage aan een uitgekristalliseerde hiërarchische structuur. Toch dient men de tegenstellingen tussen beide modellen te nuanceren. Zowel in Amsterdam,[7] Genua[8] als Antwerpen lijkt de stedelijke elite immers een schakelfunctie binnen het patronage vervuld te hebben, terwijl er in Stuart-Londen ook brandpunten waren buiten het hofmilieu.

Vertaalt men het eliteconcept van de *generalized power-holding group*[9] naar de Antwerpse situatie dan bekomt men voor de eerste helft van de eeuw een elite die ruwweg een samenspel was van twee categorieën. Ten eerste, een commerciële elite die haar machtspositie in de eerste plaats entte op economisch en sociaal kapitaal, al liet zij zich ook met het bestuur in. Ten tweede, een oud (politiek) establishment, bestaande uit gevestigde patriciërsfamilies, dat het bestuurlijke en administratieve apparaat trachtte te controleren en zich doorheen de tijd vernieuwd had door het opnemen van gearriveerde kooplui. Waar de eerste groep sociale mobiliteit nastreefde, was de tweede groep eerder gericht op reproductie van zijn positie.[10]

In deze bijdrage zullen we aangeven dat de families en personen die de elite uitmaakten, de instrumenten in handen hadden om binnen het kunstpatronage een schakelfunctie te vervullen. En dat deze functie in belangrijke mate stoelde op het bestaan van onderling verbonden netwerken. Het was immers een dicht net aan relaties dat het mogelijk maakte het politieke, sociale en culturele kapitaal van verschillende families en individuen te integreren.[11] Leden van dergelijke netwerken ontplooiden activiteiten op verschillende dimensies binnen het kunstpatronage. Niet alleen waren ze vertegenwoordigd in de institutionele beslissingscentra die de kunstpolitiek bepaalden, ook binnen het parallelle circuit van informele, sociale netwerken waren ze prominent aanwezig. Bovendien beschikten ze over voldoende financiële middelen om particulier initiatief mogelijk te maken.

Via drie onderzoekspisten wordt gepoogd het brede veld dat het kunstpatronage van de Antwerpse elite bestreek enigszins te ontsluiten. In een diachronische analyse volgen we een aantal families in de uitbouw van hun patronagenetwerk en dit gedurende de laatste decennia van de zestiende en het eerste kwart van de zeventiende eeuw. De herovering van Antwerpen in 1585 had een emigratie op gang gebracht die diepe wonden sloeg in het maatschappelijke (en culturele) weefsel. De lokale elite zag zich genoodzaakt nieuwe structuren op te bouwen en daarin nam de betekenis van de kerkelijke instellingen in sterke mate toe. De tweede piste gaat dieper in op de patronen die het patronage van de elite aannam. Daarbij wordt de aandacht geconcentreerd op de kerkelijke diensteneconomie en de proliferatie van kerkelijke instellingen. Ten slotte duiden we via het blootleggen van dwarsverbanden tussen de verschillende circuits de functie van de stedelijke elite als *gatekeeper* binnen de lokale kunstwereld.

## Piste 1: De elite en de uitbouw van patronagenetwerken in een periode van maatschappelijke wederopbouw

De herovering van Antwerpen in 1585 bracht niet alleen een diaspora op gang, ze maakte ook een einde aan de calvinistische maatschappijstructuur. Samen met de Calvinistische Republiek en veel menselijk kapitaal verdween ook waardevolle politieke en culturele infrastructuur.[12] Na de terugkeer van Antwerpen onder Spaans gezag zag een lokale elite in wording zich voor de taak gesteld nieuwe machtsstructuren uit te bouwen en het teloor gegane sociale, economische en culturele kapitaal te compenseren.

Het contextuele kader was ruw geschetst het volgende. Een economie in reconversie, die vanaf 1590 een opmerkelijk herstel inzette om in het tweede decennium van de zeventiende eeuw een fase van hoogconjunctuur te kennen.[13] Een culturele overgangsperiode, waarin men voortbouwde op het zestiende-eeuwse substraat[14] en waarin op artistiek vlak *kleine grootmeesters* als Maarten de Vos, Otto van Veen en de gebroeders Francken de brug met de generatie Rubens sloegen.[15] Maatschappelijk gezien springt vooral de groeiende macht van de kerkelijke instellingen in het oog. In enkele decennia tijd wist de Kerk zijn organisatorisch raamwerk en zijn sociale functie niet enkel her op te bouwen, maar zelfs te versterken.[16] Aan deze transformatieprocessen kan men vanuit een langetermijnperspectief nog een aristocratiserings- en regionaliseringstendens toevoegen.[17]

### 1.1. De politieke elite: circulatie of reproductie?

Politiek waren 1585 en de naweeën ervan verstrekkend. Vergelijkt men de samenstelling van de politieke elite in de periode 1586-1590 met die van de jaren voordien, dan is er duidelijk sprake van ingrijpende veranderingen. Het onder het Calvinistische bewind geïnstalleerde parallelle college van kooplieden-kolonels[18] verdween en ook het politieke personeel van de magistraat liet een radicale wissel optekenen.[19] In het licht van de zuivering die onder impuls van Farnese binnen nagenoeg alle bestuurlijke echelons plaatsvond,[20] hoeft het geen verwondering te wekken dat inzake politiek personeel de *circulatie* het op de *reproductie* haalde. Met Eduard Van der Dilft kreeg Antwerpen gedurende het eerste decennium na 1585 een burgemeester die de nieuwe koers belichaamde. Van der Dilft ontpopte zich immers tot een krachtig pleitbezorger van de Contrareformatorische actie en van patronage-activiteiten ten aanzien van de kerkelijke instellingen. Zo vaardigde hij in 1585 een verordening uit tot het herstel van Maria- en heiligenbeelden in de stad en regelde hij de teruggave van kerkelijke goederen en immobiliën.[21]

Ook andere burgemeesters en prominente wethouders konden er zich trouwens op beroepen – wat ze zeker niet nalieten te doen – afstand te hebben genomen van het Calvinistische bewind. Zo hebben we berekend dat minstens 30% van de wethouders, die in de periode 1585-1590 de dienst uitmaakte, was uitgeweken naar het buitenland of gebieden die trouw waren aan het Spaanse gezag.[22] Andere wethouders waren gevangen gezet en gefolterd.[23]

Na de verovering was het voor deze personen, die tijdens het Calvinistisch bewind een soort *tegenelite* hadden gevormd,[24] zaak hun (soms) naast elkaar opererende netwerken – met een eigen voorgeschiedenis, actieradius en zwaartepunt – op elkaar af te stemmen. Maak-

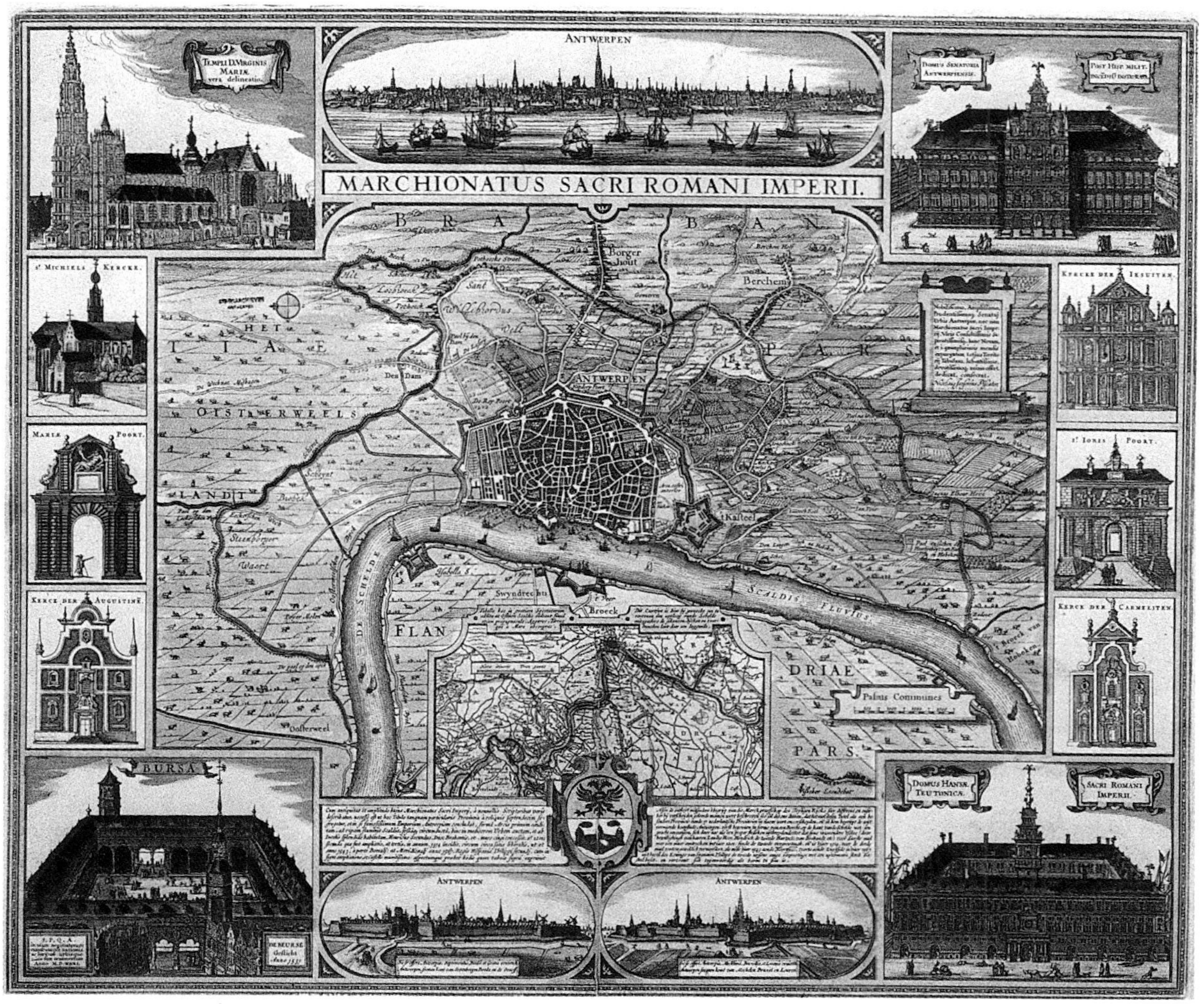


Afb. 1. Claesz. Visscher naar N. Jansenius, *Kaart van het markgraafschap Antwerpen*, 1624. Antwerpen, Stadsarchief

te de familie de basiseenheid van de stedelijke elite uit, culturele en artistieke projecten, economische lobbies en politieke facties berustten op de integratie van kapitaal en talent dat van meerdere families afkomstig was. Eenmaal deze integratie tot een goed einde gebracht, zouden leden van de *tegenelite* elkaar vinden binnen het bestuur van stad, kerkfabriek, religieuze of socio-culturele vereniging. Met het verleden nog vers in het geheugen hechtten ze aan loyaliteit. Daardoor keek men logischerwijs uit naar medewerkers en collega's die men kende of die een soortgelijke achtergrond hadden. Netwerken bleken in deze periode van contra-selectie eens te meer erg waardevolle activa. Ze beïnvloedden beslissingen en gebeurtenissen die een levensloop soms bepalend zouden sturen of een cruciale wending geven. Dit gold zowel voor leden van de *oude politieke elite* – i.e. die van voor het Calvinistische bewind – die na 1585 het toneel opnieuw poogden te betreden, als voor de *tegenelite*.

De eersten probeerden zoveel mogelijk politieke activa te recupereren. Ondermeer door te wijzen op de noodzaak aan – de door hun opgedane – bestuurlijke vaardigheden. En door te steunen op hun – door vriendschaps- en familiebanden onderbouwde – netwerken. Via een efficiënt aanwenden ervan, wisten zelfs bestuurders, die zich ten tijde van de Calvinistische Republiek door deelname aan de macht gecompromitteerd hadden verbazingwekkend veel uit de brand te slepen. Cornelis Pruynen[25] moge hierbij gelden als voorbeeld bij uitstek. Volgens de taxatielijsten van 1574 behoorde hij tot de tien meest vermogende zakenlui van de Scheldestad. En als kunst-, muziekkenner en meceen gold hij als een markante persoonlijkheid in het culturele leven van het laatste kwart van de zestiende eeuw. Pruynen had in de jaren vóór 1585 weliswaar in het schepencollege gezeteld, maar onderhield als humanist vriendschapsbanden met Torrentius lang voor diens aanstelling als bisschop in 1587. Het tweede woog zwaarder dan het eerste, want via bemiddeling van Torrentius verkreeg Pruynen gratie. Als tegenprestatie diende Pruynen een geldsom te schenken aan het college van de Sociëteit.[26] Torrentius droeg er met zijn handige politiek zeker toe bij dat Pruynen en andere koele minnaars van de Contrareformatie zich een constructieve houding aanmaten.

In tegenstelling tot deze laatsten bleef de *Keulse connectie* een dergelijke mentale ommekeer bespaard. Deze groep vooraanstaande katholieke families uit de commerciële en politieke elite had ten tijde van het Calvinistisch bewind – veelal *ter cause der catholiker religie* – in Keulen exil gezocht.[27] Terug in Antwerpen ging ze een belangrijke plaats innemen in het maatschappelijke leven. Een analyse van de uitbouw van hun netwerk laat toe de reikwijdte van een stevig net in het gereconcilieerde Antwerpen te duiden.

## 1.2. De Keulse Connectie en de uitbouw van een patronagenetwerk

Op 3 oktober 1585 trad de drieëndertigjarige Antwerpenaar Balthasar de Robiano[28] met Maria de Smidt in het huwelijk in Keulen, hoewel zowel bruid, bruidegom als de gastheer, de getuigen en de meeste gasten op het trouwfeest uit Antwerpen afkomstig waren. De Robiano was na de capitulatie van Antwerpen in augustus van dat jaar niet onmiddellijk naar de Scheldestad teruggekeerd.[29] Net als zijn gastheer Joost van den Steen – die tezamen met de gefortuneerde en invloedrijke François Vander Cruyce[30] als getuige optrad, had hij er vast nog lopende zaken af te handelen. De Antwerpse koopliedengemeenschap in exil had immers zo goed en kwaad als het ging zijn handelsactiviteiten voortgezet. Hetzelfde onzekere lot en een strijdbare katholieke geloofsovertuiging delend,[31] hadden verschillende Antwerpse families de onderlinge banden nauwer aangehaald. Waar in het economische leven de familie fungeerde als een *unit of enterprise*, zou ze eveneens een efficiënt instrument blijken voor deze zakenlui met (politieke) aspiraties. Door het aangaan van verwantschapsrelaties verzekerden de betrokkenen zich van wederzijdse verplichtingen. Religieuze instellingen en in het bijzonder de Sociëteit met haar uitgebouwd net aan sodaliteiten[32] lijken in de opbouw van dit netwerkkapitaal een beslissende rol te hebben gespeeld.

In 1588 deed De Robiano zijn intrede in het Antwerpse schepencollege. Hij trad zo in de voetsporen van zijn zwager Joost van den Steene, die in 1590 als *praepositus* van de Mariasodaliteit werd aangesteld[33] Tijdens zijn carrière binnen het college trof hij trouwens nog andere verwanten of bekenden uit Keulen aan. Maniaert Vander Cruyce bijvoorbeeld, zoon van François en evenals zijn vader een vriend van Torrentius. Ook andere families uit het commerciële milieu als De Schot, Van Breusegem, De Smidt, Boot, Moens, Goubau en Van den Broecke hadden in de Rijnstad een onderkomen gezocht. En leden van deze families zouden – de ene al sneller dan de ander – de weg naar het schepencollege vinden.[34] De families De Schot en Van Breusegem hadden hun kapitaal al in de decennia voor 1585 verworven. We zien leden van deze families dan ook al in de jaren 1590 bestuursverantwoordelijkheid opnemen.[35] De andere families – met uitzondering van De Smidt[36] – moesten hun fortuin nog grotendeels maken. Vooral Michiel Boot[37] – die trouwens net als De Robiano te Keulen in het huwelijk was getreden – toonde zich daarbij uitermate succesvol. Bij zijn dood in 1619 had hij een vermogen weten te accumuleren van om en bij de *f* 400.000.[38] Weinig zakenlui in de Scheldestad deden op dat ogenblik beter. Al is het ook Goubau, Moens en Van den Broecke voor de wind gegaan. Als zaakvoerder van een firma in expansie beheerde Jan Goubau in 1624 *f* 179.000.[39] Voor Moens en Van den Broecke zijn dergelijke exacte gegevens niet voorhanden. Van Boot en Goubau kunnen we met zekerheid stellen dat ze financieel tot de absolute top – een zeventigtal gezinnen – van de Antwerpse samenleving behoorde.[40]

Deze families uit de commerciële elite wisten hun sociaal en economisch kapitaal in politieke macht te vertalen.[41] Niet alleen binnen de magistraat, ook binnen de kerkelijke instellingen en op het daaraan geliëerde kunstpatronage gingen ze wegen.[42] De Robiano deed trouwens niet anders. Tussen 1590 en 1604 werd hij achtmaal verkozen tot schepen en in 1603 zetelde hij als binnenburgemeester. In de periode 1593 en 1595 was hij als eerste thesaurier belast met het financiële beleid van de stad. Een mandaat waarbij zijn financiële expertise hem te pas kwam.[43] Dat was niet minder het geval toen hij vanaf 1602 als opperkerkmeester van Sint-Jacob – de kerk waar zijn vader zijn laatste rustplaats gevonden had – de eindverantwoordelijkheid over de werken aan het koor droeg. Zijn rol binnen het patronage van Sint-Jacob was evenwel ruimer. Als opperkerkmeester zal hij bepaalde werken voorgefinancierd hebben en ook als donateur ondersteunde hij de artistieke projecten die de kerk de daaropvolgende decennia zou ondergaan. Verklaren politiek-strategische, familiale en religieuze motieven het engagement van De Robiano, er speelde wellicht nog iets. De Robiano kwam net als Michiel Boot immers voort uit een koopliedenmilieu waar de belangstelling voor cultuur levendig was. Het was ondermeer de interesse van De Robiano en Boot in het humanisme die het cement vormde van hun vriendschapsbanden met Lipsius en Scribani.[44]

Nam De Robiano rond de eeuwwisseling een sleutelpositie in binnen de politieke, economische en culturele milieus van de Scheldestad, de actieradius van zijn relatienetwerk zou spoedig nog toenemen. Einde jaren 1590 ondervond de regering te Brussel, extra moeilijkheden op de Antwerpse kapitaalmarkt.[45] Omwille van diens goede contacten met de Antwerpse geldmarkt viel de keuze van de aartshertogen toen ze in 1606 een nieuwe thesaurier-generaal benoemden op De Robiano.[46] In die hoedanigheid opereerde hij net als een Jan van de Wouwere[47] en een Jan de Gavarelles[48] als middelaar tussen het hof en de Antwerpse commerciële en politieke milieus.[49]

Uit hoofde van zijn functie in de centrale instellingen, was het De Robiano overigens toegelaten een adellijke titulatuur te dragen.[50] Het was de symbolische bekroning van een carrière die vorm had gekregen in en mee vorm had gegeven aan het Antwerpen van na 1585. De Robiano behoorde – net als Boot en leden van de andere genoemde families – tot de pioniersgeneratie. De generatie die in het Antwerpen van na 1585 de faciliteiten en netwerken uitbouwde. Evenals hun vaders en grootvaders voor hen poogden De Robiano en de anderen via patrimoniale structuren het verworven sociaal kapitaal in de mate van het mogelijke te institutionaliseren. Met hun nazaten die binnen de door hen vorm gegeven netwerken sleutelposities gingen innemen, deelden ze alvast twee bekommernissen: (1) het in stand houden van het netwerk dat hun van een vooraanstaande positie in het maatschappelijk leven verzekerde; (2) het consolideren van het sociale kapitaal van de familie.[51]

### Piste 2: Patronen van patronage. De elite als actor binnen het circuit van de kerkelijke instellingen

De aard van het maatschappelijk leven in het contrareformatorische Antwerpen impliceerde een structurele betrokkenheid van de stedelijke elite op het kerkelijke veld. Deze vloeide voort uit de verstrengeling tussen de profane en de religieuze levenssfeer en macht. Een verstrengeling die zich ondermeer manifesteerde in processies,[52] die als collectieve rituelen de eenheid van de stedelijke gemeenschap symboliseerden. Hun karakteristieke taal hield referenties in aan autoriteit en consensus. Ze had tot doel de bestaande orde en zijn instituties in hun macht te bevestigen.[53] Het kerkgebouw kende eenzelfde hybride karakter.[54] De belangrijkste participanten aan de processies – stedelijke autoriteiten, kapittel, corporaties, broederschappen – waren door middel van een kapel of altaar eveneens vertegenwoordigd in de kathedraalruimte.

Een kerkgebouw als dat van de kathedraal was niet alleen een liturgische ruimte, waar het mysterie van het geloof beleefd werd, waar kunstwerken als religieuze objecten het voorwerp uitmaakten van gebed en devotie. Het was tegelijk van oudsher een collectieve ruimte,[55] waar de maatschappelijke orde werd gereproduceerd en ervaren. Waar kunstwerken en hun ruimtelijke disposities het vocabularium konden worden van politieke en economische dominantie en aspiraties.[56] Daardoor werd het voor de elite een voor de hand liggende setting voor de beleving van haar geloof, voor de expressie van macht en aanzien, van vroomheid en culturele competentie.[57] Omdat de kerkelijke instellingen over het meest uitgebouwde net van communicatiekanalen binnen de collectieve ruimte beschikten, boden ze een forum bij uitstek, om de perceptie[58] en het sociale geheugen[59] te beïnvloeden.

## 2.1. Barokke vroomheid en familiale identiteit: de elite en de kerkelijke diensteneconomie

In het Antwerpen van de Contrareformatie zou de kerkelijke diensteneconomie na een aanloopperiode op volle toeren gaan draaien. Op de vroomheidsmarkt van na de reconciliatie ging het met de lekenvraag naar diensten en wat men de privatisering van de kerkelijke ruimte zou kunnen noemen in stijgende lijn. '*A sort of enclosure movement in the territory of the dead, destined to accommodate the claims of family ownership*', zo typeerde John Bossy de herdenkingscultus van welgestelden.[60]

De claim betrof tal van kerkelijke diensten – inzonderheid deze m.b.t. het dodenritueel – en de materiële cultuur die daar in het verlengde van ontstond. Zowel het celebreren van zielenmissen als het verwerven van liturgische ruimte – met het oog op het oprichten van een commemoratief monument of de inrichting van een familiekapel – maakten deel uit van deze praktijk.[61] Dergelijke behoeften werden ondersteund en gestimuleerd door campagnes van de kerkelijke overheden die gegoede burgers dienden te overtuigen geld veil te hebben voor hun zielenheil.[62] De materiële cultuur die zich op het religieuze en mentale substraat entte, genereerde een eigen dynamiek, die in belangrijke mate voortkwam uit de wisselwerking tussen demonstratie-effect en sensibiliteit voor representatie.[63]

De noodzaak tot het maken van *statusclaims* – die tot doel hadden iemands lidmaatschap van een specifieke statusgroep aan te geven – lijkt trouwens in de zeventiende eeuw te zijn toegenomen.[64] De voortschrijdende aristocratisering en culturele identiteitsvervaging tussen de stadsadel en de hogere burgerij[65] en de daarmee gepaard gaande competitieverschijnselen, voedden bij beide groepen gevoelens van onzekerheid, die in belangrijke mate te relateren zijn aan begrippen als *status honor* en *social front*.[66] *Status honor* was niet alleen cruciaal voor iemands eerbiedwaardigheid, maar al evenzeer voor diens kansen in het leven.[67]

De Antwerpse elite onderkende de verstrekkende consequenties van *status honor*, zowel in termen van politiek (in aanmerking komen voor een mandaat ...) of economisch gewicht (solvabel geacht worden ...), als de vertaling ervan naar het familiale en persoonlijke leven (keuze bij huwelijksalliantie, vriendschapsbanden ...). De sensibiliteit voor genealogie, levensstijl en representatie (*social front*) nam toe en resulteerde in het maken van *status claims*. Hetzij via statements, hetzij via gedrag[68] of symbolen en gebruik makend van materieel en/of cultureel kapitaal.[69] Het (kunst)patronage bleek vanuit dit perspectief een aangewezen instrument te zijn. In zijn verschillende gedaanten bood het immers tal van perspectieven voor de vertaling van individuele, familiale en collectieve devotie, identiteiten en waardepatronen.[70]

## 2.2. De rol van de elite bij de uitbouw van de kerkelijke infrastructuur

De kerkelijke diensteneconomie en de daaraan geliëerde kapitaalinjectie door particulieren en verenigingen lieten de kerkelijke instellingen toe wat ze op eigen kracht nooit hadden kunnen bol werken: (1) de heropbouw en proliferatie van kerkelijke infrastructuur en instellingen na de burger- en religieoorlogen; (2) het herstel, de uitbreiding en opwaardering van het kerkmeubilair en het liturgisch apparatus volgens de vormeisen van de katholieke hervormingsbeweging.[71]

Traceert men op een Antwerps stadsplan anno 1678 (afb. 2) de religieuze instellingen, dan telt men er een tachtigtal. Ze bestrijken een heel spectrum gaande van een kathedraal over parochie- en kloosterkerken tot de wijkkapel. De proliferatie van de kerkelijke instellingen was daar evenwel niet geëindigd. Kerken en kloosters hadden immers op hun beurt een ruimtelijk en institutioneel kader geboden, waarbinnen tal van activiteiten waren ontplooid: de oprichting van de Mariasodaliteiten in de schoot van de jezuïetenorde, de reactivering van ingeslapen broederschappen, de hernieuwde betrokkenheid van de corporaties op de liturgische ruimte en tal van andere initiatieven die belangrijk waren geweest bij het tot stand brengen van het kunstpatrimonium. Al evenmin biedt de momentopname uit 1678 ons informatie over de belangrijkste tempoversnelling in de heropbouw en proliferatie van de kerkelijke infrastructuur: de bouwhausse in

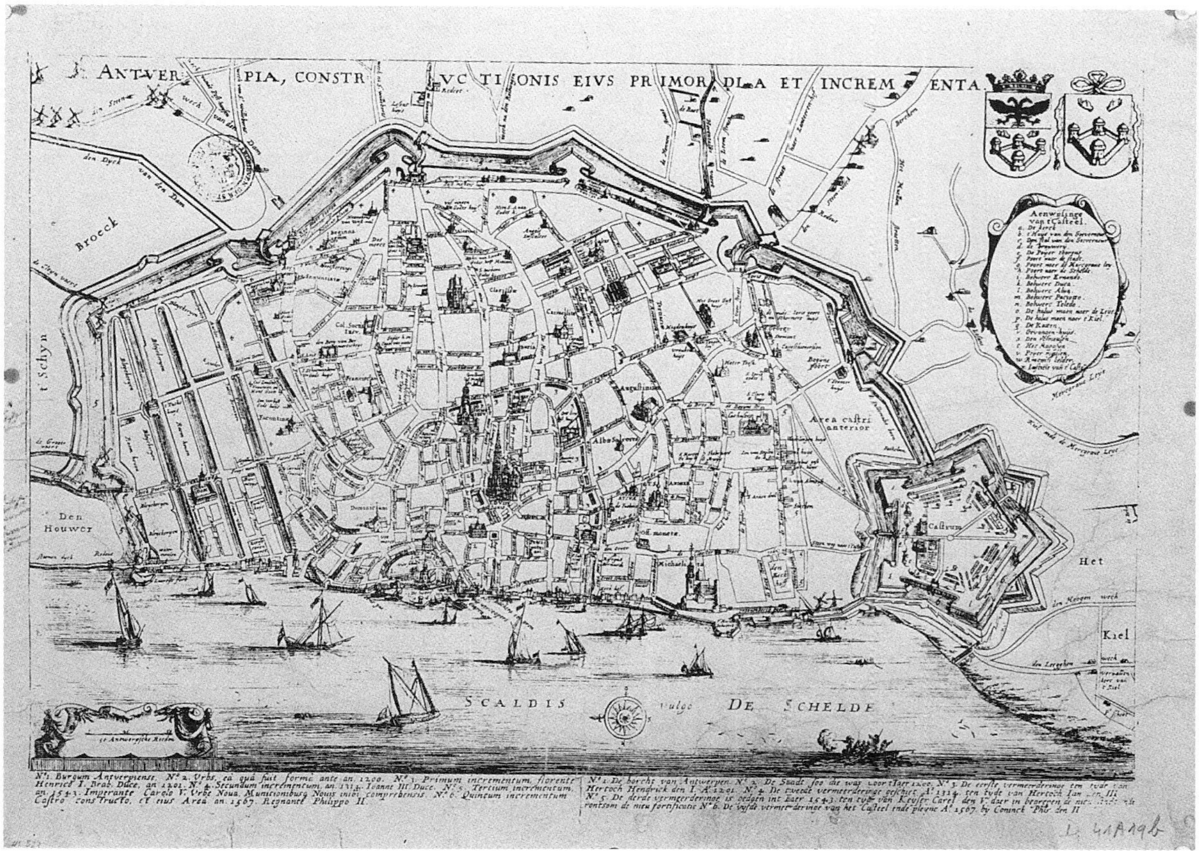


Afb. 2. Peter Verbiest, *Stadsplan van Antwerpen*, 1678. Antwerpen, Stadsarchief

het tweede en derde decennium van de zeventiende eeuw.

Binnen de tijdsspanne van deze dynamische decennia was de inplanting van talrijke kloostergemeenschappen tot stand gekomen en waren stil gelegde werken aan kerkgebouwen hervat.[72] Niet alleen de impact op de bouw- en kunstnijverheid – de nieuwe gebouwcomplexen dienden immers ook aangekleed te worden – was enorm.[73] Ook de maatschappelijke en ruimtelijke implicaties waren verstrekkend. De bouwprojecten maakten immers deel uit van een breder ruimtelijk transformatieproces, de *invasion conventuelle*. De stedenbouwkundige erfenis van de zestiende eeuw had weliswaar een ruimtelijk kader gecreëerd – waaraan Antwerpen zich tot in de negentiende eeuw gebonden zou weten[74] – dit belette niet om in de zeventiende eeuw dit geërfde kader te herdefiniëren volgens actuele eisen en normen. Waar de seculiere openbare infrastructuur geen belangrijke architectuurprojecten liet optekenen,[75] gaf het herstel van de katholieke godsdienst in zijn monopoliepositie en de daarmee gepaard gaande bouwijver en ruimtelijke expansiepolitiek Antwerpen het katholieke gelaat, zoals we dat ondermeer uit de stadsprofielen van Bonnecroÿ kennen.[76]

Een analyse van de interactie tussen dit ruimtelijke transformatieproces en de patronageactiviteiten van de elite is binnen het bestek van deze bijdrage niet mogelijk. Het betreft trouwens een uiterst complexe problematiek, die meer vragen oproept dan we in de huidige stand van ons onderzoek kunnen beantwoorden. De relatie tussen ruimtelijke en maatschappelijke constellaties is immers erg gelaagd. De wisselwerking tussen beide niveaus erg complex. We beperken ons dan ook tot een verkenning van de problematiek. Tot een analyse – die aan de hand van enkele casussen – de krachtlijnen aangeeft van de politieke en financiële inbreng van de elite bij de proliferatie van de kerkelijke instellingen. De materiële en socio-culturele invulling van de stedelijke ruimte hield enorme repercussies – van zowel economische als sociale, culturele en symbolische aard – in voor de betrokken actoren (kerkelijke en stedelijke autoriteiten, bewoners, eigenaars van immobiliën). Omdat bovendien hun belangen behoorlijk uiteen liepen, was de inzet hoog. De verschillende actoren gingen daarom over tot het mobiliseren van macht om het ruimtelijk transformatieproces in de door hen gewenste zin bij te sturen. Het aangaan van coalities met het oog op het realiseren van een groot project als de inplanting van een kerk- en kloostercomplex doet dan ook gevestigde structuren en belangen oplichten.

### 2.2.1. Politieke steun in het dossier van de inplantingen

Stellen we scherp op het aanwenden van socio-politiek, economisch en cultureel kapitaal door de stedelijke elite. Uit overtuiging, zoals in piste 1 aangegeven is, uit opportunisme of gewoon omdat het tot hun habitus was gaan behoren oriënteerden leden van de stedelijke elite hun patronage in belangrijke mate op de kerkelijke instellingen. Politiek vertaalde dit zich in de koers die het stadsbestuur voer. Werden in de periode 1577-1585 kloosterpanden door de stad geseculariseerd, gedeeltelijk afgebroken en herverkaveld,[77] de contrareformatorische bouwprojecten konden op de reële steun van de magistraat rekenen. Deze politiek leidde in de Brede Raad – het orgaan dat over de toekenning ging – meermaals tot aanvaringen tussen de magistraat enerzijds en de poorterij, de wijkmeesters en de ambachten anderzijds. De rechtstreekse subsidiëring van stadswege mocht dan niet de enige en evenmin de belangrijkste financieringsmodus van het bouwoffensief zijn, de toekenning ervan ontlokte niettemin heel wat spanningen. Tussen de kerkelijke instellingen onderling en tussen de magistraat – doorgaans de initiatiefnemer – en de corporaties die vanwege de financiële last voor de gemeenschap een gereserveerde houding aannamen. Daarnaast vormde ook de verdeelsleutel aanleiding tot verwoed lobbyen.[78]

Wanneer er beslist diende te worden over de vestiging van een nieuwe religieuze instelling, herhaalde het scenario zich. Het vinden van een geschikte locatie die de nodige inkomsten garandeerde, stuitte op gevestigde belangen van andere kerkelijke instellingen. De inplanting van een belangrijke stichting kon immers het evenwicht tussen de invloedssferen van de bestaande kerken en kloosters grondig verstoren.[79] En net als in het dossier van de financiering zag de magistraat zich ook nu geconfronteerd met tegenkanting van de poorterij, de wijkmeesters en de ambachten. Bezwaren tegen de financiële last die de stichtingen voor de stedelijke gemeenschap met zich brachten, maar ook terughoudendheid omwille van de nadelige effecten die de inplanting van een gebouwencomplex in de desbetreffende buurt kon hebben. Als de tegenkanting erg hardnekkig was, bood enkel een invloedrijk relatienetwerk uitkomst.

Hendrik van Etten trad in verschillende van dergelijke dossiers als protagonist op. Hij behoorde net als zijn vader tot de harde kern van de Antwerpse politieke elite, waarvan oude patriciërsfamilies als Van den Werve en Van Berchem de spil vormden. Ook Van Etten had zijn afkomst mee en ontpopte zich als een politiek zwaargewicht. Zo vervulde hij tussen 1585 en 1615 haast zonder onderbreking de belangrijke mandaten van schepen, binnenburgemeester of eerste thesaurier. Een machtspositie die onderbouwd werd door zijn prominente aanwezigheid in religieuze en socio-culturele organisaties en versterkt door nauwe verwantschapsrelaties met de invloedrijke families Van der Heyden en Tseraerts.[80] In 1607 – het jaar waarin hij binnenburgemeester was – wist Van Etten de Brede Raad er toe te bewegen het *Engels Huis* ter beschikking te stellen van de jezuïeten. Geen geringe prestatie, gezien ook andere kerkelijke instellingen op het gebouwencomplex aasden en de corporaties alweer bezwaren opperden.[81] In het dossier van de omstreden vestiging van de augustijnen wist hij in hetzelfde jaar samen met markgraaf Hendrik van Varick en de schepenen Paulus van Liere en Balthasar de Smidt eveneens een doorbraak te realiseren.[82] Van Etten moet een gezochte bondgenoot zijn geweest, temeer omdat hij blijkbaar kon terugvallen op een familiekapitaal en een gedeelte daarvan aanwendde bij financieringsoperaties. Zo verleende hij de annuntiaten niet alleen politieke steun bij hun vestiging in de Lange Winkelstraat in 1609, maar verschafte hij hun ook een renteloze lening van *f* 4.000.[83] Banden tussen leden van de politieke elite en religieuze instellingen resulteerden wel vaker in een strategische coalitie. Leidinggevende jezuïeten als Scribani waren zich van het belang ervan bewust en lieerden via een rekruteringspolitiek met vooraanstaanden uit commerciële en politieke middens.[84] Het legde hen geen windeieren als het erop aan kwam hun desiderata door te drukken.

### 2.2.2. Kapitaalinjectie ten tijde van de bouwhausse

De volgende te nemen klip voor nieuwe stichtingen was van financiële aard. In tegenstelling tot de reeds gevestigde kerkelijke instellingen konden ze niet terugvallen op een reeds geconsolideerd patrimonium aan onroerend goed.[85] De uitbouw van een eigen patrimonium en vastgoedbezit was slechts mogelijk via de patronage-activiteiten van de gelovige gemeenschap. Deze zijn veelal binnen de conventies van de kerkelijke diensteneconomie te situeren. Sommige particulieren doneerden evenwel enorme bedragen, die op een uitgesproken religieuze bevlogenheid duiden. Binnen de stedelijke elite waren het vooral de leden uit het commerciële milieu, die de kerkelijke instellingen in staat stelden grootse projecten ook daadwerkelijk te realiseren. Zowel door schenking van landerijen, panden of renten als door zuiver financiële bijdragen of kunstpatronage-activiteiten in de meer strikte zin van het woord. In belangrijke mate betrof het kooplieden die in de laatste decennia van de zestiende eeuw met de nodige durf en zin voor initiatief de lijnen van de economische reconversie hadden uitgezet.

Erfenissen en succesvolle commerciële activiteiten hadden Michiel Boot toegelaten op een gunstig moment grootgrondbezitter te worden. Het verwerven van grondbezit behoorde al sinds decennia tot de investeringspatronen van de Antwerpse zakenlui,[86] maar juist in de vroege jaren 1590 toen Boot de stap zette, waren de grondprijzen bijzonder laag. In de jaren 1594-1595 werd hij eigenaar van het belangrijke landbouwbedrijf *Hof van Sompeke* in Wommelgem, een landbouwgemeente bij uitstek. In het totaal zouden de landerijen en gronden van Boot 226 ha. beslaan.[87] Het platteland rond Antwerpen was door de oorlogshandelingen in de jaren 1570 en 1580 zwaar gehavend en ontvolkt, wat een scherpe daling van de grondprijs tot gevolg had. Het stelde kapitaalkrachtigen als Boot in staat om voor relatief lage bedragen op grote schaal in grond te investeren. Het agrarische herstel – dat aanving in het laatste decennium van de zestiende eeuw – zette zich tijdens het Bestand versneld door en dreef het rendement van de speculaties en investeringen op.[88] De economische opleving van de agrarische sector was één van de factoren die de financiering van de architectuur- en kunstprojecten in de stad mogelijk maakte. Zo waren niet alleen de inkomsten van de Antwerpse religieuze instellingen – met hun vaak uitgebreide landerijen op het platteland – maar ook die van families als Boot onderhevig aan conjunctuurschommelingen binnen de agrarische sector.[89]

De familie Boot doneerde samen met de families Van der Cruyce, De Smidt en Van Hove *f* 226.000 aan de Sociëteit. Deze families telden elk één of meerdere zonen die intraden en zo getuigden van het religieuze engagement dat de leden van de groep bond. De giften van de familie Houtappel – Godevaert Houtappel was de oom en voogd van Michiel Boot – beliepen minstens *f* 231.000.[90] Enorme bedragen, te meer als men in aanmerking neemt dat het totaal aan subsidies door de stad aan de Sociëteit in de periode 1585-1642 op ca. *f* 137.000 begroot wordt.[91] Tezelfdertijd verwierf de orde een aanzienlijk pakket publieke renten en een omvangrijk grondbezit.[92] De wethouder Gillis Gerardi bijvoorbeeld – die de eerste drie decennia na 1585 prominent in het schepencollege aanwezig was – legateerde de Sociëteit het *Sobrechtshof*, een hoeve met uitgestrekte landerijen te Edegem.[93] Dankzij transacties met de familie Van der Cruyce, de bankier-wethouder Urbaan van Parijs en Balthasar de Robiano verkreeg de orde in de jaren 1610-1620 aaneengesloten landerijen te Deurne en Schelle. Scribani had De Robiano immers over de streep weten te trekken om het aantrekkelijke *Venneborgh* te verkopen aan de familie Houtappel, die het vervolgens aan de Sociëteit schonk.[94]

Het profiel van de belangrijke donateurs van andere orden met bouwprojecten verschilde niet wezenlijk van wat hierboven geschetst werd. Ook hier betrof het veelal geslaagde zakenlui die hun bedrijfswinsten gedeeltelijk hadden geconsolideerd in landerijen, stedelijke immobiliën of renten. Ze beschikten daardoor over een gedifferentiëerde inkomensbasis

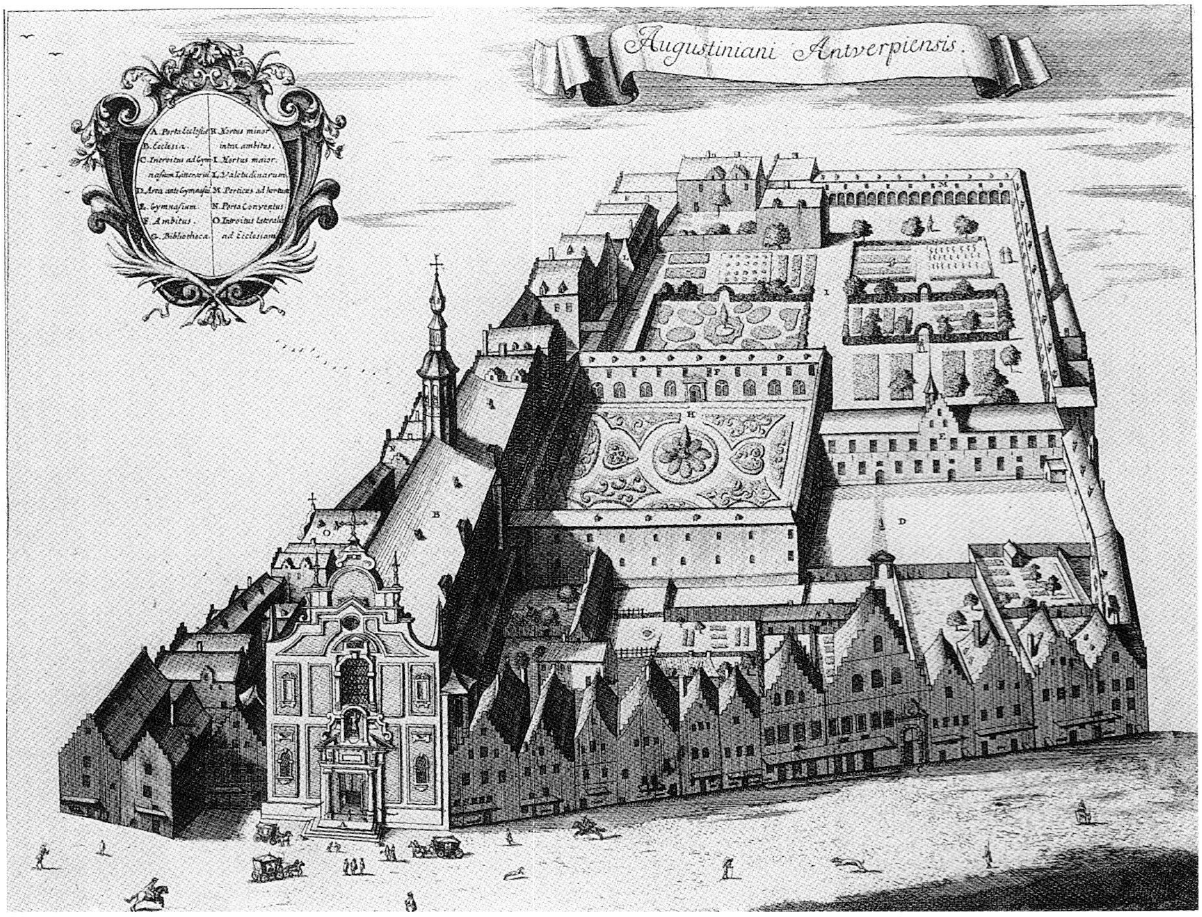


Afb. 3. Anoniem, *Sint-Augustinuskerk te Antwerpen*, in: A. Sanderus, *Chorographia sacra Brabantiæ...*, Hagae Comitum, 1727, t. II

en voldoende financiële ruimte om een optreden als donateur of borgsteller mogelijk te maken.

Bij zijn bezoek in 1611 drong de provinciaal van de augustijnen er bij de Antwerpse paters op aan een nieuwbouwproject te overwegen.[95] Het bleef wachten tot 1615 voor men tot een realisatie van de gemaakte plannen kon overgaan[96] (afb. 3). In een periode, waar het aangaan van leningen bij een vermogend individu de meest verbreide vorm van langetermijnkrediet was,[97] wekt het geen verbazing dat een orde met ambitieuze bouwplannen uitkeek naar een vermogend man om als borgsteller te fungeren. Die werd gevonden in de persoon van Hendrik Van der Goes:[98] vooraan in de zestig, kinderloos, handelaar in tapijten, wethouder, liefhebber van kunst ... en met een vermogen van ca. *f* 150.000[99] voldoende kapitaalkrachtig om zich van de taak te kwijten. Van der Goes, die in het verleden al aan de orde schenkingen had gedaan, verklaarde zich bereid en zou in de daaropvolgende jaren niet alleen grote sommen lenen, maar ook waken over het financiële beheer van het convent. De keuze voor Van der Goes bleek uitermate gelukkig.[100] Actief op de immobiliënmarkt, waar hij goede zaken gedaan had, bezat de borgsteller de nodige expertise inzake de vastgoedsector.[101] Dit zal de orde van pas zijn gekomen, toen zij aanpalende huizen opkocht om in haar gebouwencomplex te incorporeren.[102]

Net als zijn oudere broer Hendrik was Alexander van der Goes[103] een naam in de tapijthandel.[104] Met een vermogen[105] dat nauwelijks voor dat van zijn broer moest onderdoen, behoorde ook hij tot de economische top. Zoals wel meer zakenlui op leeftijd, toonde ook Alexander Van der Goes politieke interesse. Dit vertaalde zich in het uitoefenen van het wethoudersmandaat in de jaren 1620. In maart 1619 ging Alexander Van der Goes een contract aan, dat stipuleerde dat

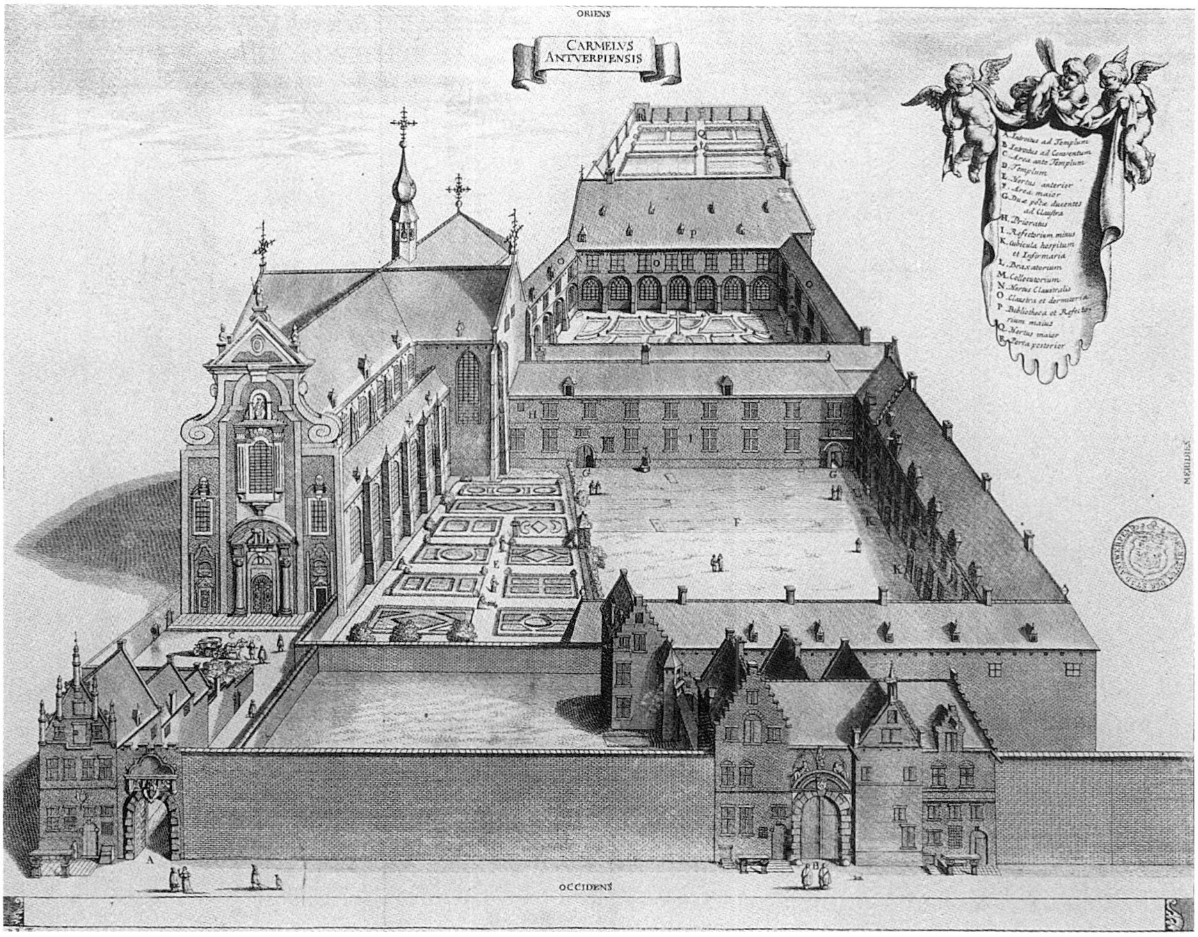


Afb. 4. Lucas Vorsterman de Jonge, *Kerk en klooster van de geschoeide karmelieten te Antwerpen*, in: A. Sanderus, *Chorographia sacra Brabantiæ...*, Bruxellae, 1659, t. II

hij de kosten van het natuurstenen lijstwerk van de voorgevel van de geschoeide karmelieten – begroot op *f* 8.500 – op zich nam.[106] (afb. 4) Enkele jaren daarvoor, in 1615, was de eerste steen gelegd voor de *Rosa Mystica*-kapel. Een project dat gefinancierd werd door de invloedrijke stadspensionaris en diplomaat Jan de Gavarelles. Deze zorgde tevens voor de symbolische bekroning door schenking van een bijna twee meter hoog Mariabeeld. Vervaardigd van massief zilver waren het beeld – dat maar liefst *f* 16.000 gekost had – en de rijk gedecoreerde kapel tot in het buitenland gerenommeerd.[107] Evenals dat van Alexander van der Goes, dat van Nicolaas Rockox[108] of dat van Godfried Houtappel beperkte het patronage van Jan de Gavarelles zich niet tot één kerkelijke instelling. Het kende een brede actieradius, die eerder dan één parochie of wijk te bestrijken, de hele stad omvatte.

### 2.2.3. Investering van menselijk kapitaal

Naast politiek-sociaal en economisch kapitaal stelde de elite ook menselijk kapitaal ter beschikking van de kerkelijke instellingen. Op deze wijze kreeg de elite greep op de machtskanalen die in het Antwerpen van de Contrareformatie aan belang zouden winnen. Zo verbond Hendrik van der Goes zijn broodnodige optreden als borgsteller aan de herverkiezing van de prior en wist deze bij de augustijnen door te drukken.[109]

Door Nicasius Bacx als eerste rector van het college aan te stellen, beoogden de augustijnen definitief af te rekenen met de vooroordelen omtrent hun geloofsorthodoxie en zich te verzekeren van enige welwillendheid in streng katholieke milieus. Nicasius was immers een zoon van Jan Bacx, die als schepen het voortouw had genomen in de strijd tegen de restanten van ketterij en hekserij.[110] Ook andere leden van elite-families trof men aan op leidinggevende posities binnen de kloosterorden. Burgemeester Andries Gerardi bijvoorbeeld was syndicus van het minderbroedersklooster en had vijf zonen die tot de orde waren toegetreden.[111] Ook de koopman-wethouder Hendrik III Moens en zijn echtgenote Maria Fourment droegen als respectievelijk syndicus en *gheestelyke moeder* bij tot de materiële welstand van de orde.[112] Moens' broer Adriaan, die theoloog was, werd dan weer door de bisschop aangesteld om het geestelijk bestuur over de kapucinessen waar te nemen. Hij bouwde het bestaande complex uit tot een klooster met kapel.[113] Evenals Hendrik III Moens die tegen het einde van zijn leven een vermogen van ca. *f* 240.000 beheerde,[114] beschikte ook Balthasar I Moretus over de nodige liquide middelen om de financiële beslommeringen en de bouwlast van de door hem als *gheestelyck vader* gepatroneerde instelling te verlichten.[115]

Ook binnen het kathedraalkapittel[116] en de kerkfabrieken waren leden van de elite prominent vertegenwoordigd. De aanwezigheid in de kerkbesturen viel niet zelden samen met de centrale plaats van elite-families binnen een lokaal netwerk zoals de wijk. In sommige zones was de socio-politieke dominantie van een aantal elite-families ook ruimtelijk duidelijk te onderkennen. Zo concentreerde het immobiliair kapitaal van de familie Schoyte zich in de Sint-Andriesparochie[117] en bezat de familie Van der Goes een gebouwencomplex in de buurt rond de Huidevettersstraat.[118] Het patronage van deze families beïnvloedde de mentale map van de mensen die de straten en pleinen bevolkten, die er passeerden, leefden en werkten.[119] Het fungeerde als kader waarin handelingen werden geïnitieerd en knopen werden doorgehakt. Te meer omdat er sprake was van een langdurige verbondenheid tussen de hierboven genoemde families en de buurt in kwestie. Door het opnemen van bestuursverantwoordelijkheid en het beoefenen van particulier kunstpatronage markeerden ze hun autoriteit binnen de wijkgemeenschap.[120]

Omdat de parochie een samenleving in het klein was, fungeerde ze als relais tussen de elite en bredere lagen van de bevolking. Een dergelijke functie vervulde ook de broederschappen. Het netwerk aan broederschappen leverde niet alleen het institutionele kader voor de betrokkenheid van de leken op de kerkelijke instellingen, het vormde tevens het raamwerk, waarin de religieuze praxis van grote delen van de Antwerpse bevolking gestalte kreeg.[121] Verder was het een structurerend element in het tot stand komen van het kunstpatrimonium. Het demonstratie-effect genereerde immers een eigen dynamiek. Ter gelegenheid van publieke manifestaties zoals processies,[122] maar ook in het patrimonium konden corporaties overgaan tot de onderlinge competitie.[123] Niet alleen was ieder broederschap een consument van kunst, het fungeerde ook als intermedium, waarlangs privé-initiatief kon plaats vinden.[124]

Binnen deze intermediaire structuren was een belangrijke rol weggelegd voor de stedelijke elite. Leden van de elite lagen aan de basis van de oprichting van broederschappen,[125] terwijl andere werden aangezocht of zich geroepen voelden om leidinggevende functies te vervullen.[126] Niet zelden lieten dergelijke personen in de kapel van het broederschap hun familiewapen in een glasraam aanbrengen[127] of dienden ze een aanvraag in om een beeld of schilderij te mogen plaatsen en voorzagen in een jaarlijkse rente.[128]

De stedelijke elite vormde de natuurlijke rekruteringsbasis voor de zogenaamde *gesloten* broederschappen. Het exclusieve karakter en het beperkte aantal leden werden bereikt door een hoge financiële instapdrempel[129] of door ledenwerving op basis van endogame coöptatie.[130] Deze broederschappen groeiden in de loop der eeuwen uit tot eerbiedwaardige instanties met een eigen traditie en geschiedenis. De sodaliteit van de latinisten bijvoorbeeld ontpopte zich als een prestigieuze vereniging, die vanaf 1654 over een eigen bibliotheek met 600 titels beschikte.[131] Lag de drempel tot toetreding hoog voor de kerngroep van het Onze-Lieve-Vrouwe-Lof en de leden van het Sint-Hubertus-,[132] Sint-Rochus-,[133] Sint-Anthonius-[134] of het Heilige Besnijdenisbroederschap,[135] lidmaatschap betekende zoveel als een (symbolisch) toegangsticket tot het Antwerpse establishment. Lidmaatschap van deze broederschappen was dan ook veel meer dan een elegante manier om 'religieus engagement' aan een gezellig samen zijn (het teerfeest) en maatschappelijk aanzien te koppelen. Deze organisaties vormden immers niet enkel een relatienetwerk op zichzelf, maar brachten een accumulatie van sociaal kapitaal tot stand. Ze zorgden immers voor een vervlechting tussen de uitgebreide netwerken van de verschillende leden. En vermits die leden zowel tot de top van de zakenwereld, de kerngroep van de magistraat, als de stadsadel behoorden, moet de impact ervan enorm geweest zijn.

### Piste 3: De elite als gatekeeper binnen de kunstwereld

De zojuist genoemde netwerken, die verschillende sferen van het maatschappelijke leven bestreken, speelden een cruciale rol in hetgeen misschien wel het grootste culturele project van Antwerpen tijdens de Contrareformatie is geweest: het behoud en uitbouw van de stad als culturele *gateway,* als centrum, waar allerlei culturele en artistieke ontwikkelingen werden gegenereerd, verwerkt en geconsumeerd.[136] Binnen deze processen speelde de elite een actieve rol, cruciaal bij de transmissie van culturele waarden. Het derde deel van deze bijdrage gaat dieper in op de rol van *gatekeeper* die de elite via haar informele en formele netwerken binnen de kunstwereld vervulde en stelt scherp op de impact van de vele dwarsverbanden.[137]

### 3.1. Informele netwerken binnen de kunstwereld

In de loop van de zestiende en zeventiende eeuw maakte de participatie van de stedelijke burgerij binnen de Antwerpse kunstwereld een nieuwe expansie door. Vormen van kunstbeleving die tot dan toe tot de aristocratie voorbehouden waren, kenden nu een wijdere verbreiding. De emancipatie van genres als het landschap, het stilleven en het portret vond te Antwerpen sneller doorgang dan elders in Noord-Europa.[138] Sommige leden van de stedelijke elite werden meer dan louter consumenten. Ze gingen zich ontpoppen tot collectioneurs en connoisseurs. De evolutie die zich eerder in Italiaanse steden als Venetië had gemanifesteerd, zette zich nu ook te Antwerpen door.

De *Iconografie*,[139] een project opgestart door Antoon van Dyck, gunt ons een blik op de Antwerpse kunstwereld in het tweede kwart van de zeventiende eeuw, daar waar de commerciële, politieke, religieuze en culturele elites elkaar troffen in het lokale kunstpatronage. De *Iconografie* bracht in een portrettengalerij naar Italiaans concept kunstenaars samen met vorsten, staatslieden en lokale prominenten: leden van de politieke, klerikale en commerciële elites.[140] Het was in dit milieu dat de humanistische traditie onder invloed van de Contrareformatie transformeerde tot een eigentijdse variant en zo een tweede adem vond. Het blikveld van de leden bleef doorgaans niet beperkt tot Antwerpen alleen. Verschillenden onder hen maakten immers deel uit van de Republiek der Letteren[141] en stonden zo in contact met geletterden en geleerden elders in Europa. Het betrof een intellectuele gemeenschap met *communicatio* als regulerend principe.[142] Een netwerk dat tastbaar werd via correspondentie, artikels in tijdschriften en andere publicaties.[143] En dat op het lokale plan concrete vormen aannam in de *sodalitates* en *collegia*, kabinetten die overal in Europa ingang vonden.[144]

Achtenswaardige panden fungeerden hierbij als ontmoetingsplaats. De *Officina Plantiniana* was zo'n trefpunt. Een *cel* van de Republiek der Letteren met een eerder informeel en ongedwongen karakter.[145] De gastheer, Balthasar I Moretus, onderhield vriendschappelijke relaties met topfiguren uit de Antwerpse administratie en politiek (o.a. Gaspar Gevartius, Philips Rubens, Nicolaas Rockox, Jan van de Wouwere, Jacob Edelheer), kunstenaars (van wie Pieter Paul Rubens ongetwijfeld de belangrijkste was) en geleerden (o.a. Justus Lipsius, Ludovicus Nonnius).[146] Personen met veelal een *peregrinatio (academica)* achter de rug en met een relatie- en correspondentienetwerk dat een internationale actieradius kende. Een van hen was zoals aangestipt Nicolaas Rockox, wiens huis *De Gulden Rinck* een ander knooppunt in de Scheldestad vormde.[147] Rockox' interesse in verschillende disciplines – recht, oudheidkunde, wetenschap, letteren – leidde niet alleen tot contacten met *geleerdenvorsten* die binnen de Republiek der Letteren een strategische positie innamen.[148] Net als ondermeer Gaspar Gevartius en Jan Brant – topmensen uit de stedelijke administratie – leverde ook Rockox een eigen wetenschappelijke bijdrage.[149] Rockox' belangstelling voor kunst lag dan weer aan de basis van een belangrijke kunst-collectie die uitmondde in een vriendschapsrelatie met Rubens.[150]

Samenkomsten *ten huize van* deden dergelijke kunstkabinetten uitgroeien tot nuclei binnen het Antwerpse *societyleven*, waar men zich op de hoogte stelde van elkaars verzamelingen en notie nam van nieuwe ideeën.[151] Het milieu hield de vinger aan de pols van culturele ontwikkelingen in het buitenland – waarvoor het als doorgeefluik en transformator fungeerde – maar stimuleerde ook innovaties in Antwerpen zelf. Niet alleen de Antwerpse leden van de Republiek der Letteren konden bogen op een internationaal relatienetwerk, de op het buitenland georiënteerde zakenlui al evenzeer. Door talrijke middelaars – denken we maar even terug aan De Robiano en Boot – werden verschillende netwerken onderling verbonden. Families als Van der Goes en Van Eycke[152] behoorden zowel tot de commerciële als de politieke elite en waren in de kunsthandel actief. Lodewijk de Roomer[153] was een andere zakenman die als middelaar optrad. Hij was niet alleen de grote man binnen het (kunst)patronage van de falcontinnen[154] – de familie De Roomer financierde de bouw en aankleding van een kapel – via zijn echtgenote Catherina Haecx was Lodewijk verbonden met Gaspar Gevartius. In het pand van De Roomer in de Keizerstraat was het voor de literaire en culturele wereld van Antwerpen en daarbuiten aangenaam toeven.[155] De band die Lodewijk met zijn broer Gaspar[156] onderhield, was waarschijnlijk nog belangrijker. Met Gaspar de Roomer had de Antwerpse elite een contactpersoon in Napels. En in feite ver daarbuiten. De Roomer domineerde immers gedurende een groot deel van zijn leven de Napolitaanse kunstscène.[157] Een netwerk van contactpersonen stelde hem in staat op grote schaal kunst te verwerven en te verhandelen. Zelf ontving hij van zijn agenten in Rome en de Nederlanden topwerken en in retour zond hij hun artistieke producten uit Napels en andere Italiaanse kunstcentra.

Het milieu van de kunstliefhebbers en connoisseurs toonde zich erg ontvankelijk voor buitenlandse invloeden en speelde een cruciale rol in de appropriatie van artistieke innovaties. Verfijnde lui als Peter Stevens en Antoon de Tassis[158] lagen aan de basis van de gunstige receptie van de portretstijl *manière grande* die Antoon van Dyck in de late jaren 1620 introduceerde.[159] Ze wisten niet alleen artistiek talent te onderkennen, maar verkeerden bovendien in de positie het ook daadwerkelijk te kunnen ondersteunen. Zo had Pieter Paul Rubens de snelle verovering van zijn aandeel binnen het marktsegment van het maatwerk mee te danken aan goede contacten met Nicolaas Rockox. Het waren immers mensen als Nicolaas Rockox en Jan Van de Wouwere die Philips en Pieter Paul Rubens binnen hun uitgebreide relatienetwerken introduceerden. Net als een Cornelis Van der Geest[160] wendde Rockox zijn invloed en kapitaal aan en bood de kunstenaar zo de uitgelezen podia om diens capaciteiten te etaleren.[161]

Vanwege hun maatschappelijke positie en culturele competentie zetelden mensen als Rockox in commissies die beslisten over artistieke projecten en gaven op die manier richting aan het Antwerpse artistieke leven. Het *commissiemecenaat* was inherent aan corporaties en broederschappen, maar ook het stadsbestuur ging bij de uitbesteding van artistieke opdrachten tot delegeren over. Vanwege de politiek-propagandistische reikwijdte werd omzichtig te werk gegaan. Bij de Blijde Intreden werden vooraanstaande wethouders met het algemene management belast, terwijl de stadssecretarissen – Johannes Bochius, later Gaspar Gevartius – het concipiëren van de iconografische programma's op zich namen. De artistieke leiding werd in handen gegeven van kunstenaars die een vertrouwensrelatie onderhielden met (leden van) de magistraat.[162] Waren de hoofdrolspelers zoals in 1635[163] – toen Nicolaas Rockox, Gaspar Gevartius en Pieter Paul Rubens het project droegen – op elkaar ingespeeld dan kon men erop vertrouwen dat de identiteit van stad en magistraat op een gewenste manier werd gerepresenteerd.

### 3.2. Formele netwerken en het institutionaliseren van sociaal en cultureel kapitaal

In de voorgaande alinea werden reeds voorbeelden aangehaald van geïnstitutionaliseerd sociaal en cultureel kapitaal. Naast constructies van tijdelijke aard, bestonden er binnen de Antwerpse kunstwereld ook instanties met een permanent karakter. Formele kanalen die de informele en tijdelijke brandpunten complementeerden. Verenigingen – zoals de confrérie van de Romanisten, het kolveniersgilde, de rederijkerskamers, het Sint-Lucasgilde en later ook de Academie – die de kunstwereld vorm gaven.

Kanunniken, gefortuneerde kooplieden, leden van de stadsadel en het wethoudersmilieu en vooraanstaande kunstenaars vervoegden de rangen van de exclusieve confrérie van de *Romanisten*.[164] Een instantie als de *Romanisten* vervulde daardoor meer dan één functie. Binnen de Antwerpse kunstwereld vormde ze – net als de rederijkerskamers en het Sint-Lucasgilde – een uitgelezen trefpunt voor potentiële opdrachtgevers en kunstenaars, die elkaar konden ontmoeten onder het houden van een *(h)eerlyck maeltyt*. Lidmaatschap van de confrérie betekende voor een kunstenaar toegang tot de relatienetwerken van de stedelijke elite, wat erg lucratief kon zijn. Het versterkte echter niet alleen zijn sociale en economische positie binnen de kunstsector. Omdat alleen meesters met een stevige reputatie en maatschappelijk aanzien toegang verwierven, bevestigde het ook zijn prestige binnen het kunstenaarsmilieu. Voor de stedelijke elite was de confrérie niet minder belangrijk. Samen met andere elitaire broederschappen en instanties met een exclusief karakter bood ze een setting waarlangs de integratie van de *homines novi* plaats vond, waarbinnen sociaal en cultureel kapitaal werden geïnstitutionaliseerd, persoonlijke en collectieve identiteiten gestalte kregen.

De ledenlijsten van deze instanties weerspiegelen dan ook in belangrijke mate de opeenvolging van generaties en elitegroepen doorheen de tijd. Het valt daarbij op hoe sommige leidende families gedurende meerdere decennia prominent aanwezig waren op het vlak van commercie, politiek, sociale aangelegenheden en patronage. De familie Van Halmale – om een voorbeeld te noemen – leverde vanaf de vijftiende eeuw schepenen en burgemeesters. Leden van families met een dergelijk lange traditie van publieke dienstbaarheid werden bij uitstek geschikt geacht om als een soort gevolmachtigde in naam van het collectief – i.e. de elite – te handelen. Eens volwassen, ging Hendrik van Halmale[165] (afb. 5) dan ook haast op grond van familielidmaatschap bestuursmandaten innemen. Ambitieus als hij was, groeide hij uit tot één van de tenoren van het politieke leven in het derde kwart van de zeventiende eeuw. Een dergelijk politiek zwaargewicht deed zich doorgaans ook binnen de socio-culturele wereld gelden. Na een conflict in 1633 binnen het bestuur van de kolveniersgilde, volgde Van Halmale Nicolaas Rockox als *hooftman* op. Een functie die hem toeliet zijn netwerkkapitaal te consolideren en prominenten – ondermeer via picturale representatie – de mogelijkheid bood tot het voeren van een imago-politiek. (afb. 6) Dit betekende niet dat alleen uiterlijke sier voor Van Halmale van belang was, want net als vele andere bestuursverantwoordelijken engageerde hij zich ook daadwerkelijk.

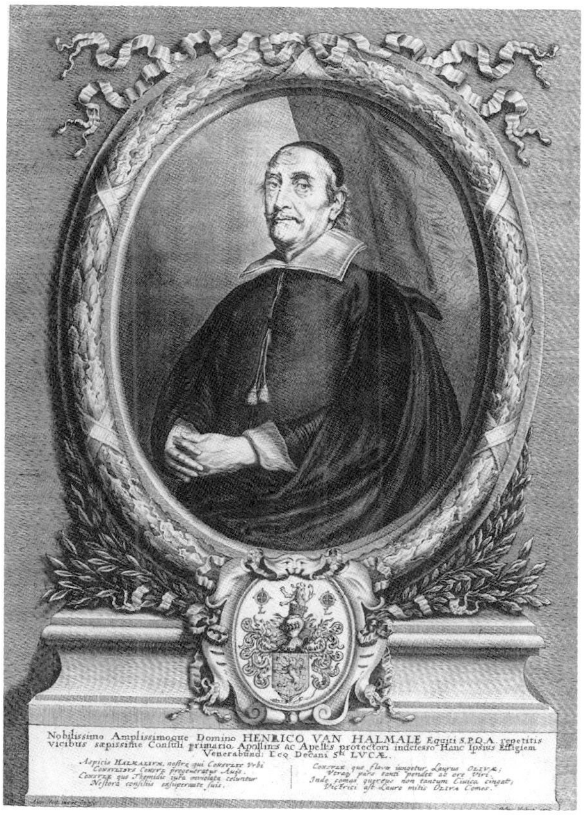

Afb. 5. Pieter Thijs, *Portret van Hendrik van Halmale*. Antwerpen, Koninklijk Museum voor Schone Kunsten

Zo zette hij in de jaren 1660 samen met David Teniers de Jonge zijn schouders onder de oprichting van de Antwerpse Academie. Het was bij het opstarten van dergelijke projecten dat het netwerkkapitaal van mensen als Van Halmale optimaal rendeerde. Omdat de Antwerpse academie anders dan het prestigieuze Parijse voorbeeld geen *nationaal* cultureel project was – dat kon terugvallen op de steun van de centrale overheid – hing veel af van de participanten die (netwerk)kapitaal inbrachten.

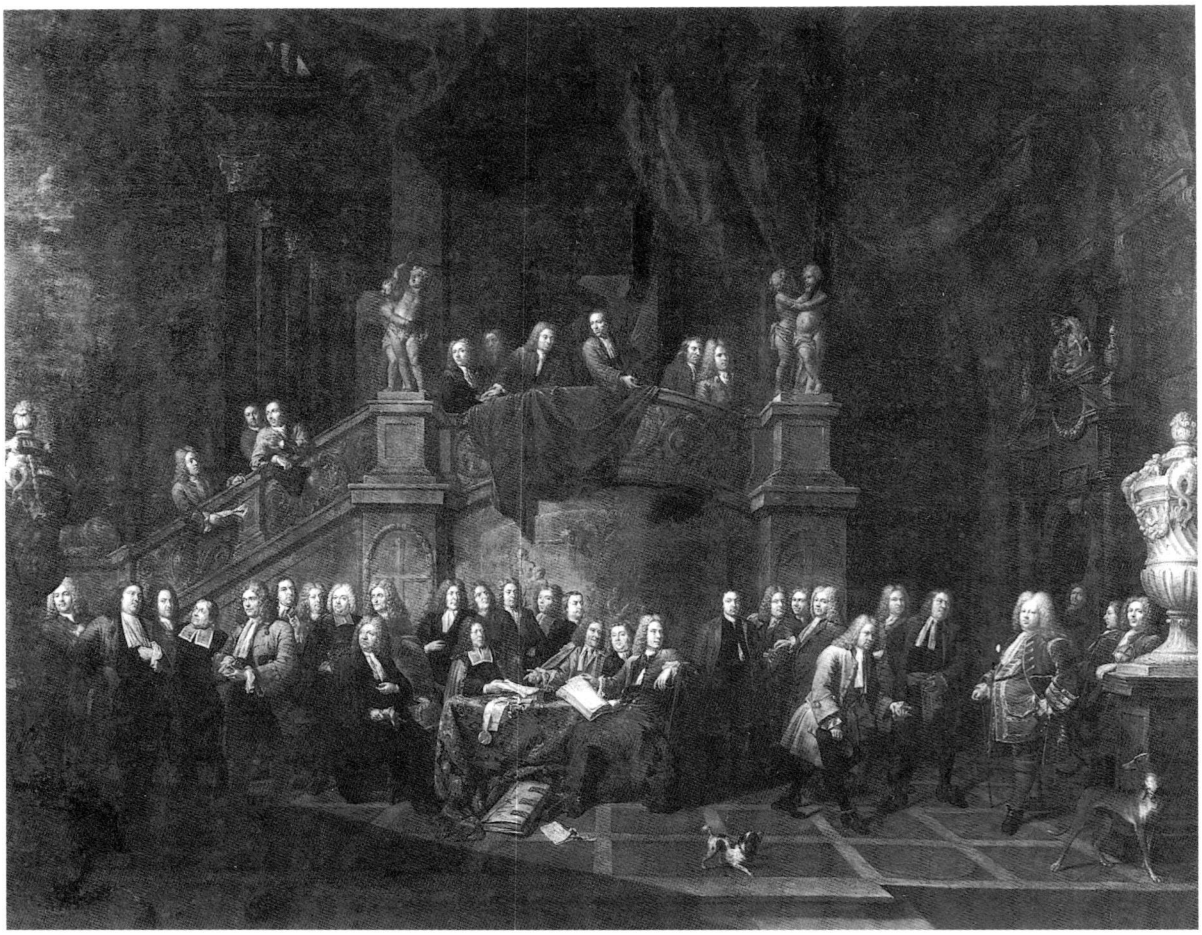

Afb. 6. P. van den Bossche, *Ontvangst van Jan-Karel de Cordes, burgemeester van Antwerpen, als hoofdman van de Jonge Voetboog, in de gildekamer.* Antwerpen, Koninklijk Museum voor Schone Kunsten

Dankzij de steun van personen binnen de magistraat kreeg men het financiële luik rond – de stad verkocht vrijbrieven – en kwam ook de vereiste infrastructuur – i.e. de bovenverdieping van de oostelijke vleugel van de Antwerpse beurs – ter beschikking.[166] Ook later nog stond de stedelijke elite voor meer dan louter het beheer in. Zo vatte Jan August van Hove, telg uit een voorname wethoudersfamilie, als hoofd van de Academie in de jaren 1740 een herstructurering aan die de gescleroseerde instelling nieuw leven moest inblazen.[167]

## Besluit

De mogelijkheid om in Antwerpen een kunstpatronage van betekenis in stand te houden was sterk gerelateerd aan (1) het aantal (actieve) participanten; (2) de onderlinge verhoudingen van de leden en de wijze waarop ze hun acties coördineerden. De aard van het maatschappelijke leven in het contrareformatorische Antwerpen impliceerde een uitgebreid patronage binnen het circuit van de kerkelijke instellingen. Een betrokkenheid op de kerkelijke diensteneconomie die concreet gestalte kreeg in de lekenvraag naar kerkelijke diensten en wat men de privatisering van de kerkelijke ruimte zou kunnen noemen. Barokke vroomheid en materiële cultuur convergeerden en creëerden een forum voor de expressie van individuele, familiale en collectieve identiteiten.

Een analyse van de op- en uitbouw van patronagenetwerken na 1585 brengt de vervlechting van de netwerken van de commerciële en politieke elites in kaart. Ook de dwarsverbanden met de klerikale top blijken talrijk te zijn geweest. De configuratie die het Antwerpse patronage aannam, vertaalde zich bij de proliferatie van de kerkelijke infrastructuur in (1) politieke steun in het dossier van de inplantingen; (2) een kapitaalinjectie ten tijde van de bouwhausse; (3) het investeren van menselijk kapitaal. De participatie van de elite in het bestuur van religieuze en sociaal-culturele instanties bevorderde de accumulatie van sociaal kapitaal en liet de institutionalisering ervan toe. Het was in de afwezigheid van strikte scheidingen tussen de sferen van economie, politiek en cultuur dat de sterkte lag van de Antwerpse elite als netwerk, als actor binnen de kunstwereld. De Antwerpse patronen van patronage maakten de stedelijke elite dan ook bij uitstek geschikt om de rol van *gatekeeper* binnen de Antwerpse kunstwereld te vervullen.

# NOTEN

* Dank aan prof. dr. Katlijne Van der Stighelen voor de kritische lezing van het artikel.

1. Een uiteenzetting van de verschillende dimensies van deze problematiek bij: F. Baudouin, 'Concept, Design and Execution. The Intervention of the Patron', in H. Vlieghe, A. Balis en C. Van de Velde, eds., *Concept, Design & Execution in Flemish Painting (1550-1700)*, Turnhout, 2000, pp. 1-26.

2. Cf. D. Rebentisch, 'Mäzenatentum: Ein Leitmotiv der frankfurter Stadtgeschichtsschreibung', in B. Kirchgässner, H.-P. Becht, eds., *Stadt und Mäzenatentum*, Sigmaringen, 1997, pp. 9-14. Zie voor een algemene inleiding op de problematiek van het kunstpatronage ook: J.H. Balfe, 'Art patronage. Perennial problems, current complications', in J.H. Balfe, ed., *Paying the piper. Causes and consequences of art patronage*, Chicago, 1993, pp. 306-324.

3. Voor het begrip kunstwereld, zie: H. Becker, *Art worlds*, Berkeley, 1982 en Idem, 'Art as a Collective Action', in A.W. Foster en J.R. Blau, eds., *Art and Society. Readings in the Sociology of the Arts*, New York, 1989, pp. 41-54.

4. De vraagstelling ontleent veel aan het veld-concept van P. Bourdieu. P. Bourdieu, *Opstellen over smaak, habitus en het veldbegrip. Gekozen door Dick Pels*, Amsterdam, 1989, pp. 171-178.

5. F. Haskell, *Patrons and Painters. A Study of the Relations between Italian Art and Society in Baroque Italy*, New Haven–Londen, 1980 (1ste ed. 1963), pp. 3-62.

6. Voor een introductie van het Stuart-patronage: D. Howarth, ed., *Art and Patronage in the Caroline Courts. Essays in Honour of Sir Oliver Millar*, Cambridge, 1993.

7. P. Burke, *Venetië en Amsterdam. Een onderzoek naar elites in de zeventiende eeuw*, Amsterdam, 1991, pp. 115-126. In 1964 wees F. Baudouin reeds op de overeenkomsten in de maatschappelijke context van de Antwerpse en Hollandse kunstconsumptie: F. Baudouin, 'Rubens' Social and Cultural Background', in *Stil und Überlieferung in der Kunst des Abendslandes. Akten des 21. Internationalen Kongresses für Kunstgeschichte in Bonn 1964*, Berlijn, 1967, pp. 9-19.

8. Zie o.a. P. Boccardo, 'Genua en zijn inwoners ten tijde van Van Dyck', in Ch. Brown en H. Vlieghe, eds., [cat. tent.] *Van Dyck 1599-1641*, Antwerpen, 1999, pp. 48-57.

9. Een overzicht van de problematiek van het elite-onderzoek bij: A. Cowan, 'Urban elites in early modern Europe: an endangered species?', *Historical Research*, LXIV, 1991, pp. 121-137; A.V. Hartmann, 'Kontinuitäten oder revolutionärer Bruch? Eliten im Übergang vom Ancien Régime zur Moderne. Eine Standortbestimmung', *Zeitschrift für Historische Forschung*, XXV, 1998, pp. 401-416.

10. B. Timmermans, *Een elite in het zeventiende-eeuwse Antwerpen. Het milieu van de wethouders (1585-1699) en de stedelijke samenleving in een periode van transformatie* (onuitgegeven licentiaatsverhandeling), Leuven, 1998.

11. Een introductie tot het onderzoek van sociale netwerken bij: A. Degenne en M. Forsé, *Introducing Social Networks*, Londen, 1999.

12. O.a. W. Brulez, 'De diaspora der Antwerpse kooplui op het einde van de 16de eeuw', *Bijdragen voor de geschiedenis der Nederlanden*, XV, 1960, pp. 279-306; J. Briels, *Zuid-Nederlanders in de Republiek, 1572-1630. Een demografische en cultuur-historische studie*, Sint-Niklaas, 1985 en Idem, *Vlaamse schilders in de Noorderlijke Nederlanden in het begin van de Gouden Eeuw, 1585-1630*, Antwerpen, 1987; O.P. Grell, *Calvinist Exiles in Tudor and Stuart England*, Aldershot 1996.

13. W. Brulez, 'Anvers de 1585 à 1650', *Vierteljahrschrift für Sozial- und Wirtschaftgeschichte*, LIV, 1967, pp. 75-99; R. Baetens, *De nazomer van Antwerpens welvaart. De diaspora en het handelshuis De Groote tijdens de 1ste helft der 17de eeuw*, Brussel, 1976, 2 dln.

14. L. Voet, 'Het literaire en geestesleven', in K. van Isacker en R. van Uytven, eds., *Antwerpen. Twaalf eeuwen geschiedenis en cultuur*, Antwerpen, 1986, pp. 192-199.

15. H. Vlieghe, *Flemish Art and Architecture 1585-1700*, New Haven-Londen, 1998, pp. 13-20.

16. J. Andriessen, 'Katholiek herstel en Contrareformatie', in Van Isacker en Van Uytven 1986 (zie noot 14), pp. 183-191; A.K.L. Thijs, *Van Geuzenstad tot katholiek bolwerk. Maatschappelijke betekenis van de Kerk in contrareformatorisch Antwerpen*, Turnhout, 1990; M.J. Marinus, *De Contrareformatie te Antwerpen (1585-1676)*, Antwerpen, 1995.

17. K. Degryse, 'The Aristocratization of the Antwerp mercantile Elite (17th-18th Century)', in C. Lesger en L. Noordegraaf, eds., *Entrepreneurs and Entrepreneurship in Early Modern Times. Merchants and Industrialists within the Orbit of the Dutch Staple Market*, Den Haag, 1995, pp. 35-40.

18. F. Prims, *De kolonellen van de 'burgersche wacht' van Antwerpen (1577-1585)*, Antwerpen, 1942. De overgrote meerderheid van de kolonels bestond uit kooplieden en financiers (23 op 27) Anders dan de *peiswillers* (zie noot 24) of iemand als François Vander Cruyce (zie infra) die een onderkomen gezocht had te Keulen, behoorden ze niet tot de top van de Antwerpse zakenwereld. Negen van hen behoorden bij de maandelijkse quotisatie van 1584-1585 tot de derde hoogste categorie, de groep van de welgestelden (in totaal 2143 personen), en tien tot de tweede hoogste, de groep van de gefortuneerden (in totaal 283 personen). Negentien van deze kooplieden-kolonels, waren in tegenstelling tot de *peiswillers* calvinisten. Als exponenten van de sterke middengroep van kooplui met sociale en politieke aspiraties maakten ze van het machtvacuüm in 1577 gebruik om het laken naar zich toe te trekken. J. Van Roey, 'De correlatie tussen het sociale beroepsmilieu en de godsdienstkeuze te Antwerpen op het einde van de XVIde eeuw' in *Bronnen voor de religieuze geschiedenis van België. Middeleeuwen en Moderne Tijden*, Leuven, 1968, pp. 243-250; H. Soly, 'Het "verraad" van de burgerij: een mythe? Enkele beschouwingen betreffende het gedragspatroon der 16de-eeuwse ondernemers', *Tijdschrift voor Geschiedenis*, IX, 1973, pp. 278-280; G. Marnef, *Antwerpen in de tijd van de Reformatie. Ondergronds protestantisme in een handelsmetropool 1550-1577*, Antwerpen-Amsterdam, 1996, pp. 31-34.

19. Stadsarchief Antwerpen, PK 1342, 1347.

20. Thijs 1991 (zie noot 16), p. 33.

21. Een van de evocaties die de nieuwe koers kracht diende bij te zetten gold de plaatsing van een Mariabeeld op het stadhuis. Het gezamenlijke initiatief van de Mariasodaliteit,

haar oprichter Costerus s.j en de magistraat, was sterk symbolisch geladen gezien het standbeeld van de lokale held Salvius Brabo ervoor moest wijken. A. Poncelet, *Histoire de la Compagnie de Jésus dans les Anciens Pays-Bas. Etablissement de la Compagnie de Jésus en Belgique et ses développements jusqu'à la fin du règne d'Albert et Isabelle*, II, Brussel, 1928, pp. 336-337; Ch. Göttler, *Die Kunst des Fegefeuers nach der Reformation. Kirchliche Schenkungen, Ablass und Almosen in Antwerpen und Bologna um 1600*, Mainz, 1996, p. 140. Op de intekenlijst ter financiering van het beeld stonden alle schepenen vermeld. R.A.E. Op de Beeck, *De Gilde van Onze-Lieve-Vrouwe-Lof in de kathedraal te Antwerpen*, Antwerpen, 1978, pp. 35-37.

22. We hebben dit voor volgende personen weten na te trekken: Blasius de Bejar, Antoon van Berchem, Andries van Breusegem, Maniaert Vander Cruyce, Jacob Dassa, Gillis Happaert, Peter van Lier, Balthasar de Robiano, François de Schot, Joost van den Steene, Jan van Stembor, Nicolaas van Stembor. Stadsarchief Antwerpen, Certificaetboek 1585, fol. 77; F. Donnet, *Les exilés anversois à Cologne (1582-1585)*, Antwerpen, 1899, passim; I. Ghijs, *De Antwerpse magistraat in een laat-humanistische en contra-reformatorische periode 1585-1621*, II (onuitgegeven licentiaatsverhandeling), Leuven, 1988.

23. Dit overkwam volgende personen: Balthasar van Vlierden, Jan de Pape, Paulus van Lier. Donnet 1899 (zie noot 22), pp. 10, 13, 60.

24. Niet iedereen distantieerde zich even vroeg of krachtdadig van het Calvinistisch bewind. De *peiswillers*, die in belangrijke mate voortkwamen uit de oude magistraat en de top van het Antwerpse commerciële milieu, formuleerden pas in oktober 1584 – drie maanden nadat Farnese een aanvang had gemaakt met het beleg van Antwerpen – hun eis tot overgave van de stad. F. Prims, 'De peiswillers', *Antverpiensia*, 7de reeks, 1934, pp. 227-234.

25. I. Ghijs, 'Cornelis Pruynen, koopman en schepen', in *Nationaal Biografisch Woordenboek*, XIII, Brussel, 1990, kol. 670-672.

26. M.J. Marinus, *Laevinius Torrentius als tweede bisschop van Antwerpen (1587-1595)*, Brussel, 1989, pp. 43, 48, 54, 180-183, 196.

27. De religietwisten in de zestiende eeuw gaven aanleiding tot verschillende golven van emigratie van afwisselend hervormden en katholieken. Het Rijnland werd voor velen een toevluchtsoord. R. Van Roosbroeck, *Emigranten. Nederlandse vluchtelingen in Duitsland (1550-1600)*, Leuven, 1968. Jan Rubens, de vader van Peter Paul, was wethouder in Antwerpen ten tijde van de beeldenstorm. In een rapport van 1566 werd hij als calvinist bestempeld en omdat er onder het bewind van Alva voor hem weinig goeds viel te verwachten, nam hij de wijk naar Keulen. Deze situatie werd bekrachtigd toen de Raad van Beroerten hem in 1570 tot verbanning veroordeelde. R. Van Roosbroeck, 'Jan Rubens', in *Nationaal Biografisch Woordenboek*, IX, Brussel, 1981, kol. 663-669. Zagen begin de jaren 1570 de hervormden zich tot emigratie genoodzaakt, dan was het onder het Calvinistisch Bewind de beurt aan de katholieken. Na 1585 zochten dan weer de Antwerpse lutheranen en calvinisten een onderkomen in Duitsland.

28. A. De Ridder, 'Baltasar de Robiano', in *Biographie Nationale*, XIX, Brussel, 1908-1910, kol. 262-263; I. Ghijs, 'Balthasar de Robiano, koopman en staatsman', in *Nationaal Biografisch Woordenboek*, XIII, Brussel, 1990, kol. 689-691.

29. Donnet 1899 (zie noot 22), p. 47.

30. François Vander Cruyce was gewezen schepen en een van de kapitaalkrachtigste Antwerpenaars van zijn tijd. Zo stond François Vander Cruyce en C^ie in 1574 als één van de meest vermogende firma's van de Scheldestad te boek en moest zij *f* 5000 bijdragen tot de verplichte lening. F.J. van den Branden, 'De Spaansche muiterij ten jare 1574', *Antwerpsch Archievenblad*, XXII (2de reeks), pp. 226-227.

31. Toen Torrentius in 1584 een week bij François Vander Cruyce te Keulen logeerde, trof hij er naar eigen zeggen deze sfeer aan. Marinus 1995 (zie noot 16), p. 159.

32. J.B. Kettenmeyer, *Die Anfänge der Marianischen Sodalität in Köln 1576-1586*, Münster, 1928.

33. Andriessen 1986 (zie noot 16), p. 183.

34. Stadsarchief Antwerpen, PK 1342, 1347.

35. Lakenhandelaar François I de Schot verwierf in de tweede helft van de zestiende eeuw een geconcentreerd grondgebied in Kontich en omstreken. Soly 1973 (zie noot 18), p. 268. In tegenstelling tot zijn oudere broer Jacob, die – als lakenhandelaar – in de sporen van vader trad en zijn jongere broer Andries – jezuïet – koos François II – jurist van opleiding – voor een bestuurlijke carrière. Tussen 1593 en 1621 zetelde hij achttienmaal als schepen. Stadsarchief Antwerpen, PK 1342, 1347; Koninklijke Bibliotheek Brussel, Fonds Goethals 1438. Genealogie van de familie De Schot. Ook Andries van Breusegem sloeg een ander pad in dan zijn vader en grootvader. Anders dan grootvader Peter van Beusegem – een specerijenhandelaar, die in 1574 tot de tien rijkste Antwerpse burgers behoorde – en vader Adriaan – die samen met zijn broers de firma verderzette – ging Andries over tot een verstandig beheer van zijn geërfde vermogen en maakte als doctor in de rechten carrière binnen het stadsbestuur. Daar maakte hij vanaf 1587 met korte onderbrekingen tot zijn dood in 1614 deel van uit. Van den Branden (zie noot 30), pp. 227, 235, 238; Soly 1973 (zie noot 18), pp. 265-266; Baetens 1976 (zie noot 13), pp. 151-153; Stadsarchief Antwerpen, PK 1347.

36. Het patroon dat de familie De Smidt laat optekenen, is minder eenduidig. In 1574 was de Cie Vincent de Smidt de firma met het grootste vermogen binnen het Antwerpse commerciële milieu. Vincent de Smidt beheerde een belangrijk patrimonium aan immobiliën en een portefeuille rentebrieven van gewicht. Van den Branden (zie noot 30), p. 226; Soly 1973 (zie noot 18), p. 264. Zoon Joseph – schoonzoon van François Vander Cruyce en zwager van Balthasar de Robiano – fungeerde van 1585 tot 1590 als onderthesaurier. Josephs neef, Balthasar, kleinzoon van Vincent, was actief als Spanjehandelaar en deed in 1602 zijn intrede binnen het schepencollege. Balthasars zonen Robert en Balthasar volgden in resp. 1627 en 1640. Stadsarchief Antwerpen, PK 1343.

37. R. Baetens, 'Michiel Boot, Antwerps koopman en schepen', in *Nationaal Biografisch Woordenboek*, VI, Brussel, 1974, kol. 44-46.

38. Ter vergelijking: Jacob Poppen, burgemeester en de meest vermogende Amsterdammer van die dagen liet bij zijn dood in 1624 *f* 920.000 na. J. de Vries en A. van der Woude, *Nederland 1500-1800. De eerste ronde van moderne economische groei*, Amsterdam, 1995, pp. 768-769. Het vermogen van de Cie Balthasar-Ferdinand De Groote bedroeg in 1635 *f* 1.593.000. Baetens 1976 (zie noot 13), pp. 140, 149.

39. Baetens 1976 (zie noot 13), p. 184.

40. R. Baetens baseerde zich op *de rekeningen en cohieren van geconsenteerde huishuurgelden* om te komen tot een alternatieve sociale stratificatie: een lijst van de duurste straten en een sociale hiërarchie in het Antwerpse woningenbestand anno 1667. J. Dambruyne herleidde de verschillende huizencategorieën tot sociale klassen en bekwam voor Antwerpen de volgende sociale structuur: 1) lage klasse (huishuurwaarde tot 80 gld.); 51%, 2) middenklasse (huishuurwaarde tussen 81 en 320 gld.); 46%, 3) topklasse (huishuurwaarde tussen 321 en 1000 gld.); 3%. Baetens 1976 (zie noot 13), pp. 274-280; J. Dambruyne, 'Conjunctuur, stratificatie en koopkracht te Gent tijdens de eerste helft van de 17de eeuw. De economische en sociale

betekenis van de rente- en woningmarkt', *Handelingen der Maatschappij voor Geschiedenis en Oudheidkunde te Gent*, XLIII, 1989, p. 14. In 1667 werden de woningen van 66 eigenaars voor meer dan 400 gld. huurwaarde aangeslagen. R. Baetens, 'Tussen hoop en vrees', in Van Isacker en Van Uytven 1986 (zie noot 14), pp. 180-181. Ruim de helft van de 60 wethouders, die we konden lokaliseren – en met name deze van mercantiele origine – resideerde in die periode in de duurste straten van de stad. 68% van hen bewoonde een pand, dat behoorde tot de hoogste huurwaardencategorie. Stadsarchief Antwerpen, Rekenkamer 2502, 2503, 2516. Ter vergelijking. In Amsterdam werden in 1631 meer dan 100 personen aangeslagen voor een vermogen van meer dan *f* 100000. J.G. Van Dillen, *Van Rijkdom en Regenten. Handboek tot economische en sociale geschiedenis van Nederland tijdens de Republiek*, Den Haag, 1970, pp. 311-312. Een vermogen, dat door de zeventigtal rijkste Antwerpenaren van die tijd ruimschoots zal zijn gehaald.

41. Michiel Boot trad in 1606 op 39-jarige leeftijd toe tot het schepencollege. Tussen 1606 en 1617 wisselde hij – afgezien van een intermezzo in de jaren 1611-1613 – de schepenfunctie af met die van eerste thesaurier. Gesteund door de politiek invloedrijke Meerse, waarvan hij deken was geweest, werd Alexander Van den Broecke in 1609 rentmeester om in 1619 een eerste maal tot schepen te worden gekozen. Het toetreden tot de magistraat door de families Moens en Goubau zou nog een generatie op zich laten wachten. Hendrik III Moens trad in 1634 een eerste maal als schepen op. Alexander Goubau volgde in 1637 en ging al snel deel uitmaken van de *inner-circle* binnen de magistraat. In de dertig jaar die volgde op zijn eerste aanstelling, fungeerde hij nog negentienmaal als schepen en bekleedde hij driemaal het mandaat van buitenburgemeester. Stadsarchief Antwerpen, PK 1342, 1343, 1347, 1350.

42. Cf. infra.

43. Voor het mandaat en de machtsinvloed van de thesaurier, zie: L. Van Buyten, 'Theorie en praktijk voor de financiele instellingen van het Ancien Régime: de verborgen aspecten van het rentmeesterschap', in *Recht en Instellingen in de oude Nederlanden tijdens de middeleeuwen en de Nieuwe Tijd. Liber Amicorum Jan Buntix*, Leuven, 1981, pp. 549-566.

44. L. Brouwers, *De brieven van Carolus Scribani (1561-1629)*, Antwerpen, 1972, pp. 160, 189 en Idem, *Het Hof van Liere van patriciërshuis tot universitaire instelling te Antwerpen 1516-1975*, Antwerpen, 1976, p. 49; Baetens 1974 (noot 37).

45. H. De Schepper, 'De katholieke Nederlanden van 1589 tot 1609', in *Algemene Geschiedenis van de Nederlanden*, VI, Haarlem, 1979, p. 285.

46. H. De Schepper, *De kollaterale raden in de katolieke Nederlanden van 1579 tot 1609. Studie van leden, instellingen en algemene politiek* (onuitgegeven doctoraatsproefschrift), Leuven, 1972, pp. 433-434.

47. Voor de rol van Van de Wouwere: E. Stols, *De Spaanse Brabanders of de handelsbetrekkingen der Zuidelijke Nederlanden met de Iberische wereld 1598-1648*, I, Brussel, 1971, p. 36.

48. F. Prims, *Jan de Gavarelles, een figuur uit de Katholieke Renaissance (1579-1645)*, Antwerpen-Utrecht, 1946; M. Van Durme, 'Jan de Gaverelle', in *Nationaal Biografisch Woordenboek*, IV, Brussel, 1970, kol. 347-359.

49. Bij felicitaties naar aanleiding van de benoeming van De Robiano, sprak de toenmalige stadspensionaris Joos de Weerdt de hoop uit dat de nieuwe thesaurier-generaal lange tijd zijn functie zou mogen bekleden '*...ten dienste van Syne Hoocheyt, vermeerderinge van tgemeyn beste van dese Nederlanden, ende int particulier, tot solagement deser desolater stadt...*' . De Robiano repliceerde daarop, dat hij niet zou nalaten '*...dese stadt ende haere vervallene saecken in alles te assisteren ende favoriseren...*'; P. Génard, 'Redevoeringen en verwelkomingen der Stadspensionarissen van Antwerpen aan de hertogen, Graven, Landvoogden, Bisschoppen en anderen, enz., van het jaar 1562 tot het jaar 1618', in *Antwerpsch Archievenblad*, 6, pp. 285-286. Het beleid en de diplomatieke missies van De Robiano zouden uitwijzen dat dit meer dan louter plichtplegingen waren.

50. L. Duerloo en P. Janssens, *Wapenboek van de Belgische Adel*, III, Brussel, 1992, p. 335.

51. Cf. M. O'Brien, *The Politics of Reproduction*, Boston, 1981 en A. Plakans, *Kinship in the Past. An Anthropology of European Family Life 1500-1900*, Oxford, 1984.

52. V. Joukes, *Processies en ommegangen in Antwerpen in de zeventiende eeuw* (onuitgegeven licentiaatsverhandeling), Leuven, 1990.

53. Alle lagen van de bevolking participeerden: de stedelijke magistraat aan het hoofd van de optocht, de corporaties, broederschappen en de clerus.. Cf. ook P. Borsay, '"All the Town's a Stage". Urban Ritual and Ceremony 1660-1800', in P. Clark, ed., *The Transformation of English Provincial Towns*, Londen, 1985, p. 239 en E. Isenmann, 'Norms and Values in the European City, 1300-1800', in P. Bickle, ed., *Resistance, Representation and Community*, Oxford-New York, 1997, p. 196. De gehanteerde beeldtaal droeg een impliciete boodschap uit, die het samenhorigheidsgevoel propageerde, vaak zonder dat de beschouwer de boodschap op het bewuste vlak kon formuleren. M. Douglas, *Implicit Meanings. Essays in Anthropology*, Londen, 1975; P. Vandenbroeck, 'Stadscultuur tussen bovengrondse eenheid en onderhuidse strijd', in J. Van der Stock, ed., [cat. tent.] *Stad in Vlaanderen. Cultuur en maatschappij 1477-1787*, Brussel, 1991, p. 79.

54. Voor de grote diversiteit aan activiteiten die een kerkruimte zoals die van de kathedraal kenmerkte: M.J. Marinus, 'De bisschoppen en hun kathedraal, 1559-1794', in W. Aerts, ed., *De Onze-Lieve-Vrouwekathedraal van Antwerpen*, Antwerpen, 1993, p. 59 en J. Van den Nieuwenhuizen, 'Leven in en om de kerk. Cultus en plechtigheden', in Ibidem, pp. 74-76.

55. Recent hebben theoretici als Solà-Morales het onderscheid tussen de categorieën publiek en privé verfijnd door aanname van het begrip collectieve ruimte. Het begrip refereert aan ontmoetingsruimten in de stad, die hoewel privaat eigendom en in die zin soms exclusief, niettemin als podium fungeren voor publieke activiteiten. M. de Solà-Morales, 'Openbare en collectieve ruimte. De verstedelijking van het privé-domein als nieuwe uitdaging', *Oase*, XXXIII, 1992, pp. 3-8.

56. Cf. B. Roeck, 'Motive bürgerlicher Kunstpatronage in der Renaissance. Beispiele aus Deutschland und Italien', Kirchgässner en Becht 1997 (zie noot 56), p. 46.

57. Voor corporaties was dit trouwens niet anders: F. Verleysen, ''Pretense Confrerieën'? Devotie als communicatie in de Antwerpse corporatieve wereld na 1585', *Tijdschrift voor Sociale Geschiedenis*, XXVI, 2001, pp. 153-174. Voor Antwerpen stelde F. Verleysen een correlatie vast tussen de plaats van de beroepsgroepen in de processie, de locatie van het ambachtsaltaar in een bepaalde kerk en de politieke inspraak van de ambachtsgilden.

58. M. Merleau-Ponty, *The Phenomenology of Perception*, Londen, 1962. Daar de sociale perceptie het gevolg is van bewuste of onbewuste processen van selectie, interpretatie en vervorming, kan ze op allerlei manieren gemanipuleerd of beïnvloed worden. W. Gallagher beklemtoonde dat menselijke activiteiten, emoties en gedachten niet louter bepaald worden door genetische voorbestemdheid, neurochemische processen, culturele geschiedenis en sociale relaties, maar eveneens door de materiële omgeving. W. Gallagher, *The Power of Place. How Our Surroundings Shape Our Thoughts, Emotions and Actions*, New York, 1993.

59. Cf. M. Halbwachs, *Les cadres sociaux de la mémoire*, Parijs, 1925; P. Hutton, *History as an Art of Memory*, Hannover-Londen, 1993; P. Burke, 'History as Social Memory', in T. Butler, ed., *Memory*, Londen, 1989, pp. 97-113.

60. J. Bossy, *Christianity in the West 1400-1700*, Oxford-New York, 1985, pp. 33-34. Vergelijk ook: S.K. Cohn, *Death and Property in Siena 1205-1800. Strategies for the Afterlife*, Baltimore, 1988, p. 97.

61. B. Timmermans, 'Barokke vroomheid en familiaal prestige. Beeldvorming, mecenaat en het commemoratieve monument in het zeventiende-eeuwse Antwerpen', *De zeventiende eeuw. Cultuur in de Nederlanden in interdisciplinair perspectief*, XVI, 2, 2000, pp. 89-99.

62. Göttler 1996 (zie noot 21), pp. 142-143; G. Vanden Bosch, *Hemel, hel en vagevuur. Preken over het hiernamaals in de Zuidelijke Nederlanden tijdens de 17de en 18de eeuw*, Leuven, 1991, pp. 71-131.

63. Timmermans 2000 (zie noot 61), pp. 90, 96-99.

64. B. Timmermans, 'The 17th century Antwerp Elite and Status Honour. The presentation of self and the manipulation of social perception', *Intersections. Yearbook for Early Modern Studies*, II, 2002, pp. 149-151.

65. K. Degryse, 'Fortuin en sociaal prestige. Enkele beschouwingen over het verraad van de burgerij tijdens het Ancien Régime', *Tijdschrift voor Geschiedenis*, III, 1977, pp. 283-293; Degryse 1995 (zie noot 17); P. Janssens, *De evolutie van de Belgische adel sinds de late middeleeuwen*, Brussel, 1998, pp. 103-107, 118-119.

66. Cf. E. Goffman, *The Presentation of Self in Everyday Life*, New York, 1959 en Idem, *Relations in Public. Microstudies of the Public Order*, New York, 1971.

67. M. Weber, *From Max Weber. Essays in sociology*, (ed. H.H. Gerth and C. Wright Mills), New York, 1946, p. 186.

68. Dit gebeurde ondermeer via consumptie- en gedragspatronen, die als een vorm van communicatie kunnen beschouwd worden. P. Burke, *The historical anthropology of early modern Italy*, Cambridge, 1987, (in het bijzonder) pp. 79-150.

69. B. Longhurs en M. Savage, 'Social Class, Consumption and the Influence of Bourdieu. Some Critical Issues ', in S. Edgell, K. Hetherington en A. Warde, eds., *Consumption Matters. The Production and Experience of Consumption*, Oxford, 1996, pp. 274-301.

70. Timmermans 2002 (zie noot 64). In de publieke en collectieve ruimte werden schenkingen of materiële getuigenissen van schenkingen door de donateur in kwestie veelal van een familiewapen en inscriptie voorzien. Vooral commemoratieve monumenten lieten toe geschiedenis te schrijven of te herschrijven. Ze voorzagen in sommige gevallen immers niet alleen in gegevens die de reconstructie van de sociale identiteit toelieten, maar maakten tevens melding van allerlei waarden en verdiensten. Timmermans 2000 (zie noot 61), pp. 89-95.

71. Voor het kerkmeubilair en zijn evolutie onder invloed van de voorschriften van het Concilie van Trente, zie: H. Bussers, 'De beeldhouwkunst', in *Antwerpen in de XVIIde eeuw*, Antwerpen, 1989, pp. 293-306.

72. (1) Nieuwbouwprojecten van o.a. augustijnen: 1615–1618 (kerk- en kloostercomplex); jezuïeten: 1615–1621 (kerkgebouw); annuntiaten: vanaf 1615 (kerk- en kloostercomplex). (2) Hervatte projecten en verbouwingswerken aan o.a. zwartzustersklooster: vanaf 1608 (uitbouw klooster met nieuwe achtervleugel en binnenkoer); Onze-Lieve-Vrouwekathedraal: 1610-1614 (vervanging houten gewelven schip door stenen gewelven), 1614 (afwerking noorderportaal), 1616 (afwerking zuiderportaal), 1619 (verfraaiing hoofdportaal); dominicanerkerk: 1618-1639 (kruisbeuk en koor); kapucijnen: 1613 (herbouwingswerken; geschoeide karmelieten: 1618-1623 (nieuwe voorgevel); Sint-Jacob: 1602-1656 (werken aan het koor, overwelving zijbeuken en –kapellen).

73. A.K.L. Thijs, De nijverheid', in *Antwerpen in de XVIIde eeuw*, Antwerpen, 1989, pp. 136-137 en Idem, 'De Antwerpse luxenijverheid: winstbejag en kunstzin', in J. Van der Stock, ed., [cat. tent.] *Antwerpen, verhaal van een metropool, 16de-17de eeuw*, Antwerpen, 1993, pp. 111-112.

74. Een overzicht bij: H. Soly, *Urbanisme en kapitalisme te Antwerpen in de 16de eeuw. De stedenbouwkundige en industriële ondernemingen van Gilbert van Schoonbeke*, Brussel, 1977 en P. Lombaerde, 'Antwerp in its golden age: "one of the largest cities in the Low countries" and "one of the best fortified in Europe"', in P. O'Brien, D. Keen, M. 't Hart en H. van der Wee, eds., *Urban Achievements in Early Modern Europe. Golden Ages in Antwerp, Amsterdam and London*, Cambridge, 2001, pp. 99-127.

75. R. Tijs, 'De bouwkunst te Antwerpen in de zeventiende eeuw', in *Antwerpen in de XVII de eeuw*, Antwerpen, 1989, pp. 273-287.

76. H. Bussers, 'Jan Baptist Bonnecroy, 17de-eeuws panoramaschilder', *Bulletin Koninklijke Musea voor Schone Kunsten van België*, 1-3, 1985-1988, pp. 168-170.

77. Het Calvinistisch bewind beoogde met de confiscatie en de gedeeltelijke afbraak van de kloosterimmobiliën en de daaraan gekoppelde opening van nieuwe straten drie doelstellingen: (1) een betere ontsluiting van oudere stadswijken; (2) het genereren van financiële opbrengsten; (3) de toepassing van het stedenbouwkundige *commoditas*-concept. Tot de gedupeerden behoorden het minderbroedersklooster, het begaardenklooster, het klooster van de clarissen en het klooster van Sint-Salvator. Na 1585 werd in teruggave van geconfisqueerde goederen voorzien en ook werden bepaalde maatregelen teruggedraaid. Wel zou de *stratenpolitiek* nog een uitloper krijgen. In 1610 werd een oude toegangssteeg, gelegen binnen het kloostercomplex van de geschoeide karmelieten, omgevormd tot een bredere toegangsweg. Deze ingreep gebeurde evenwel in samenspraak met de betrokken orde. Soly 1977 (zie noot 74), pp. 378-382; P. Lombaerde, 'Continuïteit, vernieuwingen en verschillen. Het concept van de stad in de Noorderlijke en Zuidelijke Nederlanden rond 1600', *Koninklijk Nederlandse Oudheidkundige Bond. Bulletin*, XCVIII, 1999, pp. 239-240.

78. Het was mede doordat stedelijke subsidies vaak tegen de corporaties in werden toegekend dat ze een expliciet karakter kregen. De grote verschillen tussen de toelagen aan de verschillende kerkelijke instellingen weerspiegelen duidelijke voorkeuren. Zo bleven subsidies aan de Sint-Michielsabdij nagenoeg uit, maar ontvingen de geschoeide karmelieten en de dominicanen voor de bouw van hun kerk elk *f* 18000. En werden Sint-Andries, Sint-Joris en Sint-Willibrordus eerder stiefmoederlijk behandeld, de werken aan Sint-Jacob, Sint-Walburgis en de kathedraal werden in belangrijke mate door de stad gefinancierd. Marinus 1995 (zie noot 16), pp. 77-84.

79. Zo ontlokte de poging van de jezuïeten uit 1619 om een kapel in het gebouwencomplex Hof van Liere op te richten het verzet van parochies en kloosters in de nabije omtrek. En de geschoeide karmelieten verhinderden de ongeschoeide karmelieten zich te vestigen in de Jodenstraat. Göttler 1996 (zie noot 21), pp. 220-221.

80. Stadsarchief Antwerpen, Pk 1342, 1347; GF 301; Kathedraal archief Antwerpen, 609 (2) Ledenlijsten Heilig Kruis 1570-1652.

81. L. Brouwers, *Carolus Scribani s.j., 1561-1629. Een groot man van de Contrareformatie in de Nederlanden*, Antwerpen, 1961, p. 102 en Brouwers 1976 (zie noot 44), pp. 25-27.

82. D. Leyder, *De Augustijnen te Antwerpen (1608-1797). Dagelijks leven in het klooster en op het college*, Leuven, 1996, p. 22-23.

83. F. Baudouin, 'Balthasar I Moretus, 'gheestelyck vader', en zijn verwanten, begunstigers van de Antwerpse annuntiaten', in F. De Nave en M. De Schepper, eds., *Ex Officina Plantiniana Moretum. Studies over het drukkersgeslacht Moretus*, Antwerpen, 1996, p. 137.

84. Brouwers 1961 (zie noot 81), p. 187; J. Andriessen, *De jezuïeten en het samenhorigheidsbesef in de Nederlanden, 1585-1648*, Antwerpen, 1957, pp. 100-103; Poncelet 1928 (zie noot 21), pp. 95-97. Cf. A.L. Martin, *The Jesuit Mind. The Mentality of an Elite in Early Modern France*, Ithaca-Londen, 1988, pp. 201-206, 209. Voor de aantrekkingskracht, die de jezuïeten door hun geestelijke bijstand en tolerantie t.o.v. commerciële activiteiten op Zuid-Nederlandse kooplui uitoefenden, zie: Stols 1971 (zie noot 47), pp. 393-395.

85. De kerkfabriek van de Onze-Lieve-Vrouwekathedraal bijvoorbeeld kon rekenen op jaarlijkse inkomsten, die ca. *f* 22000 beliepen en voor een groot deel voortkwamen uit een uitgebreid patrimonium aan onroerende goederen, uit de dotatie van de stedelijke overheid – 41,2% van de stedelijke subsidies aan de parochies ging naar de parochie van Onze-Lieve-Vrouw – en uit de inkomsten aan offergelden, legaten en dergelijke. Marinus 1993 (zie noot 26), pp. 47-49.

86. Soly 1973 (zie noot 18), pp. 262-280.

87. Baetens 1974 (zie noot 37); kol. 44-46; Baetens 1976 (zie noot 13), pp. 146-149; A. Sledsens, 'Hof van Sompeke of Withof', in *De aloude heerlijkheid Wommelgem. Bijdragen tot de geschiedenis van Wommelgem*, Wommelgem, 1989, pp. 55-56; F. Goris, 'Het cijnsboek van het Hof van Sompeke' in Ibidem, pp. 59-67 en J. Coolenaerts, 'De familie Boot', in Ibidem, pp. 68-72, Stadsarchief Antwerpen, T 1060 (los stuk).

88. H. van der Wee, 'The Agricultural Development of the Low Countries as revealed by the Tithe and Rent Statistics 1250-1800', in H. van der Wee en E .Van Cauwenberghe, eds., *Productivity of Land and Agricultural Innovations in the Low Countries*, Leuven, 1978, p. 13; H. van der Wee, *The Growth of the Antwerp Market and the European Economy (fourteenth-sixteenth centuries). II. Interpretations*, Den Haag, 1963, pp. 245-250, 269-272.

89. Voor de heropleving, zie: Van der Wee 1963 (zie noot 88), pp. 269-272.

90. Algemeen Rijksarchief Brussel, Jezuïeten. Vlaamse Provincie. L 600, 1438; Poncelet 1928 (zie noot 21); Brouwers 1961 (zie noot 81), p. 511; Marinus 1995 (zie noot 26), p. 159.

91. Marinus 1995 (zie noot 26), p. 81.

92. P. Coppieters, *De opheffing van de jezuïetengemeenschap te Antwerpen (1773) en de verkoop van haar bezittingen* (onuitgegeven licentiaatsverhandeling), Leuven, 1984, pp. 159, 161, 162, 179-181, 341-356.

93. Tussen 1585 en 1617 fungeerde Gillis Gerardi 24 maal als schepen of binnenburgemeester. Stadsarchief Antwerpen, Pk 1343, 1347.

94. J.B. Stockmans, *Deurne en Borgerhout*, Brecht, 1895, pp. 155, 177; Brouwers 1972 (zie noot 44), pp. 160, 189; Coppieters 1984 (zie noot 92), p. 350; M. Mouhlig, *Het Jezuïetencollege te Antwerpen in de 17de en 18de eeuw* (onuitgegeven licentiaatsverhandeling) Leuven, 1988, p. 42.

95. Leyder 1996 (zie noot 82), p. 60.

96. Voor de bouwgeschiedenis van de Sint-Augustinuskerk, zie: T. Meganck, *De kerkelijke architectuur van Wensel Cobergher (1557/61-1634) in het licht van zijn verblijf te Rome*, Brussel, 1998, pp. 96-106.

97. J.C. Riley, 'Interest Rates in Antwerp, 1664-1787', in P. Klep en E. Van Cauwenberghe, eds., *Entrepreneurship and the Transformation of the Economy (10th-20th Centuries). Essays in Honour of Herman Van der Wee*, Leuven, 1994, p. 499.

98. Voor een familiegeschiedenis: F. De Decker, 'Van der Goes', in M. Paternostre de la Mairieu, ed., *Etudes brabançonnes. Livre II. Recueil XIII des tablettes du Brabant*, s.l., 1985, pp. 13-60.

99. Stadsarchief Antwerpen, N 1490, 15/10/1618.

100. De augustijnen beschouwden Van der Goes als hun belangrijkste *patronus et maecenas* tijdens deze voor de orde bepalende projecten. Meganck 1998 (zie noot 96), p. 102.

101. Het aandeel landerijen en stedelijke immobiliën maakte ca. 40% van het volledige vermogen van Van der Goes uit. Stadsarchief Antwerpen, N 1490, 15/10/1618.

102. Tussen 1609 en 1615 kocht de orde 9 huizen. Daar was naar schatting een bedrag van ca. *f* 20000 mee gemoeid. Op basis van Leyder 1996 (zie noot 82), p. 205. Voor de aankoop van het duurste huis *Het Brandijser* dat *f* 4720 kostte, gaf Van der Goes in september 1614 *f* 3920.

103. M.b.t. Alexander van der Goes, zie: Y. Schmitz, *Les della Faille. I. Des origines au XVIIième siècle*, Brussel, 1965, pp. 193, 195, 214-216, 219-222.

104. E. Duverger, *Jan, Jacques en Frans de Moor, tapijtwevers en handelaars te Oudenaarde, Antwerpen en Gent (1560 tot ca. 1680)*, Gent, 1960, pp. 27-28 en Idem; 'De moeilijkheden van Jan Baptist van der Goes met Willem van Can en Jacques de Moor', *Bijdragen tot de Geschiedenis*, LI, 1968, pp. 69-90; Baetens 1976 (zie noot 13), pp. 123-124.

105. Stadsarchief Antwerpen, WK 1767, bundel Van der Goes (8/3/1657).

106. Stadsarchief Antwerpen, N 1490, 18/3/1619; Meganck 1998 (zie noot 96), pp. 153-154.

107. F. Prims, *Op de gronden van het Sint-Jan Berchmanscollege. Van houtmere tot carmelklooster, stapelhuis en gymnasium*, Antwerpen, 1949, pp. 48-55.

108. Voor het kunstpatronage van Nicolaas Rockox: F. Baudouin, *Nicolaas Rockocx, 'vrient en patroon' van Peter Paul Rubens*, s.l., 1977.

109. Leyder 1996 (zie noot 82), p. 62.

110. E.H.J. Reussens, 'Nicolaas Bacx', in *Biographie Nationale*, II, Brussel, 1868, kol. 22-25; L. Galesloot, 'Baxius, le dénonciateur de sorciers 1597-1598', in *Messager des sciences historiques aux archives des arts et de la bibliographie de Belgique*, 1871, pp. 80-87.

111. S. Schoutens, *Geschiedenis van het voormalig minderbroederskIooster van Antwerpen (1446-1797)*, Antwerpen, 1894, pp. 341, 342, 345-346, 251-252, 360-366. Een van zijn dochters was net als veel andere weldoeners derde-ordeling.

112. Schoutens 1894 (zie noot 111), p. 363.

113. F.H. Mertens en K.L. Torfs, *Geschiedenis van Antwerpen sedert de stichting der stad tot onze tijden*, VI, Antwerpen, 1851, pp. 76-77; *Verzameling der graf- en gedenkschriften van de provincie Antwerpen. Arrondissement Antwerpen. Zesde deel. Antwerpen. Klooster der orde van St.-Franciscus, 1e Afdeeling*, Antwerpen, 1871, p. 83.

114. Baetens 1976 (zie noot 13), pp. 198-199.

115. Een ander lid van de familie, Johanna Moerentorf, werd in 1638 moeder-overste en ook Martina Moerentorf legde kloostergeloften af. Baudouin 1996 (zie noot 83).

116. P.J. Goetschalckx, *Geschiedenis der Kanunniken van O.L.V. Kapittel te Antwerpen (1585-1700)*, Antwerpen, 1929; Marinus 1995 (noot 16), p. 106.

117. P.Visschers, *Geschiedenis van de Sint-Andrieskerk, sedert hare opkomst, tot den huidige dag*, I, Antwerpen, 1853, pp. 297-300.

118. Stadsarchief Antwerpen, N 1490, 15/10/1618 en WK 1767, bundel Van der Goes (8/3/1657).

119. Cf. D. Crouch en D. Matless, 'Refiguring Geography. The Parish Maps of Common ground', *Transactions of the Institute of British Geographers*, XXI, 1996, pp. 236-255.

120. Timmermans 2002 (zie noot 64), pp. 160-161.

121. A.K.L. Thijs, 'De Contrareformatie en het economisch transformatieproces te Antwerpen na 1585', *Bijdragen tot de Geschiedenis*, LXX, 1987, pp. 103-109.

122. Zo was het meerseniersambacht vanaf 1653 in een meningsverschil gewikkeld met de zes schuttersgilden over de plaats die ze innamen in de Onze-Lieve-Vrouwe-ommegang. Het betrof een dispuut dat verschillende jaren zou aanslepen, daar het om een bevoorrechte plaats vlak voor de magistraat ging. Joukes 1990 (zie noot 52), p. 141.

123. Toen de *oudekleerkopers* in 1682 met de beeldhouwers Norbert van den Eynde en Ludovicus Willemsens een contract afsloten, werd gestipuleerd dat het altaar dezelfde afmetingen diende te krijgen als dat van de kuipers aan de overkant. A.K.L. Thijs, 'Religieuze rituelen in het emancipatieproces van Vlaamse en Brabantse handwerksgezellen (zestiende-negentiende eeuw)', in C. Lis en H. Soly, eds., *Werken volgens de regels. Ambachten in Brabant en Vlaanderen 1500-1800*, Brussel, 1994, pp. 239-240. Voor een exacte draagwijdte van de wedijver om symbolisch kapitaal in de religieuze sfeer is het bestuderen van de interactie tussen de religieuze en de sociaal-economische en politieke aspecten erg relevant. Zie: Verleysen 2001 (zie noot 57), pp. 153-174.

124. Cf. W. Scheelen, 'De rol van de jezuïeten bij het tot stand komen van hun kunstpatrimonium', *De zeventiende eeuw*, V, 1989, pp. 60-66 en vooral J. Muller, 'Confraternity and Art in the St Jacob's Church, Antwerp. A Case Study of the Altar of the Brotherhood of St Rochus' in Vlieghe, Balis en Van de Velde 2000 (zie noot 1), pp. 97-110.

125. Zo richtte bijvoorbeeld Jan de Gavarelles in 1631 binnen de kerk van de geschoeide karmelieten het Scapulierbroederschap op. Göttler 1996 (zie noot 21), pp. 208-209.

126. Ambitieuze zakenlui en *coming men* op de politieke scène als Jacob van Eycke, Urbanus van Parijs en Jan Augustijn de Lannoy bekleedden leidinggevende functies en combineerden het lidmaatschap van verschillende confrerieën. Kathedraalarchief Antwerpen, Register 206. Ledenlijsten H. Antonius 1506-1784; Register 213. Rekeningen Sint-Hubertus en Stadsarchief Antwerpen, Kerken en kloosters 1847. En in de drie aan de augustijnerorde gelieerde broederschappen bekleedden verschillende leden van de commerciële en politieke elite bestuursfuncties (o.a. leden van de families Schoyte, Van Weerden, Stevens, Lamberti, De Cordes, Van Parijs en Moens). Leyder 1996 (zie noot 82), pp. 209-215.

127. Visschers 1853 (zie noot 117), pp. 140, 242-245, 283-285, 297-300; J. van Brabant, *Rampspoed en restauratie. Bijdrage tot de geschiedenis van de uitrusting en restauratie der Onze-Lieve-Vrouwekathedraal van Antwerpen*, Antwerpen, 1974, p. 74.

128. S. Grieten en J. Bungeneers, *De Onze-Lieve-Vrouwekathedraal. Kunstpatrimonium van het Ancien Régime*, Antwerpen, 1993, p. 498.

129. Zo varieerde het entreegeld voor de kerngroep van de Gilde van Onze-Lieve-Vrouwe-Lof van *f* 120 tot *f* 400. G. Hermans, *De Gilde van Onze-Lieve-Vrouw-Lof in de Antwerpse Onze-Lieve-Vrouwekathedraal tijdens de 17de eeuw* (onuitgegeven licentiaatsverhandeling), Leuven, 1992, pp. 61-64. Voor de entreegelden, zie: Kathedraalarchief Antwerpen, nr. 20 (vanaf 1631). De wethouders Ignatius Engelgrave en Jan Karel dela Bistrate betaalden in 1667 en 1670 respectievelijk *f* 300 en *f* 200.

130. Dit was het geval bij het prestigieuze broederschap van de Heilige Besnijdenis. Vormde het grotendeels een oligarchie in het klein met leden die voor decennia uit dezelfde (wethouders)families voortkwamen – o.a. Edward en Jan van Brecht, Hendrik en Christoffel van Etten, Karel en Gillis de Mera, Robrecht sr. en Robrecht jr. Tucher –, niettemin stelde het de rangen open voor beloftevolle *homines novi* – o.a. Michiel Boot, Ferdinand Helman, Jan Roose, Balthasar de Robiano en Jan de Ram: Stadsarchief Antwerpen, Kerken en kloosters 1847.

131. R. Mannaerts, *De artistieke expressie van de mariale devotie der Jezuïeten te Antwerpen (1562-1773). Een iconografisch onderzoek* (onuitgegeven licentiaatsverhandeling), Leuven, 1983, p. 83.

132. E. Geudens, *Het Sint-Huibrechtsgild en zijn genooten in de Onze-Lieve-Vrouwenkerk te Antwerpen (1500-1821)*, Antwerpen, 1921, pp. 84-85.

133. Muller 2000 (zie noot 124), p. 103.

134. P. Génard, *Les confréries de St. Antoine Ermite à Anvers*, Antwerpen, 1881, pp. 8, 17. Kathedraalarchief Antwerpen, Register 206 (ledenlijsten H. Anthonis 1506-1784).

135. Stadsarchief Antwerpen, Kerken en kloosters 1847.

136. A. Balis, 'Antwerpen, voedster der kunsten: haar bijdrage tot de artistieke cultuur in de zeventiende eeuw', in J. Van der Stock, ed., [cat. tent.] *Antwerpen, verhaal van een metropool, 16de-17de eeuw*, Antwerpen, 1993, pp. 118-127 en R. Baetens, 'Le rôle d'Anvers dans la transmission de valeurs culturelles au temps de son apogée (1500-1650)', in *17e Colloque international. Spa, 16-19. V. 1994. La ville et la transmission des valeurs culturelles au bas moyen âge et aux temps modernes. Actes*, Brussel, 1996, pp. 37-72. Voor de evolutie van Antwerpen naar een *consumption society*: R. Baetens en B. Blondé, 'A la recherche de l'identité sociale et de la culture matérielle de la bourgeoisie anversoise aux temps modernes', *Histoire, Economie et Société*, XIII, 1994, pp. 531-539; B. Blondé, 'The Birth of a Consumer Society ? Material culture in Antwerp, 16th-17th Century' (in druk).

137. Cf. in dit opzicht: G. Rooijakkers, 'Opereren op het snijpunt van culturen. Middelaars en media in Zuid-Nederland', p. Te Boeckhorst, p. Burke, W. Frijhoff, eds., *Cultuur en maatschappij in Nederland 1500-1800. Een historisch-antropologisch perspectief*, Heerlen, 1992, pp. 245-283.

138. A. Balis, 'De nieuwe genres en het burgerlijk mecenaat', in J. Van der Stock, ed., *Stad in Vlaanderen. Cultuur en maatschappij 1477-1787*, Brussel, 1991, pp. 237-254. Voor het proces van picturale zelfrepresentatie: K. Van der Stighelen, 'Das Porträt zwischen 1550 und 1650. Die Emanzipierung eines Genres', in E. Mai en H. Vlieghe, eds., *Von Breughel bis Rubens. Das goldenes Jahrhundert der flämischen Malerei*, Keulen, 1992, pp. 171-176.

139. *Voor een doorgedreven studie van de Iconografie*: M. Mauquoy-Hendrickx, *L'iconographie d'Antoine van Dyck. Catalogue raisonné*, Brussel, 1991. Zie ook: A. Moir, F. de Nave en C. Depauw, [cat. tent.] *Antoon van Dyck (1599-1641) & Antwerpen*, Antwerpen, 1991.

140. Het is betekenisvol, dat Van Dyck de Italiaanse perceptie van het patronage en de status van de kunstenaar op de Antwerpse situatie van toepassing achtte. Onder de prominenten treft men o.a. de wethouders Jan van de Wouwere, Alexander della Faille, Paulus van Halmale en Antoon de Tassis, Nicolaas Rockox, stadssecretaris Gaspar Gevartius aan. Evenals bisschop Jan Malderus, de clerici Albert Miraeus, Carolus Scribani en zakenlui als Peter Stevens en Cornelis van der Geest.

141. Een overzicht van het onderzoek naar de Republiek der Letteren bij: S. Neumeister en C. Wiedemann, eds., *Res Publica litteraria. Die Institutionen der Gelehrsamkeit in der frühen Neuzeit*, Wiesbaden, 1987; H. Bots en F. Waquet, *La République des Lettres*, Parijs, 1997.

142. P. Dibon, 'Communication in the Respublica Literaria of the Seventeenth Century', *Respublica Literarum. Studies in the Classical tradition*, 1, 1978, pp. 43-50; H. Bots en F. Waquet, *Commercium litterarium. La communication dans la République des Lettres 1600-1750. Forms of Communication in the Republic of letters*, Amsterdam, 1994.

143. M. Ultee, 'The Republic of Letters. Learned Correspondence 1680-1720', *The Seventeenth Century*, II, 1987, pp. 95-112.

144. M.B. Becker, *Civility and Society in Western Europe, 1300-1600*, Bloomington (Indiana), 1988, p. 12.

145. Professionele banden met de auteurs werden versterkt door het aangaan van meer persoonlijke relaties. Justus Lipsius verbleef geregeld in het Plantijnse Huis aan de Vrijdagmarkt, waar na afloop van de werkzaamheden werd nagekaart aan een goedgevulde dis: J. Materné, 'De contrareformatorische boekbusiness in Antwerpens nazomertijd. De eerste losse Moretusdrukken van Lipsius' controversiële Mariatraktaten op de Europese boekenmarkt', *Bijdragen tot de geschiedenis*, LXXXIV, 2001, p. 149. Voor de relatie tussen Balthasar I Moretus en Justus Lipsius, zie o.a.: D. Sacré, 'Balthasar I Moretus en Justus Lipsius', in F. De Nave, ed., *Justus Lipsius en het Plantijnse Huis*, Antwerpen, 1997, pp. 109-128.

146. Met hen deelde Balthasar I Moretus de *comitas*, één van de waarden, die onlosmakelijk met Lipsius' perceptie van de vriendschap verbonden was. M. Morford, *Stoics and Neostoics. Rubens and the circle of Lipsius*, Princeton, 1991, p. 53.

147. H. Van Cuyck, *Nicolaas Rockox den jongere, burgemeester van Antwerpen in de XVIIde eeuw*, Antwerpen, 1882, pp. 33-36, 43-45.

148. Onder meer Lipsius en Ortelius, van wie er vriendschapsportetten hingen in de *groote Saleth*. E. Duverger, *Antwerpse kunstinventarissen uit de zeventiende eeuw*, IV, 1636-1642, Brussel, 1989, pp. 382-386. Bovendien correspondeerde Nicolaas Rockox met Nicolas-Claude Fabri de Peiresc, die door velen als patroon bejegend werd: L.T. Sarasohn, 'Nicolas-Claude Fabri de Peiresc and the Patronage of the New Science in the Seventeenth Century', *Isis*, LXXXIV, 1993, pp. 70-90.

149. R.W. Scheller, *Nicolaas Rockox als oudheidkundige*, Antwerpen, 1978, pp. 46-55. Voor Jan Brant, zie: A. Vander Meersch, 'Jean Brandt, magistrat, philologue, commentateur', in *Biographie Nationale*, II, Brussel, 1868, kol. 905-906. Voor Gaspar Gevartius: M. Hoc, *Le déclin de l'humanisme belge. Etude sur J.G. Gevaerts, philologue et poète (1593-1666)*, Brussel, 1922.

150. Voor de relatie Rockox-Rubens: Baudouin 1977 (zie noot 108).

151. Dit blijkt uit de notities die Peter Stevens maakte. Zo noteerde hij bij een kunstenaar wie te Antwerpen in het bezit was van diens werk. Men vindt de namen terug van vooraanstaande kunstcollectioneurs en -liefhebbers. O.a. Antonio de Tassis, Gaspar van Woonsel, Sebastiaan Daems, stadspensionaris Jacob Roelants, Willem Despommereaux, Cornelis van der Geest en Jan van Meurs; zie J. Briels, 'Amor Pictoriae Artis. De Antwerpse kunsthandelaar Peeter Stevens (1590-1668) en zijn constkamer', *Jaarboek Koninklijk Museum voor Schone Kunst Antwerpen*, 1980, pp. 203-226. Voor Rubens als kunstcollectioneur: J.M. Muller, *Rubens: The Artist as collector*, Princeton (New Jersey), 1989.

152. Voor Van Eycke, zie o.a.: E. Duverger en D. Maufort, 'Giovanni Battista van Eycke en de patronen met de historie van Decius Mus van Antoon van Dyck naar inventies van Pieter Paul Rubens', *Gentse Bijdragen tot de Kunstgeschiedenis*, XXXI, 1996, pp. 97-119.

153. Zie Baetens 1976 (zie noot 13), pp. 199-200.

154. De familie moet traditioneel op de orde georiënteerd zijn geweest, want ook voor de bouw van de Sint-Jozefkapel beschikte ze reeds over een – weliswaar kleinere – kapel. Voor de aankleding van de twee kapellen deed ze een beroep op contemporaine meesters als Van Dyck, Seghers en Wildens en ook voor sculpturale decoratie had ze geld veil. Drie zussen van Lodewijk en Gaspar traden bij de falcontinnen in. De zussen maakten de falcontinnen tot hun algemene erfgenamen, Alleen al aan de metsel- en timmerwerken besteedde Lodewijk de Roomer *f* 12000. Daarnaast trok hij grote sommen uit voor de rijkelijke decoratie (marmeren altaar en sculpturen, kostbare schilderijen). Na de dood van zijn broer Lodewijk continueerde Gaspar de Roomer de patronageactiviteiten van de familie in Antwerpen. Met *f* 23000 in de jaren zestig en zeventig maakte hij onder meer de herstellingswerken aan de door brand geteisterde kapel en kerk mogelijk. Rijksarchief Antwerpen, Kerkelijk Archief Regulieren Falcon 29, twee losse stukken (01/07/1615; 22/10/1624; 05/06/1637); Falcon 81 *Register Voor de Capelle van den Heilighen Ioseph...*); Falcon 94; Falcon, charters 15 (25/05/1673 en 30/06/1673); Stadsarchief Antwerpen, Kerken en kloosters 907 (*Magno Patri Iosepho..*). In het doctoraatsproefschrift dat we voorbereiden wordt uitgebreid ingegaan op de patronageactiviteiten van de familie De Roomer.

155. M. Sabbe, *De Moretussen en hun kring*, Antwerpen, 1928, p. 65.

156. M. Vaes, 'Le séjour de Van Dyck en Italie', *Bulletin de l'Institut Belge de Rome*, IV, 1924, p. 206 en Idem, 'Corneille de Wael (1592-1667)', *Bulletin de l'Institut Belge de Rome*, V, 1925, pp. 177, 181, 182, 189-207.

157. Zijn collectie omvatte bij zijn dood maar liefst zo'n 1500 schilderijen en prenten en weerspiegelde de nauwe relaties die bestonden tussen Noord- en Zuid-Europa. Naast werk van lokale schilders trof men er o.a. ook de landschapsschilderijen van de Vlaamse schilderskolonie te Rome en oude meesters als Bassano aan.

158. I.v.m. Antoon de Tassis: F. Baudouin, 'Van Dyck's portrait of Anthonio de Tassis and his daughter Maria, both painted in 1634: an investigation report and an addendum', *Jaarboek Koninklijk Museum voor Schone Kunsten Antwerpen*, 1999, pp. 8-19. Antoon van Dyck was duidelijk een schilder die bij Antoon de Tassis in de gratie stond, want toen De Tassis zich niet langer de grote uitgaven van voorheen kon veroorloven, toonde Matthijs Musson zich gereserveerd om nog op grote schaal in Van Dycks te investeren. E. Duverger, 'Nieuwe gegevens betreffende de kunsthandel van Matthijs Musson en Marie Fourmenois te Antwerpen tusen 1633 en 1681', *Gentse Bijdragen tot de Kunstgeschiedenis*, XXI, 1968, pp. 24, 81-82.

159. Van der Stighelen 1992 (zie noot 138), pp. 178-179. I.v.m. de portretten door Antoon van Dyck in Antwerpse collecties: E. Duverger, 'Antoon van Dyck dans les inventaires anversois du XVIIe siècle relatifs à l'art', *Jaarboek Koninklijk Museum voor Schone Kunsten Antwerpen*, 1999, pp. 20-39.

160. J.S. Held, 'Artis pictoriae amator. An Antwerp Art Patron and his Collection', *Gazette des Beaux-Arts*, 1957, pp. 54-57, 60-61; A.J.J. Delen, 'Cornelis van der Geest. Een groot figuur in de geschiedenis van Antwerpen', *Antwerpen. Tijdschrift der stad Antwerpen*, 1959, pp. 59-60.

161. Zie o.a. Baudouin 1977 (zie noot 108), pp. 13-26.

162. J.P. De Bruyn, 'Officiële opdrachten aan Erasmus II Quellinus', *Jaarboek Koninklijk Museum van Schone Kunsten*

*Antwerpen*, 1983, pp. 211-260; I. Wouters, 'Het politieke schouwspel te Antwerpen in de 17de eeuw', *De zeventiende eeuw*, III, 1987, p. 41; A. Diels, *De Blijde Intrede van aartshertog Ernest van Oostenrijk te Antwerpen in 1594. Een kunstwetenschappelijke benadering* (onuitgegeven licentiaatsverhandeling), Brussel, 1994, pp. 43, 123-124.

163. J.R. Martin, *Decorations for the Pompa Introitus Ferdinandi* (*Corpus Rubenianum Ludwig Burchard*, XVI), Brussel, 1972, pp. 25-26.

164. De namen spreken voor zichzelf. Om er slechts enkele te noemen: de stadssecretarissen Johannes Bochius, Hendrik de Moy en Philips Rubens, de wethouders Hendrik van Etten, Jan van de Wouwere en Alexander Goubau, de zakenlui-wethouders Michiel Boot, Ferdinand Helman en Jacob van Eycke, de kunstenaars Otto van Veen, Jan Breughel, Hendrik van Balen, Sebastiaan Vrancx, Abraham Janssens, Frans Snyders en Pieter Paul Rubens, invloedrijke kanunikken als Cornelius de Witte en Zeghers van Hontsum.

165. Aangaande (Hendrik) van Halmale: zie o.a. H. de Ghellink Van Vaernewijck, 'Un livre de raison Anversois du XVIième siècle. Les van Halmale', *Annales de l'Académie Royale d'Archéologie de Belgique*, VI, 1904, pp. 284-384; M. Rooses, 'Portret van Hendrik van Halmale', *Onze Kunst*, I, 1901, pp. 124-130; N. De Poorter, 'Rubens "onder de wapenen". De Antwerpse schilders als gildebroeders van de kolveniers in de eerste helft van de 17de eeuw', *Jaarboek Koninklijk Museum voor Schone Kunsten Antwerpen*, 1988, pp. 224-225.

166. R.-A. d'Hulst, 'Jacob Jordaens en de Schilderskamer van de Antwerpse Academie', *Jaarboek Koninklijk Museum voor Schone Kunsten Antwerpen*, 1967, pp. 131-150; Z.Z. Filipczak, *Picturing Art in Antwerp, 1550-1700*, Princeton, 1987, pp. 164-167.

167. F. Van den Branden, *Geschiedenis van de Academie van Antwerpen*, Antwerpen, 1867, pp. 45-47; L.Th. Van Looij, 'De Antwerpse Koninklijke Academie voor Schone Kunsten', in A.W.A. Boschloo e.a., *Academies of Art between Renaissance and Romanticism. Leids Kunsthistorisch Jaarboek*, V-VI, 1986-1987, pp. 306-307.

# Rubens'Anbetung der Könige 1608 und 1628/29: die Gestaltung für verschiedene Patrone

*Barbara Welzel*

Am 9. April 1609 wurde in der Statenkamer des Rathauses zu Antwerpen der zwölfjährige Waffenstillstand zwischen den südlichen, katholischen Niederlanden und den nördlichen, protestantischen Provinzen unterzeichnet.[1] Große Hoffnungen knüpften sich an diese Vereinbarung. Seit etwa vier Jahrzehnten hatten kriegerische Auseinandersetzungen das Land überzogen und Menschen wie Land bedrängt. Für die südlichen Niederlande brach mit der Unterzeichnung des Waffenstillstandes ein beinah Goldenes Zeitalter an. Die Handelsblockaden wurden weitgehend aufgehoben. Die Friedenswünsche schienen sich zu erfüllen. Auch für Rubens ist diese Hoffnung überliefert: 'Der Frieden oder besser gesagt, der Waffenstillstand für eine lange Reihe von Jahren, wird ohne den geringsten Zweifel zustande kommen und während dieser Zeit werden unsere Länder von neuem aufblühen'.[2] Aus der Rückschau wissen wir, daß sich die wirtschaftlichen Hoffnungen nicht mehr uneingeschränkt erfüllen konnten. Antwerpen hatte seine Position als wichtigster Handelshafen an Amsterdam verloren. Das Verbot, von den südlichen Niederlanden aus mit der Neuen Welt zu handeln, wie es in den geheimen Zusatzklauseln der Cessio (der Abtretung der Niederlande aus dem spanischen Imperium unter Philipp II. an Erzherzogin Isabella und den Prinzgemahl Albrecht im Jahre 1598) verankert war, führte neben der Kontrolle der Scheldemündung durch die nördlichen Niederlande zur spürbaren Degradierung des Antwerpener Handels. Doch gleichzeitig setzte beinah unmittelbar eine kulturelle Blüte ein. Eine Fülle von künstlerischen Neuerungen kennzeichnet die nun einsetzende Glanzzeit flämischer Kunst. Gerade in der Malerei fand ein unvergleichlicher Schub innovativer Ikonographie statt. Gekoppelt war dies mit Aktivitäten der katholischen Reform, die das gesamte Territorium überzogen. Die Kunst arbeitete der Schaffung einer kollektiven Identität zu. Es galt, das Bild einer gerechten Herrschaft zu etablieren, die bestimmt war durch Frieden und Prosperität sowie durch katholische Rechtglaubigkeit.

Der Unterzeichnung des Waffenstillstandes am 9. April 1609 waren seit März Verhandlungen vorausgegangen; die Unterhändler trafen seit Januar 1609 in der Stadt ein. In der prachtigen Statenkamer des Antwerpener Rathauses sollte das Abkommen unterzeichnet werden.[3] Zur Ausstattung dieses Repräsentationsraumes gehörte seit seiner Erbauung ein Kamin. Kamine waren bekanntlich unverzichtbarer Bestandteil von Repräsentationsräumen. Sie waren weit über ihren praktischen Nutzen hinaus räumliche Auszeichnung. Der Kamin der Statenkamer wurde für das Ereignis 1609 repariert. Ebenfalls bereits vorhanden war eine Serie von 44 Porträts der früheren Herzöge von Brabant, die Anthonio de Succa gemalt hatte. Präsent war in der Porträtgalerie die dynastische Eigentradition Brabants mit seiner Hauptstadt Antwerpen. Diese lokale Tradition war durch wirtschaftliche und kulturelle Prosperität geprägt gewesen. Diesen Zustand wollte man in Antwerpen restituiert sehen; in diese Tradition sollte sich auch die Gegenwart stellen.

Neu in Auftrag gegeben wurden offenbar zwei Gemälde. Das eine stammt von Abraham Janssen und befindet sich heute – noch immer im Besitz der Stadt Antwerpen – im Museum zu Antwerpen (Abb. 1).[4] Die allegorische Darstellung zeigt Scaldis (die Schelde) et Antverpia. Das großformatige Gemälde präsentiert die beiden monumentalen Personifikationen in Untersicht und dergestalt zum Betrachter geklappt, daß es offenbar für eine hohe Anbringung, etwa als Kaminstück, bestimmt war. Der Flußgott überreicht der mit einer Stadtkrone geschmückten Antverpia ein Füllhorn. Den

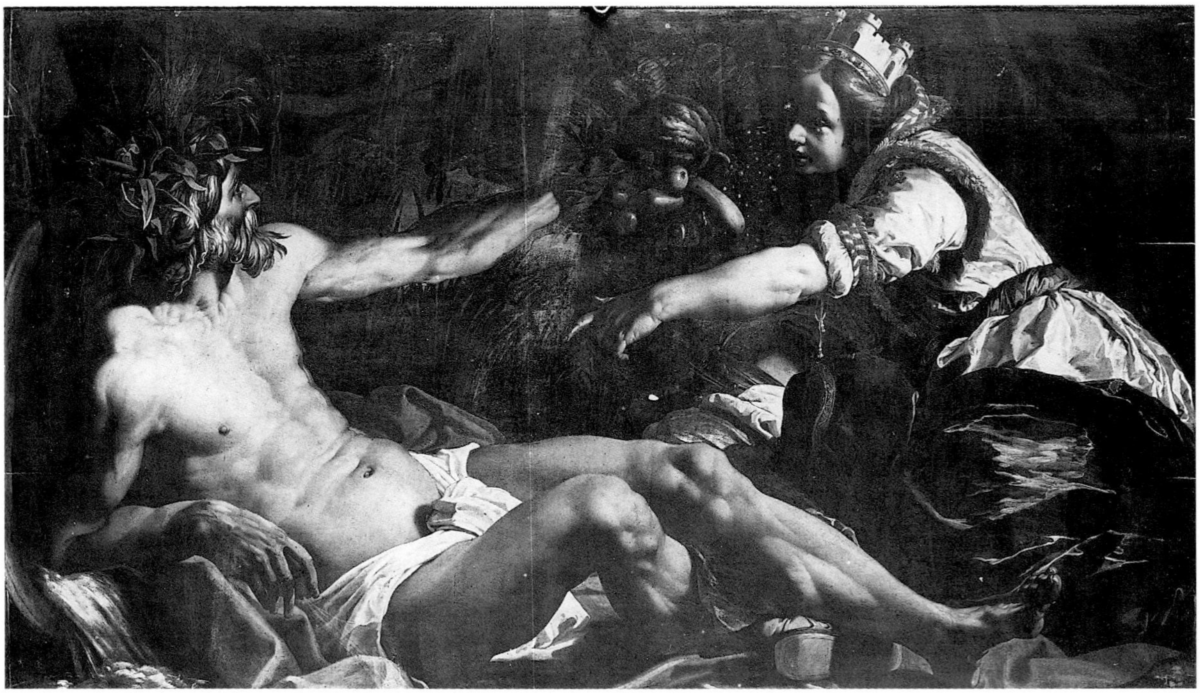

Abb. 1. Abraham Janssen, *Scaldis et Antverpia*, Antwerpen, Koninklijk Museum voor Schone Kunsten

Verhandlungs- bzw. Vertragspartnern wurde deutlich vor Augen gestellt, daß das Wohlergehen Antwerpens von der Öffnung der Schelde abhing.

Als zweites Werk wurde, so dürfen die verschiedenen Quellenüberlieferungen wohl miteinander kurzgeschlossen werden, eine großformatige Anbetung der Heiligen Drei Könige bei Peter Paul Rubens in Auftrag gegeben (Abb. 2).[5] Das Gemälde befindet sich heute im Prado in Madrid, allerdings nicht mehr in seinem ursprünglichen Zustand. Das Werk gelangte auf einem noch naher zu besprechenden Weg in die königliche Sammlung Philipps IV. in Madrid, wo Rubens ihm 1628/29 wiederbegegnete und es einer eingreifenden Überarbeitung unterzog. Für den neuen Patron schuf Rubens eine neue Version des Werkes, für die er Format, Komposition und in Teilen auch die Ikonographie veränderte. Obwohl Rubens bekanntlich regelmäßig seine eigenen Gemälde überarbeitete, läßt sich die Anbetung der Könige wohl nicht einfach in die Reihe jener Redaktionen einreihen, die ausschließlich vom Künstler verantwortet wurden. Vielmehr scheint das Gemälde in beiden Fassungen präzise auf seinen Kontext abgestimmt worden zu sein. Die Analyse seiner beiden Konzeptionen scheint daher ein Modellfall für die Untersuchung der Kommunikation zwischen Auftraggeber bzw. Patron auf der einen Seite und dem Künstler auf der anderen. Es muß erstaunen, daß diese signifikante Veränderung in der Forschung bisher kaum eingehendes Interesse gefunden hat. Die Untersuchung von Hans Devisscher interessiert sich weitestgehend nur für die frühe Fassung.[6] Die zweite Fassung ist erst kürzlich von Alexander Vergara näher analysiert worden.[7] Doch betrachten beide Autoren ihren Untersuchungsgegenstand weitgehend isoliert von seiner Umgebung. Die vergleichsweise paßgenaue Platzierung des Werkes durch Rubens, mit der der Künstler auf die räumlichen und situativen Kontexte reagierte, wird nicht näher berücksichtigt. Erst vor dieser Folie aber entfaltet die Frage nach dem Verhältnis zwischen Kunstwerk und Auftrag bzw. Künstler und Patron ihr analytisches Potential.

Im heutigen Zustand dokumentiert das Werk in Madrid die Überarbeitung durch Rubens 1628/29. Es mißt 346 x 438 cm. Dem ursprünglichen Gemälde wurden oben und rechts Streifen von 90 bzw. 107 cm angefügt. Die Antwerpener Version maß demnach etwa 256 x 331 cm. Die Komposition von 1608/09 ist in einer Ölskizze (heute Groningen; Abb.

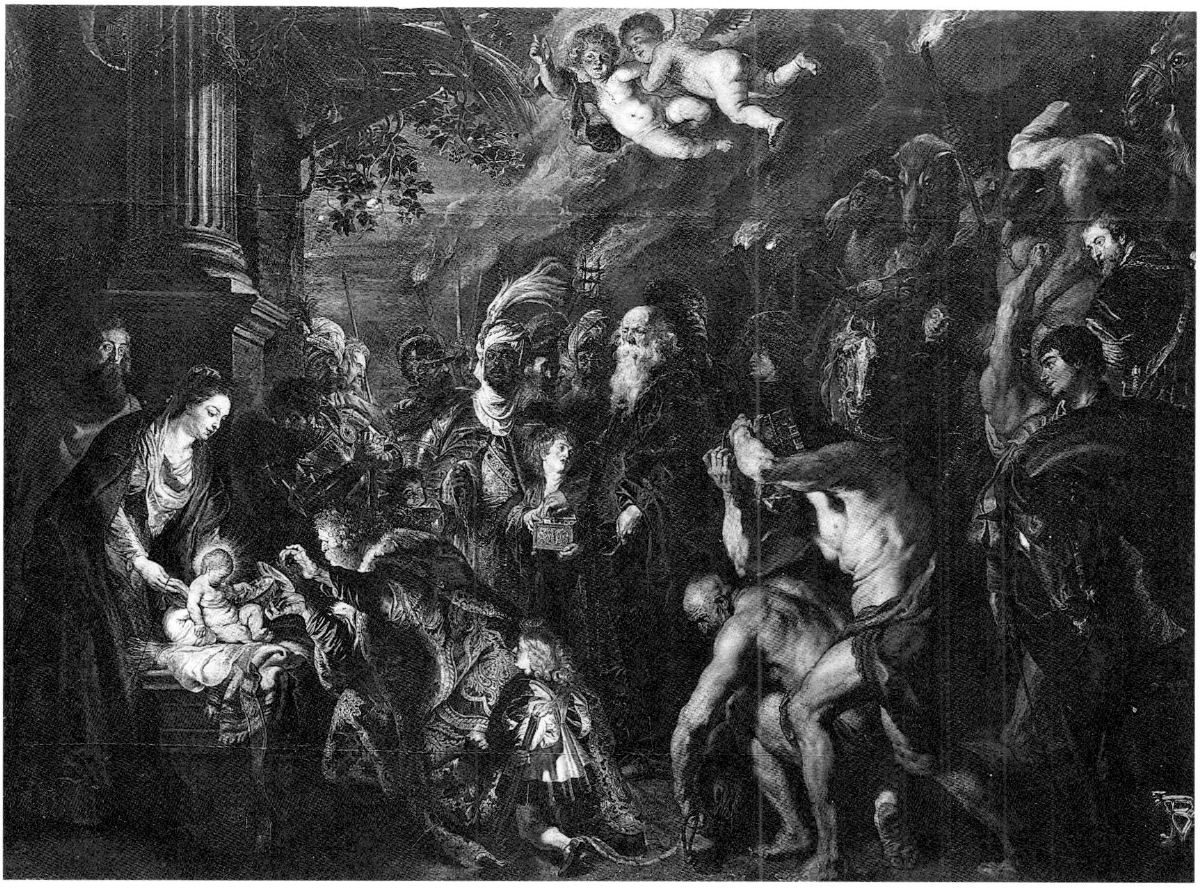

Abb. 2. Peter Paul Rubens, *Anbetung der Heiligen Drei Könige*, Madrid, Prado

3) – und in einer Kopie in Privatbesitz – überliefert.[8]

Das Gemälde zählt zu den ersten Aufträgen, die Peter Paul Rubens nach seiner Rückkehr aus Italien in den Niederlanden erhielt. Erklärungsbedürftig schien regelmäßig, daß Rubens so früh ein dergestalt öffentlicher und renommierter Auftrag anvertraut wurde. Mit Erstaunen wurde gefragt, woher denn seine künstlerischen Qualitäten so unmittelbar nach seinem Eintreffen in der Stadt bereits bekannt und vor allem anerkannt genug gewesen sein konnten. Die öffentliche Aufstellung der aus Rom mitgebrachten Version des Altarbildes für die Chiesa Nuova auf dem neu errichteten Altar in der Kapelle bei St. Michael, in der seine Mutter bestattet war, kann allein dieses Renommé nicht verursacht haben – auch wenn sich Rubens mit diesem Akt als ein Künstler darstellt, der die Tridentinischen Bildvorstellungen zu verwirklichen versteht. Künstlersoziologische Untersuchungen – etwa diejenige von Gary Schwartz zu Rembrandt[9] – haben in den letzten Jahren deutlich gemacht, daß die soziale Verflechtung in einem Patronagesystem zu den entscheidenden Faktoren gehört, die die Auftragsvergabe an einen Künstler steuern. Schon in Rom hatte Rubens als derjenige Maler gegolten, dem Erzherzog Albrecht Gemälde für seine Patronatskirche Sta. Croce anvertrauen konnte. Und schon bald nach seiner Rückkehr in die Niederlande wurde Rubens mit Porträts für das Erzherzogspaar betraut, die als Formular für die neuartigen Staatsporträts der Herrscher fungierten. Künstlersoziologisch korrespondiert die Einladung und dann folgende Ernennung zum Hofmaler. Noch in diesem Amt behielt Rubens die Verflechtung in das städtische Gefüge in Antwerpen bei. An seiner schnellen Einführung in die Antwerpener Gesellschaft unmittelbar 1608 dürfte sein Bruder Philip, der seinerseits am 10. Januar 1609 zum Stadtsekretär ernannt wurde, maßgeblichen Anteil gehabt haben. Eine gewichtige Rolle für die Auftragsvergabe dürfte sicherlich Nicolas Rockox gespielt haben.[10] Er war zu dieser Zeit 'buitenburgemeester' von Antwerpen.

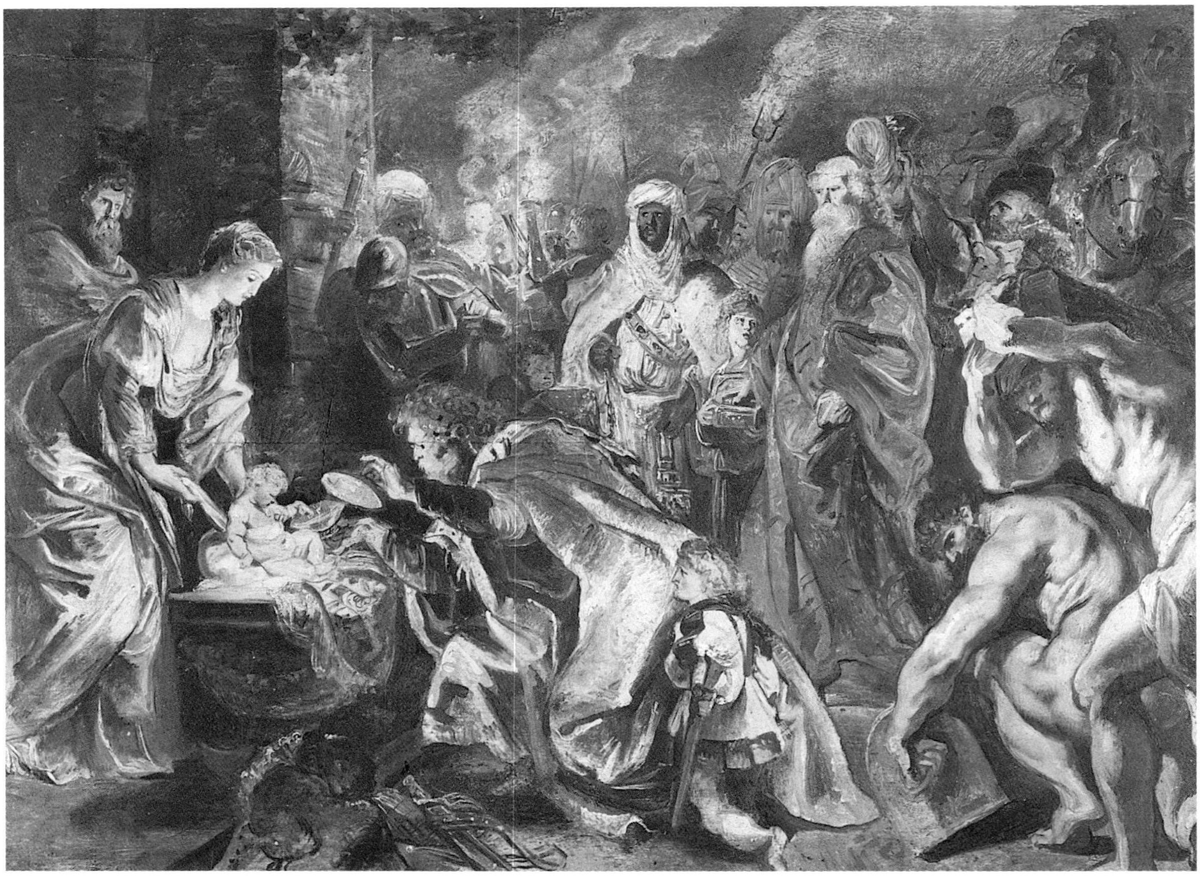

Abb. 3. Peter Paul Rubens, *Anbetung der Heiligen Drei Könige*, Groningen, Groninger Museum

In den folgenden Jahren sollte er weitere bedeutende Aufträge an Rubens vergeben. Solche gesellschaftliche Einbindung und soziale Anerkennung ist die unverzichtbare Voraussetzung für einen Auftrag wie das Dreikönigsbild für das Antwerpener Rathaus.

Ein zweiter Faktor kommt untrennbar hinzu. Rubens hatte sich offenbar bereits zu diesem Zeitpunkt – und hier dürfte die öffentliche Präsentation des Altarbildes in St. Michael keine unbeträchtliche Rolle gespielt haben – als ein Maler vorgestellt, der ikonographische Aufgaben präzise zu erfüllen wußte und mit seiner Kunstsprache die Tridentinischen Bildvorstellungen realisierte. Man konnte ihm mit anderen Worten Aufträge anvertrauen, bei denen die Selbstdarstellung und Repräsentation der Auftraggeber in einer Weise zur Anschauung gebracht werden sollten, die auch heikle und labile Konstellationen aushielt.

Die anlaßbezogene Ausstattung von Repräsentationsräumen für politische Ereignisse, namentlich für Friedensverhandlungen und Vertragsunterzeichnungen unterlag in aller Regel einem präzisen Kalkül. Die Ikonographie, mit der der Gastgeber dem Ereignis einen Rahmen gab, konnte nicht dem Zufall überlassen werden. Sie mußte vor allem auch mit diplomatischem Fingerspitzengefühl die Interessen der Parteien ausponderieren.

Immer wieder wurde mittels Bildprogrammen Politik betrieben, immer wieder auch mußten Bildprogramme verändert werden, um den Verhandlungen überhaupt eine diplomatische Chance zu geben. So wird etwa – um ein besonders sprechendes Beispiel zu zitieren – über die Verhandlungen zwischen Frankreich und England im Jahr 1384 berichtet, daß der Herzog von Berry mit der Bildausstattung des Verhandlungsortes betraut war und Tapisserien mit Schlachtendarstellungen aufhängen ließ.[11] Doch von englischer Seite wurde Protest erhoben: Wer nach Frieden trachte, dürfe nicht Krieg und Vernichtung von Städten vor Augen haben. Man entfernte schließlich die Kampfszenen und stattete den Verhandlungsort mit golddurchwirkten Tapisserien mit der

Passion Christi aus, die – wie der Chronist formuliert – den 'Herrscher des Friedens und der Eintracht' zeigten.[12]

Das bevorzugte Bildmedium für die anlaßbezogene Ausstattung von Repräsentationsraumen war, daran haben verschiedene Forschungen in den letzten Jahren nachdrücklich erinnert, die Tapisserie.[13] Gerne wählte man immer wieder – neben programmatischen Neuschöpfungen – überlieferte Werke, die ihrerseits Erinnerungsträger vorausgegangener Ereignisse geworden waren und so dazu beitrugen, das gegenwärtige Ereignis, das sie ausschmückten und kommentierten, in eine Geschichte memorierter Ereignisse einzuordnen. Eine solche Funktion der objektgebundenen Traditionsstiftung erfüllte 1609 bereits der Verhandlungsort des Antwerpener Rathauses selbst. Der Bau repräsentierte die städtische Eigentradition wie zugleich – seit der Neugestaltung des Fassadenprogrammes nach der Eroberung der Stadt durch Alexander Farnese – die Rekatholisierung unter spanischen Vorzeichen. Programmatisch war an der Fassade des Rathauses der legendäre Stadtgründer durch eine Marienstatue ersetzt worden.[14] Die Porträts der Brabanter Herzöge in der Statencamer markierten die lokale Eigentradition der Region. Das Gemälde von Abraham Janssens trat an die Stelle eines Gemäldes gleichen Themas, das 1576 zerstört worden war. Das Gemälde von Rubens fügt sich in die Tradition eines anderen Bildmediums. Sowohl das große Bildformat als auch die auf eine vergleichsweise schmale Vordergrundsbühne verteilten Figuren und vor allem deren schiere Anzahl verweisen auf das Medium Tapisserie, das – wie bereits erwähnt – als das bevorzugte Medium für die anlaßbezogene Ausstattung von Repräsentationsräumen zu gelten hat. Doch ist die Herstellung der kostbaren und angesehenen Tapisserien vergleichsweise zeitaufwendig. Der Zeitrahmen, der für die Vorbereitung der Verhandlungen 1609 zur Verfügung stand, reichte hierfür nicht aus. Das Gemälde von Rubens trat daher, so steht zu vermuten, an die Stelle einer nicht realisierbaren Tapisserie.

Die Forschung hat herausgearbeitet, wie die Bildinszenierung der Heiligen Drei Könige auf die Auftragssituation Bezug nimmt.[15] Zu nennen sind die deutlichen eucharistischen Hinweise der Darstellung, mit denen die Szene katholisch markiert wird: etwa der an einen

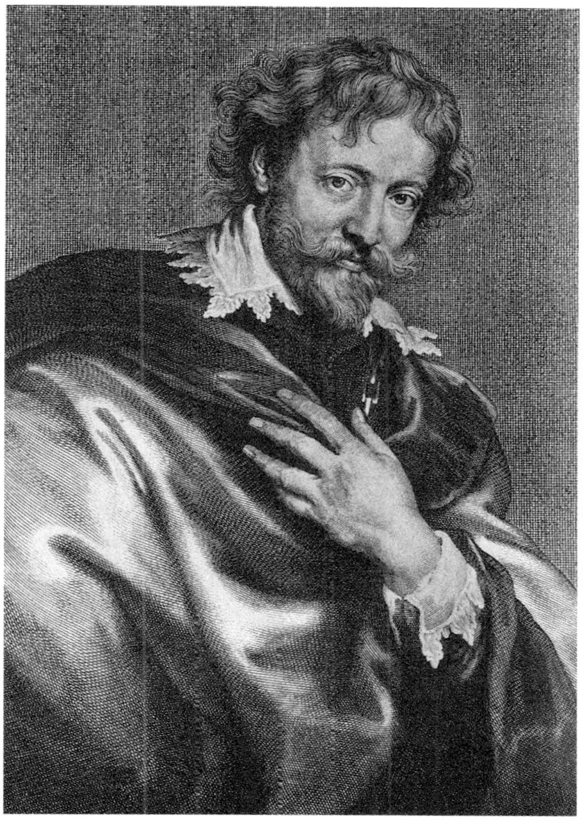

Abb.4. Paulus Pontius nach Anton van Dyck, *Porträt des Peter Paul Rubens*, Kupferstich

Altar gemahnende Stein, auf dem das Christuskind präsentiert wird, oder die priesterliche Stola, die unter ihm ausgebreitet ist. Christus gilt – wie schon die Ikonographie des französisch-englischen Friedenschlusses im ausgehenden 14. Jahrhundert gezeigt hat – als 'Herrscher des Friedens und der Eintracht'. Die Könige bringen Güter aus aller Herren Länder, ein Verweis auf die für Antwerpen erhofften Handelsgüter: Die beiden prominent gesetzten Aktfiguren schleppen Waren heran, bildzentral ist die Figur des Schwarzen gezeigt. Doch sind diese Beobachtungen um wichtige Befunde zu ergänzen. Die Heiligen Drei Könige huldigen Jesus und Maria. Maria ist Stadtpatronin und Herrin Antwerpens. Ihre Verehrung war durch die Bilderstürme verletzt worden. Die Wiederherstellung des Marienkultes war vornehmstes Ziel der Rekatholisierung.[16] Die Marienfigur des Dreikönigsbildes entfaltet in der Topographie des Veranstaltungsortes signifikante Bezüge. In der Statenkamer selbst tritt sie als typologisches Vorbild in Dialog mit Antverpia. Die Verhandlungsteilnehmer wußten, daß Maria die Patronin der Stadt sowie der Kathedrale war, weitere Marienbilder wurden in Antwerpen verehrt. Die katholischen Teilnehmer rahmten ihre diplomatischen Aktivitäten durch Gottesdienstbesuche. Alle hatten das Rathaus unter der zentralen Marienfigur hindurch betreten. Im Gewand eines christologischen Bildthemas, das auch für die protestantischen Verhandlungspartner akzeptabel sein mußte, wurde der Waffenstillstand dem Schutz der Stadtpatronin anempfohlen: der Patronin jener Antverpia, die ihr Füllhorn von der wieder zu öffnenden Schelde empfängt, der Garantin katholischer Rechtgläubigkeit und der Mutter des 'Herrschers des Friedens und der Eintracht'. Dieser Bildappell richtete sich allerdings nicht nur an die protestantischen Unterhändler. Vielmehr war er gleichermaßen an die habsburgischen Verhandlungsführer adressiert. Sie sollten die in der (durch die genannte Porträtgalerie repräsentierten) brabantischen Tradition der Stadt begründeten Hoffnungen als Ziel der Unterhandlungen – ganz wörtlich – im Blick haben. In Rubens fanden die Auftraggeber einen Künstler, der es verstand, die subtile Balance zwischen überkonfessioneller Allgemeingültigkeit des Bildthemas, katholischer Rechtgläubigkeit und gewünschtem Appell aus der Sicht Antwerpens in ein konsistentes Bild zu überführen.

Die Verhandlungen hatten Erfolg. Während die Stadtallegorie von Janssens als ortsfeste Ausstattung der Statenkamer begriffen wurde (und an diesem Ort bis in die 1880er Jahre verblieb), wurde das Dreikönigsbild von Rubens zunächst mit dem Ereignis von 1609 und den Hoffnungen auf blühenden Handel in Antwerpen assoziiert. Die Stadt Antwerpen trennte sich nur drei Jahre später von dem Werk, um noch einmal ihre spezifischen Interessen durch das Gemälde zu kommunizieren. 1612 verwendete die Stadt das Gemälde als diplomatisches Geschenk an Don Rodrigo Calderón.[17] Der Graf von Oliva besuchte am 28.8.1612 in seiner Funktion als Sonderbotschafter des spanischen Königs am erzherzoglichen Hof seine Geburtsstadt Antwerpen. Dort versprach er, Handel und Schiffahrt der Stadt zu fördern, indem er sich am spanischen Hof dafür einsetzen wollte, der Stadt das Stapelrecht für Spezereien und andere aus Spanien importierte Güter zuzuerkennen. Zum Dank und in der Hoffnung, den Forderungen damit weiter zu dienen, beschloß der Große Rat der Stadt Antwerpen (de Breede Raad) in seinen Sitzungen vom 31.8. und 1.9.1612, Don Rodrigo Calderón das Gemälde der Heiligen Drei Könige aus der Statenkamer zu schenken: 'tot eene memorie van dese stadt' – wie es im Protokoll heißt.[18] Am selben Tag offerierte der Pensionaris de Weerdt Calderón das Gemälde 'le cadeau le plus beau et le plus rare que les magistrats possédaient'.

Calderón hatte nicht lange Freude an seinem neuen Besitz. Er fiel in Ungnade und wurde 1621 hingerichtet. Sein Besitz wurde konfisziert. Das Gemälde fand Aufhahme in die königlichen Sammlungen, seit 1623 ist es im Alcázar nachweisbar, 1628/29 befand es sich in den königlichen Sommerappartements.[19] Hier nun begegnete Rubens seinem Werk 1628 wieder und unterzog es einer gründlichen Überarbeitung. Erstaunlicherweise hat erst 1999 Alejandro Vergara explizit darauf hingewiesen, daß Rubens diesen Eingriff wohl kaum in alleiniger Eigenregie vorgenommen haben kann. Er musste sich der Zustimmung Philipps IV. versichern. Die zweite Version des Dreikönigsbildes entstand also wiederum im Dialog mit einem Patron. Rubens überarbeitete die gesamte Komposition – er ergänzte etwa die Säule hinter Maria, retuschierte Gewänder und anderes mehr – und fügte oben und rechts Leinwandstreifen hinzu. Zu beobachten ist eine Intensivierung der katholischen Bildaussage sowohl in der stärkeren Betonung von Maria und ihrer Majestät als auch in der Vermehrung der eucharistischen Bildverweise.[20] Im oberen Bereich erhält das Geschehen – einhergehend mit dem gewandelten stilistischen Empfinden – eine breitere Raumzone, die die szenische Erzählung nicht mehr so eng in das Bildformat gedrängt sein läßt. Rechts fügt Rubens dem Zug der Heiligen Drei Könige weitere Reiter und ein Bildnis seiner selbst ein. In der Tradition der Künstler-Selbstporträts in der Assistenz macht sich der Maler gewissermaßen in einer Porträt-Signatur in einem monumentalen Gemälde in der Sammlung Philipps IV. präsent.[21] Diese Aussage läßt sich vor der Folie von Rubens Aufenthalt 1628/29 präzisieren. Rubens war von Erzherzogin Isabella in diplomatischer Mission nach Spanien entsandt worden, um für einen Frieden zwischen Spanien und England

Vorverhandlungen zu führen. 1629 dann wurde er – als eines der Ergebnisse seiner Reise nach Spanien – von Madrid als Unterhändler nach London geschickt. Seine diplomatische Reise an den Hof Philipps IV sollte incognito stattfinden: Rubens reiste nach außen als Hofmaler der Infantin, um Familienporträts auszuführen. Doch war der eigentliche Zweck schon früh an den anderen Höfen Europas bemerkt worden. Philipp IV. hatte sich – das ist bekannt – Isabella gegenüber sehr skeptisch über die Tatsache geäußert, daß Rubens ein Maler war. Der spanische König war in Sorge, ob ein solch eingeschränkter Status dem Ansehen der Monarchie schaden würde.[22] Wieder also traten für Rubens seine handwerkliche Tätigkeit und sein Adelstitel – der ihn allerdings nicht zu einem alteingessesenen Adligen von Geblüt machen konnte – in einen Konflikt, der für die Gesellschaft seiner Zeit rollenmäßig nicht mehr vermittelbar war. Doch antwortete er auf diese Situation mit der selbstbewußten Formulierung seiner Doppelidentität, an der er zeitlebens arbeitete.[23] In dem Selbstporträt in der Königsanbetung zeigt sich Rubens beritten als Adliger, der einen Degen führen darf. Zugleich trägt er die Kette, die ihm zum Zeichen seines Hofamtes verliehen worden war.[24] In der Überblendung des Selbstbildnisses in der Assistenz mit dem Bildformular eines aristokratischen Reiterporträts verleiht Rubens seiner Utopie Anschauung, daß beide Rollen für ihn verschmolzen werden könnten. Die Inventare des Alcázar verzeichnen das Selbstporträt nicht in ihren Einträgen zum Dreikönigsbild. Alejandro Vergara hat aus dieser wichtigen Beobachtung geschlossen, daß das Aussehen des Malers am spanischen Hof nicht bekannt gewesen sei. Rubens wählte aber ein Bildformular, das mit dem bekannten Porträtstich von Paulus Pontius für die Ikonologie Van Dycks Verbreitung finden sollte (Abb. 4).[25] Man mag daher für möglich halten, daß die Inventarschreiber das Porträt zwar erkannten, jedoch die Doppelrolle nicht zur Sprache brachten: die Doppelrolle, in der Rubens die Konventionen seiner Zeit gezielt verletzte, die er aber zugleich utopisch für sich in Anspruch nahm. Im Modus des höfischen Inventars war diese Rolle nicht benennbar, sie konnte in der sprachlichen Markierung der Ikonographie des Gemäldes keinen Ausdruck finden.

Rubens war – so dürfen wir vermuten – mit seiner in der Überarbeitung gewonnenen Bildformulierung sogar noch weiter gegangen. Die rechts eingefügten Reiter verstärken die Breitenlagerung des Bildformates. Die Wirkung des extremen Querformates, aber auch das Kunststück des weit über sein Pferd gebeugten Reiters verweisen – das ist längst beobachtet – auf Bildkompositionen Tizians, wie sie sich in bedeutender Anzahl in der Sammlung des spanischen Königs befanden. Tizian darf als der Hofmaler schlechthin habsburgischer Herrscher gelten. Seine Tätigkeit war – wie 1624 diejenige von Rubens – durch den Adelstitel belohnt worden. Es ist die Tradition Tizians als geadelter Hofmaler, in die Rubens sich am spanischen Hof stellte.

Rubens war von Philipp IV. beauftragt worden, sein Reiterporträt zu schaffen – ein Gemälde, das nicht nur in künstlerischer Auseinandersetzung mit Tizians berühmten Reiterbildnis Karls V. bei Mühlberg entstand, sondern in dem auch der Auftraggeber sich in die Tradition erfolgreicher habsburgischer Könige gestellt sehen wollte. Philipp IV. hatte Tizians Gemälde 1624 in den Alcázar überführen lassen. Rubens Gemälde fand gegenüber seinen Platz.[26] Doch suchte Rubens Tizian nicht nur zu beerben, sondern im Sinne des Künstlerwettstreites auch zu übertreffen. Bekanntlich wurde ihm ein Atelier im königlichen Palast zur Verfügung gestellt. Diese unmittelbare Nähe zwischen König und Maler ließ sich im Topos der antiken Überlieferung von Alexander und Apelles wahrnehmen. In dieser Rolle des königlichen Malers nun überarbeitete Rubens im Palast ein eigenes Werk. Die ephemere Ikonographie des Waffenstillstandes von 1609 hatte das Gemälde an seinem neuen Ort verloren. Rubens überführte mit seiner Veränderung das Gemälde zur Gänze in seine neue Funktion als Hofkunst: Das Gemälde zeigt eine biblische Historie – Werke gleichen Themas von Tizian befanden sich in derselben Sammlung. Er integrierte die aemulatio mit dem Vorbild durch die Ergänzungen rechts. Zugleich fügte er sein Selbstporträt ein. Aus der gezielten Selbstdarstellung der Stadt Antwerpen war ein Gemälde des Hofkünstlers geworden. Dieser schenkte seinem Patron nicht nur ein Selbstporträt, wie sie zur selben Zeit auch andere Fürsten begannen, für ihre fürstlichen Sammlungen zu erwerben.[27] Vielmehr mutete Rubens Philipp IV.

zugleich die Verbildlichung seiner eigenen, spezifischen Rollenutopie des Adligen, Diplomaten und Künstler zu – eine Utopie, die im Verständnis der (inventarisierenden) Zeitgenossen nicht lesbar war. Kaum selbstbewußter aber ließ sich das ursprünglich paßgenau für die Stadt Antwerpen entworfene Bild umformulieren in ein genuines Kunststück für eine höfische Sammlung. Der Maler konfrontierte seinen Patron mit seinem ambitionierten Selbstentwurf – ein Dialog, der, wenn er auch nicht in den Konventionen des spanischen Hofes aufgefangen war, so doch von Philipp IV. mitkommuniziert wurde. Andernfalls hätte dieses Bild nicht seinen prominenten Platz in der königlichen Sammlung einnehmen können. Im Bild gelang Rubens hier, was ihm in der sozialen Realität seiner Zeit doch in letzter Konsequenz verwehrt blieb. Im Bild konnte auch Philipp IV Rubens in diesem ambitionierten Rollenverständnis einen Platz an seinem Hof zugestehen.

# ANMERKUNGEN

1. Für die Diskussion der folgenden Überlegungen danke ich besonders Nils Büttner, Birgit Franke und Ulrich Heinen. Neben der allgemeinen historischen Literatur vgl. zuletzt das reiche Material, das zusammengetragen ist in: Werner Thomas und Luc Duerloo (Ed.), *Albert & Isabella 1598–1621,* Turnhout, 1998; Werner Thomas und Luc Duerloo (Ed.), [Ausstellungskatalog] *Albrecht & Isabella,* Koninklijke Musea voor Kunst en Geschiedenis, Brussel, 1998; Ursula Härting (Ed.), *Garten und Höfe der Rubenszeit,* Gustav-Lübcke-Museum, Hamm 2000–2001.

2. Brief an Johann Faber vom 10. April 1609; hier zitiert nach *Die Briefe des P.P. Rubens. Übersetzt und eingeleitet von Otto Zoff,* Wien, 1918, No. 20,

3. Floris Prims, *Het Stadhuis te Antwerpen. Geschiedenis en Beschrijving,* Antwerpen, 1930; Leo Van Puyvelde, 'La Salle des Etats à Anvers', *Standen en Landen,* XXIV, 1962, S. 115–121; Christopher Norris, 'Rubens' Adoration of the Kings of 1609', *Nederlands Kunsthistorisch Jaarboek,* XIV, 1963, S. 129–136; Hans Devisscher, *Peter Paul Rubens. Aanbidding der koningen,* Bloemendaal, 1992.

4. Öl auf Leinwand, 174 x 308 cm; Antwerpen, Koninklijk Museum voor Schone Kunsten (Eigentum der Stadt Antwerpen), Inv. 212; vgl. *Koninklijk Museum voor Schone Kunsten – Antwerpen. Departement Oude Meesters. Catalogus Schilderkunst Oude Meesters,* Antwerpen, 1988; Joost Vander Auwera, in [Ausstellungskatalog] *Antwerpen verhaal van een metropool 16de~17de eeuw,* Hessenhuis, Antwerpen 1993, Nr. 1.

5. Öl auf Leinwand, 346 x 438 cm; Madrid, Prado, Inv. 1638. Vgl. Matías Díaz Padrón, *El siglo de Rubens en el Museo del Prado. Catalogo razonado de pintura flamenca del Siglo XVII,* Barcelona, 1995, II, S. 864–867, Nr. 1638; Norris 1963 (wie Anm. 3); Hans Devisscher, in Arnout Balis et al. (Ed.), *De Vlaamse Schilderkunst in het Prado (Flandria extra muros),* Antwerpen, 1989, S. 150–153; Devisscher 1992 (wie Anm. 3). Joost Vander Auwera, 'The Artistic Relationship between Abraham Janssen and Peter Paul Rubens. Some Contextual Evidence', in *Studien zur niederländischen Kunst. Festschrift für Justus Müller Hofstede (Wallraf-Richartz-Jahrbuch,* LV), 1994, S. 227–238.

6. Devisscher 1992 (wie Anm. 3).

7. Alexander Vergara, *Rubens and his Spanish Patrons,* Cambridge, 1999, S. 19–21, 80–93.

8. Groningen, Groninger Museum, 54,5 x 76, 5 cm; Julius Held, *The Oil Sketches of Rubens,* Princeton N.J, 1980, Nr. 325. Rubens Nachfolge, Kopie der Anbetung der Heiligen Drei Könige, London, Privatbesitz; vgl. Vergara 1999 (wie Anm. 7), Abb. 40.

9. Gary Schwartz, *Rembrandt. Sämtliche Gemälde in Farbe,* Stuttgart–Zürich (1983), 1987.

10. Vgl. Frans Baudouin, *Nicolaas Rockox, 'vriendt ende patroon' van Peter Paul Rubens,* Deurne, 1977.

11. Vgl. Birgit Franke, 'Zwischen Liturgie und Zeremoniell. Ephemere Ausstattung bei Friedensverhandlungen und Fürstentreffen', in *Kunst und Liturgie im Mittelalter (Römisches Jahrbuch der Bibliotheca Hertziana,* Beiheft zu Band 33), 1999–2000, S. 205–216, hier S. 206–208.

12. M.L. Bellaguet (Ed.), *Chronique du Religieux de Saint Denys (Collection des documents inédits)* Paris, 1839–1852, II, S. 74–79.

13. Vgl. Wolfgang Brassat, *Tapisserien und Politik an den europäischen Höfen,* Berlin, 1992; Birgit Franke, 'Tapisserie – "portable grandeur" und Medium der Erzählkunst', in Birgit Franke und Barbara Welzel (Ed.), *Die Kunst der burgundischen Niederlande. Eine Einführung,* Berlin, 1997, S. 121–139; Guy Delmarcel, *Flemish Tapestries,* Tielt–London, 1999.

14. Holm Bevers, *Das Rathaus von Antwerpen (1561–1565). Architektur und Figurenprogramm,* Hildesheim–Zürich–New York, 1985, S. 55–58.

15. Zuletzt Devisscher 1992 (wie Anm. 3) mit der älteren Literatur sowie Vander Auwera 1994 (wie Anm. 5).

16. Stellvertretend: David Freedberg, 'Kunst und Gegenreformation in den südlichen Niederlanden 1560–1660', in Ekkehard Mai und Hans Vlieghe (Ed.), [Ausstellungskatalog] *Von Bruegel bis Rubens. Das goldene Jahrhundert der flämischen Malerei,* Wallraf-Richartz-Museum, Köln / Kunsthistorisches Museum, Wien 1992, S. 55–70 mit weiterer Literatur; zu nennen sind auch die wichtigen Schriften von Justus Lipsius, *Diva Virgo Hallensis. Beneficia eius et miracula fide atque ordine descripta,* Antwerpen, 1604 sowie *Diva Sichemiensis sive Aspricollis. Nova eius beneficia et admiranda,* Antwerpen 1605. Jetzt auch Cordula Schumann, *Humble Wife, Charitable Mother and Chaste Widow: Representing the Virtues of the Infanta Isabella Clara Eugenia (1599–1633),* Diss. phil. London (Courtauld Institute), 2000 sowie die Materialsammlung von Roland A.E. Op de Beeck, *De Gilde van Onze-Lieve-Vrouwe-Lof in de kathedraal van Antwerpen,* Antwerpen, 1978.

17. Zuletzt Vergara 1999 (wie Anm. 7), S. 19–28.

18. M. Rooses und Ch. Ruelens (Ed.), *Correspondance de Rubens et documents épistolaires concernant sa vie et ses œuvres, publiés, traduits, annotés par Ch. Ruelens* (I), *par Max Rooses et feu Ch. Ruelens* (II–IV), Antwerpen, 1887–1909, I, S. 206.

19. Vergara 1999 (wie Anm. 7).

20. Ausführlich bei Vergara 1999 (wie Anm. 7), S. 81.

21. Hans-Joachim Raupp, *Untersuchungen zu Künstlerbildnis und Künstlerdarstellung in den Niederlanden im 17. Jahrhundert,* Hildesheim, 1984; zum Künstlerbildnis in der Assistenz S. 243–266; zur 'genialen' Kopfwendung S. 181–220; vgl. auch Justus Müller Hofstede, 'Peter Paul Rubens 1577–1640. Selbstbildnis und Selbstverständnis', in Mai und Vlieghe 1992 (wie Anm. 16), S. 103–120, 117.

22. Brief vom 15.6.1627; Rooses und Ruelens (wie in Anm. 18), IV, Nr. 441.

23. Immer wieder hat Rubens Bildformulierungen geschaffen, die versuchen, seiner 'Doppelidentität' eine gelungene Synthese als Utopie im Bild anschaulich werden zu lassen. Dies gilt beispielsweise bereits für das frühe Doppelporträt mit Isabella in der Geisblattlaube (Alte Pinakothek, München), worauf Müller Hofstede (wie Anm. 21, hier S. 110–112) hingewiesen hat, ohne allerdings den soziologischen Konflikt auszuloten; vgl. zuletzt auch Barbara Welzel, 'Liebesgärten', Härting 2000 (wie Anm. 1), S. 49–57, 56; zum Rollenbild des Künstlers bereitet jetzt Nils Büttner eine ausführliche Untersuchung vor.

24. Stellvertretend Zirka Zaremba Filipczak, *Picturing Art in Antwerp 1550–1700,* Princeton N.J., 1987, S. 98–101.

25. Marie Mauquoy-Hendrickx, *L'Iconographie d'Antoine Van Dyck. Catalogue Raisonné,* Brüssel, (1956) 1991, no. 62.

26. Zuletzt Vergara 1999 (wie Anm. 7), S. 65–80.

27. 1623 bat der Prince of Wales (der spätere König Charles I) Rubens um ein Selbstporträt für seine Sammlung; Hans Vlieghe, *Rubens. Portraits of Identified Sitters* (*Corpus Rubenianum Ludwig Burchard,* XIX, 2). London–New York 1987, Nr. 135. Vgl. Ulrich Middeldorf und Ugo Procacci (Ed.), *Die Sammlung der Selbstbildnisse in den Uffizien,* I, *Geschichte der Sammlung,* Florenz 1971, S. 22–31.